P9-CDE-463

ORSON WELLES

By Simon Callow

BEING AN ACTOR
SHOOTING THE ACTOR
CHARLES LAUGHTON: A DIFFICULT ACTOR
ORSON WELLES: THE ROAD TO XANADU
ORSON WELLES: HELLO AMERICANS
LOVE IS WHERE IT FALLS
MY LIFE IN PIECES
CHARLES DICKENS AND THE GREAT THEATRE OF THE WORLD

ORSON WELLES

Volume 3

ONE-MAN BAND

SIMON CALLOW

VIKING

VIKING
An imprint of Penguin Random House LLC
375 Hudson Street
New York, New York 10014
penguin.com

First published in Great Britain by Jonathan Cape, an imprint of Penguin Random House UK

978-0-670-02491-9

Printed in the United States of America
1 3 5 7 9 10 8 6 4 2

Set in Bembo

For Sebastian Fox, my beloved, who made all this possible.

In memory of the secretaries who survived to tell the tale,
Ann Rogers (1907–2004) and Rita Ribolla (1908–1986).

During the prolonged applause when the curtain fell, one did ungratefully feel that one was watching a jet-propelled vampire take a bow, surrounded by the pale husks of his victims. The show is, in fact, a one-man band; and as all the world's a stage, it didn't seem odd to wonder why Mr Welles hadn't run for president instead . . . is he just a circus figure – a strong man, say, or an illusionist?

Anonymous reviewer at the first night of Welles's *Othello* at the St James Theatre London, 1951: *Third Man into Moor*

What is a man anyhow? what am I? what are you? –

If I worship one thing more than another it shall be the spread of my own body, or any part of it,
Translucent mould of me it shall be you!
Shaded ledges and rests it shall be you!
Firm masculine colter it shall be you!
Whatever goes to the tilth of me it shall be you!
You my rich blood! your milky stream pale strippings of my life!

Do I contradict myself?
Very well then I contradict myself,
(I am large, I contain multitudes.)

from Walt Whitman, *A Song of Myself*

CONTENTS

PREFACE: A WORD OF EXPLANATION

WHEN, IN 1989, my English publisher Nick Hern and I approached that splendid elder-statesman of American publishing, Aaron Asher, with a proposal to write a biography of Orson Welles, I said to him that I thought it would have to be in three volumes, the third of which, I suggested, should be a novel. He looked at me, pityingly, and said, 'If you are very lucky, you will be allowed to write this biography in two volumes, neither of which will be a novel.'

After I had written and delivered the first volume, *The Road to Xanadu*, which culminated in the release of *Citizen Kane*, I hit a rock. It was clearly going to be impossible to write the remaining forty-two years of a life which consisted of a continuous volcanic eruption of films, plays, radio programmes, journalism, painting and political interventions, without resorting to the one-damned-thing-after-another school of biography – a method I had specifically set out to avoid. With wonderful nonchalance Dan Franklin, by then my publisher at Jonathan Cape, accepted my proposal of writing a second volume which would cover exactly five years of Welles's life – five years packed with adventures and experiments in various media, but focusing above all on politics. This book was called *Hello Americans*, the title of one of Welles's many radio series in which he valiantly sought to interest the nation in its history and its place in the world. The third and final volume would trace Welles's life from 1947 when, at the end of those five largely unsuccessful years, he seemed to throw in the sponge, and stomped off to Europe. There, on and off (but mostly on), he spent the next twenty years of his life. He then returned to America, where he passionately pursued a number of projects which never reached completion – the only two films he finished from then until his death in 1985 were both in fact made in Europe.

Knowing that I had this difficult Wellesian period in my sights, friends sympathised with me – 'how sad it is,' they said, 'such a terrible decline.' But I have never shared that view. Welles did it his way. If he had modified his behaviour – if he had trimmed his sails, if he had pulled in his horns – he could have made many more films. But he would not then have been the force of nature that he was. He would just have been another film-maker. As it was, this period in Welles's life left behind him at least two films, *Touch of Evil* and *Chimes at Midnight*, that are remarkable by any standards, plus extraordinary work in several other media – but above all I looked forward to tracing that arc as Welles struck out towards the unknown region.

Such was my plan. But I was baulked by Welles himself. His prolificity during these years was so immense, the circumstances surrounding every venture (successful or unsuccessful) on which he embarked were so complex and extraordinary, and the ambitiousness of his approach to each was so unfettered, that had I attempted to encompass nearly forty years from 1947 till his death, the book would have run to considerably more than a thousand pages; just lifting it without an osteopath in attendance would have been risky. It has therefore seemed entirely logical to end this third volume with *Chimes at Midnight*, the film widely thought to be Welles's masterpiece and unquestionably his most personal work. It is also a culmination of his work in the theatre, to which – with his production of Ionesco's *Rhinoceros* – he finally bade farewell after an epoch-defining quarter of a century of provocative activity. This leaves a fourth – and truly final – volume to deal with his last two decades of unceasing exploration and experimentation, most of it in conjunction with a collaborator who was also his muse and his mistress, who inspired him to venture into territories where he had as yet never been.

★

The present volume is called *One-Man Band* for obvious reasons. Frustrated in his dealings with every studio he ever worked for, Welles made a full declaration of independence with his film of *Othello*, taking on more and more of the functions associated with film-making: raising the money, designing, editing, sometimes even shooting scenes himself. He only ever worked for a Hollywood studio – with its clearly demarcated roles and its hierarchical structure – on one more occasion after his self-exile; otherwise, he was free. But with that freedom came the possibilities of chaos, and chaos (or something very like it) was the element in which he moved for most of his remaining career.

It is a life like no other, and as before I have tried to give an impression of what it was like to live that life, and to have been part of it, to be plunged into what Micheál MacLiammóir so drolly called the Welles vortex. Welles packed more living into his life, pursued more professions, thrust out in more directions and formed more intense relationships than any twenty men put together. It is this life that has interested me, of which the *making* of movies was such a central and integral part, more than the finished results, remarkable as they often were. This sets me apart from many students of Welles for whom Welles the auteur is their sole focus. Welles would not have understood that, or approved of it. 'I'm profoundly cynical about my work and about most works I see in the world,' he told *Cahiers du Cinéma* in 1958. 'But I'm not cynical about the act of working on material . . . it's the act that interests me, not the result; and I'm taken by the result only when it gives forth the odour of human sweat or human thought.' He considered all of his work to be, as he said again and again, simply a series of experiments. His work was central to his life; each one of his major films emerged out of quite extraordinary personal circumstances and were made in the most extraordinary conditions, to the degree that the making of them is almost as fascinating as the films themselves. And that, too, would have seemed just as it should be to Welles.

He was a quintessential romantic artist: for him the experience of making his essentially subjective works – whether for the cinema or the theatre – was an end in itself. Truffaut liked to quote Welles's comment that he believed that 'a work is good to the degree that it expresses the man who created it'. And the process of creation, for him, was impossible without inspiration. Craft, skill, intelligence, planning, all admirable in themselves, were nothing without inspiration. Sometimes it came to him and sometimes it didn't. But he was always trying to provoke it, in himself and in his collaborators: always trying to storm the citadel of creativity. The romantic approach to art is as much about the artist's experience as it is about the audience's. The classical artist tries to create something objective – objectively true, objectively beautiful – and he or she is governed by a conception of fidelity: to the material, to the form and to the audience. The romantic is inspired by the idea of freedom: freedom of expression, freedom of feeling, freedom from the audience's expectations. The romantic artist says: 'Take it or leave it; this is what I feel, believe, want. Share it.' The classical artist says: 'This is a distillation of what I have understood. Use it.' The romantic artist is a child still, the classical artist, grown-up, for better or for worse, in both cases. Welles was not Michelangelo, he was Leonardo (to whom he did in fact compare himself, with all due modesty); Leonardo who, in the end, didn't care whether *The Last Supper* lasted; all he wanted was the experience of having painted it. Welles told André Bazin and Charles Bitsch in an interview with *Cahiers du Cinéma*:

> We professional experimenters have inherited an old tradition. Some of us have been the greatest of artists, but we never made our muses into our mistresses. For example, Leonardo considered himself to be a scientist who painted rather than a painter who was a scientist. Don't think that I compare myself to Leonardo; I'm trying to explain that there's a long line of people who evaluate their work according to a different hierarchy of values, almost moral values.

Occasionally (perhaps quite often) what happened with Welles on the location or in the rehearsal room was more remarkable than what ended up on the screen or on the stage. Sometimes, the process itself revealed the inadequacy of the material, human or otherwise, and he lost interest. His procedures were all his own, and they rarely fitted in with anything that a production manager or a studio executive had planned. In a sense, this approach of his was at core innocent, resembling the delight a child takes in inventing, in pretending, in transforming the materials at hand into projections of its imagination. But with the innocence of childhood sometimes came its tantrums, its evasions, its cruelty, its destructiveness. That such childlike elements were connected to a highly sophisticated, well-stocked and subtle brain is equally striking.

All this is uncommon, and needs facing head-on. Welles often behaved very badly – at work and in life – and it simply will not do to pretend that this behaviour was the fabrication of gossips or enemies. Nor is it acceptable, it seems to me, to insist that omelettes cannot be made without the breaking of eggs. One cannot simply brush this side of his nature aside as if it were irrelevant or beneath discussion, for it explains a great deal of what it was like to be around Welles, and also a great deal of what it was like to *be* Welles. And that has, from the beginning, been my quarry: not in order to judge him, but to describe him, as one might wish to describe any great natural phenomenon. Because Welles was, indeed, phenomenal, not to mention extraordinary, egregious, unprecedented. What Kenneth Tynan said of Welles early in Welles's career remains a central insight: 'A fair bravura actor, a good bravura director, but an incomparable bravura personality.'

In the twenty-five years since I started writing, Welles studies have gone through a huge revolution. In 1989 he was a prisoner of two different guerilla factions: the semioticians, blissfully deconstructing him to the point at which he would no longer have recognised himself; and the demeaners, led by the late Charles Higham, determined to give Welles his comeuppance. A new genre emerged throughout the 1980s and 1990s in the form of books by professional critics who sought to understand themselves better through their examination of Welles's place in their lives. But in recent years, something far more interesting has started to happen: individual studies of the making of the films, free from either personal animus or theoretical bias, drawing on direct documentary evidence. Supreme among these books is *Orson Welles At Work* (2008), by the French scholars François Thomas and Jean-Pierre Berthomé, which is quite simply the most illuminating book about Welles to have appeared since Richard France's *The Theatre of Orson Welles* (1977), a similarly detailed account of what Welles actually did, as opposed to simply what he produced. An even more recent book, Alberto Anile's *Orson Welles in Italy* (2013), surveying both his professional and his personal experience in that country, has shed brilliant light on one of the most revealing and intriguing periods of Welles's life by carefully examining contemporary newspaper reports and interviewing the people who worked with him. My debt to both of these books is immense.

I have been inestimably helped in understanding what was going on in Welles's life by the existence of diaries – some published, some not – kept by key participants in the making of Welles's films, notably Micheál MacLiammóir's two diaries, Charlton Heston's published diary and his memoir, and Keith Baxter's memoir, which is a primary source for information about *Chimes at Midnight* on stage and on film. In addition, I have been given free access to the unpublished diaries of two of Welles's secretaries – Ann Rogers and Rita Ribolla – and the actress Fay Compton (Emilia in *Othello*). George Fanto, Welles's cameraman on *Othello,* allowed me to read his unpublished memoir of working with Welles. I have also conducted over a hundred interviews with those who knew Welles intimately, starting in 1989; as far as I know, many of the interviewees spoke only to me, and many of them are now dead. From all of this abundant material I have tried as faithfully as possible, using a polyphony of voices, to bring Welles and his world to life. Nobody who ever met Welles doubted that they had encountered someone exceptional, and, to an unusual degree (perhaps paralleled only by the case of Dickens), people were moved to capture him in words: in letters, in interviews, in journals. It is to these testimonials that I have most frequently turned, more than to critical studies or film histories. They have often identified the connective tissue in events that have seemed otherwise isolated and illogical, and through their words things that seemed impossible or absurd began to make sense. Reading these accounts, I have begun to sense the existence of a continuous Welles, not one that simply staggers from one anecdote to another. The technique I have applied in trying to organise all this material may perhaps be compared to the way in which Welles edited his films: I have juxtaposed and woven together images, incidents, phrases, seeking (sometimes by means of echoes, sometimes sharp contradictions) to give an impression of how Welles moved through life. The greatest challenge has been to deal with the simultaneity of his activities. A month of Welles's life is worth a year, maybe a decade of anyone else's. He always seems to be, in Stephen Leacock's immortal phrase, galloping off in all directions, whether in pursuit of a woman, a film, a theatre company or a history of world economy; he's always editing, directing, acting, designing, screenwriting, making a speech, painting; in one moment paying loving homage to a long-forgotten style, in the next forging an entirely radical new one.

I have not attempted to psychoanalyse Welles, though the temptations are immense – why all those false noses? What was it about those enormous cigars? Why did he grow to such unfeasibly huge dimensions? I have not attempted it, because it is beyond my competence to do so, but also because I want to know what he *was*, rather than how he became that. The man has been my quarry, but unlike Ahab I have not sought to kill him or to stuff him, rather to capture him alive and kicking.

Captain Ahab stalks this period of Welles's life, as do King Lear and Falstaff and Don Quixote de la Mancha – mighty, mythic figures, as he was himself. The figure of Prometheus also lurks in the background: Orson bound, Orson having his liver pecked out by vengeful birds. 'The titan, however, has to undergo his punishment precisely because he continuously tries to go beyond,' in the words of Annamaria Vassalle. 'He appears to us in chains, tortured by the longing for dominating the indomitable and overwhelmed by the anguish for the inevitable lack of control over what has no limits.' My approach has changed somewhat from the one I took in *The Road to Xanadu*, in which I was determined to correct the myths that Welles and others had spun about him. Now I'm more inclined to believe that the man *was* the myth – or rather, that he grew into his own myth. He passed through the world like a figure from an old tale, a giant and a wild man, like the Orson of the early French romance. This was the authentic way for him to be; he knew of no other way. He is nothing if not egregious. Perhaps his very extraordinariness is the key to him. Peter Brook observed long ago that he was just so much bigger, so much fuller, than anyone else, that it was hard for him to deal with us, and hard for us to deal with him.

Perhaps Falstaff, also huge in every way, is really the key figure. It was the part he loved above all others, the part he played better than all others. In a life that was lived mythically one is tempted to think of him as another Ahab, a second Lear, Don Quixote born again, but in the end it is Falstaff whom he most completely resembles, both in his girth and his profound innocence. Like Falstaff he was mendacious, self-vaunting, crafty, slothful, financially dishonest, indulgent, greedy, exploitative, but like the fat knight, he is also deeply, irrepressibly on the side of life, a force of nature, ablaze with energy. His energy is astonishing and unceasing. But it would not be correct to describe him as a driven man, a Dickens or a Laurence Olivier – men whose goals were clearly defined, and whose very lives seemed to depend on achieving them. Longfellow famously described Dickens as *fato profugus* – driven, like Orestes, by Furies – and the same might have been said of Olivier. With Welles there was simply a constant supply of energy which could be squandered on anything; he seemed to give himself with equal fervour to all of his projects, whether vaudeville, radio comedy or filming the classics. It was simply in his nature, not a neurotic symptom, simply a physical or maybe a psychical condition. Also, finally, like Falstaff he was a lord of misrule, upsetting convention, upending normal practice and regular relationship; chaos followed in his wake, but the chaos was often invigorating, life-affirming, liberating – even necessary.

★

In *The Road to Xanadu*, I described the extraordinary eruption of energy, talent and personality that was the young Orson Welles and traced his impact on the theatre, on the radio and on his times; I ended the book with his arrival in Hollywood and the triumphant creation of *Citizen Kane* after an alarming period during which, despite his unprecedentedly generous contract with RKO Studios, he was unable to light on a subject which satisfied both him and the studio. *Citizen Kane*, though not a commercial success, was widely acclaimed as perhaps the greatest film that had ever been made, an astonishing achievement for a young man, barely twenty-five, who had never so much as acted in a film before, much less directed one. In *Hello Americans* I described the souring of his relations with RKO; the debacle of his aborted wartime project in Brazil, *It's All True*, and the subsequent (and to some extent consequent) mutilation by the studio of his second film for RKO, *The Magnificent Ambersons*; his increasing estrangement from Hollywood; and his refashioning of himself into, firstly, a radio entertainer, then (both in print and on the air) a political commentator. To the envious wonder of the movie-going world, he married Rita Hayworth – and then he divorced her. He made three films in this period, all critically unsuccessful: *The Stranger, The Lady from Shanghai* (with Hayworth) and *Macbeth*. He returned to the stage with *Around the World*, a spectacular musical which was a financial disaster. The book ended with Welles – heavily in debt to the Inland Revenue and disgusted with the rise of right-wing demagoguery in America – leaving the United States for Europe, where he would go on to open up new territories of artistic enterprise.

The present volume witnesses what amounts to a one-man diaspora, as he hurls himself around the globe, turning himself into an independent film-maker, running from pillar to post, balancing original work with what the French so eloquently call *travaux alimentaires*, and trying his hand at pretty much anything that will buy him a few more feet of film. Over the course of thirty years, he shoots a version of *Don Quixote*, during which time both his Quixote and his Sancho Panza die and the child heroine becomes a middle-aged woman; it is never finished. His life becomes a sort of continuous and barely contained implosion, but somehow, astonishingly, he keeps making films, among them his masterpiece, *Chimes at Midnight*, a love offering to Falstaff and his creator.

Welles told his semi-authorised biographer Barbara Leaming that when he died there would be no end of books about him. And he was right. Of concurrent and contradictory rival versions of Welles's story there is never an end. How he would have loved that! Each successive book refuses to acknowledge the discoveries of the one before. That would have amused him, too. But more remarkable yet has been his extraordinary after life: he has appeared in novels, in plays, in films. There is now a whole profession of Orson-impersonator. The man looms quite as large as his work. Like many such great figures – like Dickens, like Balzac – he seemed to know far more than us ordinary people, and at the same time far less. He was one of the most remarkable men of his time. He cannot be extinguished. The spirit goes on.

CHAPTER ONE

The Most Beautiful Baby of 1947

IT WAS money, to begin with, that drove Orson Welles to seek work in Europe. He needed to escape the pressing demands of the Internal Revenue Service, which was hounding him for back-taxes he had incurred during his recent Broadway fiasco, *Around the World*, so the offer of $100,000 to appear in Gregory Ratoff's melodrama *Black Magic* (or *Cagliostro*, as it was known in some quarters), which was about to start shooting in Italy, proved compelling. Welles, it goes without saying, played the eponymous magus – to the hilt, and beyond, on and off screen, terrorising the set with his extravagant and capricious behaviour. It was the beginning of a relatively brief period in which he played leading roles in films made in Europe; by the early 1950s he settled into occupying the high-powered cameo roles with which he continued to make his living almost to the end of his life. He was candid about his lack of interest in these parts, and indeed in acting altogether: directing was what interested him.

He was continuously erupting with projects, constantly on the lookout for ways in which to make the sort of films that interested him, in the way he wanted to make them. And America in 1947 was clearly not the place where he was going to be able to do that. If he hadn't worked it out for himself, Charlie Chaplin was on hand to tell him. Hollywood, Chaplin had announced, was dying. 'Look, if you will, at Orson Welles . . . his career and fate were decided when he said no to the Hollywood magnates. He no longer has a career or life in Hollywood.'[1] Both Chaplin and Welles (and the Russian-born Ratoff, as it happens) were under attack in a post-war America that was daily becoming more politically intolerant; all three had been denounced for their supposed communist associations, and all of them were finding it hard to work. Chaplin's *Monsieur Verdoux* – inspired by a story about a serial murderer, suggested to Chaplin by Welles – had left a nasty taste in the mouth of the American public; and Welles's most recent film, a *Macbeth* shot in twenty-seven days after a short run on stage, had been received derisively, the latest in a series of flops, not least among them the very public failure of his marriage to America's sultry sweetheart, Rita Hayworth.

So, on many levels, Welles was not at all unhappy to be out of America. Pastures new! He already had a three-film contract, signed in 1946, with the Anglo-Hungarian producer Alexander Korda, which he still hoped would come to something, though it appeared to have stalled. Their schemes had included a version of Oscar Wilde's *Salome*, which foundered because he and Korda could not agree on casting; a *War and Peace*, which it is hard to believe either of them ever took seriously (it was supposed to have been shot in Russia during the war); and a *Cyrano de Bergerac*, which was close to pre-production, but collapsed when Korda sold the rights in the play to the American actor José Ferrer. Welles continued to work on it fitfully with the designer Alexandre Trauner, fresh from his triumph with *Les Enfants du Paradis,* and the great Provençal writer Marcel Pagnol, while continuing to edit and re-edit his *Macbeth* in a variety of new versions, each more unpopular than the one before.

He was as project-fecund as ever: he kept working on his modern version of Pirandello's *Enrico Quarto* for Korda; he was talking loosely about filming *King Lear* in America and, more concretely, *Othello*, but that, he knew, he would never be able to film in America. His business partner Richard Wilson, still gallantly manning what was left of the Mercury office and continuing to steer *Macbeth* through troubled waters, had investigated the censorship position with regard to *Othello*: under the heading 'Sex', 'and listed right under "Sex perversion and White Slavery"', he found Item no. 6: 'Miscegenation (sex relationship between the black and white races) is forbidden.'[2] Wilson had had a conversation with Edward Small, the producer of *Black Magic*, about filming *Othello* in Italy; Small wanted to know if it could be done for 100 million lire (the equivalent of nearly $2 million today). Without answering this directly, Wilson reminded Small that the picture would be done entirely on location, partly in Venice, with somewhere else (probably Sicily) standing in for Cyprus, and – rather sensationally, given Welles's frequently reiterated commitment to black-and-white – that it must be in colour.[3]

Italy, where Welles remained in readiness for his next film, *Prince of Foxes,* in which he was to play Cesare Borgia, was clearly the ideal place in which to make the film, for more than purely geographical reasons. Thanks to the strict regulations governing withdrawal of money from the country, Italy was experiencing a boom in film-making: American co-productions, inflated Technicolor historical epics, for the most part; while home-grown production, encouraged by government funding, was having its neo-realistic golden age, led by Vittorio De Sica, Roberto Rossellini and Luchino Visconti. Despite post-war economic doldrums, Italy was a bracing place to be.

From the moment of his dramatic arrival in Rome in early November of 1947, six hours late, in a plane that had very nearly run out of fuel, Welles – newly slim, moustached and curly-haired for his role as Cagliostro – plunged straight into the swirling currents of Italian life. Swept away to the Excelsior Hotel, he was required to declare his race; in the hotel's register he duly entered 'Negro'.[4] His presence in Italy was not reported until two days later, accompanied by a photograph whose caption proclaimed him 'The Most Beautiful New Baby of 1947'. The following day he held a press conference, at which he was exposed for the first time to Italian Arts Reporting: questions were evenly divided between his alleged espousal of formalism (a heinous crime in neo-realist Italy) and his divorce from Rita Hayworth. In fact, the reporters knew very little about Welles, apart from his split from the most beautiful woman in the world, *Citizen Kane*, which had not yet been released in Italy, and vague rumours of *The War of the Worlds* broadcast ten years earlier. Welles brushed aside questions about Rita and elegantly deflected questions about formalism: what interested him, he said, was Italy today. He was hoping to meet both the Prime Minister and the head of the Communist Party, Palmiro Togliatti, who, as it happens, was just about to lead the newly fledged republic in a General Strike. Welles never met the Prime Minister, but he did meet Togliatti just a couple of weeks later; they had an amiable conversation over supper, which, Welles told the press, they had conducted in Spanish – a language he had picked up, he said, while fighting in the Civil War;[5] new country, new fabrications. The meal was widely reported and, indeed, photographed. What was Welles up to, one wonders? He had not hobnobbed with leading communists in the United States; indeed, he had of late been keeping a low profile, politically speaking. Did he want to make it clear that he was no Hollywood featherweight? Or was he perhaps consciously giving the finger to J. Edgar Hoover? If so, he certainly reached his target: the meeting was feverishly reported by an FBI informant, but the incident – and perhaps Welles himself – was deemed so politically insignificant that shortly afterwards his risk level was officially reduced.[6]

For the rest, he hurled himself into Roman high society and was enthusiastically welcomed, or so it seemed. In fact, the Roman *beau monde* clasped the newcomer tightly to its bosom only in order to facilitate a closer scrutiny of his flaws. Welles's particular form of exuberance was received, in certain quarters, with patrician disdain. As in Brazil in 1942, his immediate embrace of a new culture was characteristically all-consuming. He wanted to know everything, to learn the language, to celebrate its history. This enthusiasm was not wholly reciprocated. The Via Veneto pronounced that he drank too much, that he was too loud, too tall, had too many opinions, too colourfully expressed, chased Italian women too openly and dressed absurdly. He was, in fact, altogether Too American, which is ironic given his highly critical attitude to his native land, and its to him. But Welles arrived at a moment when post-war Italy had suddenly had enough of American largesse, American arrogance, American omnipresence, while still being quite keen on American money.

These attitudes all coalesced with the film Welles had come to make, *Black Magic*, the highly visible embodiment of America's presence in Italian life. It afforded work, both for the studios and all the associated ancillary trades. But it also meant that Rome was overrun by foreigners, not least the seventy or so Russian extras that Ratoff had imported, who were tramping all over the Quirinale Palace and other great monuments. The atmosphere on the film was in general somewhat deranged, by no means helped by Welles, who behaved disgracefully throughout, particularly towards the director. Cruelly whimsical, like a Nero or a Caligula, he baited Ratoff mercilessly, arguing relentlessly with him, until he would finally dismiss him with a much-repeated phrase: 'Grischa, you need a rest.' Among other caprices, Welles demanded the constant presence on set of three Muses, who were duly recruited from the unemployed population, given contracts and made to sit around looking decorative. He refused to appear at the studio until lunchtime and then quite openly directed his own scenes long into the night; Ratoff's directing was confined to the morning.[7]

It is notable that until the day he died, Welles behaved more or less badly on virtually every film he did not direct. The source of this bad behaviour was simple: humiliation. He felt that it was beneath him to appear in other, *inferior*, men's work. As much as possible, he took over any film in which he acted. He invariably rewrote his own part: in the case of *Black Magic,* he attempted – much to the dismay of the director – to turn the character of Cagliostro, a conman and lecher, into a revolutionary figure; often, as he did on *Black Magic,* he made forceful and hard-to-resist suggestions about the shooting of the scene itself. Thus traces of Welles's directorial hand are to be found, phantom-like, in many another man's film; on the whole, and insofar as it is possible to identify them with certainty, they are nothing to shout about. How could they be? The essence of a Welles film is its unique character, his personality imprinted on it from beginning to end. A quick burst of Welles in the middle of someone else's movie is meaningless, or worse: it makes the rest of the film seem dull, and exposes Welles's directorial mannerisms.

Black Magic, derived from the elder Alexandre Dumas's novel *Joseph Balsamo*, was a subject after Welles's own heart: not only was magic at its centre, but he had wanted for some years to make a film about the Dumas dynasty. He identified closely with the novelist – a giant, like himself, and, like Welles, very relaxed about other people helping to create the works that went out under his name. Dumas was a quarter black, a self-proclaimed quadroon, and that too must have fascinated Welles, who was always deeply drawn to black culture of every kind. The film's producer, Edward Small, was also a Dumas obsessive, and it is framed by Dumas *père* telling the tale to his son; who knows how Welles would have told the story, but it would surely have been more interesting than *Black Magic*. Welles's performance in the film, though he had never been, and was never again to be, in better shape physically, lacks any frisson. As the young Cagliostro, he has some of the charm and most of the energy of the young Charles Foster Kane, but – despite some very intense close-ups of his admittedly beautiful eyes – there is no sense of the magus about the performance, no sense of esoteric energy, no charisma in either the conventional or the theological senses. He makes all the right shapes, but is unable to unsettle us or to surprise us. It is an entirely conventional performance by a far from conventional-looking man. Surprisingly, given Welles's fascination with magic and the personal power many people experienced coming from him, the performance lacks force.

Welles's frustration with the film is, of course, understandable: none of the many projects he was brewing for himself to direct showed any sign of happening. And here was a great chunk of mediocrity, with eye-watering budgets and apparently limitless time lavished on it. Many people have these feelings when they work on high-budget movies. But Welles, being Welles, was unable or unwilling to conceal his feelings; he must assert his status. And anyone who failed to acknowledge it, in whatever way (perceived or actual), got it in the neck. Some years later, when Richard

Fleischer was working with him on *Crack in the Mirror*, Welles was approached by the stills photographer, who came over to show him some photos for his approval. 'Orson drew himself up as though he were a king addressing a scullery knave,' wrote Fleischer:

> 'How dare you interrupt me,' Welles said imperiously, 'while I'm talking to the director? Your pictures aren't worth looking at, anyhow. You attach too much importance to them, as though they were works of art. Well, there's no art to taking snapshots. Anybody can do it. All you need is a camera, and if you take enough pictures one of them is liable to turn out all right by sheer chance. Now leave us alone,' and he dismissed him with a wave of his hand. 'Good God, Orson,' I said, 'you treated that poor guy as though you were royalty.' 'I *am* royalty!' replied Welles.[8]

And of course he was; but, as Fleischer did not fail to point out, royalty in exile, royalty dispossessed: his regal outbursts were impotent, his victims unworthy of him.

Welles's social life was pretty rackety, slightly on the fringes of the *beau monde*. He began to create his own circle, among them a Pole named Michał Waszyñski (or Michael Washinsky as he was more commonly known), whom Welles had met on *Black Magic*, where he performed the much-needed function of interpreter. Washinsky was exactly the sort of person with whom Welles liked to surround himself: born in a Polish *shtetl*, as a young man he moved to Berlin and became assistant to the director of *Nosferatu*, the great F.W. Murnau, returning to Poland where he soon became the most prolific Polish film director of his time, shooting, it was said, one in every four films made in that country. Among them was *The Dybbuk*, the greatest of all Yiddish films. After the invasion of Poland, Washinsky escaped to Białystok, where he directed in the theatre, highly successfully; as soon as the Polish army was formed, he joined it, taking part in the Battle of Cassino, which he filmed for the army. At the end of the war he stayed in Italy, where he directed three films, after which he joined the mayhem on *Black Magic*, as an interpreter. And he and Welles instantly became bosom pals, both highly inventive fabulists, mirror images of each other, according to Washinsky's biographer: deep down, Welles longed to be a Jew from central Europe, a wandering artist with a mysterious past, while Washinsky had reinvented himself as a Catholic nobleman, universally known as The Prince and fraternally embraced as such by aristocrats. Washinsky knew everyone and could get hold of anything, and seems to have made it his business to make life very comfortable for Welles, one way and another.[9]

Welles meanwhile had acquired the unhelpful reputation in Rome of being a jinxed person – *iettatore*. During the filming of *Black Magic* the Zoppé Circus, a troupe of pyrotechnically brilliant acrobats, had pitched their tent outside the Scalera Studios, and Welles, bored with usurping Ratoff, felt irresistibly impelled to make a film of them, so he prevailed upon the production manager to set up a little shoot for him. During filming an accident occurred: while one of the Zoppé girls was flying on the trapeze, a rope broke and she fell in the middle of the track. The press reported it as an example of the sort of chaos Welles brought with him – somewhat unfairly, since, as he pointed out, she survived unharmed. This little impromptu shoot is an example of what was to become an ever more crucial part of Welles's modus operandi, one which, since Brazil, he had had little chance of practising: using the camera as a sketchpad, catching the fleeting moment, following his impulse, wherever it might take him. He claimed that Korda had asked him to make a film set in a circus, and that this Zoppé sequence would fit into it, somehow, somewhere. And who knows? It might well have done. More importantly, it kept Welles's directorial hand in, however briefly.

His projects for Korda having by this point all slipped away, he was actively looking for ways of getting *Othello* off the ground. Despite *Macbeth*'s continuing ill-favour, he was still interested in the idea of filming specially mounted stage productions, so he responded warmly to a suggestion from Bob Breen of the American National Theater and Academy (ANTA), which had produced his *Macbeth* on stage, that he might like to do something with them for the second Edinburgh International Festival of Music and Drama, in August 1948.[10] This seemed an ideal way to make the film, at much-reduced costs: $718,580 for the film, they reckoned, plus $64,000 for the play. In Hollywood it could not have been filmed for less than $2.5 million. They tried to involve Korda, who, under the terms of his contract with Welles, was already underwriting his living expenses in Italy to the tune of 3 million lire, but Korda declined, sceptical of the quality of what they would achieve for the money. Welles and Wilson forged ahead, nonetheless. On 1 March 1948 Welles was announced to play in *Othello* from 23 August to 4 September, performing at the city's oldest and most beautiful theatre, the Royal Lyceum; the Old Vic Company had graciously withdrawn its offering to allow Welles's production to take place. 'ORSON WELLES WILL BE FESTIVAL STAR,' rejoiced the *Scotsman* in a banner headline. 'His *Othello* will be eagerly awaited.' 'This year's Festival more than ever deserves the title International,' said the Glasgow *Daily Record*, 'with the inclusion of an American company in *Othello* with Orson Welles in the title role.' His career up to that point was excitedly recapitulated by local journalists; possible problems about paying for the visit were publicly agonised over, since Scotland had no dollars with which to pay the bills.

They need not have worried. Just ten weeks later the visit was making headlines again: 'FESTIVAL BLOW ORSON WELLES NOT COMING TO EDINBURGH'.[11] Welles and Wilson had decided they had too much on their plates to go straight from a theatre show into film production; fictitious difficulties over the building of the non-existent set were proffered as reasons for the withdrawal of the production, and not entirely believed. The City Fathers were far from pleased; they had already sold 61 per cent of the tickets. Edinburgh had to console itself with the transfer of a sell-out Broadway production of *Medea*: directed by John Gielgud, it starred the Scottish actress Eileen Herlie, which was not without a certain irony for Welles, since it was his determination to cast her in the proposed film of *Salome* that had caused his fallout with Korda and the demise of the project. The cancellation of the Edinburgh *Othello* also spelt the end of Welles's uneasy association with ANTA. If he was going to have anything to do with an American National Theater – and he never entirely stopped dreaming about it – it would be on his own terms, and it would have nothing to do with what he considered the sort of worthiness embodied by ANTA.

In truth, putting *Othello* on stage was never a high priority for Welles; it was always *Othello* the movie that interested him. He was now newly focused on the film because he had fallen overwhelmingly in love with a brilliant twenty-eight-year-old Italian actress called Lea Padovani, and he was determined that she would play Desdemona to his Othello. Striking rather than conventionally beautiful and somewhat on the short side, Padovani had had a huge success on stage in Rome with Cocteau's *Les Parents Terribles*, and Welles had immediately been besotted by her. He courted her unrelentingly, appearing every night at the stage door. But she was impervious to his blandishments. The more she refused him, the greater his conviction that his life was meaningless until he had conquered her. For a self-confessed Don Juan, for whom the chase was all – mere possession an anticlimax – this tactic of Padovani's was triumphantly successful; Welles remained besotted for a full year, humiliating himself ever more deeply. He told his friend Alessandro

Tasca that he had always known that one day something of the sort would happen to him, 'but I never thought it would happen when I was young'.[12] 'For him,' Padovani said years later, 'love was a delirium. He followed me everywhere, sat in his car under my window just to see me for a few moments.' This, it appears, was an entirely new experience for Welles.[13] 'Up till now,' he told his biographer, Barbara Leaming, 'I'd only ever thought of women as pleasure, like a glass of wine when you're thirsty, or a dish when you're hungry.'

Padovani broke off her engagement to a young Italian actor, and she and Welles flew to Venice to announce their engagement, stage-managed by the veteran socialite Elsa Maxwell: 'BOY WONDER AND CREATOR OF MARS INVASION TO MARRY UNKNOWN ACTRESS,' said the headline. Despite these public avowals, their relationship was unconsummated. It was nothing but turbulent, made worse, Welles believed, by their having no language in common. He went back to the United States for a month, partly out of frustration; on his return to Europe he spent a few days with Rita Hayworth, first in Cannes, then at Cap d'Antibes, during which, according to Welles, she begged him to resume their relationship. But Welles only had eyes for Padovani and, when he got back to Rome, he announced that he would be filming *Othello* with her as Desdemona; he would finance the film himself, he said. He wrote to Roger Hill back at the Todd School for any reels of film he could spare, black-and-white. And then he moved out of the Excelsior Hotel into a splendid mansion, the Casal Pilozzo in Frascati, just outside Rome, with the still-unconquered Padovani and her immediate family.

Cagliostro could scarcely have done better for himself. The mansion had but recently belonged to the former Fascist minister Giuseppe Bottai, who had built it on land on which the residence of the sister and nephew of the Emperor Trajan had stood. In the subsoil under the house were ancient cellars extending outwards for over a hundred yards; in their depths was an altar, with a tabernacle carved out of tufa soil. There Welles created his establishment, with Rita the secretary, Angelo the driver, Enrico the major-domo, and Enrico's wife, Emilia, the cook. Harriet White Medin, hired to give English lessons to Padovani, was a regular visitor to the household and reported something like a reign of terror. 'When he [Welles] bellowed his stomach would swell and his eyes would go up on the sides like a Chinese! Enrico, Emilia, Rita – everybody was going around with shaking knees because of Orson.'[14] He had a penchant for creating madcap establishments of this sort – the first house he had in Los Angeles at the start of his contract with RKO was equally colourful. When he went away, which he often did, the household, which fluctuated in size according to whom Welles had invited, lived *en prince.*

Among his guests left alone in the villa that summer of 1948 was Ernest Borneman, whom Welles had bumped into one foggy day by the Seine, and from whom he now commissioned a film treatment about Ulysses, a figure with whom the exiled, dispossessed Welles might have felt he had something in common. He had something in common with Borneman, too: the writer was the perfect paradigm of the sort of person with whom he liked to surround himself: polyglot, multidisciplinary, globe-trotting, people who had lived rich, complex, surprising, contradictory lives, but (unlike Welles) had not been widely recognised for it. Borneman was, inter alia, a crime-writer, film-maker, anthropologist, ethnomusicologist, jazz musician, jazz critic, psychoanalyst, sexologist and committed socialist. Welles's exact contemporary, he had been brought up in Berlin; as a lad he worked in Wilhelm Reich's sex clinics as well as with a world-famous ethnomusicologist; at seventeen, he escaped from the country posing as a member of the Hitler Youth (though he was in fact a member of the Communist Party) and went to England where, although he arrived speaking no word of English, he was soon making his living as a journalist. In 1937 Borneman wrote one of the great classics of detective fiction, *The Face on the Cutting-Room Floor*, following it up with an *Encyclopaedia of Jazz*. Deported to Canada during the war, he went back to London afterwards to work for the BBC, which is when he met Welles and was inevitably recruited to his entourage. Leaving his well-paid job working for UNESCO, Borneman accepted Welles's generous offer of $1,000 a week to work on *Ulysses* and duly appeared at the Casal Pilozzo with his wife, where he spent some time writing prolifically and happily enjoying the hospitality. There being no sign of any actual payment, he eventually sent Welles a telegram: 'WHAT CAN MY WIFE AND I DO TO MAKE ENDS MEET?' To this Welles replied with exquisite nonchalance: 'DEAR ERNEST LIVE SIMPLY AFFECTIONATE REGARDS ORSON WELLES.'

Such was life at the Casal Pilozzo under the reign of the Emperor Welles. When he was in residence, a critical figure in his entourage was the secretary. His favoured mode of letter-writing was rapid dictation; in addition he required someone to organise him. The burn-out rate of his secretaries was alarming: the speed of Welles's thinking, the rapidity of his changes of plan, the general chaos of his affairs – added to the rages, abuse, raillery, sarcasm and overall outrageousness of his conduct towards them – meant that few could stand the pace. Over the years a small number of remarkable women managed to stay the course. In May of 1948 Rita Ribolla, a young Viennese woman formerly married to an Italian, was handed the poisoned chalice. A remarkable linguist and currently assistant to the director of an important government agency, she suddenly found herself at the centre of Welles's operations, and since the personal and the professional were inseparable with him, that meant she was at the centre of his life. Sharp-eyed and sophisticated, she kept notes on her time with him, which give a startlingly vivid impression of what the thirty-three-year-old boy wonder was like, close up. He started as he meant to go on, when she first reported for duty at the Casal Pilozzo:

> At the far end of the terrace placed precisely in the centre between two enormous potted palms was a chaise longue. On it The Genius was reclining, draped in a flowing black robe, gazing into the setting sun. The butler theatrically announced me, he continued to gaze, I just stood there clutching the insignia of my trade. Finally the great man awoke out of his trance, turned to stare at us as if we were a mirage – then realisation must have dawned: through the orange and pink atmosphere came his voice – 'Dear Jonathan, you are missing the loveliest view, delicious food, good wines and my stimulating company, come at once.' Thus spake Zarathustra and turned back to the sunset. The butler had left and I stood there in the middle of nowhere and tried to think of a quotation which started with dear Jonathan and referred to view and food, then I noticed that my boss was trying to pierce me with his eyes. 'Your memory must be extraordinary' he said. 'Not at all, I'm afraid.' 'Then why don't you write down what I dictate?' So that's what the dear Jonathan was about: the beginning of a script, no doubt. But I was wrong, it turned out to be a cable 'What Jonathan, please?' 'What d'you mean by what Jonathan?' 'Well, he can't just be called Jonathan' 'Why not?' 'Because people usually have a last name. What's this gentleman's surname?' 'My God, don't you even know that?' 'How should I?' 'What kind of a secretary are you?' 'A new one.' 'Oh I see . . . it's Jonathan Seigneur.' I blushed, Seigneur was my secret screen idol and I'd never dreamt I could get so close to him. 'And his address?' 'Don't you even know that?' 'No.' 'Look it up in my address book.' So I looked for the butler (not far, he was hiding behind the drapes of the French window and listening) and he in turn looked for the book and there I found the address and he went to resume his stand on the terrace. 'Why haven't you

> gone yet, I want it dispatched immediately.' 'May I please have some money to do it?' 'Money???'[15]

Welles took Rita out for lunch the next day:

> He led me into the restaurant as if I were a precious porcelain figure, fussed over me like a passionate lover, managed to get the full attention of all waiters, ordered a meal which would have sufficed for a dozen hungry people and started out telling me some wonderful anecdotes. After the first course he changed to conjuring tricks. He oozed charm, ate an incredible amount of food, drank one glass of wine after the other. A one-time performance which held everyone (topped by me) spellbound. Hungry as I was, I could scarcely eat – just listen and laugh and wonder and be confused. 'Let's go,' he said, after we'd finished our coffee. I smiled and nodded affirmatively. We sat and looked expectantly at each other. Was he not going to ask for the check? 'Shall I ask for the check?' I timidly inquired. 'Of course.' Check was placed before him. He shoved it over to me. Waiter tactfully turned away. Stared at check in utter embarrassment. 'Something wrong?' Then he leaned over and whispered 'please leave a large tip for these nice waiters.' Managed to control my voice and told him I had by far not enough money with me. Furiously he asked how I dared go out with him with not enough money. Explained that I had not expected to take him out, especially not for a meal of that kind. But he had by then stomped out. Waiter was a darling and said I shouldn't cry: they knew the Signore well, men like he were too involved with creating to be bothered by such minor matters as paying which was well understood by il Padrone who was very proud and pleased to have him patronise the restaurant and was sure he'd get his money one day, anyhow. Wiped off the blue mascara running down my red face, grabbed my purse and made a fast exit. Went home and straight to bed. The only place to hide in my misery.[16]

And so it went on for three years, in a constant oscillation between delight and torment, between accusation and denial, sackings and resignations, affection and exasperation. Fascinated and appalled, Rita summed him up in a series of paradoxes: 'He calls himself a plain, simple man, but is the *ne plus ultra* of eccentricity. A complete extrovert, he refers to himself as being primarily a thinker. He can run the entire gamut of moods and feelings in a matter of minutes.

He expects to be understood without explaining, to receive without asking. But he is more of a giver than a taker. Time, money, distances mean nothing to him He does not accept no for a no, impossible for a fact.'[17] It was a relationship that Welles seems to have needed. Throughout his life, certain people – normally assistants, stage managers, press officers – were appointed to the position of sparring partner or, in extreme cases, whipping boy or girl. Sometimes they fought back. There is something of Lear's relationship to his fool about it: the king can behave foolishly, and the fool can assume regality. Welles dubbed Rita 'Miss Mud' or 'Miss Glum' and endlessly berated her for pretty well anything that happened, whether she was in any way involved with it or not. In these situations, Welles – at his best, brilliant, sophisticated, original, courageous – behaved like a monstrous adolescent or, more accurately, like a monstrous baby. And yet it was not mere caprice: there seems to have been some purpose behind all the posturing. It was a sort of test or challenge. How much would people put up with? What could he get away with? The bitch boy Eldred from *Bright Lucifer*, the spooky play the sixteen-year-old Welles wrote as some kind of self-exorcism, is somewhere there, lurking behind the civilised exterior, mocking, destroying.

★

In August of 1948, when he should have been treading the boards as Othello in Edinburgh, Welles was acting in the next big Italian–American co-production, *Prince of Foxes*, in the showy supporting role of Cesare Borgia; it was shot in Florence, Sienna and San Marino, as well as in the Scalera Studios again.[18] The Scalera brothers, Salvatore and Michele, had been slowly emerging from a cloud of disgrace: at the forefront of Mussolini's aggressive promotion of cinema during the war, churning out dozens of features and propaganda films, they were prosecuted after the fall of Mussolini for 'unjust enrichment'. They had since been busily trying to work their way back to respectability, and to that end had become involved in a number of co-productions. No doubt Michele had somewhere read about Welles's widely reported *Othello* plans; he sought out Welles and offered to produce the film. Welles delightedly accepted. Later he used to pretend that Scalera thought he was going to make a movie from Verdi's opera. What Scalera *did* think was that Welles was going to make the film with Italian actors (which would have enabled him to get government subsidies): Welles alone, he assumed, would be dubbed. This notion, which was not at all what Welles intended, mutated into a plan to shoot two versions simultaneously, in Italian and in English; that too quietly reverted to a single film in English, which would eventually be dubbed for Italy.

Meanwhile, in September 1948, there was the Venice Film Festival, in which *Macbeth* had been entered for the competition. Welles was intensely nervous about showing the film, which he had re-edited in Rome while appearing in *Black Magic*; meanwhile, Laurence Olivier's *Hamlet* had just come out in Britain and America, to pretty well unqualified acclaim, and Welles was darkly – and rightly – convinced that if you liked Olivier's film, you weren't going to like his. So he approached the festival with high trepidation. He and the perenially provocative Jean Cocteau formed a sort of anti-festival clique, clubbing together to commit what Cocteau rather wonderfully called *lèse-festival*. They had first met when the Frenchman had attended another, very different Welles *Macbeth*: the legendary all-black Voodoo production which the twenty-one-year-old Welles had directed in Harlem in 1936; Cocteau was vocal in his praise for both versions. Together in Venice, the two men behaved like two very naughty boys. Welles shocked his hosts by ostentatiously walking out of the showing of Visconti's uncompromisingly severe masterpiece, *La Terra Trema*. Like all contestants, he had a press conference, at which, under a certain amount of hostile questioning, he denounced the whole neo-realistic project (exempting only De Sica's *Shoeshine* from his strictures) as artistically dismal and politically retrograde, insisting that art required intervention; simply photographing real life was not enough. Nor, he said, could real people straight off the street – so beloved of the neo-realist directors – interpret the world; for that, you needed actors. He further attacked Giorgio Strehler's newly formed Piccolo Theatre in Milan, generally held to be a model of disciplined imagination; Welles found it bloodless. The only enthusiasm he could muster was for the great Neapolitan actor-writer-director Eduardo de Filippo, whose acting was, Welles said, 'the result not only of instinct and tradition but of research and application'.[19]

These remarks were not warmly received. Neo-realism was the prevailing aesthetic of the day, rigidly adhered to, and Italian critics and journalists of both right and left were for the most part implacably and aggressively opposed to anything that might diverge from it. To them, Welles's films, not to mention his personality, strongly smacked of the baroque, the ultimate brickbat in the contemporary critical lexicon. Criticism was polarised between the Roundhead and the Cavalier, and it was pretty clear which camp Welles belonged to. Reviewers had by now seen *Quarto Potere* (*Fourth Estate*), as *Kane* was renamed for Italy. The film had a tentative and very brief release; with few exceptions, the critics didn't care for it, seeing it as an empty display of technique and tarring it with the same brush as Welles's 1945 thriller, *The Stranger*, seen at the Venice Festival a year earlier and also disliked. Welles instinctively grasped how fundamentally irreconcilable to his work neo-realism was. For him, film was always artifice; it was a conjuring trick, an illusion. His purpose was to heighten, to distort, to intensify, to disturb perception; and for him, as he said on many occasions, editing was the supreme creative act. For an artist simply to train a camera on life was a dereliction of duty. It is perhaps a little ironic, in view of his spirited defence of acting, that so many of his own films are marred by indifferent performances, but they are nonetheless always performances; it is entirely predictable that the bovine gaze of Visconti's camera in *La Terra Trema* would drive the always mercurial Welles to distraction.

Calming down, he realised that this press conference had not gone well and would do *Macbeth* no good, so he asked for another, to explain himself more clearly. This he spectacularly failed to do. He was reported as 'gabbling uncontrollably', defending *Macbeth* as simply an alternative to mainstream Hollywood film-making, and denying any element of formalism in his work; he owed nothing, he said, to Fritz Lang or Eisenstein, nor did he feel any rivalry with *Hamlet*; but if *Macbeth* – 'produced by a small, independent outfit' – were to fail, it would, he said, be 'the end of the People's Theatre . . . mine is a small, low-budget film and I'm up against the British Empire'. If these remarks were designed to endear him or *Macbeth* to the committee, they failed. His special pleading was preposterous and transparent, said the Italian critic Tullio Kezich some years later: '*Hamlet* was produced by an Italian adventurer, Filippo del Giudice . . . who struggled to get backing for his films, as everyone did in those days.'[20]

This second press conference was a real disaster, prompting Welles to decide, in conjunction with Elsa Maxwell and the US Ambassador – as ill-advised a pair of counsellors as could be imagined – to withdraw the film from the competition. 'Why risk it?' Welles told *Daily Variety*, apparently under the assumption that only Americans would read the paper. 'It'll never be shown in Italy. Shakespeare can't be dubbed. Better keep it for an audience that understands it. Besides, they don't like me in Italy: my love for the country is unrequited. I know what they'll say, that I didn't have the guts to go up against Rank's *Hamlet*.'[21] Just as Welles feared, Olivier won the Golden Lion, with *La Terra Trema* – another triumph for neo-realism – winning an international prize. The whole episode had further soured Welles's relationship with the Italian press, which had taken another knock from Elsa Maxwell's reckless offensive on his behalf, proposing a boycott of the festival and doubting whether Italians were able to appreciate international films made in a democracy – unlike *Hamlet*, for example?

Nonetheless, while the festival was still running and he was still acting in *Prince of Foxes*, Welles took the huge gamble of starting to shoot *Othello* on location in Venice, with a camera crew headed by Alberto Fusi and Italian actors in all of the roles, except for Welles himself as the eponymous Moor, Iago, played by Welles's old chum Everett Sloane, *Kane*'s Mr Bernstein, and Bannister in *The Lady from Shanghai*, who happened to be acting with him in *Prince of Foxes*, and Emilia, who was played by Lea Padovani's English coach, Harriet White Medin. Padovani was, of course, Desdemona. Welles's flits from Florence to Rome, and Rome to Venice, including make-up changes, were achievable only because of Welles's superhuman levels of adrenalin. 'In Venice we'd elbow our way out again and down to the waiting motorboat,' wrote Rita Ribolla, who masterminded the whole operation:

> Vasco, the make-up wizard, would scarcely say 'hi' and before the boat roared around the first corner into one of the quieter canals, Borgia's beard would be off. The faster the boat whizzed, the faster Vasco worked. It took 8 to 10 minutes to get to the Hotel. It never took Vasco longer to change Borgia into Othello. When the driver slammed into reverse to stop the boat and the doorman stepped forward to hold out a helping arm, the Moor would emerge from the little cabin, step regally ashore, sweep one end of his floor length cape over the opposite shoulder and glide through the throbbing hall toward the elevator, curly head held high, beady jet black eyes staring straight ahead out of shiny black face.[22]

Lea Padovani was waiting for him:

> Upstairs, after he had folded Desdemona into his arms while we others looked discreetly into another direction, everyone would start talking at the same time – in various languages, of course. Then we'd see the rushes of the night before, afterwards scramble into boats and gondolas which took us to wherever we were shooting. If it was in the Palace of the Doges, we'd walk across Piazza San Marco and I'd often see people quickly cross themselves or put a protective hand over their startled eyes – wasn't that Venice's own

> Othello and his beautiful Desdemona in her flowing pale blue robes, flanked by the Doges in bright red, surrounded by the Nobles, calmly making their way through the masses of tourists?[23]

Padovani's English was far from perfect, which didn't matter yet because they were shooting without sound. Indeed, they were quite often shooting without Welles, who would be called away for days at a time to act in his Hollywood blockbuster, at which moments his stand-in – a giant of a man, Alfredo Lombardini, a local butcher – would substitute for him. On such occasions the shoot would be supervised by Michael Washinsky, whom Welles had appointed assistant director. The phantoms multiplied: a Welles who was not Welles, in a Welles film that was not being directed by Welles.

Othello's beautiful Desdemona was proving quite demanding. After ascertaining that the actresses would be allowed to keep their costumes, Padovani energetically objected to the lynx bordering on a cape that swept down into a long train. 'I think it would look better if it were completely lined with the fur,' she mused. 'You are perfectly right, of course it would,' replied Welles dotingly, and had it done. Obsessed by her, he ceded to her every demand, including appointing as his production manager Giorgio Papi, a married man with whom Padovani had been passionately involved throughout the period of Welles's infatuation with her. Welles's dawning realisation of this relationship was believed, by some of those who were around at the time, to be what fuelled his undentable determination to make a movie out of the most devastating account of jealousy in the whole of world literature.

Shooting abruptly came to a halt in early November, when Alexander Korda snatched Welles away from *Othello* to shoot a two-week cameo role in a film for which he would be paid the substantial fee of $100,000 – much needed, if filming was to continue. Welles could have had 10 per cent of the gross of the movie instead, which would in time (since the film in question was *The Third Man*) have meant a very large amount of money indeed, a fact that Welles never ceased to lament. But he was in a hurry; he needed the cash. He knew straight away that it was a very good screenplay, with a very good part indeed for himself, which cast its shadow over the entire film, however brief the actual screen time (just over eleven minutes), and despite (or perhaps because of) making his first appearance two-thirds of the way through the film; he also knew that Carol Reed was an excellent director, riding high on the recent international success of *The Fallen Idol*. But despite all that, Welles was determined to give Alexander Korda a hard time.

Though the great impresario had bailed him out three years earlier, at the time of his Broadway disaster *Around the World*, and had been subsidising him to the tune of 3 million lire since he had come to Italy, and though he still had an outstanding three-picture contract with him, either as director, actor-director or actor-director-writer, he felt ill-used by Korda. The cancellation of *Cyrano* rankled deeply with Welles, as did Korda's subsequent resistance to his adaptation of Pirandello's *Henry IV*, 'USING ONLY REAL LOCATIONS, SO NO STUDIO DEAL NECESSARY,' as Welles had telegrammed him: he had been ready to start lining up a cameraman and cast for it, but Korda had somehow remained unconvinced. So, out of sheer pique, though Welles had every intention of signing the contract, he made himself elusive when the time to do so arrived. Finally Korda sent his amiable brother Vincent to track Welles down.

'Two days later,' wrote Vincent's son, Michael, in his engaging memoir *Charmed Lives*, 'my father and I flew to Rome in pursuit of Orson.' In Rome, they were told at the Grand Hotel that 'Signor Welles had only just left for Florence.' In Florence, the concierge informed them that Welles had just departed for Venice, where, at the Danieli, the reception desk conveyed Welles's apologies: he had been obliged urgently to go to Naples. In Naples, naturally, they found that Welles had just parted for Capri. Once there, they saw a motorboat heading out towards the mainland at top speed. 'In the back, waving grandly to us, sat Orson, surrounded by a mound of luggage, on his way, as we soon discovered, from Naples to Nice.' They finally tracked him down to the Bonne Auberge in Cagnes-sur-Mer, where they found him 'eating the small raw artichokes of Provence, which were served with an anchovy sauce, before plunging into a steaming bouillabaisse and a roast chicken'. Welles waved them to his table, ordered more food and wine and resigned himself to his fate. Paying someone to stand watch over his door through the night, they collected Welles the following morning and got him on the plane to London, where he signed the contract and then went straight back to Rome. By now, *The Third Man* was shooting in Vienna, and Welles failed to show up for his first scene. This time Bob Dunbar, the assistant to the associate producer, was sent to fetch him; and finally, after a few more practical jokes, eyes twinkling, Welles arrived. What a naughty boy he could be, when he felt like it. And his naughtiness was by no means at an end.

What Welles didn't know was that his getting the part of Harry Lime at all – the part that was to be the most popular he ever played, in the most successful film in which he ever participated – had been very touch-and-go. Reed and Korda were keen (Korda in part because he wanted to redeem at least some of their three-picture deal contract), but Korda's American partner on the film, David O. Selznick, was bitterly opposed to Welles's involvement from the beginning. Cary Grant, Noël Coward and David Niven had already been proposed as alternatives; finally, when the two central male characters were reconceived as Americans, Robert Mitchum was keenly championed as Lime by Selznick. Welles was saved by the bell on that one when Mitchum, one of America's top grossers, was arrested for possession of marijuana, though Selznick continued to insist that casting Welles would be 'a detriment' to the picture: he was box-office poison – specially commissioned Gallup polls had proved it. 'While I do not profess knowing as much as Mr Gallup about box office values,' replied Korda in the feline tone he deployed when dealing with his pesky American running mate, 'I cannot believe him being a detriment . . . Carol thinks Orson could give a tremendous performance in this part. Picture greatly depends on Lime being extraordinary in attraction and superior in intellect.'[24]

Selznick seemed to accede, at which point Welles's *Macbeth* opened in America to villainously bad reviews, causing Selznick to exclaim that Welles would be a far more damaging name 'than has been in our worst fears to date'. How about Rex Harrison for the part? Korda drily informed Selznick that it was too late: Welles had been signed. Which, as it happened, he hadn't, though he would be soon enough. Korda was satisfied; as early as 1947 he had written a memo in which he stated his intention of making 'a photoplay, as yet untitled, to be directed by Carol Reed, starring Orson Welles'. The irony of these casting shenanigans is that the description of Harry in the novella Graham Greene wrote, before embarking on the screenplay and long before any casting was contemplated, is an almost precise description of Welles: 'Don't picture Harry Lime as a smooth scoundrel,' says Major Calloway. 'The picture I have of him on my files is an excellent one: he is caught by a street photographer with his stocky legs apart, big shoulders a little hunched, a belly that has known too much good food for too long, on his face a look of cheerful rascality, a geniality, a recognition that *his* happiness will make the world's day.'[25] On the other hand, Selznick's doubts about Welles's box-office appeal were not unfounded – that is, until *The Third Man*, which made him an international star.

Meanwhile he finally turned up, in a freezing wet Vienna in November, a week late. Reed and his first assistant director, Guy Hamilton, had filled in the time while they were waiting for Welles by shooting everything in which they could use a stand-in for Harry – Harry running away, Harry in the middle-distance, Harry and the cat; they even shot Harry's shadow. Either Hamilton or Otto Schusser, the butcher – another butcher! – who was Welles's stand-in, donned the heavy overcoat and hat in which they had chosen to disguise themselves; one or other of them would wear Harry's shoes, with Reed himself on one occasion volunteering his fingers for the shot of Harry's hand emerging from the ventilation slats of the sewer.[26] It has been estimated that Welles himself does *not* feature in a little over 30 per cent of the shots in which Harry appears. This may have set Welles a very useful precedent for his own film of *Othello*, in which, as he said, 'if you can't see the actor's face, you can be pretty certain it's not him.' In fact it would be his usual modus operandi from now on. Similarly, because of restrictions on filming in post-war Vienna, Reed and his art directors had been obliged to shoot sequences in which the geography was entirely artificial; in the immortal scene in which Harry makes his first appearance in Schreyvogelgasse, for example, when he turns the corner – except that it isn't actually him, of course – the street he appears to turn into was in reality half a mile away. This too would prove to be a very useful model for Welles.

His first shot in Vienna was to be in the sewers. When Welles realised what that entailed, he refused point-blank to descend. 'I come from California,' he is alleged to have cried. 'My throat! I'm so cold!' It is true that he suffered from various chronic respiratory conditions – asthma, hay fever, sinusitis – but the film crew was not inclined to be unduly sympathetic: the unending night-shooting, the logistical difficulties of the city itself, the non-cooperation of the various occupying authorities and the shortage of time meant they had been working around the clock, operating three units, with three cameramen, but just the one director. 'Somehow,' said Guy Hamilton, 'for 7 weeks, 3 hours sleep here, and three hours there, and lots of Benzedrine, Carol directed the whole sodding thing.'[27] A small thing like an intransigent star was not going to unsettle his calm. In the face of Welles's fastidiousness about going down into the sewer, the decision was rapidly made to reconstruct the sewers in Shepperton, where Welles was scheduled to film for a week in January. All he shot that week in November in Vienna was his first appearance in the doorway – the scene so brilliantly described in the original novella: 'a window curtain was drawn petulantly back by some sleeper he had awakened, and the light fell straight across the narrow street and lit up the features of Harry Lime'[28] – and a walk with Holly Martins (Joseph Cotten) to and from the Great Wheel in the Prater.

Welles stayed in Vienna for a week, hobnobbing with his old chum Cotten and somehow managing to get apprehended in a bar in which he was behaving somewhat noisily. 'The police of four armies have been sent to arrest me,' Welles declared, according to Sergeant Ken Sheridan, the British duty officer, in his extremely elegant official report of the incident. 'Mr Welles was a big man, and his bigness spread generously around him. He had several cronies, minions who circled and drifted around his perimeter and tried to emolliate the situation.' The Russian comrade was not amused, reported Sheridan, and kept his hand on his gun-butt. 'Mr Welles threw insults around at all of us, but as they were in American English, the Rusky never knew that he was being called a cock-sucker.' Welles was then taken to International Police HQ, which was run by Americans: 'I learned later that Mr Welles had been greeted with delight and given VIP treatment and a big booze-up with senior officers,' concluded Sergeant Sheridan.[29]

His week's work – a rather light week's work, it has to be said – completed, Welles returned to Venice and plunged immediately back into shooting *Othello*. It is not clear what exactly he shot, or whether any of it ended up in the film, but he and Trauner, now contracted to design the film, used the time to crystallise their approach; meanwhile Everett Sloane – a neurotic actor at the best of times – withdrew, no doubt finding the instability of the project too unnerving, which was probably all to the good, though the prospect of Mr Bernstein as Iago is a delectable one.

For the moment, money had to be made if the film was to happen at all. Welles, commissioned to do rewrites on *Portrait d'un Assassin* – a mad imbroglio about a crazed female impresario who forces a daredevil motorcyclist to perform the loop of death – had transferred his operation to Paris. There, comfortably holed up at the Lancaster Hotel with his old chum Charlie Lederer (currently married to the first Mrs Welles, the former Virginia Nicolson), he settled down to work. Welles was himself to have appeared in the film, which would have added considerably to the calorific content of a cast of positively life-threatening richness: Pierre Brasseur, Maria Montez, Erich von Stroheim, Arletty and Marcel Dallio (not to mention the Fratellini Brothers). In the event, Welles didn't appear in the film, and was before long being sued for 250,000 francs for not doing so by the producer Jacques Gauthier, who also demanded the return of his advance of 8,000 francs. Welles receives no credit on the film as writer, but is somewhat mysteriously listed by IMDb as having designed the film '(uncredited)'. He was everywhere that winter, his skilful fingers in many pies, a sort of celluloid odd-job man; amongst other things, reported Harriet White Medin, he supervised dubbing sessions on foreign movies, including those for *The Young Caruso*. Everything he earned was earmarked for *Othello.* On *Portrait d'un Assassin*, despite the unpleasantness of subsequent legal proceedings, not only did Welles earn a decent sum for the actual writing of the film, but one of the film's investors, Charles Phiber, a leading industrialist, agreed to underwrite *Othello* to the tune of 63 million lire.

So Welles must have approached Christmas 1948 with a mixture of feelings: a bruised heart, but the agreeable prospect of playing an excellent part in a good, well-written film, and reasonable hopes for *Othello*, if he could only secure a decent cast for it. He spent Christmas with the Cottens in their sumptuously decorated penthouse suite at the Lancaster; Cole Lesley, who had come with Noël Coward, almost at the end of his run of *Present Laughter*, in French at the Édouard VII, was another guest and received as a present a toy rabbit, which, he said, 'could hop across the room on its back legs while beating two little drums together with its front ones'. Welles, he reported, 'became insanely jealous of my rabbit and begged me to give it to him – it was four o'clock in the morning by now and the vodka had been flowing – but I couldn't bear to part with it and refused. He swore to me he would never forgive me and at the last night party of *Joyeux Chagrins* was still pointing me out to everybody as "that old meanie who won't give me his white rabbit".'[30] Rita Ribolla noted this curious trait of Welles's: 'He loves small toys, always seems to expect them as a present. Maids find (or do not find) them under beds, visitors trip over them, hostesses don't quite believe what they are seeing; now and then a child unsuccessfully tries to appropriate or successfully swaps one.'[31]

Despite these displays of perhaps rather forced high spirits, another guest, Elizabeth Montagu, who was the second production assistant on *The Third Man*, noted that 'Orson seemed unusually subdued. I suspect,' she wrote, 'he disliked playing second fiddle to the irrepressible Coward.' But the true source of the melancholy revealed itself later, when Welles recounted an anecdote concerning a young actress with whom he had been in love:

> She was then living with her parents, and as parental control was very strict, poor Orson was getting nowhere. When it became clear that he would never prise her out of the family circle, he decided that the next best thing would be to invite the entire

> family to be his guests at a luxury hotel on the Italian Riviera. His offer was gratefully accepted and soon afterwards Orson found himself paying the hotel bills, not only of his lady-love, but also of her parents, two sisters and a brother. As Orson was very much in love, he took the family group in his stride, except for the brother, whom he found obnoxious. However, the weather was still good, the sun shone brightly and long walks along the seashore with his love soon led to a tender relationship. When he proposed to her, she agreed to become secretly engaged to him.[32]

Welles rushed off to a jeweller's and the next morning, as they stood by the sea, he produced a magnificent ring, set with a huge diamond that sparkled and glittered in the sunlight:

> His fiancée tried it on and admired it, but then took it off her finger, replaced it in its box and put it in her handbag. Orson objected: 'But why? Why can't you wear it?' She smiled. 'Because I want to be absolutely sure. So, Orson, when you see me wearing it, you'll know that I truly love you.' Several days were to pass but the lady's left hand remained unadorned. Then, one moonlit evening as they walked by the sea, came a dramatic development. They had perched themselves high up on a rock to contemplate the idyllic scene. There was not a sound to be heard except for the sighing of the waves, until suddenly the silence was shattered by a hoarse cry from Orson: 'The ring, the ring! You're wearing my ring!' And indeed, there it was, his ring – and on the correct finger – sparkling in the moonlight. Orson was speechless with happiness. What a girl! And what a lovely, sensitive and romantic way to accept his proposal! He fell on his knees, covering her hands with kisses. But she recoiled. 'Not so fast, Orson, not so fast. You've got it all wrong, this doesn't mean what you think it means. No, not that at all!' Orson fell back, stunned. 'Then what does it mean?' She seemed embarrassed. 'Well, I caught my brother in my room today, he was going through my things . . .' Orson remained silent. 'Perhaps I didn't tell you, he's a habitual thief and I knew he was after the ring.' Orson didn't utter a word. 'So I felt the only thing to do was to wear it – to be on the safe side, so to speak.'[33]

Welles, recounted Elizabeth Montagu, smiled wryly as he told them this, but they were silent: it was all rather sad. 'But, I thought, anyone who can tell such a story against himself must have stature, and I soon found myself revising my opinion of Orson Welles.' This lightly embroidered story – loosely founded on elements of his relationship with Lea Padovani, crystallised into a *conte* or a parable worthy, in its way, of Guy de Maupassant or Oscar Wilde – is typical of one of Welles's most characteristic creative procedures: the fashioning of what Isak Dinesen called 'anecdotes of destiny', a phrase that perfectly describes a great deal of his work, expressing a view of the world that is at once profoundly romantic, deeply ironic and incorrigibly pessimistic.

CHAPTER TWO

Blessed and Damned

WELLES SHOT virtually all his scenes in *The Third Man* at Shepperton Studios near London during one week, the third week of January 1949. This tight schedule had been imposed on the production by Welles, claiming other commitments, though it is not at all clear what else he was doing around that time. The result was that all the sets involving him had to be ready simultaneously, and a second unit was needed in order to waste as little time as possible; on one particular day Welles worked on eight different sets. The reproduction of both the Prater Great Wheel and the sewers was a considerable challenge, both in construction and in continuity, and it is a tribute to Reed and his team that it is virtually impossible to know what is real Vienna and what is faked – the sort of *trompe l'oeil* that Welles deployed with such pleasure in his own films. He seems to have been curiously anxious during the week's shooting, creating such a tense atmosphere around himself that the crew stopped talking to him. 'Aren't I in this movie?' he asked Elizabeth Montagu plaintively. On one notable occasion, during a short section of the crucial Great Wheel sequence, she reported that 'Orson couldn't get it right, fluffing his few lines for take after take. I think there must have been twenty-five to thirty before Carol was satisfied. It was very embarrassing for all concerned and even Carol seemed unable to help him. Afterwards, Orson looked completely drained and left the studio without a word.'[1]

That evening, Montagu asked Cotten what the problem was. Cotten traced it back to their days together at the Mercury Theatre when, he said, Welles had a kind of inferiority complex about acting, 'especially with me'. There was no question, he said, that Welles was one of the greatest directors of all time, but he was uncertain of himself as an actor. 'And he knows that I know that.' This interesting complication in the relationship between the two old friends deeply informs their performances in *The Third Man*, as it had in *Citizen Kane*; the idea of betrayal, so familiar in Welles's films, is nowhere more brilliantly expressed than in his performance in Greene's deeply uneasy story; it hangs in the air between the two men. Welles 'knows that I know': Cotten sees through him, at the very least on the level of acting. Welles was often to express himself, with remarkable honesty, on the subject of his being found out – when he had the chance of meeting Isak Dinesen, the living writer he admired above all others, he ran away from it, for fear, he said, that she would see through him.

It seems extraordinary that such a prodigally gifted individual should feel so exposed, so lacking in a sense of his own worth. In the sphere of acting, the word his fellow-players use over and over again about his work as an actor is 'insecure'. Sometimes this is a matter of Welles not having learned his lines, or not having given himself time to prepare the part properly. But at a deeper level it seems that this hugely charismatic, formidably imposing man was unconvinced that he was interesting enough. Joseph Cotten was no great actor, but he was utterly at ease with his own body, and conscious of (but not in the least narcissistic about) his handsome features. This amounts to a kind of integrity, an authenticity, which Welles felt he lacked. This tension of course underlies the relationship between Charles Foster Kane and Jedediah Leland in *Citizen Kane.* Welles frequently spoke of his pride in his skills, and indeed of his natural attributes – he knew that his physical stature and his unique voice were huge assets – but more insistently he expressed dislike of his features (above all his nose) and a deep, almost existential anxiety about what he had to offer, most often choosing to hide himself behind prosthetics or, worse, histrionics.

In *The Third Man* he does neither. It is a profoundly good performance, exactly what Korda promised Selznick it would be: 'extraordinary in attraction and superior in intellect'. It is a truly dangerous performance, the depth of the cynicism constantly present just beneath the understated but irresistibly seductive, almost sexual charm. The performance is utterly, believably real, at the same time hinting at some terrible truths about the human condition. He is monstrous, somehow diabolical, this fresh-cheeked, boyish, playful figure. It is hard not to be reminded of Eldred in *Bright Lucifer*, the play Welles wrote when he was sixteen years old. Greene's Manichaean Catholicism rears its alarming head in the novella that is the source for his screenplay (and which Welles of course had read): 'for the first time,' Greene writes, 'Holly looked back through the years without admiration: as he thought [of Harry]: He's never grown up. Marlowe's devils wore squibs attached to their tails: evil was like Peter Pan – it carried with it the horrifying and horrible gift of eternal youth.' Along with his Falstaff, who is Harry Lime's exact antipode, this is incomparably Welles's best performance. And it is done without make-up. Perhaps that is why he was so insecure; but the end result is a startling, unsettling transparency.

It is interesting to speculate how much Carol Reed influenced the performance. As we have seen, it was Welles's practice to arrive on a film set with his interpretation, his make-up (which he always devised and generally executed himself), his part and even his shot list perfectly self-created, hermetically sealed and ready to be slotted into the rest of the film. He seems to have attempted to do so with Reed, but the Englishman was a canny operator, with a background in theatre (he was the illegitimate son of Sir Herbert Beerbohm Tree, the great Edwardian actor-manager) and possessed of what would nowadays be described as excellent people-skills; he was especially renowned for his ability to direct children. When Welles finally arrived on the fragrant sewer set in Shepperton, he offered Reed a suggestion as to how the scene might be shot: 'Brilliant, Orson, really brilliant!' Elizabeth Montagu reports Reed as saying. 'I wish I had thought of that!' He then paused and looked around. 'But as everything is set up to shoot it my way, we'll go ahead. And then, Orson, we'll do it again, your way . . .' After fifteen takes of doing it Reed's way, Welles had had enough. There were several other similar incidents, says Montagu, 'until Orson realised he could never win and gave up trying'.[2] Another way of expressing it, perhaps, is that after having put Reed through a series of successfully passed tests and challenges – a frequent tactic of his – Welles came to trust Reed.

On *The Third Man* he only once deployed his normal method of imposing himself on a film – rewriting – and that was a triumph, a huge contribution to the film's success. The speech he famously wrote for himself at the end of the Great Wheel scene is perfectly phrased, very funny and entirely in character; when he first spoke the lines on the set, the crew (not especially enamoured of Welles, as we have seen) laughed in all the right places. As written by Greene, the last lines of the scene had Harry replying to Holly's question 'And Anna – you won't do a thing to help?'

> 'If I could, old man, of course. But my hands are tied. If we meet again, Holly, it's you I want to see, and not the police. Remember, won't you?'

Welles amended it thus:

> 'When you make your mind up, send me a message – I'll meet you any place, any time, and when we do meet, old man, it's you I want to see, not the police . . . and don't be so gloomy . . . after all, it's not that awful – you know what the fellow said . . . In Italy for thirty years under the Borgias they had warfare, terror, murder, bloodshed – they produced Michelangelo, Leonardo da Vinci and the Renaissance. In Switzerland they had brotherly love, five hundred years of democracy and peace, and what did that produce? . . . The cuckoo clock. So long, Holly.'

Greene always openly acknowledged Welles's authorship of these famous lines; Welles in turn graciously insisted that he had cribbed them from a play by a Hungarian whose name he had forgotten, which he had seen when he was a little boy visiting Vienna with his father. To Peter Bogdanovich (with whom Welles recorded a number of conversations that became the book *This is Orson Welles*) he claimed that he had written every line that Harry uttered, but that is untrue, as the original screenplay reveals. He went further with André Bazin and Charles Bitsch in *Cahiers du Cinéma*: 'I created him all round; it was more than just a part for me. Harry Lime is without doubt a part of my creative work.' This is true enough, but only in the sense that Quasimodo is part of Charles Laughton's creative work, and Rick Blaine's part of Humphrey Bogart's. In the same interview Welles added, 'and he's a Shakespearian character too; he's very close to the Bastard in *King John*'. But what makes it remarkable in Welles's work as an actor in *The Third Man* is precisely that it *isn't* Shakespearean; it's Greenean. It has nothing of the theatre about it at all. Welles knew that he had been given such a superb entrance – appearing in the fifty-ninth minute of the film, after being referred to fifty-seven times – that he must do nothing: he must simply *be*. As for his involvement in the script, the question of authorship was always a delicate one for Welles; as it happens, the screenplay of *The Third Man*, like many, perhaps most, screenplays, is the work of several hands – Greene's, first and foremost, of course; innumerable contributions, small and large, from Reed; Jerome Chodorov's reworking of the central characters to Americanise them; unspecified contributions from Maggie Poole, wife of the playwright Rodney Ackland; and an entire substantial layer of plot (the false penicillin racket) derived by Greene from stories shown him by his friend Peter Smollett, né Smolka, the *Times* correspondent in Vienna, whom Greene knew through his close friend Kim Philby, the British spy (famously dubbed the Fourth Man in the British press).

And Welles's contributions, both thespian and verbal (he also added some well-placed lines about digestive tablets, which echo nicely with the pseudo-penicillin drugs Harry is peddling), are very much part of what makes the film so good. Like *Casablanca* and *Four Weddings and a Funeral*, it is a triumph, above all, of chemistry, which is to say, a triumph of producing: all the elements – all the contributions so carefully assembled by Korda – cohere perfectly in Reed's masterly hands. Guy Hamilton has described how ruthless Reed was in the editing process: superb sequences that would have made another man's career were extirpated without a second's thought. They didn't serve the whole, dissipated tension where it was most required, and distracted attention from the main thrust of the narrative. And Reed knew exactly what he was doing when he accepted Welles's rewrite of the end of the Great Wheel scene. If he hadn't thought it worked, he would have cut it. 'It was Carol's film, Peter,' Welles told Bogdanovich, ' – and Korda's.' This was certainly true. After a dreadful run of flaccid and insipid flops since the end of the war, Korda desperately needed this film to be a success, but the way to ensure that, as he never ceased to remind Selznick, was to enable Reed to make the film he wanted to make. It was, as it happens, the last time he and Welles attempted to work together, which is a great shame: if Welles could have worked with any producer, surely it would have been Korda. But Korda had evidently had enough; after *The Third Man* he sold Welles's contract on to the British hack film-maker Herbert Wilcox, for whom Welles appeared in two resoundingly dull potboilers.

The Third Man, it is hard not to feel, is exactly the sort of film that Welles should have been making. It is so Wellesian, in fact, that there is a widespread belief that he was somehow responsible for it, even if only by osmosis. That this was not so has been amply demonstrated here and elsewhere, though Welles himself – despite his ringing endorsement to Bogdanovich of Reed's authorship of the film (as opposed to the screenplay) – was sometimes unable to resist fuelling the suspicion, most notably in his 1958 interview in *Cahiers du Cinéma*. The interviewers, André Bazin and Charles Bitsch, told him that they felt there were sequences in the film that he had directed himself, for instance the one in front of the Great Wheel. '"Direct" is a word I must explain,' says Welles, with masterly ambiguity. 'The whole question is who takes the initiative. First of all I don't want to look as though I'm upstaging Carol Reed; secondly, he is incontestably a very competent director; thirdly he has in common with me that if someone has a good idea, he lets them get on with it; he likes to see something inspired happening, and doesn't try to put it down because it's not his, as too many little film directors do. But it's tricky to say anything about this film, because I've been very discreet, and I don't want now . . .' At which point he went on to claim that he had written the whole of Harry's dialogue.

He later felt ashamed of what he had so publicly implied, and retracted it. But in the late 1960s he was not above telling the young British actor Jonathan Lynn that when they fell behind schedule on the film, Carol Reed had given him a camera and asked him to direct some second-unit scenes, 'including the memorable scene where the cat finds Harry Lime hiding in a doorway'.[3] It was hard for Welles – humiliating, in fact – to have been part of something brilliant for which he was not responsible. He was Orson Welles, after all, Welles the wunderkind, the quadruple threat: how could he simply have given a very good performance? The point is that what Welles gave to the film is infinitely more than any rewrite, or any purported second-unit work: he gave of himself, which he was very rarely to do in his work as an actor in other men's films. And he was duly rewarded with a success unlike any he had ever experienced, or ever would again, to the extent that his identification with the part became positively irksome, though not without its advantages. It is a glimpse of the very different acting career he might have had, had he chosen ever to trust a director again.

★

After Welles finished his brief stint on *The Third Man*, he went back to Italy to start spending his $100,000 salary on resuming *Othello* – or, rather, on starting it all over again. He had shot 3,000 metres of film, nearly two hours' worth; now he dumped it all. Meanwhile, due to pressure from critics, *Kane* finally went on delayed general release in Italy, truncated and re-edited. This was RKO's delayed revenge on Welles for the detested final-cut clause in his original contract with them; when the Italian critics protested about the recutting, RKO had replied, in an official statement: 'The less films of this sort that are seen, the better: they ruin the public's taste.' Back in America, disastrous reviews of *Macbeth* prompted Republic to recut that, too. Regardless, Welles ploughed on with *Othello*; what else could he do? His immediate priority was to find an Iago, and to that end he approached his old friend Hilton Edwards, co-director of the Gate Theatre in Dublin, where in 1930 the sixteen-year-old Welles had had his start in the theatre, to persuade Micheál

MacLiammóir – Edwards's partner in life and professionally, the Gate's leading actor and chief designer, as well as a playwright and memoirist of some brilliance – to play the part.

MacLiammóir needed persuading because he had not acted on screen since 1916, when he was a boy actor and film was an altogether different medium, and because he was unconvinced that the camera would be able to cope with what he knew to be his quintessentially theatrical persona. He also had doubts as to whether he was well cast as Iago; he was after all, was he not, an *acteur noble*, a famous Hamlet and before that a Romeo to set hearts a-flutter? Could he really, he wondered, play a villain? Welles called him, to apply a little light pressure. 'Voice not changed at all,' wrote MacLiammóir in his diary.

> He said the same of me: we expressed emotion and revived memories of last farewell on quay-side at New York fifteen years ago. Said I was very ill; he said the trip and the sight of him would cure me. Said I was very old; he said so was he. (Forgot to point out that Othello was supposed to be.) Said I'd never played Iago, he said he'd never played Othello. Said I had put on weight; he said so had he, and that we'd be two Chubby Tragedians together and that he was going right out to buy yards of cheese-cloth. Said I didn't think I'd be any good on movies; he said I was born for them. (Good God!) Said I didn't see myself as villain, he said unmentionable word and that I was patently villainous in all eyes but my own and Hilton's. All this confusing but intriguing. Finally rang off and turned to H. saying I didn't think I could go.[4]

But of course he did. Not many people could resist Welles in this vein. For the next year, in the vivid, shrewd and remarkably candid diary he scrupulously kept, from the first day of filming to the last, MacLiammóir observed Welles and the progress of *Othello* from the perspective of a newcomer to the art of film-making. Simultaneously boggle- and lynx-eyed, he witnessed the madness all around him with a sort of appalled fascination; he was not to know that the shoot of *Othello* was like no other shoot in the history of the cinema. He was mesmerised by Welles; in MacLiammóir's wicked and often surreal pages, he emerges as five times larger than life and several times stranger. 'There was Orson in the doorway,' he writes of his arrival in Paris, glimpsing Welles for the first time since 1934, 'huge, expansive, round-headed, almond-eyed, clad apparently in dungarees, and miraculously unchanged . . . no bridging of the years seemed necessary: exactly as he used to be, perhaps larger and more, as it were, tropically Byzantine still, but essentially the same old darkly waltzing tree, half banyan, half oak, the Jungle and the Forest lazily pawing each other for mastery'.[5]

Welles had called MacLiammóir in late January of 1949, a few days after he had finished filming in *The Third Man*. He summoned him to Paris, where they rehearsed in various hotel rooms, perhaps not too strenuously – 'rehearsing and eating', one entry records – but rehearsals in film, however informal, are always worth their weight in gold. MacLiammóir and Welles were in agreement about the characters: 'no single trace of the Mephistophelean Iago is to be used,' wrote MacLiammóir, 'no conscious villainy; a common man, clever as a wagonload of monkeys, his thought never on the present moment but always on the move after the move after next: a business man dealing in destruction with neatness, method, and a proper pleasure in his work: the honest honest Iago reputation is accepted because it has become almost the truth . . .' Sexual dysfunction, as Welles saw it, was Iago's underlying motive: 'the immemorial hatred of life, the secret isolation of impotence under the soldier's muscles, the flabby solitude gnawing at the groins, the eye's untiring calculation'. Welles had no truck with the Christian, or perhaps more precisely the Catholic, notion of unmotivated malignancy, of diabolic negativity: it was the banality of evil that interested him in Iago. 'Any tendency to passion,' recorded MacLiammóir, 'even the expression of the onlookers' delight at the spectacle of disaster, makes for open villainy and must be crushed.' When Iago is explaining to Desdemona's gormless would-be suitor Roderigo how he will dispose of his supposed rival Cassio, he says: 'Why, by making him uncapable of his place . . .' Roderigo looks blank, and Iago, according to Welles – 'as though explaining to a child why it should brush its teeth,' as MacLiammóir puts it – adds, with a pleasant smile, 'Knocking out his brains'.

MacLiammóir's account of these rehearsals is one of the few records we have of Welles's work on a text with an actor, and it is interesting to see how detailed Welles's view of the characters and their relationship was, complex and full of psychological detail. But as always with him, his thoughts were crystallising into visual imagery: even in these preliminary rehearsals he spoke of 'the growing dependence of Othello on Iago's presence, the merging of the two men into one murderous image like a pattern of loving shadows welded'. It is further interesting to note that MacLiammóir describes Welles, before they had ever stood in front of the cameras, delivering the lines 'with a queer breathless rapidity: this treatment, with his great bulk and power, gives an extraordinary feeling of loss, of withering, diminishing, crumbling, toppling over, of a vanishing equilibrium; quite wonderful'. MacLiammóir wondered whether this was a conscious rejection by Welles of the approach he had used in *Macbeth*, 'letting us have the stuff from the wild lungs and in the manner intended', reflecting that 'people didn't like it, a verdict possibly shared by the camera, so there maybe is the answer'.

They were soon joined at rehearsals by Lea Padovani. She was 'fascinating', said MacLiammóir, 'and doesn't seem to like Desdemona at all'. A few days later she was sacked, and was back on the plane to Rome. This eruption had been a long time coming. Padovani had at last pushed Welles too far, and their relationship ended, she told Welles's biographer Charles Higham, in a spectacularly physical fight in which she finally knocked him out with a doorstop. Rita Ribolla, in her diary of events, reports a much chillier, much bleaker account of the break-up, which evidently took place not in Rome, but in Paris, where at four o'clock in the morning Welles woke Ribolla, bursting into her hotel room with a bunch of bedraggled flowers and the news that the engagement with Lea was off. 'She made a terrible scene,' Ribolla reports Welles as saying. 'Very dramatic.'

> 'What did she say?' 'That she preferred to live in a furnished room and eat spaghetti for the rest of her life than become Mrs Welles.' 'What did you say?' 'I wired you to come.' 'What are you going to do now?' 'I had you come over to tell me that.' 'I?' 'Of course, who else?' 'Do you still love her?' 'Yes. Yes. Yes.' 'Do you want to try and persuade her to change her mind?' 'No, No. No!' 'You'll wake up the entire hotel.' 'Why, is anyone asleep?' 'It's 4.40 in the morning.' 'Is it really?' 'Yes.' 'Then I suppose you want to go to bed, so I'd better go to the Bois.' 'The Bois?' 'Yes, where else can I find a bench to lay down on with my misery?'[6]

Ribolla asked what Welles wanted her to do with Lea.

> 'Get her out on the first plane back to Rome.' I called downstairs for a taxi and threw a coat over my shoulders. 'Shall we go?' I asked. He heaved himself out of the chair, up from the remnants of what once had been flowers. 'Oh dear,' he said. 'How did this happen?' I was tactful enough not to say anything. He picked them up and tried to squeeze them back into form, mumbling that they'd been so pretty, he'd gone into such trouble to find an open shop in the middle of the night, he'd hoped to give me a

little pleasure with them.

She checked Welles into the George V under her own name, then called Padovani the following morning at the Ritz, where she and Welles had been staying in interlocking rooms, to make arrangements for the flight. Padovani was dressed and packed when Ribolla arrived, and immediately demanded that the communicating door between her suite and Welles's be opened.

> 'Oh,' I said. 'Don't just stand there and oh at me,' the ex-Goddess of Love yelled, losing her attitude of bereavement entirely, 'Have it opened immediately.' She stamped her pretty slender foot with the force of a Bavarian beer-cart horse and sparks of fire shot from her then quite suddenly switched back to mournful widowhood and mumbled that I should please have it opened. I asked her why. She said that her jewels were in his room.

Eventually the jewels were recovered, and she departed with them. True to form, Welles immediately accused Ribolla of stealing them, but she was able to send him a clip from a Roman newspaper showing Padovani arriving at the airport with all her *bijouterie* in full view. 'In the nine months I was with her,' Welles said to a journalist some years afterwards, 'I paid for everything I'd done to women for twenty years.' In later years he spoke of her, sometimes affectionately, sometimes disparagingly, but it appears that it was the most intense amatory relationship of his life to that date – the first time he had met serious resistance, the first time he had been deeply wounded. Women did not get a very good report from Welles for many years thereafter.

His broken heart was the least of his worries. He now had no Desdemona. Meanwhile, Padovani's lover, Giorgio Papi, remained on board as production manager, despite having had his bag, containing contracts and 4 million lire in cash, stolen from him in a department store. Contracts were unlovely things to Welles, so he may have thought their disappearance good riddance, but the 4 million lire would certainly have come in handy. Papi was exceptionally good at his job, however, and, painful as the associations might be, Welles retained him to the very end of the shoot. He was determined to press on with the film, but the loss of his Desdemona demanded considerable rethinking; it may also be that, quite apart from the emotional distress he was enduring at Padovani's hands, Welles had finally realised that her English would never be up to

Shakespeare's verse. So began the Quest for Desdemona, which continued for some weeks. 'Have already seen three put through many of the lines but all wrong,' wrote MacLiammóir in his diary. 'Orson developing bloodshot eyes, always with him a sign of worry.'

At one point Cécile Aubry, currently the toast of the French-speaking world in Henri-Georges Clouzot's acclaimed *Manon*, accepted the role; they rehearsed briefly, she in an Inspector Clouseau-like accent ('*Why I should fear Ai know nawt, seence guilt-ee-nayss Ai know nawt*,' according to MacLiammóir's transcript), but within minutes, it seemed, she was off too, to appear in the latest American–Italian co-production blockbuster, *The Black Rose*. Where to turn now? Welles's friend Anatole Litvak invited him to see the rough-cut of the film he had just directed, *Snakepit*, featuring Betsy Blair, a rising actress noted for her fearlessly left-wing views and for her marriage to Gene Kelly. Welles immediately phoned her in Hollywood and offered her Desdemona; without the slightest persuasion, she accepted. 'His conception was of a modern young woman, a rebel against Venetian society. I'd had a glimmer of this idea myself, so I was thrilled to be on the right track.'[7]

With Desdemona finally in place, Welles invited Agnes Moorehead to play Emilia (sublime casting); Dick Wilson touchingly reported that, 'very unhappy about the prospect of playing Emilia to Betsy Blair's Desdemona', Moorehead had asked instead to be considered for Desdemona herself. Great actress though she unquestionably was, it would have been hard to imagine her as the young beauty who stole Othello's heart. 'I took it on myself to turn this suggestion down,' wrote Wilson, 'in a nice way, I assure you.' Casting Emilia was not a high priority. Welles quickly filled most of the other roles from London, including Robert Coote, fresh from Powell and Pressburger's *A Matter of Life and Death*, as Roderigo; the Irish-born Michael Laurence as Cassio; and, as Lodovico (a typically exotic Wellesian touch), Nicholas Bruce, son of the great Diaghilev ballerina Tamara Karsavina; finally he asked Hilton Edwards to play Desdemona's father, Brabantio.

Welles's fathers-in-art, Edwards and MacLiammóir, were now, as a unit, part of the team. Welles's relationship with the two men was one of some complexity, and the season he had mounted when he was nineteen at his old school in Woodstock, Illinois, with them as guest stars (MacLiammóir played Hamlet and Edwards Tsar Paul I), had further complicated it when they found themselves to be bit-part players in what seemed to them to be a festival mounted to the greater glory of Orson Welles. That was 1934; the three men had since been in touch by mail, though Welles was not best pleased with either Edwards's telegram congratulating him on his performance 'as Count Dracula' in *Jane Eyre* or MacLiammóir's 1946 autobiography, *All for Hecuba*, which told a rather different story about Welles's early break at the Gate Theatre from the one Welles himself had been telling. But he never ceased to acknowledge their importance in his life and work, the poetic intensity of MacLiammóir's acting and his peerless command of language, as well as Edwards's mastery of stage-craft, more particularly the radical use of light by which Welles had been so profoundly influenced. For their part, they were glad of the money: the Gate had had a troubled existence for some time and they were personally on their uppers. Moreover, Edwards was keen to learn about film. MacLiammóir had had tea with the ancient Madame Maud Gonne MacBride, Yeats's great legendary love, and she had vatically enjoined him to find out how to make films 'for Ireland'. Welles's *Othello* may not have been the best training ground.

MacLiammóir – unlike many of his colleagues – had in his possession the thing Welles least liked anyone to have: a contract. It confirmed that he was to be paid 1.5 million French francs, to cover three weeks rehearsal and ten weeks shooting. The document prudently stipulated that 'for any further work over and above this period, the artist shall receive payment pro rata'; all expenses were also to be paid. In time, this document came to seem like nothing but a cruel mockery. Meanwhile the great adventure commenced. Or nearly. Just as shooting was about to begin, everything stopped, again. Welles had run out of money, and he agreed to appear, for his now statutory fee of $100,000, in yet another American–Italian blockbuster, the same one, in fact, for which Cécile Aubry had deserted *Othello*: *The Black Rose*, in which she played the title-role of a fourteenth-century virgin; Welles gave his Mongol warlord, Bayan of the Hundred Eyes – no acting required, if we are to believe Harriet White Medin's description of his behaviour in the Casal Pilozzo, just an enjoyable dip into the make-up box. Copper-coloured, with puffy eyes, he languidly exhales the dialogue, the character's mind apparently elsewhere. This may have had something to do with his own preoccupation with finding suitable locations for *Othello*. *The Black Rose* was shooting in Morocco; when Trauner heard this, he urged Welles to take a detour to Mogador, a little down the coast from inland Meknes, where he was then shooting, as a likely site for the many scenes set in Cyprus – the bulk of the play, in fact, so it was a crucial location. Welles found Mogador perfect beyond his wildest imaginings, with its fortress, its ocean, its starkness and the almost complete absence of the modern world. First occupied by the British – Drake had Christmas lunch there in 1577 – then by the Berbers and lastly by the French, Mogador lost its purpose when the port was shifted to Casablanca; the arrival of the *Othello* film crew was, says Nicholas Shakespeare in his essay on the town, 'more or less the last occasion anything happened in Mogador'.[8]

Just before it did – like a distant hubbub from another planet – the *New York Times* brought news of Senator Jack Tenney's State Senate Committee on Un-American Activities Report, which listed individuals 'who followed or appeased some of the Communist Party line program over a long period of time'. The list included Charlie Chaplin, Frank Sinatra, Thomas Mann, Dashiell Hammett, Danny Kaye, Maurice Chevalier, Henry Wallace and Orson Welles. Most of those on the list responded: Sinatra said that 'this statement is the product of liars, and liars to me make very un-American leaders'. 'I don't know what they're talking about,' said the great bandleader Artie Shaw. 'I don't think they do either.' Katharine Hepburn 'refused to dignify Mr Tenney's un-American accusation with a reply'.[9] There was no response at all from Welles. Perhaps he didn't know that he was even on the list. Perhaps, obsessed by trying to film his seventeenth-century story of the corrosive effects of jealousy, he no longer cared.

Welles had assembled the crew for *Othello* largely from the Italian–American films in which he had recently acted: Washinsky, the first assistant director, as we have seen, he met on *Black Magic*; the director of photography, with whom he had also worked on *Black Magic* in his dual capacity as star and unofficial director, was the great Anchise Brizzi, who had shot the Italian film that Welles admired above all others, *Shoe-Shine*. Brizzi's associate was Alberto Fusi, who had filmed the sequences in Venice with Padovani the previous year; their junior was Oberdan Troiani, at the very beginning of his career. Giorgio Papi, also from *Black Magic*, though still nominally production manager, had decided that Morocco was not for him (apart from anything else, his mistress, Padovani, wasn't there). So Welles had hired, seemingly at random, an American called Cunningham, who was the inventor of a type of magnetic recording tape, the possibilities of which of course thrilled Welles, but whose qualifications for getting permits, arranging transportation and so on were non-existent; in the end, even the magnetic tape turned out not to have worked, leaving then without so much as a guide track for the footage. Trauner arranged for a Frenchman, Julien Derode (who would later go on to coproduce *The Day of the Jackal* and *Julia*), to take charge of the day-to-day running of the production, which he did, with more or less cooperation from Welles and the rest of the crew. Welles had also summoned another colleague from an earlier time, the Hungarian cameraman George Fanto, with whom he had shot the superb Jangadeiros section of his aborted film *It's All True* in Brazil. 'ARE YOU AVAILABLE TO FLY IMMEDIATELY CASABLANCA,' came the telegram. 'REPLY HOTEL DE PARIS, MOGADOR.'[10] Fanto, who had been in Rio making educational programmes for a series called *Native Brazilians*, was on the next flight out.

He arrived at the same time as MacLiammóir, Hilton Edwards, Betsy Blair and Robert Coote; dinner was already under way at the Hotel de Paris. 'Squeezed together at one long table in the dining room', wrote Fanto, 'were the cast, the technicians, French and Moroccan dignitaries, members of the international press, Shakespearean scholars. They wore costumes, kaftans, uniforms, suits and leisurewear.' This was paradise for Welles; back to the palmy days of *It's All True*: immersion in another culture, another world. 'The table was loaded with African lobster, lamb stew with couscous, lots of wine and only water for the Moroccans. Everybody competed for Welles's attention. He could and did deal with all, sitting at the head of the table . . . nothing escaped Welles's attention as he was endowed with a perception which was a combination of antenna, radar and computer.'[11] He spotted MacLiammóir, and 'rose thunderously from hordes of tumultuous diners and swept towards me waving his napkin like a flag and crying, "Welcome, welcome, dearest Micheál!" Then, folding me in bear-like embrace, stopped dead suddenly to say "Hey! what have you been doing? You've put on about six pounds. God dammit, I engaged you to play Iago and here you come Waddling In To Do It!"' Thus publicly shamed, MacLiammóir picked guiltily at his supper, after which Welles took him on a tour of the moonlit fortress town. 'Pacing up and down under the moon, I learned of his endless difficulties about money, Italian wardrobe, and cost of labour: everything as I see it is against him before he starts, but his courage, like everything else about him, imagination, egotism, generosity, ruthlessness, forbearance, impatience, sensitivity, grossness and vision, is magnificently out of proportion. His position at the moment is grotesque in its lack of stability and even likelihood, but he will win through and all at the end will fall into his hands, the bright-winged old gorilla.'[12] MacLiammóir's confidence was to be sorely tried.

It is no accident that the published version of his diary is entitled (quoting from Iago's advice to Roderigo) *Put Money in Thy Purse*. Money was at the core of their problems, from beginning to end. Welles was now on his own: Scalera had pulled out of their co-production. The Italians would simply distribute. 'The film', said a press release, 'will be produced by Mr Welles at his own expense,'[13] as chilling a phrase as can be imagined. It is hard to think of any major director who is not independently wealthy or has a studio of their own who had ever contemplated such a thing. The reality kicked in immediately. On the very first day of rehearsals, 10 June, the entire male wardrobe, ordered from the house of Peruzzi in Florence, failed to appear because of non-payment of bills. Betsy Blair was in the production office when Welles and Trauner arrived in some agitation. 'Orson pleaded on the phone to Florence; he shouted and threatened and appealed in the name of Art, civilized values, and future work. It was to no avail. If there was no cash on the table, no costumes would be on the plane. And there was no cash.'[14]

The first scheduled scene was the murder of Roderigo, which Welles had planned to shoot in the street. There seemed no way forward; even the improvised costumes were not yet ready. After sketching in silence for a while, Trauner, says Betsy Blair, quietly suggested that they shoot the scene in a Turkish bath, with the actors in towels. 'Orson roared with joy,' says Blair. 'He threw his arms around Trauner, picked him up, and danced from table to table.' MacLiammóir reports it differently: Welles had the inspiration himself during a sleepless night. It seems, in fact, that Trauner had already designed a Turkish bath months earlier, shrewdly supposing that there would be a use for one. It's possible that Welles chose to make it seem as if they were at a complete impasse (though the absence of nearly all the male principals' costumes constitutes a very real impasse) in order to pull a brilliant solution out of the hat, instilling the principle of improvisation in the minds of his cast and crew; either way, the scene as shot has a fantastic sense of *sprezzatura*, a freshness and a sense of being made up as it goes along, which is everything Welles wanted in a film. And this extemporising spirit is what he sought above all else in his collaborators.

Fanto described Trauner as 'a wizard when it came to executing ideas which Welles came up with under stress'. He found a perfect location for the Turkish bath, under the rampart of the fortress that was used by the locals as a fish-market, and he rapidly transformed it, to great visual effect. 'It was a place with vaults on two levels,' said Trauner. 'I just needed to install some gratings. We had no smoke machines, so we used incense. As you can imagine, the mingled fumes of incense and fish were rather striking.' As usual, Welles demonstrated what he wanted by making sketches. His drawings, said Trauner, showed his very good visual sense. 'He never denied the decorative aspect, but he stripped it down. He was one of the first to strip characters . . .

his visions were a painter's visions. Like Eisenstein's.'[15] In the absence of the costumes from Rome, Trauner got the Jewish tailors of Mogador to run them up from whatever materials they had to hand. They made fake armour with sardine cans, while the local tannery made shoes, jerkins and uniforms. The simple, homespun character of the clothes thus conjured up proved to be an improvement over what had been envisaged by Trauner and Welles. 'When we needed a chain for Desdemona's handbag,' Trauner said, 'I liberated the toilet chains from the hotel, which did the trick perfectly.' When the money was at last released, the costumes arrived from Italy, embroidered and brocaded. 'We gave them to the extras; otherwise they would have clashed with the simplicity of the local materials.'[16] Mogador was doing very well out of the film: 'the whole town mucked in as extras,' reported Nicholas Shakespeare, 'each person rewarded with a daily ration of two dirhams, a tin of sardines, some Coca-Cola and some bread'.

Welles was now quite literally making it up as he went along, responding to the environment, constantly looking for ways of intensifying the drama by visual means; the text, he felt, would look after itself, at least as long as he and MacLiammóir were speaking it. MacLiammóir was astonished at the frenzy of the process, as well he might have been. Not since the early days of cinema – when Abel Gance would hike up the adrenalin levels by firing pistols into the air over the actors' heads – had a director been so mercurial, so personally involved in the physical process of filming. The extremely lively sequence in which Cassio gets drunk turned, according to MacLiammóir, 'into a real Orgy' because Washinsky, out-Wellesing Welles, let loose a few barrels of red wine among hordes of Jewish extras:

> The Arabs stuck to Coca-Cola . . . Hilton, nothing loath to help in this sort of scene, rushed up and down on one side of the harbour armed with a stout stick and yelling directions in English with some scattered but vivacious ejaculations in French, with Washinsky on the other side screaming in any language that came into his head. Orson stood on a rickety pile of boxes and stood behind the camera yelling in American and Italian . . . as Bob, Michael and I dashed about among the crowd bawling what we could of Shakespeare's lines and being slapped, pinched and pushed and winked at by now totally inebriated Israelite soldiers.[17]

Welles seemed to have no predetermined plan and rarely completed a scene, preferring to shoot fragments – 'pieces of a puzzle', in the words of Jean-Pierre Berthomé, 'to which only he had the answer'.[18] He never actually appeared in front of the camera himself unless it was unavoidable. He was understandably preoccupied with all the other elements for which he was responsible, but in addition he was nervous of acting with his fellow-actors, or even committing to a performance; nonetheless he appeared on the set in full make-up. At the end of every day, Troiani, the assistant cameraman, had a blacker face than Welles, because whenever Welles peered through the viewfinder to see a new set-up, he left his make-up on it.

The crew were shooting on an old-style heavy Mitchell News Camera. 'It took a quarter of an hour to get the thing right,' reported Troiani, 'because Welles would maybe want a tower in the distance to be seen between two strands of hair. The actor had to be absolutely motionless.'[19] Then one of the new Caméflex cameras arrived: Welles was among the first to use it; the delighted manufacturer, Éclair, sent someone to photograph him doing so. Introduced just two years earlier, it was a shoulder-held portable 35mm camera with instant-change magazines, and it offered Welles exactly the freedom he craved; now he could follow his impulses. The director of photography, Anchise Brizzi – patrician and classical, impeccable in his three-piece suit in the midday Moroccan sun – loathed Welles's way of working, as did his associate Fusi. Troiani reports that Welles would ask Brizzi if the shot was okay. 'It's okay,' he would reply, 'though to my way of thinking . . . ' 'I'll shoot the whole goddam movie again if I have to,' Welles used to retort, 'just tell me was it good or not?'[20]

Eventually the two cameramen had had enough and walked out. Papi advised Troiani that if he followed suit, he'd end up at the bottom of the ocean, which was persuasive enough to make him stay, but only as assistant cameraman. Troiani concluded that being Welles's director of photography would be a nightmare, but he loved the way Welles worked, constantly building shots to create an effect on the viewer – unlike Visconti, for example, who, as far as Troiani was concerned, had 'no conception of cinema at all; it was just filmed theatre'. After *Othello*, Troiani had no time for anyone but Welles in fact: 'for me, if they didn't live up to Welles, they were nobody'.[21] Trauner described the atmosphere of the shoot as 'rather Elizabethan – perhaps more Elizabethan than the film itself'.

They had all been living in their hotel in the nearby city of Safi for some three or four weeks; no bills had been paid, so, there was only one thing for it, wrote George Fanto: 'you have to show that you're not poor so you order more and more extravagant dishes'. This was a perfectly Hungarian modus operandi, one that Alexander Korda had used all his life. Fanto's very rich mother had come to stay in the hotel, and she kept the staff sweet with tips, cigarettes and expensive confectionery. 'We were a small team during filming,' wrote Fanto. 'We had unending discussions from dusk to dawn, flung ourselves into major philosophical debates with Orson who suffered from insomnia. These conversations would go on till 3 in the morning and resume at 6. Between us – with MacLiammóir and Hilton – we had plenty of things to fight about. Very lively it was, very animated.'[22] It is notable that of the cinematographers, only Fanto was part of this lively band.

Before he walked out, Brizzi had shot tests on Betsy Blair; she was asked simply to speak the phrase 'Welcome, My Lord Othello, to Cyprus' a number of times over the course of two days' shooting on the ramparts. She was having a splendid time in Mogador and adored sitting with everyone in the evenings, listening while Welles regaled them with his visions of *Othello* and projects to come – among them what sounds like a rather enticing musical version of *The Tempest* with Louis Armstrong as Caliban. Then suddenly filming stopped and Welles disappeared. Blair got a note that she was to pack without telling anyone; Welles would be waiting for her in a hotel in Casablanca. He received her in his bed in huge white silk pyjamas and vividly described how dire the financial circumstances were. 'Any disappointment I might have felt was dissolved in sympathy for him. He said he knew I'd want to get back to Gene and Kerry and not hang around Rome while he scrabbled for finance. As soon as it was in place, he'd summon me back.' He was very excited, he said, about their 'characterization'. He'd keep her posted at all times. Oh, and by the way, could she buy her own ticket back to LA? It would be reimbursed, of course.[23] Of course it wasn't: and of course she never heard from him again. Welles had decided, he told MacLiammóir, that Blair was 'too modern' – the very reason he had cast her. Clearly he had no easy answer to the crucial question of what kind of a woman Desdemona was; no doubt his recent experience with Lea Padovani had deeply confused his view. The rest of the cast were told she had been sent on holiday to Paris. In due course Fanto, who had taken on some of the tasks of the production manager, wrote to Blair to tell her the truth, explaining that Welles was only trying to serve the film, and Shakespeare. Some time later he got a reply from her: 'I am no longer angry with Orson,' she wrote. 'I don't think he's a bastard, as a matter of fact I quite agree with you.'[24]

Filming had not of course closed down; it continued, after a fashion, as Welles publicly pondered how to shoot the film. 'Orson beautifully dressed up and painted a dark chocolate brown,' noted MacLiammóir:

> paced to and fro for hours thinking it all out on the edge of the farthest watch tower, among a thicket of cannons and anxious shivering technicians, black rocks and leaping waves below, and a tempest howling overhead. Finally with warnings frantically hissed and shrieked at us by everyone, we assume stout leather belts to which ropes are attached, and held fast by Marc, Pierrot and other members of the French crew (Arabs being considered too emotional for the job) hang at right angles from the battlements in order to play the scene, camera at dizzy levels conveying sense of terror and (not wholly unfounded) feeling of physical danger . . . as neither of us could hear the other speak and as we were both continually engaged in pulling portions of our clothes out of our mouths whither the wild winds had tossed them, intimate and rather spicy information proffered by Iago was difficult.[25]

At least Welles no longer had to carry in his head the whole of what he had shot: the film finally had a continuity supervisor, known as Gouzy. They also had an Emilia, Fay Compton; had it not been for the lack of a Desdemona – details, details – they would have had a full cast. Compton was a very distinguished British actress, with a famously vivacious private life, noted for her classical work and not without experience in film; she had appeared with some success for Carol Reed in *Odd Man Out*. She arrived in Safi full of trepidation, having taken the job against the advice of her agent; London was awash with rumours about the production and, sure enough, on arrival at the hotel she found a gang of actors on the brink of mutiny. Someone immediately showed her a clipping in a French newspaper reporting that Welles had no money, and that the film would never be made. Certain that the experience would be, at the very least, interesting, she too decided to keep a diary. Called to Mogador the following day, she met Welles, 'who seems really pleased to meet me', she confided in her diary. She had drinks with MacLiammóir and Edwards and was driven back to Safi with them in Welles's car, swigging from MacLiammóir's bottle of brandy. 'Much laughter and many stories told.' There were more drinks, then more.

The next day Compton started filming – the handkerchief scene – and, back in the hotel, she seized the opportunity to press her contract into Welles's hand; thus cornered, he then 'got off', she told dear diary, 'with French tootsie actress in hotel'. In his absence, she settled in for her first proper gossip with the actors, discovering that they and the crew had only got any money at all because they refused to move from Rome until they were paid. MacLiammóir had received nothing, having being offered a slice of the film instead, which he didn't want. 'And rightly too. It may never be finished or shown.' Compton concluded that 'Orson has apparently mucked everything up.' The following day they shot more of the handkerchief scene, and later, at supper, where he joined them after he had, again, 'dallied with his tootsie', she found herself falling under his spell. 'An overwhelming personality with a capital E ego. Incredible energy and vitality . . . as a director is very patient, *very* helpful . . . as he says, to be good in films, you must not so much act as *think* . . . very much the same as Carol's method.'[26]

Three days later, just as she was getting into her stride, the production was suddenly closed down and the camera crew released, with the expectation of further shooting in three weeks' time in Venice. Welles, MacLiammóir and Edwards all fell ill with bronchitic ailments. Fay Compton told her diary that she hoped the film would be made, 'if only to stop the "I told you so"s'. Orson, she said, was 'a Great Titan against The World'[27] (which, she added, not unperceptively, was how he saw himself). MacLiammóir and Edwards found themselves back in Paris – 'habitual feeling of having never left Paris descends' – and were introduced by Julien Derode to the new Desdemona, the French-Canadian actress Suzanne Cloutier, whom Welles had seen in Duvivier's *Au Royaume des Cieux*; she had also just acted in Marcel Carné's *Juliette*, as yet unreleased. 'Feel sure', wrote MacLiammóir, 'somewhere in her There is Steel. Interesting; I smell Ham, Character, Individuality, and above all, Indestructible Will, and prophesy that Orson will have trouble with her (as she no doubt with him).'[28] MacLiammóir's prophetic soul did not deceive him.

CHAPTER THREE

Der Dritter Mann Persönlich

FAY COMPTON returned to London, where gossip about the film was raging more fiercely than ever. Robert Coote had gone to Rome, whence he telegraphed her: 'DARLING PLEASE DO NOT COME HERE. IT'S EVER SO NASTY' and followed it up with a postcard saying, 'they have no news, no money, drinks, gals, clothes or future. What *is* happening?'[1] He sent Welles a cable asking whether the film had been abandoned. Lee Cresell sent Compton a card saying that not a shot of film had been done and that everyone was in the usual state of nervous collapse. Her agent told her that the whole thing was 'a washout'. Then suddenly, at a day's notice, she was summoned, and made the difficult journey from Northolt via Milan and thence to Venice by train.

There was no one to meet her. Compton got to the Europa Hotel, where she had been told to find Welles, but he was not in; she tried calling MacLiammóir, at which point Welles arrived, astonished that she was there, but delighted. Flowing over with bonhomie, he gave her his room overlooking the Grand Canal; he, MacLiammóir and Edwards then took her to Harry's Bar. From there they all took a gondola back to the hotel, but Welles got off at a nightclub, 'where he is meeting some Tootsie, I imagine,' she steamily informed her diary. The following day was less agreeable. They all met for dinner, along with Suzanne Cloutier, Nicholas Bruce and Robert Coote, who moaned about his hotel room. Welles – 'nervy and depressed' – attacked Coote for his constant grumbling, then turned on MacLiammóir for being late and not apologising, and for slacking throughout the day. Edwards arrived and pitched in. Such was the mood among the actors in Venice, in August 1949. 'Oh dear!' sighs Compton to her journal.[2]

Anchise Brizzi having departed with Alberto Fusi, G.R. Aldo took over as cinematographer for the Venice shoot. He had been director of photography on Visconti's masterpiece *La Terra Trema*; no doubt Welles refrained from mentioning that he had walked out of the film in disgust when he saw it at the Venice Festival two years earlier. Aldo shared the position of director of photography with Alvaro Mancori, the assistant cameraman on *Black Magic* and an *Othello* veteran: he had shot some of the Venetian sequences a year earlier. Aldo didn't last long this time round: once, according to Mancori, he told Welles that a shot he proposed wouldn't work. 'Shoot the picture,' roared Welles. 'I'll worry about what works and what doesn't. Nothing's impossible. I'll cut it if it doesn't work out.' Shortly afterwards Aldo departed. Mancori was careful not to make the same mistake. He observed Welles closely. 'Welles had a terrible character. Frightening if riled. A bully. If he bellowed at you, he did no more than that. But if he was quiet . . . watch out. A strange animal indeed.' He came to respect Welles nonetheless, despite his being, as Mancori put it, 'full of little manias', which included always blaming someone else: the actors, the crew or, as often as not, the cameraman.

With what Mancori described as his 360-degree vision, Welles missed nothing.[3] As an actor, he was always conscious of his exact position. In one shot that involved the old-fashioned Parvo Debrie camera, he could catch sight of himself in a mirror that lit up when the lens changed; while he was acting he would check in the mirror to see whether his framing was right. He didn't hesitate to make the operators repeat camera moves over and over again, which drove them mad, but he knew exactly what he wanted. His ingenuity was limitless: 'lances held aloft by an array of soldiers were small splinters in thimbles on each finger of a hand,' writes Alberto Anile in his indispensable *Orson Welles in Italy*. 'A sheet flapping next to a basin of water was a sail on the Mediterranean sea.' At such moments Welles rediscovered his childlike delight in the medium, reminding himself that it was, as he had so memorably remarked when he first went to RKO, 'the best electric train set a boy ever had'.

As only an Italian perhaps would, Mancori even grudgingly admired Welles's outlandishly capricious behaviour on the set, because he carried it off with such flourish. He would call the entire crew and actors for nine in the morning, and then show up at six in the evening surrounded by pretty women and a chap playing the accordion. 'What can you do with a man like that?' asked Mancori plaintively. It takes a nearly superhuman level of chutzpah to behave in this fashion on a film set, which at the best of times is a seething mass of resentments and mutinies waiting to happen. It is a gauntlet thrown down, an explicit assertion of personal status, which says: 'Defy me if you dare.' It is behaviour designed to provoke. And provocation was one of Welles's central strategies – a technique, in fact. 'If everything's going well,' said Trauner, 'you can rely on him to come up with something that throws everything into doubt. It's subconscious.'[4] It is a tactic that breeds adrenalin and counteracts complacency; it was deeply embedded in Welles's temperament.

On *Othello* the particular target of this approach was Suzanne Cloutier. It has been suggested (by her, among others) that Welles wanted to have sex with her, and that his subsequent behaviour towards her was an extended punishment for her having rejected of him. Welles was perfectly capable of behaving in that way, but it seems that with Cloutier it was less to do with sex than with a fundamental temperamental hostility. As MacLiammóir has indicated, she was at core made of steel, despite the little black rag doll that accompanied her everywhere and her unceasing attempts at artless girlishness. MacLiammóir's reproduction of her conversation gives a vivid sense of what it was about her that enraged Welles: 'She had too much heart, that was her secret. She meant psychically speaking in the main, because she was, in the main, a psychical person. Sometimes she didn't believe she was of this earth at all, especially when her heartbeats made her feel she was nothing more or less than a Bird. All that was purely spiritual. As for physical side, well, her heart was the wonder and despair of every specialist in Paris, to say nothing of Ottawa, Hollywood and other centres of learning.'

Welles instinctively sensed resistance. His methods of breaking Cloutier down were unrelenting, worthy of *The Taming of the Shrew*. 'He had the habit of nibbling pumpkin,' reported Mancori, 'and he would spit the seeds at her as she was doing her part. He knew what the camera would and wouldn't pick up. He wanted her to speak perfect Shakespearean English while he spat at her, poor woman.' MacLiammóir records the battle of wills between them – Welles scornfully dubbed her 'Schnucks' – but spares the harsh details revealed by Mancori. On one occasion she was keen to visit her ailing mother in London. Welles refused point-blank. Taking pity on her, Mancori quietly checked the schedule: she was in the clear for a few days. She went. As it happens, Welles went to London too, and one evening chanced to walk into the restaurant in which Cloutier was dining. She burst into tears; he beat his fists on the table and roared at her, 'I told you not to come! Who told you to come?' Eventually she admitted it was Mancori. Welles confronted him: 'You did something that went against my wishes. I had said no because . . . I know why I didn't want her to go!'[5]

Cloutier spent a great deal of her time during the film in tears, but Welles never really got to her. She was wrapped up in a cotton-wool ball of her own self-obsession. She and Welles had something in common – they were both fabulists, masters of self-reinvention. When her future husband, Peter Ustinov, first met her, she told him that her mother was a German Jew and that her father was a Native American, neither of which was even remotely true. In later years Cloutier pretended that she and Welles had got on very well, and that they remained close friends; this was not true, though at the very end of filming they had arrived at a kind of truce.

For once Welles, normally violently opposed to spectators on a film set, allowed glamorous visitors to watch while they worked, perhaps thinking he might be able to get some much-needed money out of them: 'Astonishing figure arrives,' reported Fay Compton in her diary. 'Cross between Witch in fairy-tale and one-time telephone cover – turns out to be Diana Duff Cooper with a more than usually offensive staring society group. Their manners are really *alarming*.' This was Lady Diana Cooper, the great socialite and one-time heroine of Max Reinhardt's legendary production of *The Miracle*. The next visitor was Welles's co-star and sparring partner from *Jane Eyre*, Joan Fontaine, and then Joseph Cotten turned up for lunch with Welles, which threw Cloutier into a terrible state: 'Desdemona tied up with nerves and therefore unable to speak, let alone act,' noted the relentless Compton. 'Nervy and touchy as hell over her hair etc. . . .' Both Cotten and Fontaine (as a page), but not Lady Diana, were slipped into a shot, so successfully disguised that they are invisible in the finished film. The scene they were shooting – four minutes long at the most, shot in the cloister of a Byzantine church – went on endlessly till they ran out of light, whereupon Welles turned it into a night-shoot, but it still wouldn't come right. It was *Death in Venice* weather, the heat from the notorious *sirocco* all but unbearable, causing Hilton Edwards acute distress. 'Am amazed at Orson's patience in the face of maddening situations,' confided Fay Compton to her diary. 'Also have great respect for him as director and love working for him.'[6]

A day later, Welles disappeared; it was left to Fanto to tell the actors that the rest of the film would be shot in Rome, at the Scalera Studios, where Trauner had built an elaborate set reproducing parts of Mogador and Venice. Compton had to be back in London to do a play, so she was anxious at the chaos that seemed to have overtaken the film, with very little being shot; in fact what they did mostly was reshooting, because Welles thought what they had was too pretty. Compton's affection and respect for Welles grew daily: she was exactly the sort of actor Welles loved, a feisty pro, with no grand ideas about herself, but an absolute determination to get it right. 'Orson has thought of brilliant but devilish way to do villainy speech. I am ashamed to say it took me 25 takes to get it. Orson doesn't seem to mind.' She had not yet been paid, but on she went. The following night they shot through a storm. Then it was discovered that the last two intricate shots had been on dud negative. 'Our half-witted script girl loses the other half and can't give Orson any of the information he needs as to what is good and what isn't. Nobody will take blame. Eventually, assistant cameraman, Fusi, is blamed and sacked, and taken back again. Storm raging through all this.' There was no more film left: the plane bringing fresh supplies had broken down at Cannes. 'Orson raging – naturally – but still behaving a jolly sight better than most people would.'

The following day Welles told her that he had seen the rushes and that she was 'sensational' and that the crew referred to her as *la Duse Inglese*, after the greatest of all Italian actresses, Eleonora Duse. *En passant*, Welles confessed to her that he had developed an intense dislike for Suzanne Cloutier. 'She's a silly little thing,' Compton admitted, 'and selfish and stubborn, but has a nice side to her and I don't think she deserves such loathing.' The following day she changed her mind: 'Last shot of day with Suzanne. Help! Perfectly simple shot but of course she repeatedly muffs it. She's had all day to learn one line – won't listen to Orson – combination of stupidity and stubbornness – and dares to say she is tired. Gets told off by Orson – rightly . . . at last we finish and go home. Suzanne in tears in car.' At the dinner break, Welles went off to Rome on a date and didn't come back for three hours, leaving the actors and the crew kicking their heels. 'Naughty,' writes the doting Miss Compton, more than half-admiringly. Rome was in the grip of a heatwave; the electricity was down in the city and two old generators were blowing hot air into an already stifling studio. When Welles returned to the studio, an electrical storm suddenly blew up; he ordered the cameramen to shoot it: who knows, he said, what use he might not put it to? Finally, at the end of the week, and in good time to get to her rehearsals in London, Compton was discharged, garlanded with praise and presents; it was her birthday. 'What an extraordinary experience this has been. Wouldn't have missed it for the world.'[7]

Two days later, on 19 September 1949, shooting was again suspended. MacLiammóir and Edwards – Rosencrantz and Guildenstern to Welles's Hamlet – hung about, as they had done so often since *Othello* began, in a sort of upholstered limbo, dining and drinking and visiting theatres in Europe's finest watering holes (Paris,

Berlin, Brussels) until next called upon to make an appearance. The call finally came in October, when MacLiammóir was summoned to Viterbo, a little to the north of Rome, for a few days' filming. They did reverse shots on a scene filmed three months earlier in Safi, and the death of Desdemona, upon completing which Welles abruptly sped off, in full make-up, back to Rome. The shoot then moved to Venice, 'cold, wave-ridden, echoing to the sound of bells and distant footsteps and the lapping of water on the marble, inexorably beautiful in the mirrored autumn twilight', as MacLiammóir moodily put it, convinced now that if he and Edwards – who had joined him for various scenes as Brabantio – ever again played on a real stage in Dublin, 'it would be a miracle'. The Italian shooting was completed in a month, some of it shot with Welles *in absentia* while he searched for new locations; on such occasions, Washinsky directed.

Once filming was complete, MacLiammóir, Edwards and Cloutier were flown first to Marseilles, en route – as they believed – for Morocco again; but instead of North Africa, they were transported to the idyllic artists' colony at Saint-Paul-de-Vence in Provence, where they were greeted gloomily by Welles, who immediately set off for Paris. A few days later they joined him there. No explanation was ever offered for any of these bewildering peregrinations. Their lives had turned into a major-key rehash of *Waiting for Godot*, with a dash of Kafka – major key because they were excellently fed and watered and the locations were all charming, but the sense of disorientation was acute. They were beginning to doubt whether they would see Dublin that Christmas: 'feel sure that Orson has plans for large Christmas tree in market-place at Mogador, entertainment probably to include brief but startling appearance of O himself as Santa Claus'. As if in defiance of the chaotic reality, Welles made a public announcement that *Othello* had completed filming and that he would soon be starting work on *Ulysses*, which was certainly putting a brave face on things.

The truth of the matter was that he was increasingly anxious about money; his last earnings had been in April, on *The Black Rose*. With no handy $100,000 on offer from a passing blockbuster, he had started to think in terms of a theatre tour, to kick off in Paris and then to play such centres as Brussels, Antwerp, Lille and Amsterdam. It would consist of a double bill comprising *The Importance of Being Earnest* (slightly cut) and Marlowe's *Dr Faustus* (savagely cut). Edwards would direct *Earnest* and play Canon Chasuble and Marlowe's Prologue; Welles would direct *Faustus* and play Algernon Moncrieff and Faustus; while MacLiammóir would play Jack Worthing and Mephistopheles, having by now presumably accepted that villainy was well within his range. Suzanne Cloutier would play Cecily and – 'poor child', remarks MacLiammóir – Helen of Troy, while Fay Compton, if they could get her back, would be Lady Bracknell. They would ask Dior to design the costumes and André Derain to do the set. Of course they would.

After a few more days of ebullient planning, still at the stage where everything seems possible – Dior? *pourquoi pas?* Derain? *mais naturellement* – Edwards and MacLiammóir gratefully returned, just in time for Christmas, to Dublin, where a card from Welles was waiting for them: 'Miss you badly already and hope for wonderful things in New Year.' There were affectionate phone calls on Christmas Day, but no certainty as to what was going to happen next. Welles wrote to them from the Hotel Lancaster in Paris, by no means encouragingly: 'As 1949 prepares to die of old age I want to acknowledge that I've made it pretty awful for both of you. Come what may (and it probably will) you deserve to know how earnestly I'm going to balance the budget before next Christmas . . .'[8] But then, in the New Year, something wonderful happened, just as Welles had hoped: the French-Algerian financier/producer Edmond Tenoudji of Films Marceau came through with 12 million francs in exchange for the French distribution rights, so filming could resume.

★

In mid-January 1950, MacLiammóir was duly summoned to Mogador, which was reached, as usual, by slow and exhausting steps via Paris and Fez. There were some changes of personnel: George Fanto was now sole director of photography; young Patrice Dally (who would later assist on *Rififi*) replaced Washinsky as assistant director; and James Allan was art director in place of Trauner. Welles himself did not appear for ten days and, when he did, it was with a lovely Swedish actress on his arm, a very classy tootsie indeed, dubbed by MacLiammóir 'Belle of Stockholm'. For the most part, filming was focused and productive; with the aid of photographs and print-outs of footage, Welles and Fanto had worked out in advance exactly what was needed to complete the film. Time was limited, money tight. None of the other actors, apart from the irrepressible 'Schnucks', were present. Everyone and anyone was liable to be enlisted into lending a back, a shoulder or a neck, supposedly belonging to Cassio, Montano or Roderigo. Welles was in bonhomous form, which may have been not unconnected to the presence at his side of 'Belle of Stockholm', with whom from time to time he would slip off. 'Orson disappeared to unknown destination,' wrote MacLiammóir. 'Maybe the Moon but suspect Casablanca.' On such occasions Welles would leave long and detailed instructions as to precisely what he wanted shot.

> 'Canons from the wall as already established . . . if there is a windless day, remove the flags from the standards because they would look ridiculous without wind. The camera doesn't move from Othello to the castle but from the castle, through the wall, to Othello; the opposite of what would seem logical . . . hand held camera following the flight of seagulls for the idea of delirium . . . shot of canons firing and Othello rising to his feet after epileptic fit: use English film . . . DON'T FORGET THE CANONS DON'T FORGET THE CANONS.'

All this, said Mancori, 'in imperfect Italian'.[9]

The mood darkened somewhat when the unit transferred to Mazagan, to the north of Mogador where Welles had discovered a fifteenth-century Portuguese cistern of striking appearance, outside which he had decided to take a wide-shot of the brawl between Cassio, Montano and Roderigo (all played by doubles, of course); later, Desdemona would meet her end there. 'Its beauty, of undeniable and bewildering quality,' wrote MacLiammóir, 'only equalled by its enormous size, foetid, clinging air, and general aspect of nameless doom.' Transforming it into a filmable location was a huge labour, which Welles entrusted to George Fanto, who had now become de facto production manager, as well as director of photography. Fanto set to work, day and night, with his crew, restoring columns, filling the cistern with water into which, somewhat riskily, he put aniline dye to make it sparkle, and building interlocking platforms to keep the lights and cables out of the water. 'It took endless hours of work with unskilled Moroccan labour.'[10] Finally, suffering from laryngitis and a high fever, he took himself off to the hotel, much to Welles's freely expressed vexation. His reproaches greatly upset Fanto. Welles wrote him a note later that night, telling him that he deeply appreciated how much he had sacrificed to keep on working in the cistern, but, 'my dear George, it does not justify the general (that's you) walking off the set because you're hungry or tired or sick'. Next day he sent him another, longer letter. It is a remarkable document in many ways. Welles begins by apologizing to Fanto for his bullying, assuring him that, if Fanto should ever take 'the human risk' of working with him again, he would not be subjected to such behaviour. He recognizes that any cameraman working on such a tight schedule would need strength of character, and even more so when having to accommodate what Welles acknowledges to be his often unreasonable demands. Pushing, Welles explains, is often a necessary expedient, if never a pleasant one.

He acknowledges, however, that his method of carrying out such pushing may not be the right one for Fanto – is, in fact, 'obviously all wrong.'

> But there's no use my pretending that under these present conditions my style of pushing on a set is going to change. And when any shot (an exterior without lighting especially) isn't ready after nearly two hours I'm afraid I'll be heard from, nor am I likely to welcome replies in terms of marital difficulties, divorces and such personal items.

Welles refuses to regard such talk as 'courageous,' lamenting, as he had done at the time, the introduction of the personal note whenever he feels the need to crack the whip. In response to Fanto's plea that such measures should be avoided, Welles comments, 'I'd very much like to be able to throw that instrument away, but the shorter the budget the longer the whip.' He hardly needs, he says, to remind Fanto that their budget is as short as they come, that they are 'nerve-rackingly enough at the dead-end of [their] money and indeed of money-making possibilities.' They have to stay on schedule; there is no option.

Welles again asserts his deep and warm friendship with Fanto, but goes on to make it clear that he does not regard the matter in hand as being either of friendship or even of good will. He will be tactful, he says, in his future dealings with Fanto, but bluntly warns him that if Fanto ever falls behind in his work as he had done the day before, 'I will break my promise.'

Welles ends by saying that it would delight him if Fanto were not to decide against working under such conditions, protesting again that he wants Fanto to know how enormously he regrets his part in the previous day's unpleasantness.

It is the letter of a monomaniac, a man for whom no rules, no human considerations exist when there is a film to be made. He demanded the maximum of himself – that much no one could deny – and he expected the same of all his partners in the work: he has an almost Christ-like expectation that those who work for him will be ready to abandon mother, wife, child: He that loveth father or mother more than me is not worthy of me: and he that loveth son or daughter more than me is not worthy of me. Welles is the way, the truth and the life: he who is not with him is against him. For a man of a religious disposition like Fanto, it was an irresistible call. In an age long before health-and-safety regulations, Welles expected that his cohorts would risk everything for the film. For him. It is the language of a commander rallying the troops – Henry V, Patton. And it is true that Welles was waging war on all fronts, and that, for the film, it was a matter of life and death. And there would always be people who were ready to take, as Welles so pithily put it, the human risk of working with him.

There is a postscript to the letter:

> If you aren't better, don't come to work till you are. If you determine to get up – then you must *stay up*.

Fanto got up; and he stayed up. Who wouldn't have?

As it happens, it was Hilton Edwards who actually directed the sequence in the cistern. Welles genuinely wanted his old boss to try his hand at the medium, insisting, as he always had done, that there was no skill to directing movies that couldn't be picked up by an intelligent person in a morning, but also convinced that a stage director as imaginative and forceful as Edwards undoubtedly was, would be an excellent film director. Edwards was shyly determined to give it a stab; Welles very seriously proposed during the making of *Othello* that Edwards should direct a film of *Julius Caesar* with Welles as Brutus. There is no question that Welles meant this sincerely; but the offer was another manifestation of the complicated relationship that he had with Edwards and MacLiammóir, indissoluble partners in life and in art (though no longer, for many years past, in bed). Edwards was to all outward appearances a hearty, vigorously masculine man, MacLiammóir a feline aesthete with something uncanny about him, witty, eloquent and unnervingly intuitive. Welles was instinctively drawn to Edwards, with whom he made common cause, sometimes to the exclusion of MacLiammóir: he and Edwards – sensible men of the world, practical, efficient, capable – mocking MacLiammóir's vanity, his apparent illogicality, his inability to handle the electrical or mechanical apparatuses of the twentieth century.

MacLiammóir watched, bided his time, made mental notes – and written ones, too, in the diary he religiously kept, day in and day out, in Irish, as a protection against prying eyes. 'Why is it, I wonder,' wrote Welles in the surprisingly candid Foreword to *Put Money in Thy Purse*:

> that most of us who are Micheál Mac Liammóir's friends – having never been his victims – are so very certain that at any minute we might be? . . . In company, that Micheál of ours doesn't slash or slaughter, or even prick, but lavishly spreads about him, instead, the pleasant oils and balms of good humour. He is an entertainer rather than a conquistador, a good companion, who could certainly scratch, but who prefers to purr . . . I now reveal his true, his darkest secret. It is simple almost to the point of squalor: he keeps a diary!

Welles's friendship with the partners was a deep one, one of the deepest of his life, a potent brew of something almost filial with something nearly sexual, but it had endured (and was again to endure) some very rough patches, at which *Put Money in Thy Purse* only hints. Rocky times were to come.

Meanwhile there was the bravura opening sequence of *Othello* to be shot: the funeral processions of Othello and Desdemona, and what MacLiammóir fearfully referred to as the Cage Scene, in which Iago is roughly hauled up to the top of the ramparts in a wooden crate as Othello and Desdemona are carried off in their coffins. 'This Orson's invention and I've been dreading it for months.' As he was hauled up, the local population stood in respectful silence; as he descended, they applauded. After that it was down to the Cistern, 'the Underworld', as MacLiammóir named it, 'gazing camera left with tense expression at nobody at all, turning, twisting, peering through windows, and getting myself kicked, prodded, slapped, pushed, and trodden on by extras till I was black and blue'; and then back to the ramparts, to be dragged along at the end of a piece of rope with what he called the dog-collar round his neck, tugged and jerked back and forth and sideways. The final sequence on which MacLiammóir worked was the intricate travelling shot in the scene that preceded Othello's epileptic fit. There were seven takes, MacLiammóir noted, and it was by now 7 March; after the last take, Welles announced, 'Mr MacLiammóir, I am happy to tell you you are now an out-of-work actor. You have finished Iago.' Like many other things to do with the film of *Othello*, this valediction proved to be illusory, but for the time being it inspired MacLiammóir to a celestial vision of his 'friends and fellow-adventurers', which forms the last paragraph of *Put Money in Thy Purse*:

> Already I see them in my mind's eye as if painted on a gauze, through which the back-stage lighting will presently shine, revealing other scenes and other characters . . . Trauner and Dally and Brizzi and dear Fanto and the rest of them standing in serried ranks, the banners of their trades a-flutter stiffly above their heads. And behind and beyond them all is Orson, mysteriously grimacing as he lolls towards them with hands outstretched, waving Godspeed from his rolling banks of cumulus and thunder-cloud, the Painted Lightning forked ambiguously behind his head.

Welles had no such sense of celestial harmony. His first job, once he was back in Rome, was to raise money to start to put all this together; not to mention paying the cast and, indeed, Trauner. All local sources of revenue had dried up. He discovered that his old friend Darryl Zanuck was holidaying at Cap d'Antibes and so, in a reckless gesture, he climbed into a cab and told the driver to take him to the French Riviera. Once he'd found Zanuck at supper with friends, Welles knelt before him and begged for help. Zanuck offered him nearly 200 million lire in exchange for 50 per cent of the English-language distribution rights. Italian currency restrictions meant that he had to justify the amount with the authorities, which Papi, still production manager (but no longer Padovani's lover), duly arranged, at the same time applying for financing for an extra ten weeks' shooting. No wonder the Painted Lightning in MacLiammóir's vision had forked *ambiguously* behind Welles's head. The final tableau was far from achieved.

Welles himself went to Taormina, taking with him the script of *Ulysses* – not the version over which Borneman had so long toiled, but a rival version to be produced by Dino De Laurentiis and directed by the great German director G.W. Pabst, with Greta Garbo coming out of her decade-long retirement to play Penelope, and Welles himself in the title-role. He hummed and hawed long enough to convince De Laurentiis that he was going to go ahead with his own version, and was duly paid a lot of money not to do so. But however much Welles got from De Laurentiis, it was not enough to take *Othello* forward or to cover his debts, despite the dribble of funds being slowly released from 20th Century Fox. Welles was gently but embarrassingly reminded of what he owed MacLiammóir and, to a lesser tune, Edwards, both of whom were in desperate trouble financially: they believed – with the perfect financial innocence that had characterised the whole of their always perilous tenure of the Gate Theatre – that they would be paid for the whole period of their work on the film, rather than just the days they had actually filmed.

As a way of killing a number of birds with one stone, Welles began to turn again to the plans for a theatre evening, about which he and Edwards and MacLiammóir had become so excited the previous December. MacLiammóir had said then that he and Welles were longing 'to trumpet about on a stage again', which was certainly true for MacLiammóir and probably true for Welles. It was presumably in Taormina that he ran up the two plays that he proposed they should do – not the bewilderingly improbable double bill of *The Importance of Being Earnest* and *Dr Faustus* that he had originally suggested, but an entirely new play satirising Hollywood, called *The Unthinking Lobster*, and a new version of the Faust story, incorporating chunks of Marlowe and Milton plus a pinch of Dante, all washed down with a lot of Welles. To this he gave the name *Time Runs* ('The stars move still,' says Faustus as he dies, 'time runs, the clock will strike / The Devil will come and Faustus must be damn'd'). He called the double bill *The Blessed and the Damned*, and they represent Welles's first and only attempt at playwriting since his two boyhood efforts, written before he was seventeen; he had long ago shown himself to be a play-editor of genius, but that of course is a very different skill.

Welles had somewhere along the line hooked up with an ambitious young French producer called Georges Beaume, who in turn had an association with Pierre Beteille, the owner of the splendid Édouard VII Theatre off the boulevard des Capucines: they would do the plays there in mid-June of 1951. Welles immediately approached MacLiammóir and Edwards; MacLiammóir turned him down, pointedly preferring to judge an amateur drama festival in Kerry, but Edwards – out of affection for Welles, no doubt, but also in the hope of recovering some of the money they were still owed and so desperately needed – signed up to play the Archbishop in the first play and Mephistophilis in the second, to design the light and generally supervise the production. Somewhat surprisingly, Welles invited Suzanne Cloutier to play Helen of Troy in *Time Runs* and, more fittingly, Miss Pratt the secretary who becomes a star in *The Unthinking Lobster*; she was flush from her recent success in Julien Duvivier's *Au royaume des cieux*, which might have helped the box office. It certainly needed help: the rest of the cast was assembled from inexperienced young Americans drifting through Paris. Duke Ellington, no less, had agreed to write the score, which one might have thought would have created something of a stir, but curiously little was made of it.

The management had a challenge on its hands anyway, trying to sell two plays in English during the summer, when half of the theatres were closed and most of the population had decamped to the coast. Welles's fame was the only pull. He was indeed *très connu* in France: *Le Troisième Homme*, which had won the Grand Prix in Cannes the year before, was as big a hit in Paris as it was everywhere else, and Welles had come out of it particularly well, as Truman Capote, who happened to be in Paris at the time, noted in a letter that reveals something of the general view of Welles's acting: 'saw the most wonderful movie. Carol Reed's *The Third Man*. Orson Welles is in it – superbly, believe it or not.'[12] Welles had a powerfully articulate following among young French film-makers, but their fine words, alas, buttered no parsnips. Nonetheless, Beaume managed to whip up a storm in the press with some remarkable claims: 'It's almost certain', reported a breathless *Parisien libéré*, 'that Orson Welles will be performing four of his own plays on a Paris stage. Such is the excitement', it continued, 'that Box Offices will be set up in Paris, in London and in New York.'[13] *L'Aurore* easily topped that: 'The announcement of the show has created such excitement in the artistic world, that an aeronautical company has arranged special flights between Paris and Rome and London and Paris.' The forthcoming Paris premiere of *Black Magic* added still more mysterious and glamorous dimensions to Welles's profile: it was promised that Welles, *in person*, would adjudicate – while lunching with a few famous friends – a sensational trial of wits between two eminent fakirs as to which could stay buried underground in a coffin the longest. 'Cagliostro-Welles will give 50,000 francs to the winner.'[14] Encounters with the Press were lined up on a daily basis, but the journalists who interviewed him found the cause of all this excitement in surly form.

'Orson Welles is rehearsing in a dilapidated theatre,' reported *France-Soir*. 'He's in a foul temper. He's had no voice for two days, is wrapped up in a heavy winter coat, communicates with the actors through his stage manager and only parts his lips in order to shout at someone.' For the photo, the interviewer reported, Welles presented his back to the camera as in *The Third Man*, 'then he turns round and fixes the lens with his staring bug-eyes. Orson', he continues cattily, 'is, like Louis XIV, staying at Versailles. Why doesn't he sleep at the Palace one night? He deserves no less.'[15] In early rehearsals Welles had been rather more cheerful, 'but then,' wrote Jenifer

Howard, the young American actress who was playing the gossip columnist in *The Unthinking Lobster*, 'things began to unravel, and Orson became increasingly distracted and, at times, thoroughly fed up and bored with the lot of us'.[16] He was put out all over again, as he been on *Othello*, by Suzanne Cloutier. Rehearsals became very haphazard. The actors would arrive for a 10 a.m. call; Welles would show up at 5 p.m. 'We might, or we might not, get a run-through. He was just as likely to sit round joking and telling wonderful stories for an hour and then take us all out for dinner. Sometimes work wouldn't start till ten or eleven at night at which point little or less than little was achieved.'

Hilton Edwards took over the rehearsals when Welles disappeared, which was increasingly often. Sometimes – not always – he was with the French film editor Jean Sacha, trying to make sense of the fifteen hours of material he had had developed from the *Othello* footage. Then suddenly he became interested in *The Blessed and the Damned* again. He and Edwards had seen a young black American singer in cabaret and were instantly overwhelmed by her; she had formerly been part of the Katherine Dunham Dance Company, she was called Eartha Kitt and Welles knew that he must have her. 'A huge domineering-looking hombre-giant stepped his way towards me,' she wrote in her autobiography. 'I felt the electrifying waves of his personality hit me as he drew nearer. "Can you learn fast? We open on Saturday."'[17] He immediately sacked Suzanne Cloutier from the part of Helen of Troy, which he rewrote for Kitt, doubling it in size, and from then on all his energy and enthusiasm were given over to working on those scenes; *The Unthinking Lobster*, in which she did not appear, was given scant attention.

'He could not tolerate ignorance of any kind. If one was not quick enough, Orson lost patience,' wrote Kitt. 'The quicker one was to receive what Orson had to give, the better his creative powers were.'[18] The one thing Welles could never tolerate was slowness. He had wanted to sack Stanley Cortez on *The Magnificent Ambersons* for what he called his 'criminal slowness'; George Fanto had suffered the lash of his whip for the same offence. But Kitt was not just quick – she was electric. 'Those rehearsals were grand to watch,' said Jenifer Howard. 'His size and dark power were amazingly balanced by her cat-like grace and her lightness and quickness.'[19] Often, Welles would dismiss the rest of the cast and the two of them would paint the set together, as they ran lines, and then they'd go and dine with Hilton Edwards. 'They would eat huge meals,' said Kitt's biographer, 'and the men would discuss Plato or Camus and get up from the table to declaim speeches from Shakespeare.'[20] Kitt listened and learned. Then she and he would walk together through Paris and watch the sun come up over the Champs-Elysées, as they finally headed back to her hotel. 'He would take me to my door,' she wrote, 'ring the bell and say, "*À demain.*"' Kitt's biographer has his doubts that things ended there.

The burden of the music, naturally, fell on her, increasingly so as Welles realised what an astonishing vocal instrument she possessed. Halfway through rehearsals he had tracked down Duke Ellington to Milan and asked him to write five songs for the show. Ellington was happy to oblige: it was, he said, 'one of the most extravagant gestures of flattery I have ever received', from 'a man of genius who happens to be a very dear friend of mine, Orson Welles . . .'[21] He soon knocked off the songs (or, more likely, his composing partner, Billy Strayhorn, did), recorded them and sent them to Welles; a week later Welles called again: now he needed twenty-eight incidental music cues. Ellington was in Stockholm; Hilton Edwards was accordingly despatched there, only a week before the show was due to open, to work on them with Ellington and Strayhorn, which he did, acting out all the parts for them and hurrying back to Paris with what they had written. Strayhorn came with him, and set new lyrics for the show as quickly as Welles could come up with them.

Technical rehearsals were, as usual with Welles, a nightmare, because he only really started to function creatively when he had everything at his disposal – the set, the light, the sound, the short film he had shot for the beginning of *The Unthinking Lobster*; there was also Micheál MacLiammóir's recording of the opening and closing speeches of *Time Runs* to slot in. The opening was put off once, twice, three times. 'The audience for last night was told that evening dress was obligatory,' star reporter René MacColl told the readers of the London *Daily Express*, which, like several London newspapers, was following events keenly:

> When beautifully-gowned women and men in dinner-jackets arrived in the theatre they were turned away. Tonight in the darkened auditorium, I found thirty-five-year-old Orson Welles in a blue turtle-neck sweater rehearsing the *Brainless Lobster* company. He said: 'I have been ready to open for a week. I don't know what all this is about.' At this point a girl came to the foot of the stage and said, 'Mr Welles, those dresses are still not ready.' 'Never mind,' said Welles. 'Trouble?' he went on. 'Well, only a bit. We have had difficulties with the French technicians – they just don't

> get our methods. They like to improvise. I hate improvising . . . but everything is ready.' A young man came up and said, 'Orson, we just can't come to an arrangement about the piano.' 'Well,' said Orson, 'they can't have any more money. That's final.' An ornamental curtain was lowered onto the set. Welles gestured at it moodily, 'Look,' he said. 'Not a patch on how I envisaged it. When you order pink it comes out mauve. Heart-breaking. Then the scenery is put in the alley. I have not left the theatre for three days and nights. But we are all ready. You understand?'[22]

Finally, after all these mighty labours, they opened and were politely received. Eartha Kitt remembers taking ten curtain calls, and an ecstatic press. It was: for *her*. About the plays the critics were less certain. Many reviewers were frank about the inadequacy of their own English; most thought the first play was an amusing enough squib, but that *Time Runs* was probably rather more interesting. It was all guess-work. Eartha Kitt certainly captivated them, but they were *absolument bouleversé* by Welles. As well they might have been, given the build-up he received in the programme booklet. First was a typical pen-portrait by Cocteau:

> Orson Welles is a giant with the face of a child, a tree filled with birds and shadows, a dog who has broken loose and gone to sleep in the flower bed. An active loafer, a wise madman, a solitary surrounded by humanity, a student who sleeps during the lesson. A strategy: pretending to be drunk to be simply left alone. Seemingly better than anyone else, he can use a nonchalant attitude of real strength, apparently drifting but guided by a half-opened eye. This attitude of an abandoned hulk, and that of a sleepy bear, protects him from the cold fever of the motion picture world. An attitude which made him move on, made him leave Hollywood, and carried him to other lands and other horizons.[23]

Welles provoked this sort of writing, especially among the French. His friend and unofficial PR man, Maurice Bessy, contributed a piece that starts:

> He comes on stage and nothing exists but his presence. He offers the spectacle of his strength and of his intelligence, an untamed strength with an indefinable something that is malicious and incurable. A raw strength, chiselled in granite. He appears and we experience the gasp of emotion that scorches the air in a moment

> of danger . . . we know that his soul fits a unique being of supple genius and breeding. We know that he acts and gives himself as a man; and receives with the soul of a woman . . . he is the most worldly of bohemians and the most tender of Don Juans.

The piece ends: 'He is alone on this earth. Alone with a few pieces of baggage. Cherish him because he is not made in the same cast as the everyday man, because he is part of an extra group, a challenge to God.' Georges Beaume's piece, entitled 'Orson Among Us', as if he were the Lord's anointed, told the possibly bemused Parisian theatregoer that at a time when vapidity was everywhere, Welles was, 'along with Malraux, Picasso and Lawrence of Arabia, if not the highest, then certainly the most modern manifestation of the demon of the absolute'.[24]

The critical fraternity understandably felt the need to rise to the challenge of all this ecstatic prose. The temptation to out-Cocteau Cocteau proved irresistible: 'The arrival of Welles on the Parisian stage – this bear with the face of a fallen angel lolling among the clouds – is a revelation. For us, this theatrical manifestation of his is more convincing than what we know of him from films . . . however infinitely indefinable, he is himself, 4-dimensional, splendid, unusable, you either reject him or embrace him, like thunder or mandragora.' At least Cocteau had the excuse of being an opium addict; what were these chaps on? 'He's the last of the *monstres sacrés*. A super-*monstre sacré*, in fact, because he combines the jobs of designer, author, director, actor. He has Orson-Welles syndrome . . . an *enfant terrible* (Cocteau's son, perhaps?) who is also Prospero, Caliban, Ariel, he demands love or hate.' This same critic, however, had his feet sufficiently on the ground to end his review: 'I would by the way like to know why the ticket prices have been doubled at the Édouard VII,'[25] which may offer a clue as to why nobody, alas, came to see the show.

Anglophones, and in particular American tourists, may have been rather put off by Art Buchwald's 'Paris after Dark' column in the *International Herald Tribune*:

> Orson Welles has many personal grievances against Hollywood. In his new play *The Unthinking Lobster* . . . [he] gets most of them off his chest. It has gags aimed at a few of the Brown Derby crowd, and a sophomoric message that left the audience embarrassed as well as cold . . . instead of a rapier, the author-actor uses a sledge-hammer to get his point across . . . unimaginative sets and the less said about the

> staging the better. Welles's revenge boomerangs, and *The Unthinking Lobster* becomes a satire of Orson Welles doing a satire on Hollywood.

On the other hand, he said, '*Time Runs* . . . has a great deal of good theatre value and saves the evening from being entirely wasted.'[26] Micheál MacLiammóir, visiting the play for the first time, described it as 'a worry' and asked himself (in the diary that would later be published as *Each Actor on His Ass*) whether it could be because of what he called 'the curiously suffocating darkness that hovers over it, a sense of foreboding and damnation brilliantly stated, that turns the evening into a brooding vulture'.

★

The first and much lighter of the two plays, *The Unthinking Lobster*, is in effect a curtain-raiser, a broad boulevard satire on Hollywood, a subject to which Welles was irresistibly drawn and to which he kept reverting throughout his career, despite his frequent and very public dismissals of the place. The satire, as Art Buchwald rightly suggests, is fairly scattergun, taking in rather more than Hollywood. Welles insisted in interviews that it was not about movies at all: it was, he said, 'about the conditions in which grace' – in the theological sense of the word – 'can exist'. The premise is droll enough: Hollywood is in the grip of religious fever; Jake Behoovian, boss of the Zitz-Cosmic studio, decides to make a film about St Anne de Beaumont, a French-Canadian peasant who cures the sick and infirm of French Canada, tossing aside their crutches and bandages – clearly a wicked send-up of Suzanne Cloutier in her more rapturous moments. The film is being directed by a certain Sporcacione, an Italian semi-documentarian – Welles's dig at the neo-realists – who has decided that, for greater verisimilitude, the disabled should be played by the disabled. The star, however, has dropped out, and so Behoovian's secretary, Miss Pratt (Cloutier), agrees to stand in for her. In the course of filming she actually cures the cripples: a miracle, in Hollywood! An archbishop is summoned to check her credentials; he determines that the secretary is an authentic saint. Hollywood falls apart: people no longer take meetings – they pray. To sort things out, an Archangel descends and strikes a deal: if Hollywood makes no more movies about heaven, heaven will make no more miracles in Hollywood.

It's slight stuff, though just sometimes Welles seems to be edging towards something deeper: the Archbishop asks Nancy Pratt, the celluloid saint, 'You believe you love God?' And she answers, 'Despite miracles. Despite cheap paintings, relics, bad sweating, bleeding, groaning statues, yes. You say that I have committed the sin of pride.

But I can't lie to you: I love Him. The world, full of ugliness, is in agony. I don't love that.' Mostly Welles seizes the opportunity to get some aperçus off his chest: Behoovian (played by Welles) is given the line with which Welles delighted to bait Italian journalists: 'As for Italy – I forget who said it – Italy's a nation of actors, the least good of whom are the professional ones.' The fake Archduke, who runs the exclusive Hollywood eatery called Chez Chi-chi, says of theatre acting: 'Well, it's not exactly normal. But what's normal about painting your face and showing it in public? It's a little deranged, frankly. Like making love. And a good actor is a good lover . . . like a lover, he tries to conceal the embarrassing reality; what he does to achieve that is truly ridiculous. Oh, it's not easy! Six nights of partying, plus matinées.' Which perhaps tells us more about Welles's attitude to love-making than to the theatre.

There is a rather half-hearted attempt to link this first play to its Faustian companion piece: 'What d'you want me to do?' says Zitz, of the contract that has been offered to him, 'sign it in blood?' And there are some sub-Pirandellian meta-theatrical musings: 'For us artists, every performance contains a whole lifetime of virtue and sin,' says the phoney Archduke. 'Every exit is a death. And the fall of the curtain is as . . . final as the Last Judgement. Heaven, for us, is suspended on a painted drop at our backs, and there's no hell beneath us – it's in front of us . . . where we're looking. For us, where we were looking during the play no longer exists.'

The piece is a *jeu d'esprit* – a trifle – but it is nonetheless part of Welles's capacious range of enthusiasms. In the telling phrase of Bill Krohn, Welles was not a radical; he was a man of many nostalgias. Throughout his career in the theatre and on radio and on television, though not on film, he indulged in his passion for past forms – among other things, low comedy, high comedy, screwball comedy, spectaculars, farce, to say nothing of magic. For the most part it has to be admitted that, magic aside, he had no real gift for any of these things. *The Unthinking Lobster* attempts a peculiarly French form, the light comedy of ideas, but the form demands, paradoxically enough, a certain rigour, which is here absent; neither the ideas nor the comedy quite work. Welles's conviction that he had examined the question of the conditions under which Grace can flourish – why not in a Hollywood studio? – is mistaken. He obviously wants to have fun, too, but doesn't quite manage to: both the dialogue and the invention are more than a little tired. He was once again pursuing the ignis fatuus of his life, the quest for popular success. The motive was partly financial, but also, quite simply, because he liked to make people laugh. With *The Unthinking Lobster*, on the whole he failed in this ambition.

Time Runs – 'an old legend in a new mixture' – is another matter. Owing something to Welles's mentor and friend Thornton Wilder, it presents Faust sometimes as his medieval self, sometimes as modern man; it meditates on the human condition in a collage of pregnant phrases from great writers – mostly Marlowe, whose *Dr Faustus* Welles had directed with such electrifying results in New York in 1936. These passages are linked by wistful connecting sequences by Welles himself, the whole thing underpinned and woven together by the music Welles loved above all other: jazz. It is scarcely a play at all, being, as Welles's chum Cocteau might have said, not so much a text as a pretext, offering opportunities for production. The piece changed radically in rehearsals and during production, though the essential form remained the same: a voice-over at the beginning tells us that there has been a great catastrophe and that we are in 'the last year of the first Age after Christ'. A chorus of 'three intelligent negro girls' tells the story of Faust. Mephistophilis appears as a friar and makes himself known to Faustus, which causes the girls to sing:

Hungry little trouble
Damned in a bubble
Yearning to be
Be or be free
All that you see
Is all about me.

One of the intelligent Negro girls turns into Helen of Troy, who, after a long chunk of Marlowe, becomes his wife in modern times:

FAUSTUS: You know, there's some nice operas about me, too. I'm getting famous darling.

He goes to the club.

HELEN: I'll leave the light on in the hall.
FAUSTUS: Is your love strong enough to save me?
HELEN: No, I can't save you. You'd better let out the cat.

He is unfaithful to her, and begins to devote himself to his inventions.

FAUSTUS: The god I serve is mine own appetite.

CHORUS: Don Giovanni Faustus loved the ladies
Made him a bargain to go down to Hades
Lived him a life compounded of sin
Went to perdition but couldn't get in.

FAUSTUS: I want to go to the moon.

A group of curiosity-seekers, 'such as form in front of a prison before an execution', arranges itself across the stage. They discuss Faustus and his culpability. One of them has a package that ticks. Helen (Faust's wife) says that it's one of his inventions:

HELEN: He was not evil. Evil is evil things. Hunger is evil and disease. He only wanted time to fight them. He isn't ready to die . . . he hated death and darkness: is that wicked? He made weapons to use against them – I know, I know, he also made weapons to use against himself . . .

The chorus then comments, in some rather flat Eliotese:

CHORUS: In the absence of Heaven as a tragic fact
We in this terrible century cannot laugh
At blessedness. It is not to be mocked.
Heaven's an old joke with its harps and halos
But even we must respect the state of grace.

Faustus shouts out Marlowe's great desperate cry to the universe: 'Stand still, you ever-moving spheres of heaven . . . I'll burn my books. Ah, Mephistophilis!' At the end, the bell having tolled twelve, and as Helen reprises her odd little ditty 'Hungry little trouble / Damned in a bubble', Faustus addresses the audience in Welles's words:

I refuse to be insane. I share that common dignity
I do not claim the sanctuary of the madhouse.
I hold myself responsible. Do not think
I stumbled into the pit. I dug it myself.
Go home now and pray for the damned.
Pray for the living souls removed
From the community of life.
Pray for the free man who damned himself.
Go in haste for damnation is contagious.

And the Voice from the beginning leaves us with Marlowe:

> Cut is the branch that might have grown full straight
> And burned is Apollo's laurel bough,
> That sometime grew with this learned man.
> Faustus is gone . . .
> *Terminat hora diem, terminat author opus.*

All the lights dim except for one, which focuses on the ticking package we have seen several times already. 'The theatre is filled with the sound of slow ticking.' Like many in 1951, and for some time to come, Welles was deeply disturbed by the atom-bomb and its fateful possibilities; but the piece is infused with a more general sense of melancholy, not to say pessimism, which MacLiammóir so acutely perceived: the sense of 'foreboding and damnation' that is quite profound with Welles, an underlying apprehension, so precociously present in *Bright Lucifer*, of a fundamental wrongness, a lurking evil, an Original Sin, perhaps, which dogs so many of his characters – the source of the guilt that Welles always insisted was unassuageable, which had to be acknowledged and faced, not expunged. But *Time Runs* is too leaky a vessel to contain any real response to this idea. No doubt the stage production created a certain atmosphere: 'He plays beautifully with light,' said *Le Figaro*, 'a real head-banger for the chief electrician, and he creates a diabolical rhythm which does credit to Welles the stage director, proving himself a rival for any of our stage Titans.' But it is a poor piece of writing, a reminder that Welles always worked best with existing structures and stories: here he is trying to create something that has the freedom and spontaneity of jazz, and he fails.

He rapidly lost interest in the show, no doubt discouraged by the poor houses. Francis Koval interviewed him for *Sight and Sound* one evening: 'that night the curtain rose twenty minutes late in the Paris theatre where Orson Welles was the main attraction . . . the angry audience, stamping their feet impatiently, fortunately never suspected that my own dinner-table interview with Welles had been the cause of that delay'.[27] Around the same time Welles was visited backstage by the noted English journalist and photographer Daniel Farson:

> People drifted in and out. One man announced, 'I'm the only person I've met who likes the first play better than the second.' 'That's the way it is,' said Welles in the sing-song voice of Kane. 'Some people enjoy the first play, some the second. No one

enjoys them both.' The man and the two women with him laughed sycophantically, but the mood changed when the man asked how the play was doing. 'Since Korea, you know, the theatres are half-empty.' Welles disappeared behind a screen, emerging in his underclothes with a glass of champagne. Another young man came in, examined the bowl of roses and the empty magnum. 'A pity they're so faded,' Welles said of the first, and, 'A greater pity that the champagne has faded too.' He flashed a smile and walked out.

Farson, an acute observer and commentator, describing him (as, inevitably, the French had done) as a *monstre sacré*, acutely remarked that Welles possessed all the qualities of the breed in abundance: 'gusto, a strange retention of innocence, and a grand irreverence. And, of course,' he added, 'the brilliance.' Farson wanted to know if Welles ever wanted to return to the United States. 'After an embarrassing silence, he said, "It seems so blunt to say just 'no'. Anyhow, not for the moment."'[28] Farson had obviously touched a nerve. And, indeed, the last line of Welles's curriculum vitae in the theatre programme at the Édouard VII states baldly: '1947: He comes to Europe, where he has remained ever since.'

Welles's relationship with Eartha Kitt during the run of the show suffered from the presence, first in town and then in the stalls, of her on–off boyfriend, the great Josh White, guitarist, singer, civil-rights activist – a man after Welles's own heart, with whom he had been associated politically, standing side-by-side with him on many a Popular Front platform, and someone who, like Welles, had been, in the expressive FBI phrase of the time, a 'Premature anti-Fascist'. Now White was just a rival, so when Welles came to the great scene from Marlowe's *Dr Faustus* that begins, 'Was this the face that launched a thousand ships?', he seized Kitt's face and on the line 'Make me immortal with a kiss' sank his teeth into her lower lip so fiercely that it bled. Afterwards she hurled her tiny body at his vast bulk, punching and kicking, but it made no impact. 'Why did you do it?' she asked. 'Oh, I was just in that mood,' he told her, and walked off. White overheard what had happened, but Welles was already in his chauffeur-driven car and sped off. After that, Kitt refrained from her nightly visits to his dressing room, 'though I missed the old yell of "Kitt, are you ready?"'[29] Welles meanwhile spent his days working on a screenplay about sexual obsession; he called it *Lovelife*.

The show closed early at the Édouard VII. Now, dragging his

ever-bewildered colleagues from the Gate Theatre with him, Welles suddenly plunged into a six-week tour of Allied-occupied Germany with a new show cobbled together from fragments of *The Blessed and the Damned* and pretty well anything else he could think of on the spur of the moment. The primary objective was, of course, to make money, but there was another reason: Welles's political self, largely dormant during his Italian sojourn, had suddenly reawoken and he enthusiastically accepted an offer from *France Dimanche* to write a series of articles on the situation in post-war Germany. This would be a return to the glory days of his syndicated column for the *New York Post*, sending despatches from South America and the lynching belt of the United States, and he took it very seriously indeed.

CHAPTER FOUR

Citizen Coon

MACLIAMMÓIR, HIS sulk over, now joined them. The show they took with them to Germany in August 1950 was a sort of buffet of dramatic titbits devised by Hilton Edwards: very sensibly, *The Unthinking Lobster* had been dropped altogether and *Time Runs* substantially cut and rearranged for three actors and a small chorus, drawn from the young American actors in *The Blessed and the Damned*, who also doubled as stage management and wardrobe assistants. George Fanto, fresh from filming *Othello*, joined them as 'factotum, collector, disburser, paymaster, interpreter, agent', as well as designing the lighting for the show – an ambitious forty-eight lighting cues in all. In what MacLiammóir called the 'mixed salad' that followed, he and Welles and one of the kids performed a surreally compressed version of *The Importance of Being Earnest*, in which Welles got the chance to play Lady Bracknell, or at least to speak the best of her lines in the mouth of Algernon Moncrieff; MacLiammóir played Jack Worthing, and young Lee Zimmer played both of the butlers. This was followed by the death of King Henry VI (MacLiammóir) from Part Three of the play of the same name, with Welles as the murderous Richard of Gloucester, a part he had last played at the age of fifteen, in *Winter of Discontent*, his own adaptation of Shakespeare's history plays, at the Todd School in Woodstock, Illinois. For the tour, he wore, said MacLiammóir, 'the largest Hump ever seen outside the deserts of Arabia or the Zoo'. Eartha Kitt sang sultry songs from *Time Runs*, with Welles doing soliloquies from Marlowe's play, after which he performed magic tricks, introduced by MacLiammóir in German.

The show was billed as *An Evening with Orson Welles*. It all sounds rather entertaining, an old-time Variety Bill, with Classical Recitations and Conjuring; it cannot often have happened, however, that the two were performed by the same man. First stop was Frankfurt, where a cocktail party was thrown for them in the gardens of the American Club. The poster, it seems, claimed that they would be performing Goethe's *Faust*. Welles cleared up the confusion that had been caused. 'No, not Goethe,' said Welles, 'just me' – though that of course was not strictly true, either. The news hadn't reached all of the audience that night: expecting Gretchen at the Spinning Wheel, they were deeply bewildered by Eartha Kitt's bluesy asides; nonetheless, the show played to good houses in a post-war Germany starved of contact with English-speaking culture.

The minds of the principal performers were not entirely focused on the show, however. MacLiammóir, who had known Germany well before the war – had, indeed, with Edwards, brought back to Ireland news of the exciting developments in modern German theatre – viewed the current state of the country with apprehensive melancholy, fearing and assuming a lurch towards communism. Welles was keenly observing the scene too, and what he saw was quite the opposite. He saw – everywhere, it seemed to him – clear signs that Nazism, far from having been extirpated, was renascent. He and MacLiammóir and Fanto paid a rather moody visit to Hitler's holiday hideaway at Berchtesgaden: 'all is bright, shining, clean, picturesque and quaint,' wrote MacLiammóir in *Each Actor on His Ass*. 'It's absolute Hell.'

After Frankfurt, they played a profitable week in Hamburg, then moved on to Munich. Here Welles had been invited by Neo-Film Productions GmbH to produce a German film in Germany: 'such a decision of yours', they wrote to him, 'would contribute more to an international understanding as it may be possible by many a politician or statesman'.[1] Welles replied that only by shooting something would he be able to determine how well equipped the studios were, and so, to MacLiammóir's mystification – 'Orson suddenly smitten with barking decision to make short films of *Importance* and *Henry and Gloucester*' – they were swept away after the show one night to the enormous Geisengeige Studios just outside the city and shot until dawn.

'O. seemed happy about it and was, as always, at the top of his form when there are cameras about,' wrote MacLiammóir, 'especially in small hours of morning.' But Welles found the facilities inadequate, so not only did he declare the short films to have been a waste of time, but he also declined the offer of making the proposed German film, which might have opened up all sorts of remarkable possibilities for him, both creative and financial. Welles's increasing dismay at what he saw – or thought he saw – all around him in Germany had confirmed his dislike of the country. This feeling was by no means mitigated by his being besieged wherever he went by people who, spotting his unmistakable outline – Harry Lime being at least physically indistinguishable from Orson Welles – shouted, '*Der Dritte Mann! Der Dritte Mann!*' at him. 'O. gave them the famous Welles stare, which is something between that of a dying bull and a voodoo mask,' observed MacLiammóir, 'and said in firm and unfaltering English that nothing on earth was more nauseating to his soul than to be called The Third Man, and that the next lady who did so would unhesitatingly be put to death.'[2] Even more vexing was the propensity of café bands to strike up Anton Karas's maddeningly catchy little 'Harry Lime Theme' the moment Welles entered the place. 'Graham Greene created him,' said the American advertising campaign for *The Third Man*, 'Carol Reed brought him to life . . . Alida Valli sought him . . . and Karas's music followed him wherever he went.' How right they were.

An Evening with Orson Welles played half a week each in Düsseldorf and Bad Oeynhausen, the headquarters of the occupying British Army of the Rhine; finally, in early September, they arrived in Berlin, where Welles addressed a room full of German journalists, theatre and film critics – 'the cream of Berlin's "Chelsea Set"', according to the *Daily Telegraph*. Welles refused to rise to the critical bait, preferring to make jokes, which only succeeded in baffling his earnest interviewers. 'What is wrong with this country anyway?' he asked. 'They haven't made a decent film since the war.' 'Are you planning to go to Hollywood, Mr Welles?' 'No, nor am I planning to die. But both are inevitable – and about as attractive.' 'What is wrong with the film industry as a whole?' 'It's becoming increasingly nationalistic, more divided and less forceful. In Germany there is only slavish imitation of Hollywood.' An American journalist asked, 'You don't like Hollywood, do you?' 'Did I say that? I like Europe and I've a lot more to learn here.' 'What do you think of yourself, Herr Welles?' 'That's none of your business.' 'Have you a message for us?' 'Message? Who? Me?'[3]

He certainly had a message for the readers of *France Dimanche*. His articles had been coming out at regular intervals during the tour and had caused quite a stir, which is exactly what they were intended to do. The following year he condensed the articles into a piece for the distinguished London magazine *The Fortnightly Review*, and in this form (under the title 'Thoughts on Germany') they constitute one of the most remarkable examples of Welles's polemical writing, very much in the manner of his pieces from the mid-1940s in the *New York Post* and, later on radio, in the form of *Orson Welles's Commentaries*. His starting point was the possible rearmament of Germany, and his analysis probing, if a little overheated:

> I was beginning to realise how times have changed. The Germans themselves have changed from a problem to a hope. Most of the

> other people who were saying that Europe must be saved from a strong Germany were saying that only a strong Germany can save Europe . . . we are preparing to encourage the Germans to fight (or at least impress the Russians). That makes sense. But to encourage fascism is something else. We now find ourselves faced with spending a great deal more than before to keep Germany – the part we are responsible for – from going communist. We came to make Germany free of Hitlerism; we're staying to keep it free of Stalinism.[4]

This was touchy territory, as he well knew. The idea that the victorious Allies were 'encouraging Fascism' was, in 1950, fiercely provocative, but provocation, as we have seen, was Welles's key modus operandi.

He begins his essay, as he often did in his *New York Post* columns, by way of an encounter with a powerful man, in this case the celebrated armaments manufacturer Fritz Mandl, then visiting from Buenos Aires, where he had been supplying munitions to the Argentinian dictator, Juan Perón. Welles happened to be sitting near him in a bar. The portrait he paints of Mandl is of a piece with the gallery of corrupt men-of-power central to so many of his films: Kane, Bannister, Arkadin, Quinlan, Clay.

> The eyes in the sharply-drawn, solid-looking head, are set in a questing expression. They are the eyes of a shrewd hunter, but you surprise in them a curious pallid emptiness – a dead spot. It as though the centre of a target were painted white, or like the vacuum in the heart of a tornado. It makes him look dangerous.

Mandl, who was being fawned over by a group of bankers, was brooding out loud over the Third World War:

> Brooding is the word, not gloating. Zaharoff used to gloat. But then there were different wars and he never expected the Red Russians to win any of them. Mandl says they're bound to win this next one.

Welles had long been fascinated by Sir Basil Zaharoff, the so-called 'Merchant of Death', the famous arms dealer and arts philanthropist of obscure Greek origin, who had made millions out of the First World War. Mandl was a more thuggish variation on the same theme; both of them contributed something to Welles's character Gregory Arkadin. Mandl was one of the most sinister figures of the Western Hemisphere, according to Ralph Bellamy in the *Reader's Digest*: 'Menace Number One to the peace of the Hemisphere . . . weapons of destruction fascinate [Mandl]', sending him, Bellamy reports, into raptures over some new land mines 'which tear off the feet of advancing soldiers'. Much of this, which Welles appears to have swallowed hook, line and sinker, was FBI propaganda. But sensational reports of Mandl's social life were true enough – he was a compulsive womaniser, party-thrower and later alcoholic wife-beater, with connections at the very highest level. He had, famously, been married to Hedy Lamarr, star of the film *Ecstasy*, but she had run away from him. Much of this, too, fed into Welles's film *Mr Arkadin*. In his 'Thoughts on Germany' Welles allows himself a moment's contact with 'the dead-eyed man': Mandl's cigar had gone out and Welles lit it for him. 'He thanked me and we smiled at one another. After all, why not? We've got something in common; we've both been married in our time to movie stars.' All of Welles's mingled repulsion and attraction to power is to be found in that moment.

He moves on from Mandl, a representative of international capital with a vested interest in waging war on 'the Red Russians', to approach his main theme: the German character and how dangerous it is. He describes a car journey in which he is driven by 'a girl' – a rather politically progressive girl, it seems – who has views about her fellow-countrymen: 'Every German driver simply must on the road pass every other German driver,' she tells Welles. He endows his Germans, even the ones he admires, with funny foreign locutions. He doesn't imitate their accents, but he lets us know that they talk kinda funny. 'He is eager his home to get back to, and there to be stuffing himself with noodle soup,' continues 'the girl':

> 'He wants to be the first. Every German wants to be the first. The German feels naked without a uniform. He needs to march with lots of other Germans or he gets sulky. Also he must have somebody to bully. And always – always – lots of noodle soup. There's no cure for it. No cure at all for being German. Occupation, education – nothing does any good. This is a country of noodle-souper men.'

This 'girl' is clearly the ventriloquial conduit for Welles's own table-talk. When he speaks in his own voice, the view is pretty much the same, just without the funny locutions:

> As mystic, musician and militarist, the German has made himself deeply felt. He has physical courage, creative imagination and a tendency to burst into tears. We all know about his blood-lust, his death-wish and his marvellous sentimental capacity for keeping the festival of Christmas, and let's be frank about it: we're sick to death of him. Also he seems to be fairly sick of himself. What's to be done? If the German doesn't like himself, he can't amount to anything in the world, and when he does manage to persuade himself that he's somebody, doesn't he then start persuading the rest of us – and in such a wise that we all wish he'd never been born? Answer: he does and we do.

This is the tone familiar from Welles's radio *Commentaries*: rising hysteria riding on a steady rhetorical build, delivered in a curiously personal tone, as if he himself had suffered directly from what he is describing. It was a tone first heard in his 1945 broadcast *Officer X*, championing the black veteran Isaac Woodard, who had been blinded by an unnamed policeman in the American Deep South. This was the broadcast that provided the matrix for Welles in this mode, with its closing threat: 'Officer X, we know who you are. We're coming to get you.' In his 'Thoughts on Germany', as if having caught himself at it, Welles switches to another voice: a bluff Yankee businessman, who says of the German: 'He never was any good. Honest, maybe, but nutty. Look at the Nazis and the nudists. All of them.' Welles the commentator resumes: 'The chief topic in Germany is the German. It's very like patients in a sanatorium discussing their ailments. Germans do really seem to look upon their race as an affliction.' He allows a modicum of reasonableness to another of his cast of voices, 'a poet': 'Germans are all dreaming of a united Germany,' he says. 'But if there's anything new about the dream it's that our highest and most secret hope is that the worst of the battles which make that dream come true will be fought by others – and fought elsewhere.' Having allowed this 'poet' a sensible opinion, Welles then slaps an off-the-peg racial tag onto him, too: 'The poet turned to the waiter. "Bring me some noodle soup," he said.'

The last section of this unnerving piece describes a pre-dawn visit by Welles to a bar in Frankfurt; he was evidently in need of sobering up – 'I was drinking coffee.' He describes the scene: 'It was past dawn and it felt like it. The band had groaned out its last stale set of American hit-tunes when suddenly they began playing the *Horst Wessel* . . .' Bashing out the official Nazi anthem has become common practice, he tells us, to get people up on their feet and off home. 'But then people began singing the words and one character near me went so far as to accompany his vocalizing with the Nazi salute.' He understands, he says, that after the Nazi era people are spiritually impoverished: millions of Germans are incurably Hitler-bent. 'You can't blame a night club crowd for wanting to hear something more German than *Oklahoma*. It's just too bad that the only substitute they could think of was the *Horst Wessel*. Something had to be done about that Nazi salute, of course, but I couldn't think just what.' He describes himself sitting there, 'a confessed premature anti-Fascist . . . pop-eyed, mouth agape and doing nothing while some great roaring boor poisoned the air with Nazi war chants and stuck his stiff arm in my face.' Then a young woman proves herself 'that rarest of German birds: an authentic anti-Nazi', by pulling some flowers out of a vase which she then throws at the Nazi's head. Whereupon, says Welles, 'yelling like a crazy Indian, an immense female, a good executive type for a concentration camp, rushed from behind the door and seized the markswoman from behind. When she was quite safely pinioned and helpless, her outraged victim – a large man – stepped to her side and, whilst the crowd cheered, commenced striking her in the face.' At this point, Our Hero shakes himself together and steps in. *Kapow!* 'I must tell you that one Nazi is one tooth less pretty than he was. And, I'm happy to add, he kept standing again and again and asking for more. It was altogether satisfactory and remains one of the nicest memories of my German trip.' When Welles leaves, having of course refused compensation of any kind, the Young Woman stands up and gives him the bunch of flowers that she removed from the vase before she hurled it – what is this? An out-take from *Casablanca*?

Calming down a little, Welles notes that the only reason no one in the bar fought back was because he was 'a member of an occupying power'. 'But I couldn't help nursing my loss of pride with the reflection that the Germans are forever making it impossible for us to avoid knocking them down, and – worse still – making us feel guilty for doing it.' There is something deeply disturbing about all of this, the sense of personal animus, and it is worth remembering that until the Japanese bombs landed in Pearl Harbor, two years after the Second World War began, Welles had toed the Popular Front line of non-intervention in what was perceived to be a British imperialist war. Now his rabid anti-German stance out-Churchilled anything Churchill had said during the war. 'His most recent set-back is popularly supposed to have taught Fritz to abhor the sight of uniforms and forever after loathe the sound of march music,' Welles continues. 'Tourists from the victorious democracies can't seem to get over their astonishment at finding German instincts less damaged than German cities. The truth is that human nature in this forest land is neither an invention of Dr Goebbels nor an easy target for bombs.'

What is noteworthy is Welles's presumption of inbred – one might say genetic – patterns of behaviour, and the violence (verbal and physical) that this presumption brings forth from him. In 1945, having seen film from the newly liberated concentration camps, he had written in *Free Press*: 'the newsreels testify to the fact of quite another sort of death, quite another level of decay. This is a putrefaction of the soul, a perfect spiritual garbage. For some years now we have been calling it Fascism. The stench is unendurable.' Four years on, Welles was still raging inside, refusing to accept that anything fundamental had changed and determined to expose the uncured cancer at the heart of German life. Unquestionably there were Nazis who survived Germany's defeat unscathed; some even thrived. Welles does not target them: it is the whole German people he has in his sights. The episode in the Frankfurt bar feels confected, a fabrication based on selected details he might have observed, or something heard at a dinner party and then elaborated – a perfectly reasonable procedure for an artist, though not necessarily for a political analyst. But he whips himself up to believe it, engineering emotion in himself to such a degree that, as in his *Orson Welles Commentaries* broadcasts a few years earlier, the actual subject – the outrage in question – is left behind and it becomes all about him. Who or what was it that he was purportedly punching again and again and again in that bar? An embodiment of something malign in humankind? In him?

'Thoughts on Germany' comes to an end on a note of highly weighted ambiguity, with Welles hearing 'the plaintive piping cries of young children at play in a bombed building'. Little boys – about four years old, he guesses – 'dropped in Berlin after the last bomb. I may have imagined it, but did they really seem to be playing soldiers?' Why is it, he asks, 'that if you lose a war, you're supposed to lose your faults with it? Can a people be expected to surrender up their personality?'

These are dark, disturbing, unforgiving thoughts, very much part of Welles's *Weltanschauung* (as he presumably would not have put it). He was brought up a Lutheran, but often claimed to have been raised a Catholic: his sense of Original Sin and unassuageable guilt are certainly highly developed (as, of course, was his belief in the immutability of character, famously expressed by him in *Mr Arkadin* in the fable of the scorpion and the frog. 'Why did you poison me?' cries the frog to the scorpion as they both sink into the river, across which he was carrying them. 'It's in my character,' replies the scorpion). All of this adds up to a degree of fatalism in Welles's outlook, a sense that we cannot change, that we are doomed by our destiny to behave in a certain way, and that nothing short of divine intervention can prevent it. He detested psychoanalysis, whose purpose he saw as the elimination of guilt. Guilt, he insisted, must be lived with, not resolved. This, of course, accounts for his fascination with the Christian notion of Grace, with which he toyed so very lightly in *The Unthinking Lobster* – Grace, the divine antidote to Original Sin, 'the love and mercy given to us by God because God desires us to have it,' as defined by the Wesleyans, 'not because of anything we have done to earn it'. Guilt and grace (in many different manifestations) are central to this thinking, and underpin Welles's 'Thoughts on Germany'. There is, too, more than a dash of the character Welles played on radio in the 1930s, Lamont Cranston, otherwise known as The Shadow: 'Who knows what evil lurks in the hearts of man? *The Shadow knows*.'

Not that the readers of his *France Dimanche* articles – entitled 'The Noodle-soupermen' – would have been aware of any of that; but they were suitably shocked and alarmed, as they no doubt hoped they would be, by this report from the creator of the infamous *War of the Worlds* broadcast. News of the articles soon filtered through to Germany and, when it did, all hell broke loose, to the extent that in November 1950, 20th Century Fox were obliged to withdraw *Prince of Foxes* from exhibition in the Rhineland-Palatinate, a sizeable territory representing substantial earnings. 'Our company', read the official statement accompanying the film's withdrawal, 'is astonished at how Welles has frivolously and superficially passed judgement on an entire people – we repeat, Welles has no permanent contract with us.' 'Our company', it is worth noting, was the very company that had just advanced Welles 200 million lire to enable him to complete *Othello*. As ever, Welles was deeply indifferent to his own best interests.

The storm over the *France-Dimanche* continued to rage, causing Welles to issue a less than fulsome *démenti*. He didn't want his name, he said, to be involved in 'terrible misunderstandings' due to misquotations. It was not true, he protested, that he hated

Germany; on the contrary, a large part of the German press was engaged in spreading the rumour that he was hated in Germany.' Anything he might have said, he insisted, was entirely based on what Germans themselves had told him about Germany. 'If a German tells me that all Germans are incurable due to certain dangerous tendencies, then I must object to this point in the same way I object to those racial theories by which the Germans once tried to overwhelm us.' At which unworthy point, he beat a retreat. He was impatient to get back to Rome and *Othello.* 'These lowering skies,' he said to MacLiammóir in Brussels, 'this soft sugary food, these earnest tearful people, this great Northern gloom, after such a lot of it all, dearest Micheál, don't you feel that Italy perhaps . . . ?'[5] He and Hilton felt that deeply, but they needed with some urgency to return to the lowering skies of Dublin, which they duly did – the money due to them for *Othello* still unpaid. Edwards wrote to Welles from Ireland to inform him that they were on the brink of collapse: 'the bank has stopped all payments of course and a writ of attachment on our personal belongings is to be issued in fourteen days . . .'[6] Welles responded by sending £800, but, as Edwards remarked in his acknowledgement of the sum, it did no more than 'stave off the more voracious of the wolves'.[7] Welles also agreed to narrate, and make a token appearance in, a short film that Edwards would direct, but this generous offer scarcely affected their financial position.

★

Welles, meanwhile, embarked on what he stated categorically would be the final shooting on *Othello*, in Rome, in Venice and in Pavia; MacLiammóir was suddenly summoned from Dublin, Cloutier from Paris. Welles had been picking up shots on and off throughout the year, some of them considerably more than pick-ups in fact: he now reshot some crucial sections of the film's bravura opening sequence behind the Scalera Studios, near the Appian Way, conjuring up astonishing images from the most modest of elements. 'It was almost a bare set, with scattered platforms, vertical props spaced 10 and 50 feet away from each other, and dry-stone walls,' according to the composer Francesco Lavagnino, by then working with Welles on the score. 'A little further away, there was a small house, and, close to a basin of water, what looked like a hanging laundry. At the right moment, the sun hit the water and suddenly there was the port of Cyprus. Soldiers on the platforms gave the perspective, the reflection of the water on the walls showed the sheet as a sail, the walls themselves as a pier and the basin as the Mediterranean.'[8]

Welles had begun the process of distilling the thousands of feet of film he had shot into a coherent entity; for him, music was always a crucial part of that process. Lavagnino, intrigued by photographs he had seen of Welles directing *Othello* on location, secured a meeting with him – at 2 a.m., at Welles's insistence. Inevitably, Welles failed to show up. When they did finally meet, Lavagnino played for him and 'he sat there, all ears, he looked like a child'. Lavagnino discovered that, with Welles, the music might lead the film just as easily as the film led the music. He had written something for the murder of Roderigo in the hammam: 'It was real melodrama. As Orson and I sat there thinking about it, we each had an idea which, we confessed, we didn't dare to propose. We counted to three, then we blurted out at the same time: "Mandolins!"' Building on this, Welles had another idea: he wanted the music to build to a crescendo and then break up, leaving just the dissonant sound of all the instruments untuning. 'He kept waving to me to go on and on with the music.' He needed it because he had had an idea of inserting a shot of lute-players into the scene and suddenly seen how to do it. This is how he and Bernard Herrmann had worked together on *Citizen Kane* and *The Magnificent Ambersons*: making the piece on the hoof, all the elements interacting with each other in a chemical – almost an alchemical – process.

This sequence, the murder of Roderigo, is of course one of the great triumphs of the film, musically, dramatically, cinematically. With Lavagnino, Welles had found a true collaborator and co-creator, someone who responded to his essentially musical instincts – a rare event on his films. Welles was musically literate: he had grown up around music. His mother was a distinguished pianist; he himself had played the piano as a boy; his guardian, Dr Bernstein, had a long and passionate relationship with the great soprano Edith Mason; and Welles had attended the summer operas in Highland Park (and written alarmingly precocious reviews of them). So when he spoke of music, he knew what he was taking about. More importantly, he saw music as the essential art – everything in film and theatre, he insisted, should have musical form, a musical shape, and his work was governed at a deep level by that idea. It was Welles who had the very effective idea, that at the murderous climax of the film each of the instruments accompanying the theme associated with Desdemona should one by one fall silent, until only the flute would be left playing it. Not that the work was easy: Lavagnino described their time together as 'delightful hell'. He had to compose music to mere snippets of film, bits and pieces that had been edited 'by two or three different people at different times'. Welles would listen over and over again, until suddenly something – often the most unlikely thing – would inspire him. He was, he told Lavagnino, 'like one of those whores who was indifferent to some Herculean client and then gets turned on by a simple nobody who comes around at the right time'.

Welles and Lavagnino were sufficiently in tune with each other that the moment they stood in front of the large orchestra and chorus of 200 they had assembled, they knew it was all wrong – 'like touristic Tchaikovsky,' said Lavagnino – and that they must start all over again. Lavagnino hunted down 'the only harpsichord in Rome' (surely not?), then recast the grandiloquent funeral music in the opening sequence for just sixteen instruments and twelve voices, strategically placing three microphones in specific spots to create aural perspective. Tragically, this exquisite detail can no longer be heard in currently available copies: in the 1990s, in an act of misguided filial piety, the soundtrack was re-recorded with a live orchestra and chorus – the Chicago Symphony Orchestra and Chorus, no less – without reference either to the original score or the way it had been recorded.

By late November of 1950 Welles was confident enough in what he was doing with *Othello* to call a press conference – 'in fluent and picturesque Italian', according to *Corriere della Sera*[9] – to announce the film. It was, he said, 'another Shakespeare, this time closer to the time and spirit of the play. Perhaps *Othello* will be less Shakespearean than *Macbeth*, but it will be more Elizabethan,' adding, in a sly autobiographical joke about his own experience in Italy, that it described 'the conflict of a brutal, instinctive foreigner and Venetian power and culture'. He took pains not to be overweening. 'I don't know if I have got it right this time either. Or even if there is a right way. I don't make films, I carry out experiments. Everything I do is experimental.' This particular experiment, he said, would be released in June 1951; shooting for his next film, *Ulysses*, would commence shortly. This was a standard ploy of Welles's: he never announced a finished project without announcing at least one more to follow it.

In fact *Othello* was far from finished. Never mind the editing, there was yet more shooting to do. In December 1950, Fay Compton, defying a sceptical agent and paying her own way, got herself to Venice, as requested. To her amazement, she was put up at the five-star Bauer Grünwald Hotel. Welles gave her a terrific greeting. 'Impression I get', she wrote in her diary, 'is that Orson more inconsiderate than before – keeping up till all hours to shoot his own close-ups and everyone being on call at all hours all the time. But as usual *extremely* nice and most considerate to me.' Her agent – the very powerful Al Parker – had sent him several cables and letters that were, she felt, unnecessarily rude, though 'O takes it very well.' On several nights she went to the studio to dub her part; one night she read the part of Iago off camera for Welles. The equipment was so poor that they could only dub when they were not shooting on one of the two stages. 'Suzanne and I trying to remember what we did 14 months ago,' she wrote. 'Following day sound has been traced and sorted. Mistakes such as Willow Song in Cyprus scene!! Do song all over again. *Hope* with success.'

The reason for these blunders was that Welles's American editor, Lou Lindsay, with whom he had worked on *Macbeth*, had now gone, and the new cutter was reaching the end of his tether – was, as Compton put it, 'obviously going mad!' The vast cache of three years' intermittent filming was in a state of complete disorder; only Welles knew what he needed. Sometimes they were simply unable to find what they had shot. One afternoon Welles suddenly asked for a repeated shot of Emilia. 'So make up and dress once more.'[10] Finally, as a preparation for his dubbing of Cloutier, he asked Compton to make a tape of the part of Desdemona, which she did the day she left, 14 December. To her astonishment, before she went, she was paid in full, including the return fare that she had paid out of her own pocket. A couple of days later everyone else went home for Christmas – the third Christmas of shooting.

⋆

At the beginning of 1951, Welles was working full-time on cutting the film: a rabid dog had bitten him, which confined him to Italy, curtailing the habitual multiplicity of his activities. He had been editing *Othello* intermittently from the beginning of shooting, with an international assortment of editors, among them the Frenchman Jean Sacha, the Italian Renzo Lucidi and the Hungarian Jenõ Csepreghy, otherwise known as John Shepridge; in Venice in December 1950, as Fay Compton tells us, he had been working with the American Lou Lindsay. Apart from the vast quantity of disparate material that he had to organise into coherent and expressive form, he was faced with the problem of half a dozen different emulsions of the film itself, none of which matched: he had got stock from wherever he could, especially at the beginning of the shoot. The sound was an almost total write-off; Cunningham's magnetic tape, still in its infancy, proved almost entirely unusable. A massive programme of dubbing was now unavoidable, a dreary prospect in many ways, but with the redeeming possibility of improving or changing performances. Actors were yanked in from all over the world to redo their dialogue; when they couldn't come or when Welles thought their work could be improved upon, he did it himself; thus Bob Coote, who had so irritated Welles with his typically English negativity about everything, is unmistakably voiced by his director, with the result that the character Roderigo becomes even more of a puppet than usual.

From the moment Welles shot his first professional film – as part of his 1938 Mercury Theatre production of *Too Much Johnson* – he had been intoxicated with the infinite possibilities of editing. Although desperately keen to get *Othello* into circulation, he rejoiced in the new freedom he had created for himself: no producer breathing down his neck, no studio apparatchik reporting back on him, no hidebound editor trying to impose rules on him. He had a taste of this on the final version of *Macbeth*. Now he was absolutely in charge, for the first time. And because of the astonishing amount of material they had shot, he had plenty with which to follow his inspiration; he was free to fine-tune it in a way he had not been able to do since *Kane*. In the process he became aware of what he felt was still missing, and he wanted to change his approach to certain things, particularly regarding the part of Desdemona. So back to Mogador they went in April 1951, just Welles and Cloutier and a camera crew of one: George Fanto. 'Suzanne coped well with the harsh realities of the Spartan military outpost,' Fanto wrote in his memoir. 'Without fuss she acted in love scenes with Welles/Othello in parts of the decaying fortress of Mogador which was used as latrine by the natives. Cloutier deserved much credit for us being able to finish her sequences in five weeks within the allotted budget.' On the last day of *Othello* she told David Robinson, 'I had to be script, make-up, messenger; Fanto producer and business manager.' Eventually, it was done. 'I shall never forget Orson's face when we did the last shot, and it was the end at last,' said Cloutier. 'We all cried.'[11]

Back to the editing suite in Rome, where he worked with Renzo Lucidi. 'There is always a better way' was Welles's endlessly repeated mantra, as they picked and unpicked sequences – always, it seemed to Lucidi, ending up with their first ideas. On and on they toiled, to the point where, by the end of the summer, they felt it was ready for submission to that year's Venice Film Festival; on the strength of the film having been accepted, Orson Welles Productions, a new outfit conjured into being by the endlessly versatile Fanto, did a deal with Loew's International Corporation for the remaining 50 per cent of US and Commonwealth rights. Welles said he needed 100 million lire to complete the movie, which was a little alarming since the deal was signed on 24 August and the film was due to be shown in Venice on 1 September.

CHAPTER FIVE

Man of Mystery

WHILE THE negotiations over the distribution rights for the film of *Othello* were taking place, Welles was in London, where he had been engaged by Laurence Olivier Productions (LOP) to direct and act in a production of *Othello* the play, to be presented at the magnificent St James Theatre, where Olivier and his then-wife Vivien Leigh were triumphantly ensconced in Shakespeare's *Antony and Cleopatra* in repertory with Shaw's *Caesar and Cleopatra*. Olivier's invitation was perhaps a little surprising. 'You're going to play Othello?' an incredulous John Gielgud said to Welles, bumping into him at a party. 'In London? On *stage*?'

Welles was scarcely a Shakespearean novice, of course. All of theatrical London knew about the Fascist *Julius Caesar* of 1937, which had hit the front pages of the world's newspapers and which the great British impresario C.B. Cochran had unsuccessfully tried to bring to the Royal Albert Hall just before the war. No, what was really surprising about the invitation was that Welles's *Macbeth* had recently opened in England to villainously bad reviews, which had invariably contrasted it unfavourably with Olivier's *Hamlet*, and Welles, as we have seen, had taken this very badly. The two men had known each other since the late 1930s, when they had appeared together on radio under Welles's direction in a very jolly version of P.C. Wren's *Beau Geste* as part of the Campbell Playhouse season of adaptations, but since then Welles's standing in the world had been steadily slipping, while Olivier's rose inexorably. He had become a major film star with *Rebecca* and *Wuthering Heights*, returning to England in the early years of the war, where, in collaboration with Ralph Richardson, he had turned the Old Vic into the forum of the nation, earning himself the title of the world's greatest classical actor, and a knighthood.

This was the man who now invited Welles to perform one of the most daunting roles in the Shakespearean canon. The deal had been brokered by Sandor Gorlinsky, the theatrical agent, who having seen *The Blessed and the Damned* in Paris the year before had clearly not rated its chances in London, but wanted to do something with Welles: *Othello* must have seemed like an obvious choice. There was great interest in London in the film's progress, into which British actors like Robert Coote and Fay Compton had disappeared for long periods, coming back with hair-raising stories of madness and mayhem; and in April 1951, while Welles and Suzanne Cloutier were shooting the very last shots of the film in Mogador, *Picture Post* had featured the film on its cover, with a splendid, lavishly illustrated four-page spread inside, in which it was revealed that the film might not be seen 'for some months' (five years, as it turned out).[1] *Othello* was, said the *Post*, more ambitious than *Macbeth*. 'It is the first film since *Citizen Kane* that Welles has made as he wanted to, free from the dictates of Hollywood policy. Though it was made economically, he had to fight hard to get the money. It is an indication of his faith in it that he contributed to the budget himself from salaries earned acting in other films.' This unaccustomedly warm and enthusiastic piece was accompanied by superb photographs, further whetting the appetite of the British public for the already legendary, though as yet unseen, film.

Welles made his first appearance on the British stage in June 1951, at the London Palladium not in blank verse but on a variety bill, in a tribute to the late great comedian Sid Field, in the congenial company of the Crazy Gang, Judy Garland (an old girlfriend of Welles's), Danny Kaye, Peter Ustinov (now married to Suzanne Cloutier), his new boss, Laurence Olivier, and, in drag, Richard Attenborough, Jack Buchanan and Douglas Fairbanks, Jr. Welles's contribution was to saw Elizabeth Taylor in half. A few days after the gala came the widely reported announcement that 'Sir Laurence Olivier will present *Third Man* star Orson Welles in *Othello*'. There was rivalry between this production and the Old Vic's forthcoming version of the play. *Theatre World* humorously invited Welles to withdraw in favour of the Old Vic, quipping that 'two blacks don't make a white'. It was not the first racist gag that would be bandied about on the subject of the play. 'Meanwhile,' burbled *Theatre World*, 'we are curious to see the film he has made of it. We have recovered sufficiently from his film of *Macbeth* to stand it.'

He was suddenly everywhere in England: the radio series *The Adventures of Harry Lime*, with Welles in the title-role and directing, was about to start transmission with huge success on the BBC. In the pre-credit sequence, Karas's familiar little zither tune clattered away until a gunshot rang out. Those who knew how much Welles detested the tune might have surmised that he had killed Karas, but no: 'That was the shot that killed Harry Lime,' Welles would say. 'He died in a sewer beneath Vienna, as those of you know who saw the movie *The Third Man*. Yes, that was the end of Harry Lime . . . but it was not the beginning. Harry Lime had many lives . . . and I can recount all of them. How do I know? Very simple. Because my name is Harry Lime.'

Welles had been persuaded to revive the character with whom his name was now so annoyingly synonymous by an extremely sharp operator called Harry Alan Towers, another of those shady figures to whom Welles was ineluctably drawn, and who were ineluctably drawn to him. Ten years after their collaboration, Towers was arrested, charged with operating a vice-ring at a New York hotel; his girlfriend, in her statement to the FBI, claimed that Towers was a Soviet agent responsible for providing compromising information on individuals for the benefit of the USSR. Later he was linked with a vice-ring at the United Nations; for some years he produced soft-porn films. That was a little way in the future. At this earlier, less steamy point in his career, Towers – through his irresistibly named company, Towers of London – had cannily bought the rights to the character of Harry Lime from Graham Greene, and offered Welles a great deal of money to appear in and direct a series of fifty-two episodes recounting Harry's early escapades.

At no point did Welles think of *The Adventures of Harry Lime* as anything other than a way of making a quick buck, though his performance is effortlessly charismatic: he remained an incomparable radio actor, engaging, witty, suggestive, with an extraordinary gift of creating instant intimacy with the listener. He usually wrote the introductory sequences himself. This Harry – affable, worldly-wise, wry, of course – is a much less hard-edged one than Greene's. The scripts were the work of a team of writers that included Welles's screenwriter for the long-since-abandoned *Ulysses*, Ernest Borneman, who had the rare distinction of having finally received all the money Welles owed him. Welles expended very little time and thought on the series, but some episodes interested him more than others and he would tinker with them; in some cases, they acquired lives of their own. One, 'The Dead Candidate', he turned into a screenplay called *VIP*, which he unsuccessfully tried to sell to Korda; his Paris friend Maurice Bessy later novelised it under the name *Une Grosse Légume*. Another, 'Greek Meets Greek', was one of the sources for Welles's film *Mr Arkadin*. Another fifteen were turned into short stories, three of which bear Welles's name, though it is unclear whether he actually wrote them.

He recorded several shows a day, sometimes as many as ten, urging on his little company of actors on to sharp and creditable accounts of their various shady characters. They often recorded in Paris, and the atmosphere was uproarious, with everyone playing two or three parts, while Welles bawled out colourful commentary on their work. As a young actress, Elaine Dundy often appeared on the programme; once Welles, after quickly casting the episode from the available pool of actors, proposed that they record the script without rehearsing, without even a read-through, which was splendid until she came to a point where she was about to have to play a scene with herself. 'This is ridiculous,' Welles roared at the producer in the sound booth. 'Where are all the other actors?' 'Don't you remember, Orson?' replied the producer. 'You sacked them all at lunchtime.'[2]

Though he did it for money, Welles loved the genre: all his life he travelled with a suitcase full of pulp fiction, thrillers, gangster stories, crime stories, which he consumed at a rate of two or three a day. He claimed to have written these kinds of stories for cheap magazines as a teenager in Spain. Narrative (and narrative is everything in these kind of yarns) was Welles's obsession. Asked by Leslie Megahey what was most important to him as a film-maker, he replied: 'Story, story, story.'[3] These little potboiling tales were almost pure narrative, and they had to grip from beginning to end; what anyone thought of them afterwards was neither here nor there. It was a very particular skill. 'He was always critical of the writers,' Towers said,

> 'and on occasions he suggested to me that maybe he would write some of the scripts. He asked me how much we paid and I told him, and a few weeks later six scripts arrived and I paid him. And the shows were, I wouldn't say that much better, but Orson was happy and I was happy, until I had a ring at my doorbell one morning and was confronted by a gentleman called Mr Ernest Borneman, who was complete with carbon copies of Mr Welles's scripts which he told me he had written and for which he hadn't been paid. That same afternoon I was in the studio with Orson and mentioned this occurrence; Orson looked me straight in the eye and said "Don't pay him, they were very bad scripts."'[4]

Popular though they were, *The Adventures of Harry Lime* was a mere sideline for Welles. The programmes were made whenever he had the time to do them. They went out every week for a year, so they had to be sure that there was always at least one episode in hand. But the main business was *Othello.* He was making the programme throughout the pre-production, the rehearsals, the tour and the London run of the play. For once he had strong back-up in the form of Laurence Olivier Productions, who were particularly skilful at casting. Welles had only two requirements: he wanted actors who had not been in the play before – who, ideally, had not acted in Shakespeare before; and he wanted them to be short. And indeed all of his leading actors were small of stature. The Australian actor Peter Finch, whom Olivier had just directed in *Daphne Laureola*, was asked to play Iago; he was not tall. Gudrun Ure, invited to play Desdemona, was a discovery of Olivier's from the Citizens' Theatre in Glasgow and was positively tiny. Maxine Audley (5' 1"), who had been appearing with Olivier and Leigh in the two Cleopatra plays, but chose not to go on the forthcoming US tour with them, was cast as Emilia. Small she might have been, but she had a guilty secret: not only had she played in Shakespeare (most recently Charmian in *Antony and Cleopatra*), she had actually played the part of Emilia before, which she took considerable pains to conceal from Welles. It is notable that none of these three principals remotely resembled the actors who played the equivalent roles in the film. No doubt Welles was trying to reconceive the play for the theatre. Indeed, his approach in the film was so fundamentally cinematic that it was irrelevant to any imaginable production of the play. It would have been like trying to put *Citizen Kane* on stage.

The designer he was given was one of the most admired in the British theatre, John Gielgud's favoured collaborator, Margaret ('Percy') Harris, of the famous design team known collectively as Motley; she was noted for the exquisite simplicity of her work, its clarity and lightness and elegance – not, perhaps, especially Wellesian qualities. In fact, his notion for the setting was very straightforward: he wanted a great brown velvet cloth, which would extend to the top of the proscenium arch and divide the stage into two halves; the action would be played in whichever half was exposed, while the scene-change took place behind the curtain. Apart from that, the design elements were very simple: a rostrum, a window, a drape, a few columns, to be realigned for each new scene.

Design meetings at Harris's studio were unconventional. Welles would arrive at eleven, having been in the hands of his masseurs for a good two hours beforehand, whereupon the studio would be invaded by Italian lawyers advising him on the suit he had taken out against a journalist who had accused him in print of being drunk while directing. On three separate occasions, Welles had failed to show up in court for the case he had brought, and the judiciary was becoming somewhat agitated. Eventually the case was tried with him *in absentia* and he was fined 5,000 lire (a bagatelle) for contempt of court. Even when Harris's studio emptied of these extremely vocal advisers, Welles found it hard to concentrate on the matter in hand. On one occasion, a child on his bike was playing rather noisily in the yard just below the window of Harris's second-floor studio. Welles said he couldn't work if the child was going to make so much noise; Harris said there was nothing she could do about it. Welles, jaw grimly set, said there was something *he* could do about it, and he went to the window and stared out of it, silently. After a few minutes the child stopped making any noise. 'I told you I'd stop him,' said Welles. The following day, Harris heard that the child had suddenly fallen ill while playing. In time he recovered, but he never played in that yard again, and certainly never made any noise. It must be stressed that Percy Harris was one of the most down-to-earth, practical, rational people who ever lived, and was still, forty years later, at a loss to explain these events. Slightly chastened, she resumed her work, trying to give Welles what he wanted, but feeling that she never really did. Even more strongly than his musical instincts, Welles's visual instincts were highly developed, and it took a certain kind of designer to enjoy translating his sketches into physical form; Harris was not one of them.[5]

Two more actors joined the core team before rehearsals began in August: Basil Lord, a seasoned farceur, as Roderigo, and John Van Eyssen, whose first Shakespeare play this was, as Cassio; the rest of the cast joined after three weeks. Rehearsals proceeded in high spirits and with many anecdotal breaks; Welles was particularly keen on John Barrymore stories, especially the one about the time Barrymore, playing Hamlet, hurled his Ophelia into the wings with savage force one night, bruising her badly. When she asked him why, he replied, 'You looked so pure.' This story, oft-told, always made Welles roar. 'He so obviously wanted to be Barrymore,' Maxine Audley thought: elegant, fearless, passionate, impulsive.[6] As far as *Othello* was concerned, he seemed to have no overarching conception of the play or, if he did, he failed to share it with them or explain why, indeed, he wanted to do it at all. He was fertile with views of the characters, however, as he had been with MacLiammóir during their early rehearsals for the film. He had very strong views, in particular, about Desdemona, whom he saw as essentially submissive and doll-like, which was very much how he had directed Suzanne Cloutier in the role. Ure was of another view, but did her best to play the character according to Welles's lights.

Welles was determined to get the actors to free themselves up. 'I think he was probably the first person who ever said to me "Don't mind if you make an asshole of yourself",' said Audley. 'He said "You must make a noise when Peter stabs you in the back."

And I said "I'm afraid of making a funny noise." He said, "It doesn't matter, do it, make a fool of yourself." I was rather ladylike I think, I was rather *Shakespearian*, and he knocked that out of me, he made me much more down to earth than I had been in Shakespeare.' He pushed Finch towards rat-like qualities, emphasising the disparity in height between them. 'He staged it beautifully,' said Audley. 'It was terrific to look at.' But he was very firm with Finch, Ure and Audley that they must never touch him. This was scarcely an issue in rehearsals, because Welles himself rarely (if ever) acted with them, preferring to sit behind his desk, organising the action. His understudy, Michael Godfrey, stood in for him. Welles appointed him his whipping boy very early on, bullying him remorselessly.

Ure concluded that Welles was anxious and insecure. 'He had wanted to do this all his life and he was now getting the opportunity and he was terrified, absolutely terrified.'[7] He confided in her his conviction that the public didn't like him. 'Now it does not help any actor to go on stage convinced that the public don't like you because you'll start ten miles back,' said Ure. But she felt that he was right. 'The West End theatrical public were out gunning for him. Somebody would come out of a doorway and try to trip him up. Like a lot of big men he'd stand at a bar, now he wouldn't have hurt a fly . . . and people would try to pick a fight, they'd come up, they'd deliberately come up at the bar and try to goad him to react.' She sensed great loneliness in the man. 'You don't expect to be rehearsing in the evenings but with Orson you were, that is Finchy and I were. We went back to his flat in Park Lane very often where I poured out large whiskies and Orson would pace up and down and talk and this would go on until about midnight because he didn't want to be left alone.'

★

Two weeks into rehearsals, Welles disappeared, leaving the actors to their own devices. He was going to a party in Italy, he said, airily. It was true; he was. But first there was the small matter of delivering a copy of *Othello* to the Venice Film Festival. He arrived in Venice at the end of August without the film, which he intimated had been held up by Italian customs; the director of the festival furiously and publicly denied this. Welles then proposed that the Italian version, prepared under someone else's direction and dubbed by Italian actors, should be shown. It was duly sent for. Journalists waited for news while Welles and the projectionist went through it reel by reel. They discovered that it was totally out of synch, the calibration unacceptable. Bowing to the inevitable, Welles withdrew the film on the morning of the day it was to have been shown. To cancel one film you have entered in the film festival may be regarded as a misfortune; to cancel two looks like carelessness. Venice was not best pleased. Welles, rather bravely, called a press conference to apologise. Contrite and dressed in white, every now and then lifting his eyes heavenwards and speaking Italian 'with a childish lilt', reported the *Corriere della Sera*, he said: 'Other directors move on, but I'm stuck. This film is my last chance and I can't afford to make the wrong move.' The film was finished, he said, but the only copy he could get hold of was not good enough: it needed accurate fixing and printing. It was, moreover, dubbed into Italian: he should have the right, he said, as both author and leading actor, to show the film with his own voice, 'and not the voice of another actor, however good'.[8] The journalists, spoiling for a fight, were taken aback and even, to some extent, won over: this was a new Welles, plaintive and touching, little-boy Orson, begging for mercy. It was unnerving and left them feeling slightly cheated, outmanoeuvred, the victims of a conjuring trick. Some suggested that he no longer wanted to enter the film for Venice, but was waiting for Cannes, where he was more likely to be appreciated. It did nothing to win their respect, even though, grudgingly, they extended their sympathy.

Welles now headed for his party – right in the centre of Venice, as it happens, at the magnificent baroque Palazzo Labia just off the Grand Canal. This was no ordinary party, it was the party to end all parties, the most glamorous social event of the post-war period, perhaps of the century: *Le Bal Oriental*, a masked costume ball thrown by Don Carlos de Beistegui y de Yturbe, the diminutive Mexican multimillionaire who had only ever visited Mexico twice, and then only briefly. The guest list, a sort of amalgam of the *Almanach de Gotha* and *Variety* magazine, included the Aga Khan III, Barbara Hutton, Gene Tierney, Countess Jacqueline de Ribes, Count Armand de La Rochefoucauld, Paul-Louis Weiller, Cecil Beaton, Gala Dalí, Baron de Chabrol, Desmond Guinness, Alexis von Rosenberg, Baron de Redé, Prince and Princess Chavchavadze, Patricia Lopez-Willshaw, Fulco di Verdura, the Duchess of Devonshire, Princess Natalia Pavlovna Paley, Nelson Seabra, Aimée de Heeren, Princess Ghislaine de Polignac, Princess del Drago, Princess Gabrielle Arenberg, Hélène Rochas, Princess Caetani, Princess Colonna, Prince Mathieu de Brancovan and many others. About thirty of the costumes had been designed by Pierre Cardin; the ball was his breakthrough. Christian Dior and Salvador Dalí designed each other's costumes. Lady Diana Cooper came as Cleopatra, Daisy Fellowes as the Queen of Africa, Jacques Fath was *le Roi Soleil* and Arturo Lopez-Willshaw did a striking turn as the Emperor of China with his boyfriend, the Baron de Redé, as the Boy Emperor.

Welles, whose costume had, inevitably, failed to materialise, came as no one in particular, swathed in silk, his pillbox hat topped with a vast and floppy feather. The tiny reclusive, misanthropic host, Don Carlos himself, bewigged and bedizened, his scarlet robes flowing gorgeously about him, towered above his guests in his sixteen-inch platform soles. Members of the Marquis de Cuevas's ballet troupe danced sarabands and minuets; the firemen of Venice formed a human pyramid, four rows high, in the central room of the palace; a troupe of giants entered; and there were two jazz bands. It could have been directed by Fellini, with designs by Tiepolo. Venice, impoverished and glum since the war, was delighted to be the scene of so much conspicuous consumption. All of this Welles stored away in his mind until it re-emerged in *Mr Arkadin*.

★

When Welles returned to *Othello* rehearsals after his eventful week away, he demanded a run-through of the play; afterwards he roundly told the company that they were all dreadful. By now the rest of the actors had joined them, and rehearsals had moved to the Ambassadors Theatre. The little world of London theatre was agog with rumours and anecdotes from the rehearsals; the latest Orson stories immediately did the rounds, with suitable embellishments. To the delight of the ghouls, all was clearly not well. Welles was frustrated, he told the actors; he felt they were too obedient, too efficient, too passionless. Their sheer Englishness was a burden to him. In 'Thoughts on Germany', which had appeared a couple of months before rehearsals began, he had offered some sharp thoughts about national characteristics. The cold-blooded Britisher, he said, was an invention of the nineteenth century; a hundred years before, the Englishman had been notorious for his effusiveness. 'In any mask, there are holes to look through, and behind that stupid elaborately official face we catch in some lights the gypsy glitter of eyes belonging to the real Englishman grinning out at the rest of us – the eyes of Falstaff and of Hamlet. The eyes of crazy sea-dogs and wily statesmen – of a desperate, tender-hearted, naïve and demoniac people who are the world's greatest poets, its first humourists, and most thorough-going madmen.'[9] To revive this antic spirit in the pleasant, hard-working, cooperative members of his *Othello* company, Welles applied some shock tactics.

Rehearsing the play on the tiny stage of the Ambassadors Theatre, he got hold of a twenty-foot pole used for adjusting the lights and pushed the actors around with it: 'To hell with The Method!' he roared. 'This is the Welles way: act, you sons of bitches!'[10] Perhaps it was a desire to convey to the actors the gargantuan nature of Elizabethan appetite that inspired him to have his meals brought in every day from the Ivy Restaurant opposite: he continued directing as he sat gorging in the stalls, addressing the cast through a megaphone. The actors were now struggling rather badly, precisely because he remained in the stalls. His hapless understudy – abused, mocked, roughly shoved around with the lighting pole – was playing Othello; Welles himself never set foot on the stage, which meant that the actors had no idea what sort of a performance he was going to give and were thus unable to create their own characters in relation to his. This can conceivably work on film; indeed, the film he had just shot was made on exactly that principle. But a theatre production is not made in the editing suite; it has to evolve as a whole. Everyone is interrelated. The transitions between scenes are crucial; the unfolding narrative is the responsibility of every single actor, however small his or her part. Unlike a film, a play is not a mosaic: it is a living organism in which all the constituent parts have been surgically connected to ensure that the blood flows through it, animating the whole, connecting the beginning to the end and all that lies between. This did not happen during rehearsals of *Othello*, with the result that the actors, as they headed out on the road – to Newcastle, and its the beautiful Theatre Royal – viewed the approaching first performance with fear in their hearts.

Their anxieties were amplified when they got there and found a wholly incompetent crew making an absolute mess of the set. These were the LOP team, and their incompetence was legendary: the big problem, according to Percy Harris, was that 'there was really nobody sober enough to get the production on.' Harris suggested that Welles ask her then brother-in-law, George Devine – later to be one of the great men of the English theatre of the twentieth century when he founded the English Stage Company at the Royal Court Theatre – to take over the physical production, which he did, occupying himself with the lighting and the functioning of the great brown-velvet front curtain, 'the wipe', as Welles called it, which was the central element of the set, and which almost never drew back when it should. The setting was relatively straightforward, consisting of an arrangement of rostrums and columns, a staircase and a flying window, but they were all large pieces; manoeuvring them into place depended on very specific coordination. It was the actors who had to move them: starting on Sunday night, they slogged away till five the following morning; as they left the theatre, Gudrun Ure saw the lines of people already queuing for tickets and wondered what sort of a show they were going to get later that night.

Newcastle was wildly excited about the production. Journalists who interviewed Welles were above all exercised by the question of whether people would expect him to be Harry Lime when they came into the theatre. 'What does it matter what they think when they come in?' roared Welles. 'It's what they think when they come out that matters.'[11] He had hired a trainer to get him into shape for the part. This was Fred Vallecca, who, reported the *Chronicle*, had boxed with Sugar Ray Robinson and Aly Khan, 'and he has also taken on crocodiles'. Fred, whom Welles had met in Rome, was not just a trainer, he was a fan. 'Orson Welles knows how to take care of himself,' said Fred, 'and has more energy than any of them. He loves the theatre. He is a great actor and the most interesting person I know.'[12]

Earlier in the week the *Newcastle Evening News* had watched with awe as Welles consumed two complete meals one after another during the course of the interview, soberly reporting his claim that he was playing Othello because he had already played most of the other Shakespearean parts (he had, in fact, professionally performed exactly seven Shakespeare parts on stage – Hamlet's dead father, Claudius, Mercutio, Tybalt, Brutus, Falstaff and Macbeth – plus a twenty-five-minute King Lear on radio). He enthusiastically described the tour that would follow the London run of the production: Bruges was fine – wonderful audiences; Rome and Vienna were fine; and then there was Stockholm (for Christmas), with parties and snow and torches and maybe even reindeer. Was it a good idea, they wanted to know, to direct *and* star in a play? It was not, Welles admitted, after a moment's thought. His fellow-actors may have agreed with him. He reflected on his approach to theatre. 'When I do the unorthodox,' he said, 'it is because I don't know or have forgotten the orthodox. When people say I break tradition it is usually because I don't know what the tradition is.' He added that he was terrified of one line in *Othello*: 'where shall I go?' 'It's a grand opportunity,' he said, 'for someone in the gallery to shout "Back to America".'[13]

The audience never shouted out any such thing, though the actors might well have been tempted to do so. Having finally been released at 5 a.m., they were called for 11.30 later that morning; Welles failed to show up because, he said, he was tired. Consequently they never had a full dress rehearsal, simply skipping from one lighting cue to another, which meant they had never run the play at all before meeting the public. That night Ure was so terrified that she had to be slapped to get her on stage. Everything that could go wrong did go wrong: the curtain stuck, the pieces of the set ended up in the wrong place, the flying pieces became intertwined. Never having run the play fully, even in the rehearsal room, Welles – who now appeared on stage for the first time – came on from wherever he thought might be best, without reference to anything the understudy had done, speaking whatever lines came into his head, some but by no means all of them from *Othello*, and rarely in the right order. The result was certainly lively, but more often than not it meant that the actors found themselves in darkness, though Welles invariably managed to locate his own light.

The set, with its high platforms, took a certain amount of negotiating, which Welles, never especially adroit at stage movement, found even more challenging than usual, since he had elected to wear massive platform soles, adding two or three inches to his regular 6' 3". His black make-up, which was also new to his fellow-actors, kept melting; every time he left the stage it needed to be refreshed by his diminutive dresser, Becky Martin, who was obliged to stand on stepladders in order to sponge it on, at the same time proffering him a bottle of brandy, from which he would gratefully swig, causing him to sweat even more. By the time he came to murder Desdemona, he was perspiring so profusely that Ure too was black from head to toe. By now Welles was scarcely in control of himself. 'The mattress had slipped with his unexpected weight so that my head was against the edge of the wood,' remembered Ure, 'so he took me and went bang, bang, bang and my head went bang, bang, bang and the audience were screaming and I was left with half my back hanging over the rostrum; it was quite high, it must have been three, four feet off the ground.'[14] The incident made it into the newspapers. 'Maybe I got excited,' Welles admitted to a reporter from the *Evening News* in the bar afterwards. 'It was in a good cause', gamely added Ure, '(rubbing her neck).'[15] The *Evening Chronicle*, reviewing the production, noticed nothing untoward. They found it 'fine and forthright: no frills, no nonsense', and Welles himself 'a grand, towering Othello' who 'declaimed with eloquence'.[16]

With the first night out of the way, work continued on a production that was still undergoing a sustained nervous breakdown. There were nightly note sessions on stage after each performance – 'requiems', Gudrun Ure called them – in which Welles would give astoundingly detailed and accurate corrections to the actors and stage crew, followed by rather livelier sessions after in the Turk's Head, the legendary theatrical hotel, beloved of touring companies. Here the company would repair to Welles's suite to drink themselves to a standstill, bystanders at a raconteurial Olympics, in which the chief – the only – contenders were Othello and Iago: Welles v. Finch. Finch was usually the victor: his stories of the Australian Bush trumped Welles's theatrical yarns; as often as not Welles would drift off to sleep, and Finch and Maxine Audley and the rest of the gang would continue to carouse, which eventually caused the entire company to be barred from the hotel. And not only the *Othello* company – all actors, much to the displeasure of Gladys Cooper, arriving the following week with Noël Coward to do his new play, *Relative Values.*

Out of favour with hotel managements the company might be, but it was immensely popular with play-goers; audiences were large and enthusiastic. One stage-struck fifteen-year-old, Brian Blacklock, was mesmerised, not only by Welles's performance ('we cowered in the stalls lest his shadow fall on us – or his eye'), but also by the haunting music, 'provided by a rather fluting troupe of invisible musicians . . . right up to the penultimate scene in the last act, when a faint but lyrical melody breathed in the background. And then the final scene . . . Welles whooped and thundered, then stooped like some monstrous hawk upon its prey, and stifled his wife – all to the same melody, now augmented, and so atmospheric.' At the curtain call, Welles unexpectedly came to the footlights:

> 'Ladies and gentlemen,' he said, 'in the next-to-last scene some of you may have heard some music in the background. It was from a man with a trumpet, playing in the street outside the stage-door. I sent my dresser out to give him a pound to go away. Which he did. Unhappily, he returned, bringing his friends with him . . . Ladies and gentlemen, tonight History has been made: for the first time in any theatre in the world, Desdemona was done to death to the strains of "Melancholy Baby".'[17]

The unaugmented score, played by the 'rather fluting troupe of invisible musicians', relayed on stage via a Panotrope, was the soundtrack of the movie and it was, apart from Welles himself, the only element that the stage production and the movie had in common. A number of the notices for the second and last leg of the tour, in Manchester, were impressed by the effect of the music: 'clavichord and a choral chant which brought the final curtain down'. But Manchester's reviewers, though respectful, were less sweepingly enthusiastic than Newcastle's, expressing reservations about Welles's performance, which would be echoed by many

London critics: 'He is perplexed and also pathetic; sometimes there are hints almost of a puzzled boy,' wrote the *Guardian*.[18] Welles began, according to the *Evening News*, magnificently: 'all negro and no Moor, this Othello had the bulk of a heavyweight boxer' (thank you, Fred Vallecca); 'he rose to his greatest heights in the scenes where Iago's poison took effect and rarely has the turning of that tortured mind against Desdemona been better shown.' But then 'much of the power seemed to go out of him'.[19]

A slight bafflement hangs over the reviews. The same critic felt that the production was straining too hard to be a movie: 'the hand that had rocked the film sets was trying to rule another world'. The *Oldham Chronicle* was altogether blunter: 'not the most suspicious critic could have conceived that the production would bore. In this alone, Mr Welles has maintained his reputation for being unexpected.'[20] The company continued to work on the production, the hour-long 'requiems' continued after each show, and a new company manager, Laurence Olivier's personal favourite, Diana Boddington, came on board and took things in hand.

> I went round and met Orson Welles, and I said 'I'm pleased to meet you', so he said 'what do you think?' So I said 'well one thing that worried me very much,' I said straight away, 'You cannot have lights showing like that.' And he said 'Would you mind waiting a minute', so I went out, and Lovat Fraser went in and he came out again and said 'My God, you've really upset him', and I said 'What's he said?' '"You're going to put that Boddington woman back on the next train to London", so I think you'd better go in and explain yourself.' So I went in again and I said 'Mr Welles I understand you're a bit upset about what I said but I'm a very honest person and say exactly what I think and that is what I think' and he said 'Diana, we're going to get on,' just like that, 'I know we're going to get on,' and we got on for 9 years.[21]

Under Boddington's skilful stage management, the production became more and more fluid, and Welles more and more confident of the text, but there were no significant changes; the matrix had now been fixed.

★

On to London. Many of his colleagues noted Welles's rising levels of anxiety. He appeared remote from the company. Since the anecdotal contests in Newcastle, they had had very little contact with him, apart from the nightly note-marathons in Manchester, during which, clad in a dressing gown, he would swig from a bottle of brandy while they sat there, parched. He had total recall of every aspect of the performance – lights, sound, positions, tempo, inflection – and disgorged himself of all of his observations at leisure. By the time they got to London, the physical production was running smoothly and the company was essentially doing what they were told to do. It was his own performance on which Welles was focused, conscious of the comparisons that would inevitably be made, and of the fact that he was acting in Laurence Olivier's theatre, under Laurence Olivier's management. He changed his physical appearance, going from Moor to Berber: on the road, black-skinned, with romantically ruffled shiny Caucasian hair, his nose *au naturel*, his chin unadorned; in the West End, bull-like, ageing, short-haired, hook-nosed, goatee-bearded, lighter-complexioned. The pre-publicity emphasised his Shakespearean credentials, adding a few more roles to his imaginary CV: King John, Angelo, Coriolanus and Richard III (which, admittedly, he had played at the age of fourteen). The 1936 Harlem *Macbeth*'s three-month run had now become three years, and Welles was alleged to have directed *The Tempest* at the Federal Theatre, which he had not. Expectations were running uncomfortably high.

The first night at the St James Theatre was exactly that: there were no previews, no time to get accustomed to the majestic dimensions of the auditorium; they just had to plunge in. *Le tout Londres* was there, including royalty, both British (the Duchess of Kent) and Hollywood (Jenifer Jones, Judy Holliday and David O. Selznick), along with half the actors in the business. The Oliviers were blessedly absent, having gone on a cruise to recover from the exertions of their recent New York season, sending Welles a pair of gold cufflinks engraved with the letter O and a card that read, 'To our very own boy with the love, wishes and pride of his Mom & Pop' – their running joke about his great size compared with their merely average dimensions. Despite a bronchial and unusually ill-behaved audience, and a slightly recalcitrant wipe-curtain, the production went as well as could have been hoped for; it was so rapturously received that, after six curtain calls, Welles was moved to make a speech in which he said the production was the realisation of a twenty-year ambition, adding, oddly, that he hoped he had been a success, 'because the play has already been a success for several seasons'.

The reviews were perfectly respectable, in some cases enthusiastic: 'An Othello of Pathos,' cried the *Telegraph*;[22] 'Orson is a Great Othello,' averred the *Herald*.[23] There was universal acknowledgement of Welles's initial physical impact, of the richness of his voice, of the tenderness and gentleness he showed in the role, of his restraint. But the enthusiasm was tempered. English critical discourse of the period tended to box-ticking: did the actor have the correct pathos? Did his voice have the right notes in it? Did he shape the part so that the climaxes landed properly? Was he sufficiently noble? In most of these departments, Welles was felt to have failed. The phrase that recurred was 'smouldering volcano'; or, as *The Stage* more elegantly put it, 'to sit through this production is an experience akin to waiting for a threatening thunderstorm that never arrives in full fury'.[24] There was a general feeling of frustration: 'Orson Welles's Othello was in some ways the most extraordinary theatrical performance of the year,' wrote Stephen Williams in the *Evening News*:

> Here was a magnificent figure of a man, with a presence that overwhelmed one with its majesty, 'An eye like Mars to threaten and command,' and a voice that hummed and vibrated like a bass cello. And what did he do with these prodigious gifts? He missed tremendous chances, he either misquoted or threw away some of the most sonorous lines in the language; he seems almost unaware of those pieces of savage, blistering invective with which the demented Moor lacerates his feelings. *Othello* is a great tragedy; it was a greater tragedy to see all this superb, superabundant vitality kept in leash, this volcanic energy so unnaturally prevented from loosing itself.[25]

This was not simply the arrogance of an insular critical establishment: it was felt both by audiences and his fellow-players. Something in the performance failed to ignite. From a visual point of view, it worked splendidly. 'He had a great flair,' said Percy Harris, 'for looking very magnificent.' More than that, Welles had an extraordinary presence; the image of the character was potent. 'He looks like some dark monster invading us from Mars,' said Harold Hobson in the *Sunday Times*, 'or a deep-sea diver, or a creature emerging from a fantastical coal mine.'[26] T.C. Worsley memorably wrote in the *New Statesman*:

> this huge, goaded figure rolls onto the stage with a dreadful fog of menace and horror, thickening, wave after wave, with each successive entrance. The very deliberation of his movements, of his great lifted head and rolling bloodshot eye, and the deep slow notes rumbled from his massive chest, pile up the sense of inevitability almost to the point of the unbearable. In the end we long (and isn't this the point of tragedy?) for the tension to be burst.

This could be a review of a great actor-manager of the previous century and stands as an eloquent tribute to the physical and, indeed, psychic impact of Welles, which should never be taken for granted: he was a phenomenon. 'Mr Welles', Worsley continued, 'gave off an aura of terror such I have seen no actor before produce.'[27]

But to climb the mountain called *Othello*, neither physical appearance nor charisma nor even inspiration will suffice. It requires unrelenting hard work, mentally, physically and vocally. Welles seems never entirely to have mastered the text, so inevitably he was always enslaved to it, never able to ride it, always hanging on for dear life, or putting on the brakes to slow the play down to the speed of his own thought rather than Othello's. He was also unable to reveal the character's detailed progression through the play or indeed its hidden strata. The sections that he had incorporated into the film were naturally the ones he knew best – most notably the scenes in which Iago poisons Othello's mind: the first was 'the superb moment of this production', said Worsley, 'which brings us to the interval at the highest pitch of expectation'.[28] But the second act proved harder to sustain. In the phrase of actor-laddies of yesteryear, he lacked puff: the stamina, both physical and vocal, demanded by these great roles. He was, in a word, unprepared. Fred Vallecca had melted away in Newcastle, and now Welles was simply out of shape. 'He was terribly fat and he was terribly soft, there was no resilience physically,' said Percy Harris, who was called on to dress him for a few nights when Welles's dresser was ill. 'His shoulders were quite round, and his hips, and his general shape. Nothing stayed on, so the trousers were sort of buttoned onto this strap, and then the jacket. The shirt then had to be on an elastic and had to be outside the trousers, and then the jacket had to be buttoned through too, so it was a sort of waist length jacket. And it had to be buttoned through onto it so that it all stayed on. And then to keep the cloaks on! He had various cloaks, that was very difficult.'[29] She sent her assistant, Christopher Morahan, to a Newcastle lingerie manufacturer for a corset for Welles, 'and of course,' remembered Morahan, 'they didn't believe the measurements. They said there must be some mistake here and then I explained it was for Orson Welles and then they understood perfectly, and ran one up for him.'[30]

Welles was scarcely in better shape vocally, having taken no care of his peerless instrument; *The Blessed and the Damned* had not challenged him in that way, much less *An Evening with Orson Welles*, and his last appearance on stage before that had been *Around the World*, which had simply been a lot of shouting. His lack of flexibility, allied to his native sonorousness, led to monotony. Not long after the production closed, Olivier – who had returned to England soon after *Othello*'s opening night – observed this of Welles's performance: 'Anything that might be said to have detracted from his Othello was purely on the technical side, and was due to his being out of practice physically. The extra special kind of breath control, and in true fact simply the athlete's training necessary for the weightier Shakespearean roles, let him down on the big speeches and high-flying scenes.' He went on to say that 'it would of course have been better for him, as it is always better for anybody embroiled in one of these parts, to have somebody else direct the play for him, but it is Orson's magician's training that makes him want to handle the whole works. One day I feel certain that his talent for pure acting will receive the recognition and acclamation that it merits.'[31]

Again and again, this view was repeated: Welles the director had let down Welles the actor. He had not allowed himself to be directed on stage by anyone since he was nineteen, when he played first Mercutio, then Tybalt for Guthrie McClintic. 'If ever Mister Welles chooses to play the role again and subjects himself to the discipline of being directed by a Benthall or a Gielgud,' opined the *News Chronicle* of Welles's *Othello*, 'then fight, bribe or bludgeon your way into the theatre, for that will be a performance echoing down the ages.'[32] Not only when he was rehearsing, but during the run itself, more than half of Welles's mind was on his fellow-actors, the lighting, the stage machinery. The slow, selfish growth of a performance within an actor over the course of rehearsal and performance never happened for him.

The physical production of *Othello* was mostly dismissed as simultaneously dull and hyperactive; Welles's tinkering with the text – changing words, reordering scenes, inventing silent action – was sniffily disapproved of, although within a decade such things would become commonplace at the future National Theatre and Royal Shakespeare Company. The curious effect of his artificially induced proportions was noted with puzzlement: in some quarters, this giant Othello's relationship with a Desdemona who was just over five foot tall was considered grotesque. His altitude literally set this Othello apart from all the others, a situation compounded by his instruction to his fellow-actors never to touch him or approach him too closely – an old-time actor-manager's demand. The result was to isolate Othello. Whether this was Welles's conception of the character or was simply the outcome of his desire to dominate absolutely, this isolation had a secondary but very significant consequence: he was unable to form any detailed relationships with the other characters, which meant that he was condemned to repeat the image he first presented.

In the review that dominated all the others, that of Kenneth Tynan in the *Evening Standard*, one terrible noun was slapped down on the table: 'No doubt about it, Orson Welles has the courage of his restrictions. In last night's boldly staged *Othello* at the St James's Theatre, he gave a performance brave and glorious to the eye; but it was the performance of a magnificent amateur.'[33] 'EVENING PAPERS ARE FINE,' Welles telegraphed Olivier the day after the first night, 'BUT TYNAN SAYS I'M AN AMATEUR STOP WIRE INSTRUCTIONS.' The *Standard*'s headline – now distressing merely to quote – was, even for 1951, a bit of a shocker: '*CITIZEN COON*'. In this production, Tynan said, 'a whole generation was on trial. If Welles was wrong, if a contemporary approach to Shakespeare in his thunderbolt hands failed, then we were all wrong.' In fact, almost uniquely among his fellow-critics, Tynan found the production, with its hints of Berliner Ensemble style, admirable.

> He sacrificed much to give us a *credible* account of a play which bristles with illogicalities. The conception was visually flawless – Cassio's drunk scene became a vivid blaze of mutiny, and the killing of Desdemona with crimson awnings over a white couch, and the high rostrum towering behind, can never have looked more splendid.

But Welles's own performance dismayed him. It was, Tynan said:

> a huge shrug. He was grand and gross, and wore some garish costumes superbly. His close-cropped head was starkly military, and he never looked in need of a banjo. But his voice, a musical instrument in one octave, lacked range; he toyed moodily with every inflection. His face expressed wryness and strangulation but little else. And his body relaxation frequently verged on sloth. Above all, he never built to a vocal climax: he positively waded through the great speeches, pausing before the stronger words like a landing craft breasting a swell . . . Welles's Othello is the lordly and mannered performance we saw in *Citizen Kane*, slightly adapted.[34]

A couple of nights after this review appeared, Tynan went backstage to say hello to Welles and was astonished to be turned away. 'Welles uttered one word with a bellow that shook everything in the room that was made of glass,' wrote Tynan's then-wife Elaine Dundy: 'Out!'[35] Like many a critic before him and since, Tynan failed to understand that his darts, so blithely fired off, actually drew blood.

He and Welles knew each other: Welles had written the

'Introductory Letter' to Tynan's bobby-dazzling first book, *He that Plays the King*: Tynan, he wrote, had 'materialized out of a puff of Paris fog, handed me the manuscript of this book and before vanishing somehow bamboozled me into reading it and writing this'. He must be, said Welles, 'some sort of a magician' – praise indeed, coming from Welles. Tynan, twenty-three at the time, had been obsessed by Welles since boyhood, an obsession that lasted for the remaining thirty years of his brief, brilliant life, and produced some of the most vivid, contentious writing ever penned about Welles. Aged fourteen, he had written to a friend, after seeing *Citizen Kane* on the first day of its release in Birmingham, that he was 'dazzled by its narrative virtuosity' and its 'shocking but always relevant cuts, its brilliantly orchestrated dialogue, and its use of deep focus in sound as well as vision';[36] the following year, after seeing *The Magnificent Ambersons*, he wrote to Welles, who – astonishingly – replied to him, explaining that the studio had cut it without his consent. 'The picture suffered from all this meddling, but your letter', Welles added gracefully, 'makes me feel the result perhaps wasn't as disastrous as I'd feared.' But it was *Kane* that had knocked Tynan sideways: he saw the film five times during its week-long run, once with his eyes shut to prove to himself that the soundtrack was expressive enough to be listened to in its own right.

The impact of Welles on the young Tynan gives a vivid sense of what he meant to that generation: the exhilaration, the youthful confidence, all the rules stood on their head. At the end of 1943, now sixteen, Tynan wrote about Welles in his school magazine, under the heading 'The New Playboy of the Western World': 'He is a gross and glorious director of motion pictures, the like of which we have not seen since the great days of the German cinema; he reproduces life as it is sometimes seen in winged dreams . . . watch him well, for he is a major prophet, with the hopes of a generation clinging to his heels.'[37] On Tynan's bedroom wall hung photographs of Salvador Dalí, Jean Cocteau, Max Ernst, Pablo Picasso, Charles Baudelaire, Sit Henry Irving, Walt Whitman – and Welles; he affected a new pose: 'arrogance, bass voice, hanging lower lip. Which reads o-r-s-o-n.'[38]

Tynan was a natural idolater and, like most such, he was harsh on his gods, as Welles discovered a week after the opening of *Othello* at the St James Theatre, when 'Orson Welles as I see Him' appeared in a magazine called *The Sketch*. Discernible through the curlicues of the young Tynan's verbal embroideries is a sharp, cruel snapshot of Welles in full flood at thirty-six:

> In these lean years he has fattened and, in repose, resembles a landed whale. The body slumps like an inflated embryo; the eyes glower without meaning; the nose is a button; the head tilts sumptuously back as if reclining on a houri's shoulder. One's impression is of a becalmed luxury liner. But speech transfigures him: the pedigree mane of the fighting bull bristles, and he lunges forward, breasting his paragraphs like a surf-rider, bouncing over your interpolated breakers of 'But – ' and 'Don't you think – ' 'Negro actors are all untalented,' he will assert: 'They're musicians, but nothing else. Paul Robeson was just Brian Aherne in black-face.' A minute later: 'There's no problem about *The Cocktail Party*; it's a straight commercial play, with a comic climax that Saki used and Evelyn Waugh used – the surprising martyrdom of a well-bred lady in exotic surroundings.' What does he read most? 'You'll think me pompous, but P.G. Wodehouse. Imagine it: a benign comic artist in the twentieth century. Nothing about personal irritations, the stuff Benchley and Dorothy Parker write about: simply a perfect, impersonal, benevolent style.' Shakespeare: 'I think Oxford wrote Shakespeare. If you don't agree, there are some funny coincidences to explain away . . .'[39]

Welles's conversation, says Tynan, has 'the enlivening sciolism of Robert L. Ripley's "Believe it or Not"; he has a wonderfully catalogued library of snap judgments.' So far, so amiable. Then comes the summing up, another of the premature obituaries Welles had been receiving at regular intervals since *Kane*:

> Since *Citizen Kane* his search for new openings has been somehow desultory. His affection for Europe has qualified, dimmed, even muzzled his earlier forthright certainties; and he may develop into an uproarious armchair voyeur. As with Coleridge, a blockage of undigested experience has dammed up creativeness; only the tonic bile of criticism filters through to us. The changed Welles is a connoisseur – that social, wine-wise, stomach-sensitive creature without whom art could never be understood, but by whom it is so rarely hammered out. In broadening, he has become flattened; possibly the blind, instinctive upper-cut of theatrical effectiveness is even now beyond his reach. To his friends he overflows and is Johnsonian; but that contemporary who said that Welles is 'necessarily careless' of his genius may not have been wholly wrong.[40]

Tynan had clearly not seen him in action on the set of *Othello* in Mogador or Venice. It is characteristic of many of Welles's commentators that they select one or other of the many Welleses as quintessential, but the mystery of the man is that all the Welleses coexist; all are true. Welles himself was no doubt irritated by the latest verdict from this young whippersnapper whom he had encouraged, but it was something else earlier in the piece that really upset him, and was still upsetting him thirty years later: the phrase 'blubber shoulders'. Welles told Tynan's widow, Kathleen, 'That made me a permanently fat man. I'd been in training, I ate nothing. I thought if I have "blubber shoulders" after what I've been going through, to hell with it!' Their friendship survived, mostly because Tynan wanted it to: as Kathleen Tynan notes, her husband was in search of a father figure, a father whom he could use as a punchbag without fear of forfeiting his love.[41]

This was not at all pleasing to Welles, who spent a great deal of his life avoiding the responsibilities of fatherhood, both actual and projected. He absolutely refused to extend paternal leadership to his company at the St James Theatre. Despite better-than-average notices, morale generally dwindled; Welles seemed increasingly uninterested in the play or the part, and had little contact with the actors. Sometimes there were confrontations. One night Welles hurled the bag of coins that Othello throws at Emilia so vigorously that it hit Maxine Audley in the face, drawing blood. After the curtain had fallen, she marched over to him and slapped him as hard as she knew how, 'and everybody in the theatre came and shook me warmly by the hand and said, "we've all been longing to do that"'. The following day Welles called her to the stage before the performance and, without a word of apology, set about analysing what had gone wrong. 'He had me come on with a handful of coins, he made the gesture of throwing and as he threw I raised my hand and dropped the coins. He wanted that gasp from the audience. And it got the gasp,' she said, admiringly. 'He made it into a conjuring trick.' [42]

One night with Gudrun Ure, he struck her hard across the face with a parchment; a few nights later he struck her with it three times in a row, reducing her to tears. 'We got to the curtain and, all smiles, he came down and he said "that was just great" and I looked at him and I said "Orson you shouldn't do that, that is very bad" and he said "but why?" and I said "if you don't know, I can't tell you". But it was just disastrous, just no comprehension of what was wrong with it.' The actors never saw him before or after the show: instead he gave them audible directions during it: 'Quicker, quicker. Get ON with it. Move left. Stop. Quieter.' His own performance was increasingly slapdash and mechanical. Once – and once only, according to Gudrun Ure – he focused himself; he had spotted Laurence Olivier at the back of the stalls. 'And it was marvellous. Never again.'[43]

★

His energies and his focus were elsewhere. He struck a new deal with Harry Alan Towers, the producer of *The Adventures of Harry Lime*, to remake a radio series called *Secrets of Scotland Yard*, to which Towers gave the new name *The Black Museum*. Welles would simply introduce the fifty-two programmes, for which Towers would pay him 'quite a substantial amount of money for a comparatively short period of his time'. The contract was signed in the back of a cab after the second night of *Othello*. Welles was not in a good mood: he had read most of the notices by now. 'He muttered to me in the taxi "Have you got the contract, Harry?" and I said "Yes" and held it out to him together with the pen. He signed it with the comment "Lower than this I cannot stoop."'[44] The money, paid up front – though Towers inevitably spent the following year chasing Welles around Europe to record his contributions – was immediately ploughed into yet more editing of *Othello*, specifically on the soundtrack.

Welles took particular pleasure in replacing Suzanne Cloutier's voice with that of Gudrun Ure; he himself, having already revoiced Robert Coote's Roderigo in its entirety, now dubbed some of Michael Laurence's Cassio, Jean Davis's Montano and even MacLiammóir's – admittedly extremely imitable – Iago. All this was in preparation for the film's world premiere in Rome on 29 November, followed by the Milan premiere the day after. Welles was on stage in London, and therefore not present, which was perhaps just as well, given the volatile nature of his relationship with the Italian press. There was nonetheless a certain fanfare around the openings – both charity galas – and in Rome an aeroplane blazoned the name of the film on the sky in vapour-clouds: there it stood for a glorious moment, till it dissolved into the empyrean, an all-too-precise metaphor for the film's subsequent history. Even on this, its first outing, it disappeared without a trace after four days, being swiftly replaced by a whacky comedy with a resonant title: *Mago per Forza – The Reluctant Magician*.

In its consideration of *Othello*, the Italian critical fraternity plunged in along sharply divided lines, their discourse far removed from the homespun commentary that the English-speaking press would offer. Much of the discussion hinged on whether or not Welles's work could be described as baroque, a heinous offence for the neo-realist followers of Benedetto Croce. 'The more baroque the artist, the bigger the effect and the less the substance,' in the words of the great realist novelist Alberto Moravia.[45] For the pro-baroque faction, Welles's latest offering was a triumph, revealing him as 'a follower of Tintoretto and El Greco, bringing together the rationalism of Pascal and the labyrinth of Theseus';[46] the hard left, meanwhile, toeing Moscow's line, dismissed him for his formalism. There was general, if qualified, admiration for the film's vitality: 'a film', said *Oggi*, 'narrated with all the means that the cinema has at its disposal'.[47] Welles's scourge, Aristarco, the journalist he had taken to court but failed to prosecute, said the same thing from a different angle: Welles, said Aristarco, was 'a hedonist, narcissistically indulging his extravagant camera positions, both as director and as actor . . . anxious to dazzle at all costs', which gave the film 'a revolutionary-seeming appearance without a revolutionary content'. It fell to Moravia to state the core case against Welles: 'You could say that, like some fish, he is unable to plumb the depths but must stay close to the surface to breathe. Hence his need to make a big splash . . . it seems that Welles believes that the job of the artist is to dumbfound rather than win over and move. This is due to his inability to penetrate the depths of art or life.'[48]

In one shape or another, from *Citizen Kane* to *F For Fake*, this was the accusation: all form and no content; all surface and no substance. Avoiding this framework of judgement altogether, Vittorio Bonicelli in *Il Tempo*, reviving a familiar comparison, daringly struck a heretical note: 'there is more Shakespeare in the "arrogance" and "ribaldry" of Orson Welles than in the refined academic work of Laurence Olivier. (Here endeth my reputation.)'[49] It is piquant that, at the time of this review, the ribald and arrogant Welles was acting under the management of the refined, academic Olivier; indeed, the programme for *Othello* at the St James carried an advertisement for the latter's film of *Hamlet*.

★

The run of the play was coming to an end, and Welles was keen to start re-re-editing the film in preparation for the following year's Cannes Film Festival, into which it had been entered. He had no desire to embark on the stage production's European tour, about which he had spoken so expansively in Newcastle. The company was scarcely heartbroken at the news; Laurence Olivier Productions, on the other hand, was less cheerful: they had hoped to recoup some of their losses on the show by taking it to New York. *Othello* in London ran for just eleven weeks: the average weekly income had been £1,500, average weekly expenditure £2,500. Lovat Fraser, the general manager for LOP, having sounded Welles out, quickly came to the conclusion that, *Othello* was 'a thing of the past' for him, and that he would not fulfil his obligations by playing in New York; shortly afterwards Fraser received a letter from Welles saying how much he wanted to do the show in New York and on tour in America, but that he was, alas, waiting on a film. At this point Olivier himself stepped into the discussion, and wrote to Welles, iron hand in velvet glove, in an entirely characteristic example of his silky determination, masked by faux-jocularity – a mode with which Welles would later, to his cost, become very familiar:

> Our dearest little boy, Viv and I have both been so dying to see you. I have been wanting to pick you up and hug you and swing you round and dance you up and down on my knee and even go bird-nesting with you to show you in some tiny measure how sweet and generous was your dear thought about that wonderful fridge in New York, for which I thought of you with gratitude every night of the God-damned run. We are simply longing to see you. When is this going to be possible please. – Now I have to write to you about a ridiculous business detail. Have you ever any intention of going to New York with *Othello*? Because if not, I think it would be a good idea for us to sell the costumes. We don't want to do this if there is any likelihood at all of your being able to fulfil your promised intention of going to New York in the piece, because that will be our only possibility of our really getting our losses back. Have a think, dear chum, and let us know. We really long to see you; we really do. Always your devoted Larry.[50]

Olivier's steely focus, which had already won him the more or less uncontested title of the greatest actor in the world, was a quality entirely lacking in Welles, whose apparent self-confidence masked a disabling insecurity and an utter lack of guile, the quality he later described in Olivier as 'peasant cunning'.[51]

He had in fact long ago given up any idea of playing Othello in America: for Welles, the stage show was, as Lovat Fraser correctly divined, 'a thing of the past'. After it closed, making way for *Snow White and the Seven Dwarves*, Welles went to Dublin to visit Micheál MacLiammóir and Hilton Edwards, and was greeted by a wholly unexpected storm of protest engineered by the Catholic Cinema and Theatre Patrons' Association, loudly proclaiming Welles a communist – 'Stalin's Star', shrieked the placards picketing the Gate

Theatre when he attended a performance of Maura Laverty's *Tolka Row* there. At the interval Welles's jaunty wave to the picketers out of the window was greeted with outraged cries and shaken fists; fuel was added to the flames by the play's author, whisky glass in hand, regaling the crowd with a spirited rendition of 'The Red Flag'. At the end of the show Welles was called on to make a speech, and he spoke of how moved he was to be standing on the stage where he had made his debut twenty-one years earlier, and lamented – to loud applause – that the demonstration had interfered with 'the tribute to so fine a play'.[52] He departed by the fire-escape, leaving Hilton Edwards to calm things down by informing reporters (quite accurately) that, far from being a communist, Welles had spent his whole life trying to be a capitalist. The remark may have been tinged by a certain grim irony for him, since MacLiammóir and Edwards were on the brink of bankruptcy, still struggling with debts incurred during their two years of working on *Othello*. This financial misunderstanding would simmer and bubble underneath the relationship for many years; to the bitter end, in fact.

★

One of Welles's many tokens of reparation was to have taken part, as promised, earlier in 1951, in a short film written and directed by Edwards and produced by MacLiammóir. *Return to Glennascaul: A Story Told in Dublin*, a charming and skilful ghost movie in its own right – it was nominated for an Academy Award as Best Short Film of 1954 – also functions as a kind of pendant to *Othello*. The film begins with Welles in silhouette, supposedly doing a take for *Othello*. The speech is carefully chosen: Othello as a teller of tall tales, describing his wooing of Desdemona with stories of his exotic experiences among the anthropophagi and 'men whose heads / Do grow beneath their shoulders'. 'Put your hat on straight, Mike,' says a lightly bearded Welles, presumably to MacLiammóir, before the take, but he soon cuts himself off – 'I can't get this thing right, let's break for lunch.' The movie set is littered with arc lights, one of which catches him, his giant shadow showing him lighting a cigarette. The shadow-Welles turns to us, blacking out the screen, and introduces himself on the soundtrack as 'Orson Welles – your obedient servant', promising to tell us a story from 'the haunted land of Ireland', which 'purportedly happened to me'. He has come to Dublin, he tells us, to talk *Othello* business with Hilton Edwards, 'the producer and director of the film that follows'. He promises to disappear from the story very soon: getting back from the making of one movie, as he puts it, to the making of another – 'my own' – for which he is, 'I'm afraid, still wearing my *Othello* beard'.

He disappears soon enough, as promised, but – like Harry Lime – effortlessly dominates the film. At the beginning of the story he is driving through the night when he comes across someone whose car has broken down; he offers the man a lift and they fall to chatting, which enables Welles to make a delicious meta-filmic joke. The man is having trouble with his distributor, he says. 'I'm having trouble with my distributor, too,' says Welles, with a sly grin. The man, Sean Merriman (Michael Laurence – Cassio in Welles's film of *Othello*), tells the story of two women, mother and daughter, whom he picked up at this same spot a year ago. He dropped them off at their house, Glennascaul – 'the glen of shadows', Welles's voice-over tells us, while the story plays out on the screen. The women invite him in. Everything about both the house and the women is strangely old-fashioned. Merriman shows them his cigarette case, which belonged to an uncle of his who died in China; it is inscribed to him from a certain Lucy. After having a drink, Merriman departs, remembering too late that he has left his cigarette case in Glennascaul. The following day he goes back, but finds the house boarded up and for sale. An estate agent tells him that the owners – a mother and her daughter – died some years before. He gets a key and, brushing aside the cobwebs, retrieves his cigarette case. The film cuts back to Welles and Merriman in the car, examining the case. The point of the story, Merriman tells him, is that the daughter's name was Lucy. Welles, spooked, scoots off in the car, speeding past two elderly ladies hoping for a lift. 'Did you see who that was?' asks one, and the other replies, 'Yes, but I don't believe it.'

The film, though modest in its scope, is quintessential Welles. The teasing prologue on the movie set plays, as Welles loved to play, with Pirandellian tropes – what is fiction, what is truth? – putting himself into the frame, literally and metaphorically; it is vintage Welles, as is the instant immediacy of the voice-over: swift, quizzical, wry, both confidential and unsettling. The story itself is exactly the sort of thing Welles adored. And the cinematography seems to bear Welles's touch in every frame. The opening sequence purporting to have been shot on the *Othello* set bears a strong resemblance to the witty trailers Welles shot for *Citizen Kane* and *The Magnificent Ambersons*, even down to a sign on the wall that says: OTHELLO MERCURY FILMS, while the film proper, with its expressionist lighting and sharp definition of black and white, its leisurely camera moves and its rarefied performances, not unlike those in *Ambersons*, is quintessentially Wellesian.

There appear to be no records of the filming, so it is impossible to determine how many days Welles spent shooting in Ireland; it is equally impossible to know how much of the script he was responsible for, if any. His voice-over is so utterly characteristic that it is hard not to feel his hand in it. But Edwards and MacLiammóir had known Welles and worked with him for over twenty years and were perfectly capable of writing Wellesian periods to order. As far as the cinematography is concerned, Edwards was steeped in the lighting that evolved in Berlin in the 1920s and 1930s; and his cameraman, George Fleishmann (who had crash-landed in Ireland on a reconnaissance mission in 1942 and decided to stay), had been born in Austria and trained at the Berlin Film Academy, photographing documentaries in Germany before the Second World War, including – as a camera operator – Leni Riefenstahl's *Olympia* (1936). What is startling is how the film presages Welles's later work – in particular the short television film *The Fountain of Youth* from 1958 and *F For Fake*; both of these (and *Return to Glennascaul*, whoever was responsible for it), with their playful narratorial interventions, are in essence filmic transpositions of Welles's radio work of the 1930s. As so often with Welles, his innovations prove to have deep roots in the past.

CHAPTER SIX

Reason Not the Need

His sojourn in the British Isles over, Welles returned to Italy, to Rome, the nearest thing he knew to home. From there, at the end of January 1952, he announced his next film, *Mr Arkadin*, which he had been germinating all through the previous year, while he was editing *Othello* and playing in the West End. His first attempt at the screenplay was written in Casablanca in March 1951, and seems to have been directly inspired by his relationship with Michael Olian, an international financier of extreme dubiousness. Welles, according to a detailed exposé of Olian by the star investigative journalist Michael Stern in *True* magazine,[1] had visited Olian's Roman residence, the Villa Madama – designed by Raphael, no less – for dinner one night and stayed for a year. Olian was Welles's kind of guy: having had a heart attack, he was instructed by his doctor to give up smoking, drinking and the more vigorous kind of female companionship. 'You know what I did when he told me that? I went out and smoked five packs of cigarettes a day and drank three bottles of champagne at a sitting.' His hospitality was on a stupendous scale, catering with scientific precision to the needs and desires of his guests. Olian and Welles were seen everywhere together in the less salubrious Roman watering-holes, but pleasure, though always welcome, was not Welles's sole reason for cultivating Olian, who had lately become a commanding figure in the Italian film industry. Welles needed $35,000 to complete the last few days of shooting in Mogador for *Othello*; Olian, for whom this sort of money was peanuts, gave him $200,000 in exchange for first recoupment rights in England and the United States, plus 50 per cent general ownership. The *Othello* cake was being sliced into too many pieces. The figures scarcely seem to add up, but in a sense it was all theoretical: the film never recouped, so no one was due anything. Welles's friendship with Olian came to an inevitable end 'because', says Stern, 'the chief facet in Welles's genius is his ability to run through a bankroll, his own included'. Stern overheard a blazing if somewhat one-sided row between the two men, in which Olian accused Welles of being a fool, 'while the embarrassed actor-director tried desperately to mollify him with "Tu as raison, Michel"'.

Welles was of course deeply fascinated by Olian, a Lithuanian by birth, who, as Michael Stern put it, 'changed his nationality as lightly as some people change a suit of clothes'. At one point or another he had passports from Italy, Russia, Latvia and the League of Nations and nationality status resulting from residence in France, Germany and Switzerland. He started as a petty criminal in Riga, functioned as a money-changer in Berlin in the Twenties and had established himself in France as a financier by the Thirties. 'His attitude to the law', Stern drily remarks, 'is highly individual . . . and he is noted for his highly original approach to government matters,' bribing his way out of any inconvenient situation. During the war he was in Switzerland, earning the gratitude of his friends Himmler and Goering by personally supervising their Swiss bank accounts. Olian's name, says Stern, is totally unknown in America, but

> it is entirely likely that it will compare favourably in fame with such professional mystery men as George Dawson, Basil Zaharoff and Aristotle Socrates Onassis, for at this writing, the military attachés of several friendly governments, the French Sûreté, the Swiss government, our own Central Intelligence Agency and the congressional investigating committee . . . are scrutinising his present activities.

Welles became intrigued by the dramatic potential of all of these mystery men, to whom he seemed so easily to relate. The film he was going to make would be drawn, he said, from an 'unpublished crime novel' of his and would deal with the misadventures of an arms dealer 'along the lines of Basil Zaharoff'. For obvious reasons there was no mention of Michael Olian.

★

1952 was, by Wellesian standards, uneventful. He turned down an offer from La Scala to direct two Verdi operas (*Macbeth* and *Othello*, inevitably) and another from the Metropolitan Opera in New York to direct *Porgy and Bess*; the latter offer was presumably a belated response to the Harlem *Macbeth*, or even *Native Son*, the electrifying adaptation of Richard Wright's novel he had staged in New York in 1941. It is a curious fact that Welles, so often (and not entirely inaccurately) described as operatic in his approach, never attempted to work in that medium. Only a year later, as we shall see, he staged a ballet, but he seems almost pointedly to have avoided directing opera, despite his precocious exposure to and appreciation of it as the seven-year-old correspondent of the *Ravinia Chronicle*. The matchless sequence in *Citizen Kane* in which Susan Alexander Kane attempts to sing an aria from Bernard Herrmann's glorious Massenet pastiche, *Salâmmbo,* embodies the whole gesture of French Romantic opera in a few short minutes and should have had every intendant in the world reaching for their phones. But it never happened.

Othello, the most consciously operatic of Welles's films, was entered for the Cannes Festival in May of 1952 and, to the outrage of the Italians present, won the Palme d'Or, which it shared with Renato Castellani's winsome *Due soldi di Speranza* (*Two Penn'orth of Hope*). As he went to the platform to pick up his award, to the strains of a band bashing out a march from a forgotten French operetta in lieu of the Moroccan national anthem (Morocco being the nominal country of origin of the film but possessed of no known anthem), he was roundly booed and jeered at, and not just by the Italians: the French national press pronounced the film 'more old hat than *L'Arroseur Arosé*'. Welles, with his love of slapstick and his passion for early cinema, may have been wryly amused by the reference to Louis Lumière's one-minute one-reeler, the very first film comedy, but it scarcely helped to promote the film's fortunes. Not even a coveted Palme d'Or (or half of one) was enough to secure distribution in America.

As James Naremore has remarked, even among Wellesians, *Othello* is a film more admired than loved.[2] The fact that it exists at all, and has a clear artistic coherence, is a miracle, given the circumstances of its creation, but something crucial is absent from it. The staging is brilliant, from the famous opening shots on the coffins of Othello and Desdemona, as the Rachmaninovian chords pound away, then the intersecting planes of the cortège itself, with another procession on the horizon and the soldiers with their halberds and flags on the upper level of the ramparts at yet another angle, creating a frame of visceral dynamism all achieved, as we know, by astonishing ingenuities of perspective, a triumph of *trompe l'oeil*. Dissolves show us the dead bodies being veiled, with soldiers in close-up in the foreground. Iago is suddenly dragged across the frame in apparently bright daylight where everything before has been darkling, to be thrown into a cage. There is a disorientating and disturbing extreme close-up of his inscrutable eye, then his point of view of the funeral procession, at which the cage yanks him upward, twisting and revolving until we see only his silhouette. The singing on the soundtrack turns to the chanting of a requiem mass. All this functions as an overture, exactly, in fact, as overtures often work in the opera house, giving you a glimpse of the whole piece, starting, as does the prelude to Act One of *Carmen*, for example, at the end. Then a title card on parchment tells us that we're about to see *The Tragedy of Othello* then another proclaims *A Motion Picture adaptation of the play by William Shakespeare*, under which Welles in voiceover, backed by twiddling mandolins, describes the elopement of Desdemona in the works of the tale by Cinzio on which Shakespeare based his play. He introduces Iago, who is first heard off screen, his distorted, echoing voice urgently whispering: 'I have told thee again and again and again: I hate the Moor'; what we see on the screen is a chapel. This is all brilliant, wholly cinematic, a startling translation of the plot and the world of *Othello* into cinema.

What it is not is dramatic. It is a response to themes and characters of the play, but it does not engage us with the story; it has no actuality. It is like a great visual tone-poem, the sort of thing Tchaikovsky or indeed Dvořák (who wrote a splendid *Othello* overture) so effectively created in music; it is decidedly not operatic, in the way that Verdi's treatment of the same story is. This is compounded by the performances. MacLiammóir, despite all his and Welles's best intentions, is villainy incarnate. The whole feel of his performance is oddly Victorian: with the oily, silky, insinuating quality, more subdued than one would expect, that for the Victorians denoted villainy. This, you feel, is how Sir Henry Irving might have played Iago – which is hardly surprising, since MacLiammóir's Shakespearean career started in 1912, when he appeared in *Macbeth* not with Irving (who was by then dead) but with his great rival, Sir Herbert Beerbohm Tree. It is in many ways a fascinating performance, superbly spoken, but there is no surprise in it, no possibility that anyone could be taken in by him. He presents a constant, undeveloping image, as does Suzanne Cloutier as Desdemona. And above all, Welles, despite his magnificent presence, his strength, his clarity and his intelligence, fails to engage us. From as early as the speech to the senate – 'most potent, grave and reverend signors' – when Othello cleverly and wittily wins them over with the story of his courtship of Desdemona, Welles adopts the curious narcoleptic manner that reviewers of his stage performance so regularly commented on, the great general tranced, led on by he knows not what, both bewildered and innocent. 'This is an Othello who is obviously "perplexed in the extreme",' the *Manchester Guardian* had written: 'one fancies that there is the phrase from which Mr Welles drew most of his reading for the part.' Perhaps he did; but it is unhelpful to the story, and fatally diminishes the range and intensity of what Othello feels. In addition, there is a curiously misplaced boyishness about Welles's Othello; it sometimes looks as if he might burst into childish tears.

None of this makes any interpretive sense, so one can only conclude that it is due to the limitations of Welles's acting. The result is that one believes in nothing about the man – his love for Desdemona, his dread of losing her, his murderous jealousy. None of it rings true. So one is compelled to wonder why Welles chose to tell this story, if the emotions in it were not ones he could engage with, or ones he was equipped to portray. It is as if he felt the need to damp himself down in order to be truthful. Which is odd, coming from the man who told Peter Bogdanovich that 'there simply isn't such a thing as movie acting . . . all this talk about the special technique required for acting to the camera is sheer bollocks. Stage actors are supposed to be too big. Well, Cagney was a stage actor and nobody was ever bigger than that. He came on in the movies as though he were playing to the gallery in an opera house . . . he played right at the top of his bent, but he was always *true*.'[3] The acerbic Anglo-American critic Eric Bentley, reviewing the film on its American release, put the case with characteristic trenchancy: Welles 'never acts, he is photographed – from near, from far, from above, from below, right side up, upside down, against battlements, through gratings, and the difference of angle and background only emphasises the flatness of that profile, the rigidity of those lips, the dullness of those eyes, the utter inexpressiveness and anti-theatricality of a man who, God save the mark! was born a theatrical genius.'[4] It is a harsh fact that whether due to a conception of the great tragic figures (because the same is true of his Macbeth), or whether it is simply because of the circumstances of the film's creation and his preoccupation with all the thousand things that directors have to worry about, Welles gives an inert, almost cataleptic performance of Othello which deeply undermines the audacity, originality and swagger of his film.

Despite the French newspapers' rejection of *Othello*, there was a growing body of writing and thinking about Welles among the film-making community in France which marked the beginnings of a fascination with his work that would before long burgeon into a full-blown love affair. As early as 1946, the third edition of *Revue de Cinéma* prominently featured Welles, offering illustrated extracts from the screenplays of *The Magnificent Ambersons* and *Citizen Kane*, whose apparently diffracted narrative is proved to have an iron logic, as well as a digest in translation of Roy Alexander Fowler's useful pioneering pamphlet *Orson Welles: A First Biography*, which had just appeared in Britain. Two years later, along with Pabst, Castellani and Alberto Lattuada, Welles was interviewed by Jean Desternes at the Venice Film Festival; the theme was, inevitably, realism, with Welles expansively expounding the argument against. Clearly his French interviewer relishes his epigrammatic manner, his taste for paradox, his pleasure in arguing from first principles, his willingness to cause offence. 'We must distinguish between realism and reality,' he says, *ex cathedra*. 'People who talk about the neo-realism of my films must be joking . . . Eisenstein and I are children of the same father – Griffith. But we've taken different paths and are no longer related – except insofar as we've both turned our backs on realism. Realism has no existence for me, it doesn't interest me at all.'[5] There would be a great deal more in this vein over the years.

Even in (then) much less theoretically based Britain, there was interest in Welles's ideas as opposed to his persona; in an interview with Francis Koval in 1950 in *Sight and Sound*, after proffering a somewhat disingenuous endorsement of neo-realism, Welles declares that critics have absurdly overrated the importance of the image in films: words, he says, are the crucial element, story the supreme imperative – not for its anecdotal value: 'it is more a combination of human factors and basic ideas that makes a subject worth putting on the screen.' Koval is one of the few interviewers then or since to acknowledge Welles's interlocutory mischievousness, quoting André Bazin, one of Welles's earliest admirers, and a prime proponent of the idea that a film must belong entirely to its director, on the subject: 'Among his many qualities, Welles possesses a genius for bluffing, which he regards as one of the fine arts, in the same league as conjuring, theatre or cinema.' As if to prove it, the interview ends with Welles announcing his next script, *Lovelife*, a picture about sexual obsession: 'despite the subject, it will not be endangered by any censorship. It will be so respectable that families will take their children to see it without the slightest hesitation. But if I succeed – the picture will shock every adult with human feelings and social conscience.' He solemnly assured another interviewer that he rose at 6.30 every morning to write a book on the history of international organisations and their growth. It deals, he says, with the question of the nation versus the international idea. 'The complete human being, with his highly developed curiosity and his orneriness, is in peril all over the world. That's the great thing that's going on. A man should be allowed to be crazy if he wants to be, to stay in bed one morning if he feels it good, or thumb his nose at a sacred image. Conformism to certain stencils of thought – that's what worries me.'[6] The book if it ever existed never saw the light of day. But Welles's anticipation of anti-globalisation is striking.

He was also, he said, at work on a screenplay entitled *Caesar!* in which his *Third Man* co-stars Trevor Howard and Alida Valli would play, respectively, the title role and Calpurnia; the film would be directed, he claimed, by Hilton Edwards, but if Welles was simply producing it, he had a very hands-on conception of what that meant. He planned to shoot the film in Eur, the spectral, unfinished development built in the south of Rome in 1942 to celebrate twenty years of Mussolini's Fascist rule – an inspired location, with its sterile faux-Roman streetscapes defying all attempt at animation; accordingly he and Oberdan Troiani, his cameraman from *Othello*, conducted a thorough recce, with Troiani taking copious photographs. Nothing, alas, came of the project, though Welles was to return to *Julius Caesar* again. Around the same time he signed a contract with Olympic Films in Rome to produce, direct and star in two films to be made in Italy in both English and Italian. The first was to tell the story of Benvenuto Cellini, the Florentine sculptor, silversmith and rakehell; the other was *Operation Cinderella*, about a Hollywood crew dividing an Italian village when it descends on a location near Naples to shoot a Renaissance film: denounce it though he might, Hollywood was never far from Welles's mind, the demi-paradise from which he had been ejected. Screen tests were done for *Cellini*, casting allegedly complete. He had a co-writer for *Cinderella*, Piero Rognoli, but he was disinclined to work on the screenplay, preferring to entertain visitors and backers by acting out scenes from the movie under arc lights magically rigged up in the garden of his house. The production company paid him 50 million lire, but it all came to nothing.

Needing yet more money, he accepted a dreadful part in a dreadful film, on which he behaved dreadfully. The film was *Trent's Last Case*, from the crime classic by E.C. Bentley, and the producer/director was Herbert Wilcox, neatly described by Michael Kustow as 'the middle-class master of British cinema but a commanding figure in the demoralised post-war industry'.[7] Wilcox had bought out what was left of the long-term contract Korda had with Welles, out of which only *The Third Man* had resulted – a triumph, of course, but one too time-consuming and tiresome for Korda to risk repeating. As it happens, Wilcox and Welles had met in Hollywood: Wilcox by chance had seen some of the *Kane* rushes, and had sought Welles out to tell him what a huge success he would have. 'That's the first kind word I've had in Hollywood,' Welles told him. 'I'll do anything for you, if you ever want me to – for nothing.'[8] In fact, Wilcox paid him handsomely to play the murder victim, Sigsbee Manderson, which he does in a classic Welles make-up – aquiline nose, thin lips, staring, almost puppet-like eyes. To characterise the menacing nature of his relationship with his wife (played by Margaret Lockwood) Welles kisses her with alarming force: like Eartha Kitt, she ended up with bruised lips, but, unlike Miss Kitt, she accepted it philosophically. 'The scene came out alright on the screen,' Miss Lockwood, then reigning queen of British film, told Peter Noble, 'so I guess I shouldn't complain.'[9] The film was a considerable box-office success on both sides of the Atlantic. He made a second film, *Three Cases of Murder*, for Wilcox, who described the experience of working with him with surprising candour: 'As an artist Orson is a superman but as a person he is too beset by abstractions and he tries to do too many things to have any satisfactory human relationships. It's difficult to like Orson,' Wilcox told Noble, 'because he does his best to make you actively dislike him.'[10]

If this was indeed his objective, he succeeded beyond his wildest dreams on his next film, *L'Uomo, la bestia e la virtù*. The screenplay was drawn from the Pirandello play of the same name; Welles was cast as the Beast – Captain Perella, a coarse Neapolitan sea-captain. Perella comes home to his wife (Virtue), who, unknown to him, is pregnant from another man (the Man); they gull him into having sex with her so the child can be passed off as his. The film was essentially a vehicle for the Neapolitan comic genius Totò, who plays the prissy professor, Paolino di Vico, with whom the wife is having the affair; the wife herself, Assunta, was played by the distinguished French actress Viviane Romance, more usually to be found playing *femmes fatales*. The film was directed by Totò's regular director, Steno; together they had made some of the most successful films in the history of the Italian cinema. Welles was of course familiar with Pirandello's work, having written a screenplay freely based on the great Sicilian writer's masterpiece, *Enrico IV*, with its unsettling interrogation of illusion and reality, madness and sanity. *L'Uomo, la bestia e la virtù* is a very different kettle of fish, a sexy comic fable, almost like something out of Boccaccio, and Welles, who bravely insisted on playing the part in Italian, entered into it with some commitment, devising an extraordinary make-up for himself, perhaps Neptunian in intention, but satyr-like in effect, with tumbling brown locks, arched eyebrows and curly beard. He essays an Italian body-language, too, with much gesturing of hands; only the presence of Totò, one of the cinema's supreme masters of physical expression, in the league of Keaton or Chaplin, slightly undermines his authenticity. It's a big, spirited performance, a remarkable physical transformation, made all the more complete because in the end they dubbed him, so the voice that emerges from his lips is not one of the most instantly recognisable vocal instruments of all time, but that of a rough Italian sailor.

Welles was cast in the film at the last moment by Carlo Ponti, who co-produced the film with Dino De Laurentiis; he was paid 3 million lire a day, three times what Totò himself was earning, though there was no question on the set who was the star. 'He was always addressed as your Highness,' Welles told Peter Bogdanovich. As a matter of fact, the comedian, born in a shabby suburb of Naples, was perfectly entitled to being so addressed, since he was, technically speaking, not only an Imperial Highness, but also – in a list of titles which reads like the dramatis personae of an early Shakespeare comedy – a Palatine Count, a Knight of the Holy Roman Empire, the Exarch of Ravenna, Duke of Macedonia and Illyria, Prince of Constantinople, Cilicia, Thessaly, Pontus, Moldavia, Dardania, Peloponnesus, Count of Cyprus and Epirus, Count and the Duke of Drivasto and Durazzo. The joke pretty quickly wore thin for Welles, who was annoyed by the long hours imposed by the director, by the permanent presence on set of Viviane Romance's Egyptian-born husband supplying his wife with constant rewrites, and by the sheer indignity of having to act in a vehicle conceived for an Italian clown and bearing daily less resemblance to anything which might have come from the pen of Pirandello. For the most part Welles sat on the set, unapproachable and tetchy; everything, it seemed, was a problem.

At this point, he discovered that his contract contained a penalty clause: he was entitled to a handsome supplement whenever shooting overran. So he began to take longer and longer over his make-up, particularly his beard, interrupting shots to keep making small adjustments to it. It didn't take Ponti long, after paying the penalty once or twice, to realise what Welles was up to; soon they were openly at loggerheads, Ponti refusing to pay the overtime. One day, three days before the end of the shoot, Welles snapped, called the producers and walked out, leaving his bags at the hotel, along with a letter in which he thanked Steno and the screenwriter, Lucio Fulci, 'followed,' said Fulci, 'by a series of Sons of a Bitch and Fuck You's for the producers'.[11] Welles's remaining scenes were shot from behind with a body double; they auctioned his bags.

It was, notes Anile, the end of Welles's turbulent six-year-long relationship with the Italian film industry. He now had burned his bridges as an actor; as a director he was unbankable. The following year, as if symbolically, Scalera, having failed to convince the authorities that *Othello* was an Italian film, went into receivership.

★

But if it was the end of Welles's professional life in Italy, it was the beginning of a personal relationship which would endure, with vicissitudes, to the end of his life. Sometime in 1952, Welles had seen and been smitten by a darkly pretty twenty-four-year-old actress called Paola Mori, and before long they were closely involved. His feelings for her were romantic and highly charged; this, he felt, was The One. 'Friend,' he said to a perceived rival, the actor Walter Chiari, 'leave her alone. You're just toying with her. I need her . . . I love her.'[12] Mori's family home at the Villa Fregene, near the Roman seaside, became his base. Mori had been born in Italian Somaliland, where her father was a colonial official; her mother was the Contessa di Girifalco. During the Second World War, when British Somaliland invaded its Italian neighbour, Paola, her sister and her mother were interned for a year (during which time Paola learned rather good English). Shortly after, the family was reunited in Italy, and they went to live in Fregene. With her simple strength and innate distinction, Paola was something new in Welles's life: a restraining, calming influence – up to a point. She acted as a very necessary buffer between him and the world. He was becoming more and more impatient with his life, a state of mind which tends to be self-generating. The wry resignation, the amused self-knowledge he demonstrated in interviews, was rarely glimpsed by those who worked with him, though he was still able to command the loyalty and even the love of his colleagues. The divine *furor* was so palpable, his passion to create, to make something new, something exciting, something beautiful, in addition to his obvious skill and inspiration, outweighed for many of his actors and technicians the impatience, the surliness, the bullying, the impulsive and contradictory instructions. As often with Welles, one senses something archaic about him. He behaves like some great tribal chieftain, a warlord of art, riding roughshod over the niceties of conventional behaviour, sometimes sulking in his tent, sometimes rousing his people to great heights, now making huge strategic decisions off the cuff, now mysteriously absenting himself. The egotism is so massive that it becomes epic, universal. We may try to psychoanalyse Welles, but perhaps it is better to accept him as a phenomenon, unparalleled, a law unto himself – because he accepts no other law. Like Oscar Wilde he is an antinomian, born for the exception, not for the rule. Boundaries, definitions, limitations are unknown to him, and intolerable. 'What's worth fighting for?' he wrote in a magazine article that year. 'A flag? A class? An idea? A system? No, only man, with his variety and his complexity, his sheer limitlessness, is worth fighting for.' This is both very modern and very ancient, sentiments that would not have been strange to Walt Whitman.

In April of 1953, as it happens, Welles was invited by the BBC to record extracts from Walt Whitman's *A Song of Myself* from his sprawling masterpiece, *Leaves of Grass.* Welles and Whitman are a perfect match: the poet's unconfined metre suits Welles wonderfully, the ecstatic rhetoric, the emotional resonance, the exploratory, celebratory self-intoxication, can never have been better realised. The poem must have struck profound chords with him: again and again, as he reads, Whitman seems to speak for Welles.

> Do I contradict myself?
> Very well then I contradict myself,
> (I am large, I contain multitudes.)

Or:

> The spotted hawk swoops by and accuses
> me, he complains of my gab, my loitering.
> I too am not a bit tamed, I too am
> untranslatable,
> I sound my barbaric yawp over the roofs
> of the world.

Might not Welles just as well have cried out:

> Turbulent, fleshy, sensual, eating, drinking
> and breeding,
> No sentimentalist, no stander above men
> and women or apart from them,
> No more modest than immodest.
>
> Unscrew the locks from the doors!
> Unscrew the doors themselves from their
> jambs!

The BBC recording is the zenith of his poetry reading, not merely sonorous but deeply felt, a perfect congruence of reader and poet.

★

Later that same year, Welles was invited by the Edinburgh International Festival (which clearly bore no grudges for the shenanigans over *Othello* five years earlier) to deliver a lecture. To accompany it, he showed the first reel of *Othello* and the last of *Macbeth*. The lecture was entitled 'The Third Audience'; in it Welles edged a little closer to television, announcing that 'movies are dying, dying, dying.'[13] The problem, he said, was that between the minority avant-garde and the mass-market ('the sixty million people'), there was a gap. 'We have to find a way of making films – and here television may help us – by which, if two million people see them, we have a return for our money; which involves the creation of a true international audience and a struggle,' he declared, reverting to his Popular Front rhetoric of the Thirties and Forties, 'with the mysterious national forces in the world which call themselves governments.' He did not, he said, blame Hollywood; that would have been old-fashioned. Rome had turned itself into a small Hollywood, and England had fallen flat on its face trying to do so. Then, in an aside, he made one of his calculated provocations, a hand-grenade lobbed lightly into the conversation; it must have played very well in Scotland. 'England,' he said, 'is the only film industry without a tradition.' Hitchcock, Korda, Powell, Thorold Dickinson, all casually thrown onto the scrapheap by Welles. 'They were making films in Stockholm, Budapest and Copenhagen forty years ago, but they were not making them in London.'

By way of introduction to the extracts from *Macbeth* and *Othello*, he said, 'I do not know whether a happy marriage can exist between Shakespeare and the screen. I certainly know that I did not succeed in making one.' But he defended the attempt as a means of getting away from banality. 'There are many questions that cannot be discussed in front of sixty million people', he said, and returning to 'our classics' was a way of addressing them. He excused his *Macbeth* on the grounds that it was shot in twenty-three days and should have been judged accordingly, as 'a kind of violently sketched charcoal drawing of a great play', while *Othello* was a 'free and vigorous' adaptation of the play, comparable in its freedom and vigour, he said, to what Verdi and his librettist Boïto had done with it. Then, finally, he turned to television, 'an exciting thing because it is in the hands of the first generation'. But it could never, he said, be a substitute for film: 'it will never give the director the scope that the film camera can give him. Television,' he said, 'is an actor's medium . . . but the great power of film, the use of image as such, will always belong to the cinema.' This is the same Orson Welles, of course, who, only three years earlier, had told Francis Koval how absurdly film critics overrated the image. Does he contradict himself? Very well then, he contradicts himself.

Welles would soon be finding out at first hand about the medium he had so far held in such scant regard. But meanwhile, there was another unknown medium to be cracked: ballet. Welles had in his time been a great connoisseur of ballerinas, but not necessarily because of their terpsichorean gifts. No doubt he was charmed when, at supper one night early in 1953, Roland Petit, the brilliant showman-choreographer who created the Ballets de Paris, asked him to make a piece for one of the company's stars, Colette Marchand, for their forthcoming season in September at the massive Stoll Theatre off Kingsway. Welles was to design the set and costumes and devise the scenario; Petit would choreograph, to a score by the precociously gifted Jean-Michel Damase. The basic idea came quickly: Welles had been reading a book about the murals in the caves of Lascaux in south-western France – only opened to the public five years earlier – and had become fascinated by the idea of the mammoths depicted in the paintings whose bones were embedded in the surrounding ice. He imagined a young woman similarly frozen; she is discovered and put on display in a fairground. A young man falls in love with her, which melts the ice, liberating her; she kisses him, whereupon he in turn freezes. It is another of those riddling fables scattered throughout Welles's *oeuvre*. In his programme note for the London season, he described it as 'a kind of parable showing that two people are never in love with each other to the same degree', which may have been sobering for Paola Mori to read.

A certain amount of mystery surrounded the project. The company's press release announced *Le Loup*, with a libretto by Jean Anouilh and a score by Dutilleux, which became one of Petit's biggest triumphs and 'another by Orson Welles'. Making up the quadruple bill were two more short ballets, Gosvsky's *La Perle* and the satirical romp *Deuil en 24 heures*. 'Nothing is yet known about Mr Welles's ballet,' said the release, 'not even its title.' Welles himself seemed a little vague about the whole project. The young designer Richard Negri was seconded to help him realise his ideas. Welles was in ebullient form – 'umpteen activities going on and constantly interrupted by phone calls from all sides of the globe', according to Negri[14] – and he and Petit worked very happily together. His set was on a grand scale, consisting of huge sacking drapes with paintings of mammoths in fluorescent paint which, with the use of black light, would appear spectrally in the dark, while a great canopy would sweep up to reveal the block of ice containing the girl, who, nestling on a black velvet ledge, appeared to be suspended inside it. Both the tripods supporting the drapes and the concealing canopy were vast. The engineering problems posed by this were handed over to Negri: 'The whole lot was left entirely on one's plate.' He found a specialist in stage effects, and together they laboured day and night in a tiny room in the Stoll; they were still working when the curtain was due to go up on the first night, which it finally did half an hour late. 'From Orson Welles', wrote *Dance and Dancers*,

> we have come to expect something spectacular whatever he does – whether it be films, the theatre, or his choice of escort for the evening. The audience assembled for his first ballet expected anything to happen. In fact, had he walked through the auditorium leading a family of rattle-snakes with diamond collars, no one would have been very surprised. Even the interminable wait before the curtain rose . . . seemed some kind of Wellesery.[15]

When the piece finally started, the action proved to be very simple: a fairground barker announces that on his Arctic voyages a professor of archaeology has discovered a girl encased in a block of ice; the professor then draws back a curtain to reveal the block. A young man passes by; bewitched by the lady, he switches off the ice-machine. Flames and smoke fill the stage. They dance, and as they dance, she thaws. Realising her power, she enslaves him. The professor closes the curtains, but the lady draws them open again: there, frozen inside the block of ice, is the young man who loved her. Curtain.

All went well on the first night until the great canopy which was to reveal the young man now frozen in the ice block caught on the edge of the structure. The *Daily Express* gossip columnist was tailing Welles in the wings, from where he was watching the show. 'It should have been fun,' he said, 'but it's hell.' 'As the ballet went on Welles could not stand on his feet. He got down on his knees and leaned on his stick. And then he laid down full-length on the boards and cupped his head in his hand.' When the canopy stuck, there was general panic. 'Then the great voice of Welles rose up: "Continuez! Continuez! Let it tear! Let it tear! C'est magnifique!"'[16] The effect, Richard Negri conceded, was indeed very striking: 'what happened, which was rather marvellous in one way, is that the canopy then sort of unpeeled in a spiral, you see, and dropped.' Welles had often remarked that a director's job was to supervise accidents; now he was in his element. It was a very expensive accident, as it happens: the canopy had to be remade every night, and it never spiralled out in quite the same way ever again. But at least for that performance, in September 1953, they had a triumph: the ballet ended to a great roar of applause; Welles, hobbling on stage with a stick because of a sprained ankle, took great delight in acknowledging it. Such occasions were all too rare in his life.

The reviews, though mixed, were lively. The *Express*'s man said: 'The new ballet by Orson Welles is terrific. Ballet is so often namby-pamby. Welles shows how exciting it can be – given a first-class new idea.'[17] The most controversial aspect of the piece proved to be the prologue Welles had written and – unmistakably – delivered from off stage through a microphone, 'in which', said the *Daily Telegraph*, 'he has pretentious things to say about the gradual closing in of the ice that is to engulf the world'. It seems to bear some family resemblance to the speech Micheál MacLiammóir recorded for *Time Runs*, with its apocalyptic intimations, and introduced, thought the *Telegraph*, 'a crude and jarring note . . . to a poetic conception'.[18] The *Times Educational Supplement*, less charitable, commented that 'it was hard to imagine that, without his programme note, we would ever have known what Mr Welles intended us to think.'[19]

In Paris, *Une Femme dans la glâce* was not a success ('very badly lit,' said Welles, 'as everything always is in Paris'). 'I think they threw it in the Seine,' said Negri. 'It was never heard of again.' It is an odd-man-out in Welles's work, though deeply interesting and highly characteristic. Fable is one of the forms to which Welles was most often drawn, especially the fable which distils a bitter truth. This particular story seems not at all to demonstrate what Welles claimed in his programme note: far from showing that people are never in love to the same degree, it shows man as a helpless victim of woman, tragically fated to perish when he liberates her with his love. Welles was much given, especially during the 1950s, to statements about women, which, though no worse than the routine misogyny of the period, are certainly no better: 'I hate women. I hate them generally, not in particular but in an abstract way. I hate them because one never learns anything about them. They are inscrutable.' Bafflement and frustration seem at the root of these feelings. 'A woman's love may be more mature but is never as intense as a man's . . . women cannot bear to be fooled. Men love it. The more intelligent they are, the more amused they are at being fooled. A woman gets angry if she doesn't know how the thing is done.' Woman was adrift, he felt. 'She has the vote. She has independence and she still has not decided what she really wants to be.'[20] All part of the standard contemporary battle-of-the-sexes discourse, perhaps a little more flamboyantly expressed, but Welles reverted to the subject with remarkable frequency. It was, at the very least, a subject of compelling concern to him, of which *Lady in the Ice* is a fairly explicit expression.

The ballet also brings us apocalyptic Welles, in the introductory ruminations on the forthcoming ice age (before the war it was British imperialism, after it neo-Nazism; then it was the atom-bomb, in time it would be the H-bomb), but most strikingly, it brings us *First Person Singular* Welles, the author entering the frame of his story and addressing the audience directly, a genre that Bill Kronshaw, borrowing from Northrop Frye, calls epos. This mode, which Welles explored extensively in his radio work of the Thirties, and in the trailers of his movies, was to become increasingly important in his work – the author/director shaping, introducing, mediating, qualifying the story. Welles as guide, as commentator. Everything filtered through Welles.

★

Meanwhile, Welles had met up again with his old mentor, Ludovicu Brecher, the former Soviet agent of Polish birth and Rumanian upbringing, who, under the name Louis Dolivet, had been a close associate of Jean Moulin, the great hero of the French Resistance. A few years later, Dolivet, by then in America, had met Welles through Beatrice Straight (whom he shortly afterwards married) and, finding Welles desperate to become politically active, had undertaken his political education, grooming him for high office, actively encouraging him to stand as Secretary General to the newly formed United Nations. After 1945 and the conference which established the UN, Welles went off the boil politically, and in 1947, as we know, he left America for an extended leave of absence. That same year of growing right-wing paranoia, Dolivet was denounced in a Washington newspaper for his communist past. He finally left for Europe after the breakdown of his marriage to Beatrice Straight, who had financed his magazines and his activities; when he tried to return to the United States after the sudden and mysterious death of their son by drowning, he was refused readmittance. He returned to Paris, where he continued his political activities, in very much the same vein as he had before. In 1953, he was appointed editor of a new monthly journal, *Démocratie Combattante*, whose political director was Henri Laugier, one of the authors of the Universal Declaration of Human Rights, and a co-founder of the World Health Organization, UNESCO and UNICEF; the magazine's president was the distinguished trade unionist Léon Jouhaux, a Nobel Prize-winner and co-creator of the International Labour Organization. Despite its pedigree, *Démocratie Combattante* folded with the September/October edition (no. 6/7), but not before publishing an article by Welles, who had run into Dolivet again. The article, which took as its theme the question of systems, was a throwback to the Welles of his ill-fated *New York Post* daily column:

> You always hear the notion that such and such a system has not been entirely developed or pushed to its logical conclusion. Thank God! It's one of the blessings of humanity that no system has ever achieved total success. For it's an established fact that the complete victory of an efficient system has always meant the burning of the books. Certain systems burn more, others burn only the best, and that's the only difference.

He purveys a sort of despairing rhetoric, a last rallying cry in the face of the inevitable. It is tinged with deep political pessimism:

> It is too late for the barricades – they have either collapsed about our heads or been trampled beneath our feet. The revolution too has become a system. In this second half of a century that organised the conquest of the material world and the slavery of the spirit, we must seek not methods but men. We must seek not strength among our leaders, nor discipline in the ranks, but the greatest possible number of human beings. Let us defend ourselves before all defence becomes impossible, let us move to the offensive before we lose forever the only values worth fighting for.

No sooner were Welles and Dolivet reunited than they began to plan a 'Foundation For a New Humanism', to embrace all their activities, artistic, literary and political. It would be financed by films which Welles would direct. Dolivet, who had never had anything to do with film before, would produce, and a screenplay that Welles had been working on earlier that year would be their first outing. In September they signed an agreement, and in December Welles sold the screenplay, which he called *Masquerade*, to Filmorsa, the company they formed. Shooting would begin in January 1954.

★

Before that, having established what he hoped would be a new phase in his life as a director, Welles briefly broke his self-exile and returned to America – not to Hollywood, to New York, to a new medium and an old sparring partner: William Shakespeare. He also had, in Peter Brook, as all too rarely for him, a director he greatly admired. The two men had met, in quintessentially Wellesian fashion, on the overnight cross-Channel ferry from Ostend to Dover. Welles, wrapped in a cloak and sporting a large black fedora, had loomed up out of the fog which, Brook said, seemed to proceed from his cigar. He appeared immediately to know who the younger man was, and to have seen all his ground-breaking productions; Brook in turn praised Welles extravagantly. Brook, ten years younger, was almost as much of a prodigy as Welles had been. At Oxford University, he had caused a stir with a production of Marlowe's *Dr Faustus*, largely because he had secured the services of the notorious Satanist Aleister Crowley as occult adviser on the play. After Oxford, at the age of twenty, he discovered an equally young Paul Scofield at the Birmingham Repertory Theatre; together they stormed the Shakespearean heavens. At the age of twenty-two he was appointed director of productions at Covent Garden Opera, famously collaborating with Salvador Dalí on a scandalous production of Richard Strauss's *Salome*; at twenty-five, he transformed John Gielgud's approach to Shakespeare in radical productions (the ones Welles had seen) of *Measure for Measure* and *The Winter's Tale* at the Shakespeare Memorial Theatre in Stratford-upon-Avon. The two men fell happily into conversation on the ferry, and started laying plans to work together; in fact, in 1947, eight years before Brook did *Titus Andronicus* with Olivier, he had asked Welles to play the part for him at Stratford, but Welles had been otherwise engaged. It was perfectly natural, then, that when Brook, in 1953, was asked by Robert Saudek of the Ford Foundation's Radio-Theatre Workshop to do something for his trail-blazing arts television programme *Omnibus*, Brook should suggest *King Lear* with Welles in the title role. Saudek leapt at the suggestion, even though Welles's reputation in his own country, in 1953, was somewhat cloudy.

He had, to all intents and purposes, been absent for six years, during a time of political turmoil and crisis in which many of his fellow-actors had been harassed and in some cases indicted. Welles had occasionally been mentioned in connection with his left-leaning colleagues, but his voice, hitherto so eloquent, so insistent, championing the social democratic corner right up to the moment of his departure, had not been heard, neither in self-defence nor in denunciation of the witch hunt. Professionally, he was viewed by America with bemused fascination. His films of *Macbeth* and *The Lady from Shanghai* had been released there and critically dismissed, but more in sorrow than in anger. News of his activities in Europe was scant. From time to time, rumours of a return would spread: in 1952, for example, he was firmly announced as bringing the London production of *Othello* to Broadway, in repertory with *The Merchant of Venice*, in which, of course, he would have given his Shylock; nothing more was ever heard of it. There was a general perception that, *Citizen Kane* notwithstanding, Welles's real destiny was not in movies at all, but as a classical actor-manager; sometimes he even thought so himself, as long as he could be everything else, too of course. His time at the Federal Theatre Project – the Harlem *Macbeth* and *Dr Faustus* – and the Mercury Theatre – *Julius Caesar* and *The Shoemaker's Holiday* – still lived in the memory of New Yorkers as part of a golden age of theatre, the classics new-minted. The wave of emotionally and sexually supercharged young actors emerging from Lee Strasberg's Studio had shown no interest in the great classical tradition which in America stretched back to the Booths and down to the Barrymores. This gap, people felt, needed to be filled. America expected. It is not without irony, then, that Welles's return to America and to the classics should have been stage-managed by an Englishman.

Despite some anxiety about possible complications in his tax situation, the project was irresistible to Welles: *Lear* had been in his sights for some time; he played the part seven years earlier, trombone-toned to begin with, then flutingly melodramatic in madness, in a thirty-minute radio digest of the play on the *Mercury Summer Theatre of the Air*, and was keen to have another go at it. But beyond that, *Omnibus* was exactly the sort of enterprise he passionately believed in. He had strong feelings about education; in interviews he was wont to remark that what he really wanted was to give everything up and concentrate on the really important task of harnessing film to education. *Omnibus* – wonderfully described by Saudek as 'a variety show of the intellect' – was specifically conceived as part of the cultural Cold War, to shake America out of its consumerist conformism and aid the development of 'mature, wise and responsible citizens'. If that programme seems somewhat paternalistic, the execution of the programme was anything but. With the Anglo-American Alistair Cooke – informed but informal, master of the finely judged off-the-cuff introduction – as master of ceremonies, the touch was light without being lightweight, exactly what Welles had attempted on his own *Almanac* radio show of the 1940s, and with much the same mixture of elements. *Omnibus*'s opening show, in 1952, gave an excellent indication of how it meant to go on: it began with a little Gilbert and Sullivan, moved on to *The Trial of Ann Boleyn*, a new play by Maxwell Anderson starring Rex Harrison and Lili Palmer, then featured some dancers from Haiti and an adaptation of a short story by Saroyan, before showing the first moving images of X-rays of the human digestive system, and ended up with a respectful celebration of Veterans' Day. Over its nine-year span it would feature, inter alia, Stokowski conducting Britten, the young and unknown James Dean acting, Mike Nichols and Elaine May's first outing on television and Leonard Bernstein's analysis of Beethoven's Fifth Symphony. 'The world was too full of wonderful things,' said Saudek, 'and television too few of them.' *King Lear*, in *Omnibus*'s second year of transmission, was a huge and bold leap into the unknown for the programme: the entire ninety minutes was to be given over to one item. The show had an unprecedented budget: initial reports suggest $150,000, but that was later modified to $78,000 – still a vast sum for television; Welles himself was paid partly in cash, partly in travel, and partly 'very high' expenses.

Television was something about which Welles was increasingly if cautiously enthusiastic, though he hadn't yet worked out, he said, what it really was. Explaining why he was doing *King Lear*, he told the *New Yorker* that he wanted 'to find out something about television here. I've never seen an American television show.' Having hitherto only toyed with the idea, he now started thinking about it seriously. Believing that every medium had a unique character, and that one medium should never attempt what was another medium's preserve, he came to the conclusion that what was particular to television was its capacity to purvey fact: a perfect educational and documentary medium, then, but one which he thought would never be suitable for story-telling. His view, however, was shifting; in a couple of years, indeed, he would find a very brilliant way of telling stories on television. Now, in collaboration with his clever young director, he was prepared to take a gamble on *King Lear*. He was young for the part – thirty-eight, though you might have been forgiven for thinking him older: European cuisine had bulked him out considerably and he was now weighing in at 275 pounds. It was an obvious part for him; as he often remarked, referring to the old division of actors into types, he was a 'King actor'. Lear, he told an interviewer, was the only one of Shakespeare's heroic characters he hadn't played (not quite accurate: there was still Coriolanus, not to mention Titus Andronicus). And he was genuinely keen to work with Brook: 'he is the best director for Shakespeare,' he said, magnanimously.

But Welles was notoriously difficult. How, the press wanted to know, would young Brook fare? When the *New York Times* sat in on rehearsals for *King Lear*, it was disappointed to find that 'not once did Mr Welles, famous on two continents for more self-esteem than humbleness, lose his temper or threaten to have anyone ejected from the hall.'[21] It was all very low-key, the *Times* found: Welles – 'who appears not to walk but to shuffle with an air of relaxed pomposity'

– wandered into the scene with Regan and Goneril, puffing on his cigar the while, 'seemingly listening to the others only for his cues'. He took direction, said the *Times*, 'graciously', making jokes and the occasional suggestion. 'Rehearsals meant Orson and me swapping ideas,' remembered Brook, 'trying, changing and discarding them with such relish that up to the last minute the poor performers had no idea where they were, especially as I was slashing the text as we went on.' This was exactly the atmosphere Welles loved, the old Mercury Theatre atmosphere. The *Times* watched a rehearsal of the scene in which Lear and his fool come upon what they take to be a lunatic called Poor Tom. 'Obviously the actor was enjoying himself immensely as all three roared away at one another,' reported the *Times*. 'When he bellowed the loudest, Mr Welles's oval face resembled that of a baby yelling its head off for attention. Apparently,' added the paper's Val Adams, sadly, 'his old time flamboyant spirit was satisfied to settle for the scenery-chewing role afforded by *King Lear*.' The *New Yorker* was luckier: Welles obviously took to the interviewer and behaved with altogether more exuberance, despite being injected by a doctor as they spoke: 'Infected throat. Antibiotics. Evil mixtures. I don't understand them at all. You have to yell such a lot in this show! Hoot and holler! I've been abroad since 1948. I came back to do *Lear* . . . I thought it'd be a good idea to do Lear, because with the big beard no one can say I'm bad. They can't even see me.' On the whole, the American press regarded Welles as a strange beast just arrived from another planet, or perhaps another era, who might at any moment run amok.

In the trailer put out a week before the programme was transmitted, a chain-smoking Alistair Cooke is almost tremulous as he announces Brook ('brought over from London') and Welles ('in his first television appearance'). Brook, throwing out directions in his very pukka English accent – 'No, no, d'you remember? We were going to do it *quietly*' – puckishly supervises a rehearsal of a graphically-staged account of the gouging out of Gloucester's eyes, after which the cast dissolve into merry laughter. 'Could we see Mr Welles?' asks Cooke, plaintively, 'thirteen million people want to see Mr Welles.' 'Ah, you're asking a lot,' says Brook, 'this is the scene just before Lear appears, but I'm afraid we're going to have to ask you to go.' Which he obediently does, with Welles still unglimpsed. During the last week of rehearsals, the room where they were working began to resemble a zoo. Lear's hundred knights were to have falcons on their arms and great hunting dogs and Irish wolfhounds at their side; these canine and avian co-stars now appeared. The choosing of the right falcons became a major challenge, 'so for three days of rehearsal there were about nine or ten of these great birds sitting in the dark', their heads shrouded in black hoods; Welles himself brought on the body of a deer, a real, dead deer. Brook had opposed it, but Welles overruled him. At the dress rehearsal, a dog-handler appeared with a matching pair of immense, magnificent, pure-white Borzoi which had been contracted at considerable expense. 'Mr Welles narrowed his eyes,' recollected Robert Saudek. '"Get rid of those dogs," he growled.' The star had instantly detected an intolerable risk of being upstaged.[22] To add to the circus atmosphere, a section of the rehearsal room was set apart for sponsors and clients who sat and watched all of this, awestruck.

Brook's credit reads 'staged by Peter Brook'; the official television director was Andrew McCullough, a young *Omnibus* staffer (later responsible for episodes of *Lassie*, *The Fugitive* and *The Donna Reed Show*). But earlier, in the rehearsal room, according to Robert MacCauley, playing sundry lords, Welles, seamlessly and with effortless authority, had taken over command of the camera plot, prescribing lenses, shots, moves.[23] There was no confrontation, no loss of face, no comment; Welles simply did what Welles knew how to do better than anyone. And rehearsals continued. Welles's fellow-actors were on the whole a very accomplished group, many of whom had distinguished pasts and some of whom would have successful futures. Cordelia was played by Natasha Parry; she was married to Peter Brook. Her sisters Goneril and Regan were played by, respectively, Beatrice Straight had and Margaret Phillips; Miss Straight had just come from the Broadway premiere of *The Crucible* for which she had won a Tony Award for her performance, while Miss Phillips had just been playing Portia at the City Center in New York. Arnold Moss was Albany; his finest hour was to come later, when he played Kodos the Executioner in *Star Trek*. David J. Stewart, playing the highly augmented role of Oswald, Regan's servant (he is given the best of the excised role of Edmund), had just won the Clarence Derwent Award for creating the part of Baron de Charlus in Tennessee Williams's *Camino Real*, though, to his chagrin, he became most famous for his role in *Murder, Inc.* A large number of the cast were British in origin, among them Frederic Worlock as Gloucester (later the Judge in *Perry Mason*), and Bramwell Fletcher as Kent. Fletcher had starred, as long ago as 1931, opposite John Barrymore in the film of *Svengali*, which would certainly have endeared him to Welles. Scott Forbes's strikingly handsome Cornwall was British, too, though he later became an American television

Welles in Paris, 1950, with his Othello semi-beard
(Photograph Robert Doisneau).

The secretaries:
Michael Washinsky (left),
Welles (descending stairs) and
Rita Ribolla (right) filming *Othello*,
Venice 1950 (*above*); Welles and
Mrs Rogers, London, 1955 (*right*).

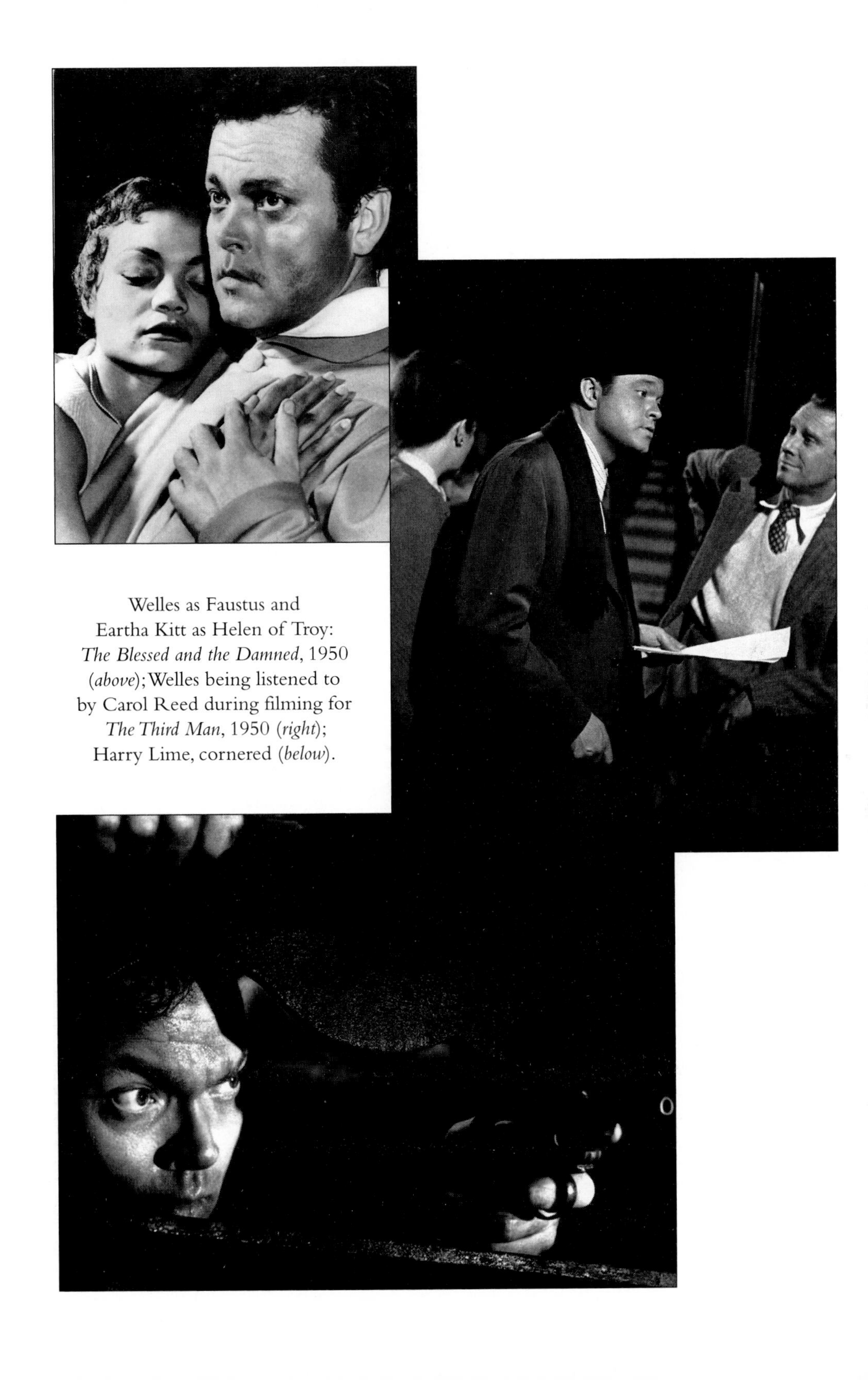

Welles as Faustus and
Eartha Kitt as Helen of Troy:
The Blessed and the Damned, 1950
(*above*); Welles being listened to
by Carol Reed during filming for
The Third Man, 1950 (*right*);
Harry Lime, cornered (*below*).

Othello as seen in London, 1951 (*bottom left*); Welles (Othello) and Peter Finch (Iago), drawn by Ronald Searle for *Punch* (*below*); *Othello*, original version: with Gudrun Ure (Desdemona) in Newcastle-upon-Tyne (*right*); St James's Theatre, embellished by Welles, just before the end of the run, December 1951 (*bottom right*).

Man, Beast and Virtue: Welles as the beast, 1953 (*top*);
'The Final Problem': Gielgud as Sherlock Holmes, Welles as Moriarty,
Ralph Richardson as Dr Watson, London, 1955 (*bottom*).

Welles and Paola Mori at their wedding, Caxton Hall, London, 1955; Welles with Paola Mori and Beatrice Welles, London, 1960 (*below right*); Welles with his daughter Rebecca, Vienna, 1955 (*below*).

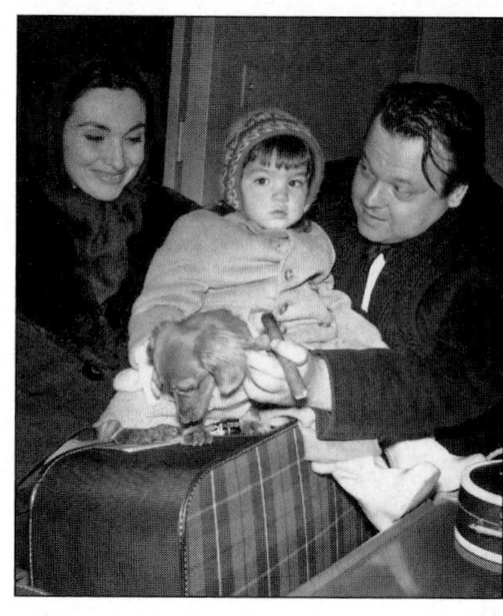

Moby-Dick press conference, Dress Circle bar, Duke of York's Theatre, June 1955 (*left*); sketch by Welles for his make-up as the Guv'nor/Captain Ahab (*below*).

Welles in costume and as the Guv'nor/Ahab (*above* and *right*).

Moby-Dick: Welles as the Guv'nor/Ahab with Joan Plowright as Miss Jenkins/Pip, London, 1955 (*left*); Welles directing *Moby-Dick*, Duke of York's Theatre, London, 1955 (*below*).

star as the hero in *The Adventures of Jim Bowie*. The superb English actor Alan Badel, playing Lear's Fool, was on the brink of an international stardom that never quite came: he had just played, to great acclaim, John the Baptist in William Dieterle's *Salome*, in which the former Mrs Orson Welles, Rita Hayworth, played the title role. Badel and Welles had only just been acting together in a mediocre Herbert Wilcox film called *Three Cases of Murder*, which may have accounted for his presence in *Lear*. The baffling role of Poor Tom – baffling, that is to say, when the character who is pretending to be Poor Tom, Edgar, has been excised from the play – falls to Welles's old boss, colleague and sparring partner, Micheál MacLiammóir; it is to be presumed that his being cast was one of the ways in which Welles tried to remedy the penury into which MacLiammóir and Edwards had fallen as a result of their two-year adventure on *Othello*.

In the build-up to transmission, the mood in the rehearsal room was buoyant. On the whole, said a candid *Omnibus* employee immediately after the transmission, Welles behaved better than they had expected, except, he added, for demanding hand-made gloves ($75), a silk velvet costume, and real ocean-wet seaweed for his scene with Gloucester.[24]

The broadcast itself, however, was very nearly scuppered. *Omnibus*, uniquely among TV programmes, did not have sponsors: it had subscribers (in this case, Scott Paper Company, Greyhound Buses and AMF). Thanks to its generous endowment from the Ford Foundation, *Omnibus* was able to sell space for advertisements and place them where they chose. There *Omnibus* had the advantage over Welles's later radio programmes, all of which were very much beholden to their sponsors (the *Mercury King Lear* is interrupted by a good deal of rhapsodising over Pabst's Blue Ribbon beer). In the trailer for *Lear*, Cooke draws attention to the remarkable fact that the transmission is not going to be interrupted by any 'messages' from their subscribers. In fact, the subscribers had fully intended to have two commercial breaks, but Brook and Welles had point-blank refused; the subscribers likewise dug their heels in and were only convinced, at the last possible moment, by Brook's canny argument that they would gain huge kudos if it were known that they had eschewed commercials to allow the flow of the great tragedy to proceed uninterrupted. He was right: it did. On the night, before the transmission proper began, Greyhound Buses had a nice leisurely opportunity to laud itself, without any reference to what the audience was about to see.

Presently, Cooke appeared and gave a highly intelligent introduction to the play, after which the play ran uninterrupted for its duration. The introduction drew attention to Shakespeare's growing melancholy in the wake of his son's death, with Cooke noting that the play was thought baffling for two centuries after it had been written, that the eighteenth century thought it disorderly and the nineteenth century found it morbid. He hoped that in the context of what he called the barbarities of the twentieth century, the audience would learn more from Shakespeare's pessimism than from the optimism of lesser men. This was 1953, after all: the Cold War had just taken an alarming new turn with the US's new emphasis on nuclear weaponry and McCarthy's demented anti-communism was still rampant.

The introduction perhaps promises too much in terms of contemporary relevance. The production is a decently staged, very well-spoken (largely English-accented, in fact) account of what was left of the play after Brook's cuts, by a group of on the whole very accomplished actors, in 'period' costumes; the sets are simple and effective, moving from the interiors of Lear's court and his daughter's castle to the exteriors – Lear, the Fool and Poor Tom meet in a kind of expressionistically painted windmill – ending up on the sea coast at Dover. The excision of the so-called subplot – the story concerning the two sons of the Earl of Gloucester, Edgar, legitimate, and Edmund, not – rips out a huge part of the play's meaning and (especially once Lear has taken to the heath) a great deal of its narrative coherence. This was of course inevitable in reducing the play to transmittable length. In the trailer for the transmission, Brook impishly pretends to believe that it is an improvement. 'The subplot is only there,' he says, eyes twinkling, 'because Elizabethan actors didn't have intermissions, so they needed a rest.' The cinematography on a large number of cameras is somewhat excitable, but the sang-froid of the operators (and, indeed, of the actors, led by Welles) on this lengthy and demanding live transmission is remarkable. The energy and danger is unmistakable. The television director, Andrew McCullough, was clearly on a high. 'As I sat at the control panels,' reports Brook of the transmission itself, 'I saw him intoxicated with the possibilities of the new medium, cutting wildly from one camera to another.'[25] Things go wrong, speeches occasionally overlap, moustaches come adrift. TV drama, at this time and for some decades hence, was rehearsed exactly like a play, so the actors in *Lear* have a sense of the overall rhythm of the piece, are secure in their lines and work together as a team. It is, in fact, rather like a very good repertory performance, with some of the actors merely competent, while others are outstanding – Beatrice Straight, for example, Margaret Phillips, Bramwell Fletcher, and notably Badel and MacLiammóir, who both make strong impressions, even if Badel (who affects a sort of falsetto) is more or less incomprehensible and MacLiammóir, due to the cuts, utterly unfathomable (as well as being five years older than his own father in the play).

The show of course begins and ends – literally, in this version – with Lear. The word extraordinary barely begins to do justice to Welles's work, which is on the most epic scale conceivable, physically and vocally, though not, perhaps, emotionally. It exists in a different world of expression from that of his colleagues, having a distinct feeling of the nineteenth century about it, though it is so stylised that it is sometimes closer to Kabuki or Noh. The make-up is sensational: in the first scene he is unrecognisable, his own button nose encased in a large, aquiline putty proboscis, his beard copiously covering a jaw which juts pugnaciously forward, his eyes monstrously made-up to enhance what the *New York Times* called his 3-D eyes. In addition, he wears a sort of balaclava, on top of which is a crown; the collar of his cloak sweeps up behind his head, framing it in white. This is his first look. In addition, he wore, as he had done in the London *Othello*, platform boots, making him more than ever a figure out of myth or fairy tale. In the next scene, he wears a long coat and a flat cap, lending him a somewhat Holbeinish appearance, à la Henry VIII. Later, he takes off the cap and just wears the balaclava, which he finally loses on the heath, liberating a fine head of hair, giving him a Mosaic look – early Charlton Heston – or, increasingly, a feeling of Captain Ahab before the mast, his eyes quite frighteningly protrusive. For the scene with Gloucester, his head is draped in that fresh seaweed; he looks like something from the Palace of Monsters in Bomarzo. Much mock was made by critics of his physical appearance – 'facially', said the *New Yorker*, 'Mr Welles resembled a man who had been haled off a park bench and hastily pressed into service as a department-store Santa Claus.'[26] Very few Lears use make-up at all, beyond a beard; most are concerned to pare down as much as possible, as Lear commences on his journey towards essence. Welles's make-up inevitably and perhaps intentionally has a distancing effect.

Vocally, he is magnificent in terms of phrasing, diction and dynamic range: he can whisper or roar, and all points in between, and he is almost always audible, and always comprehensible. Line after famous line sings out with perfect clarity. What he lacks is a sense either of the lived life contained in the line, or of poetic feeling. Whenever rhetoric is called for he is supreme. The result, though, is that one is scarcely moved at all. Like many Lears, he gets better and better as he goes on, and his final scenes with Cordelia, both alive and dead, are most delicately played, though they remain stubbornly unmoving. Nonetheless, by the end one has a sense of a mighty force having shuffled off its mortal coil. It is an awesome spectacle, like the death of a bull or a dinosaur, but not a particularly human one. Welles again seems not to bring anything of himself to the role; it is hard to know why he is playing the part, other than that, as Edmund Hillary so memorably remarked of Mount Everest, it is there.

Once Lear is dead, we are returned to the studios, and some messages from 'one of our patient subscribers': 'New Scotties with wet strength added!' Presently Cooke congratulates a bestubbled Brook, who graciously thanks everyone and heads for his hotel, where, he later revealed, he slept for an entire day and night. Then the credits roll over Virgil Thomson's threnodic postlude, with muted trumpets and pizzicato strings, and Alistair Cooke, getting into the theatrical spirit, bows silently.

The reviews were on the whole very favourable, especially for Welles, though not necessarily in the terms he would have liked: 'Orson Welles, a great ham of an actor, undertook the role of King Lear, a great ham of a part, and was I thought, enormously impressive,' said the *Herald Tribune*. 'No other part is big enough for Welles, who suffers from gigantism of manner and mind.'[27] Elsewhere, though, he was praised for his 'power, heart and sheer artistry'. His arrival on the television screen was warmly welcomed. Comparing him to a confidently patient boxer who lets his opponent flail away for eight or nine rounds and then calmly steps in to finish the fight with one blow, the same reviewer said: 'Orson Welles burst into television a couple of Sundays ago, and knocked everything for a loop . . . establishing a new high for the medium.'[28] Brook's production and the other actors were generally admired. It was the play that got it in the neck: 'Welles's achievement is even more remarkable when you consider that *Lear* is, in many ways, a ridiculous play.'[29] As if they were young Victorian ladies, the critics were outraged by one incident in particular: 'the gouging out of the eyes is the most ghoulish and revolting bit of business ever seen on any stage or screen . . . bad taste is bad taste, and a Shakespearean wrapping makes it no less reprehensible.'[30] But Welles triumphed: 'Altogether it was a memorable hour and a half and I hope Mr Welles proposes to tarry in this country long enough to do a few more plays on television.'[31] That was not to be: he had a film to start in Europe. But *Omnibus* reported one of its 'major mail pulls' for *King Lear*, and it was hoped, they said, that he might 'become identified' with future *Omnibus* performances, on Steinbeck, perhaps, or Hemingway. That, too, was not to be. 'There is a tide in the affairs of men,' as Brutus remarks in *Julius Caesar*,

> Which, taken at the flood, leads on to fortune;
> Omitted, all the voyage of their life
> Is bound in shallows and in miseries.
> On such a full sea are we now afloat,
> And we must take the current when it serves,
> Or lose our ventures.

This was surely such a moment in Welles's life. And it passed. Television got on very well without him, and he returned to his consuming obsession, the thing he thought his proper work: making movies.

'The chief justification for the production', Richard Watts Jr, of the *New York Post* ended his review, 'was Orson Welles's performance. It is quite possible that he is the King Lear the theatre has been waiting for.'[32] That, too, was not to be. He did indeed play King Lear in New York, but it was very much *not* the King Lear the theatre had been waiting for. It was a *King Lear* which they ransacked the critical thesaurus to denounce. But meanwhile, the *Omnibus Lear* was one of Welles's rare critical honeymoons.

CHAPTER SEVEN

The Scorpion and the Frog

1954 BEGAN promisingly, with Welles back in harness, directing the film briefly called *Masquerade*, now known again as *Mr Arkadin*. Despite the existence of Filmorsa, the company Welles and Dolivet had set up, the financial underpinning of the new film was as precarious as *Othello*'s. Welles managed to find a Spanish co-producer for a three-picture deal, but before long this man fell out; he found a replacement, Producciones Hispano Film, who were, however, only prepared to back *Mr Arkadin*, and only if it were mostly shot in Spain instead of Italy, as in the screenplay. Welles accordingly relocated much of the film to Spain, a country he knew and loved; the masked-ball scene, instead of being (like Beistegui's ball) Venetian, became Goya-themed.

Filming started in late January; editing began immediately, with two British technicians, Bill Morton and Derek Parsons, working day and night so that Welles could have access to them at all times – an extraordinary extravagance, perhaps designed to avoid the perpetual need for reshooting that had characterised *Othello*: if he could identify what he needed immediately, he could shoot it before moving location. This was especially important since many of his large and distinguished cast were hired only for a day or two; if reshooting were necessary it was vital to do it before they disappeared. In fact Welles could congratulate himself that he was already ahead of the game, having seized the opportunity of a break in shooting on *L'Uomo, la bestia e la virtù* the year before to persuade the producers – with whom he was still then on talking terms – to let him have the use of the crew for a few days in lieu of his salary; the method he had evolved on *Othello* of assembling his film shard by shard was now second nature to him. With a junior assistant director on the Pirandello film, a wiry, ruthlessly efficient young man named Sergio Leone, Welles filmed a scene in which a thief runs away from the police by dashing in front of a speeding train. He had asked Leone to find him an extra 'with the most terrifying thief's face imaginable'. The man he found was a dead ringer for Mussolini, which delighted Welles

– 'the world's biggest thief!' he cried.[1] They shot for three days, with Welles urging the man to run ever closer to the front of the train. The shot made its way into the film.

But despite this head-start, the shoot was problematic from the first day: 'just anguish,' he told Bogdanovich, 'from beginning to end'.[2] This is uncommon with Welles's films. The high levels of adrenalin he generated normally swept everyone up. Mad and often physically arduous though the shooting of *Othello* had been, there was a kind of excitement, a sense of adventure, which, for all except diehard whiners like Robert Coote, made it at the very least a memorable experience. But *Mr Arkadin* was a joyless slog. Welles had little respect for his crew, who were resentful, slow and lacking in proficiency; for their part, they were unaccustomed to being told how to do their job by the director. After the experience of *Othello*, Welles knew exactly what he wanted and how it had to be achieved, however unorthodox it might be. He knew more about their cameras than the crew did, and could see little point in going through the charade of coaxing them into doing what he wanted: he simply cut to the chase and told them.

The cinematographer was Jean Bourgoin, a Renoir veteran, and later director of photography for Jacques Tati, but he had no interest in Welles's experiments and simply executed the angles and used the lenses that were asked of him. Then there was the red-tape. Post-war Europe was bedevilled by petty bureaucracy, constantly hemming Welles in and holding him up. The rushes were developed in a French laboratory. 'Can you imagine', he lamented in a piece he wrote for *Film Culture* with the somewhat grandiose title 'For a Universal Cinema', 'that I had to have a special authorization for every bit of film, even if only 20 yards long, that arrived from Spain?' He remonstrated with the authorities, but to no avail. 'One might convince a tribal chief from Darkest Africa – but officialdom will remain as deaf to the oratory of Demosthenes as to the reasonings of Descartes.' Even getting work permits for his international crew was a nightmare.[3]

But the problems ran deeper than that, beginning with the screenplay. Screenplays for Welles were very much a starting point, and could – and would – be changed according to circumstances or fresh inspiration. Hitherto he had always worked from a source: a novel (*The Magnificent Ambersons*, *The Lady from Shanghai*), an original screenplay (*The Stranger*, *Citizen Kane*), a play (*Macbeth*, *Othello*). In the case of *Mr Arkadin* the ur-material is almost as elusive as Gregory Arkadin himself. Since as early as 1951, Welles had been telling people that he was working on a novel about a famous arms-dealer;

he had been seen typing what he said was the manuscript. He airily referred to this same novel in various interviews, and made a very clear public announcement, as we have seen, about making a film derived from it; he went to Casablanca to write it, after staying with Mike Olian, partly, no doubt, inspired by prolonged exposure to a real-life conman. But Basil Zaharoff – 'Europe's Man of Mystery', as he was widely known – the international swindler and munitions dealer of Greek origins who ended his long and lurid life covered in honours, not least a knighthood of the British Empire – was the primary model. Welles had been fascinated by him since at least 1936, when, in Sidney Kingsley's stage play *Ten Million Ghosts*, he had, as a twenty-year-old, played a character clearly based on him. Zaharoff was equally clearly the inspiration for one of the *Harry Lime* radio scripts Welles produced for Harry Alan Towers in 1952; the episode's title, 'Man of Mystery', made the connection pretty explicit. For the radio script, Welles rechristened him Gregory Arkadian, with its obvious echo of Olian's name, and he stands in the long line of powerful, unknowable, empty men Welles was drawn to portraying: Kurtz in *Heart of Darkness*, Kane, Charles Rankin in *The Stranger*, Cagliostro, Mr Clay in *The Immortal Story*. He was equally drawn to these men in life, Olian and Fritz Mandl among them: simultaneously attracted and repulsed by them.

Many of the *Harry Lime* scripts are journeyman work, redeemed only by the deftness of a hard-working cast, a sprinkling of self-knowing hokum and Welles's unique throwaway charms, honed on radio shows in which he performed in the 1940s. 'Man of Mystery', broadcast in April of 1952, is on a different level. It opens with the curiously haunting image – somehow especially powerful on radio – of an empty plane flying in the skies above France, after which the plot is swiftly and skilfully established: Arkadian, a great international magnate, hires Harry Lime to find out about his past, so that, unbeknown to Lime, he can systematically wipe out anyone who had ever known him as the petty criminal he was, to prevent his daughter Raina from finding out about his shabby origins. It is virtually impossible to attribute authorship to any of the episodes of *The Adventures of Harry Lime*, though Welles certainly edited them all, but it seems more than likely that Welles had had an idea for a movie and seized the opportunity to give it a dry run on radio. The question is whether this radio play derived from Welles's purported novel, or whether it was simply whipped up by him and his team of writers as part of the production line of weekly broadcasts. Meanwhile, even before the transmission of 'Man of Mystery', Welles had completed a screenplay he called *Masquerade*, which is essentially an elaboration of the radio play, and indeed uses many lines from it. Or is it? Are they perhaps both taken from the mysterious novel-in-progress?

The screenplay starts, as does the radio play, with the puzzle of the empty plane. It then essentially follows the course of 'Man of Mystery', adding a couple of subplots and incidents from 'Greek Meets Greek' and 'The Golden Fleece', other episodes of *The Adventures of Harry Lime*. Completely new is a spectacular first meeting between Arkadin (who in the translation from radio to screen has lost the third 'a' in his name) and the investigator he hires (who is now named Guy Dusmenil). Their rendezvous takes place at a fancy dress ball in Venice, obviously modelled on the legendary *Bal Oriental* at which Welles had been a guest two years earlier, and which gives the screenplay its title. It also includes excursions to the various figures of Arkadin's past, now scattered across the globe. The screenplay bears an epigraph from Ralph Waldo Emerson – famous, haunting lines from his essay on *Compensation* (which also makes an appearance in Welles's film *The Stranger*). They are words that powerfully express Welles's own feelings about guilt:

> Commit a crime and the earth is made of glass. Commit a crime and it seems as if a coat of snow fell on the ground, such as reveals in the woods the track of every partridge and fox and squirrel and mole. You cannot recall the spoken word, you cannot wipe out the foot-track, you cannot draw up the ladder, so as to leave no inlet or clew. Some damning circumstance always transpires. The laws and substances of nature – water, snow, wind, gravitation – become penalties to the thief.[4]

The crucial difference between 'Man of Mystery' and *Masquerade* is that in the radio play the investigator is, of course, Harry Lime (Welles); for the screenplay, a new investigator was required. In *Masquerade* this is Guy Dusmenil, an elegant gentleman detective. By the time they started shooting, *Masquerade* had again become *Mr Arkadin* and Dusmenil had become Guy Van Stratten, a more rugged and troubled figure than his predecessor. Despite the glittering succession of cameo roles that the script calls for – the figures from Arkadin's past who have to be eliminated – there is a triangle at the centre of the screenplay on which the film stands or falls: Arkadin, Van Stratten and Raina. Obviously Welles was going to play Arkadin, but he took a huge gamble on the other two parts. As Raina, the daughter whose love and respect Arkadin so desperately seeks to secure, he cast his lover, Paola Mori, who had had the slenderest experience of acting; and, as Van Stratten – the engine of the plot, and increasingly Arkadin's prey – he cast one of the actors who had worked with him on the *Harry Lime* radio series, Robert Arden, who up to that point had had a very modest, if solid career as one of the small pool of American actors working in London. At the time, Arden was playing the supporting role of Rusty Charlie in the London production of *Guys and Dolls*; at first he assumed that the urgent messages left for him at the stage door of the London Coliseum were a prank, but eventually he called back and was astonished to be offered what he took to be the leading role ('I was in every scene!') in Orson Welles's latest film. A day later, Welles's secretary sent him a one-way plane ticket for Madrid, with a request to buy himself an appropriate wardrobe for the part, for which he would, he was assured, be reimbursed.[5] As always, Welles was supremely confident in his ability to draw what he needed from any actor. Arden had some film and television experience, but nothing that could possibly have prepared him for what was to follow.

The moment he arrived at the airport, Arden was whisked away to Welles's hotel; the door of Welles's room was opened by the actor playing Jacob Zouk, Welles's old colleague Akim Tamiroff – 'welcome to Madrid, Spain!' – and off they went, Arden, Welles, Tamiroff and Mrs Tamiroff (Tamara Shane, also in the movie) for a bibulous supper at Horcher's, Madrid's finest restaurant. Then, when it was well past midnight, they went straight to the studio and shot the scenes between Zouk and Van Stratten well into the small hours. When they reconvened the following afternoon, Welles announced that he had had an idea: he would reframe the film within a flashback structure – the whole film would in fact be a series of flashbacks, told by Van Stratten to persuade Jacob Zouk to run for his life. Arden, in his innocence, asked Welles whether that meant they would have to shoot the material again. No, Welles patiently told him, what they had shot was fine: he would just redub it.

This instability of the basic material was new in Welles's work. In *Othello* he had adapted to changing circumstances and allowed himself to be inspired by what a location might offer. But the story of *Othello* is the story of *Othello*, whatever slant you might put on it, and the words are all by Shakespeare; in the case of *Mr Arkadin*, it was never entirely clear what story Welles wanted to tell, and since he never signed off on a definitive version of the film, it is virtually impossible to know how it might have ended up. There are, in fact, as Jonathan Rosenbaum has brilliantly established, seven versions of *Mr Arkadin*, some supervised by Welles, others not, many of them almost identical but for different dialogue dubbed over the same scene, without any real correlation between the words and the actors' lips – a somewhat surreal experience. This multiplicity of versions makes the film hog-heaven for Welles scholars, affording endless opportunities for playing the great sport of 'what if?' More interestingly, it offers a glimpse of Welles in the act of creation, shaping and remaking his raw material as a sculptor or a painter might, searching for the form and meaning of what it is that he is creating. It is perhaps especially interesting that, with *Mr Arkadin*, he never seems quite to have answered those questions.

What sort of film did the quondam collaborators Dolivet and Welles want to make for their first venture – apart, that is, from one that made money, a primary objective, since the whole point of their partnership was to subsidise the Foundation for a New Humanism? Did they intend the film to be politically challenging, a critique of capitalism? Or should we take seriously Welles's later claims that Arkadin is really Stalin (like the Generalissimo, Akim Athabadze – Arkadin's real name – is Georgian by birth)? But why would the former communist agent Dolivet want to make an anti-Stalin allegory during the bitterest phase of the Cold War? (Stalin had died in February 1953.) Or is the film simply supposed to amuse, a subversion of the detective genre?

The *Masquerade* screenplay as it stands contains a number of highly suggestive elements, ideas and gestures to which Welles was always drawn. It is, for a start, hokum – an idiom that Welles loved. Throughout his radio career, up to and including *The Adventures of Harry Lime*, he had taken an innocent delight in yarns, especially thrillers, which provided opportunities for suspense, atmosphere and character acting of the ripest variety; *Journey into Fear* is a rare example of this among his films, though both at RKO and later on he had worked on a number of projects of a similar kind. These pieces are the radiophonic and cinematic equivalent of conjuring tricks – delicious, outrageous and leaving more than a whiff of chicanery behind them. Another, more sophisticated Welles could not fail to pick up on any deeper resonances that these artless tales might contain, and so from time to time there is a sudden modulation, a shadow of significance will fall, political or philosophical, but it is largely unexplored. It simply contributes another colour, another strand in the tapestry. Often this is achieved by the time-honoured mechanism of the introduction of a fable or exemplary tale into the piece: in *Masquerade* it is Arkadin's famous speech about the scorpion and the frog, which has passed into the collective consciousness – often attributed to Aesop, though it seems to have been entirely original to Welles:

> This scorpion wanted to cross a river, so he asked the frog to carry him. No, said the frog, no thank you. If I let you on my back you may sting me and the sting of the scorpion is death. Now, where, asked the scorpion, is the logic in that? For scorpions always try to be logical. If I sting you, you will die. I will drown. So, the frog was convinced and allowed the scorpion on his back. But, just in the middle of the river, he felt a terrible pain and realized that, after all, the scorpion had stung him. 'Logic!' Cried the dying frog as he started under, bearing the scorpion down with him. 'There is no logic in this!' 'I know,' said the scorpion, 'but I can't help it – it's my character.'[6]

In the film this has the weight of a central illumination – a comment, it seems, on the immutability of character. But the film seems determined to disprove the proposition: is it in Arkadin's character to kill himself? Is it in character for Van Stratten – the hard-boiled adventurer – to risk his own life by trying to save Jacob Zouk? Of course the question of identity had always been of deep interest to Welles, who had, from an early age, fantasticated his own past, inventing a family tree, mythologising his own childhood and casting doubt on his paternity, and suggesting to various people at various times that his mother had had affairs with King Edward VII (who died in 1910, five years before Welles was born) and the great bass Fyodor Chaliapin (nowhere near Chicago in 1914). A line from 'Man of Mystery' survived (with variations) in every version of the story: 'Where did I come from? . . . that's my real secret, Mr Lime. I don't know who I am.' Amnesia features in a number of Welles's unrealised projects – *Henry IV*, from Pirandello, and *Carnaval*, the proposed framing device for the *It's all True* footage, among them – and with it comes the crucial Wellesian question of authenticity. All stimulating, richly interesting ideas, but almost none of them come home to roost in *Mr Arkadin* in any of its versions.

Nor do they need to – if Welles was making, as he seems to have set out to make, a delicious diversion, a black comedy that comes to a climax, of all the good days in the year (as Dickens would say), on Christmas Day. Creative artists often divide their work up into categories: François Truffaut spoke of his left-handed and his right-handed films; Éric Rohmer contrasts his fables with his realistic stories; Jean Anouilh has pink plays and black plays; Graham Greene categorises some of his works as entertainments, others as novels. Welles's films, too, fall into different genres. Few of them are out-and-out comedies, pure light entertainment. But Welles loved to entertain, and much of his art, like his conversation, can be considered a series of provocations, none of them to be probed too deeply. So with *Mr Arkadin*. Almost everything about the film – the visual vocabulary, the musical score, the cameo performances – is a manifestation of what Bertolt Brecht contemptuously called 'the culinary arts': its purpose is to tickle the palate, to delight and to divert. Its essential problem is in its execution, the absence of a 'Lubitsch Touch', or the naughty wit of a Billy Wilder. This is partly to do with the tiresome circumstances in which the film was made and the inadequacy of the crew; partly because of Welles's preferred method of filming, where close-ups were left to last, making interplay between him and the other actors impossible; partly because of the way in which he reconceived the film as it went on. Mostly it is to do with the writing. The dialogue is for the most part formulaic, and often clumsy, but more importantly, there seems to be no clear through-line, so the film resolves itself into a series of attitudes – gestures that have no coherent meaning.

As it happens, we have a clue as to what kind of film he wanted to make in the form of a novel that appeared under his name, first in serialised form in French in *France-Soir* and then, translated into English, in the London *Daily Express*, until it finally came out in hard covers in 1955 – again first in France, then in England, translated by the journalist Robert Kee. 'It is perhaps surprising', says the blurb for the English edition, 'that Orson Welles, so phenomenally active and versatile in the arts, has not written a novel before.'[7] Indeed it is, but *Mr Arkadin: The Novel* was not it. The book was written in March of 1954, when filming had been under way for over a month, by Welles's chum and sometime publicist, Maurice Bessy, an *homme de lettres* at large who had written additional dialogue for a number of films. He had approached Dolivet for permission to write the novel on the basis of the then-current screenplay, a copy of which he had; Welles would get sole credit for authorship. The novel Bessy ghosted gives us, therefore, a glimpse of Welles's thinking about the film at the time of shooting.

Narrated by Van Stratten, it reads remarkably well, and illuminates things in the film that are otherwise unexplained or unmotivated. In the novel, for example, the strangely cryptic shot of Van Stratten's ex-girlfriend Mily lying immobile on the beach (which in some versions is the opening shot of the film) is fully explained: there is a knife between her shoulder-blades, exactly the death Arkadin has just inflicted on Jacob Zouk. Likewise, the oddly arbitrary appearance of the *penitentes*, pilgrims dressed, as Mily says in the movie, in Ku Klux Klan hoods and gowns, is made equally clear in the novel: they are votaries of San Tirso, the patron saint of the village where Arkadin has his castle. The procession honours Our Lady of Despair for saving the saint, who had doubted God's mercy. 'You will spend the rest of your life in repentance,' Our Lady had told Tirso, 'in regaining that mercy of which you had doubted.' In the novel the procession of pilgrims is followed by the arrival of the consecrated Host 'amidst a brilliance of white candles. There was always a remission for the sins of man,' says Van Stratten, narrating – something that Welles devoutly hoped was true. This moment of grace does not occur in the film, where there is guilt, but no absolution. It seems this is another theme that Welles would have liked to have explored, another autobiographical resonance: towards the end of the film, during Arkadin's encounter with Van Stratten in Munich in the Frauenkirche, Arkadin asks whether he's gone there to pray 'for both of us'. In the novel, like Scarpia in Puccini's *Tosca*, even as Arkadin engages in a menacing exchange with Van Stratten, he is crossing himself like a good Catholic. This eschatological framework continues to the very end of the novel: 'My father was my father,' says Raina. 'That's all. And I loved him.' Van Stratten comments that 'Arkadin, who knew everything, who could do anything, hadn't understood that. Like Tirso, who had doubts about divine mercy and divine love, he didn't put faith in the indulgence and tenderness of a daughter. Like Tirso, he threw himself into emptiness.' Is this Bessy, or Welles? Either way, it is absent from the film, to its great disadvantage. There is no evidence that Welles believed in God, but ample evidence that he had an essentially religious cast of mind, not so very different from Graham Greene's. He may have been shy of expressing it; certainly in the film it is largely absent.

In the novel Arkadin is described by Van Stratten as massive, 'overtopping me by a good head and a half'; in a suggestive phrase with interesting reverberations for Welles himself, he is described as possessing a 'deliberate' massiveness. Arkadin's voice, says Van Stratten, was 'almost inhumanly soft. Thus I imagined did savage priests chant their spells when carrying out some bloody rite. Neither spite nor pity. Complete attention combined with a curious detachment' – which recalls Welles's vision of Mr Kurtz in the film of

Heart of Darkness that he never made: the dangerous voice, the voice that must not be listened to, the voice of the hollow man. Arkadin's face is 'as immobile as granite', his eyes 'of a subtlety and a depth which were truly disconcerting'. All of which perfectly expresses Welles's performance and tells us that it was a conscious choice. Again and again, the novel compares Arkadin to mythic figures: 'he reminded me of that bearded and lecherous centaur caressing a young girl . . . at Berne,' says Van Stratten. Raina says that he deliberately tried to look like God, like Jupiter, like Bluebeard; as in the film, a young assistant compares him to Neptune.

None of this is in the radio play, or in *Masquerade*. It seems to have been at least partially provoked by Welles's decision to use the magnificent castle of Alcázar in Segovia as Arkadin's castle. 'A real fairy-tale castle,' says Van Stratten in the book, 'with turrets and a winding road and ramparts draped in ivy. A fairy tale, but not the one in which the princess marries the prince and lives happily ever after. This was the castle of the magician or the wicked ogre.' In his shooting style, and especially perhaps in his own make-up, Welles seems to have chosen to emphasise this fairy-tale aspect of the story, consciously embodying the fabulous: the limitlessly rich and powerful father guarding his beautiful daughter from the dangerously attractive commoner. To this end Welles – as he had done in *Othello* on stage and *King Lear* on television – increases his already towering height with the use of platform soles, shoots himself from low angles, and adorns his face with hair and a beard that almost covers it, lending it a curious resemblance to Jean Marais's lion-face as la Bête in Cocteau's *Beauty and the Beast*, but which – unlike Marais's beard – simply seems stuck on. 'The first time I saw *Mr Arkadin*,' writes Gary Giddins, one of the film's most astute commentators, 'I assumed that Welles's wig and beard, the kind of thing you expect to see in a high school production of *Faust*, were part of Arkadin's masquerade costume, and was thus stymied by his wearing them throughout.'[8] Curiously enough, in the novel, Raina says of her father, 'My father wears his power as he wears his beard; it's all a trick, to make him seem like God.' It is, to put it mildly, highly theatrical.

This stylised approach sits very oddly with the modern-day thriller that surrounds it, and the rackety assortment of ex-criminals that Van Stratten discovers in their respective dens. Here the idiom is, as Welles himself said, Dickensian, and Welles had made sure that he commanded the services, for a day or two at a time, of some of the ripest performers on the face of the earth: the Russians Akim Tamiroff and Mischa Auer; Grégoire Aslan and Suzanne Flon from France; the great Greek actress Katina Paxinou, aquiline and heavy-lidded; and one of the greatest of all British actors, Michael Redgrave. Welles had hoped for Michel Simon, Alida Valli, Ingrid Bergman, Marlene Dietrich, but the cast he actually got for these parts is eye-wateringly wonderful.

Each of them creates a credible world of his or her own, each blessed with the experience and richly matured expressive gifts to bring the Higher Hokum to life, each adding an individual fantasy to their creations: Aslan, dying with his face to the ground; cadaverous Auer and his monstrously magnified eye in the flea circus; Redgrave, sleazy in hairnet, flirting with his cats and teasing Van Stratten with possible purchases (among them a 'teleoscope', as he irresistibly pronounces it); Flon, who had also played the part in 'Man of Mystery', beguiling and world-weary as Baroness Nagel; Paxinou superbly commanding and entirely credible in her love of the young Arkadin – or Akim Athabadze, as she knew him; Tamiroff, kvetchy and wheedling as Jacob Zouk, funny and utterly credible, a clown-tramp, a Jewish Beckett with overtones of Zero Mostel; Peter van Eyck (who had once been a production manager for Welles at the Mercury Theatre), elegant and filled with bitter melancholy as Thaddeus; even Frédéric O'Brady (the original radio Arkadian), his scene cruelly truncated in the editing suite, but entirely credibly in the grip of cold turkey as he gibbers on board the ship – all brilliantly shot by Welles, in each case creating a visual gesture that crystallises the character and the situation. It is a superb suite of scenes, as are the action shots at the dock and the street scenes in Munich, especially the climax at Christmas. (In the attic in which Van Stratten finds Zouk, an upended canvas of Hitler sits on top of a pile of rubbish, put there by the Welles of 'Thoughts on Germany'.) Earlier the real-life actor/cabaret artist Gordon Heath makes a charming appearance as himself, in the manner of Hoagy Carmichael in *To Have and Have Not*; even Dolivet appears on screen for thirty seconds. In all of this one feels that Welles is having fun – not least, no doubt, because he himself is in none of these scenes. Here are many of the ingredients of a very classy, somewhat Carol Reedish/ Graham Greeneish entertainment; and the vivacious and ever-inventive score by Jean Renoir's regular composer, Paul Misraki, one of the great figures of French post-war film, points in the same direction, with its swirling glissandi and international flavour.

And then there are the three central performances. Paola Mori, neatly revoiced by the British actress Billie Whitelaw, is perfectly pleasant as Arkadin's daughter Raina, though nothing more. It's a wonder the performance is as good as it is, given what she was up against – firstly, an incoherent storyline for her character; secondly, being directed by her boyfriend (who happened to be Orson Welles); and finally, Robert Arden. Arden was a charming man and became a skilful actor, but, as he said himself, he was not ready for the role of Guy Van Stratten, where he had to tread a tricky line between hard-bitten brashness and animal attractiveness, neither of which qualities were his by nature. It's a part for Humphrey Bogart or Frank Sinatra. In *Masquerade* Guy Dusmenil is described as 'charming and attractive'; in the novel Van Stratten is given a detailed and credible background – a freeloading mother; a father conned into paying for his education, despite dubious evidence of paternity; a youth spent bumming around the watering-holes of Europe; a war in which he served with distinction; a career in petty crime. It's a part predicated on easy charm and heartless calculation, and the plot entirely hinges on him convincing us, first, of his ability to make Raina fall in love with him – which is, on the showing of the film, incomprehensible – and, second, of a deep underlying resemblance between himself and Arkadin, who was, he says, 'once something like me'; this is profoundly unconvincing in any version of the film, but is dealt a death-blow by the photograph of the young Arkadin/Athabadze that Sophie shows Van Stratten – Welles photoshopped to look irresistibly powerful and gorgeous, elegantly tailored and sporting a splendid moustache. This photograph, incidentally, deals another death-blow to a different branch of the narrative – why would Arkadin not want his daughter to know that he was once that dashing, sexy young man? Paxinou's unerring acting at this point evokes him and the deep love they had with absolute conviction. All we are left with by way of Van Stratten's supposed resemblance to Arkadin is the fact that at some point they both changed their names.

The essential problem with Arden's acting is simply that he had no confidence, unlike his seniors: he is clearly hanging on by his teeth, concentrating fiercely and barking out his lines. Perhaps that had worked for him as Rusty Charlie in *Guys and Dolls*, or perhaps Welles found the one thing he could do with any conviction and got him to do it over and over again. Even when Van Stratten discovers that his girlfriend has been murdered by Arkadin, all Arden can do is bark. The surviving footage of Welles directing him off camera is profoundly discouraging: Welles gives Arden his inflections, which he imitates, but never fills with life. It is painful to witness. During the all-important scene where Arkadin commissions Van Stratten to investigate him, softening him up with booze, Welles insisted on using real alcohol, with predictably lamentable results.

No doubt Arden was not helped by the fact that frequently it was not Welles he was acting with: as often as not, a Spanish assistant director was off camera, reading the lines with minimal comprehension, and so even just engaging with his fellow-actor, which in itself can sometimes make a scene work, was denied him.

Arden wasn't wrong about one thing: Van Stratten is the leading character in the film. The potential of the part, as revealed in the book, is startling; as Robert Polito says in his masterly introduction to a recent reissue: 'the enhancement of Guy Van Stratten is the artful wonder of the novel'.[9] Had Arden been a better actor, or better able to cope, he might have been able to import some of that into the script; and had he done so, it might have helped Welles's own performance, which, as well as being highly stylised, is apparently hermetically sealed, consisting of a series of fixed grimaces and stares, devoid of any credible impulse or emotion. The mainspring of the plot, Arkadin's love for his daughter, is entirely unbelievable, nor do we see any hint of the vulnerability of which Van Stratten speaks in the novelisation: 'this absurd but keen feeling of pity which had affected me, too, several times when I was with Arkadin'. Perhaps if Welles had read the novel – something he denied ever having done – it might have improved his performance. It is full of acting notes: after Arkadin says, 'Raina is very important to me,' Van Stratten observes: 'There was something on which I could not quite put my fingers in the way he said that. I felt somehow he had nearly revealed to me the one chink in his armour of money, the one crack in the granite of his power. "More important than anything else on earth." Yes, a note of sadness, even of fear.' The equivalent moment in the film never happens. The words are said, but the feeling is absent.

No doubt, given time and a sufficient number of retakes, Welles might have made something more coherent and indeed cohesive of the material; perhaps if he had even longer to edit it, he might have found a unity of style, though it is hard to know what he could have done with the three central performances. The film has a unique atmosphere and is full of curious autobiographical echoes, which makes it feel highly personal in its rather stylised way. The parallels with *Citizen Kane* are so obvious as to make them seem intended: both films begin at the end of the story, both are investigations into the life of a magnate, both have flashback structures. Arkadin's castle is Xanadu by another means: 'Arkadin had bought it, restored it, decorated it,' says Van Stratten as the novel's narrator. 'All in the best of taste and no detail wrong. And yet it was all wrong. Maybe one was too conscious of the vast amount of money which had been spent on it.' And in the last reel of the film it is scarcely possible to hear Welles bellow, 'I am Gregory Arkadin!' in the airport at Barcelona and not hear Kane roaring at Boss Jim W. Geddys, 'I'm Charles Foster Kane. I'm no cheap, crooked politician, trying to save himself from the consequences of his crimes.'

Though there is scarcely a direct comparison to be made between Welles and Arkadin, since at least as early as 1962 Arkadin's Aesopian fable has been seen (first by the independent film distributor Daniel Talbot) as an allegory of Welles's career. Parker Tyler, in a highly influential essay, further interpreted it as a parable for his life as 'a Big Experimental Cult hero':

> The scorpion must cross a stream (i.e., Welles must make a film) but to do so he must enlist the help of a frog (it is easy to imagine a producer or a backer as a frog). But 'Ah,' says the frog to the scorpion, 'your sting brings death! So why should I carry you across?' – that is, why should a producer listen to Welles's blandishments when notoriously he is a maker of expensive films that 'sink' their backers? The scorpion then reasons: 'Now, look. If I sting you, you will die, that's true, but if you die, I will drown – so why should I sting you?' The frog-producer (once again!) is convinced by this wily argument, swims across with the scorpion on his back ('Camera!') and duly gets stung. Before he sinks to his death, he has time, however, to ask the scorpion: 'Why?' The scorpion-director makes this answer, the only one he can make: 'Because it is my character.' Thus, adapted to the present theme, it is Welles's character to make films, even if he must perish with his backers.[10]

Certainly in the case of *Mr Arkadin* Welles's relationship with the backers – or, more precisely, with the producer – very quickly started to go badly wrong. It is possible that Dolivet's inexperience in film was partly to blame. Certainly he was unable to cope with Welles's erratic schedules, his prolonged absences and constant changes of mind. As far as Welles was concerned, he was frustrated by the crew, increasingly nostalgic for the efficiency and diligence of American technicians, and deeply exasperated by working with his two over-parted leading actors. Moreover he was shooting a Spanish version of the film simultaneously, using Spanish actresses for the roles of Sophie and Baroness Nagel. The pressure was immense. Patricia Medina, the Anglo-American actress playing Mily, who (moonlighting from her contract with Columbia) filmed for a heady ten days, reported looking blankly at a bare set that was intended to be a suite on Arkadin's yacht; the following morning when they shot the scene, Welles had personally furnished the set with items from his hotel, transforming it into the acme of luxury.[11] He liked improvising, of course, but not when he was obliged to do so because of the inadequacy of the team. Dissatisfied with the results he was getting, he constantly sought reshoots, on the French Riviera, in Munich and back in Spain; in mid-June in Paris, five months after shooting had begun, Renzo Lucidi started editing in earnest: he had a staggering fifty-five hours' worth of film to work with; *Citizen Kane*, by contrast, had essentially been edited in the camera. Meanwhile, Dolivet threatened to take over the film unless Welles honoured the deadlines he had agreed.

Shooting came to an end on 26 June 1954; Welles signed a new contract with Filmorsa, to whom he granted his exclusive services till the end of 1956, assigning his recent screenplays to the company as collateral on which to raise new investment – an astonishing vote of confidence in the fledgling company and a testament, apparently, to his confidence in his relationship with Dolivet. By August the Spanish version was finished. It had been submitted as Spain's entry in the Venice Film Festival, but it was withdrawn, another in the long line of Wellesian withdrawals. Welles threw himself into shooting the shots still missing from the English-language version, in a Paris studio and on the Riviera: these included the scenes with the Baroness, Sophie and Oscar. He also finally added Misraki's score. He had only given general indications to the composer as to what he wanted for each scene, and now he cut and patched it as he deemed appropriate. The music and the uses to which it is put are, as Jonathan Rosenbaum has observed, one of the most successful elements in the film; Welles's instinct in these matters was exemplary. But it is a very different notion of composing for film from Bernard Herrmann's: Herrmann needed precise timings, he needed to see the film, he needed to receive, and he expected to give, input. He was Welles's partner in the enterprise. Now Welles was in sole command: an absolute monarch of celluloid.

But work was not proceeding quickly enough for Dolivet: in October he issued a two-week ultimatum. It passed. Welles was given a new and final deadline: Christmas. Christmas came and went. In January 1955 Dolivet formally instructed Welles to stay away from the editing suite, which he did, though he continued to work with Lucidi at long distance. Surprisingly, this was not the end of the road for the partnership of Welles and Dolivet; they continued to plan future projects. In October, they had started pre-production for their next venture, a post-atomic version of the Noah story, going so far as to start casting and scheduling the film. This project (an old subject of Welles's) petered out, but in late January, while still banished from the editing suite, Welles – underwritten by Filmorsa – did some tests, in colour, for a new project. It was the first time he had worked with colour since 1942 in Brazil, and it would be more than ten years before he came back to it; it was also his first engagement with a subject that he would never again be able to let alone, *Don Quixote.*

It seems that the spur for making the test was interest from CBS in a film somehow related to Cervantes's epic; it was to last half an hour. One might as well attempt the Bible in ten minutes. Welles had the inspired idea of plonking Quixote and his doughty man, Sancho Panza, into the modern world. He called it *Don Quixote Passes By*, casting two recent graduates of the *Mr Arkadin* school of hard knocks, Mischa Auer and Akim Tamiroff (Quixote and Sancho Panza, respectively – obvious but inspired casting), and setting them loose in the Bois de Boulogne on a crisp winter's day. The stills taken on the day are superb. CBS, it appears, were unimpressed with the results and there the project ended for the moment. But Welles had been bitten by the *Quixote* bug and would come back to the venture again. And again. Meanwhile *Mr Arkadin* was ready, in a version put together by Lucidi and Dolivet, with some telephonic input from Welles.

Nobody seemed to want it.

CHAPTER EIGHT

The Most Telegenic Character

DESPITE THE somewhat mixed impression made by his *Othello* at the St James Theatre, Welles continued to have a very high profile in Britain; he had made a powerful impression as a guest star in a couple of unremarkable British films for Herbert Wilcox and remained a very big beast on the international scene. In mid-January of 1955 he was invited to appear on a somewhat gladiatorial BBC programme called *Press Conference*: 'personalities who make the news answer questions impromptu from men who write the news,' the announcer tells us, in her cut-glass accent. Previous victims had included Sir Anthony Eden, shortly to succeed Winston Churchill as Prime Minister. It was Welles's first appearance on British television, and the larger public's first experience of his unique personal charms. It was, indeed, Welles's first appearance as himself on television anywhere, the forerunner of the hundreds and hundreds of interviews in that medium that he would give over the next thirty years. He proves to be an absolute master of the situation, wittily and gracefully deflecting the distinctly boorish questions of a team made up of star British journalists of the time: John Beavan, Elizabeth Frank, René MacColl, William Hardcastle.

'Why have you avoided television when you've seized every other medium?' asks one of them. 'Just a question of terror,' Welles replies, irresistibly wrinkling his brow. 'Can it be good?' 'It is already very good, as interesting as the cinema is today. I think we're going to find new forms in television, and revisit old forms, to rediscover the story-teller, for example. I do feel that television is going up a blind alley when it makes imitation movies.'

They ask him about his career – 'your amusing and wonderful life', as MacColl superciliously calls it – but he brushes it aside: 'I'm not very interesting on the subject, you know.' He's terrified, he says, about what they'll think about *Othello* when it comes out. He talks about the as-yet-unreleased *Mr Arkadin*: 'It's in that dangerous condition when in the morning I think it's splendid. In the evening, I wonder.' He describes it as 'a tragedy, with melodramatic and comic adornments. It isn't a thriller. Oh, that makes it sounds as if it isn't thrilling – I'm doing a rather poor job of selling it here.' He talks about his desire to return to politics – 'Adlai Stevens is a distant relative. But I kept quiet about that during the recent campaign. I figured it was the least I could do to help the Democratic party' – and about his conviction that the police are destroying civil liberties all over the world, a comment that caused a considerable stir in the newspapers.

Asked about his favourite actresses, Welles quite surprisingly nominates Greta Garbo. Then something electrifying happens. One of the journalists wonders whether what he calls 'the quiet school of acting', as personified on the English stage by Sir Gerald du Maurier, isn't going out of fashion. 'It can't go out of fashion,' says Welles, 'as long as there's that's machine there' – and he points to the camera, staring straight into the lens with a look so frank, so intimate, so playful and so seductive that he seems to leap straight into one's front room, and television suddenly becomes the most brilliant form of communication ever invented. Sixty years later, one feels in direct personal contact with the man; in the background his prickly interlocutors are by now visibly purring with pleasure, vanquished by his charm.

He made another conquest on the programme. It was produced by an ex-BBC publicity officer-turned-producer, Huw Wheldon, who was in time to become one of the commanding figures in British arts broadcasting. Welles had played his usual hide-and-seek games with Wheldon prior to the programme, not showing up till the last possible moment; when he finally did, they calmed themselves down by drinking a great deal of Scotch whisky. Welles was entirely unimpaired by it, but the moment the cameras started to roll, Wheldon says he knew he had made 'a first-rate error'. The panel was 'wrong', he said, in a letter to his father written the next day. 'I had forgotten that, theatricality or no, unreliability or no, [Welles] was a big man . . . a really outstanding man, a singular & a great person, whose stature would not respond to the twittering tempo of what I had set up.'[1] He was doing, he continued remorsefully, 'a shoddy injustice to one of the most remarkable people I have ever met'.

Throughout his life, Welles hit certain people with the force of a hammer blow – Roger Hill, John Houseman, George Schaefer, Richard Wilson, George Fanto – people who immediately saw beyond his external bravura and did everything they could to serve his genius, wayward though it might be. He did not always treat them well, but for the most part they remained devoted. Wheldon immediately joined their ranks: 'being in a room with Orson Welles,' he said, 'was like sharing a room with a cathedral'. From the time of *Press Conference* forward, he was Welles's doughtiest champion at the BBC, and indeed not much later produced for it one of the most engaging and original items in Welles's entire output, *Orson Welles's Sketch Book*. 'The BBC have captured Orson Welles, one of the world's foremost personalities,' rejoiced *TV Mirror*, 'for six 15-minute programmes in which the ebullient young American actor-writer-producer will talk about everything from ballet to bullfighting, from magic to murder, illustrated by his own sketches, drawn while you watch':[2] a perfectly reasonable summary of the programmes, but one that barely begins to convey the charm and ease – the playful complicity – of Welles's performance.

The set-up is very simple: Welles, formally dressed in dinner jacket and bow tie, is seen sketching a head – perhaps his own? – then he scratches it out. But in the first programme, in a typically Wellesian gesture, he starts out by disavowing the device:

> I hope you haven't gathered from the title of this that you're in for a televised art exhibit. The sketchbook part of it is frankly just a prop. A prop is a stage term . . . there are props in real life. We put our hands to our face, light a cigarette, that sort of thing. In other words a prop is what it means in the dictionary: it is something to prop ourselves with. It is a crutch, something to lean on. So the sketchbook is exactly that – it is a prop. It is something for me to turn to when I lose the thread and something for you to look at beside my face which ought to come as a nice break in the horrid monotony.

Seamlessly he starts story-telling: about his early days in Hollywood, about his time at the Gate, all the old stories, honed and refined. But his telling of them is self-deprecatory, confessional, wry. He chats inconsequentially away, but the effect is hypnotic, like a magician's patter. He amuses himself, eyes twinkling, brow irresistibly dimpled. His intelligence is palpable, and he addresses his audience as similarly intelligent equals. There is in fact a faint whiff of deviltry in the air: like a fireside chat with Harry Lime. One doesn't believe a word of it, but one simply has to watch him. This is Welles's fabled table-talk in particularly pure form: the presence of other people in the studio – an interviewer, a fellow-guest – would have diluted the experience. It is his gift for instant intimacy that is so remarkable, as it had been on radio, and as it reportedly was in life. A crucial part of his brilliance is to appear to be talking very personally to each viewer. 'Mr Welles treated the cameras as old friends,' remarked the *Daily Telegraph*. 'In a quiet and casual manner, he gathered his audience around his feet as if he were at their fireside and proved that the art of story-telling can remain unaffected by the mechanics of television.'[3]

He improvised these pieces, always arriving at his conclusion at exactly the last possible second; the sketches were really introduced because, as he tells us, the cameramen had to change the film every few minutes. He plays with an almost 3-D effect when he reaches over to place the sketch on its stand – you feel as if it might poke you in the eye – but once again, as he had done in *Press Conference*, he reserves his most startling effect for a look into camera. After describing the impact on him of his first exposure to the Dublin public, at the Gate Theatre, he says: 'But on that first night I made a discovery. I learnt that an audience can be a fierce creature which can turn suddenly dangerous.' And he looks at us, the viewers, straight into our eyes, as if he could discern the danger out there: far into the back of our brains he looks, quietly alarmed at what he sees. Then he lets us down gently:

> That fierceness is generally in defence of the fragile miracle which is expected every evening in the theatre. The audience defends that miracle, the artists preside over it, nobody performs that miracle, everybody contributes to it and above all it must not be treated lightly. Respect in the presence of that miracle is part of the normal respect of the professional for his job.

Not, it has to be said, that respect for the 'fragile miracle' was something for which he had been specially noted when he himself appeared in the theatre. But by the time he has finished his first *Sketch Book*, we are eating out of his hand.

It is a real kind of wizardry, a very particular kind of charisma. And of course it is Welles unadorned, unhampered by his having to play a character – although one may presume that his persona is indeed a characterisation, a very conscious self-presentation; needless to say, this Welles was not available twenty-four hours a day. Even here, though, he is ahead of us, deftly pulling the carpet from underneath our feet. 'You may have wondered why I look so peculiar on the television,' he says at the beginning of the second *Sketch Book*, 'and it's partly, I must confess to you, the fact that you see my nose as it is. In most of the films that I appear in I put on a false nose, usually as large as I can find.' He draws no conclusion from this, and offers no explanation for it, though it could certainly be said of him as an actor that he suffers from a kind of inverse Pinocchio effect: the larger his nose, the less truthful he becomes. But this Welles – button-nosed Welles, vulnerable, human Welles – in this Welles we trust. As the *Sketch Books* progress, he becomes less boyishly bashful and more explicitly political. He returns to the anxieties about the police state that he had expressed in *Press Conference*:

> We are told we should co-operate with the authorities. I don't want to overthrow law. On the contrary I want to bring the policeman to law. Obviously individual effort won't do any good. There is nothing the individual can do about protecting the individual. I should like it very much if somebody would form a great big organisation for the protection of the individual. They'd have offices at every frontier. That way when we get to frontiers and are asked to fill out a form we can say no. And they would say ah but it is the regulations and we would say very well see our lawyer because if there were enough of us our dues would pay for the best lawyers. We could bring to court these invasions of privacy.

This was bold stuff for anxiously conformist 1950s Britain, when policemen were still 'bobbies' helping old ladies across the road, and when most people believed that the great big organisation for the protection of the individual that Welles was proposing already existed: it was called the State. In another episode he recounts the story of Isaac Woodard, the black soldier blinded by a policeman ('Officer X') in a state in the deep south of America. He ranges over an almost promiscuously wide range of topics, opining engagingly on whatever topic comes to him, sometimes treading on dangerous ground, as when he meditates on national characteristics:

> We think the English are cold, of course they aren't. We think they are sane. Of course they aren't exactly sane, they are wonderfully mad and a people of genius. They pretend to be sane to conceal from the world their immense plans and schemes. And we think the Italians are lazy. Imagine! The Italians lazy! They work like beavers, they like work. When I lived in Rome, I had some people build a wall for me. They worked all week and then

> on Sunday they brought their wives to show them the wall they were building. It was a very exciting thing to show off the work they were involved in. The Germans are supposed to be phlegmatic. I don't know how we can think of the Germans as being phlegmatic after what we have been through in the last fifteen years but we still do. And we think Americans are silent. Silent! Look at me! Fifteen minutes' uninterrupted talk.

In his sixth and final *Sketch Book*, Welles abandons any pretence of sketching because, as he tells us, the programme is being transmitted from a studio, in real time, so there is no need to provide a cover for reel-changes. He's no longer wearing a dinner jacket and bow tie; instead he affects tweeds. He's just come from lunch in the country with the Oliviers, he tells us, where the talk turned, inevitably, to actors and acting, and he reads out an amusing letter by Mrs Siddons about the audience in the theatre. All this is a shameless but irresistible device to enable him to talk about the play he's currently doing, *Moby-Dick*, which opened only a few days earlier. Playing to this lively and exciting West End audience, he says, has been a wonderful experience – a public that likes the theatre for its own sake and likes acting for its own sake. As he drives to his theatre every night, he says, he passes in front of a statue of Sir Henry Irving, which stands in front of a hotel called the Garrick Hotel. 'Now there isn't a city in the world where there is a statue to an actor and a hotel named after an actor right next to each other. That is nice for an actor as it makes you feel you are in a profession that is taken seriously and gives pleasure and interest to people.' He is of course word-spinning. But he never falters, never hesitates. Sometimes he takes a moment to think about what he's saying, but even that is charming: one seems to see inside his mind. And then – twinkle, twinkle, little Orson – he's off on the next perfectly formed sentence, which turns out to be part of a perfectly formed paragraph.

He signs off this final episode with a valediction that is unquestionably heartfelt, but still playful: the magician insisting on the transparency of his procedures. He's actually just filling in time, he tells us:

> I have been watching the clock and I see that I have about 40 seconds to say goodnight to you in those remaining seconds that I have. What a privilege and pleasure to be speaking on the television in England. Because here I am talking to you and before I

> began to speak not only did I have no idea what I was going to say but neither did the BBC. I might have founded a new religion or attempted to overthrow your government. You don't know what I might have done.

What he says is no more than the truth: there was no medium in America in 1955 for which that would have been true.

> And how nice it was of you just to let me talk to you and how grateful I am for that experience and for playing in your theatre and how much I look forward to the resumption of all these experiments next year if I may please. Goodnight.

Neither experiment was resumed. He never acted on the English stage again after *Moby-Dick*, and *Orson Welles's Sketch Book* was not recommissioned, though it had been an immense success, and remains a remarkable example of what television can do. 'If Orson Welles were to join one or other of the two main political parties, I guarantee that some 15 minutes of him on television would sway the electorate for his side,' proclaimed the London *Evening News*. 'This is by way of saying that Mr Welles is the most telegenic character who has ever appeared on our screens.'[4]

Talking heads had not been unknown on British television heretofore, but they were stiff affairs, essentially lectures. No one before Welles had understood the essential characteristic of television, its intimacy. It went into people's homes, as radio had done before it, but with the additional dimension of a personal presence. It was *First Person Singular* in three dimensions and could – and should – be a real encounter, even if, in Welles's hands, a gratifyingly subversive one. Having instantly mastered the form, Welles's enthusiasm for the programme quickly evaporated and he became restless. At some point during recording for the show, he found that he'd run out of ink for his sketch, whereupon he threw down his pen in irritation. Wheldon left the control gallery to propitiate him, but by the time he reached the set, he was told that Welles had left for Paris: the charming ironist encountered by viewers had become a petulant child. By the last programme, which went out live, Welles was seemingly already bored with the limitations of the *Sketch Book* format. Before long, however, he would take the lessons he had learned from it and weave them into something much more complex.

Meanwhile, the programme's success led to another televisual venture for him, this time for a new and rival broadcaster. After years of resistance, Parliament had finally conceded that the BBC's monopoly should be challenged by some enlivening commercial competition; 22 September 1955 was the day designated for the launch of the new channel, and among the glittering offerings on that momentous day would be the first of Welles's new programmes, which were to be called *Around the World with Orson Welles*, thirteen half-hour programmes commissioned by Associated-Rediffusion, the company to which the franchise for London and the south of England had been awarded by the newly convened Independent Television Authority. 'ORSON WELLES WILL STAR FOR RIVAL TV,'[5] shouted the headlines. His every move was news.

He was even briefly back on radio. The latest venture of the roguish radiophonic impresario Harry Alan Towers was a highly successful series of Sherlock Holmes adaptations starring the patrician duo of Sir John Gielgud, as Holmes, and Sir Ralph Richardson, as Watson. For the last episode, 'The Final Problem', Towers asked Welles to appear as the dastardly Professor Moriarty, pushing Holmes over the Reichenbach Falls, which he did with commendable elegance and restraint. On the day of the recording he took the two knights out to lunch. 'Orson was so avuncular and shouted and laughed so loud the whole restaurant was staring at us,' recollected Gielgud. 'It was just like two little boys at Eton who had been taken out at half-term by their benevolent uncle.'[6]

★

During the period in which the *Sketch Book* was being transmitted, Welles rather suddenly married Paola Mori at the splendid Caxton Hall in the City of Westminster – not only the site of many glitzy show-business weddings, but also the starting place of one of the greatest of the suffragette protests. The spirit of Mrs Pankhurst seems not to have infected Paola. 'I will organise Mr Welles as soon as I marry him,' she told a reporter. 'We understand each other so well that if we go to a restaurant, we can sit and eat without uttering a word, perfectly happy.' Welles silent at the dinner table is a difficult image to conjure up. Welles, for his part, said: 'I take marriage seriously. I am sure I've found the right girl for me. She knows how to soften my rough edges, a gift more precious than gold.'

The wedding took place just two days after Welles's fortieth birthday; the two events may have been connected in his mind. The ceremony, which lasted all of twenty minutes, appears to have been somewhat precipitately arranged: Paola called Mr Prince, the registrar, at 7 a.m. on 8 May 1955 and asked if they could be married at 8.30. 'I changed out of my golfing clothes,' said the imperturbable Mr P, 'and back into my office dress. I was in Caxton Hall in time to greet the pair as they came up the back door.' Peter Brook and his wife, Natasha Parry, a close friend of Paola – she was staying with Natasha's parents – were up at the crack of dawn to witness the wedding; the earliness of the hour may have been not unconnected to the bride being some four months pregnant. Nonetheless there were two press photographers present, at whom Welles, twitching the collar of his brown tweed jacket, 'scowled happily'.[7]

There was no question of a honeymoon. At the time of the wedding Welles was in the midst of preparing for his stage version of *Moby-Dick*, a project that had been long brewing with him.

His first attempt at it had been in 1946, when he planned a version of the novel on disc, to be adapted by his chum Brainerd Duffield, with Charles Laughton as Captain Ahab; this never happened, but that same year Duffield readapted the material into a thirty-minute radio play for Welles's final American radio drama series, *Mercury Summer Theatre of the Air*. Welles played Ahab, blustering and roaring above the ocean to rather generalised effect. The performance (and indeed the broadcast) is all lungs and no heart, perhaps because even while recording the radio version he had started to conceive of a much more interesting way of doing it. He now saw it as an oratorio, as he put it, with a large chorus and orchestra, and singing and dancing. Shortly after the broadcast Duffield produced a remarkable outline of the show Welles had in mind, under the fanciful heading *Antepast* (= antipasto, a starter or taste-tickler).[8] The document is reminiscent, in its prancing erudition and cheeky showmanship, of the glory days of the research unit of the Mercury Theatre and its successor at RKO.

> Recognition and acceptance of the work of a great creator seldom come in his own generation and usually only after the passage of considerable time. Melville, the untimeliest of the American Titans, has only lately been properly appraised. A multiple personality, driven by neuroses to create works of libidinal intensity, he was inevitably rejected by the chill philistinism of his age. The novels of his maturity are grandly symbolical, allegorical, full of fantasies and abstractions. He enunciated Freudian truths in an era which made prudery a fetish. He renounced the sterile and spurious orthodoxies of Victorian tradition and entered a realm of the pure irrational. His theme, the apocalypse and doom of civilisation, was unwelcome and he lived and died a

magnificent failure.

Who exactly, one wonders, is speaking? And who, precisely, are we talking about?

The document discusses Captain Ahab, the figure by whom Welles had for so long been obsessed. 'He is of course the externalisation of Melville's own inner conflicts.' How one loves that 'of course'.

> He is one of the strongest images in all literature. His ego passes from the objective world into the unconscious and back to the outer world. He ranges from the narcissist reveries of twilight consciousness through physical activations of trag-melodrama [*sic*], arriving by spiritual transit at the eventual apotheosis. His quest is involved with the basic rhythms of the universe, the rhythms of life and death.

Not the sort of stuff that could be readily encompassed within a thirty-minute radio drama. 'Because of the novel's content, fraught as it is with intangibles, with non-literal sequences, any ordinary representational form is out of the question.' Welles – 'not the least energetic of Melville's admirers' – has imagined 'an oratorio production of real vitality and function'. The entire theatrical vocabulary, it seemed, would be deployed to give the work its fullest voice and expression. Melody, symphonic and choral, movement, dance-gesture, light and colour – all would blend in patterns to kindle the spectator's latent responses. 'Now, with the creative intelligence of Welles as producer and star, an original score especially composed by Bernard Herrmann, and words contrived from Melville by Brainerd Duffield, the project is a challenge of significant force and potentiality.' No kidding. It was nothing if not ambitious, a Wagnerian *Gesamtkunstwerk*, a Reinhardtian epic, a piece of total theatre, the Living Theatre's *Frankenstein avant la lettre*.

> *Twang of harpoon!*

says the script.

> AHAB: The jaw! The jaw! Oh!

> MEN: Cries of terror.

> *Music. Crunching as boat is splintered. Churning of water, tremendous shim-*

> *mering climax, diminishing into a series of harp glissandos, leaving gentle bubbling of water then deep rippling chorus suggesting the engulfed ship.*

There are Dances, there are Hymns, there are big formal groupings; the proposal even supplies a breakdown of musical leitmotiven (including one, piquantly enough, for *Rose-bud*, the fragrant ship which the *Pequod* at one point encounters).

It is perhaps unsurprising to find Welles in 1946, just on the point of creating his mega-vaudevillian Broadway musical *Around the World*, thinking of *Moby-Dick* in equally spectacular terms. However, the description of the stage itself – the *schema*, as the proposal, highfalutin to the last, insists – indicates a different kind of scenic vocabulary, one less immersive than suggestive:

> At center back, a bare-boned structure to represent the ship. Ladders lead to a railed deck. A bowsprit pointed toward the audience. A mast, ropes, and crow's-nest near the masthead. The stage is otherwise unfurnished. A long row of steps along the apron which will sometimes accommodate singers. An orchestra. A cyclorama.

In fact, apart from the last three items, the design as such is not a million miles away, in its essentials, from Welles's London *Moby-Dick* of eight years later, though that was performed not in the sort of epic space that the *Antepast* seems to envisage, but in a tiny West End theatre.

The show that the proposal describes had been commissioned by a formidable consortium consisting of the San Francisco Theatre Association, in conjunction with Alexander Korda, the Comédie-Française and the great London impresario C.B. Cochran, all of whom were poised to receive it at the end of 1947. Welles nonchalantly deferred it – on account, he said, of the large amount of rehearsal it would take – to April 1948 in London and the following month in Paris. This was the last that was heard of *Moby-Dick* until 1955, by which time Welles's thinking about it had undergone a 180-degree revolution.

CHAPTER NINE

Call Me Ishmael

IT IS not entirely clear when Welles came back to the idea of *Moby-Dick*. He may well have been prompted by John Huston's invitation to him in 1954 to play Father Mapple in his film of the novel. Huston had expressed an interest in Welles for the role of Ahab, the part for which nature seemed to have intended him, but the producers, the Mirisch brothers, were never going to approve of him, not least on commercial grounds; instead they imposed the clean-cut, chisel-jawed Gregory Peck on Huston. By way of consolation, Huston threw Welles the tasty morsel of Mapple, whose stupendous sermon on the subject of Jonah and the whale is one of the great set-pieces of the book. Huston and his screenwriter, Ray Bradbury, had failed to reduce the great sermon to a filmable length, so he asked Welles to undertake the job, which he did with his usual brilliant editorial instinct. He was booked for a single day at Shepperton Studios, for which, to the astonishment of the British press, he was paid a rumoured £2,000 ('I got more than £2,000,' he told the stunned *Press Conference* team, 'and I will take less'; in fact he was paid $10,000).

On the day of shooting, once he had struggled up to the top of his marine pulpit, Welles told Huston that he was as nervous as he'd ever been. 'Would you like to rehearse?' asked Huston. No, replied Welles, but could he have a drink? Huston provided a bottle of brandy 'for him to visit', and then they went for a take.[1] Welles was word-perfect and pitch-perfect. They did another take, for good luck, but it was the first that they used. The performance is one of Welles's most successful on film; Melville and Welles are as good a match as Whitman and Welles. He is somehow inside the rhetoric: his mastery of the phrasing is absolute and his vocal attack superb, triumphing over the cinematic inertness of the sequence as shot by Huston's cameraman, Oswald Morris. Welles's self-designed, highly sculpted make-up on this occasion works brilliantly too, the high brow, severe nose and out-jutting beard lending his features the quality of an engraving or a woodcut. In his performance one has a glimpse of the film of *Moby-Dick* that Welles might have made. 'Orson's performance was so nearly flawless', wrote Huston, 'as to make me optimistic about the rest of the shooting. I should not have been.'[2] The film, which took three years to make, was not a success at any level: artistic, critical or financial.

Welles's relationship with Huston was largely amicable, but inevitably complex. Every relationship with Welles was complex, but this one was especially so, because Welles had known and deeply loved Huston's father, the great actor Walter Huston – the father who had abandoned Huston at an early age; they later had a reconciliation, but Welles's almost filial devotion to Walter was a complication for Huston, Jr. He was nine years older than Welles, but their lives and careers were oddly parallel. Their first films appeared in the same year, 1942, but *The Maltese Falcon* and *Citizen Kane* had very different trajectories: *Kane* failing commercially and leading in short order to the demise of Welles's Hollywood career, *The Maltese Falcon* a commercial triumph, leading on to so many job offers for Huston that he never got round to making the planned sequel to the film.

Welles came to direct his only Hollywood box-office success, *The Stranger* (1945), because Huston stepped down to direct another movie. He liked and respected Huston, though he was not, in Welles's view, a specially gifted director; Huston saw Welles as a self-defeating genius. Both men were flamboyant hell-raisers, but Welles's was infinitely the more complex and contradictory personality. The strikingly parallel lines of their careers would from time to time converge, right to the very end, when Huston played a character very like Welles, in Welles's last, unfinished film.

Huston was pretty well fearless, but he would never have dreamed of trying to put *Moby-Dick* on stage. For Welles, it was a challenge he must face. The version he finally brought to fruition – *Moby-Dick Rehearsed* – is an exercise in pure theatre, celebrating the artifice and imaginative scope of the stage, presenting the piece as a rehearsal-room run-through of a dramatisation of the novel, given by an American nineteenth-century theatre company. It is by far his most successful attempt at playwriting, filled with the contradictions that make him such a distinctive figure. It is a bold and experimental approach to putting an epic novel on stage, which at the same time celebrates the vanished world of the old-time actor-manager; it is an attempt to address one of the densest, most resonant works in all of American literature, while striving to be thrillingly entertaining. It is breathtakingly spectacular, using the simplest of means; grittily realistic and a triumph of illusion.

The prologue to the play sets up the basic premise: an actor-manager, variously referred to as the Old Man and the Guv'nor, has decided to try out an adaptation of *Moby-Dick* written by his son, also an actor, who will play Ishmael. The acting company – who are playing *King Lear* by night – are far from enthusiastic about the play, which they have now been rehearsing for some time. There is much banter between the actors, especially about the young actor-adapter. 'The Guv'nor should never have allowed you to go to university. God deliver the theatre from educated actors!' Welles, of course, never went to university, and had all the autodidact's scorn for those who did. The theatre, he believed, was not about imparting knowledge or telling people what to do. 'My god, gentlemen, how would you like to listen to uplifting lectures from your cook?' cries the Guv'nor (Welles's part, needless to say). 'When it is theatre – the theatre is poetry. True, when we do chestnuts like *Spartacus* or *The Bells*, we don't speak it, but we try to make it. After all, that's our profession; one in which nothing is absolutely required except an actor – and of course he only needs an audience.' One of the younger actors chips in: 'and when the audience decides it doesn't need us – ' 'Boy, they NEVER need us,' roars the Guv'nor. 'Nobody ever needed the theatre, at all, except the people up on the stage. Did you ever hear of an unemployed audience?'

Having asserted his authority, he instructs the company to run through the show: no props, no costumes and no stopping, unless and until they break down. 'Or until our friends out there decide they've had enough. This time we're asking for quite a bit of extra co-operation from them,' he says, peering out into the auditorium. And then he makes a Shakespearean allusion, which tells us what he's up to: the novel may be Victorian, but the stagecraft is Elizabethan:

> Piece out our imperfections with your mind;
> Think – when we speak of whale-boats,
> whales and oceans,
> That you see them –

The actors rush about getting ready. 'What exactly do you want me to DO?' begs the most serious actor in the company. 'DO?' bellows the Guv'nor. 'Stand six feet away and do your damnedest!' The overhead work-light suddenly switches off; the actress plays 'hurry music' on the harmonium, there is a flurry of efficient chair-moving and other preparations; then – at a signal from the stage manager – the movement freezes and, after a short silence, the play begins. One of the actors plays a mouth-organ, and the stage manager reads out the stage directions.

> *Scene: the wharf in Nantucket, the whaling ship* Pequod *in the background. The owner, Mr Peleg, discovered. Enter to him Ishmael.*

The actors go about their work on a more or less bare stage, using whatever means come to hand, improvising costumes and props, piling boxes on top of each other, swinging on the ropes hanging from the flies; the framing device is discarded until the very last seconds of the show, and a straightforward, pithy, hard-driven digest of the novel plays out in two acts, the first culminating in the spotting of the whale, the second in Ahab's great cry, as he harpoons his quarry: 'Stern all! The white whale spouts thick blood!'

The dialogue is written in the sort of blank verse into which so much of Melville's prose naturally falls. The play hurtles along, the only serious pause being for Father Mapple's sermon, given in more or less the cut Welles made for Huston's film. The parts are evenly divided; it is, with the exception of Ahab and Starbuck, very much a company piece, requiring a flexible and versatile ensemble. It is Melville fast and furious, not Melville mystical or even especially metaphorical. Needless to say, the chapter-long meditations on whaling have gone, as has the homoerotic intensity of the relationship between Ishmael and Queequeg. Welles tilts the relationship between Ahab and Pip, the cabin boy, to give it overtones of King Lear and his fool, as a gesture, presumably, towards the idea of the company performing the two plays in tandem in repertory. In effect, it has become a play about the corrosive power of obsession. There is no room for the sort of Freudian resonances envisaged in the proposed oratorio version. As a text, it is above all concerned to offer opportunities to the actors – very much the sort of thing that the Mercury Theatre of old would have taken on with relish: a piece for performance.

The play reached the London stage via the good offices of the writer Wolf Mankowitz, whom Welles had met in Paris and with whom he instantly hit it off. Mankowitz was another of those modern Renaissance men to whom Welles was naturally drawn: born into poverty in the Jewish East End, he had gone on to Cambridge as a student of the formidable F.R. Leavis, became a world authority on Wedgwood china and proprietor of an exclusive porcelain shop in Piccadilly, all the while writing highly successful novels, plays and screenplays mostly based on his early years in the

East End; the year before *Moby-Dick*, Carol Reed directed *A Kid for Two Farthings*, adapted by Mankowitz from his own novel. He was witty, vivacious, erudite and deliberately provocative, and seems, until the Soviet invasion of Hungary, to have been a dedicated and recruiting member of the Communist Party; he ticked every one of Welles's boxes.

Their friendship was cemented one bibulous night in Paris when they ended up in the sumptuous apartment by the place de l'Opéra that Dolivet had hired for Welles during the editing of *Mr Arkadin*, and Mankowitz watched spellbound while Welles cut together the *Don Quixote* footage he had shot in the Bois de Boulogne. For a while Mankowitz took on himself – as so many had done, and would again give it – the task of giving Welles's career the push that he himself seemed unable or unwilling to do. They determined to work together: Mankowitz had a business partnership with the theatre manager Oscar Lewenstein, who not so very much later would be instrumental in creating the English Stage Company at the Royal Court Theatre, which would change the face of the British theatre. Mankowitz suggested that he, Lewenstein and Welles should stage a season of plays: an adaptation of *The Sun Also Rises* with Marlene Dietrich, a play of Mankowitz's for Welles and Akim Tamiroff, and *Moby-Dick*. And because Welles was yet again broke, Mankowitz suggested that he, Mankowitz, should serialise *Mr Arkadin*, not from the novel, but direct from the screenplay, for *Paris-Soir* and the London *Daily Express*, and did highly lucrative deals for both on Welles's behalf; after which he took the idea of *Orson Welles's Sketch Book* (a notion he claimed to have conceived)[3] to Huw Wheldon, who was only too delighted to work with his idol and even secured a substantial advance from the BBC, 'something they had never done before – or since'.

Mankowitz and Lewenstein were tyro producers with very little money. They soon shelved the more ambitious idea of a repertory season, settling for *Moby-Dick* alone. Welles suggested they team up with two American producers he knew, Henry M. Margolis, a theatre-loving industrialist and restaurant owner, and Martin Gabel, actor and producer, Cassius to Welles's Brutus at the Mercury Theatre nearly twenty years earlier; together Gabel and Margolis had had substantial successes on Broadway with *Tiger at the Gates* and *Reclining Figure*. *Moby-Dick* was costed at a modest £3,000, and they stumped up the entire sum, for which they also got the film and television rights; Welles had agreed to put in £1,000, but that never materialised.

The Duke of York's Theatre was free for the limited four weeks of the run; it suited Welles perfectly, with its capacity of 650 and a distinguished history, including the world premiere of *Peter Pan* and the production of David Belasco's *Madama Butterfly* that Puccini happened to see when he was looking for a new subject. If the production was successful, announced the publicity release, then later in the year a new repertory company headed by Orson Welles under the management of Wolf Mankowitz and Oscar Lewenstein would be created. 'Welles believes', the release continued, 'that by doing the plays with as little scenery as possible and actors doubling parts, it will be economically possible to produce more plays and not rely on the smash-hit.' In this he was a decade or two ahead of his time.[4]

Despite all this fanfare, Welles, ever resistant to being tied down, declined to sign his contract; Lewenstein refused to commit to the Duke of York's unless he did: '[Welles] said this showed no faith in him and I had to confess that I didn't have total faith.' Welles angrily made to sign the contract without reading it. Lewenstein insisted that he must; with bitter reluctance, Welles acceded. This strange and typical rite of passage over, casting went forward. Lewenstein knew the theatrical scene intimately and secured a remarkable group of actors for Welles, the cream of young British talent, all of whom went on to national (and in some cases international) fame: Patrick McGoohan, Gordon Jackson, Kenneth Williams, Wensley Pithey, Peter Sallis and – the only woman in the cast – Joan Plowright.

Welles had seen Plowright for the part of Bianca in *Othello* in 1951: 'When I'd finished,' she wrote to her parents, 'he walked slowly towards the stage and stopped and looked at me and said in a deep voice which shook the theatre, "Who are you, you're very good, who are you, what have you done?" Honestly, he did!'[5] Plowright was too young for Bianca, he said, but he promised to remember her; and, four years later, he did. In *Moby-Dick* she was cast as Miss Jenkins, the actress playing Cordelia who, in the play-within-the-play, takes the part of Pip, the *Pequod*'s black cabin boy – 'and if you could also play the harmonium,' Welles said to her, 'that would be helpful' – warning her that it would be like nothing she had ever done, or seen, before.[6]

Not everyone had such an agreeable experience. McGoohan, fresh from his acclaimed performance in the West End in *Serious Charge* at the Garrick Theatre, entered the auditorium:

> All lights were on the stage; the rest of the theatre was a black abyss with Welles out there, listening. I started to read and then I

heard two voices, Welles and somebody next to him discussing production costs. So I stopped and Welles immediately boomed out 'Why did you stop?' I said 'I thought you might want to listen to me.' Welles snapped, 'I can listen and talk at the same time. Keep reading.' It happened again. 'Mr Welles,' shouted McGoohan, throwing down his script, 'you can stuff *Moby-Dick*.' 'Mr McGoohan,' shouted back Welles, 'Will you play Starbuck?'

He had chosen his cast, as McGoohan said, 'from repertory and character actors. There were no "names" among us. We worked as a team, and Orson drove us to find the exact force of the play much as Captain Ahab drove his crew to find the white whale which had taken off his leg.'[7]

For his exercise in total theatre, Welles was surrounded by a gifted support team – a music director (Anthony Collins, famous for his score for *Tom Brown's Schooldays*, who had also, rather less brilliantly, composed the music for *Trent's Last Case*); a choreographer (William Chappell, the noted dancer, designer and director); and a lighting adviser – none other than Hilton Edwards, who performed his task for £75, yet more reparation for the *Othello* deficit. Welles himself was on £8 a week, plus £100 a day expenses, a staggering amount in 1955. This was doled out to him in cash by a hapless youth snatched from obscurity on the switchboard of the King's Theatre, Hammersmith, where rehearsals were being conducted. This young chap, Gareth Bogarde (Dirk's younger brother, as it happens), was quietly manning his phones when a roaring Welles strode into the theatre, demanded to be moved from his present hotel and then strode off. Immediate hubbub. Where should they put him?

'Gareth,' the company manager said, 'get him into an American hotel, he's an American.' So I got a taxi to Harry Meadow's Club where he was staying. I went there and I said, 'I've come to move Mr. Orson Welles's belongings.' And he said, 'It's about fucking time you did!' And he said, 'Are you paying?' And I said 'I don't know anything about money or bills or anything but I simply have to pack his clothes.' And he said, 'Yeah, well you'll find a lot to pack, sonny.' And then I was shown upstairs and he had got two suites and he used to move from one to another throughout the night. He couldn't sleep in one bed for very long so he'd then get up and walk about and then go into the other suite, which had a big adjoining doorway. And he'd lie all over the bed in there for a bit. And there were crumpled old underpants and

> socks and bits and pieces. And his passport was there. Everything was there. A huge trunk that was full of old 'Penguins' and penny dreadfuls. His life was there.[8]

Bogarde dutifully packed Welles's bags and transferred them to the Butler, an American hotel. On the strength of this triumph, he was appointed Welles's gopher. 'You'll have to look after this man,' Oscar Lewenstein said. 'He needs somebody to run errands. And he needs somebody to get him here to the theatre and get all the actors and artists and everybody together and he needs somebody to take him to bed and put him away at night because he gets out of hand. Do you want to do that?' And Bogarde said, 'Yeah, it sounds great!' Bogarde was soon disabused of that notion, on being instantly plunged into the chaos that was Welles's life. 'What should I get you, Mr Welles?' To which Welles would reply, 'Don't ask stupid questions, Mr Bogarde, Sir.' On discovering that he was Dirk's brother, Welles invariably referred to him as 'Mr Bogarde, Sir'.

His first task was to move Welles into a new hotel, where – Welles's reputation evidently preceding him – he was asked for a deposit. Bogarde approached Welles:

> I had to go to him in his room, and I was terrified of him. He was a very frightening man. And I said, 'The management wants some money, Mr. Welles, and I know you have what I gave you this morning . . . uh do you have any left?' And he said, 'No I don't have any money. You know I don't have any money.' He was very cross. And then he said, 'Take them my watch and find my things in my trunk. There's money in my trunk.' And so we went through all of his trunks and there was about five hundred quid from French banks and some German money and stuff. And I took handfuls of this foreign currency and went down to management and tightened my tie. 'I have some money from Mr. Welles,' I said. 'Take this in good faith.' I gave him the money and the watch. And they thought it was very strange. Obviously they were aware. Anyway, we moved him in and then he sent down for another bed. He broke the bed – the first night the bed was bust and I remember spending hours on the phone to The Dorchester and they eventually did a deal, and they sent him over a king-sized bed.[9]

Then there was the time Welles asked Bogarde to get him a flat, with one end of the apartment higher than the other to create a sort of stage. Bogarde went to Harrods and said, 'Mr Welles is looking for a flat.' And they said, 'We're very sorry, but we don't do business with Mr Orson Welles.' He hadn't paid any bills. On another occasion, the head waiter at the Caprice restaurant in St James's rang up and asked whether somebody could go up to Montpellier Place (where Welles and Paola had been staying the year before) and collect all the silver that belonged to the Caprice. Could Bogarde organise something like that? Welles had been ill, it transpired, and all his meals had been sent over on huge silver platters from the Caprice every day – lunch and dinner. Bogarde duly returned all the engraved silver platters. 'There was an enormous collection of them. The maître d' came out and said, "We've been waiting for these for months!"'

Most often Bogarde got it wrong. When Paola's mother came to stay, Welles told him to find a bigger room for him, and to get his mother-in-law a room in the hotel as well. 'And I said, "Well, I'll try and get you all on the same floor." And he looked absolutely enraged. "I don't want her anywhere near me! My God, don't put her on the same floor! Put her on the roof for Christ's sake!"' But Bogarde did finally get something right: Welles said, 'Marlene Dietrich is coming to London, Mr Bogarde, Sir, so you will send her flowers – roses.' Without hesitation, Bogarde went across to a flower shop and asked them, 'How many red roses do you have in this shop?'

> And the woman said, 'Enough, I'm sure.' And I said, 'Will you please send all of them to Miss Marlene Dietrich at the Dorchester Hotel.' So 80 dozen roses went and he was thrilled with that. He said, 'The roses were sensational, Mr Bogarde, Sir. You did a good job.' Which was the only bit of praise I ever got.

By now the play was about to open, and Bogarde's job was over. He never got paid. His salary was supposed to have come from Welles's daily £150, but that had always mysteriously disappeared by the end of the day. All through his time with Welles, Bogarde contrived to sit in on rehearsals and was constantly astounded at his tormentor's energy and brilliance with the actors. 'And it would go on and on and on. And he was wonderful – he was a wonderful director! That was entirely different. That's why he was worth working for.'

Rehearsals were long, arduous and chaotic. 'Some days,' wrote Joan Plowright, 'Orson would be in a thundering bad temper, changing scenes and dialogue all the time and working the actors into the night. Other days he would be chuckling and wreathed in cherubic smiles as some kind of order began to emerge. On yet other days he would suddenly abandon us altogether, being forced to dodge the attempts of exasperated creditors to have their writs served upon him.'[10] On one of these occasions, Mankowitz donned Welles's unmistakable black overcoat and fedora hat and led a process-server off the scent while Welles escaped out of the back door.[11] But sometimes he was absent just in order to be absent: 'he would be away doing something or other, you never knew quite what,' said Oscar Lewenstein. 'He's a very mysterious person and he intended to make a mystery of everything. He never told any one person everything that he was doing so you always had a feeling there were a whole number of other things going on . . . he seemed to have built up a great array of secret arrangements to highlight very little. You always had a terrible feeling that he was going to need to be in Barcelona the day we were opening and very often he was.'[12]

After each of these mysterious absences, Plowright says, Welles would be back, recharged, with huge hampers of food from Fortnum & Mason, 'chomp his way through two chickens, pâté de foie gras, quails' eggs and succulent pastries, and down a bottle or two of Chablis without a care in the world'.[13] The *Daily Mail* came to rehearsals one day and found a more abstemious Welles:

> Mr Welles was obviously going through a creative phase: he had run out of cigars (I counted nine stubs on his ashtray) and he was drinking endless supplies of black coffee from a green beaker. He hacked out stabs of dialogue and passed new lines round the players like slices of cake. All day he had been sending relays of new dialogue to a typing bureau. As I came away he had his scouts out looking for an actor who could climb ropes and play the mouth-organ.[14]

Morale was good during rehearsals: when he was in the vein, Welles could break the company up. When Gordon Jackson spoke his opening line on the stage for the first time – 'Call me Ishmael!' – Welles shouted back from the stalls, 'And if a man answers, hang up!' In his autobiography Kenneth Williams, a brilliant, bitter actor of sublime comic gifts, spoke warmly of working with Welles, who for his part said he couldn't rehearse with Williams because he made him laugh too much; finally they hired an extra rehearsal room so that the two of them could work together alone.[15] But in his posthumously published *Diaries*, Williams expressed himself with rancour: 'I wish to God I had never *seen* this rotten play, and Orson Welles and the whole filthy tribe of sycophantic bastards connected with this bogus rubbish . . . Orson Welles may be a brilliant "personality", but he knows nothing about producing a play. His *lack* of ability is bitterly apparent.'

He resents the entire team: 'The latest madness from the Welles–Chappell–Edwards trio is *rocking* the cast. We have to play all the scenes staggering at regular intervals to suggest the motion of a ship. The result is an effective impression of inebriation. Hours and hours are wasted on this kind of nonsense. Everyone is embarrassed by such stupidity.'[16] This of what was universally agreed to be the most effective moment in the production. As the saying goes: there's one in every company.

Until they left the King's Theatre in Hammersmith and started work at the Duke of York's, most rehearsals were conducted by Hilton Edwards and Billy Chappell, and involved the elaborate choreography simulating the movement of the boat that Kenneth Williams had so derided. The cast found this tedious to rehearse, although when they eventually discovered the effect it had on the audience, they were glad enough of the hard, painstaking slog they had put into mastering it. But when Welles was present, it was a different story. Surrounded by his young team, he clearly felt much more at ease than he had done with the rather starrier, West Endish cast of *Othello*, and without the unsettling figure of Laurence Olivier hovering in the wings. With his *Moby-Dick* gang there was never any doubt about who was in charge, but though he had a dozen different creative ideas a minute, recollected McGoohan, 'he wanted ours too. Anyone could make a suggestion, from the electrician to the leading actor. "Good! That's a better idea than mine. Come on, let's try it."'

When Welles was convinced of the rightness of a sequence, he would stop at nothing to make it work. One three-line sequence defeated them. They had begun rehearsals at ten that morning. By quarter to ten at night even Welles's devoted crew were near mutiny. They looked at each other and, by common unspoken consent, they all went across the road to the pub. Within minutes Welles was there, ordering drinks for them, 'and turning on such a force of personality that, actors as we were,' said McGoohan, 'we became a captive audience, helpless with laughter at his anecdotes and stories'. Then, without a word, he led them back 'like lambs' to the theatre, where they stayed till 5 a.m., working on the same three-line sequence.[17] This was the spirit of the Mercury reborn in St Martin's Lane. And Welles was really beginning to enjoy himself. Just before the opening, he told the London *Daily Telegraph* that he intended to make his headquarters in England and work, for the main part, in the theatre. With bigger and bigger screens, he says, the actor in films is dwarfed: he cannot compete with the Rocky Mountains. 'I feel that the day of the actor is returning. What I want more than anything is to run a repertory theatre.'[18]

As was his usual practice, Welles never played the part of Ahab during rehearsals, handing it over to his understudy; he only acted with the company in the opening sequence, in which he appeared as the Guv'nor, and for Father Mapple's speech, which he evidently enjoyed doing – and which he knew, which was not necessarily the case with Ahab's text, as became evident during the technical rehearsals. These rose to great heights of chaos, as Welles made the production on the hoof, enormously elaborating the supposedly simple ropes and blocks that the text called for, and demanding ever more, and ever more complex, lights, which Mankowitz had to comb London to find. In the end, all of this cost as much as (if not more than) a conventional realistic design might have done. In addition, Welles kept rearranging the sequence of scenes until no one knew what was going on, so that by the time of the first performance (no previews in 1955, of course) the adrenalin was positively nuclear, not least Welles's own.

A dauntingly brilliant audience was expected – among them Marlene Dietrich and the brilliant comedienne Judy Holliday, once the Mercury Theatre's switchboard operator. On that first night the company had rehearsed from 11 a.m. to 2 p.m.; it had a short break; then rehearsed again till six, with Welles constantly fine-tuning and indeed changing things; the curtain went up at seven. All his efforts were nearly undone by the cheery informality of working practices in the London theatre of the period. Just before the curtain went up, he received a brief visit from the theatre's follow-spot operator. That afternoon Welles had called a special rehearsal to take the man through the dozens of carefully orchestrated cues, each one laboriously repeated until he could fade out or bump up the light promptly and on cue. The man now dropped into the dressing room, shook Welles by the hand and said, 'Pleasure to have met you, Mr Welles. Tata for now. Not to worry – my mate Alf'll be on the light tonight.'[19]

The prologue went splendidly, especially the moment when, cloaked and fedora-hatted and sporting a fine aquiline nose, Welles made his mythic first entrance as the Guv'nor, in a brilliantly devised cue, suddenly appearing out of the darkness in a luminous cloud of cigar smoke. When the play proper began, the lighting operator – old Alf, presumably – got his cues out of synch. The ship's crew appeared thrillingly lit among the rigging, but after a moment the light suddenly disappeared, leaving the sailors shouting at each other in the dark, while on the lower deck a blinking Ahab and Pip the cabin boy sat brilliantly illuminated but mute. They swiftly launched into their scene, whereupon the lights immediately switched off them and onto the silent sailors, now crouching below, waiting to make their next entrance. Welles cut in half the scene with Pip, so that finally the lighting operator could catch up with himself.

Meanwhile, Welles's false nose began to part company with his real one; his attempts to return it to its moorings being increasingly unsuccessful, he ripped it off, hurling it to the floor, presenting the audience with the surprising spectacle of an Ahab who had undergone sudden cosmetic surgery. A further menace now declared itself in the form of Mrs Welles – Paola, Contessa di Girifalco – who had taken it upon herself to stand in the wings with the script and whenever (as quite often proved to be the case) Welles was unable to remember his next line, she would sing it out to him in a crystal-clear, Italian-accented voice audible on the other side of St Martin's Lane. This might have been helpful, but Welles was much given to significant pauses, which Mrs W interpreted as failures of memory. Eventually, in an aside, he despatched Pip the cabin boy to silence her.

None of this disturbed the audience in the least. They understood perfectly well, as Joan Plowright observed, that Captain Ahab was also the actor-manager directing what was a rehearsal; so, for all they knew, anything that happened could have been in the script. At the intermission, the crew created the whaling ship by setting a rostrum in the auditorium. 'Well-dressed spectators shrank in their seats from the proximity of burly perspiration,' wrote Kenneth Williams in *Just Williams*. One lady's box of chocolates got squashed on her lap, at which she protested loudly; and the spectators in the circle completely lost sight of the cast. 'They rose in their seats to extend their view, provoking cries of "Sit down!" from those seated behind. Orson, with his hand raised for the harpoon, was roaring "Shut up!" to the audience between his vengeful curses, and we eventually returned to the stage amidst considerable confusion.'

Nonetheless, the sea-chase went splendidly well, the climax riveting, the theatre in almost complete darkness except for a single light on Welles's face; at last, when the tension was all but unbearable, he launched the harpoon, but the rope attached to the harpoon somehow twined itself round Ahab's leg, dragging him into the water; down they went together, Ahab and the whale and the rest of the crew, leaving only Ishmael (Gordon Jackson) solemnly describing the scene as the lights gradually faded to black. After a long silent pause, the stage lights began to come up again, revealing Welles not as Ahab, but as the Guv'nor. Taking out a cigar and lighting it, he walked over to the prompt corner, picked up the script of the play, closed it and then, turning back to one of the stagehands, said, 'You can bring down the curtain.' Peter Sallis, playing the stage manager and a dozen other parts, remembered:

> 'As [the curtain] touches the floor the audience stand and they are shouting and they are clapping and they are cheering, our audience that Orson, by sheer willpower I would say, has won over. He's had a bit of help from others in the cast, of course, but it begins to dawn on us all that this is Orson's night. It's the first time we've actually seen him or heard him get it right and it's magical. We line up for our curtain call, and we're just in one line with Orson in the middle, and although we don't turn inwards, I think mentally we all do, we all bow invisibly to Orson. It is his night.'[20]

★

Moby-Dick took London by storm. In later life Welles thought it the best thing he had ever done in any medium; certainly he received the best reviews he had had since the early days at the Federal Theatre Project and the Mercury. Even the *New York Times* reported transatlantically: 'Welles *Moby-Dick* admired in London.'[21] Elizabeth Frank, one of the journalists who had cross-examined Welles with such amused condescension on *Press Conference* at the beginning of the year, rather finely said in the *News Chronicle*: 'As Captain Ahab, Welles has devoured the essence of the living theatre, the lustiness of the Elizabethans, and the fearless innocent eye of the barnstorming Victorians.'[22] There was a general sense that he had found a perfect vehicle for his ideas, and a subject that was big enough and rugged enough for his supercharged theatricality. 'It takes an Orson Welles', said the *Daily Mail*, 'to conjure a ferocious sea drama out of a background of clothes baskets, packing cases and scraps of irrelevant scenery and to send us away with the feeling that we, too, have been grappling for our lives with that whale.'[23]

The *Express*, mysteriously describing Welles as 'the laughing jumbo of Europe's gay spots', hailed the play – though its 'reckless melodrama' veered between 'the nonsensical and the flabbergasting' – 'the biggest theatrical thunder in years'.[24] Welles's own performance, despite his impressive voice and impressive face, was, *The Times* felt, inexpressive, nor did he truly dominate the scene;[25] Welles's fan T.C. Worsley of the *Financial Times*, hailing the production as 'the purest make-believe, the purest theatre, all embodied out of the imagination alone' and admiring the company, which acted 'with every muscle, and bring it triumphantly off', was also oddly disappointed by Welles himself.[26] In the circumstances, it is astonishing that Welles did as well as he did; even he admitted to Richard Watts Jr of the *New York Times*, after the performance, that 'he has been so busy with the other aspects of his Melville enterprise that he hasn't had a chance yet to work out his portrayal of Ahab completely. It is clear', continued Watts, 'that he is still feeling his way tentatively through the tumultuous role, and there are times when he is inclined to rumble ominously rather than act. But even now there are flashes of enormous power in his playing, and all the gusto that makes him a fascinating stage figure.'[27]

It is hard to imagine a more terrifying ordeal for an actor than to expose himself to a role like Othello or Ahab or Lear without being properly prepared for it. It is as if occupying himself with the needs of the physical production and his fellow-actors put off the moment of actually engaging with the awful demands of his own role, so that at the crunch point, all he could do was screw up his eyes and trust in God, like some mad bungee-jumper, but without a safety cord. This is not courage, it is not a challenge: it is fear and denial. The astonishing thing is that, with nothing but intelligence and personality and stamina, Welles was able to do it at all; and that sometimes, but not always, the excitement of the production was in some way enhanced by the extreme uncertainty of the leading actor. Not for everyone, however. 'The boy wonder pulled out all his theatrical tricks,' said Robert Otway in the *Sunday Graphic*, 'and only succeeded in proving that he was middle-aged. Yes, I was saddened by it all. Miserable, chiefly, at the sight of a one-man band who hasn't yet learned that it's better to play one instrument perfectly than to be competent at the lot . . . watch him closely for long and monotony creeps in. He isn't supple and he isn't expressive. The real trouble, I suppose,' he concluded, 'is simply this: Mr Welles hasn't the genius to control his own abilities.'[28]

On the other side of the Atlantic, the influential expatriate English critic Eric Bentley dismissed the show as an example of what he calls 'American style' productions: there are, he says, no flesh-and-blood people on stage, 'there is only a tormented

Caravaggist scene, of dangling ropes and shadows and sweat and staring eyes: toiling amateurism brought to a pitch of frenzy'.[29] That word again: amateurism. Nobody, favourable or unfavourable, seems to have got what Welles was after. Until the Sunday papers appeared.

The review Welles was most interested in – Tynan, now at the *Observer* – transcended all the others, good or bad. As if in recompense for his review of *Othello* ('CITIZEN COON'), the critic pulled out all the stops in celebration of the man who was once, and to some degree remained, his idol. Tynan began:

> At this stage of his career it is absurd to expect Orson Welles to attempt anything less than the impossible. It is all that is left to him. Mere possible things, like Proust or *War and Peace*, would confine him. He must choose *Moby-Dick*, a book whose setting is the open sea, whose hero is more mountain than man and more symbol than either, and whose villain is the supremely unstageable whale . . . yet out of all these impossibilities, Mr Welles has fashioned a piece of pure theatrical megalomania. A sustained assault on the senses which dwarfs anything London has seen since perhaps the Great Fire.

Then, in a comparison that would have deeply gratified Welles, he continued: 'It was exactly fifty years ago last Wednesday that Irving made his last appearance in London. I doubt if anyone since then has left his mark more indelibly on every second of a London production than Mr Welles has on this of *Moby-Dick*.' In another reference that would have pleased Welles enormously, he says, 'The technique with which Thornton Wilder evoked "Our Town" is used to evoke "Our Universe."'

Tynan focuses admiringly on Welles's use of sound – hardly surprising for the critic who noted of *Citizen Kane* that listening to the film with one's eyes shut is as rewarding an experience as watching it. But the review is not an unqualified panegyric. Tynan praises the other actors, but hesitates when he comes to Welles. 'In aspect, he is a Leviathan plus. He has a voice of bottled thunder, so deeply encasked that one thinks of those liquor advertisements which boast that not a drop is sold till it's seven years old' – a strangely prophetic line, foreseeing the Welles who, a quarter of a century later, would assure us that Paul Masson sold no wine before its time. 'The trouble is that everything he does is on such a vast scale that it quickly becomes monotonous. He is too big for the boots of any part. He reminds one of Macaulay's conversation, as Carlyle described it: "Very well for a while, but one wouldn't live under Niagara." Emotion of any kind he expresses by thrusting out his chin and knitting his eyebrows. Between these twin promontories there juts out a false and quite unnecessary nose.' Then Tynan makes one of the best jokes of his career: 'Sir Laurence Olivier began his film of *Hamlet* with the statement that it was "the tragedy of a man who could not make up his mind." At one point Mr Welles's new appendage started to leave its moorings, and *Moby-Dick* nearly became the tragedy of a man who could not make up his nose.' He concludes on an exhilaratingly positive, even crusading note:

> Earlier in the evening, as the actor-manager, he makes what seems to be a final statement on the relationship of actor to audience: 'Did you ever,' he says, 'hear of an unemployed audience?' It is a good line; but the truth is that British audiences have been unemployed far too long. If they wish to exert themselves, to have their minds set whirling and their eyes dazzling at sheer theatrical virtuosity, *Moby-Dick* is their opportunity. With it the theatre becomes once more a house of magic.[30]

Every word of this peroration would have been music to Welles's ears, especially, perhaps, the final phrase.

Many of those who saw the show agreed with Tynan's review. The young Peter Hall, already on the first rung of a career that would make him the dominant figure in the British theatre for twenty-five years, thought it the best production he had ever seen (he thought *Othello* the worst);[31] and the young designer Tony Walton, one of the great innovators of twentieth-century theatre design, saw the production over and over again. But these enthusiastic responses did not, alas, translate into ticket sales. The advance for the show had been poor, to begin with, and business built slowly; only the last few performances of the short run actually sold out, which is surprising: the small theatre held only 650 seats. The cognoscenti came, and pronounced the play thrilling; but, as with so many of Welles's films, the general public were not drawn to it. His celebrity, which was immense – he generated publicity just by walking into a room – was not of a kind that made people want to see his work; even his new television fame failed to boost sales. Despite the exhilaration of the production, its imagination and its physical commitment, to say nothing of Welles's charisma and towering presence, it was, at its heart, a deeply nostalgic event, a reinvention of the nineteenth-century theatre; and in England in 1955 a theatre revolution was drawing rapidly nearer.

Only a month after *Moby-Dick* closed, just 500 yards up the road, at the Arts Theatre, *Waiting for Godot* began its first English-language run, and the startled West End public was suddenly confronted with the avant-garde at its most uncompromising. The play opened to worse advances than those for *Moby-Dick*, and people walked out at every performance, but the play steadily gained ground, radically changing the idea of what might be expected from a play; it transferred to larger theatre and ran for six months. Meanwhile, Joan Littlewood, an earthily brilliant genius intent on destroying the bourgeois dominance of theatre, staged and appeared eponymously in the first British production of Brecht's *Mother Courage*, which took the theatre in another, more overtly political direction; and only a year later John Osborne's *Look Back in Anger* put recognisable contemporary young men and women on the stage. In this company, Welles's theatrical tour de force seemed rather pointless to the arbiters of taste, but equally failed to please the traditional West End audience, who expected sumptuous sets and glamorous stars. Despite its *hommage* to the theatrical past, *Moby-Dick* was in certain ways ahead of its time, notably in its Poor Theatre ethos – no props, no costumes, no sets – and in the emphasis on the ensemble. By the 1960s every regional theatre in Britain was doing productions in the style of *Moby-Dick* – they were, in fact, quite often doing *Moby-Dick* – partly for aesthetic reasons, partly out of economic ones and sometimes from political considerations. As so often, Welles was out of synch with his time.

As usual with him, he considered the show to be a permanent work-in-progress, and during its short run he continued shuffling scenes and rewriting to the last performance, more often than not without notifying anyone else. 'He would sometimes reel off a great speech that we had never heard before,' wrote Joan Plowright. 'Having worked on his adaptation for several years, there were obviously chunks of it that had not been included in the present version, and which he would revert to without any warning when the fancy took him.'[32] On one occasion Peter Sallis was standing in the semi-darkness with Wensley Pithey and Patrick McGoohan, waiting for Ahab:

> And then there emerged behind the packing cases, what at first looked like a white mop, and then it went on and it was obvious

> that there was going to be a face. There were two enormous great white eyebrows. There were two tiny holes where the eyes were, and then this white moustache and beard, which out father-christmased Father Christmas. It went down to his navel. Orson, for it was indeed he, said, 'There are whales hereabouts, I smell 'em. Look sharp for the whales, all of ya, and if ya see a white one, split ya lungs for 'im.' I had to say to McGoohan, 'What do you think of that, now, Mr Starbuck? Ain't there a small drop o' something queer about that, eh?' We managed to get through it, but it was a glorious moment.[33]

On another occasion Kenneth Williams, as the carpenter Elijah, had a long speech about carving Ahab a false leg made from ivory. Welles suddenly leaned over his kneeling figure and muttered, 'Get off.' 'I rose muttering a lame ad lib, "God bless you, Captain," and backed away into the wings with the scene unfinished.' Joan Plowright was waiting for her next scene:

> She rushed on saying her line, 'Oh Captain put thy hand in mine, the black and white together . . .' with such incoherent haste that Orson was quite taken aback, but Joan rattled on with the speed of a Gatling gun about white being black and black becoming white, till it sounded like a high-speed detergent commercial.

Afterwards Williams went to Welles's dressing room and asked why he had cut the dialogue so drastically. '"You bored me," he said shortly, and if there's a snappy answer to that I haven't found it.'[34]

But he was equally capable of sudden inspiration. On one occasion, says Plowright, he gave a magnificent performance, 'full of such passion and power and depth of sorrow that we actors were all mesmerized and felt we were in the presence of a wayward genius. He couldn't always do it like that; if he wasn't in the mood his wicked sense of mischief would reassert itself.'[35] He affected not to be distressed by the poor business, telling Plowright, 'there'll be the hits when everybody is excited about you, in parts you were born to play, and everyone loves you. The other times there will always be a percentage of the audience, perhaps very small, sometimes a bit bigger, who don't go for your chemistry. There's nothing to be done about that. But if they don't go for your chemistry, make sure they admire your skill.'

In truth, Welles harboured a deep conviction that 'the general public don't like me', as he had said to Gudrun Ure. There was a sense of loneliness about the man: Joan Plowright had a curiously touching vision of him one night after a show at the Duke of York's Theatre. Paola was kneeling on the floor with a basin of water, bathing his feet. 'He was gazing down at her with the grateful eyes of a small boy, when I stopped by to say goodnight. "Where are you going, Snooks?" he asked me. (He had christened me Snooks on the second day of rehearsal.)' If Plowright had known that this is what Welles and MacLiammóir had venomously dubbed Suzanne Cloutier on *Othello*, she might not have been quite so touched. 'It was perhaps the two bottles of wine under my arm that had prompted the question. I told him we were having a cheese-and-wine party in Kenneth's flat. "Why wasn't I invited?" he asked plaintively . . . he looked so vulnerable and deflated that I felt I could willingly have joined Paola on the floor and helped to bathe his swollen feet.'[36]

For the most part, though, he was glad to be part of the London theatre; a week after the opening of *Moby-Dick* he took part in *The Night of a Hundred Stars*, a midnight charity gala, in which, rather oddly, he acted with Richard Attenborough in a scene from Attenborough's recent hit film, *The Guinea Pig*. And Welles was seen in all the familiar actors' eating haunts, like Le Caprice, where one night he ran into the man who had launched him on his spectacular career in the Federal Theatre in 1936, but whom he now regarded as his mortal foe, John Houseman. They hugged each other as if there were nothing but love and good memories between them. Houseman told Welles how eager he was to see *Moby-Dick*, 'about which I had heard and read such good things'. He was not sure, he said, which night he was coming because he was waiting to hear from Stratford, where Laurence Olivier was playing *Macbeth*, 'to which it was virtually impossible to buy a ticket'. The glasses on the table suddenly leapt and crashed as a huge fist slammed onto the table. 'Orson was on his feet. His eyes were glazed and his face had the sweaty gray-whiteness of his great furies. Very quietly and intently, underlining each word as though addressing a child or a half-wit, he said, "*It is more difficult to get seats for* Moby-Dick *than it is for* Macbeth. For twenty years, you sonofabitch, you've been trying to humiliate and destroy me! You've never stopped, have you? And you're still at it!"' Houseman headed for the door, his wife on his arm. 'Behind us I could hear Orson howling . . . that I'd better not stick my filthy nose into his theatre; if I did he'd come down off the stage and personally throw me out!'

Houseman saw the show the following night. 'It had all the

excitement and magic that were Orson's special theatrical virtues.'[37] But he didn't go backstage afterwards. In fact, they didn't see or speak to each other again for another twenty-five years, and then only on television, sitting on a couch on a chat show, after which they shook hands and went their separate ways.

★

Someone else who never made it backstage after *Moby-Dick*, though not for want of trying, was Louis Dolivet, *Mr Arkadin*'s unhappy producer. His relationship with Welles, strained since Dolivet had required him to be absent from the editing suite in order to get a signed-off copy of the film, had broken down irretrievably. Welles refused point-blank to have anything to do with him. This may in some measure be connected with Paola Mori's open dislike of Dolivet, who had been uncomplimentary about her performance in the film, which now had a life of its own, quite separate from Welles.

The novel (written, as we know, by Maurice Bessy) had come out under Welles's name, and the film, in effect edited by Dolivet, had been signed up for distribution by Warner Bros, who requested a new title for it. Welles himself supplied it – *Confidential Report* – though one of the other titles by which he sometimes referred to it might have been a little more alluring: *Arkadin the Adventurer.* Dolivet, smarting from the financial losses he had incurred, formally proposed that Welles might like to assume full ownership of the film by paying back the cash investment and settling outstanding debts; unsurprisingly, Welles declined the offer. Still the *Arkadin* roadshow rolled on, like the film's pilotless plane: early in August a five-part serialisation of *Confidential Report*, allegedly specially written by Welles, but more probably by Mankowitz, appeared in the London *Daily Express.* It's scarcely more than a simple precis of the film, with little character or flavour. A few days later there was the gala world premiere in London of what Welles called the 'selling copy' of *Confidential Report*; Dolivet and Bob Arden were there, but Welles and Paola Mori (the film's leading lady, after all) were conspicuously absent. The reviewers were underwhelmed, but not unduly contemptuous: 'it is, *qua* plot, quite a good plot; it has a beginning, a middle and an end, though they don't come in that order, and plausibility is a word in some other language. But Welles is far too big,' said *Punch*. 'He bulges out of the interstices of the plot, he fills the auditorium . . . ah, well, it's certainly an exciting film to see, provided you don't let yourself get mad at it.'[38]

Welles also skipped the premiere of the Spanish version in Madrid, with the two rather disappointing Spanish actresses who replaced Flon and Paxinou as the Baroness and Sophie. He appears, in fact, to have given up on the film. He ignored the February 1956 re-edit, which cut the whole flashback structure; he did not show up at Cannes in April when this version was shown there.

But still the *Arkadin* machine ran on autonomously: in May 1956 the British *Argosy* magazine published a condensed version of the novelisation under the title *Dark Journey*: 'Welles's bow as a major novelist,' says the magazine. 'A new milestone in Mr Welles's contribution to entertainment.' And then eventually the novel itself came out in England and the US, translated – though this of course could not be acknowledged – by Robert Kee from a French version of a screenplay written in English. The novelisation is an anomaly: an improvement on the original – no masterpiece, to be sure, but consistent and engaging, and with a certain emotional force. But Welles disowned it utterly. *Mr Arkadin* and everything connected with it was a sham and a disaster, and Welles generally preferred not to think about it. 'My old dream of being able to make enough capital outside of America to pay my debts and get a fresh start before returning to residency there', he wrote to Dolivet, 'is completely shattered', a remark which, as François Thomas has pointed out, is a very clear indication that Welles was not in Europe from choice, leading the carefree life of an independent film-maker. No: his eye was very clearly on America – which to all intents and purposes still meant Hollywood – where he could make films to a standard that would satisfy him.

★

Welles's health was not good by 1955. His bulk was growing daily, with attendant ill-effects on his always troublesome joints and feet. During the rehearsal period Gareth Bogarde had arranged for a nurse to give him an injection every night 'to get the excess fluid out of his body', a somewhat doubtful prognosis; every morning, likewise, he had to be given another jab to get him on his feet. 'He'd be rolling about on this collapsing bed,' said Wolf Mankowitz, 'with a sort of evil-looking "dead" face, a nurse hovering around with a huge syringe to give him this huge injection.'[39] He took a wide range of medicaments – among them vitamin E- and B-complexes and cow urine – to counteract his many afflictions, which included severe asthma and frequent tonsillitis, neither of which would have been in any way assisted by his habit of puffing through a large box of Romeo y Julieta cigars every day.

His energy remained prodigious, renewed by occasional retreats to his bed – the real explanation of many of his mysterious absences. There he read, wrote, sketched, planned, staved off the world. Paola was his chief buffer against its depredations, but he needed a dedicated professional to organise him properly. Gareth Bogarde had been a stopgap who did his best; just before *Moby-Dick* opened, Oscar Lewenstein replaced him with a formidable woman who became, on and off, the lynchpin of his operation and, after his death, the fierce guardian of his reputation. Ann Rogers was nearly fifty, married with a young son; she had been born in America, then came to England, where she was brought up bilingually by her German stepfather. Before the war she ran her own translation agency in London, later monitoring the Italian Abyssinian invasion for the Foreign Office; afterwards she successfully set up the Promotion Department of the *Times Literary Supplement* and *Times Educational Supplement* and then joined forces with a leading theatrical publicity agency. And it was while she was working for this organisation that Oscar Lewenstein suggested she might like to help out with Welles. 'She was a sort of "body" that we introduced to stand between Orson and us,' said Wolf Mankowitz, 'to take some of the blows.'[40]

Their encounter is revealing, firstly of the effect Welles had on people, but secondly of his modus operandi at the beginning of a relationship. He would throw down a gauntlet to test a person's mettle, to try to ascertain whether he or she was worthy of his attention. Mrs Rogers met him at his hotel. He arrived *deus ex machina*. 'He came down in the lift, alone. I thought he was extraordinarily youthful looking and light on his feet. There's this big man easily moving out of the little lift to me who was waiting for him on a bench and he said "Are you Mrs Rogers? I like you". So I said "and I like you" which wasn't like me at all: I didn't usually show my hand so quickly. I loved the look of him. And he exuded . . . personality's the only word to use but a magnetism. I was attached to him from then on.' They took a taxi to the theatre; Welles asked her to get some copies of *Antony and Cleopatra*. When Mrs Rogers arrived at the theatre with them, Welles took her to his dressing room and told her that he was going to direct some half-hour television broadcasts of Shakespeare plays. Among the plays was *Antony and Cleopatra*. 'I want you to cut out all the dead wood,' he said, handing her a copy. And then, turning to leave, he said, 'end on an up note'. 'I thought, my God, who does he think I am?' recalled Mrs Rogers. 'But it was a test to see if he could faze me and to see how calm I would remain and I didn't react at all. I just said "yes".' The following day he brought her some tape recordings he'd made in Vienna; half of them were in German. 'And he said he didn't know how I'd manage about that, I'd have to get somebody to translate. I said "I can do that". He said "what?" I said "yes, I can do that" and I did. He would demand the impossible or ask you to get the impossible or to find the impossible and you did it. And I thought my poor old brain has never been so exercised before. Isn't this wonderful, aren't I lucky!'

He handed everything over to her:

> He would look in these great big trouser pockets and have a handful of notes and would give them to me and say 'get this, get that' and I realised that he'd been doing that with other people before and he must have been defrauded and robbed or deceived and that was when I made up my mind that there was only one way to deal with him and that's always to tell him the truth. Always to answer every question he asked me truthfully, which I did; sometimes about my husband and my family or about actors and actresses or what people had confided in me. It would be the truth without any opinion of mine and he knew that he could rely on me and be absolutely honest and then I could enjoy it and I did.

She made a number of very clear decisions at the beginning of their relationship, and abided by them to the end. She noted all outgoings and all money coming in and opened a Swiss bank account. 'I made up my mind that there's only one way to deal with him and that would be to be absolutely scrupulously honest and then I could sleep at night and I would have the advantage.' Welles somehow understood this: he later described Mrs Rogers as someone who had made a conscious decision to be good – that she was one of the few people on earth who strove to be good. 'I had to be. I don't know where I would have been if I hadn't been so straight.' Goodness was, of course, a central concern of Welles's, though his interest in evil may have had a slightly higher profile.

Mrs Rogers introduced a much sought-after element of structure and formality into a life that was largely without boundaries. 'I reckoned I would not call him Orson until he asked me to and so therefore I wouldn't ask him to call me anything else but Mrs Rogers. So Mrs Rogers it was.' As she acknowledged to herself, she adored him, but she scrupulously observed the proprieties; and so her relationship with Welles lasted to the end, and well beyond: to the day she died. 'In any other world I would, I suppose, and if I had been a different kind of person I could say I was in love with him, but I don't think I was.'

Welles was utterly intrigued by her self-containment. 'He just dug it up, my life. He would wander about in my bedroom when I wasn't looking; our bedroom, my husband's and my bedroom, taking in whether there were two single beds or a double bed.' He asked her for the keys to her house when they went on a winter holiday. She said, 'I'm sorry I can't leave the keys with you because the insurance won't permit it and my husband had said no, I mustn't do so.' To which Welles replied, 'I don't know how you ever came to marry that man. I think he's a horrible man and I'm surprised that you should pay so much attention. After everything I have done for him.' In fact it was Mrs Rogers who had made the decision about the house. 'He had one of his crews in my garden at five o'clock one morning with all the equipment and they left the front door wide open in Warwick Avenue and went off while we were still asleep in our beds and that's not good enough.' She was one of the few people who ever said no to Welles and survived to tell the tale.[41]

So, with the parameters of the relationship firmly established, she set to work. Her immediate task after he had opened in *Moby-Dick* was to facilitate the two very promising projects he had in hand, both for television: the film of the play; and *Around the World with Orson Welles*, the documentary travel series for Associated-Rediffusion, which would launch Independent Television Broadcasting in the United Kingdom. Television loomed large in Welles's life in 1955, or rather, it looked as if it would: the day *Moby-Dick* closed after its brief run, 9 July, the *New York Times* announced: 'WELLES TO STAGE TV COLOR SERIES'.[42] He would also, it reported, head all-star casts in CBS productions to begin in the autumn. 'CBS confirms that Welles is signed to direct and star in a series of elaborate color television shows based on contemporary or classical plays and novels.' *Antony and Cleopatra* was presumably to be one of the classical plays. But first up, the press release stated confidently, would be *Trilby*, with Welles as Svengali: back to the Higher Hokum again – nineteenth-century theatre at that, Welles's comfort zone. Theodore Sills would be in charge of the series, which Harry Saltzman (later to distribute *Chimes at Midnight*) would produce. Not another word was heard of this immensely promising project. It seems that Welles was flirting with television, still not entirely clear as to how to position himself in relation to it. It was still generally regarded as an inferior, second-rate medium and would for some years continue to be; movies were the only serious activity for a grown-up film-maker. Welles partly shared that view, and partly sensed huge potential. But for what? When he finally came to terms with the medium, it would be with all his old freshness and zest. In 1949 Dick Wilson had advised him to cut his teeth on English television.[43] Which, six years later, he did. Up to a point.

CHAPTER TEN

Around the World Again

AROUND THE *World with Orson Welles* was an inspired idea, or so it seemed. No one could have been better qualified to make such a series. Welles had already been *Around the World*, of course, once on stage and twice on radio, courtesy of Jules Verne. But in real life he was a born globetrotter: as a boy, he had very nearly put a girdle round the earth, as his alcoholic father's travelling companion and occasional carer: they crossed Europe, passing through France, Spain, Germany and Hungary, and going as far as China and Japan; he sent vivacious reports back to a Ravinia newspaper. Dick Welles died when Welles was fifteen; only a year later he made his own way to Ireland, ostensibly to paint, but actually in the hope of finding work as an actor. Only a year later, after a brief spell back in Chicago, he took off again, once more on his own, to Morocco, where – he claimed – he enjoyed the hospitality of the legendary tribal chieftain known as the Glaoui, moving on to Spain and ending up in Seville, where he said he fought bulls.

Welles's meteoric theatrical career then kept him in America till 1942, when, having made *Citizen Kane* and *The Magnificent Ambersons*, he spent some months of that fateful year in Brazil, shooting what was intended to be a contribution to the US government's South American wartime Good Neighborhood initiative. An insatiable xenophile, Welles had immediately fallen in love with the country and its history, shooting thousands and thousands of feet of film, covering the carnival in Rio and the poverty-stricken *favelas*, then moving to the sandy northern coastal city of Fortaleza. Welles was overwhelmed by the potential of the material he found all around him, and *It's All True*, the film he tried to make there, spiralled out of control; he came home under a cloud which never entirely dispersed. Five years later he moved to Europe, moving constantly between Italy, France, Spain and Germany, with extended visits to Britain. He was a citizen of the world as well as a film-maker of proven, if fitful, brilliance, and a series of travel documentaries written and directed by him is one of the best ideas British television ever had.

If the potential was limitless, the budget was not. The schedule proposed for *Around the World with Orson Welles* was very tight. The series would be co-produced by Filmorsa, because Welles, as we have seen, was under exclusive contract to them for three years. In the end it was Filmorsa and Dolivet (with whom Welles was scarcely on speaking terms) who put up most of the cash and took ultimate responsibility for delivering the films. Welles had a reasonable lead-time to prepare his thirteen half-hour documentaries, which were commissioned in January for transmission in September. He sketched out a number of fairly obvious initial possibilities: Rome, Paris, Madrid and (not taking his British audience very far round the world at all) London; Vienna, with its Harry Lime associations, chose itself. Welles quickly knocked off a few days' filming there in February 1955 for an episode that he called 'Revisiting Vienna'; it was the sound tapes from this that were the ones he handed to Ann Rogers at their first meeting.

Then, in mid-May, just after he had got married and just before rehearsals for *Moby-Dick* began, he embarked on something much more challenging: he had got wind of the retrial of a violently controversial case concerning a triple murder in rural France. In January 1953 the distinguished seventy-five-year-old British nutritionist Sir Jack Drummond, along with his wife Anne and his daughter Elizabeth, were camping in the hamlet of Lurs in south-eastern France when they were brutally murdered; a local farmer, Gaston Dominici, also seventy-five, confessed to the crime and was duly condemned to be guillotined. His story did not, however, add up in any way, and he later recanted his confession. A huge petition resulted in the reopening of the trial. The story had caused a particularly huge scandal in Britain: Jack Drummond was a very distinguished scientist, who had masterminded British nutritional policy during the war and was, at the time of his death, research director of that great national institution, Boots the Chemist. The subject was a perfect, sensational opening for Welles's series of travelogues for Independent Television, a bold statement that would instantly dispel any sense that these were going to be harmless home movies.

His arrival with his cameras at the scene of the inquiry stirred up the controversy all over again. Many local people, including the civic authorities, were critical of Welles's involvement, claiming that it would be prejudicial to a calm reconsideration of the events of two years earlier. Questions were asked in Parliament, there were critical newspaper articles and protests, and threats to refuse to allow any film that Welles shot to leave the country – all of which was of course grist to Welles's mill: 'he didn't give a shit,' reported his cameraman, admiringly.[1] His approach, he told *France-Soir*, was to allow each of the witnesses to reveal what they knew in turn, so that everyone watching would be able to form his or her own opinion, like the members of a jury in a murder trial. No wonder the authorities resented this subversion of due legal process. The latent demagogue in Welles was always lurking, ready to emerge at the slightest provocation.

He filmed in Lurs on 10–15 May, deploying two cameras: an Arriflex, noiseless, light and flexible – a news camera, in fact, but without sound – and a much heavier one, which shot synchronous sound. This was the first time this method had been used. For *The Dominici Affair*, unlike the other films in the series, Welles was striving above all for a sense of actuality, which the swiftly responsive Arriflex would allow him to create; he was especially keen to establish his presence on screen as a sort of impassioned bystander, asking all the questions, actually being on the spot. He encouraged his cameraman, Alain Pol, to put him in the frame, even if it was just an ear, a shoulder, the tip of his cigar, so that it was unquestionably Orson Welles conducting the investigation. 'I followed him,' said Pol, 'like a dog follows its master.' Pol was impressed by Welles's certainty about what he wanted, not only specifying the lens and the shot with great precision, but also being able to gauge the angle of a filter, not by looking through the camera, but by looking at the reflection on the lens. '"Too much sky", he'd say, and he was always right', which proved, Pol concluded, 'that he was not just a great director, but a great technician'.

Stylistically, Welles seems to have been interested above all in generating energy with the frequent use of whip-pans, and in the free hand-held feel of certain shots. He encouraged the *France-Soir* journalist Jacques Chapus, who had been obsessively covering the case from the beginning, to reconstruct the events leading up to the crime, and indeed to act out the crime itself, with great physical abandon, as the camera follows him wherever he goes. Give or take a few shots of the ravishing Hautes-Pyrénées landscape, Welles seemed uninterested in characteristic Wellesian framings or camera angles. 'Television is nothing more than illustrated radio,' he told *Cahiers du Cinéma*, still wrestling with the question of what the medium was. 'The word has primacy; the images are unimportant.'[2] This is another Welles, not Welles the artist: it is Welles the reporter, Welles the dramatiser of democracy, Welles the people's tribune. He enters into the role with relish.

After his allotted six days of shooting, Welles had gone back to

London to start rehearsals for *Moby-Dick*, leaving Pol, whom he trusted implicitly, to shoot any useful pickup shots that might occur to him. The play opened in mid-June, whereupon he turned his attention to further episodes in the series. He had asked his friend Lael Wertenbaker to write two episodes of *Around the World with Orson Welles* for him: one about women in Spain, the other about the French Basque country. She told him that she had never seen television, to which he replied: 'All the better.'[3] Predictably, Welles was more interested in the script about the Basque country – a culture and a cause upon which he now became a world authority overnight. He had a notion that the episode should be framed around him supposedly visiting the son of a friend – Wertenbaker's eleven-year-old, Chris, to be precise – who would be, in Wertenbaker's phrase, 'Orson's local host and sidekick and translator' (from Euskara, the local tongue). Wertenbaker was a distinguished American journalist who in a couple of years would become famous – notorious, even – for her memoir, *Death of a Man*, in which she described how she assisted her ailing husband Charles to end his life. Welles had met Charles in 1953, for an interview to which neither man had been looking forward, only to find that they were enchanted by one other; he had visited them frequently in the small fishing village of Ciboure where they lived, near the Spanish border on the Basque coast of France.

Endless telegrams and letters flew back and forth between them during the run of *Moby-Dick*; the moment the show closed, Welles arrived in Ciboure with two cameramen and a sound truck, approved the script and nominated Wertenbaker as his assistant director, and little Chris as his talent scout. They shot scenes for a day and a half, then Welles abruptly announced he was leaving to join Paola in Italy: they were, he said, to 'get on with it'. Fortunately the technicians he had brought with him were top-flight. 'I knew what I wanted,' Wertenbaker wrote, 'they knew how to get it.' After ten days, Welles suddenly appeared in Bordeaux for a day. Wertenbaker sent a chauffeur-driven car to pick him up and take him to a location in the interior of the Basque country. He was in grumpy form – tired, he said, of speaking French; he did not, moreover, like the chauffeur. He would ride instead in her tiny Hillman Minx, which she would drive. Knowing that they were well over budget, Wertenbaker proposed dismissing the other car. No, Welles said, he might need it. 'So an empty limousine was tooled up and down the narrow mountain roads and into remote villages and back all that long day.'

They got most of what they needed that day, with Welles scowling and growling at everyone; the remainder of the pickups – Welles's side of the interviews with other people and his conversations with Chris – were shot outside Paris a little later, in Alain Pol's garden on the Seine, where they found neutral backgrounds to match the Basque settings of the original encounters. The material was good enough, Welles decided, to justify two episodes, which it certainly did. In these episodes there is no question of the kind of *verité* reportage that characterised *The Dominici Affair*; here he rejoiced in his more usual artifice, in visual prestidigitation. When he and Chris were purportedly watching *pelota* in Ciboure, they were in fact – hey presto! – in Paris, with Welles's driver and Wertenbaker pitching a ball at each other off screen to provide them with eye-lines; the fandango Welles and Chris were supposedly watching was hilariously rendered off screen by Wertenbaker, which amused and relaxed both Welles and his youthful *cicerone*: 'Orson at his most charming,' wrote Wertenbaker, 'with a wholly natural eleven-year-old boy.' Then, in a studio outside Paris, she watched, astonished, as Welles cut the Basque footage they had shot – 'thousands of strips hanging from pegs' – into a seamless and authentic-seeming programme. This was Welles in his element. 'His visual memory was astounding,' she wrote. Even the hard-bitten and resentful technicians, who had not yet been paid – they never would be, as it happens – applauded as he performed his marvels. By August the two Basque episodes were as near as dammit complete.

But time was running out. Transmission date for the first episode was 22 September. Welles zipped over to Paris to shoot some eccentrics, including Isadora Duncan's brother in a toga; he went to Spain and shot a bullfight; he went down to that grand old music hall, the Hackney Empire in the east of London, and talked to the local housewives; he went to the Royal Hospital in Chelsea to talk to some Chelsea Pensioners (the octogenarian and nonagenarian retired soldiers seemed not to have the slightest idea who he was). In these episodes, or potential episodes, he did not appear in most of the shots himself, but spoke from behind the camera, so from time to time he would make his way back to Alain Pol's garden on the Seine and shoot large numbers of drop-in linking sequences, improvising all-purpose lighting effects that suited quite different episodes equally well – flickering lights on his face stood in for reactions both to fireworks in Saint-Germain-des-Prés and candlelit processions in the Basque country.

From August to September, Welles edited round the clock, mostly in Paris. Alain Pol noted, awed, that he worked from 6 p.m. to noon, fuelled only by Scotch whisky. From time to time he would get up to use the toilet; occasionally he'd smoke a cigar. Otherwise he cut through the night and into the following day. The technicians were baffled by what he was doing with the film; it didn't seem to make any sense. Finally he would show it to them. 'Well?' he'd say. 'And it was marvellous,' said Pol. 'Alas, he didn't always do the editing.' Sometimes it was one of the journeymen studio cutters. Or Dolivet – officially the producer, answerable directly to Rediffusion – would demand a change, and on those occasions, said Pol, Welles would go into a black rage. He was always willing to accept suggestions from below, but never from above, and, to his inexpressible chagrin, once again somebody else was in charge.

Now panic was in the air. Despite his Herculean editing stints, he had run out of time. *The Dominici Affair*, which was always to have been the first programme, was close to completion, but at the last moment the French government, as they had threatened they would, stopped it from leaving the country, 'until it had been submitted to the official committee for the control of films', stated the Minister of Industry and Commerce, 'and approved by them'. Welles went public, claiming he had been accused of corrupting witnesses. 'Nonsense. The trial has been over for months. I have a right to use a movie camera as surely as a journalist uses his typewriter.' According to Lael Wertenbaker, Welles secreted a copy of the film in his luggage and headed for London, but Rediffusion's lawyers refused to let the company so much as touch the illegal film; this received widespread publicity, but the impasse was total, and *The Dominici Affair* sat in its sealed cans until, more than forty years later, the documentary director Christophe Cognet put together everything that could be found, along with interviews with many of the participants. It is deeply ironic that Welles's career as a television director should start with the impoundment of his first film.

In the absence of the first episode, Rediffusion had to withdraw *Around the World with Orson Welles* from its glittering launch, promising that it would start soon. The nation was now waiting with bated breath. Welles called Wertenbaker in Paris to tell her that she had seventy-two hours to complete editing the first Basque episode, which she would then have to fly over with personally, in time for transmission. He told her he would pretend to be in Paris, but would in fact be hiding out in London, because if he came over and worked on the film himself he would never finish it. 'Know thyself!' remarks Wertenbaker, who, with her three cutting-room technicians, worked straight through those seventy-two hours, whereupon the boss of the LTC studio where they had done the round-the-clock editing refused to release the film and soundtrack until Welles paid the 7 million francs he owed them. Wertenbaker argued that if Welles's Rediffusion contract was broken, they would never get a franc. 'They had only one chance (slim, as we all knew) to collect, and that was to release this film.' Which they did, barely in time for her to make the last possible plane to London. Needless to say, no one was ever paid – not the studios, not the technicians, and of course not Wertenbaker.

It was under those perfectly Wellesian circumstances that *Around the World with Orson Welles* made its appearance on 7 October 1955 with 'Pays Basque I (The Basque Countries)'. The programme was well liked, as was its sequel, and indeed the series in general and Welles in particular. Neither the audience nor the television commentators were to know that well over half the episodes had been cobbled together by Louis Dolivet and various editors from the bits and pieces Welles had shot; that half of the footage was from stock; and that when Welles was on screen he was rarely where he purported to be. The two Basque films are the nearest to what he originally had in mind, and they have charm, imagination and a certain passionate dignity. In fact, in the Basque region itself the films have become – to deploy a tiresomely overused word – almost literally iconic, as both celebration and rallying point. The remaining four episodes (all he ever completed) have less to recommend them, despite the engaging quirkiness of the oddball characters Welles chose to interview in Saint-Germain-des-Prés, the grave charm of his faintly surreal conversations with the old soldiers in Chelsea, the chirpiness and honesty of the housewives in Hackney, and the drama he conjures out of an empty *corrida* in Madrid. They are for the most part scrappy, clumsy and a bit flat-footed, though Welles himself, bashful and confiding, always charms, almost as if he were sharing with the viewer a private joke at the manifest imperfections of the programmes.

'Madrid Bullfight', the third in the series, is something else. It caused a sensation, not because of Welles's opinions or indeed his approach, but simply because of the subject matter. The fact that half the programme (to the intense annoyance of Rediffusion) consisted of a commentary by Kenneth Tynan and his then-wife Elaine Dundy – also passionate aficionados of bullfighting – only stoked the flames: Tynan and controversy were old bedfellows; his book *Bull Fever* had just come out, to roars of disapproval from some quarters. The moment Welles's programme was announced, in fact, the Animal Defence League was up on its hind legs to protest, threatening writs. The board of directors of Associated-Rediffusion was convened, to see what was being spoken of as 'the most controversial programme ever'. Small cuts were promised and the programme was preceded by a statement saying, 'if any of you have very strong prejudices against this contest between man and beast and feel that the spectacle may be unnerving to you, we are giving you this warning. But we hope you will stay with us.'[4] Welles's old gift for spooking the public had not deserted him. The programme is a remarkable document in many ways. The Tynans, who open and close it, give a brisk account of the training of the bulls and the rituals of the *corrida*, striking a curious tone, enthusiastically confronting the reality of a bullfight head-on. 'Twenty-three thousand people are going to see a cruel spectacle, but not for a cruel reason.' Ingeniously concealing his severe stutter, Tynan talks about the death of the bull and the danger to the matadors with the blithe heartlessness of a precocious adolescent, celebrating the 'sparkle and gaiety of the crowd'; Dundy describes the mules as 'the undertakers of the bullfight, carrying away the dead bulls'. They are shocked and excited when Manolo Vázquez, the young matador, is gored by a bull that is then immediately killed.

To twenty-first-century sensibilities, this is upsetting, but infinitely more disturbing is Welles's contribution. He is seen taking his place in the packed *corrida*, and he delivers his commentary supposedly from among the crowd, but in fact in pickup shots in which his face is framed by the ropes demarcating the rows of seats, and a few extras behind him; he brilliantly conveys the impression that he is delivering his reflections while watching the fight itself. Occasionally he turns to look into the camera, sharing his thoughts with us with startling directness. And, as always, he is utterly indifferent to trivial matters like continuity: when he apparently turns round in his seat to buy a flower, he is wearing a different suit, a different bow tie and a different haircut. His commentary is a mine of information, encyclopaedic in his knowledge of the sport, its history and its significance, and seamlessly eloquent, which is all the more remarkable for clearly having been improvised. His tone is one of flattering intimacy – 'you know all this old stuff,' he seems to be saying, 'I'm just reminding you of it' – but he endows it with the particular colour he brought to Harry Lime in *The Third Man*: an odd smiling ruefulness, a tender melancholy in the face of the awful reality of human life.

He describes the bullfight as a tragedy in three acts, invariably referring to the matador as 'the killer of bulls'; recounting the history of modern bullfighting, he tells us of an innovation that made it possible to kill a bull face-to-face – 'as you will see', he tells us solemnly. Watching it is like sharing a box at the bullfight with Harry Lime, feeling oneself gently but inexorably infected by his diabolical world-view. When Tynan speaks of cruelty, he is self-consciously cynical and wilfully daring; but Welles really chills the blood. Both are playing themselves, of course, but Welles's is a profound assumption, Tynan's a posture. 'Perhaps,' says Dundy, at the end of the programme, 'we've given you some idea of what it is that makes people like Orson and ourselves go to the bullfight when we're in Spain.' 'It's a fever,' says Tynan, nicely plugging his book, 'and as far as anyone knows, it's incurable.' Dundy laughs merrily. Reviewing the programme, the *Daily Telegraph* thought that 'thousands must have been sickened' by the 'barbaric spectacle'. The Tynans and Welles, 'though not exactly gloating over the performance, created the impression that bullfighting was a commendable affair'. Particularly offensive, thought the *Telegraph*, was the insertion of an advertisement halfway through 'suggesting brightly that everyone would be having a wonderful time, and would enjoy a glass of wine just as much as this programme'.[5] Welcome, Britain, to commercial television.

Welles, as it happens, was not around to comment on the furore; he had done a runner, slipping out of the country in mid-October, leaving behind him no forwarding address, and only three more episodes. Dolivet, raging impotently, had taken to communicating through his accountant, who passed on the message that Welles must complete the series as per the contract or buy Dolivet out of his Filmorsa contract. Response came there none.

'Revisiting Vienna', the final programme (the sixth of the announced thirteen), was transmitted in December. It is a shoddy piece of work, shamelessly trading on Welles's *Third Man* connection, opening and closing with Anton Karas playing the zither in the *Stube* he had bought on his profits from the film, with a dreadful daub of the stubbled Harry Lime fleeing the cops on the wall behind him. Then Welles freely associates, to no discernible purpose, in front of first the newly rebuilt Wiener Staatsoper, then the Hotel Sacher, at which point the true theme of the episode emerges – cakes, at every mention of which (and there are many) Welles's eyes fill with yearning. The scenes in the kitchen of the Café Demel are semi-pornographic, Welles drooling over the rows and rows of glistening newly made *Torten*. He interviews the septuagenarian *patronne*, and here the dialogue becomes really steamy. Like someone at an Alcoholics Anonymous meeting – 'my name is Orson Welles and I'm a cakeaholic' – he confesses that 'if there was any hope for my figure I said good-bye to it in Demel's'. It's a feeble, if pawkily charming end to a series that offered Welles remarkable opportunities, but with which he quickly grew impatient. *The Dominici Affair* and the two Basque films are genuinely interesting experiments in very different genres, which point to real possibilities that he chose not to explore. Instead he retreated, as so often in his life, to the theatre, back to New York, his first theatrical stamping ground, the scene of his earliest and in some ways his greatest triumphs.

He left behind him the torso of his third British television venture of 1955, *Moby-Dick: The Movie*, on which, astonishingly, he was engaged at the same time as trying to throw together *Around the World with Orson Welles*. Filming the Melville book was part of the deal he had made with Henry Margolis and Martin Gabel in order to get the play on at the Duke of York's. It would be the opposite of Huston's pulverisingly literal version (then still unreleased), and would reproduce something of the physical intensity and abrupt cuts that had made the stage show so startling – like reading Melville by lightning. Most of the shooting took place over the space of a week at the old Scala Theatre in Fitzrovia and at the Hackney Empire (featured by Welles in his London episode of *Around the World with Orson Welles*, no doubt in a break from filming *Moby-Dick*) and featured most of the original cast, including Kenneth Williams, whose entry in his diary for the last night of the stage show was entirely consistent: 'Last 2 shows of this ghastly play. Party after, onstage. Awfully drear.'[6] A week later, he and his fellow-actors were in front of the cameras, without Joan Plowright (Welles cast a young black lad in the part) and with Christopher Lee, still on the bottom rung of his profession, as a new recruit. Welles seems to have had no clear plan for shooting. 'Action,' Lee overheard him say to the cameraman, who replied, 'Mr Welles, I haven't got a set-up yet.'[7] 'Find one and surprise me,' snapped Welles. He was as responsive as ever to the inspiration of the moment. At the Empire one day, a maintenance man opened the sun-light at the top of the building. 'The effect was startling,' wrote Peter Sallis:

> It was Wagnerian. This great shaft of incandescent light shining down from this circular hole in the roof on to the stalls below. It was as if somebody had turned a searchlight on its head. Orson stopped. He stopped everybody, and without issuing any instruc-

> tions or any particular note, he started to go round grabbing up wooden chairs and tables and things, and placing them in the centre of this beam of light, right over the stalls. It was clear what he was up to, and we all helped him and finally built this kind of trestle table, and then he got Gordon Jackson and me to go through both our parts in this shaft of light.[8]

Welles shot a great deal very quickly, but nothing on himself. At the end of the week's shooting he gave himself over to *Around the World with Orson Welles*, though sometimes he managed to combine the two projects. Patrick McGoohan was sent to complete a sequence for *Moby-Dick* and came across Welles in the studio surrounded by models, 'little bits of Paris and Madrid and Barcelona', according to Peter Sallis, against which he filmed his pieces to camera.

This too was abandoned when Welles returned to America in October 1955. The footage went missing almost immediately, though there are persistent rumours of sightings. It represents another path not followed by Welles: the reimagining of a stage show in film terms, much more radical than the attempt he made in *Macbeth*, where the film was shot under strict studio conditions and its physical realisation was utterly different from the stage production. With *Moby-Dick* it seems that, in an attempt to convey the physical excitement of the show, Welles intended to push his improvisational approach even further than he had on *Around the World with Orson Welles.* He came back to the material – to Melville's novel, at any rate – twenty-five years later when he shot a number of sequences, including Father Mapple's sermon. That attempt too was abandoned; his confrontation with the great white whale never found celluloid form. For the time being, he went back to another of his lifelong obsessions, *King Lear*, a play which embodied in particularly stark form many of the ideas that preoccupied him throughout his life: the corrosiveness of power, the death of innocence, the fragility of hope, the reality of evil. The truncated television version had been a huge success for him; now he wanted to crown that with the play in the theatre. As an actor, he felt that it was a role he had to undertake, and on stage – the role of roles, the one he was born to play, the one with which he most identified. By pleasing (or perhaps ominous) coincidence, his new young wife was just about to give birth to a baby girl, making him, like Lear, a father to three daughters.

CHAPTER ELEVEN

The Schizo King

WELLES HAD been very eager for the baby (named Beatrice, after Welles's mother) to be born on American soil, which she was, on 13 November 1955, and was thus, as he had intended, a fully fledged American citizen. This may have betokened a genuine nostalgia for his homeland; Europe had been proving increasingly frustrating and he seemed to be pursuing a sort of scorched-earth policy there, burning bridges behind him with reckless abandon.

His return home had been provoked by an offer from the dynamic Jean Dalrymple of New York's City Center, a public theatre which had since 1943 pursued its mission – very much in the spirit of the old Federal Theatre Project – of bringing the best in the performing arts to the people at reasonable prices. Welles had supported it in the past, taking part in galas and fund-raisers for it, and so when, in early 1955, it found itself in one of its regular financial crises, Dalrymple took herself off to Europe to persuade Welles to stage *Moby-Dick Rehearsed* there – a rather brilliant idea: the huge flamboyant auditorium would have been a ideal setting for Welles's dazzling experiment in physical theatre. To make the offer more attractive, Dalrymple proposed that he should do the show in repertory with *King Lear*, the play, after all, that the *Moby-Dick* company was supposedly touring. But Gabel and Margolis didn't want to do *Moby-Dick* at the City Center, they wanted to do it on Broadway. Instead, though José Ferrer had done a slapstick version of the play at the City Center a few years earlier, Welles proposed to do Ben Jonson's *Volpone* in tandem with *Lear.* Fourteen *Lear* copies of each play were duly sent out from London to New York. *Twelfth Night* seems to have been in the air too. Another play that occurs frequently in Ann Rogers's memos about the City Center season is *The Cherry Orchard* – an astonishing thought, though what is *The Magnificent Ambersons* but American Chekhov? All Welles's talk about wanting to start a theatre company had been deeply sincere, although England was clearly no longer the chosen location for it: the

London season, with Dietrich in *The Sun Also Rises* and a play by Wolf Mankowitz, had gently faded away.

Henry Margolis, despite having lost his investment on *Moby-Dick* and not even having a film to show for it at the end, as promised in the contract, continued to indulge his romance with the theatre by investing in the proposed season. Perhaps a little perversely, considering that this was his comeback to the American stage, Welles planned to surround himself with a largely British company. While he was shooting *Around the World with Orson Welles* and the *Moby-Dick* film he had gathered together a cast of good young actors – Sheila Burrell, Jack May, Edgar Wreford, Hazel Penwarden and (the most interesting of them all) Donald Pleasence, who was slated to play the Fool in *Lear* – but he neglected to make any arrangements for their American work permits. Once Welles had returned to America, Mrs Rogers negotiated a volley of rapidly crossing transatlantic telegrams, silograms and cables, trying to establish the actors' legal right to work on the New York stage. Welles had also asked his recent Starbuck, Patrick McGoohan, and the London-based Canadian actor John Colicos to join the company. They were constantly being put on red alert, then stood down, with Welles becoming more and more impatient and the actors more and more frustrated. 'I refuse to be a puppet, to be hung up by a string,' McGoohan furiously told Ann Rogers, 'and, when I am wanted, to be dusted off and used, even if I am only an actor.'[1] In the event, neither he nor any of the other British actors made the transatlantic journey; at the end of November the US immigration office refused them visas on the grounds that they fell short of being 'of distinguished merit and ability',[2] which was a little humiliating for them and, indeed, for the actors by whom they were eventually replaced, who now knew that they were certainly not first choice. So Welles's bold new venture was mired in controversy from the start, with vigorous protests from the indigenous acting community, who were unimpressed by his argument that 'I wanted to prime the pump with actors who had been doing Shakespeare for years.'[3]

Even without that unfortunate start, his return to the New York stage after a nine-year absence – though unquestionably Big News – was scarcely the Return of the Prodigal. He, and everyone else, was very much aware that he was on probation. The influential critic Walter Kerr, writing in *Theatre Arts* in 1952, while Welles was in Europe, had set the tone in a savage and widely read piece headed 'Wonder Boy Welles', which summed up what many people in America thought about him: 'Orson Welles once made a picture

– *The Magnificent Ambersons* – about a boy who got his comeuppance,' wrote Kerr. 'Mr Welles's own comeuppance is now a matter of record.'[4] At thirty-six, Welles had been through at least three careers, he said: spectacular success in theatre, in radio and in films.

> 'Of each spectacular success he has made an equally spectacular mess. His fourth career – that of international joke, and possibly the youngest living has-been – has occupied him for the past five or six years, and threatens to become the only one by which he will be remembered and dismissed.' He also seems to have fallen into the unattractive habit of explaining to the press, in pained tones, that a good many of these debacles were caused by mechanical breakdowns, hostile environment factors, evil spirits, or just about anything except his inability to assay, and make judicious use of, his own personal equipment . . . even those of us who do remember the good, the promising, the exciting things about Orson Welles are not much inclined to say so any more. We have a feeling that our earlier enthusiasm may not have been justified, that we may have been taken in.

Welles was not without talent, Kerr concedes, as director, producer and scenarist:

> In fact, the only thing that was ever seriously wrong with Orson Welles was his unfortunate notion that he was an actor. Everybody's talent stops some place, and Welles's covers a lot of ground before it gets winded. But it does stop. It stops somewhere just short of the footlights.

If Welles were willing to throw in the towel as an actor, Kerr concludes, 'it's my guess that he could find plenty of work to occupy him in the American theatre. There is some possibility that he will return to this country soon . . . and it will be nice to see him back, provided,' he viciously concludes, 'we don't have to see him.'

The publicity that greeted Welles's return, four years after Kerr's hatchet job, was immense, but scarcely bedecked with bunting. 'WELLES IS BACK IN FULL CRISIS', cried the *New York Herald Tribune*. 'Orson Welles is jittering from one end of his vast bulk to the other because he opens on Thursday at the City Center.'[5] Welles was ready to come back to New York, reported Don Ross, to establish a repertory theatre like his old Mercury Theatre, 'which flourished here in 1937 and 1938 and greatly added to the joy of life'. But, asks Ross bluntly, 'does New

York want Mr Welles to return?' Welles's company, he said, would do plays by the Greeks, Shakespeare, Molière, the dramatists of the Restoration and the nineteenth century, plus 'some new plays by people like Christopher Fry and T.S. Eliot'. It would be theatre of poetry, Welles said, instead of prose. 'In New York there is the theatre of prose and music, but the theatre of poetry is incidental and accidental, rather than being a part of the city's life.' It would be non-profit-making, absorbing part of the Broadway theatre and the best of the people working in the off-Broadway theatre. Who would pay for it? wonders Ross. 'The foundations and the dough boys are interested,' Welles replies vaguely.

'Of course,' he added, 'I can louse the whole thing up with a bad *King Lear*.' Lear was his favourite part, he confessed, which he had been waiting to play all his life. 'He is 40,' Ross drily observes. This was, Welles said, the most important show of his life, and he hated having to open in the biggest town in the world without more time for rehearsal. The plan had originally been to tour *King Lear*, and it would tour if it succeeded at the City Center. Ross seems lightly sceptical of the whole enterprise. Welles's $3 million deal with CBS, he reports, has fallen through, due, 'some say', to his 'whimsical demands'. Some people, Ross continues, regard Welles as 'a ticking time-bomb'; but the man before him in his hotel suite – vodka glass in hand, with pretty young Mrs Welles gliding about, and Snowflake, their little Maltese dog, wagging its tail – 'does not tick'. And at Schumer's Rehearsal Hall 'the actors say he does not tick. Maybe', Ross concludes, clearly disheartened, 'he never did.' The *World-Telegram* was equally miffed: 'Orson Welles has been back from Europe for five weeks, and the town has not exploded, burned down or disintegrated.' Welles wryly says that he never was that kind of fellow. It was all made up by newspaper and magazine writers; he has never been temperamental. 'The bondage of what used to be written about me is over now.'

This *gravitas* offensive reached its apogee on the *Ed Murrow Show*, where a mellow, sweetly reasonable Welles, after introducing his wife and showing pictures of his baby, was seen padding about in his suite at the Sulgrave Hotel, clutching what appear to be designs for *King Lear*, answering Murrow's friendly questions with due deliberation, in his own good time.[6] This is no Wonder Boy, but a paterfamilias, a good-humoured sage who has been around a bit. 'Is it nice to be home?' asks Murrow. 'It's *wonderful* to be home,' purrs Welles, talking about the lure of the theatre, how he can't live without it, 'even in the years when I've slummed with other mediums'. Would he describe himself as unpredictable? 'I'd describe show business as unpredictable, Ed.' Politically, he sees himself as 'very much for individuals and opposed to conformists, members of a gang'. Murrow wants to know whether Welles thinks television has lived up to its potential. 'Well, no, I don't, Ed. It's a medium maybe as important as the printing press when it popped up on the cultural horizon. I think there are new forms that haven't even been attempted on television and that it's solidifying and crystallising too quickly.' 'Muscle-bound in its infancy?' asks Murrow. 'Yes,' replies Welles, with an irresistible smile, 'middle-aged when it's still young.'

This much-admired and much-commented-on interview nearly never happened. Welles wanted to do it after the show had opened, but Murrow went out live at 10–10.30 p.m., before *Lear*'s final curtain fell; moreover, he felt that his room at the Volney Hotel was not big enough. Finally, Henry Margolis, with great good grace, vacated his own very large suite at the Sulgrave and handed it over to Welles and family. Not, however, before the newspapers had got wind of his elusiveness: 'it's not unusual for us to begin working on a subject's home on Monday for a Friday telecast,' someone from CBS told the *New York Herald Tribune*. 'What is unusual is to have a subject who doesn't know where he lives.'[7]

In Welles's universe, even giving an interview became fraught with complexity. Richard Maney, the press officer on the show, remarked that Welles always brought 'excitement and confusion with him wherever he went'. There was no lack of excitement around *King Lear*, and a fair mount of confusion. It was publicly launched by no less illustrious a personage than Mayor Wagner, who, with Welles at his side on the stage of the City Center, announced both *King Lear* and *Volpone*. A day or two later Welles and Jackie Gleason, who was riding high on the huge success of *The Jackie Gleason Show*, had a long dinner at Toots Shor's Restaurant, during which they argued over which of them should play Volpone in Jonson's play and which Volpone's sidekick Mosca; the excited producers called Maney and told him to write a press release. 'It doesn't matter who'll write the press release,' said Maney. 'Who's gonna write the retraction?'[8] Shortly afterwards, *Volpone* disappeared without trace.

Ironically, it could well have been that *Volpone* might have proved a better calling card than *King Lear*. Welles's plans for it seem highly entertaining: he commissioned a score from Marc Blitzstein, which was 'really a kind of musical,' said the composer, 'with songs, numbers, dances, production-pieces. The harpsichord is the centre of the instrumental ensemble.' Blitzstein had taken Stravinsky's *Soldier's Tale* as his model: 'gay, tart, heartless, brilliant, juicy, stylish, popularvenetio-serenadeo pieces'.[9] It is unclear how much of the text Welles would have retained, but on the face of it, Jonson, with his brilliant virtuoso language and his archetypal characters, would have been right up his street; and Jonson was a novelty in New York, which – despite Welles's apparent belief that the city was bereft of the bard – had seen rather a lot of Shakespeare lately, not least a warmly received production of *King Lear* four years earlier, directed by the man Welles thought of as his nemesis, John Houseman, with a company made up (as Jonathan Rosenbaum has pointed out) largely of ex-Mercury actors.

At the City Center itself, not long before Welles was making these pronouncements about the dearth of Shakespeare in New York, major productions of *Othello* and *King Henry IV, Part One* had been seen and respectfully received. Welles's main point, of course, was true: there was, neither in New York nor anywhere else in the United States of America, a company devoted to performing the classics. This, he said, was his current mission: 'he believes', reported *Cue* magazine, 'Broadway has the greatest talent pool in the world. But this, he avers, is no substitute for doing a job steadily, and American actors do not steadily play the classics. With a repertory company, he would work nine months of the year, take three off to make the necessary big money to keep the company afloat.'[10] Welles summed it up: 'The great works of literature are not given as many performances nowadays as they deserve. I believe that if there is any useful contribution I can make, I should.' The notion of this classical company under Welles's leadership is a dizzying prospect, and could indeed have made a major contribution to the American theatre of the 1950s, though the words 'doing a job steadily' do not seem to describe any other project in which Welles had previously been involved.

In all this blaze of publicity about *King Lear*, and in all of his utterances about the play and the part, Welles never actually explains what it is about either that interests him. He had indeed been thinking about the play for some time: on the back of his 1946 broadcast, the following year he had sketched out a scheme for a version of the play that was, according to the notes, 'arranged for production as a play with music in continuous performance on a bare stage with a curtain', which sounds like a nod to Brecht and the austere stagings of his Berliner Ensemble; Welles was, of course, to use the device of the curtain a few years later in the *Othello* at the St James Theatre in London. The 1947 version of *King Lear* covers sixty-six loosely typed pages in six sections, of which only the fifth is missing; each has an epigraph quoted from the play and a designated season: 'PART THE FIRST: "The younger rises when the old doth fall." Early summer. PART THE SECOND: "O let me not be mad, sweet heaven." Early Fall', and so on. The last line of this version is 'O she's dead.'[11] Both concise and epic, it is a scheme for the play, rather than a version or even a view of it, but it has some sort of visionary Blakeian quality, underpinned by the changing seasons.

It may be that this basic outline was in Welles's mind as he contemplated staging the play in New York, but if so, he never shared it with anyone. He was notably unforthcoming about the play, the part, or his view of either. 'Towering' and 'tremendous' are words that recur when he talks about the play; while in his *New York Times* piece, 'Tackling Lear',[12] he simply calls the character 'the old thunderer', the closest to a description of the mad old king he offers. 'It strikes me, after almost a quarter of a century in theatre service,' he wrote in his *New York Times* article, 'as high time that I make my first attempt at the play and the role. If I don't now, when – at least in America – will I be able to do it again?' He admits that the chances of getting it right first time round are slender: 'let those who will come to hear, see and judge this year's essay remember that there are no tenors who would care to be remembered for their first season's Tristan and few bassos whose Boris Godunov was born at full scale in the first opera house where it was attempted.' He hopes, finally, that if his new *Lear* should be considered redundant, it would not discourage 'the founding, as soon as may be, of a solid theatre establishment'. It is an uneasy, defensive piece, giving a potential theatregoer no clear impression of what he or she might be likely see, should they choose to buy a ticket; it seems, in fact, to be a plea for clemency addressed to the critics. It is also a little ungallant to Jean Dalrymple, the doughty and skilful director of the City Center. She it was, Welles says, who persuaded Messrs Margolis and Gabel 'to forgo commercial considerations in the interests of a short season at the City Center, whose budget unhappily cannot be stretched to include *Volpone*'. In fact, when she saw the projected budget for *King Lear* alone, she demanded that it be halved. Even so, it cost twice as much as any other production in the City Center's history. One thing that Welles's production was definitely going to be about, it was clear from the beginning, was size – an exercise, like much of Welles's work, in gigantism.

The theatre itself was (and is) massive. A cavernous former Mecca of the quasi-masonic Ancient Order of the Nobles of the Mystic Shrine, it had a capacity of 2,800; Welles set out to make it appear even bigger than usual, persuading Dalrymple – at considerable expense, involving riggers and carpenters on overtime – to remove the swagging that masked the top of the curtain so that, when it rose, it entirely disappeared behind the crown of the plaster proscenium, resulting in a monumentally tall and bare frame for the action. The stage was occupied by huge interlocking platforms, not unlike the ones he used in London for *Othello,* but sloping; these were pushed into place by soldiers and courtiers. Most of the action took place on these sloping platforms, isolated by lights, a vast number of which were required, including some of the City Center's geriatric house-circuits. Everything, including the props and the furniture, was on a massive scale – swords were four times as large as usual; as in the television broadcast, when Lear came on he had a hooded falcon on his wrist, and when his men joined him, they lugged a large deer on with them. Behind the platforms was a great black velvet backcloth, the full depth and width of the soaring back wall of the stage, on which were painted, in colour, motifs from Piranesi's celebrated etchings of prisons, the *Carceri d'invenzione*, cunningly underlit to offer darkly glowing visions of nameless horrors in the great black pit of the stage. These designs were essentially Welles's work, though the settings were attributed to Theodore Cooper, an amiable and hard-working television designer; the costumes – in what is loosely known as the Ancient British style – were by City Center regular Robert Fletcher, likewise working from sketches by Welles. Liking Fletcher's thoughts about the play, Welles took him aback by asking him to audition for the highly challenging role of Edgar, normally thought of as a stepping stone to the part of Hamlet. Fletcher had acted before, but nothing remotely as demanding as Edgar. Welles gave him the part. 'He was no great shakes as an actor,' drily noted the stage manager, John Maxtone-Graham, 'though he was beautifully costumed.' Fletcher had earlier designed the clothes for *Othello* and *Henry IV*, *Part One* at City Center; much later he was to gain immortality by designing the costumes for *Star Wars.*

The remaining members of Welles's creative team were musicians. Blitzstein wrote the score – 'not Wagnerian heroic,' Welles told him – and was joined by two of Blitzstein's colleagues, Otto Luening and Vladimir Ussachevsky, pioneers of *musique concrète*, who were already mildly notorious after demonstrating their work on television. Welles was looking for what he called 'symbolic abstract effects'. Sceptical of it at first, he rapidly became enchanted with the possibilities of this new form, and would frequently leave rehearsals to slope off to Luening and Ussachevsky's studio to engender ever more arcane sounds. The result, according to one of the baffled actors, was 'like an airport runway with planes taking off and landing'.[13] In addition Welles commissioned a special tape consisting only of sub-audio frequencies to induce discomfort in the audience during the mad scenes, making them perspire and feel agitated; in fact, in performance the carefully plotted cues often went for nothing, because Welles and the other actors varied the pace of their delivery. Working on the sound took an inordinate amount of Welles's time, not least because, thanks to union regulations, he was not permitted to speak to the operators directly.

Union regulations of one sort or another blighted Welles's experience on *King Lear*, and contributed to his general feeling that the good old days of theatre were swiftly vanishing. He was conscious that in New York – unlike London, whose own, rather different revolution was nigh – there had been a radical change in the way actors saw themselves and their work. The Method was in full swing: the free, unstructured expression of emotion was at a premium. Welles had no truck with this: it was the realism he so loathed all over again. 'I prefer communication to mumbling, twitching, "realisation", etc.,' said Welles. 'Communication is more related to Maurice Chevalier and the circus.'[14] He pointed the finger, not at Lee Strasberg or the teachers of the Studio, but at Stanislavsky, who, he said, was 'a genius – and an amateur. Most of his followers are merely amateurs.' In particular he thought that in America the approach to Shakespeare had gone from the effete – as practised on the Broadway stage by the English-born actor Maurice Evans and his director, Margaret Webster, both of whom he cordially despised – to the internally overwrought, as recommended by Strasberg. In Welles's view, classical acting was essentially extrovert: 'The Shakespeare actor is closer to Ethel Merman and Bert Lahr than you think.' His mission was to save Shakespeare for America.

*

On the first day of rehearsals in Schumer's Furniture Depository (a cut-price rehearsal room on 65th Street, with a noisy elevator that opened directly into the room, lousy acoustics and nothing to sit on but old aeroplane seats), Welles presented his edited version of the play, two hours and twenty minutes played without intermission, including a few interpolations from other plays, *Twelfth Night* among them. He lovingly addressed his cast of seventeen actors and twelve extras, telling them they were the nucleus of the company of classical actors he had so long dreamed of; that they were, indeed, the New Mercury Company. Many of them were, in fact, well versed in the classics: John Colicos, who was playing Edmund, had only months ago been playing the part of Lear himself, at the Old Vic in London, no less; the British actor Roy Dean, playing Kent, had appeared in no fewer than twenty-six Shakespeare plays from 1943 to 1947 (in addition to being British national hurdling champion in 1948). The Gloucester, young Lester Rawlins, had appeared in *Othello* and *Henry IV, Part One* at City Center earlier that season; as had the Cornwall, Thayer David, who had also done *The Taming of the Shrew* directed by the dreaded Margaret Webster. Sorrell Booke, later to be nationally famous as Boss Hogg in *The Dukes of Hazzard*, was a graduate of both Harvard and Yale and was immersed in Elizabethan literature; Alvin Epstein, as the Fool, a student of Martha Graham, had come from the famous Decroux School of Physical Mime, and had just played the Fool in Hebrew at the Habima Theatre in Tel Aviv. Even Robert Fletcher, as Edgar, had appeared in *Love's Labour's Lost* and *The Merchant of Venice*; and Jack Aronson, walking on as this and that, had studied at the Old Vic School in London.

The three women were scarcely less classically experienced: Welles's Regan was Geraldine Fitzgerald, Ellie Dunn to his Captain Shotover at the Mercury before the war, and now a considerable film star; the Goneril was Sylvia Short, married to Fritz Weaver, who had just played Portia out of town; and Cordelia was the radiant Swedish film star Viveca Lindfors, fresh from a huge triumph in *Anastasia* on Broadway, and had earlier appeared in a show called *Introducing Will Shakespeare*. It was no mean company; there was still great excitement at the idea of working with Welles.

How it all started to go wrong – and it did, horribly – is a familiar story. First of all, as usual, Welles rarely played Lear in rehearsal. He preferred to delegate the part to someone else. The someone else in this instance was an actor called Pernell Roberts (later famous in the television series *Bonanza*), another very experienced Shakespearean. He was not Welles's understudy, but was in fact playing the Duke of Burgundy and had never been formally asked to depute for Welles. So one day when Welles said, 'Here, Pernell, you take the book,' Roberts refused, saying, 'Why, if I don't get extra pay? You want me to do this, you pay me for it.'[15] Perhaps he was feeling cocky, having lately won a Drama Desk Award for an off-Broadway *Macbeth*. After lunch, he was dismissed in full view of the company.

Shortly afterwards there was another bloodletting. The elderly stage manager tried to arrange an inaugural Equity meeting, which had to take place, according to Equity rules, during rehearsal hours. When Welles discovered this, he erupted in a black rage, ranting against bureaucracy: whenever he had to fill in official forms, he said, he made up numbers or lied or left things out. The Equity meeting went ahead, but the stage manager, shaken, handed in his notice and the very raw, young assistant stage manager, John Maxtone-Graham, took over – an important appointment, as it happens, because Welles had started absenting himself from the rehearsals and Maxtone-Graham was obliged to run scenes with the actors, who were not best pleased at being abandoned. On the rare occasions when Welles was in attendance, he sat at his desk, often looking bored, doodling all day long with a rapidograph pen someone had given him, evidently wishing himself elsewhere.

Just occasionally he was moved to get up and demonstrate, and then it could be electrifying. One day he suggested that Thayer David should play the Earl of Cornwall 'like a terrifying Nazi official with life-or-death powers'[16] and got up to show him how to do it, brilliantly. He carefully orchestrated group scenes and reactions as he had so cleverly done at the Mercury, the old Saxe-Meiningen methods of disciplined teamwork, which he had been practising since he was a fourteen-year-old martinet at Todd School for Boys; the results were often astonishing. It must have been on one of these days that the piercingly intelligent and brutally tough critic of the *New Republic* magazine, Eric Bentley, sat in on rehearsals. Bentley had written about Welles savagely enough in the past, so it is surprising that Welles even allowed him into his rehearsal room. But what Bentley – who, as we have seen, described the London *Moby-Dick* as 'toiling amateurism brought to a pitch of frenzy' – saw at Schumer's impressed him: 'I saw nothing of the Welles of popular mythology, undisciplined, perverse or just plain drunken . . . neither grandiose nor feverish, he spoke the language of common-sense, and gave the actors tips based on a veteran's know-how and a theatre-poet's inspirations.'[17] He admired the way Welles absorbed the inspiration of the minute, not sticking to a preconceived staging, but integrating what he had imagined with what he saw before him. Why, then, Bentley asked himself, were the end results not better? 'Mr Welles has always been tempted to turn the theatre into a Notion and Novelty store . . . this is the cheap and childish side of Mr Welles. His real talent is not even in that direction, but, as I have hinted, starting from sound and sober craftsmanship, culminates in effects which, while they are audacious, can also be dignified and grand. There was a grandeur in the best moments of his *King Lear* far surpassing anything in Guthrie's *Tamburlaine.*' But most importantly, said Bentley, Welles should never both act in a play and direct it.

It is extraordinary how Welles never came to terms with this simple and self-evident proposition. He never really gave himself a chance in the theatre. It was still common for the leading actor to direct the play – Gielgud and Olivier both did it. But they at least made sure that they were in absolute command of their texts, and they were always available to the other actors. It is a matter of deep regret that Welles never worked on a play with, say, Peter Brook, with whom he had such a warm relationship and with whom he had had a rare happy professional experience. The reason he avoided acting with his fellow-actors during rehearsals was the same reason, that, in his films, he shot as many of his own scenes as he could after the other actors had departed: he was, he admitted to the cameraman Edmond Richard, deeply shy of submitting his performance to their appraising eyes. In the theatre, he was eventually bound to act with his fellow-company members, but he deferred the moment for as long as humanly possible. For the same reason, he did not wish to expose himself to the probing attention of a director over the weeks of rehearsal. In movies, his practice was to learn the lines, show up and, with a minimum of interchange with the director, do his scene or scenes in as few takes as possible. Welles was fundamentally insecure as an actor, which makes his persistent returns to the theatre either foolhardy or very brave.

All actors to some extent feel insecure; their salvation lies, generally, in the script, a constant source of information and inspiration, and in their fellow-actors. A certain *esprit de corps* almost always prevails because, like the members of a human pyramid, everyone depends on everyone else. And a problem shared is a problem halved. Welles denied himself both these comforts, first because his relationship to his own lines was so tenuous – it was the last call on his attention – and second because he put off engaging with his fellow-players. And in the *King Lear* company he had no chums, no peers; there was no one he admired, nobody to raise the adrenalin levels for him. His occasional efforts at communication failed, as when, for example, he would join the cast for lunch, but never offered to chip in. He found himself, as so often, alone.

His old colleague Emerson Crocker, appointed assistant director, walked out early on, when it became apparent that Welles wanted to use him as his whipping boy, someone he could shout at and punish; as Crocker left the room, Welles shouted at his departing back: 'you should never argue with a man with a microphone.'[18] Welles was warm enough with Geraldine Fitzgerald, and even shared an interpretative note with her: 'nature,' he said to her, 'abhors a vacuum, and Lear, when he gives everything away to his daughters, had created a political vacuum. And into that vacuum, in his experience, always steps the spear.' So after the court had dispersed, after Lear had divided the kingdom among his daughters, and the sisters had met and parted, Welles left the stage totally empty:

> There was nothing on it, nothing at all. He got rid of all the thrones, he got rid of everything, and it was just there, just a dirty, empty stage. And nothing happened at all, and the audience got a little bit nervous. And then very, very soft-footedly, starting at the very back – it was a very, very big, deep theatre – comes Edmund the bastard, and he comes down front and says, 'Thou nature art my goddess'. It was so thrilling, even though the audience didn't know what the concept was, but they knew that something terrible had happened.[19]

Welles allowed Fitzgerald's fifteen-year-old son, Michael Lindsay-Hogg, to sit in on rehearsals; there at least he had a fan: 'he was glorious at that time,' wrote Lindsay-Hogg in *Luck and Circumstance.* 'Forty years old, tall, broad, dressed in black, starting to be heavy but not nearly with the weight which must have partly killed him. But there was something else to him, a kind of emanation of energy and intelligence, curiosity, and originality.' Entranced, the boy watched him work. 'He'd catch my eye often, winking sometimes, sometimes a smile. Or, if one of the actors was not doing a good job, he'd look at me and roll his eyes.'[20]

The mood in the room was not good. Welles had almost immediately decided he'd made a mistake in casting Viveca Lindfors, who suffered in his eyes from being two things: 1) Swedish, with a heavy accent; and 2) a devout follower of the Method. He made no attempt to conceal his contempt for her. In her desperate struggle with the language, she hired a Shakespearean coach, which only provoked more scorn from Welles. The company were scarcely kinder to her, going into corners to mock her accent. But if they had no time for Lindfors, they had even less for Welles. 'There was a lot of hatred of Orson in the room,' said Alvin Epstein, who was personally very happy to be told what to do, as were John Colicos and Roy Dean; others, in that heady dawn of Method exploration and actors' self-examination, found it intolerable.

At the end of three weeks the disgruntled company moved into the theatre for technical rehearsals, whereupon Welles disappeared into the blackness of the auditorium and addressed the actors through a megaphone; often he would come up onto the stage to adjust a light himself, or set a sound cue, or shift a piece of scenery, and then disappear back into the stalls. In the midst of all this technical activity, he would, just occasionally, make personal contact with an actor; once, completely out of the blue, he approached a particularly unhappy-looking extra playing a knight; this was Julian Barry, later to be the author of the Broadway hit *Lenny*. 'Do you know what this play is all about?' Welles asked him. 'The play is about a noble knight who sees that the king is making a terrible mistake and he wants to tell him that, but he is not high enough in the court to be able to approach the king and speak with him.'[21] A parable, perhaps, of the relationship between a very important and famous director and an extra. But whatever their feelings about rehearsing with him, the company were deeply impressed by Welles's lighting; often his most striking effects were achieved with great economy: 'using a few key instruments,' recollected Maxtone-Graham, 'he created a marvellous Gothic mood in that cavernous theatre.'[22] He made particularly striking use of follow-spots, isolating individuals so that, on their great sloping platforms, they appeared to be suspended in space; the Piranesi patterns on the backcloth likewise seemed to be three-dimensional, free-standing objects.

And all the while, Welles was putting off the awful moment at which he would actually have to play King Lear.

When he finally donned the costume and emerged in the extraordinary quasi-expressionist make-up he had devised for the character, he was completely unaccustomed to negotiating the ever-changing set and its treacherous planes, and ill-adjusted to the Stygian gloom that prevailed backstage. There was, as usual with Welles, no dress rehearsal, though at least he had a number of public previews. At the first of these, adrenalised and under-rehearsed (a treacherous combination), he stood at the tip of one of the slopes, which jutted out like the prow of a ship, cried out, 'O Fool, I shall go mad,' and scooped up Epstein by the back of his neck and raced upstage down the platform. 'My feet are hardly touching the ground,' said Epstein:

> because I have this two hundred and twenty five pounds behind me going as fast as he can go, holding me up in the air. I'm really not controlling the movement at all. And we're heading into the wings and the wings consist of a series of black velour cloths, hiding steel girder lighting posts. Frames to which are attached lighting instruments and he heads for one of those that he thinks is a curtain because he hasn't done it often enough.

> He's raising his arm so I know what he thinks. He thinks it's a curtain, he can push it aside, and I know it's a steel girder. And I was wriggling madly not to be crushed against the steel girder. And I managed but of course he didn't. He went slam into it. I got out of the way and he went smack into it like that.[23]

In the general kerfuffle, Welles sprained his ankle and – a bit of a tradition with him, this – lost his false nose. Next day the nose was restored and Welles made his way across the set a little more circumspectly, now weighed down with a heavy surgical boot. Accidents continued to happen as the extras and stage crew groped away in the semi-darkness, trying to find the many-coloured marks on the stage that were the temporary resting place for the platforms. At a later preview, the platform representing Dover beach moved too fast and too far, jutting right out into the auditorium. Oblivious of this, Lester Rawlins, as the blinded Gloucester, jumped – ending up not on the expected apron of the stage, but in the lap of a woman in the front row. Gamely he continued with his next line, which happened to be 'Have I fallen or no?'[24]

Over the course of the six previews the production got sharper and quicker, and Welles became nimbler with the boot he was still obliged to wear. Finally 12 January 1956 arrived, a real first night at which the press were actually present. Quite understandably, Welles seems to have succumbed to heavy nerves: the jury was assembling for what he had called 'the most important show of my life'. By some absurd caprice of fate – or perhaps it had been carefully planned – *Citizen Kane* was playing for a rare revival at the 55th Street Playhouse, an art-house cinema just opposite the City Center, allowing the incoming audience to remind themselves of the competition Welles was up against: himself.

It seems that the combination of anxiety about the play and the performance and pain from his ankle led Welles to administer some alcoholic medication to himself over the course of the evening. By the final curtain, 'the measured ringing cadences of Lear had metamorphosed into the slightly drunken, nasal bray of Charles Foster Kane,' noted Welles's stage manager, John Maxtone-Graham. 'Either as a result of painkillers or whiskey or both, Welles as Lear was slurring his lines quite badly.'[25] Nor was he always able to remember them – when he staggered in with the dead Cordelia in his arms, he repeated Lear's 'Howl' many times more than Shakespeare's prescribed four, until at last he remembered the next phrase. Welles told Barbara Leaming that what had thrown him that evening was the applause that greeted his entrance: 'It was so enormous and so long and so sustained that it completely disoriented me.'[26]

A few nights later he identified a different problem when speaking to the audience at the City Center: on the first night, he said, 'I began to believe the play, to believe it so terrifyingly that I ceased to communicate with the audience.'[27] This question of what was fake and what was real – the conflict between giving in to one's unconscious and controlling it – had haunted Welles for many years. It is something all actors have to deal with, but for Welles it was deeply problematic. He seemed nervous of his own underlying emotions, clumsy in handling them. The great classical roles, of course, call for intense engagement with the most powerful of human emotions in peculiarly distilled form. The part of King Lear, especially his rapidly developing madness, forces the actor to engage with things that most people would rather avoid; if you open yourself to them too nakedly, it can be dangerous, both to yourself and to the play. For the most part, Welles kept a large distance between himself and the emotions of the character; at the New York City Center on 12 January 1956, his own feelings and those of King Lear had become dangerously interconnected.

At the curtain call, which was generously applauded, a tired and emotional Welles held up a hand and made a speech in which he expressed his pleasure at being home, an unusually simple sentiment for him. He then walked back with Alvin Epstein across the set, turned a corner and broke his one remaining good ankle. There are other accounts, the most entertaining being Maxtone-Graham's that when Marlene Dietrich, who had been in the audience, entered his dressing room, Welles said to his wife, 'Paola, say hello to the most beautiful woman in the world,' and Paola knocked him to the ground. As often with Welles stories, the most amusing version is the one to go for; either way, Welles, having been legless in one sense during the performance, was now legless in another.

The following day, the actors were summoned to the stage and told that, for obvious reasons, Welles couldn't go on as Lear, but he wanted to spare the City Center any loss of revenue, so he would talk to the audience, explain what had happened, tell a few stories, perhaps read a few speeches from *Lear*. The actors were welcome to stay and listen. Few did, unsurprisingly; they had heard all the stories, and wanted to do the play, not listen to Welles in extract.

There was no announcement before the curtain went up so, when it did, the audience was astonished to see, not a palace in Ancient Britain and a mad old king, but a fresh-faced Welles in a lounge suit sitting comfortably in a wheelchair with a table and a carafe of water at his side. 'Ladies and gentlemen, I am Orson Welles,' he said, 'and there will be no performance of *King Lear* this evening. We will not dance *The Red Shoes*.'[28] He then told them that he had exactly quarter of an hour to prevent them from going for a refund, after which time the box office would be closed, and that he proposed doing so by telling them jokes and performing conjuring tricks: 75 per cent of the audience elected to stay. As the remaining 25 per cent vacated their seats, a voice called from way, way up in the balcony: 'It's kind of lonely up here. Can we come down?' They did, and Welles engaged his slightly dwindled audience effortlessly, as only he could. With genuine humility (and Welles's humility was absolutely genuine) he confided in them his conviction that the show had not gone well the night before because of his excessive belief in the character and his situation, and then he spoke a number of the speeches as he felt they should have gone, and those who were present felt they had never heard Lear more movingly or beautifully spoken. He kept them spellbound for an hour and a half, and they went home happy.

The reviews had by now come out. They were not, on the whole, good. The tone was sorrowful rather than angry; as usual, they were not so much reviews as enquiries into the Welles problem. The *New York Times* – then, as now, the crucial review – made an interesting distinction: 'Mr Welles has a genius for the theatre. It is fine to have him back again. And it is easy to appreciate his attack on the problems of staging a fiery Elizabethan drama. But the attack has left Shakespeare prostrate. Mr Welles's talent does not equal his genius.' For all the flair and energy of the staging, Welles did not, the *Times* felt, get inside the character of Lear, 'nor does his production get into the heart of the poem'.[29] The *New York Herald Tribune* was surprised and disappointed by how unexciting it all was: 'an evening of hope deferred and valiant efforts but mildly rewarded'.[30] Like many other critics, the *Saturday Review* attacked Welles's speaking of the verse, describing it as coming not in 'the torrents of emotion and word music that it is but in fitful splashes like a faulty spigot when a bit of air has got into the plumbing'. Instead of a stimulating beginning to Welles's projected repertory season, what emerged was 'a heavy and meaningless thing that resembles bad, old-fashioned opera more than it does a fresh approach to the classics'.[31]

Walter Kerr, who five years earlier had so forcefully delivered his negative verdict on Welles, seemed inclined to be more generous. He vividly describes the scene in which Lear divides the kingdom up. A gigantic map is brought on: 'As [Lear] begs Cordelia for a loving word, the map is stretched taut and tempting across his breast. Then when Cordelia has stuck to her guns, he charges right through, splitting Britain open like a paper-hoop in a three ring circus. And when he has finished lashing his daughter with his tongue, he slashes at her with the remnants of the map.' Kerr gives a sense of Welles's radical lighting effects: when Lear and the Fool made for the heath, Welles bathed himself in a deep blue spotlight, while the Fool – 'looking like a donkey-eared Pinocchio' – stared up into a green one, as violent flashes of pure white streak the ruined arches and pitted windows behind them. And at Lear's sobering realisation that he is a man more sinned against than sinning, 'the Fool sang Feste's song from the end of *Twelfth Night*, "The rain it raineth every day", an extraordinary juxtaposition of different worlds.'

Kerr makes all this sound rather interesting. Inevitably, there is a *but* coming: 'but every effect is a bequest of Mr Welles's inventive but much too conniving mind. His heart seems to have nothing to say.' The result, Kerr says, is 'an intelligent automaton at centre stage'. And he has imposed the same 'hard-driven monotony' on the rest of the company, 'all of them . . . divested of feeling, of intimacy, of direct personality'.[32] This is a consistent accusation against his acting, on both sides of the Atlantic, and it is something recognisable from his work as an actor on screen. Wolcott Gibbs, the *New Yorker*'s man, under the heading 'The Schizo King' – it is not entirely clear whether the headline refers to Lear or to Welles – acutely suggests that 'the secret of Mr Welles may be that he is under some inward compulsion to create something larger, more cryptic, and more various than any the author had in mind'.[33] Welles's enthusiasm and energy were not in doubt, said Gibbs, but his performance of Lear was 'almost continuously self-defeating'. The majority verdict was clear. Welles had been weighed in the balance and found wanting, both as director and as actor.

One critic, however, came to a radically different verdict. Richard Hayes wrote in *Commonweal* that as he did not belong to the generation for which Welles appeared to have been 'a traumatic experience' he had approached the production 'untrammelled by the expectations and suppositions of prejudice'. It was not all, for him, 'the meagre failure the newspaper critics might have led one to anticipate, but a *Lear* of much intelligence and ingenuity'. Though he found it lacking in personal resonance, it had 'inward moments of some beauty and depth'. He questioned his colleagues' reactions: was there not, he asked, 'something punishing and harsh in the meagre critical and popular response to Mr Welles's elaborate production? How do we make the prodigy pay for his early audacities long after he has sloughed them off?' If Welles was not the absolute Lear of his generation, at least he came out of the attempt 'with a brighter honour than so many of his contemporaries who have settled for such mild victories. Quite possibly he does lack "a sense of direction" as we so consistently remind him, yet at least his confusion is the distress of plenty, not poverty.'[34]

A balanced appraisal: it is true that Welles never settles for the easy option. It is also true that he was to some extent in thrall to his own generation, who found it hard to forgive him for not having had the career they had projected for him, nor had he yet – either in America or in England – connected to a younger generation. This *King Lear* was hopelessly old-fashioned to the young and simply flat-footed to the middle-aged; but for the latter group, it was not merely disappointing, it was heartbreaking. On the first night at City Center, Paula Laurence and José Ferrer sat together: Laurence had been Welles's Helen of Troy in the 1937 *Dr Faustus*, and Ferrer was then a shining beacon of classical acting on the Broadway stage. After the curtain fell on the first night, they remained in the stalls when the rest of the audience had left and wept.[35]

Welles himself took the reviews, as he took all reviews, on the chin. The day after his one-man performance the company was called in to restage the entire production to accommodate the wheelchair. Certain effects became impossible – Welles could never negotiate the sloping platforms, for example, not even pushed by Alvin Epstein ('Miss Bedpan', as Epstein thereafter called himself, after Sheridan Whiteside's nurse in *The Man Who Came to Dinner*, another play featuring a grumpy old man in a wheelchair). Remarkably enough, the general view among the company was that the production, and his own performance, took a huge turn for the better once Welles was in his wheelchair. He rapidly mastered its possibilities 'and got incredibly adept with it, as you might imagine', according to Geraldine Fitzgerald. 'He'd hardly had it an hour before he could have been in one of Chaplin's shows.'[36] But it went further than that. In the wheelchair, said Viveca Lindfors, 'his performance improved extraordinarily, as if confinement forced him to use a deeper, more private part of himself and give up the image of the giant Welles.'[37] This observation touches profoundly on the wellsprings of Welles's behaviour, the constant need to assert and emphasise the very thing he had for nothing: his scale, which runs parallel to his constant need to assert his versatility. If he didn't assert his size, he would feel small; if he didn't advertise his multifaceted brilliance, people would think him ordinary. Here, in the wheelchair, through no fault of his own, he had to acknowledge his limitations: no one could blame him for simply playing the character and the situation. In many senses, he had taken the weight off himself.

Interestingly, he made no attempt to customise the wheelchair, to dull down its high chromium shine. He wasn't King Lear: he was clearly an actor with two damaged ankles in a wheelchair. The burden of impersonation had been lifted from him: now he could just speak the lines with truth and engagement, as he had done when he was talking to the audience in his lounge suit. (It is notable that Richard Hayes's friendly and sympathetic review in *Commonweal* was of a performance in the wheelchair.) Welles spotted another gain in the situation, another theatrical opportunity. Every night, before the curtain went up, he made an announcement through an off-stage microphone: 'Ladies and gentlemen, there is a tradition in the Chinese theatre that the prop man, however active on stage, is invisible. That is the way I hope you will look at King Lear's wheelchair.'[38] This statement engendered a perfectly Brechtian state of mind in the audience: do not expect any illusions; everything you see will be true. An illusion in itself, of course, and thus a perfectly Wellesian moment, too.

It was a bold piece of showmanship, both enlivening and imaginative: the sort of thing that wakes an audience up rather than immersing them in emotion or atmosphere, preventing them from surrendering their critical intellects. During the performances, Welles was, as ever, constantly aware of the other actors' work and, as he had done in London during the run of *Moby-Dick*, he communicated his desires to them as directly as possible, on stage. Speed was his main note. 'Get the lead out of your ass, Epstein!' he barked at his colleague one night;[39] and when Sorrell Booke, as Albany, tried, just once, on the very last night, not to gabble his speeches at the end of the play, the dead body of King Lear roared profanities at him till he got up to speed.[40] Clearly Welles by now was enjoying himself. One night earlier in the run, Maxtone-Graham became aware during the scene on the heath that amongst all the wild utterances pouring out of Lear and the Fool, Welles was screaming, 'John! JOHN!! JOHN!!! SWITCH SIXTEEN IS NOT ON,' which it wasn't. This was Welles at full throttle in his playpen.[41]

Finally, after just twenty-six performances, it was all over. Welles had a last drink with some of the actors on the deserted stage, before leaving City Center for ever. He had been ferried back and forth between the Sulgrave and the theatre each night in an extremely expensive Keefe & Keefe ambulance, paid for, once again, by long-suffering Jean Dalrymple, who had also provided him with a paid assistant to minimise his inconvenience. As he left the theatre that last night, Tom Clancy, who had been playing Curan, pushed him out onto the loading dock and helped him down to the pavement. Once there, Welles rose miraculously from his wheelchair, folded it up, hurled it into the back of the ambulance and walked unassisted and without difficulty to the front seat. 'With a signature cigar jutting from his face,' reported Maxtone-Graham, 'he called out an obscene farewell to City Center and Jean Dalrymple and was driven off into the night.'[42] It crossed the minds of more than one of the actors that the whole ankle thing had been a fraud, a cover up job. Welles was already moving on. Another failure: his dream of the New Mercury Theatre melted into air, into thin air; his hopes of a triumphant homecoming dashed. *Tant pis!* He would come back to *King Lear* in another medium, in another form. On, on.

For the City Center, it was less easy to move on. Shortly after *Lear* closed, the *New York Times* reported on a City Center press conference at which there was an unusually frank admission that Welles's production had brought the public arts body to its knees, as a result of excess expenditure: the set doubled its appointed budget, with an overall production cost twice that of any previous show (which is rather remarkable, considering the number of musicals and operas performed there). In addition, Welles's ambulance had cost $1,000, to say nothing of the assistant; the twenty-six stagehands had further swollen the tally. The cancellation of the tour meant the income from that – had it happened, Margolis and Gabel would have paid $3,000 a week to City Center – had not materialised. Business had initially been good, but fell off after news of the broken/sprained ankles got out. The run had grossed $90,000 against a projected take of $150,000. Because of this failure, the ballet and opera seasons were curtailed respectively to four and three weeks. The City Center, the *Times* report concludes, was uncertain of how to survive.

In the end the City of New York bailed it out, but it had been a scary, near-death experience for them.[43] This terrible public drubbing, along with the reviews, pretty well put paid to whatever hopes Welles might have entertained of future work in the New York theatre; the detailed analysis of his over-spending only confirmed a disastrous reputation in that area. It was not a noble failure, just another manifestation of what Eric Bentley had called his gift and need for Being A Headliner. The publicity generated by the production and its attendant ills was indeed immense, especially after his accidents, but, as a slogan, 'the Wheelchair *Lear*' sold no tickets. It was publicity for publicity's sake. The danger was that the story of Orson Welles was increasingly becoming a chapter, not in the history of the performing arts, but in that of publicity. Brooks Atkinson of the *New York Times* returned to the fray two weeks later to worry again about the performance, concluding that, despite his gifts, Welles lacked 'the perceptions of an artist'.[44] George Jean Nathan (the original of *All About Eve*'s acidulous Addison de Witt), observing fondly that it was impossible to refrain from admiring Welles for 'taking more chances than even a wealthy, amorous widow with delusions of desirability', compared him to the great quick-change artist Leopoldo Fregoli: Welles, he says, 'can emerge from behind a screen in rapid order as a stage, musical comedy, television, radio or movie actor, stage or film director, producer, writer, press-agent, vaudeville sleight-of-hand artist or apparently anything else, short, as of this moment, of a strip-tease artist'.[45]

CHAPTER TWELVE

Orson Welles, Television Needs You

As if deliberately tipping his hat at George Jean Nathan, Welles's next engagement after *King Lear* closed was to perform a scene from the play (with cast) on the *Ed Sullivan Show*, alongside Lucille Ball, Desi Arnaz, a ventriloquist, the Four Ames Brothers, Rodgers and Hammerstein. As if that were not enough variety, the day following the *Sullivan Show* he went straight to Las Vegas, where for three weeks he filled the Riviera Hotel's Clover Room with an ambitious act which was an unqualified success; unqualified successes came rarely in Welles's life. The initial impulse was, inevitably, economic: though he had cost the City Center dearly, his own salary had been a token $85 a week; with a new daughter to maintain, he needed serious money – and quickly. Welles had been alerted to the fact that the Mafiosi who had turned the formerly staid desert resort into Sin City had begun to pay big bucks to big-name entertainers. This turned out to be no exaggeration: he was offered $45,000 for the three-week engagement, which was due to start on 25 February. According to *Daily Variety*, the Riviera Hotel's new entertainment director (whose predecessor had been blown up in his car by a dynamite bomb placed there by his employers) had asked Welles what kind of an act he had in mind. 'Don't you worry, Mr Goffstein,' Welles had replied. 'It will be the most dramatic performance ever presented in Las Vegas' – which strongly suggests he hadn't thought about it yet.

Needless to say, he was delighted to have the opportunity to present himself before the public as a magician – the favourite, he always claimed, of his many manifestations; over the half-decade since he had last performed a conjuring trick in public, he had religiously kept au fait with the latest developments. But he was not just offering magic – he had a killer card up his sleeve, which none of his rivals could provide: readings from Shakespeare. In short, it was *An Evening with Orson Welles* by another name. He was very relaxed about it. He got a nasty shock when he, Paola and Beatrice arrived in Las Vegas and he saw the Clover Room, which was to the average cabaret venue what the City Center was to a telephone box. It was vast – far too big for the modest array of mentalist tricks he'd planned. The show was due to open in three days: he moved quickly, and soon enough, through his extensive magic network, he found the help he needed. The Kirkhams, Kirk and Phyllis, performers and innovators themselves, supplied him with the big illusions he knew he required and were contracted to assist him on stage during the act. He selected three of their biggest illusions: the Broom Suspension, the Temple of Benares and the immortally named Duck Vanish, and, under Kirkham's tutelage, he quickly mastered them.

When Welles stumbled upon the Clover Room's state-of-the-art revolving stage, he seized on the idea of using it to give a 360-degree demonstration of the magical apparatuses – something no one had ever done before. As in any other sphere in which he worked, he took control of all the elements, changing the orchestra's repertory and arranging the supporting acts. And all the while, Kirk Kirkham told Bart Whaley, he was aware that Welles was 'absolutely petrified'.[1] Perhaps that accounts for his decision at the very last minute to replace Phyllis Kirkham with Paola in the Temple of Benares, an illusion that demanded complicated box-hopping. Paola was deeply disinclined to do it, but Welles relentlessly urged her on and on, until finally she ripped her dress trying to get from one box to another; to calm her sobbing, he relieved her of the job, reverting to Phyllis Kirkham as rehearsed. Was he trying to punish Paola in some way? Or did he genuinely not understand how difficult and frightening a thing he was asking of her? Or was it simply a displacement activity to divert his anxiety away from the performance he was about to give? Whichever it was – and it may have been a combination of all three – it is a striking instance of the curious lack of empathy that Welles sometimes manifested: a tendency to treat people as machines.

As always in these situations, once he was in front of the audience in his own persona, his incomparable rapport with them took over. The ducks got out of their box, the music cues were all over the place, and the volunteers from the audience took an eternity to get up on stage and go back to their seats, but, despite running for an astonishing seventy-five minutes, the show was a palpable hit. 'A phantasmagoria of magico, mindreading, levitation and closing dramatic reading of Shakespeare' was *Variety*'s verdict, noting nothing wrong with it that some judicious trimming and tightening would not put right. By the following night, Welles the master editor had cut it down to twenty-five minutes of pure gold. It opened with the Broom Suspension, 'a sock start for the razzledazzle to follow', then there was a sensational prediction of the answer to television's *$64,000 Question* and then there were mind-reading stunts; the mental telepathy tricks, *Variety* magazine inimitably remarked, 'also grabbed big kudosing'.

But the climax of the show was not the magic at all: it was, improbably enough, the Shakespeare that really wowed the gamblers, the gangsters and their guests and the smattering of showbiz figures who constituted Welles's audience. Mark Antony's funeral oration from *Julius Caesar* was a warm-up for what an admiring *Variety* called 'a solid piece of biz – makeup onstage and donning costume for the w.k. [well known] Shylock speech from *Merchant of Venice*'. It is to be wondered just how w.k. 'Hath not a Jew eyes?' was to Welles's audience. Perhaps it came to them with the force of revelation. After it, he was brought back for many bows. The local reviewer, 'Willard', was deeply struck by this: 'it would not be out of the realm of possibility whatsoever to foresee several shows in the three-frame booking dominated more and more by these.' Moreover, he added, a full twenty-five minutes of Welles doing scenes from Shakespeare or readings from other classics, 'or even the racing Form', would be received with 'tumultuous applause'. Welles had conquered Las Vegas, which impressed Willard: 'it took Orson Welles plenty of courage to undertake the Las Vegas trek . . . actors, per se, have not fared too well in these parts.'[2]

All in all, it is one of the more remarkable episodes in a life made up of extraordinary events. Coming hot on the footsteps of *King Lear*, it is almost bewildering, suggesting a range of sympathies and abilities that are virtually unprecedented. The fact that the *Lear* was a qualified failure, and the cabaret act an almost unqualified success, is neither here nor there; the fact that the director of *Citizen Kane* acquitted himself with distinction as a magician in a place where the greatest magicians regularly appeared is striking, but not deeply significant; what is truly mind-boggling is the fact that he performed Shakespeare in a nightclub on the Las Vegas strip, to 'tumultuous applause'. Moreover, the manner in which he did it – setting the scene as he made himself up, only speaking in character when the make-up was complete – is a piece of meta-theatricality of real originality. He did the same thing later on television on the Dean Martin Show, this time as Falstaff, and it is a little piece of genius, utterly spell-binding, a histrionic conjuring trick – intellectual cabaret, ontological *trompe l'oeil*. As Bart Whaley, writing from the illuminating perspective of being an authority on magic, remarks, 'he had broken with stage tradition and dared to expose, and thereby teach, a trick of the theatrical trade, the very mechanics of illusion'.[3] It is not necessarily great acting, but as performance it is sublime – entirely external, but an exhilarating celebration of shape-shifting, and a piece of bravura that is somewhere close to the essence of theatrical gesture, seamlessly blending Shakespeare and showmanship; no wonder Brecht admired Welles so much.

Flatteringly, he was asked to do two extra shows the night after he officially closed, so that the Clover Room could present some competition to two other acts opening that night: Dean Martin and Jerry Lewis at the Sands and, by an exquisite irony, Eartha Kitt, with whom Welles had last performed in *An Evening with Orson Welles* on its European tour; she was opening, with great success, at El Rancho. And then in April Welles was off to Hollywood, after all these years, to play the John Barrymore part in a television remake of the Hecht–MacArthur stage hit *Twentieth Century*; he did this to earn his standard $100,000 (no mean sum in 1956: approximately $850,000 today), but mostly to put his foot back in the door. The sentimental association with his old chum Barrymore was no disincentive, either.

Meanwhile, as a direct result of their reunion on the *Ed Sullivan Show*, Lucille Ball and Desi Arnaz, suddenly major players in television with the shrewdly managed success of *I Love Lucy*, suggested that Welles should do something for their company, Desilu. Welles had always been a fan of Ball's work: in 1940, he had proposed her for the lead in his adaptation of *The Smiler with a Knife*, one of the many doomed projects he fielded at RKO before at last hitting on *Citizen Kane*. RKO turned her down, but Welles had maintained a friendly relationship with her and Arnaz when they were both disgruntled contract players there. Ball had appeared several times on radio with Welles on CBS's *Orson Welles Almanac*, doing the sort of simple skit Welles adored: once, playing his secretary, Miss Grimace, she says: 'That'll be all.' 'That'll be all *who*?' replies Welles, haughtily. 'That'll be all, Fatso.' Very big laugh. Now she and Desi were in a position to help him, and when they met up again on the *Sullivan Show*, Arnaz asked Welles to come out to Desilu and do something with them. 'They still had great faith and confidence that Orson was a great creator,' Bernard Weitzman, Desilu's head of business and legal affairs, told Ben Walters, 'and a star, and a genius.'[4] Arnaz, with his sharp eye on the future of television, had noted the success of anthology series like *Alfred Hitchcock Presents*, launched just six months earlier, and proposed something similar for Welles, except with a different notion of the host's relationship to the programme:

> If we could accomplish the effect of you, as the host, in front of the television set in the viewer's living room, telling them what is happening or about to happen behind you, it would be much more intimate and we wouldn't have to be in the same set all the time. What do you think?[5]

This was music to Welles's ears, of course, a further extension of the *First Person Singular* idea, building on his extraordinary personal charm and capacity for instant intimacy with the viewer: much preferable to acting, which he regarded as a chore, and one, moreover, that made him anxious. Being obediently ours was as easy for Welles as falling off a log; he readily agreed to shoot a pilot programme with this format. The idea he offered them was *Volpone*, an extension or perhaps a contraction of the version he had been planning with Marc Blitzstein for City Center, with the additional element that the actors would bring on elements of the set and then take them off again.

The idea was greeted with little short of panic by his new partners: 'You can't do this script,' Arnaz's executives told Welles. 'It's outrageous. The networks would laugh you out of the business.'[6] It was Weitzman who, after going through the lists of optioned short stories, came up with John Collier's darkly humorous tale 'Youth from Vienna'.[7] Collier's story features a young endocrinologist, Humphrey, who falls for a Broadway star, Carolyn Coates, to whom he becomes engaged; he spends a great deal of his time away from her, studying in Vienna with the world's leading authority on glands. After three years' absence, he comes back to find Carolyn in love with Alan, a glamorous young tennis player. They determine to marry; Humphrey offers them what seems to be a generous wedding present: one of three phials of an elixir of youth, which he and his teacher have managed to formulate. But with it comes a warning: to be effective, the whole phial has to be consumed, which leaves the young couple with a dilemma – which of them is to take it? The plot is brilliantly worked out to create maximum mayhem in their lives, destroying their love; finally Carolyn returns to the endocrinologist, who reveals that the elixir was a fake all along.

The story immediately tickled Welles's fancy, perfectly reflecting his own taste for fatalistic fables in which human beings are caught, spider-like, in webs of their own weaving. The English-born but US-domiciled Collier had a particularly mordant world-view, expressed in an idiom that is both whimsical and needle-sharp, and verges on – and sometimes wholly embraces – the transgressive: his first book, *His Monkey Wife*, concerns the consummated relationship between a colonial administrator and a rather attractive primate named Emily. 'Youth from Vienna' is less shocking, but if anything more savage. Welles set to work on the pilot straight away, and produced a screenplay, entitled *The Fountain of Youth*, that is a masterpiece of adaptation, evidencing all of his editorial command. The story, already concise, is made yet more linear; wisely, Welles retains a great deal of Collier's original text, sensibly deferring to mainstream American sensibilities: he refrains, for example, from quoting Collier's account of the endocrinologist's courtship of the star:

> You may imagine the effect of this gaunt, gauche, hollow-cheeked young man, in altogether the wrong sort of jacket, sitting among that well-groomed crowd, lecturing a popular idol of twenty-three on the effects of certain unsavoury juices upon horrible insane little girls, who wallowed in their own dung. Of course, she fell wildly, madly, head-over-heels in love with him, and before the month was out it was announced they were engaged to be married.

Welles's interventions in the story are noteworthy. He makes the scientist considerably older than the starlet, which turns it into a slightly different story – a rather more conventional one, the revenge of an older man on the young, instead of a young man on his more beautiful contemporaries; he introduces the idea of the fountain of youth, along with a passing reference to Juan Ponce de Léon, who allegedly discovered Florida while looking for the mythic fountain; and – again perfectly wisely – he somewhat alters the narratorial tone to incorporate his own wry seen-it-all, man-of-the-world manner, which is rather different from Collier's acidulousness. It is, after all, 'Orson Welles speaking', as he says at the beginning of the film:

> How would you like to stay just as young as you are and not grow a day older for the next two hundred years? Oh, I'm not plugging some miracle new cosmetic. The question is actually faced by the three characters in our story, two men and a girl. The eternal triangle plus eternal youth add up to a whacky little

romance which we'll bring you, if we may, in just a few seconds.

It isn't Collier – nothing *whacky* about *his* world – but it is vintage Welles, and irresistibly engaging, filled with all his plump, twinkling melancholy at the folly and sadness of human affairs. From the beginning, he plays delightfully with us and with the medium. He said of *The Fountain of Youth* that, of all his films, it is his only comedy. If not exactly that, then it is – along with *F For Fake* – his most playful, and playfulness is one of the essences of Welles that only gets an occasional look-in in his major films. It seems, on the strength of his work for British television and this little masterpiece, that he felt he could let his hair down in a medium that as yet had no classics, no real form, and could become whatever you wanted it to be. It is also worth noting that he had superb source material on which to draw.

Desilu provided him with excellent back-up, mostly drawn from the *I Love Lucy* team. The young Chilean art director Claudio Guzman provided him with the very simple settings that he needed: convinced that the medium could never match the cinema visually, he set out to create a sort of collage world of elements, a shorthand of location and mood, in which the story could move at the speed of light. The supervising editor, Dann Cahn, who had been part of Welles's team on *Macbeth* ten years earlier, felt relaxed enough to be able make suggestions: a striking early shot of a light turning into the camera was his idea. As he had done on *Kane* and every other situation in which he felt relaxed, Welles happily gave permission to his collaborators to contribute ideas. Essentially, though, he had conceived the whole thing in his mind – the use of stills in the manner, as Ben Walters observes, of a *photo-roman*; the over-dubbing of his voice as the characters' lips move, or alternatively their voices coming out of Welles's lips: 'oh,' says Welles, but in Joi Lansing's voice, 'darling, what's all this about eternal youth?' The back-projection can suddenly transform a scene: Humphrey, newly returned from Vienna, stands at the dockside, the lights briefly go down to silhouette, and when they go up again he's in a restaurant and the waiter is relieving him of his overcoat. Welles steps into the frame, almost rudely sometimes, blotting out the characters. There is a delectable lightness of touch to the whole thing, the only conceivable misjudgement a sequence when the starlet contemplates the phial before drinking it. Welles speaks some of the remarkable paragraph in which Collier describes her experience:

> She stood and watched her reflection, and, in the stillness and silence of the apartment, she could feel and almost hear the remorseful erosion of time. Moment after moment, particles of skin wore away, hair follicles broke, splintered, and decayed, like the roots of dead trees. All those little tubes and miles of thread-like channels in the inner organs were silted up like doomed rivers. And the glands, the all-important glands were choking and clogging and falling apart. And she felt her marriage was falling apart, and Alan would be gone, and life would be gone.

In the film, as Welles speaks and Carolyn Coates looks into the mirror, she sees her face decay in a series of anatomical images. As realised, it seems a little schematic, almost like a PowerPoint presentation of decay; but the sequence still casts an authentically deathly chill over the otherwise merrily mordant proceedings. By all accounts, Welles had a delightful time during the brief four-day shoot. There was a composer-pianist on the set during the shoot and Welles would suggest a musical gesture, or a particular rhythm, to fit the scene; music too functions as a shorthand. When they recorded the soundtrack, Welles would propose certain instrumental effects. Whether this entirely justifies his credit as being responsible for 'musical arrangement' is uncertain.

The actors all give excellent accounts of themselves, especially perhaps Dan Tobin as the scientist, droll and steely; Joi Lansing, more often seen in a bikini than, as here, fully clad, lacks the carefree quality that Collier vividly describes, but is in every physical sense perfect for Welles's purposes (on screen and off, apparently). Billy House, memorable in Welles's *The Stranger*, makes a charming contribution; and the *I Love Lucy* regular Marjorie Bennett appears as a sort of conflation of Hedda Hopper and Louella Parsons. The pulchritudinous Rick Jason (later to be famous as Platoon Leader Second Lieutenant Gil Hanley in the series *Combat!*) gives a striking account of Alan Brodie, the tennis champion, but his relationship with Welles was not the best: 'Orson had, among other objectionable habits, a maddening one of walking away from you as you were in conversation with him,' wrote Jason in his memoir, *Scrapbooks of My Mind*.

> He'd talk to you over his shoulder and you found yourself trying to keep up with his stride as you spoke. One day he did it to me for the fourth or fifth time. I stopped, put two fingers in my mouth and let out a whistle that would frighten a banshee. He stopped, turned to me and said, 'Something the matter? Spit it

> out.' 'When we're conversing, will you kindly not walk away from me.' Absently he said, 'Was I doing that? Sorry.' (He wasn't sorry a bit.) He cleared his throat and said, 'What is it you wanted?' I stared at him. 'Nothing,' I said, turned and walked away.

But for the most part it was fun – the best fun Welles had had for a long time; the sort of fun he had been used to on the radio shows in the old *Campbell Playhouse* days, freewheeling, inventive, discovering ever more of the medium. Desi Arnaz gently made it clear to Welles that Desilu had no slack in their budgets: 'Orson, I know that you are partly responsible for breaking RKO Studios. You went to Brazil to do a picture, shot a million feet of film and never made the picture, and you couldn't have cared less. But I am not RKO. This is my Babalu money, so don't you fuck around with it.' [8]Thereafter Arnaz maintained a respectful distance as producer. Welles duly came in on schedule and only $5,000 over budget, and everyone who saw the film adored it, including the network executives who had it in their power to buy it, and indeed to authorise more episodes; at the end of *The Fountain of Youth*, indeed, Welles promises a second film – *Green Thoughts*, also adapted from Collier, a 'spook story', says Welles, of 'a man-eating Tiger Orchid'.

It never happened. Arnaz and company had overestimated the networks' stomach for risk of any kind. According to Weitzman, though they liked the film, they and the advertising agencies refused to believe that Welles could duplicate its success, especially on a weekly basis:

> They'd say, 'Mm, you know, we'd love to have it if it was somebody other than Orson Welles. He doesn't know much about television, and we don't really trust him. He didn't pay his taxes, they shipped him out of the country, and what did he do when he was in Europe? He did a couple of things, but nothing comparable to *Citizen Kane*.'[9]

Television was indeed, just as Welles had told Ed Murrow, already ossifying in its infancy. NBC's daringly highbrow president, Sylvester Weaver, was ousted in favour of a successor who proudly espoused 'what we call a schedule of meat-and-potatoes'. For Welles, it was Groundhog Day again: he had been here before, with Charles Koerner at RKO fifteen years earlier, trumpeting his notorious watchword: 'Showmanship before genius' – though, God knows, Welles had nothing against showmanship; indeed, *The Fountain of*

Youth was a fine example of it. When it was finally transmitted, two years later, as part of NBC's *Colgate Theatre* – a one-off series of unaired pilot programmes rushed in to replace the allegedly rigged game show *Dotto* – it was scarcely accompanied by fanfares, though the preview in the *New York World-Telegram and Sun* said that 'once you've seen it, you'll know why it was never bought. It's too daring, imaginative and funny to be confused with the stodgy fare they think TV audiences want.' The review the following morning had the simple headline: 'ORSON WELLES, TV NEEDS YOU':

> Mr Welles may, as his detractors say, be the prime ham of the Western world. He may also be a snob, a spendthrift and a poseur. His temper may be terrible, his self-infatuation hopeless. But his presence on the home screen last night projected excitement, gaiety and a note of quality that's most rare for these times.

In a summer, the reviewers says, that had 'all the excitement of a rummage sale', Welles's 'small caprice' was all the more to be treasured. 'It has humor. It had bold and unusual techniques. And it had great charm. Heavens, it even had a moral . . . now why can't we see Mr Welles every week?'[10] Remarkably, the programme won the prestigious Peabody Award, based at the University of Georgia; and the citation, spoken by the publisher and humourist Bennett Cerf, sums up the film eloquently and precisely: 'To Orson Welles, for the wit, originality, and insouciance of *The Fountain Of Youth*, NBC, one of the merriest, most irreverent half-hours of the year 1958, this special Peabody Award is given.'

The Award was too little and too late to influence Welles's career in television. If, in 1958, American television needed him, in time he came to need it much more: to the day he died, he pursued it ardently, abjectly and with scant reciprocation. By 1958, when he might have made a difference, each of the opportunities that could have led to something in the new medium – *Omnibus*, the CBS spectaculars, Desilu's projected anthology series – had come to nothing, due to a familiar combination of Welles's reputation, his obstinacy and his elusiveness. He did, in fact, make one further foray into American television, which manifested all of these elements. It was shot in 1957, to a commission from ABC's Jim Aubrey, as part of a planned weekly series, for which he was to be paid $200,000. Welles was slow to deliver, however. Aubrey told Arnaz that he would have to go out to Italy to track him down. 'I wondered how soon it would be before you had to go to Italy,' said Arnaz. 'How much has Orson spent already?' 'Over two hundred thousand dollars and we haven't seen one fucking foot of film yet.' Aubrey went to Italy. About three weeks later he came back. 'What happened in Italy?' asked Arnaz. 'Can you believe this?' said Aubrey. 'He wouldn't even see me.'[11] Eventually the first episode of the projected series, variously entitled *Portrait of Gina* or *Viva Italia*, was delivered, but immediately rejected. Leonard Goldenson, Aubrey's superior, described it as 'very poorly done' and 'little more than a home movie', and returned it to Welles, who dragged the cans around Europe with him for a while, finally leaving them behind in a hotel room in the Ritz Hotel in Paris, where they repined in the lost and found department till the early 1980s.

Welles's desire to rid himself of the film is understandable. It recycles all the familiar tropes of his documentary style, but this time around with neither charm nor inventiveness. Even his own persona, such a reliable standby in a crisis, falls flat. He seems to have an underlying point to make, which is about the ingratitude of the Italians, something from which he undoubtedly felt he had suffered, but it makes for a very curmudgeonly interlocutor. Seen in the twenty-first century, the film also suffers from a drooling heavy-breathing commentary on 'the ladies of Italy', as the camera roams over various posters and paintings featuring parts of their semi-clothed anatomies. In fact the tone of the piece is that of a gossip column, underlined by an over-vivacious score consisting of every notable piece of Italian music from Rossini to 'Funiculì, Funiculà', although from time to time, for no discernible reason, Harry Lime's zither-theme makes an appearance. The Italian-bashing starts in earnest pretty quickly: Welles tells us that Rossano Brazzi (the biggest Italian star of the day internationally) isn't *disliked* in Italy, but he certainly isn't adored there; Brazzi concurs wryly, noting that the greatest of all Italian actresses, Eleanora Duse – worshipped everywhere else in the world – played to half-empty houses in her native land. And Caruso said he'd die in Italy, but never sing there. And so it goes on. Paola Mori is roped in to tell us that Italians don't like going to see shows: they prefer to make a show of themselves. Welles interviews Vittorio De Sica – 'one of the few directors in Italy who deserves to be called great' – who tells us that his films are always flops in Italy.

Welles sets off for Subiaco, where Gina Lollobrigida – the ostensible subject of the film – was born. The people of Subiaco aren't proud of her success, we learn; in fact they're not very nice people at all. A pen pal of Gina's is located; from her we discover that, as a child, Gina was unhappy, had few friends and couldn't get away quickly enough. 'Fifteen hundred years ago,' says Welles, 'history took leave of Subiaco, never to return: we'll take our cue from history. And from Gina – she left town in a hurry: let's follow suit.' Finally we meet her. It was her first appearance on television; quite a coup. She is ravishing to behold, but evidently furious about many things: the newspapers, the public, the government. 'What do the papers do to destroy you?' prompts Welles. 'EVERYTHING!' she cries back. 'Why are people so nasty to you?' She shrugs: 'Italy is a strange country.' 'A strange country,' repeats Welles, adding, with patent insincerity, 'but adorable – the people are adorable.' And he bids us farewell (for once not obediently ours) with the word *ciao*. '*Ciao* for now.' It was *ciao* for good for the series.

The programme is a remarkable and unusual example of Welles unadrenalised, unable to summon up any enthusiasm for the task in hand. The camera work is absolutely routine; he can't even get animated by the idea of playing 'Orson Welles'. The programme bears the same relationship to his better television work as *Mr Arkadin* does to *Citizen Kane*; its feebleness is all the more astonishing in such close proximity to *The Fountain of Youth*. It closed the last door on any fruitful relationship that he might have had with American television.

⋆

While Welles was working for Desilu, two years earlier, he had, at his own suggestion, stayed with the Arnazes in Hollywood: not a happy time for them. He remained there for ten weeks, 'but it seemed like ten years', according to Lucille Ball. He occupied the guest house, but regarded the rest of the house as an annexe to it. 'He had the servants hopping,' she told her neighbour, Jim Brochu, who wrote it all down. 'He'd walk in the living room, all in black with his big cigar blowing, and scare the hell out of the kids. I heard Little Desi crying one afternoon, and I thought, "Orson's home."'[12]

Ball was not the first person to find Welles reminding her of Sheridan Whiteside in *The Man Who Came to Dinner.* She claimed, half-seriously, that in order to get him out of the house she invited him to do an episode of *I Love Lucy*, which he duly did. The premise of 'Lucy Meets Orson Welles' goes back as far as the *Orson Welles Almanac Shows* – further, in fact, right back to Welles standing in for Jack Benny on Benny's own show: as in *I Love Lucy*, he gave his much-recycled performance of himself as a disdainful Great Thespian – a performance he was not entirely averse to giving in real life. In this case, 'Orson Welles' is in need of an assistant for his magic act and asks Ricky if Lucy will oblige. She, meanwhile, assumes that, on the strength of her unforgettable Juliet at school, Welles wants her to perform Shakespeare with him. After much toing and froing she does end up, of course, assisting him in his magic act – though not before he has given her and Ricky a glimpse of his genius as a Shakespearean, in a heavily rhetorical account of Romeo's soliloquy in Juliet's tomb in the last act of the play, 'Ah, dear Juliet, why art thou yet so fair?' Ricky and Lucy are duly awed, after which the plot then limply climaxes with the magic act, in which Lucy assists Welles in the same Broom Suspension effect he had just successfully performed in Las Vegas.

The act requires a great deal from the assistant, as it happens, including considerable powers of abdominal control; this had not been explained to Lucy. It was, she told Brichu, the most painful experience of her life, worse than childbirth. 'It felt like the broom was up my ass, and I had to stay on the goddamned thing for at least five minutes,' which lends a certain retrospective poignancy to Welles's line 'The Princess will feel nothing!' and an unmistakable urgency to Lucy's last line: 'Romeo, wherefore art thou, Romeo? Romeo, get me down from here.' The show was, she told Brichu, 'a stinker', and it is hard to disagree. For all Welles's longing to be part of the world of comedy (attempts to do so would recur almost to his dying day), it is not where he belongs; or perhaps, to be more precise, he never found a comic persona that could integrate with anyone else.

Welles's next engagement in his re-establishment of himself in America was a Hollywood B-movie, *Man in the Shadow.* Welles's agents proposed him for the film's heavy, Renchler, for $60,000, rather less than his going rate, but he urgently needed it. The studio – astonished – agreed, though it was rather more than their going rate. Up to that point the film, produced by Albert Zugsmith for Universal, had been, in Zugsmith's words, 'a lousy little Jeff Chandler movie'; now it was 'a big, big picture'.[13] In truth, it was never just a lousy little picture: it is a serious account of racism on the Mexican–American border and of the tyranny and corruption of wealth. It is also shot in CinemaScope, and no CinemaScope movie was ever a lousy little movie: lousy, perhaps, but not little. Moreover Chandler (who, by curious chance, had – as a singer – very successfully preceded Welles at the Riviera Club in Las Vegas a year earlier) was only held back from being a major star by his contract with Universal; when he left them, he swiftly rose to the front rank. And Jack Arnold, who was slated to direct, although scarcely D.W. Griffith, had had some considerable success with *The Creature from the Black Lagoon*, *The Incredible Shrinking Man* and *It Came from Outer Space*, all superb examples of their genre (and all produced by Welles's old whipping boy from Mercury days, William Alland – Thompson the reporter in *Citizen Kane*).

Clearly, though, Welles's presence in the cast raised the temperature, especially on the first day: he showed up on the set, according to Zugsmith, with a fistful of closely typed pages, saying, 'You'll be interested to see the changes for today.' Welles and Zugsmith had already met, in the wardrobe department: Welles had demanded the use of his own make-up artist and Zugsmith had refused. Reasonably and pleasantly, Welles asked again for the man; he was, Welles said, the only one who understood his 'nose problem', and Zugsmith, charmed by this display of vulnerability, graciously acceded. The rewrite situation was less easily resolved. By the time Zugsmith arrived at the set on that first morning they were already shooting the scene, in Welles's rewritten version. Zugsmith went over and told him he thought it was a great improvement, but that it would really help everyone if they could have the scene the night before shooting. Over vodka and his favourite cigar, Welles agreed that he and Zugsmith would rewrite the following day's scenes every night, which is how it happened. The director, Jack Arnold, seems to have been surprisingly compliant with this usurpation of his authority, but he and Welles had a contretemps that same first day of shooting, a stand-off that was clearly in the nature of a test. They were shooting the last scene of the picture, where all the townspeople went out to Renchler's ranch and started chasing him. Arnold wanted a shot, he told Lawrence French, in which Welles, running away, would be tripped up:

> I had a mattress that was out of camera range to catch him, and as I was setting up the shot Orson came over to me and looked at me with piercing eyes and said with that deep sonorous voice of his, 'Mr Arnold, exactly what are you doing?' I told him: 'In this scene you're going to trip and fall onto a mattress that's off-camera.' He said, 'Oh no, I can't do that. That's not going to work.' I said, 'Mr Welles, you are a genius and a wonderful director, but I'm making this picture and it's my name that will be on it, so if it's the last shot I make, it's going to be in this movie.'[14]

And so it was. The film is well made, well and interestingly shot and on the whole well acted. The weakest spot, alas, is Welles's performance, his expressive powers as so often blocked by his nose. The easy communicativeness of *The Fountain of Youth* or the wit of Harry Lime are strait-jacketed; he wears a mask, but it is not a mask that liberates, it only confines. Every line he utters simply restates the character – there is no sense whatever of immediacy, of what the American stage actor William Gillette so precisely described as the illusion of the first time; no sense that the character might possibly have responded differently. Welles's Renchler technically fulfils the function of the heavy, but he has no actuality, so there is no danger, no surprise, no life. There is nothing for us to discover: Welles tells us at every turn exactly what to think about the character and his actions. Interestingly enough, Welles asked Arnold if in a certain sequence he could be filmed from below; Arnold agreed, and they shot the sequence as Welles proposed. It does not appear in the finished film; it would have no doubt stood out as stylised. But Welles was right: for his performances in this vein to have life (and there were many, many more such performances to come) a degree of distortion in the filming is called for, producing a heightened expressiveness, the grotesque danger and energy of fable or fairy tale. Filmed in the missionary position, as it were, Welles's Renchler is like opera without music – like a vampire in the daylight. It is stranded, beached, lacking the element that brings it to life.

By comparison, Jeff Chandler, certainly a lesser figure in every way than Welles, is alive and involving; we care for him, we follow his story – and a very good one it is. It has often been pointed out that *Man in the Shadow* is a sort of companion piece to *Touch of Evil*: both are studies of racism; both turn, symbolically, on a badge. Ben Sadler, Chandler's character, has his stripped from him, while Welles's Quinlan tenders his in pique. The big difference between the films is, of course, that *Touch of Evil* is a work of idiosyncratic genius, as opposed to a good solid achievement.

CHAPTER THIRTEEN

Venice of America

THERE ARE a number of versions of how Welles came to direct *Touch of Evil*. Al Zugsmith's is perhaps the most colourful: on the last night of shooting *Man in the Shadow* in 1956, he told Todd McCarthy and Charles Flynn – in the anthology of film history and criticism, *Kings of the Bs* – that he and Welles got together to celebrate their successful working relationship. Welles said he'd like to direct a movie for Zugsmith. 'What's the worst script you've got?' he asked. Zugsmith handed him *Badge of Evil*, adapted by Paul Monash from a recently published novel by 'Whit Masterson' (a pseudonym for the successful novel-writing team of Bob Wade and Bill Miller), which Universal had optioned. Welles asked for two weeks to write a new screenplay, which he duly delivered; he and Zugsmith then went through it together, trimming it down to size. 'The studios aren't interested in artistic product,' observes Zugsmith. 'Orson', he adds, piously, 'is primarily an artist, a great one.'[1] There is no mention in this account of Welles being cast as Quinlan.

Welles himself recollected it quite differently when talking to Peter Bogdanovich: after *Man in the Shadow*, he said, Universal sent him a script – 'a very bad one' – featuring a crooked detective they wanted him to play. 'I was still wondering whether I could afford *not* to make it when they called up Chuck Heston and said, "Here's a script – we'd like you to read it. We have Welles." And Heston misunderstood them and said, "Well, any picture that Welles directs, I'll make."' And so, according to Welles, they asked him to direct it.[2] Heston's own story is significantly, if subtly different: he read the script on Boxing Day 1956 and the conversation with the studio the following day went, he says, like this:

> 'This really depends on who directs it. Who's going to direct it?' They said, 'We don't know who's going to direct it, but we have Orson Welles to play the heavy.' And I said, 'Well, you know, he's a pretty good director. Why don't you have him direct it?' And

you'd think I'd suggested my mother direct it. But they came back and they said, 'Well, yes. Okay.'[3]

Heston is much the most reliable of the three witnesses: he kept a daily journal throughout the period, which, though perhaps not as surreally entertaining as Micheál MacLiammóir's *Othello* journal, *Put Money in Thy Purse*, gives – along with the relevant chapters of his autobiography, *In the Arena* – a very clear guide to the tangled history, especially in its murky post-production period, of the last film Welles directed in America.

The almost grudging manner in which Universal had accepted Welles as director was reflected in his being paid neither to direct nor to rewrite the film: he did the whole thing for his relatively modest actor's salary. It was well worth it to him. This was exactly what he needed; exactly what he had come back from Europe for a year earlier – not television, not the stage, not Las Vegas; he wanted to direct a film, in Hollywood. He had earlier been announced as directing his pal Charlie Lederer's script from 'Tip on a Dead Jockey' for MGM, but it had fallen through. *Badge of Evil* was a better option: a major Hollywood film with a star of the highest magnitude; *The Ten Commandments* had opened in October 1956 and Heston was now a household name.

Welles instantly saw the potential in the material: the Monash screenplay's story of corruption and betrayal spoke to his preoccupations loud and clear. In fact, as François Thomas and Jean-Pierre Berthomé have shown, he retained a great deal of Monash's work: Monash was no hack, either as writer or producer; in 1958, the year *Touch of Evil* appeared, he picked up an Emmy Award; a year later, he wrote and produced the pilot for the TV series *The Untouchables*. Welles retained many of the changes Monash had made to the extremely readable, hard-hitting original novel, *Badge of Evil*, which he claimed not to have read until after he'd shot the film; in fact he incorporated elements from the novel that Monash had not thought to include. The result was a screenplay that was exceptionally well grounded, a sturdy springboard for the story Welles wanted to tell, centring on the struggle between a veteran cop in the grip of an entrenched racism because his wife was killed by a Mexican, a man so convinced of his own intuition that he forges evidence to support it, and an idealistic young district attorney who stands for the letter of the law.

Welles and Heston quickly got acquainted, Welles overwhelming the very serious and proper new young star with his charm: 'He filled the room with his voice, his energy . . . with *himself*,' Heston wrote in *In the Arena*. 'He gave me a very large malt whiskey splashed with water, and mesmerised me for an afternoon.' Heston had just turned down a lot of money to appear in a television special; for *Badge of Evil*, as it was still known, he would get an unreliable 7.5 per cent of the gross, but he was excited by the prospect of working with Welles. 'I think we have a chance at a better picture than almost any I could make now,' he told his journal. 'I'm bound to learn a great deal from Welles, in any case. I think he has what I need now.'[4]

Heston was immensely impressed by the new screenplay. Welles had done his rewrite in less than a week, adding layers to his own character, Hank Quinlan; crucially relocating the action to a Mexican–American border town; and changing the name and nationality of the investigating attorney (Heston's character): he would now be a Mexican called Vargas, they decided, whereas his wife – Mexican in the novel – would be an upper-class gringa; these changes intensify and dramatise the racist undercurrent already present in both screenplay and novel. The revised screenplay was palpably the work of the man who, eleven years earlier, had bravely and passionately taken up the cause of the real-life blinded black veteran Isaac Woodard. As he had said frequently in his interviews in Europe, nothing upset Welles more than the abuse of police powers, and his commitment to the idea of racial equality had been unwavering, from as early as his 1936 Harlem *Macbeth*. It may well be, too, that he was responding to the mood in America in early 1957: when he started filming *Badge of Evil*, the National Association for the Advancement of Colored People – Welles's old comrades-in-arms on the Isaac Woodard campaign – had just initiated the actions that would culminate six months later in the extraordinary scenes in Little Rock, Arkansas, in which a thousand paratroopers escorted nine black students into a desegregated school. Of course the border town in *Touch of Evil* is in Mexico, but racism is racism, and in America, in 1957, it was endemic.

The studio was resistant to the idea of shooting on location at the border itself ('they wanted Orson where they could keep an eye on him,' says Heston),[5] which prompted Welles to one of his great creative leaps: he found a location outside Los Angeles, which he would make into his own border town, shooting it selectively, to create its reality in the camera. The place was Venice, California, known as 'the Slum by the sea', with its low-rent, rundown bungalows that were attractive to immigrants (among them a number of Holocaust survivors) and a lot of arty young kids; their hangouts were frequently raided by the police. There, fifty years earlier, the quixotic philanthropist Abbot Kinney had built what he called

'Venice of America', at vast expense – a people's Xanadu on water, with a network of canals and bridges and streets faithfully reproducing those of Venice itself. It had been a sort of mirage, gondolas and gondoliers on the Californian coast, and it had evaporated soon enough, with the Great Crash. In that same year oil was discovered, derricks and refineries were installed in vast numbers and it was suddenly a boom-town. This too was short-lived. But, though many of the canals had been filled in and most of the bridges pulled down, a picturesque few had remained, along with whole blocks of ornate and faithfully reproduced Venetian arcades, loured over by the cranes and derricks. Out of this haunted, shabby environment, with its myriad ghosts, Welles fashioned his Las Robles, a Mexican border town like none other, a *capriccio* made up of disparate and incongruous elements, each with its own potent echoes.

Welles knew how important this film was to him, and he embarked on it with intense focus, flair and cunning. This last was necessary, he felt, because he was working for a boss again. Louis Dolivet, his last producer, whom he had thought a friend, had turned into a boss – a vengeful one, at that, who would continue pursuing Welles for some years. But here at Universal he was working for real old-style Studio Bosses: in this instance, Edward Muhl, a decent, civilised fellow, but a studio man through and through, who started as secretary to the founder of Universal, Carl Laemmle; now he was head of production at Universal International and would remain in that job until 1973, through thick and thin (and there was rather a lot of both). To Welles, Muhl was The Enemy. It was nothing personal: Muhl simply represented authority, and authority threatened autonomy. Authority was determined to contain Welles, to limit him, to tell him what to do. Heston saw what was going on. 'Orson had an odd blind spot,' he observed. 'He was infinitely charming with his crew and actors, but I've seen him deliberately insult studio heads. Very dumb. Those are the guys with the money. If they won't give you any, you don't get to make any movies.'[6]

This simple truth was not one Welles was ever going to embrace. On this occasion his deep-seated sense of Us Against Them stimulated him into a brilliantly executed *coup de théâtre*. In cahoots with the actors, he rehearsed – in his own house, unbeknown to the studio – a particularly complex single-shot sequence: the scene in the crowded apartment of the prime suspect, Sanchez, which involved people going back and forth, talking over each other, moving in and out of the rooms of the apartment as Vargas begins to suspect that Sanchez is not getting a fair hearing. The studio sensed something was going on: 'they seem to fear what I hope,' wrote Heston in his diary for 7 February 1957, ten days before shooting began: 'that he'll make an offbeat film out of what they'd planned as a predictable little programmer.' The studio's anxiety was all grist to Welles's mill. Heston vividly catches the drama of it: on the first day of shooting, 18 February, 'we never turned a camera all morning or all afternoon, then the studio brass started gathering in the shadows in anxious little knots. By the time we began filming at a quarter to six, I know they'd written off the whole day. At seven-forty, Orson said, "OK, print. That's a wrap on this set. We're two days ahead of schedule."' They had shot, as Heston records, twelve pages in one take, as well as inserts, two-shots and over-the-shoulder shots: 'the whole scene in one, moving through three rooms, with seven speaking parts'. This mightily impressed the studio brass, just as it was intended to; from then on they left Welles to his own devices – exactly the result he had wanted.

Welles's adrenalin was now at full flood; he mined every scene for its cinematic potential, constantly adapting to changing circumstances, ceaselessly inventing, pushing the crew, the actors and himself as far as possible. This was Welles in his absolute element, leaving his signature on every frame, every performance, every location. Heston's journal again captures the exhilaration of the experience, the sense of freedom from received practice, in his account of a scene between Heston's Vargas and Mort Mills's Schwartz, which was set in a car. This would normally have been shot in the studio, against back-projection, but Welles wanted to do it in a real car, driving down a real alley – no easy matter in 1957. The cinematographer rigged up the shot, cramming the back of the car with batteries and strapping the camera to a wooden platform on the hood; the recording unit twisted their cables around the seats and taped mikes to the dashboard. There was no room on the car for a camera operator or a sound mixer. 'Someone suggested cutting the front off the car and towing the rear half behind a truck large enough to carry a crew,' says Heston. Welles was outraged. 'Nonsense!' he shouted. 'These boys can shoot it without a crew.' At the prospect, 'these boys' really became boys. Catching Welles's spirit of derring-do, Heston drove half a mile down the alley and said, 'Turn over.' Mills flipped the right switches, checked the appropriate dials. 'Speed.' Heston revved up the car's engine and shouted, 'Action!' and they were off. When they got down to the end of the alley, Welles said, 'How was it?' Heston said, 'Perfect! I'd like one more.'[7] The shot is exhilarating: the roof is down, the wind blows on their shirts, the adrenalin is sky-high – perhaps higher, to be strict about it, than the scene calls for. But the excitement of seeing the streets hurtling by behind the two men is irresistible. Heston proudly claimed that it was the first time a dialogue scene had been shot in a moving car. 'We had a marvellous time,' he wrote, which he did – and they all did, from the beginning of the shoot to the end.

Part of the exhilaration Welles felt while shooting *Touch of Evil* was due to his having a superb technical crew at his disposal, who could handle anything he threw at them. He and the cinematographer, Russell Metty, were old colleagues: Metty had been a 'contrast consultant' on *Citizen Kane* as far back as 1941; later, on *The Magnificent Ambersons*, he had shot some of the additional material required by RKO while Welles was still in Brazil; and in 1946 he had been Welles's director of photography on his most overtly commercial picture, *The Stranger*. Metty's work on the film, culminating in the superb Grand Guignol finale at the top of the clock tower, is very striking, especially in his bold carving-up of shadow and light; not for nothing had he once been a contrast consultant. It was with *The Stranger* that Metty had come into his own as a cinematographer: thrilled by his swiftness, impressed by his ideas, Welles had given him his head. After *The Stranger*, Metty formed a long and fruitful partnership with the German-American director Douglas Sirk, as different a director from Welles as could possibly be imagined; Metty evolved a distinct style for him, emphasising emotional ambience and shooting in colour; but, reunited with Welles, he immediately fell back into his stride, returning to black-and-white with all his old mastery.

Their collaboration on *Touch of Evil* is on a par with Welles's relationship with Greg Toland on *Kane*: creative, inventive, playful, entirely mutual. Between them, Metty and Welles summon up a definitive world, one of the greatest of all moviescapes, integrating an expressionist vocabulary of low and skewed angles and distorting lenses into the more humdrum vernacular of cop movies, plunging the audience into the characters' nightmarish experience. There was genuine give-and-take between director and cinematographer: Welles, for example, always acknowledged that the idea of shooting the film's classic opening sequence in a nearly continuous tracking shot had been Metty's; he immediately saw its potential and pushed it as far as it could go. And, as with *Kane*, Welles's delight in the medium and his refusal to be confined by any perceived limitations is embodied in the very fabric of the film, so that generations of film-makers have been inspired by it to make movies themselves: murky though the world it discloses may be, every frame of *Touch of Evil* celebrates the art of film.

There was excitement around the project from the beginning; actors queued up to be in it. Heston as Vargas, of course, had been cast by Universal; as was Susan Vargas, Janet Leigh, who had been proving herself in a multitude of genres, not least in romantic vehicles with her then-husband Tony Curtis. She gave herself eagerly to the experience of working with Welles: 'It started with rehearsals,' she said. 'We rehearsed two weeks prior to shooting, which was unusual. We rewrote most of the dialogue, all of us, which was also unusual, and Mr Welles always wanted our input. It was a collective effort, and there was such a surge of participation, of creativity, of energy. You could feel the pulse growing as we rehearsed.'[8] To a large extent, Welles framed the roles of the Vargases around the actors he had been given. He encouraged Heston – tall, athletic and commanding, but oddly inflexible – to look as Mexican as he could; the effect is striking, though not notably Hispanic: Heston remains merely tall, athletic, commanding and oddly inflexible. But Welles integrates him brilliantly into the texture of the film, keeping him moving as much as possible, part of the group, denying him any dramatic solo *moments*; Leigh, who broke her arm before shooting began, but gamely carried on, is fresh and sassy and very credibly in love with her husband (alas, Heston refrains from showing comparable tenderness towards her). They are the innocents in a world of desperadoes and oddballs.

Here Welles drew around him an astonishing repertory of character actors, or in some cases just characters, a troupe to match the one he assembled for *Mr Arkadin*. As the would-be gang-leader, Uncle Joe Grandi, Welles's chum Akim Tamiroff (an *Arkadin* veteran, of course) is as richly layered as ever, masterfully pitching his performance between slapstick – with an ever-shifting wig and uncertain command over his gang – and genuine menace; Dennis Weaver, fresh from starring on television as Chester in *Gunsmoke*, presents a nervy, twitchy night-watchman, who seems to be in perpetual motion, dancing a St Vitus's dance in and out of the motel, alternately appalled and attracted by Leigh's Susan Vargas. The character of the night-watchman was a late addition to the script, and Welles encouraged Weaver to push himself into new territory as an actor. His scenes were for the most part improvised, but he was anxious to adhere to what he and Welles had discussed in terms of character:

> I told Orson I was having trouble staying in the room and still being true to the selection we had decided on. I had an impulse to run and he asked what was stopping me. I said according to the script I've got to stay in the room. He told me the script

must yield to the truth . . . 'so run!'[9]

The performance sometimes tips over into pantomime – as does Tamiroff's occasionally – which suggests a dimension of the film that Welles chose not to push as far as he might have done. But throughout the film there is always a sense of freedom, of spontaneity. 'You felt you were inventing something as you went along,' Janet Leigh remembered, fondly. 'Mr Welles wanted to seize every moment. He didn't want one bland moment. He made you feel you were involved in a wonderful event that was happening before your eyes.'

Ray Collins and Jo Cotten bring up the rear on behalf of the old Mercury company – Cotten as a police surgeon, kitted out with spectacles and a luxuriant moustache, which disguise him as effectively as the same props aged him in *Citizen Kane* – not at all, that is. Collins is his usual credible self; and it is a moment of note when the three of them (Collins, Cotten and Welles) share a screen again after all those years. Mercedes McCambridge, roped in at the last moment, is quite unnerving as the seemingly gay biker in the sequence in the motel in which the gang menaces Susan. Welles had suddenly summoned the actress to the set one day. 'Did I have a pair of black slacks and a black sweater? Sure I had. Did I have a black leather jacket? I said I wouldn't be caught dead in a black leather jacket. He said never mind, come anyhow. I went.'[10] He put her in the make-up chair, cut her hair, rubbed black shoe-polish into it till it turned into a mass of black ringlets, blackened a small mole on the side of her face and rubbed more polish into her eyebrows. He told her to affect a gruff Mexican accent, burst into the motel room with the gang and say that she would hang around and watch. It took one take; she was back home in Bel Air by 4 p.m. that afternoon. This, too, is Welles in his element, joyously playing with the best electric train set a boy ever had: being able to summon actors and mould them into pleasing and interesting shapes. It's his toy theatre come back to life; it's him and his juvenile thespians at Todd all over again. And it is an integral part of the brilliance of *Touch of Evil*.

Luxury casting beyond the dreams of Mammon comes in the form of Zsa Zsa Gabor as the hostess of a bar briefly visited, and, supremely, in Marlene Dietrich's Tana, the bordello keeper. Of indeterminate nationality, she seems to be the only employee in the place, impassively dealing out the truth, purveying a sense of fatalism without judgement: the very quality Dietrich expressed so potently in her stage act. This is her in Josef von Sternberg mode, with black wig (it had been made for Elizabeth Taylor) and a trim, timeless body. She is somehow detached from the action and yet full of brilliantly subdued emotion, providing a plangent descant to the turmoil and destruction all around her. She was rightly proud of her delivery of the famous last lines of the film: 'He was some kind of a man. What does it matter what you say about people?', which places the whole drama that has preceded it *sub specie aeternitatis*. But for Quinlan, Tana represents some sort of past happiness – so distantly past that there can be no memory of it, just an association. The idiotic pianola tune that invariably heralds and accompanies her appearances takes Quinlan into a dream of that prelapsarian state of innocence and happiness which lies at the heart of so much of Welles's work: Kane's carefree tobogganing childhood, the Ambersons' golden days of wealth and elegance, Michael O'Hara's life before he set eyes on Elsa Bannister, Falstaff's reverie of Merrie England – and Welles's very own and private Eden, the hotel at Grand Detour, near Springfield, Illinois, the demi-paradise over which (in his soft-focused memory) his father had presided. Just such a pianola might have played there as tinkles away in Tana's establishment, recycling the same idiotic tune over and over again: the heart's history arrested, stopped as surely as Miss Havisham's clocks, never moving forward, forever stuck in a groove.

Dietrich brings an unfathomable depth to what has passed between her and Quinlan. We can know nothing of it, of those whole weeks at a time when he would stay there, drunk. Perhaps there is something more personal lurking in the background, something between the two actors themselves. Dietrich told *Esquire* magazine that she had been 'crazy' about Welles in the Forties, when he was sawing her up in *The Mercury Wonder Show*. 'I was just crazy about him – we were great friends – but nothing . . . because Orson doesn't like blonde women. He only likes dark women. And suddenly when he saw me in this dark wig, he looked at me with new eyes. Was this Marlene?' Harry Lime-like, her effect on the film is out of all proportion to the amount of screen time she occupies.

It is not rare in Welles's films for one actor to break away from the overall gesture of the film to embody a distilled human truth, functioning as a kind of choric figure: in *The Magnificent Ambersons* it is Agnes Moorehead, in *The Lady from Shanghai* it is Glenn Anders. In *Touch of Evil* there are two actors who do this – Dietrich, and Joseph Calleia, playing Quinlan's deceived colleague, Menzies. Calleia's haunted features figure more and more prominently on screen as the truth about Quinlan increasingly dawns on him, along with the knowledge that he must betray him. Welles spoke beautifully about Calleia, whom he had seen on the Broadway stage when he was a boy, and who, though he rarely played a leading part, was, Welles believed, one of the best actors in the business. 'You play next to him,' Welles said, 'and you just feel the thing that you do with a big actor – this dynamo going on.'[11] Calleia's abundant inner life casts a growing spell over the film as it comes to its climax, bringing to vividly personal life Welles's sempiternal subject: betrayal.

Quinlan, *Touch of Evil*'s betrayed anti-hero, is one of Welles's most extreme physical characterisations. There is no suggestion of bulk, either in the original novel or in Monash's screenplay; he is simply lame as a result of a bullet in the leg, a bullet intended for his fellow-officer, Menzies. In Welles's re-imaging his reformed alcoholism has driven him to seek consolation in candy bars, which he must have been consuming by the wagonload. He's so fat that Tana doesn't recognise him at first. 'You're a mess, honey,' she tells him, factually, when she does. Bud Westmore, from the distinguished dynasty of Hollywood make-up artists, had devised with Welles as gross and ugly a visage for Quinlan as possible, with Welles's large eyes reduced to little rodent-like peepers, his own nose covered with a long ski-slope of a conk, the face weighed down with puffy jowls, the mouth at once slobbery and slitty. Welles was far from slim at the time, but he added massive padding to his bulk. This hobbling man-mountain, this slag-heap of iniquity – it demands a Shakespearean vocabulary of insults to do justice to him. And, indeed, Quinlan is a dystopian Falstaff, one who – unlike the Fat Knight – is not witty in himself, nor is 'the cause that wit is in other men': he is beyond wit, deserving only of Tana's deep astonishment. But this man is dangerous; dangerous above all because he places his intuition above the evidence. He is every cop, like Officer X, who has come to believe that he is justice. He is not corrupt in the financial sense: his corruption is a form of vanity, the vanity of those who believe themselves infallible. And he is also a man out for revenge: revenge on the race that killed his wife, a loss that we are given to understand has destroyed his life. All of this is brilliantly, vividly conveyed – spelled out, one might say – in Welles's performance, which, invariably shot from below, is overwhelmingly impressive.

And yet it does not stir us, as Calleia or Dietrich stir us; it does not move us, or even provoke us to anger – 'such things should not be!' It is monumental in a way that the performances in *Ivan the Terrible* (equally huge, equally schematic, it would seem) are not: with Eisenstein, the living human being is still at the centre of the performance. Welles's Quinlan is an unforgettable portrait of corruption, physical and moral, but it is not a living one. If there is an actor whom he resembles, it is Dietrich's old sparring partner in *The Blue Angel*, Emil Jannings, a performer likewise given to creating extraordinary shapes that he filled, not with lived life, but with a wealth of detail and a selection of off-the-peg emotions. It is worth recollecting Walter Kerr's words about Welles's King Lear: 'every effect is a bequest of Mr Welles's inventive but much too conniving mind. His heart seems to have nothing to say.' A year later, at a press conference in Brussels, Welles made a remarkable admission: 'I do not feel myself,' he said, 'essentially a cinema actor; my faculties as an actor are better in the theatre. I have to make an enormous effort to create the appropriate cinematic effect which in a true cinema actor is instinct. I have to go through a complex mental process to get the effect Gary Cooper gets when he breathes, that Raimu gets just by his presence, and what's more, I'm not even sure I succeed.'[12] What is curious is that the film Welles made is the opposite of his performance: mercurial, fluid, inventive, constantly morphing stylistically in dream-like fashion.

Once Welles's creativity was engaged, he followed it to the limits. He had increasingly shifted shooting away from the studio and out to Venice or to bleak, flat Palmdale in northern California (where most of the motel sequences are shot); on an impulse, he decided one rainy night to shoot a sequence in the hotel elevator, getting the athletic Heston to race up the stairs in real time to meet it at the end of its journey (the first-ever such shot in a film, according to Heston, a great *Guinness Book of Records* man). 'Not tough to do today, with battery powered sound and camera,' notes Heston in *In the Arena*, 'but a real killer shot in 1957, with light and sound cables hanging three stories down the elevator shaft.' The same night, Welles and Heston were relieving their bladders in the hotel's basement cellar: 'Wouldn't this be a great place to do that scene in the file room with you and Joe Calleia?' said Welles. Zipping up, Heston replied, 'It sure would. But isn't that scheduled for Friday, back in the studio? They'll have the set built by now. Besides, Joe isn't even called tonight. It's two a.m.; he'll be dead asleep. We've got three more pages to shoot up on the third floor anyway. That'll take the rest of the night.' 'Nonsense! He'll be better if he's confused. That's what the scene's about,' roared Welles, his eyes gleaming.[13]

Calleia was sent for; the two remaining set-ups were quickly despatched, and they shot the scene, with a groggy, baffled Calleia, to superb effect: Heston drives the scene forward, as Calleia drifts in and out of focus. This is a kind of Method filming, the only sort of Method-anything that Welles countenanced. The cellar of the hotel, moreover, proves to be a superb location, a sort of shiny Fritz Lang prison, like something out of *Metropolis*. The final sequence of the film, as Vargas follows Quinlan and Menzies over and under bridges and through water, his recording device in his hand, and the sharp angles of the derricks soaring up into the black night, evokes the world of the Piranesi dungeons that Welles had hoped to summon up for his *King Lear* at the City Center.

They had shot fifteen nights one after another, but, swept along by exhilaration at what they were doing, everyone held up. Word had spread to the front office, as it always will do; Heston reported that you had to come early to get a seat for the showing of the rushes. Even the Universal press office seemed to have got the hang of it. Their initial press release rejoices in Welles's unconventional approach, telling the whole legendary story, more or less accurately: the first day's shooting, the opening tracking shot, the relocation of the scene in the DA's office, the choice of Venice as location.

> Within a week after rolling the initial take, Orson had broken every rule in the book . . . refusing the easy-to shoot-in 'wild walls' of a sound stage which can be moved or removed for any camera angle, Welles deliberately picked the second story bedroom of a dilapidated hotel for the room occupied by Janet Leigh and another room in the same building for the back office in police headquarters. 'Unheard of,' stammered technicians. 'Nonsense,' Welles bellowed. 'Tear out the wall to bring up the lights and take the camera up from the street on a derrick!'[14]

This was a new way of writing about Welles, less concerned with who he was than with what he did, and how he did it. The press release continued:

> While construction and destruction was in progress, Orson, the minute-miser, called for an Éclair camerette, had it loaded with 400 feet of film and, by means of this ingenious hand camera, had himself, 'Chuck' Heston, Ray Collins and Harry Shannon shot entering the elevator, riding up in it and exiting it to walk down the hall. The fact that he had been the first director to successfully do a long take in a moving elevator was too time-consuming for Welles to ponder. Outside, a cast automobile waited for the precedent-breaker to make history again. He prepared to shoot a chase scene without a cameraman.[15]

If this narrative, especially with its emphasis on Welles the 'minute-miser' and Welles the 'precedent-breaker', had established itself, the studio bosses might have been a great deal more relaxed about him. 'Improvising a signal knocking system from himself to the operator, he took off, careening through the community in a manner reminiscent of the old silent days.' It is Chaplin who is being invoked here, but it could have been Griffith, early DeMille, von Stroheim, Abel Gance: as always, Welles was trying to replicate the high creative energy of the early days of a medium that had become stale. Universal's anonymous press officer can't have been the only person in Hollywood to get the point of Welles: he even gets the camaraderie on the set, especially the complicity between leading man and director. 'Some carefree, inspired directors re-write scenes between takes. Obeying his dramatic intuition, Welles ad-libbed much of his re-write in the middle of a take. Only the most adept trouper could survive these rigors opposite this mercurial individual. Such a trouper', the press release adds, 'is Charlton Heston.'

He and Welles were, Heston felt, getting closer and closer: this was their baby. After shooting the complex scene with the bugging device in the water, they cracked open a bottle of brandy and drank it in the car outside Welles's house. 'We more or less agreed on partnership,' confided Heston to his diary, 'which seems a very exciting prospect to me.'[16] Welles suggested an eco-apocalyptic novel, *Earth Abides*, which interested Heston, but at that point, had Welles wanted to direct the Los Angeles telephone directory, Heston would have agreed to be in it. Welles was reaching parts of him that no other director had. 'My son took his first steps one year ago today,' he wrote in his diary, 'and I almost feel I'm only beginning to do the same [as an actor] on this film. Orson is certainly the most exciting director I've ever worked with . . . God, maybe it will all begin to happen now.'[17]

The last shot was, unusually, the last shot of the film, Quinlan's watery death; they finished filming at dawn. It was 1 April. The schedule was a mere week behind, and they were a nugatory 3 per cent over budget. Welles and Heston had a celebratory drink or three in the trailer, then took the last magnum of champagne with them and found a place that would provide them with bacon and eggs to go with it. 'It was a hell of a picture to work on,' Heston noted. 'I can't believe it won't be fine.' Then they had a steak and watched *Lady from Shanghai* on TV. 'It's good,' noted Heston, 'but not as good as ours, I think.'[18] This was the apogee of their relationship, the consummation of the romance of film-making; it was also the end of the good news for *Touch of Evil*.

As early as 7 March, three weeks after filming had begun, Welles had shown Heston two or three reels of roughly cut-together footage. Welles had just fired his cutter, but 'even mis-edited', said Heston, 'it looked special'. Now, after the briefest pause, Welles set to work in earnest with his new editor, the experienced and amenable Virgil Vogel, whose last job as an editor this was to be; he had just begun to direct, which he went on doing for the rest of his life. Welles never visited the cutting room, but saw cut scenes on the big screen, after which he would issue detailed notes. Some of these dictated notes survive, showing the needle-sharp detail in which he worked:

> Dub the line 'I told you I brought you up here for a reason'. One light flash too many in my trip towards Tamiroff with the stocking before I choke him. I suggest we cut Janet. It's just a little long – my trip from the bed to Akim to choke him. After first shot of Tamiroff dead – use the same piece of Janet that is there now, but before she rises. Then return to his face blown up so that the eyes are even bigger for a flash. Then repeat moment of her and have her rise screaming. Shot of the old lady talking and the people shouting: all that must be before the entrance of Chuck Heston and the car. There should be absolutely no jeering at the girl once Chuck Heston comes in.[19]

Welles next briefly met Henry Mancini, then under contract to Universal, to talk about the score. Welles's presence on the Universal lot 'that gave you Bonzo, Francis the Mule, Ma and Pa Kettle, countless horrible horse operas, and all those awful Creature pictures that Herman Stein and I scored' seemed wildly incongruous to Mancini, who had read the impressively detailed three-page letter Welles had written for Joseph Gershenson, the head of the music department, outlining his expectations of the score. The letter made it clear that he didn't want any scoring at all as such – 'that is to say, underscore,' as Mancini put it, 'the disembodied music that comes from nowhere behind a scene to enhance or establish mood'. All the music, Welles said, had to be what was technically known as source music, occurring naturally within the action, from a visible source – a juke-box, an orchestra, a radio or, indeed, a player-piano; it should be a mixture of rock and roll and Latin jazz, where needed, to capture the feeling and effect of a modern Mexican border town. As it turns out, this is exactly what Mancini had planned to do, which was just as well, since he got very little out of the meeting arranged with Welles, who, in cape and hat and furiously smoking a long Montecristo cigar, was already in high dudgeon with Zugsmith. 'It seemed,' said Mancini, 'as if doom, the wrath of hell, was invading the music department.' At the height of his rage Welles snapped around, looked at the composer, pointed a long finger at him – he had met him just half an hour earlier – and said from a great height, 'Who's he?' Mancini put his head down and got on with his work.[20]

Welles continued supervising the editing, consciously creating a nightmarish atmosphere, disjunct, jagged, menacing, arrhythmic. He alternated leisurely long sequences with abrupt ones, sometimes – as in the scenes in the motel – suspending linearity altogether. After nearly two months he took a brief leave of absence at the beginning of June to go to New York, to do a few conjuring tricks for a very large sum of money on the *Steve Allen Show*; while he was gone, Virgil Vogel was replaced by Aaron Stell, until recently a television editor. Stell asked to be allowed to do his own cut without supervision from Welles, who agreed, while continuing to dub the film with his usual creativity. 'Orson continues to amaze me with the ideas he has,' wrote Heston in his diary. 'He created a climax for me in the bar scene that wasn't in the printed footage, simply having me dub a speech in four little places. Whatever happens, I am in his debt.'[21]

Meanwhile, Welles and Heston were still looking for a new project to work on together. Welles proposed Conrad's *Lord Jim* and the recent British novel *The Singer Not the Song* (again set in Mexico) as possible projects; then, towards the end of June, Welles had a more concrete suggestion, a reversion to an old project: he had drummed up some cash, including $25,000 from Frank Sinatra, to make a television special from *Don Quixote* and asked Heston to play the title-role; Heston was sorely tempted, although he had already signed to make his next film, *The Big Country*, for William Wyler. Meanwhile, in mid-July, Aaron Stell's cut of *Touch of Evil* was shown to the studio executives, who were unimpressed with it. Ernest Nims, Welles's editor on *The Stranger* and now head of post-production at Universal, was called in to fix it with Virgil Vogel. This was ominous news for Welles: Nims, under direct instructions from Sam Spiegel, had shortened *The Stranger* by a crucial twenty minutes – the key twenty minutes of the film, Welles believed, rendering it fatally incoherent. But he was by now urgently trying to assemble his team for *Quixote* and urging Heston to come to Mexico with him. Heston's agent, Herman Citron, thought the whole thing was madness, 'and so do I, really,' wrote Heston in his journal. 'But Orson is impossible to resist, especially with a part like this.'[22]

Welles had a madcap plan whereby the *Quixote* cast and crew could all enter Mexico on tourist permits, then pay a fine when they were found out. Eventually Heston conceded that it would be impossible: he wouldn't be able to get his passport back in time to return for shooting on *The Big Country*, so Welles went off without him, leaving detailed instructions with Nims for the work on *Touch of Evil* and firing off a letter to Edward Muhl complaining that the film had been 'jerked away' from him.

CHAPTER FOURTEEN

The Return of Awesome Welles

AFTER BEING briefly reunited with the wonderful equipment and superb technicians of a major Hollywood studio, as well as reacquainting himself with the concept of budgetary and time constraints, Welles found himself, with *Don Quixote*, back to the freedom and uncertainty of independent film-making. He had, it is true, a producer – the Russian émigré Óscar Dancigers, who had given Luis Buñuel, in flight first from Falangist Spain and then from neurotically anti-communist post-war America, a career in Mexico – but his relationship to Welles was purely that of a facilitator. Welles's approach to *Quixote* was radical: he determined to improvise the movie, which would mostly be shot on silent 16mm equipment; in fact, he would be reverting to the shooting style of the great silent-film comedians.

The scenario had changed since the tests he had shot in Paris two years earlier for *Don Quixote Passes By*, the aborted thirty-minute film he was going to make for CBS. In the new version Welles would appear, as himself, in conversation with a young American girl called – nudge, nudge – Dulcie. Welles would tell her the story of Quixote and Sancho Panza, whom she would then meet, later relaying her adventures back to Welles. As Dulcie, Welles cast Patty McCormack, fresh from her stage and screen triumphs in *The Bad Seed*, laden with nominations (Oscar and Golden Globe for Best Supporting Actress) and a coveted prize: the Milky Star Award for Best Juvenile. Akim Tamiroff came straight from *Touch of Evil* to play Sancho Panza, the role he was put on earth to play, while as Quixote – in the absence of Mischa Auer, who was otherwise engaged in Europe – Welles cast Francisco Reiguera, a Spanish actor and writer who had been in Hollywood as early as 1917, but had returned to Spain, only to leave it again after the triumph of the Fascists in the Spanish Civil War. If Tamiroff was born to play Panza, then Reiguera *was* Quixote: emaciated, intense, otherworldly.

Welles had selected scenes from the novel, which the actors rehearsed, but only, he said to André Bazin, so they would know their characters. 'Then we went out into the street and we played, not Cervantes, but an improvisation backed up by these rehearsals, by the memory of the characters.'[1] It is astonishing that Welles was able to give himself over to this other world, a sportive world of children and innocents and madmen, while the dark vision of life that he had so fervently and imaginatively fashioned for Universal International only a few months earlier was laid out on the slab, being nipped and tucked by mere journeymen, dutifully enacting the will of their ignorant masters. But Welles had been ensorcelled by Cervantes's world, and when he tore himself away from it at the end of August to return to Hollywood, to view what Nims and company had done with *Touch of Evil*, he hastened back as quickly as he could, promising to send notes on what he had seen. The notes never arrived, or perhaps they were never sent.

By now, having done as much on *Quixote* as he wanted to do for the time being, Welles refocused on *Touch of Evil*. As if waking up to reality from a dream, he took stock of the situation, suddenly appalled about what was happening to his film. He refused to take calls from the studio, or even from Heston. He finally came back to California at the end of October, eight crucial weeks after he had departed. Eventually he left a message for Edward Muhl, promising to have a talk with him 'in a couple of days'. Anger and pride possessed him; but he was behaving tactically, too, as he saw it. As far as he was concerned, he was now at war with the studio bosses. But this was a war he could never win, as he might have known from previous experience.

Meanwhile Heston saw the result of Nims's work, a rough-cut which, he felt, had 'flaws'; nonetheless, he said, 'there are some truly marvellous things in the film. Orson's enormous talent is evident throughout.'[2] Rick Schmidlin, who masterminded the superb restoration that a retrospectively remorseful Universal paid for, forty years later, came to the conclusion that Nims thought he was doing Welles a favour; in fact, what he was really doing was destroying him. '*The Stranger* was Welles's most commercial film,' said Schmidlin, 'and I think Nims was trying to give Welles another commercial film, but it didn't work because Nims didn't have Welles's blueprint in mind.'[3] Nor, of course, did Welles himself, till he saw the work in front of him. He sent Muhl a letter detailing everything he thought was wrong with the rough-cut. The studio, for its part, wanted some reshoots, for the sake of clarity. Welles met Heston and told him he was happy to do retakes, 'and do them free as well',[4] then wired Muhl to tell him that he would be available every night to work with Nims; Muhl wrote back by return to say that Nims would be available any night Welles chose to stop by.

This seems not to have happened. Welles wrote to Heston that he had had no response from Muhl to his offer to do reshoots. Everything now depended on Heston, said Welles: would he agree to do reshoots with someone else directing? 'Your position is really quite strong,' continued Welles, 'since you accepted the picture only on condition that I directed it and you will be entirely in your rights if you insist that since I am not available, the studio must abide by that condition.' On his original copy of the letter, Heston scrawled 'NOT TRUE' against Welles's claim that he had only accepted to do the picture if Welles directed it; he had simply suggested Welles as director, and Universal had agreed. Welles pressed on: he saw that Heston was his only chance. 'You have a financial interest in the film and it would be foolish not to protect that interest. I have made a very generous offer to Muhl and it can only be turned down arbitrarily with a self-admitted attitude of ill-will.' If Muhl says no, then 'I would have to insist on having my name as director and author removed from the credits and would have no choice but to conduct an intensive publicity campaign explaining my own position.' This being the case, he adds, Heston has urgent financial reasons 'to require that the film be completed by the man with whom you contracted to make it'. He ends, 'Love, Orson'.[5]

Heston understandably began to squirm under this pressure. Welles was beginning to thrash around. He thought he could outwit the studio because they were stupid, and because he was in the right. But, from the studio's point of view, he wasn't. They commissioned him to make a commercially viable piece of popular entertainment: he wanted to make a work of art. They had no objection to art, as long as it sold. But in Welles's case, as far as they could see, artistic simply meant obscure. The more creative he got, especially in post-production, the further down the drain their profits went. This was vexing to Universal, because they liked what he had done, in general. But he seemed to them to be perversely determined to make it inaccessible, even clumsy – to make it look as if it had been ineptly made. From their point of view. They wanted to helped him, and help the film. But time was money, and they were already vastly over their post-production budget. On 11 November Heston realised that, paid or unpaid, 'it becomes obvious that they really don't want Orson to do the work for whatever reason. Partly, I suppose, because of the 300 G overage on the budget. Partly because they don't like the way he made the film, I suppose.' After a conversation with his agent about the retakes, it became apparent to Heston that 'my legal position is that I have to do them anyway, which gets me out of a horny dilemma, but doesn't please me'.[6]

Meanwhile, Edward Muhl replied to Welles in a letter whose tone, if a little weary, is measured and wry, and notably courteous in his rehearsal of the whole sorry saga. 'There seems to be', he says, 'a disposition on the part of some of us involved in the matter of *Touch of Evil* to make a ponderous project out of the completion of the picture, whereas ordinary experience, many time repeated, indicates that this is no more than a simple matter of solving a series of not very intricate problems by the application of simple practical intelligence.'[7] These remarks rather neatly sum up what divides Welles from producers in general. They see a set of 'not very intricate problems', which they have the wisdom and experience to settle effortlessly. Welles sees an opportunity to do something new, something beautiful, something that makes a contribution to the art of film and that doesn't just reproduce the last successful movie.

In his letter Muhl – who was not without a sense of humour – imagines a state of war over *Touch of Evil*, with the production of a great number of White Papers, which would serve as the basis for some youngster's PhD thesis on 'The Unfinished War between Orson Welles and Universal, 1956–1959'. He humorously notes that the cutting and finishing period on the picture is running second only to *Jet Pilot* (which, directed by Howard Hughes when he owned Universal, had taken seven years from start to release). The last day of shooting on *Touch of Evil* had been 1 April. After four months of editing, Muhl had asked, he said, to see the picture. On 22 July he received a communication from Welles in Mexico in which there was, as he puts it, 'a muffled tone of anguish' because Welles 'felt that the picture had been jerked from his hands'. Muhl had replied to this letter on 24 July, suggesting that when Welles returned from Mexico they should have a talk, and at the same time informing him that he had assigned Ernest Nims as cutter, 'to get the picture in absolutely final shape for preview'. Muhl had then asked Welles to say if he agreed with this or if he had an alternative suggestion. Welles, having seen the picture with Nims, said he would make a number of suggestions in writing and transmit them to Muhl. 'You, or someone connected to you was notified approximately three weeks after this that those suggestions had not arrived.' They had finally appeared on 4 November. Then, abandoning the tone of sweet reasonableness, Muhl's letter cut to the chase: the film had now, with the substantial expenditure on editing, cost some $1,100,000: that is to say, $300,000 (roughly 30 per cent) over budget. He and his fellow-executives had 'carefully' screened the picture many times; some 60 or 70 per cent of Welles's suggestions in his letter of 4 November had been implemented, said Muhl, as well as one of Heston's.

What they were now proposing, Muhl told Welles, was to shoot seven script-pages of additional film to 'repair certain chaotic sections in the telling of this story which we believed was intended to be told'. First and foremost, they wanted to 'straighten out and reduce the cryptic quality of the opening reels of the picture' and to effect 'other improvements' that they felt were necessary. This, said Muhl, would cost $20,000, excluding dubbing. They would be getting another director to do it, he remarked, 'so as to assure to as great an extent as possible, the obtaining of this needed material without, if possible, spending more than this allocated sum on a picture which is already over-priced'. The formal legalistic language sought to conceal the enormity of what he was proposing. 'It is my definite feeling that this will not impair the fine creative contribution you have already made to the picture which I duly appreciate.' What was he talking about? The *entire picture* was Welles's fine creative contribution. 'I would like you to go along with this plan sympathetically, if you possibly can, and give us any assistance that it is possible for you to give with the players or any other personnel involved. Upon the completion and incorporation of the material, I will be very pleased to show you the picture in the form which we consider complete, and to receive any editorial contribution you may wish to suggest, or, conversely, to amiably endure your criticism, however the situation may evolve.' Muhl was addressing Welles like a liberal parent talking to a naughty child who has been grounded – this, to the director of *Citizen Kane.* Finally, stiffly, he added, 'the foregoing is as nearly as it can be made to do, an honest statement of my feelings and I hope you respect it'. It was not a statement of feelings at all: it was a fait accompli.

How had things come to this pass? What had happened to the huge excitement and admiration that had surrounded Welles by the end of shooting? Clearly shooting is a very different phenomenon from post-production. During the shoot, exhilaration and energy were paramount; anything that slowed down the process had to be eliminated (like prissiness about sound, for example). The more that could be improvised, the better. Editing, however, was an entirely different matter. The possibilities were endless; a frame more or less could transform a sequence. But it was, by its nature, a slow, painstaking process. And one from which it was necessary to keep stepping back.

Welles invoked a Spanish word to describe what that meant:

querencia. He described it to Mrs Rogers as 'a place where one feels secure, from which one's strength of character is drawn. The place in the ring where the wounded bull goes to renew his strength and centre himself, ready for a fresh charge. A place in which we know exactly who we are. The place from which we speak our deepest beliefs.'[8] It is the zone of real creativity. That, of course, was not a place to which any studio boss was going to allow his film-makers to go: not on his dollar. Chaplin had done exactly that: when he needed time to create, he simply suspended work on the film until inspiration came. Unless and until Welles, like Chaplin, owned his own studio, he would never get that time. But it is a strange art form where the work can be taken away from the artist and handed over to others to finish: this does not happen with a poem, a painting, a symphony or a sculpture. Welles was doomed to work in a sphere where money was the central determining factor and where instant results were required. It was his tragedy that he lacked the gift of working conceptually, to conceive his work in his head. His inspiration came from what he saw in front of his eyes; his genius depended on being able to improvise and interact with the material, during filming and after it. It was a costly process, and after he left RKO in 1942, no one was prepared to pick up the tab.

The retakes went ahead. Heston experienced 'a deep moral ache', but his lawyers were clear: he had to do it. He tried to call Welles, but failed to get him. Then he wired him, which finally provoked an emotional reply, replete with underlinings and capital letters.

> <u>The studio can have no possible excuse for refusing your request that you be directed by the man whose participation in this project was your first and fundamental condition for being in it.</u>

He finishes by summing up in the 'baldest possible terms': unless the studio is stopped they will wreck the picture –

> AND I MEAN WRECK IT BECAUSE IT IS NOT THE KIND OF ONE-TWO-THREE ABC VARIETY OF PRODUCT THAT CAN BE <u>SLIGHTLY WRECKED</u>.

Without his help, Welles says, the result will be very much less satisfactory than the most routine film, not just something less than Heston had hoped it would be, but '<u>GENUINELY BAD</u>.' Critics all over the world will say it is bad, says Welles, and he will have to explain himself to the critics. He envisages a terrible fight: as things are with him in the film industry he simply cannot afford to sustain such a blow, which means that even if Heston chooses to give up the fight, Welles has no choice at all. 'As far as I'm concerned the fight will just be beginning. I dread it and I'm heartsick at the idea of having to involve you. But you really cannot avoid some involvement – now or later.' Heston thinks of himself as helpless against the studio, but, says Welles, 'you aren't helpless at all, and it's well within your own power to save much of a rather large investment of time, money and – yes – love.' He can do this by getting a little tough. If he doesn't then Welles will have to get very tough later – 'and that will be very tough indeed on everybody.' It could be Lear speaking: 'I will have such revenges on you both / That all the world shall – I will do such things / What they are, yet I know not: but they shall be / The terrors of the earth...' The fight he is talking about, he says, is not one that he imagines he can win. 'It's a fight everybody must lose. You can be decisive in avoiding it, and in making up your mind you must consider well that it's not a fight I can afford to refuse. Much love as always Orson.' He was on the brink of hysteria: terrified that he'd blown it – his return to Hollywood, and the movie. And he had – up to a point. The truth is it would probably have been a flop even if he'd edited it from beginning to end, exactly as he wanted it. It's private, quirky, bizarre. One for posterity.

On the strength of this letter, Heston pulled out of the shooting scheduled for the following day, agreeing to pay for it himself. It cost him $8,000 ($68,000 today): a rather large sop to his conscience. But he knew he had to do it. The following day, after he showed up for the reshoots, under the circumspect direction of Harry Keller, veteran of over twenty Westerns and some episodic television, Heston confided to his journal: 'I have done worse work in the movies than this day's retakes, but I don't remember feeling worse . . . I was able to talk them out of one change.'[10]

The next day Welles wrote him a letter that is simultaneously menacing and playful, oddly reminiscent of Arkadin toying with Guy Van Stratten. Welles has heard, he says, that both Heston and Janet Leigh have been increasingly cooperative with Keller. He acknowledges that, since the new dialogue was not 'absolute hogwash', Keller himself was not altogether incompetent, and the additional shooting would necessarily involve a substantial amount of 'close footage on both you bums', their participation in the project was not unreasonable. However, he says, the reality is that the reshoots will destroy the picture. The actual process may have turned out to be a bit less crude than they had all feared, but the fact is, Welles grimly insists, that it is no longer his film. He begs Heston 'not to permit the merry stimulation of work to interfere with that air of reticence you had sworn to maintain.' Not only are they doing things to his picture – adding things, reworking it, reshaping it – but he's locked out, locked out of Eden, the only Eden he knows. He's a child cast out of the nursery: the games have suddenly stopped, the caper's over, the fun has finished, he's banned from the playground, feeling what Falstaff feels by the end of the second part of King Henry IV.

Now distinctly more menacing than affectionate, Welles continues his letter with a merciless portrait of Heston as a goody-goody – 'cooperative Chuck' – highly respected by all his colleagues, a professional who is disciplined on the set and 'wildly eager' to make the shooting smooth both for his fellow actors and for the film's executives: 'In a word,' says Welles, 'he's the Eagle Scout of the Screen Actors' Guild.' Welles urges Heston to 'leave his uniform and flag in the dressing room.' He doesn't go so far as to propose, he says, that the actor should 'growl and snap at the folks', but he does implore him at the very least to avoid giving any indication publicly that he thinks the reshoots are of any value or are contributing to making the film clearer – even if, Welles adds naughtily, those happened to be Heston's actual sentiments. He should avoid any opportunity, whether on the set or in the commissary, of granting 'any element of justice' to the reshoots, since anything he might say to that effect would be seized on by the producers, just as it had been in the past. 'There's nothing I can do about meeting the excitations of the close-up lens,' Welles ends, 'but I can implore you to curb your peace-making instincts and to maintain an aloof and non-committal silence. That goes for Janet, too, dammit. In a word, keep your yap shut. Much love Orson.'

The tone – passive-aggressive-playful – is uncomfortable, on the edge of being threatening, underpinned by a sense of Welles having spies on the set: the Shadow Knows. This feeling comes from deep hurt, a sense of betrayal in fact: they're collaborating with the enemy, as he insists on seeing all producers and executives. 'To Orson,' Heston told James Naremore, 'if you had an office and a secretary, you were the ENEMY.'[12] For Welles, Heston and Leigh had sold their souls for a couple of tawdry close-ups.

On 5 December, having been shown the latest version of the film, he tried a new tack, presenting Muhl with a now-famous fifty-eight-page memorandum, in which he identified everything in the film he thought could, and should, be changed. It reveals an astonishingly detailed grasp of the material, frame by frame, and a formidable sense of how to use and integrate the elements he had often created off the cuff. The tone is perfectly judged; he rarely writes from an Olympian position of omniscience or infallibility: sometimes, indeed, he criticises his own work. Noting that the editors have restored a line which he cut from a scene between Vargas and Susan ('Don't be morbid . . .'), he says:

> The present editing not only retains this line, but the cut between Vargas's leading Susan off-scene and their next two-shot is very rough. The original editing of this particular little section was really quite effective and I honestly can't see what, from any point of view, has been accomplished by tearing it up and re-building it in this form. In terms of clarity, nothing is gained; considerable excitement has been lost and an unpleasant line (which I regret having written) has been put back in.[13]

Again and again his comments show his original editing choices to have been made simply in order to tell the story better, 'to aid clarity and improve the narrative line', as he says at one point. Welles's commitment to narrative – which of course includes sometimes deliberately destabilising it – is at the core of his project as an artist: he conceives of human affairs as a series of self-contradicting and often ironic events, the frog and the scorpion being the paradigm of all such narratives. All his stories are (in the words of the title of a collection by one of his most admired authors, Isak Dinesen) anecdotes of destiny. *Touch of Evil* is no exception. It ends with a series of ironies: in order to track down a cop who has been forging evidence, because that is the only way the guilty will be brought to justice, Vargas uses a recording device that he despises but must deploy, because it's the only way he'll get the evidence that will put Quinlan in prison. And at the very end of the film we discover that the prime suspect, Sanchez, the son-in-law of the man who was blown up, has confessed: he did plant the bomb. Quinlan's intuition was right. For these ironies to register, it is vital that the story is crystal-clear at every turn. Welles's explanation of his approach is almost naively straightforward: he wants the audience to identify with 'the leading man and woman', he says:

> What's vital is that both stories – the leading man's and the

> leading woman's – be kept equally and continuously alive; each scene, as we move back and forth across the border, should play at roughly equal lengths leading up to the moment at the hotel when the lovers meet again. This simple but drastic improvement . . . will put the identification with the characters in a just proportion and in a form which I'm sure you'll admit, if you're willing to try it, is irresistibly interesting. No point concerning anything in the picture is made with such urgency and such confidence as this. Do please – please give it a fair try.

It is an extraordinary document, in itself, as an example of Welles's mastery of form and his awareness of the precise meaning and weight of every element in the film, but also because of the circumstances in which it was written: a world-class director of proven brilliance on his knees before an executive who had never shot a single frame of film in his life, begging him not to introduce any radical changes into the film, but simply to allow him to refine and clarify what is already there. Oh, and to contain any damage the reshooting may have done:

> In the light of the decision to deny me permission to direct these scenes, to write the dialogue for them or to collaborate in that writing, or indeed even to be present during your discussions of the matter, I must, of course, face the strong probability that I am the very last person whose opinion will be likely to carry any weight with you.

He is by now calm enough to know that simply trying to get the film out in the least damaged form is the only practical, achievable result. 'I want the picture to be as effective as possible – and now, of course, that means effective in *your terms*.' At the end of the memo he writes in considerable detail about the soundtrack – 'the rather sadly neglected dimension of the sound track' – so carefully conceived by him and so wantonly unpicked by them:

> For the close angle of the chase, the plan was for a quite interesting pattern of newscasts to be heard on the radios of the two cars and in the two languages. When Vargas switched stations, there was to be a dreamy, old-fashioned Mexican waltz to take the place of the announcer's excited chatter, and thus underscore our short love scene with a sentimental note, nicely combining 'local color' and, in realistic terms, perfectly justified. This pattern

> was to be rudely broken by the aggressive siren of Quinlan's car, and then – after Vargas's departure in that car – the gently picturesque lullaby would soothe Susan toward sleep as Menzies drove off with her.

The usurpation of Welles's intentions for the soundtrack begins with the first frame. Henry Mancini had declared himself in favour of Welles's policy of using only source music, but the irresistibly visceral score he wrote for the opening tracking shot, with its underpinning Mexican rhythms, rasping horns, piercing trumpets and slinky winds, is the opposite in effect to what Welles had in mind. Here, in a nutshell, is the Universal view versus the Welles view: something punchy, effective, instantly graspable versus something subtle, sophisticated, complex. You pays your money and you takes your choice.

In the memo, Welles reveals his sophistication at full stretch – a sensibility of immense subtlety and imagination, not one seeking instant solutions. It took him time to get to these ideas, and further time to execute them to his satisfaction; we cannot know what *Touch of Evil* would have been like, had he been given full licence to do what he wanted to do with the material. It could have become an entirely different film. Any film-maker knows, as he films, that the same script could result in a dozen different movies. And of course with Welles, as with many great film-makers, there is no such thing as the script, the screenplay – there is only the film, the film forged in the director's mind, in the shoot and in the editing suite, of which Welles so memorably observed: 'this is where the film is made.' It was, for Welles, a dangerous seduction, which he was not always able to resist. With *Touch of Evil*, the film was taken out of his hands. Heston and others maintained that the finished result was not so very different from what Welles had in mind; but Rick Schmidlin, attempting to restore the film to something like its original state, used Welles's memo – and Welles's memo alone – as his guide, and he found that, without exception, every single one of Welles's suggestions not only worked but had a transforming effect not just on the scene, but on the film itself. The memo ends with an impassioned plea:

> At the very end, I had a particular arrangement of short cuts building up to Quinlan's collapse into the water of the canal. This involved the closing of the recording device, the backing up of Quinlan, his dead body dropping into the water, and other moving shots arranged in a very fast crescendo. As I left it, this brief

> montage, although not exactly as I wanted it, was quite close to being right. I honestly believe it was – or would have been – one of the most striking things I've ever had anything to do with. I close this memo with a very earnest plea that you consent to this brief visual pattern to which I gave so many long days of work.

As it happens, Edward Muhl was not indifferent to Welles's passionate plea. He wired him to say that the majority of changes in the memo would be implemented; would he turn up for dubbing on Wednesday? Welles was suspicious. He wrote to Heston like a seasoned tactician: 'What interpretation are we to put on this?'[14] The possibilities were: first, that they were afraid he wouldn't go for the dubbing session unless they agreed to changes; second, that 'a certain throbbing of war drums' had reached their ears at last, and they intended to make a convincing show of cooperating with his suggestions, in the hope of spiking Welles's guns; third, that they were in a state of 'utter demoralisation'. The studio was indeed in crisis. Hundreds of employees, as Welles rightly said, were being fired from the studio, and the rumours of Muhl being next for the chop continued to spread. 'In such an atmosphere of decay and despair, maybe the sheer force of energy – which they now see I am prepared to put into this fight – has awed them into momentary compliance.' There were two more possibilities: the constructive spirit of the memo amounted to a strong weapon, which they did not wish to have used against them; or they had all been genuinely converted and were hastening to put the majority of the points into effect. This last possibility, Welles drily observed, was the least likely.

He was clearly rather enjoying all of this, and began to fashion strategies to take advantage of what he perceived to be the weakness of the studio's position. Nothing so naive for him as accepting Muhl's statement at face value and cooperating with him to make sure the film was as good as it could be made. No, Welles was playing a longer game. In fact he rather wished that Muhl and company had continued to be as 'muleish' as Heston had found them to be, over whether Welles would be allowed to do the reshoots or not. Nonetheless, he had a master plan that would result in getting the picture '*really right*', as he put it:

> There is a thing called the Decca Company which owns Universal, and I have a plan of battle based on this very interesting fact. There is a lot of money tied up in our picture, and the argument that its potential importance, as a box office attrac-

> tion, has been compromised by arbitrary and ignorant behaviour would certainly carry much weight with the stockholders. It's my best guess that Muhl and Company are going to try to put up the most convincing display of cooperation they can manage, in order to protect themselves . . .

These are the fantasies of the powerless: fearless confrontations, cunning ruses, killer facts, chicanery exposed, authority trounced, virtue rewarded. It gives a vivid glimpse of Welles's profound innocence of the way the world works. As it happens, before long Universal International was saved by selling off a large studio and eventually being taken over by MCA, after which they had a run of successful movies, many of them starring Doris Day; Edward Muhl remained head of production until 1969. In the context of these tectonic upheavals, *Touch of Evil* was a tiny, barely noticed speck on the horizon. Would its destiny have been other, had Welles taken a more conciliatory line, expended a little more effort on cultivating and charming what Heston called the 'studio brass'? Flattered them a little? Impossible to know. Such things were beneath him. Thinking that Welles needed to be protected against himself, Heston offered to set him up with his very powerful agent, Herman Citron of MCA. They met: 'I'm so honoured to meet you,' said Citron. 'May I call you Orson?' To which the reply came: 'Mr Welles will do.'[15] He remained unrepresented. It was, as the scorpion observed, in his nature to behave as he did.

In December, Welles went to Europe (to shoot *Portrait of Gina*, of all things), and he stayed there. He was thus not present when in January 1958 *Touch of Evil* was sneaked into a cinema in Pacific Palisades for a preview; incorporating about half of his notes in the December memorandum, it lasted some 109 minutes. It was not liked. When it went on release, in February, it was as the B-half of a double bill of which the A-half was *The Female Animal* – shot by Russell Metty, directed by Harry Keller, produced by Albert Zugsmith and starring Hedy Lamarr, ex-Mrs Fritz Mandl. On this outing *Touch of Evil* lasted ninety-four minutes, much of the excised material being Harry Keller's reshoots; Welles's memo had pointed up so many inconsistencies in them that Universal decided that it would be easier simply to drop them all.

The whole business was uncannily like a rerun of the *Magnificent Ambersons* fiasco, even down to being slipped into the mainstream on a double bill. In both cases, the studio reacted adversely to what Welles had filmed. 'They don't like the way he made the film, I suppose,' a baffled Heston confided in his diary.[16] Even Welles was somewhat baffled. 'The picture was just too dark and strange for them,' he told Peter Bogdanovich. 'It's the only trouble I've ever had that I can't begin to fathom. The picture rocked them in some funny way . . . They were deeply shocked – they felt insulted by the film in a funny way. And hurt and injured – I'd taken them for some kind of awful ride.'[17] With both *The Magnificent Ambersons* and *Touch of Evil*, the studio was in trouble, in need of a hit, and sensed that the film Welles had made for them was out of step with the zeitgeist. In each case, their instinct was to modify it in some way, to normalise it, to try to turn it into something belonging to a recognisable genre: to make *The Magnificent Ambersons* a simple family saga; to turn *Touch of Evil* into a movie about a bent cop. When their tampering resulted in something that was neither itself nor quite anything else, they abandoned the movie in question, which is really the saddest thing that can ever happen to a film. To fail is one thing, but to be rejected by your own studio – to be a waif, an orphan – is a harsh fate for any film, which needs all the help it can get.

Even the reviewers were conscious of the second-class status the film was being accorded by its studio. '*Touch of Evil* came creeping quietly into the theaters a few weeks ago,' wrote Gerald Weales in the *Reporter*. 'No fanfare. No publicity. Universal International dumped *Touch of Evil* into the neighborhood theaters in New York . . . as though they wanted to get the film off their hands in a hurry.'[18] In the *New Republic*, Stanley Kauffmann asked: 'Are there so many pictures available today that this one has to be released furtively?' As it happens, Kauffmann found that the film, 'while not in the same galaxy with *Kane*', is 'an exceptionally good thriller stunningly directed'.[19] And, rather more importantly for the film's sales, the *New York Times* – announcing that, 'thanks to Orson Welles, nobody, and we mean nobody, will nap during *Touch of Evil*, which opened yesterday at R.K.O. theatres. Just try' – went on to describe the film as 'an obvious but brilliant bag of tricks. Using a superlative camera (manned by Russell Metty) like a black-snake whip, he lashes the action right into the spectator's eye . . . where Mr Welles soundly succeeds is in generating enough sinister electricity for three such yarns and in generally staging it like a wild, murky nightmare . . .'[20]

Still Universal did nothing to promote it; like RKO in 1942, they just wanted rid of Welles. 'I was so sure I was going to go on making a lot of pictures at Universal,' Welles told Bogdanovich, 'when suddenly I was fired from the lot. A terribly traumatic experience.

Because I was so sure. They went out of their way to compliment me every night for the rushes, and "When are you going to sign a four to five picture contract with us? Please come and see us." Every day they kept asking me to sign the contract. Then they saw the cut version and barred me from the lot.'[21] Janet Leigh remained angry about it, forty years later: 'Even now I think: What have we been robbed of? What have we been cheated of? We might have had five more masterpieces. We'll never know. It's a shame.'[22] The truth is that the movie would probably have been a flop even if Welles had edited it from beginning to end, exactly as he wanted it. It's private, quirky, bizarre. One for posterity. Welles was deeply disappointed, though he never puzzled out why or how it might have happened. 'It was sad for me it turned out that way,' he told Bogdanovich, 'because I was ready to settle down in America.'[23]

Instead, he went back to Europe. He remained friendly with Heston, but nothing practical came out of their relationship; certainly no 'partnership' of the kind they had spoken of that drunken night in Welles's car. He returned, agentless, to his *travaux alimentaires* – in this case the secondary role of a bullish TV commentator in John Huston's *The Roots of Heaven*.

It was while he was shooting it in Paris that he got an entirely unexpected invitation to attend the International Film Festival, which was part of the very high-profile Brussels World Fair of that year; *Touch of Evil* received its European premiere at the festival. To his astonishment and that of Universal, which had done everything it could to prevent the film from being entered, it won the International Critics' Prize, and Welles won a separate award for his Life's Work. The film was an immense success, both with the critics (especially the French critics associated with *Cahiers du Cinéma*) and with the public. As acutely described by Sarah Nilsen in *Projecting America*, this outcome was deeply displeasing to the organisers of the American contribution to the World Fair: giving publicity to the dystopian vision of America purveyed by *Touch of Evil* was not the reason President Eisenhower had secured emergency funding from Congress for what he considered 'by far the most significant opportunity for the United States to use culture as an asset to the nation's foreign policy'. What they had in mind was Walt Disney's fifteen-minute *America the Beautiful* in 360-degree Circarama, offering a whistle-stop tour of the nation, encompassing both the Grand Canyon and Ford's Rouge River automobile factory, 'America depicted as a singular, unified organism,' as Nilsen says, 'pulsating with the heartbeat of a booming capitalist economy'.[24] It certainly did the trick. 'With the ending,' reported the *Los Angeles Times*, 'there is a loud applause . . . from persons of many countries . . . yes, even a few Russian visitors'.[25] That was what Eisenhower had in mind, not a forensic probe of the diseased underbelly of the American Dream.

But if Welles displeased his fellow-countrymen (or at least their elected representatives), he delighted his hosts and the European press in general. As Nilsen points out, 1958 was a pivotal year for Europe, marking its emergence from austerity and a return to both prosperity and self-respect. France in particular, having just installed Charles de Gaulle as premier of the tottering Fourth Republic (during the last week of the Brussels World Fair, as it happens), began to assert itself on the world stage; for the first time since the end of the war, American hegemony was seriously threatened. Nilsen makes an interesting, if slightly overheated case for *Touch of Evil* as a parable of the decline of the old America (Quinlan), imperilled by the vitality of its neighbours (the Mexicans). 'A bomb literally explodes open the relations that will drive the narrative. At the height of the Cold War, atomic bombs were omnipresent in the minds of most spectators and clearly also in Welles's,' she says. 'The film was a nightmare vision of America collapsing under the panic and fears produced by the racial, sexual and gender changes transforming the outdated America of Quinlan and his cronies.'[26] This reading is consistent with Welles's own political views – he was deeply preoccupied by the bomb – though it is not necessarily the film he thought he had made. For him, the crucial figure was Vargas. 'The things said by Vargas are what I would say myself,' Welles told André Bazin in Cannes, a month before he went to Brussels. 'He talks like a man brought up in the classic liberal tradition, which is absolutely my attitude. So that's the angle the film should be seen from; everything Vargas says, I say. Also, is it better to see a murderer go unpunished, or the police being authorized to abuse their power? If one had to choose, I'd rather see crime going unpunished. That is my point of view.'[27]

Welles's success in Brussels and the warmth of his personal reception marked a new phase in his European profile as a film-maker; from now on, especially in France, but also in Britain, Germany and even Italy, he was admired, analysed, interviewed, idolised. He enjoyed it greatly, almost invariably agreeing with the questioner's interpretation of his work, however arcane; he even sometimes advanced a few interpretations of his own work that had just occurred to him. It was a favourite pastime: the exchange of theor--ies, the definition of genres, the interpretation of life. It was glorious table-talk, for him, in which everything and its opposite were simultaneously true; the cigar smoke hangs in the air; there is always another bottle of good wine on hand, and the talk flows on and on. 'I strongly believe,' he told Bazin and Bitsch in Cannes, expansively 'that a critic knows more about an artist's work than the artist himself; but at the same time he knows less; it's even the function of the critic to know simultaneously more and less than the artist.' Enjoyable though all this was, Welles knew it would not get him one inch closer to being asked to direct a film. And, as he knew, it emphasised the huge transatlantic gap of perception about him, though even he can scarcely have imagined that he would never again direct a film in his own country.

★

For Welles, 1958 was a year for winning awards: the two at Brussels, and the Peabody Award for *The Fountain of Youth*, both to do with past work – in the case of *The Fountain of Youth*, long past. Meanwhile there was money to be made, and thus acting to be done, which he found increasingly disagreeable, especially since he found himself being directed by men with, as he saw it, less title to the director's chair than he.

In December of 1957, while locked in mortal combat with Universal over *Touch of Evil*, he had been acting for 20th Century Fox in a film whipped together from three Faulkner novels and drenched in a great deal of essence of Tennessee Williams. The director was Martin Ritt, a former teacher at Lee Strasberg's Studio, and thus, in Welles's view, second cousin to Satan. The press department of 20th Century Fox, like their counterparts at Universal, had obviously decided that instead of trying to conceal Welles's antics during filming, they should make a feature of them. Accordingly, in February of 1958, an article appeared in *Life* magazine under the heading 'The Return of Awesome Welles'. 'Two weeks after we started,' Ritt told the reporter, 'you could lay bets we would never finish. Such rows!' Welles, said *Life*, 'approaches every movie scene with the Olympian omnipotence of the director, even when – as in the latest and biggest of his Hollywood films – he is not the director'. They quoted him as saying: 'There was a note of suspicion: I did not know what kind of monkeyshines I would have to put up with and the cast did not know what kind of caprices they would have to put up with from me.' 'But,' stated *Life*, 'from one battle to the next, they worked out the problem. The result is rich acting by Welles as a blustery plantation owner and a first-rate movie full of sex, fun and barn burnings.' Enough said.

The part of Cy Sedgewick, television reporter, in *The Roots of*

Heaven followed, relatively painlessly (his chum John Huston was directing), and then, later in the year, Welles appeared in *Compulsion*, an altogether more rewarding undertaking. In this light fictionalisation of the notorious Leopold and Loeb case, Welles was cast to play Jonathan Wilk, squarely based on Clarence Darrow, the real-life advocate who successfully defended the murderous youths. Richard Fleischer, hot from his success with *20,000 Leagues Under the Sea*, was approached to direct the film. 'When I learned that Orson Welles had already been cast as Darrow, my tongue was hanging out,' said the fearless Fleischer. 'I would kill to do this movie.'[28]

Welles only appears in the last third of the film, and then mostly in the courtroom, and he was available for exactly ten days, with no leeway: the day before shooting started he had been driven to Hollywood from Mexico, where he had been shooting more sequences for *Don Quixote*; and at midnight on the day shooting ended, he was booked onto a boat leaving Long Beach for China, where he would appear in *Ferry to Hong Kong* for the English director Lewis Gilbert. Fleischer, a shrewd, witty writer, left a well-observed and illuminating record of working with Welles in his post-*Touch of Evil* directorial hiatus. He quickly worked out how best to handle him. 'There was no fooling him about the mystique of directing. He knew what you were going to do as soon as you started to do it,' wrote Fleischer. 'Since he knew as much about directing as I did, and was a bona fide genius in the bargain, I thought more than twice about how I was going to handle every scene he was in.' It worked: Welles never once interfered with Fleischer's work as director. 'He was the actor, I was the director, and that was that. We developed a wonderful working relationship based on mutual respect.' But Fleischer was aware that Welles must be feeling great envy of him. 'They send me the worst, the most impossible, the most ridiculous pieces of crap you've ever read,' Welles told him. 'They say to themselves, "Welles is a genius. Maybe he can do something with this mess. And we can get him cheap, too." They're so bad that even I wouldn't do them.' Welles's underlying frustration manifested itself only once with Fleischer: he had asked Welles to leave the scene by the left. Welles wanted to exit by the right. 'I'm sorry, Orson,' said Fleischer, 'you can't.'

> 'Why not?' 'Well, you may have noticed that there is no wall on the right-hand side.' He looked and thought for a moment. Then the jealousy and the challenge came out. 'Do you know

what I would do if I were directing this picture?' 'No, I don't. What would you do?' 'I'd wait until they built me a wall.' 'That,' I said, 'is why I am directing this picture and you are not.'

Welles, Fleischer discovered, had his idiosyncrasies as an actor. In close-ups and reverses he preferred not to have the other actor off camera. He played the entire scene just as though the actor were there, reacting to non-existent dialogue, responding with his own, interrupting, overlapping, laughing, growing angry, exactly as though there were someone there speaking to him. When he absolutely had to act with another actor, he would avoid eye-contact; if he happened to catch the actor's eye, he forgot his lines. In an early courtroom sequence he had no difficulty playing to the extras who filled the jury benches, but looking into the eyes of E.G. Marshall, to whom a lot of the speech was directed, was so difficult for Welles that he finally asked him to close his eyes when he was addressing him; he asked the same of all the assistant DAs sitting next to Marshall. 'There they were,' says Fleischer, 'all lined up, listening intently, with their eyes closed. It was a ludicrous but memorable sight. It seemed to me that the image he was facing would have been more distracting than having them looking at him, but no, Orson breezed through the speeches without any trouble at all.'

Because of the shortness of time, Fleischer devised a complex set-up for the final climactic summing up in which all three cameras shot everything in one direction, then they all moved round and shot the next segment, and so on, until they'd done the complete 360 degrees. 'It was like throwing a large jigsaw puzzle into the air and planning it so all the pieces would fall in exactly the right place, with all of them fitted together perfectly.' The final three minutes of the speech would be done in one long shot. Each time Fleischer suggested doing the final shot, Welles reacted 'like a horse to a rattlesnake, rearing up with panic in his eyes'. Finally Fleischer asked him what the trouble was. 'Stage fright! I'm scared to death of that scene. Please, let's do it the last thing.' Finally the day came. Welles asked if they could rehearse it technically till it was perfect, which they did for some hours. Then he rehearsed it alone for ninety minutes. And then they shot it. 'It was deeply moving. It was Orson Welles at his best. There was spontaneous and prolonged applause from the crew when I quietly said, "Cut. Print." I stood up and applauded, too. Orson came over and embraced me.' At the end of the following day – Welles's last – there was a little reception for him, which he attended in high good humour.

Meanwhile, in the production office, a sheriff deputed by the IRS was waiting to impound Welles's entire salary for the film against outstanding tax. The producer, Darryl Zanuck, had the onerous task of breaking the news to Welles – especially tricky because they needed the actor to do some dubbing on the scene he had filmed the previous day, the all-important final peroration. Welles took it surprisingly calmly, then went with the producer, director, editor and camera crew into the viewing theatre, where they looked at the rushes of the scene they had shot the day before. Welles had been sitting alone near the front of the theatre, with everybody else ten rows back. The screening came to an end:

> He rose from his seat looking like an Old Testament version of God in all His wrath. 'That is the worst film I have ever seen in my life,' he declaimed. 'It is a disgrace. You should all be ashamed of yourselves for being associated with it!' There seemed to be small black clouds, with little flashes of forked lightning, roiling about his brow as he stepped into the aisle and started to pace. His voice supplied the necessary thunder. 'It is a total disaster from beginning to end. I am shocked and dismayed by what I've seen,' he roared. We sat there immobile, hypnotized.

Then he attacked Fleischer: how could he have selected such poor angles? Didn't he know better than to show him in a chest-size figure that made him look like a character in a Punch-and-Judy show? Couldn't he see that the American flag behind him in the rear of the courtroom distracted from his speech? It was the cameraman's turn next. 'Hardly pausing for breath,' reported Fleischer, 'heaping acid invective and vile criticism on our heads . . . he finally stormed out of the theater.' They ran after him, finally tracking him down back in the viewing theatre, where he did the dubbing 'in a cold fury', perfunctorily but efficiently. Then it came to the final twenty seconds, where there was a clearly audible camera hum on the soundtrack. 'I refuse to loop this scene,' said Welles. 'This is a matter for the Screen Actors' Guild,' he said. 'And with that,' says Fleischer, 'he left and never came back. He got on a boat and went to China' (where he proceeded to torment Lewis Gilbert, the director of *Ferry to Hong Kong*, who described it as his 'nightmare film', entirely because of Welles's intransigence).[29] Even Fleischer, who had had a stimulating, enjoyable time with Welles on *Compulsion*, was astonished that 'he was willing to harm the picture as well as himself by walking away from the opportunity to make it right. For all his brilliance, his genius, his intellect, he was at this moment an immature, unreasonable juvenile, cutting off his fake nose to spite what? Himself? Me? The movie business that wouldn't let him direct? It didn't make sense to me then and it doesn't make sense to me now.' Fleischer wondered whether 'maybe, just maybe, it's the basic genetic, tragic flaw that brought this movie giant down'.

A few weeks later, Welles wrote to Fleischer apologising for his behaviour on the last day of the film, asking for his 'forgiveness and understanding'.[30]

It is worth relaying this incident, firstly because it is one of many, many similar scenes throughout Welles's career as a film actor; and secondly because Fleischer is a friendly witness, admiring and sympathetic – to a remarkable degree, in that he worked with Welles again, on *Crack in the Mirror*, on which Welles again behaved very, very badly. 'You think you did a great job on *Compulsion*, don't you?' he said to Fleischer one Saturday evening after shooting a scene in *Crack in the Mirror*. 'You're taking a lot of credit for very little. All you've got is one outstanding performance that made you and the whole picture look good.' 'Orson,' replied Fleischer:

> 'I want to tell you something. I think it's one hell of a fine picture and I'm proud of it. I've never been proud of a picture before, but I am of this one. And I'll tell you something else. I'm not going to let you spoil it for me.' We stared at each other, then he said quietly, 'You're right. You're absolutely right. I shouldn't have said that. I'm sorry. I apologize.'

He behaves badly; he apologises. It is a recurring pattern, though he rarely apologises to anyone without power. Mostly what is at issue is a matter of status. He is being humiliated, diminished, disregarded in some way. The offender seems not to understand who or what he is; the offence, in essence, is lese-majesty. Like many another analyst of Welles's career, Fleischer sees *Kane* as the root of the problem: 'The magnificent achievement of *Citizen Kane* and its disappointing aftermath must have been like a worm constantly and painfully eating away at his insides.' Welles, he says, was like a king in exile 'who still considered himself king'.

Fleischer describes another incident: an even more extreme manifestation of this sense of outraged dignity. Welles was on the set, about to commence his cross-examination of Diana Varsi as Ruth Evans. The unit publicity man walked onto the set. Welles caught sight of him, 'a tall, blond fellow in his thirties,' says Fleischer, 'with a puffy face. He was a tasty dish to set before the king.' Welles roared at him: 'What are you trying to do, ruin me, you incompetent nitwit?' He had told the man to cancel his appointment with the gossip columnist Hedda Hopper, which the publicist had done, but an hour later. Welles was bellowing now:

> 'An hour later! You called her an hour later! It should have been done immediately. Have you no comprehension of urgency or priority? Didn't this seem important to you? What you did was totally irresponsible, inefficient, and lazy! Did you have the sense to send her flowers? Can't you think for yourself, you witless oaf, or has your calling destroyed your brain? Are you so unqualified that you have to be told how to do your job? An ape could be trained to do it better. All you're doing is keeping a monkey out of work.'

The publicity man finally managed to call out in some anger, says Fleischer, tears running down his face, 'You're not a very nice person, Mr Welles!' 'Don't you tell me what kind of person I am,' bawled Welles. 'Look to yourself, you nincompoop. You are an irresponsible and unreliable fool whose inadequacy is equalled only by his ineptness. You are a member of an overpaid and under-talented profession, and I want you to leave this stage and never show your face around me again.'

At which point, says Fleischer, Welles seamlessly went into the cross-examination of Varsi:

> It was a tour de force for Orson, a display of dazzling virtuosity. He had shown us a flash of royal purple. The whole thing, from start to finish, was a bravura performance. He had captured us, manipulated us, and finally entertained us, if you can call the spectacle of a Christian being eaten by the king of beasts entertaining. When he reached his last line, 'No further questions,' he knew he had us in the palm of his hand. He turned and sailed off to his dressing room like a mighty dreadnought under full steam and never looked back. Curtain.

This is the behaviour of a man in hell – behaviour stemming from impotent rage at his situation, behaviour of which, only minutes later, he must be profoundly ashamed, knowing that its assertion of power and vitality provides a temporary and meaningless rush of adrenalin, at the expense of someone utterly unable to defend himself. It is the eternal recourse of the bully, and it is ugly, irredeemably ugly. Whether it is, as Fleischer claims, the manifestation of 'a tragic genetic flaw' is another matter. But it is to be doubted, even if it were, whether that was what – in Fleischer's phrase – brought 'this movie giant down'. The reason Welles never again worked in Hollywood as a director is not that he was ungovernable, but that the work he produced failed to fit into any of the categories that sales departments could market. Once his creative juices were stirred, he was incapable of working formulaically: he had to follow his impulses.

Touch of Evil was so nearly a great cop movie, but it had Welles's stamp all over it, to a degree that alienated the average viewer. 'I did it my way' might as well have been the epitaph of his career as much as his proudest boast. Acting in other men's films, however much he might rewrite the dialogue or try to influence the camera angles, could only be frustrating. With rare exceptions, pretty well every time Welles appeared in another man's film, it turned ugly. The best plan was to squeeze his role into the shortest possible time, so that he had no opportunity to indulge in the full horror of his situation. 'You know,' he said laughingly to Fleischer on the set of *Compulsion*, 'you're being very lucky with me on this picture.' 'Really?' asked Fleischer. 'How come?' 'You've only got me for a short time,' Welles said. 'If I'm on a picture too long I get bored. Then I can cause problems.'

After *Ferry to Hong Kong*, in which Welles appears in a self-designed make-up apparently representing W.C. Fields as Quasimodo and sporting an enterprisingly 'off' British accent, he turned up in *David and Goliath*, a ludicrous Franco-Italian co-production in which he plays a raddled King Saul, alongside a Yugoslavian beefcake David and an Italian circus giant called Kronos as Goliath. Welles bashfully confessed to Peter Bogdanovich that he had directed his own scenes, but presumably (to judge from them) this would merely have involved the most perfunctory indication of where the cameras might be. Welles's performance is broad, in every sense, though it is worth noting that neither in this role nor any of the many other comparable parts in which he is accused of chewing the scenery does he raise his voice. Like the great Victorian stars, he speaks slowly and softly, creating time and space around himself. It is unquestionably ham, but it is very thinly sliced.

This embarrassment of a film was quickly eclipsed by the success of *Compulsion*, for which he shared the Best Actor Prize at Cannes with Dean Stockwell and Bradford Dillman; Welles delivers the courtroom summing-up speech like a great operatic scena, with a remarkable dynamic range and a masterful command of pace, powerfully dominating murmurs and protest from the public gallery, sinking to great inward intimacy in his addresses to the judge. It is rhetorical, properly so, and in the same way that Darrow's great original summing-up was, but there is no doubting the character's sincerity – or, indeed, Welles's. Commonly cast as thugs, tyrants and villains, he is generally called on to express the opposite of his own views. Welles could readily identify with Wilk/Darrow's anti-capital-punishment sentiments, which chimed exactly with his statement of what he calls 'the classic liberal tradition' in his 1958 interview with Bazin and Bitsch. The speech struck such a chord with the public that it was released separately on a bestselling 45 rpm extended play record, which must be the last time such a thing occurred with a Hollywood movie.

The principal reason Welles had made *David and Goliath*, apart from the substantial emolument, was to avail himself of the loan of equipment from the film company (the fragrantly named Beaver-Champion Attractions Inc.), so that he could shoot more of *Don Quixote*, which was in a state of continuous evolution; the new material was shot in Manziana, just outside Rome, where Welles was giving his King Saul at Cinecittà. *Quixote* had by now become what it would be for the rest of his days: Welles's creative lifeline, the repository of his artistic conscience. He had to answer to no one for it. He could shoot it in his own good time, following the implications of the story, the better he understood it; he could endlessly experiment with editing. Whenever he made a decent killing with a part, a sizeable portion of it was invested in *Quixote* – his notebook, his diary, his cinematic letter to himself.

CHAPTER FIFTEEN

Everyone Loves the Fellow Who's Smiling

WHEN HIS sense of self-esteem was running low, Welles generally turned back to the theatre. He had been in discussion with Hilton Edwards for some time about possible collaborations with the Gate Theatre; they had continued these discussions when they worked together in the dreaded *David and Goliath*, in which – no doubt at Welles's suggestion – Edwards had been engaged to play the Prophet Samuel, which he does with appropriately vatic intensity, like something out of an illustrated Victorian Old Testament, the pseudo-biblical phrases rolling nobly off his tongue. He must have felt that the end result was not entirely satisfactory, since his performance is credited to one Edward Hilton. But at least it gave him a chance to nail Welles down to a commitment for the coming season.

The relationship between Welles and Edwards was complex and deep. Visiting Welles in Dublin, Richard Fleischer was astonished to see the overweening Welles – the terror of stills photographers and press representatives everywhere – reduced to a schoolboy in Edwards's presence. Edwards was Welles's first and only master in the theatre, and Welles constantly looked for opportunities to work with him; Edwards, for his part, saw Welles as an extraordinary, world-beating personality and a fountain of almost too many wonderful ideas, but a constant source of stimulation. Over the now thirty-five years of their friendship, they had endured a number of challenging experiences – above all, the financial meltdown caused by Edwards's and MacLiammóir's participation in *Othello* and the general chaos that prevailed on *The Blessed and the Damned* – but when Welles called for him, Edwards always answered, most recently on *Moby-Dick* in London. They were chums, comrades-in-arms. The relationship between Welles and MacLiammóir was, on both sides, much more ambivalent, Welles believing that MacLiammóir (whom he freely admitted was a great actor and an extraordinary creative personality) held Edwards in a witch-like spell, while MacLiammóir was darkly suspicious that Welles used

Edwards for his own selfish purposes. It is not entirely fortuitous that the deal for Welles's latest venture with the partners was finally sealed while MacLiammóir was away in America playing Don Pedro to John Gielgud's Benedick in *Much Ado About Nothing* on Broadway.

In fact, discussions had started in June of 1959, when Welles's idea for a one-man show in which he would play Falstaff had evolved into the notion of a two-handed play, exploring the relationship between Falstaff and Prince Hal. Welles had long been obsessed by the figure of Falstaff. *Winter of Discontent*, the adaptation of the three parts of *Henry VI* and *Richard III* that he had staged at the Todd School as a schoolboy, had been intended as the first part of an evening whose second part would have culminated in *Henry V*; the central character of this part would have been none other than Sir John Falstaff, played by none other than Orson Welles, aged fourteen. Time and money ran out in 1929, but nearly ten years later Welles, now at the head of the Mercury Theatre, returned to the idea with a script called *Five Kings*, which was essentially Part Two of *Winter of Discontent*. Welles at last got to play Falstaff, but the production – heavily dependent on a capricious revolving stage – was not a success; nor was Welles's Falstaff greatly admired. He refused to give up on it, though, insisting on putting the costumes and the set (all seventeen tons of it) into storage. After nearly ten years, it was clear that nothing was going to happen to it, and in 1946 Welles finally acceded to Dick Wilson's request to be allowed to sell it off. But only a year later, he got wind of a production of a version of the Falstaff story by his old Mercury colleague Richard Baer and shot off a furious protest; Baer hastily wrote back to reassure him that his production was nothing to do with *Five Kings*: it was 'a slight improvement on my own version which I did at Princeton as an undergraduate.'[1]

Falstaff was his, Welles felt, as of right; but unlike the other great characters he had attempted, he was not simply motivated by the challenge of cracking a huge role: his feelings for Falstaff were much more personal. Welles saw the fat knight as a member of an endangered and rapidly disappearing species: an individualist, a sensualist, a yea-sayer, representing Merrie England, that prelapsarian state of being of which the last traces had all but disappeared with the coming of industrialisation – which had, indeed, already begun to disappear in Shakespeare's own time, as the all-encompassing Elizabethan state wrapped its tentacles around the nation and the old ways disappeared under the pressure of new laws, stricter controls. Falstaff is oblivious of the threat of this encroachment. He carries on regardless, devoid of the sense of guilt that haunts modern man; he is, in fact, essentially innocent. Welles goes one step further: he is not just innocent, he is good. And then Welles goes yet one more step. Falstaff is essentially motivated by love – love of life, and, most poignantly, love of Hal. Inevitably, from Welles's perspective, he will be betrayed.

It is a striking and an original reading of Falstaff, which almost completely omits the character's comic dimension, seen by theatrical tradition as central; Welles told Peter Bogdanovich that he saw the character as 'tragic'. In fact, he seems to have related to the play in an intensely autobiographical and highly complex way. Of course he identified with Falstaff, the man of insatiable appetite; but he connected equally strongly with Hal – Hal who uses life-embracing Falstaff to humanise himself, casting him as a warm, loving, permissive substitute for his cold, austere father. At the end of the play Hal rejects this 'bad' drunken father, just as Welles rejected his own 'bad' drunken father; Hal's devastating words to Falstaff as he discards him – 'I know thee not, old man' – could just as easily have been uttered by Welles to his father Dick when, egged on by Roger Hill, he refused to meet him unless he stopped drinking; not much later, Dick died without ever seeing his son again. In 'My Father Wore Black Spats', the extraordinary autobiographical fragment he wrote for French *Vogue* towards the end of his life, Welles said: 'I killed my father',[2] which is no more literally true than saying that Hal killed Falstaff, which Welles insisted he had.

All of this was swirling around inside Welles when he approached the character of Falstaff again, after a gap of twenty years. The plan was to do the two-handed play Welles and Edwards had been discussing at the Dublin Theatre Festival, in September of 1959, for two weeks; this was duly announced. The Dublin impresario and theatre producer Louis Elliman would produce it; Hilton Edwards would direct it; and one of the Gate's regular designers, Molly McEwen, was to design it. When McEwan pulled out because of other commitments, Welles assumed responsibility for designing both costumes and sets. Welles was now back at home with Paola and Beatrice in Fregene. Edwards, obviously wishing to move things along, wrote to him, offering to sketch out a rough version of the play, which by now had grown again, evolving into a full-cast event that would comprise virtually all of Falstaff's scenes from *Henry IV, Parts One* and *Two* shaped into two halves, linked by material from *Henry V* and *Richard II*. Welles, digging deeper into the material, was now ambitiously trying to encompass not just Falstaff's story, but the birth of the modern political world – the triumph of realpolitik over the chivalric ideal.

Three weeks later, Welles sent Edwards a copy of what he now called *Chimes at Midnight*, suggesting that they should do the play in tandem with *The Merchant of Venice.* With the play he included some notes 'not on *staging* – but on what you call *essence* . . . on what I think the play is *about*'.[3] They give a vivid sense of his directorial approach, his sharp understanding of the play and his constant awareness of the audience's engagement with the characters and their story: here he is discussing adding the scene between Lady Percy and her husband, Hotspur (Act Three, Scene Three of *Henry IV*, *Part One*): 'LADY PERCY MAKES HOTSPUR REAL,' he says, in capitals. 'The more real he is, and the more sympathetic as a human being – the better our first act pays off from every point of view . . . I believe that an important part of Shakespeare's plan for PART ONE was to make Hotspur actually more sympathetic than Hal.' A striking thought: 'THE DEATH OF HOTSPUR,' he goes on at the top of his voice, 'IS MORE THAN MERE CLIMAX. It introduces the note of tragedy on which all of PART TWO is based. It makes the final comment on chivalry WHICH IS THE SUBJECT OF PART ONE.' Welles has a remarkably integrated view of the plays: Hotspur's death, he says, 'represents the death of the chivalric idea . . . and also of course it marks a tremendous change in the development of Hal's character. It is not only that he kills his great challenger in single combat (just as he will kill his great friend in the end) BUT THAT THE PERSON HE KILLS BE REAL AND ATTRACTIVE TO US AS A PERSON.' Which brings Welles back to Lady Percy: 'without his wife, Hotspur is greatly lessened as a human figure – as a person we care about, and mourn over when he dies.' This is very much joined-up thinking about the play. But then his showman's instincts assert themselves: 'WITHOUT HOTSPUR'S WIFE WE HAVE NO ATTRACTIVE FEMALE IN THE WHOLE DAMN EVENING ********* Alright, enough of that!'

The creative temperature was rising; flickerings of theatrical glory were appearing on the horizon. And then, as so often with Welles, it was all snuffed out – on this occasion, because of his commitment to a film whose dates were suddenly brought forward: his second for Richard Fleischer, *Crack in the Mirror*; it was produced by Darryl Zanuck, who had saved *Othello*'s bacon at a critical moment, and to whom Welles accordingly felt morally indebted. He would have to pull out of the Dublin Festival, he wrote to Edwards, or at the very most do just two performances of *Chimes at Midnight*, which made no sense whatever financially.[4] He promised to pay for the production himself. But *Chimes at Midnight* was just the tip of the iceberg: Welles had been made a director of Dublin Gate Productions, and he and MacLiammóir and Edwards had been planning a series of shows, films and television productions, all of which would now be imperilled by the demise of *Chimes at Midnight.* He proposed various ways around the problem – shifting dates, and so on – most of which would require him to subsidise the venture personally. The letter shows him to have proposed a major programme with the Gate, his old capacity for engendering projects and whipping up enthusiasm for them in no way diminished.

For Edwards and MacLiammóir it was all deadly earnest; for Welles it was great sport. Just talking about things is no fun – you have to believe that they're actually going to happen. And before you know where you are, you have a whole year's work planned out in some detail. There had been, for example, serious discussion of him doing a play based on the great Liam O'Flaherty novel *The Informer*, set at the time of the Irish Free State, though Welles was not convinced, preferring a story-telling compilation called *Tales from the Irish Hills*; and at one point he was going to play Willy Loman in *Death of a Salesman* for them. For a small outfit like Edmóir (Edwards and MacLiammóir's production company), planning a season like this was life-and-death stuff: no $100,000 cameos for them, if things fell through. In fact Welles had committed a sum of money to Dublin Gate Productions, out of which Edwards was to be paid a retainer, which Welles now increased. Despite the chaos and anxiety he had just unleashed, Welles's letter to Edwards shows real tenderness and affection. He signs off 'I love you, Orson': the O of Orson is smudged, and next to it he has written the phrase 'blotting his copybook again'.

Edwards acted swiftly: he pulled *Chimes at Midnight* out of the theatre festival, at no cost to Welles, but at the small price of him promising to put in a personal appearance after one of the shows in the festival, or on a Sunday. 'I had to take an awful lot of insulting gabble from small fry that I was bluffing,' wrote Edwards, 'or that you had no intention of coming at all. This, as you can imagine, made me very angry and I ripped up bellies left and right and swore on the Bible, the Talmud, the Koran and the Dublin telephone Directory in that order, that they lied in their teeth.'[5] Edwards then proposed a post-Christmas opening for *Chimes at Midnight* at the Gaiety Theatre. 'If,' he continues, 'now that you see it, in all its horror it goes beyond your intention or your convenience we are surely old friends enough for you to have a second thought upon the matter with "no offence gave or took".' Welles was still definitely on for *Chimes at Midnight*; and he honoured Edwards's promise by breezing in from Paris on the last Saturday of the festival at the end of September, showing up at midnight, 'a burly man in a baggy dinner suit,' reported the *Daily Telegraph's* man in Dublin, 'with a little fringe of beard that made him look in his own words "like something between Edward VII and an unsuccessful gold miner"'.[6] He entertained his packed audience by resorting to the tried-and-tested formula: some Shakespeare, then questions and answers. He talked about *Don Quixote* – 'I had to finance it myself because it's pretty difficult to get a bank to put up money for a film that's mostly in your head' – and said he was sorry not to have been able to do *Chimes at Midnight* at the festival, but then 'it's Theatre Festival here the whole year round'. All very charming, and warmly received: no sign of the Catholic Cinema and Theatre Patrons' Association, no pickets denouncing Stalin's Star.

He retreated back to Paris and *Crack in the Mirror*, playing the double role of a prosperous attorney and a disturbed working-class man, the former rather more convincingly than the latter; meanwhile, Louis Elliman budgeted the show, determining that the only way it could break even would be to do six extra weeks, in addition to the four scheduled weeks in Dublin. Belfast could take it for two, then they would need four weeks in English provincial cities, ending up in the West End of London. Simultaneously, as part of the familiar Wellesian pattern, another producer, the Dutchman Jan de Blieck, having got a sniff of all this, proposed a two-production European tour, starting in Paris and then going on to the Benelux countries.

Edwards got on with trying to cast the play. Maxine Audley, Welles's feisty Emilia from nearly a decade earlier, was asked to play Portia and Lady Percy; she was not unwilling, but it was uncertain whether they could afford her. An offer for the parts of Hal and either Bassanio or Antonio was put in to Patrick McGoohan, who swiftly turned them down; and a general call was put out for a Mistress Quickly: 'For this I would like someone who is practically a variety artist in talent.'[7] Edwards is writing, but it seems to be Welles who is speaking. The question of who was actually directing the show was never clearly resolved; eventually Edwards was officially credited with the production ('Staged by Hilton Edwards'), though Welles was clearly the *fons et origo* of the whole venture.

By now Jan de Blieck had added Germany to the European

tour, which rendered *The Merchant of Venice* unsuitable: Welles had doubts about the viability of the play so soon after the end of the war. 'The picture of a Jew to be published just now is not Shylock,' Welles told the *Daily Express*. 'The Jewish story to be told just now is not the one about the pound of flesh. Not so long ago six million Jews were murdered. I think I know what Shakespeare would have felt about that story. I only wish he were alive to write it.' In its place, Welles proposed doing *Twelfth Night* in the spirit of P.G. Wodehouse (one of his favourite authors), with himself as Jeeves-Malvolio, surrounded by Orsino-Bertie Wooster and an assortment of Drones. Edwards would be Sir Toby Belch. 'Toby as an Edwardian rakehell with curled white mustachios, a monocle and a top hat,' he wrote to Hilton Edwards. 'Ought to be great fun for you.'[8] By any standards it is astonishing that, just three weeks from the beginning of rehearsals, they were unsure of the second play in their season – the play, indeed, with which they intended to open in Belfast. At one point Webster's *Duchess of Malfi* raised its decadent head. Edwards was by no means averse to risk, but all this free-flowing adrenalin was beginning to make him feel ill; in fact he was ill, having had a fall, and was confined to quarters with a temperature of 104. From his sickbed, he uttered a *cri de cœur*:

> I have a suggestion which will probably make you open the sprinkler stop-valves on me and leave me on the apron singing *Abide with Me*. However I will risk it. Wouldjever consider concentrating for the moment on one show, *Chimes*, which is the readiest; spending an all-out effort on it; devoting yourself selflessly to your acting of Falstaff, so that without dissipating energies we could deliver one slap-up production instead of two shaky ones?

Sanity prevailed; *Twelfth Night* – or would it be *The Duchess of Malfi*? – was deferred till *Chimes at Midnight* had opened. Rehearsals began at the YMCA in London in late January. The cast Welles and Edwards had assembled was for the most part young and eager, with a characteristic admixture of the ancient and eccentric. Auditions had created the same stir as his two previous West End productions, but the actors willing to work for a minimum wage and embark on an as-yet-unspecified tour were inevitably going to be less established than the ones he had approached for his stage productions of *Othello* and *Moby-Dick*. They arrived in dribs and drabs. Welles went about the process of casting with characteristic originality; he was, as ever, determined to avoid mere competence. First on the scene was Keith Baxter, who was twenty-seven years old, a couple of years out of RADA (his training having been interrupted by two years of National Service in Korea). He had a few small film roles to his name, one of them in Powell and Pressburger's then-notorious *Peeping Tom*, but was currently engaged in bottle-washing at Simpson's restaurant in the Strand. He joined the long queue of hopefuls at the New Theatre in the hope that the smallish but lively part of Prince Hal's edgy sidekick, Ned Poins, might still be available. Instead he was astonished to come away with the crucial role of Hal, equal in length and importance to the part of Falstaff. Thelma Ruby, thirty-five at the time, an established comedienne with extensive experience in revue but none in classical theatre, was cast as Mistress Quickly (fulfilling the Edwards/Welles criteria for the role); Welles was especially delighted that, like Baxter, she had never done Shakespeare before. Leonard Fenton, a civil engineer in his mid-thirties who had just decided on acting as his career, had been sent along by his new agent, with no expectations of being cast:

> Came into this little room, Hilton was sitting behind this big desk, Orson was standing against the wall. They both said hello, a sort of cursory hello, and Hilton did all the talking. Said we're looking for a Bardolph, we want him played in an old Cockney dialect. Said, there aren't any long speeches so we would like you to read a speech of Falstaff's as Bardolph, in a Cockney dialect. So they gave it to me to look at and I started reading it and then suddenly Orson said, 'Of course that's the way that line should be read.' And I thought is he sending me up? But he wasn't, he wasn't. And I got through it, got to the end and Hilton said, 'thank you very much, very good, thank you. Well, we've got your agent's name and number.' And Orson said 'What do you mean get in touch, we want him.'[9]

Anne Cunningham, twenty-three, proved to be something of a free spirit. She auditioned with the Rumour speech from *Henry IV, Part Two*. 'I jumped about and then I did somersaults and I rode my legs in the air and I threw apples about and it was really very, very odd.' In the middle of the speech Welles shouted out that it was a 'very *interesting* reading. Have you done Shakespeare?'

> And I said, 'Oh yes, I've just done *Romeo and Juliet*.' So he said, 'Oh, did you play Juliet?' and I said no. He said, 'Well, you're too young for the mother, what did you play,' and I said, and I really said in all seriousness, 'I didn't actually have a line, but I had a line addressed to me, "she that makes dainty I warrant you, she, I'll swear, hath corns." I mean, I wasn't a walk-on or an extra, it was really quite important.'[10]

He roared with laughter and said, 'I've got to have this girl, I mean, in my company.' He cast her as Chorus (a somewhat undefined role in the still-being-written *Chimes at Midnight*) and as Viola in *Twelfth Night*.

Everybody was to be cross-cast between the two plays; Baxter was to be Orsino and Ruby Maria. This cross-casting caused difficulties for young Peter Bartlett, fresh from playing Claudio in *Much Ado About Nothing* at the Open Air Theatre in Regent's Park: he joined the company to play as cast, and by default ended up playing Hal's younger brother John of Lancaster, a part that was supposed to double with Viola's twin, Sebastian, in *Twelfth Night*. Alas, Bartlett in no way resembled Anne Cunningham, so 'they put me through a fortnight of torment because young men kept coming round all trying to look like Anne Cunningham and my knowing that if they did they would take away my John of Lancaster from me.'[11] No Anne Cunningham lookalikes appeared, so Bartlett kept his John of Lancaster. Aubrey Morris, a short young-old character actor with an interestingly lyrical-comical, slightly grotesque quality, was cast as Justice Silence and Curio in *Twelfth Night*; Justice Shallow was played by Keith Marsh, equally short. Shorter than both of them by a head was Henry Woolf, who played Nym; he was to play Feste in *Twelfth Night*. Lady Percy, whose inclusion in *Chimes at Midnight* Welles had set so much store by, was to be played by Zinnia Charlton (who would also play Olivia), and Doll Tearsheet by the Australian actress Shirley Cameron. By far the most exotic member of the company, and thus irresistible to Welles, was Terence Greenidge, playing the very sober role of the Lord Chief Justice, and the rather more choleric one of the Earl of Northumberland. Barbadian by origin, a founder-member of the Hypocrites Club at Oxford, co-author and director with Evelyn Waugh of the scandalous film *Scarlet Woman: An Ecclesiastical Melodrama*, in which he also appears as Father Murphy, SJ ('a very beautiful priest'), Greenidge was the author of some slim volumes of verse, a collection of *Four Plays for Pacifists* and a critical study of modern university life, *Degenerate Oxford?*

(1930). No Wellesian company was complete without at least one actor with a similarly exotic curriculum vitae.

Two members of the cast were there for what might be called Hiltonic reasons: twenty-seven-year-old Patrick Bedford, a strikingly handsome actor from the backstreets of Dublin, played Poins and Davy, Shallow's man; he was Edwards's current boyfriend, part of the complicated ménage maintained by Edwards and MacLiammóir at Harcourt Terrace, their elegant Georgian home in Dublin. The other actor proposed by Edwards – attached as assistant to the directors, and featuring as Gower and Feeble, among sundry other spit-and-cough roles – was Geraldine Fitzgerald's son, Michael Lindsay-Hogg, now nineteen years old and nominally studying at Oxford University, but grounded in Dublin with his mother because of debts run up during his first term. He was of course delighted to be liberated from the Dublin suburbs by Edwards's suggestion that he join the *Chimes at Midnight* company. The critical role of King Henry IV, almost equal in importance to the roles of Falstaff and Hal, was to be played by Reginald Jarman ('pro-tem', Welles's casting notes say: he was confidently expecting to inveigle MacLiammóir into playing the part when he came back from America, just before opening night in Belfast). Jarman was a veteran of the Gate, and an old pal of Edwards's – solid, pipe-smoking, deaf: 'I'm deaf in this ear, old boy,' he told Baxter, 'speak in *this* ear.' When Baxter approached Jarman's other ear, he found a huge deaf-aid. 'I cover it up with a cunning disguise,' cried Jarman, triumphantly. The disguise was several layers of Elastoplast and his own rather bad wig.[12] Two crucial parts were still uncast by the time of the first read-through of the play: Pistol and Hotspur. Julian Glover was very nearly cast in the role, but made it a condition that his new wife would also join the company. This was Eileen Atkins; a missed opportunity there.

At the first rehearsal they read the play through, recollected Thelma Ruby:

> and Hilton said there was a whole pile of drawings of where he wanted everyone to move and how he wanted everything done. It was all, he said, thought out and it was carefully planned and then he said, 'Now, I'd like you to work this way with me, I'd like you, if you have any suggestions and you want to change anything to do it afterwards, but first of all I would like to do the plan as I've planned it.' And Orson said, 'If I can do that then the rest of them can.'[13]

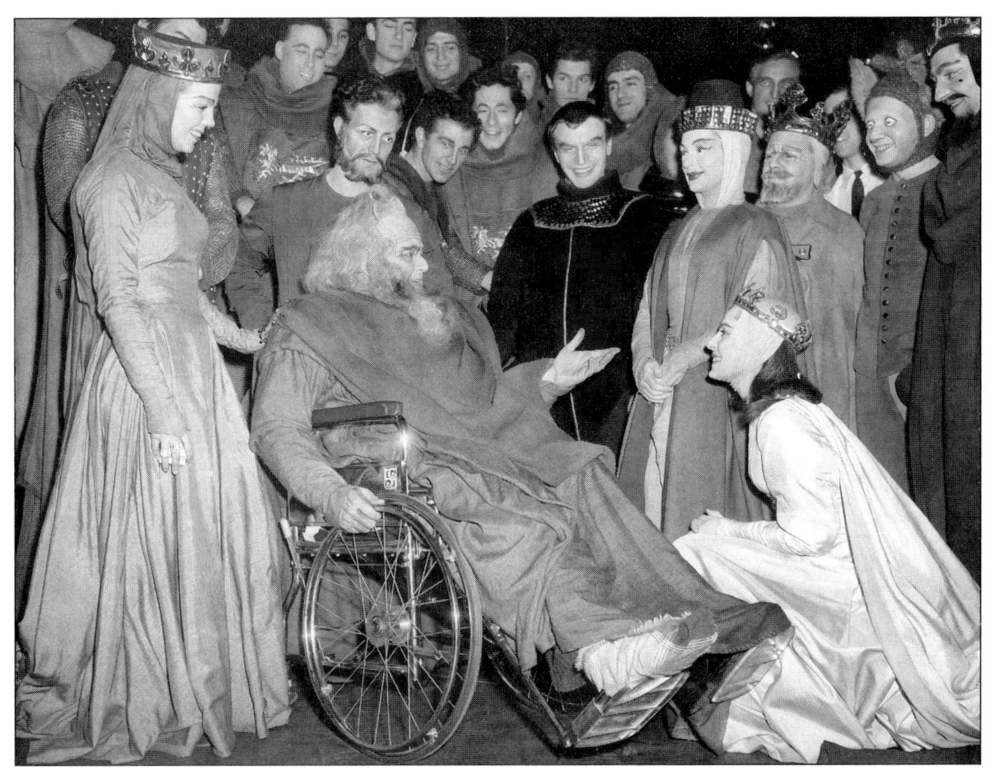

Wheelchair-bound *King Lear* New York, 1956: left to right: Geraldine Fitzgerald, Welles, Roy Dean, John Colicos, Viveca Lindfors (*above*).

Welles as Mr Arkadin, 1956 (*above*); Welles as Father Mapple in John Huston's *Moby-Dick*, 1956 (*right*).

Welles as Hank Quinlan in *Touch of Evil*, 1958 (*left*); Welles, Charlton and Lydia Heston, Hollywood, 1957 (*below*).

Welles telling tales in *An Arabian Night*, Associated Television, 1960 (*right*); Welles carrying the motion at the Oxford Union, Oxford University, 1960 (*below*).

Chimes at Midnight on stage, Belfast Grand Opera House, 1960:
Keith Marsh (Justice Shallow), Welles (Falstaff), Aubrey Morris (Justice Silence), (*above*); Keith Baxter (King Henry V), Welles (Falstaff), Terence Greenidge (Archbishop of Canterbury) (*below*).

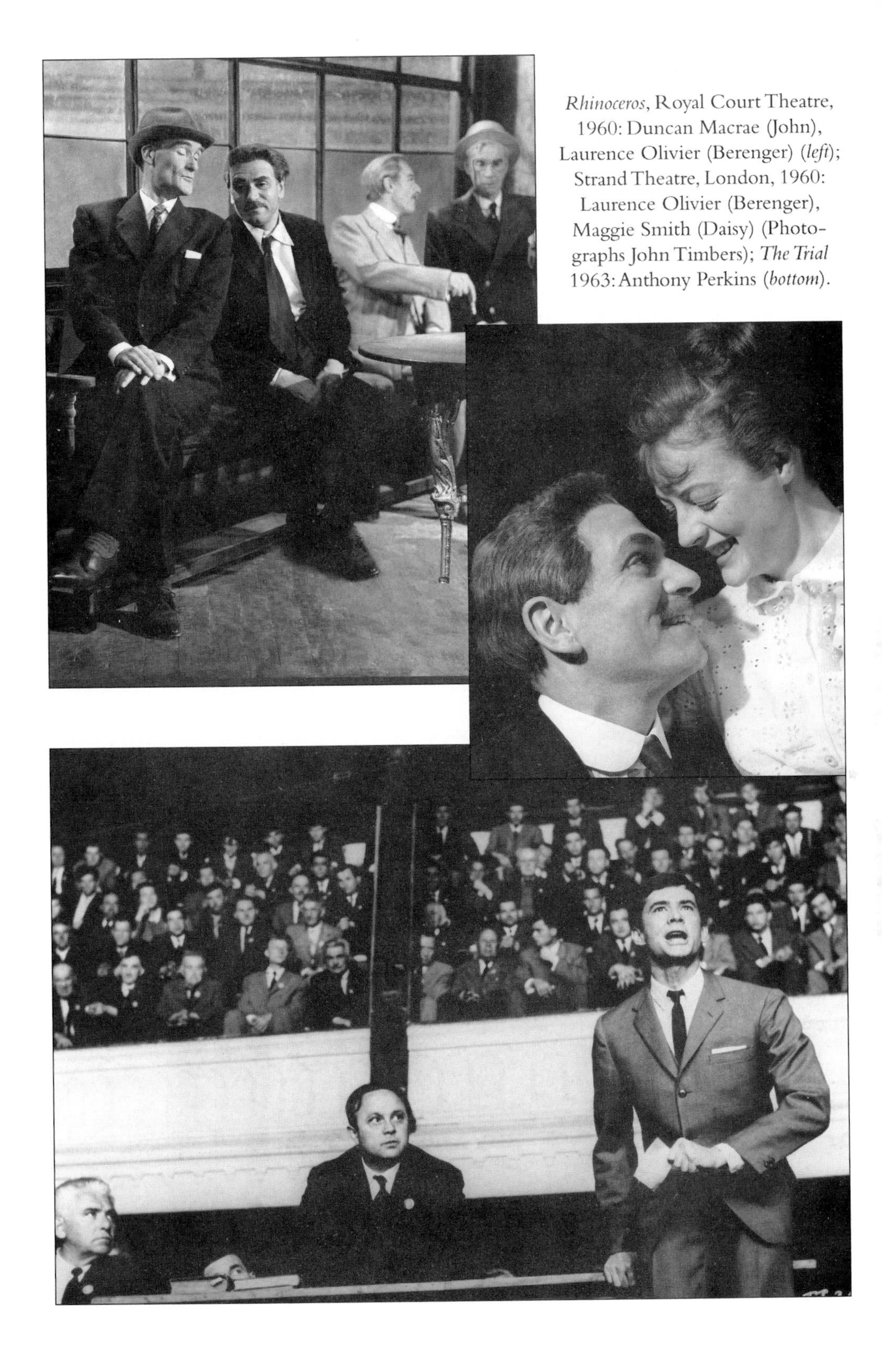

Rhinoceros, Royal Court Theatre, 1960: Duncan Macrae (John), Laurence Olivier (Berenger) (*left*); Strand Theatre, London, 1960: Laurence Olivier (Berenger), Maggie Smith (Daisy) (Photographs John Timbers); *The Trial* 1963: Anthony Perkins (*bottom*).

Chimes at Midnight film, location photographs, 1964: Keith Baxter (King Henry V), Welles (*above*); Keith Baxter (Henry V), Welles, Jeremy Rowe (John of Lancaster) (*top right*); Welles, Keith Baxter, John Gielgud (*below right*); Welles, Norman Rodway (Hotspur) (*right*) (Photographs Nicholas Tikhomiroff).

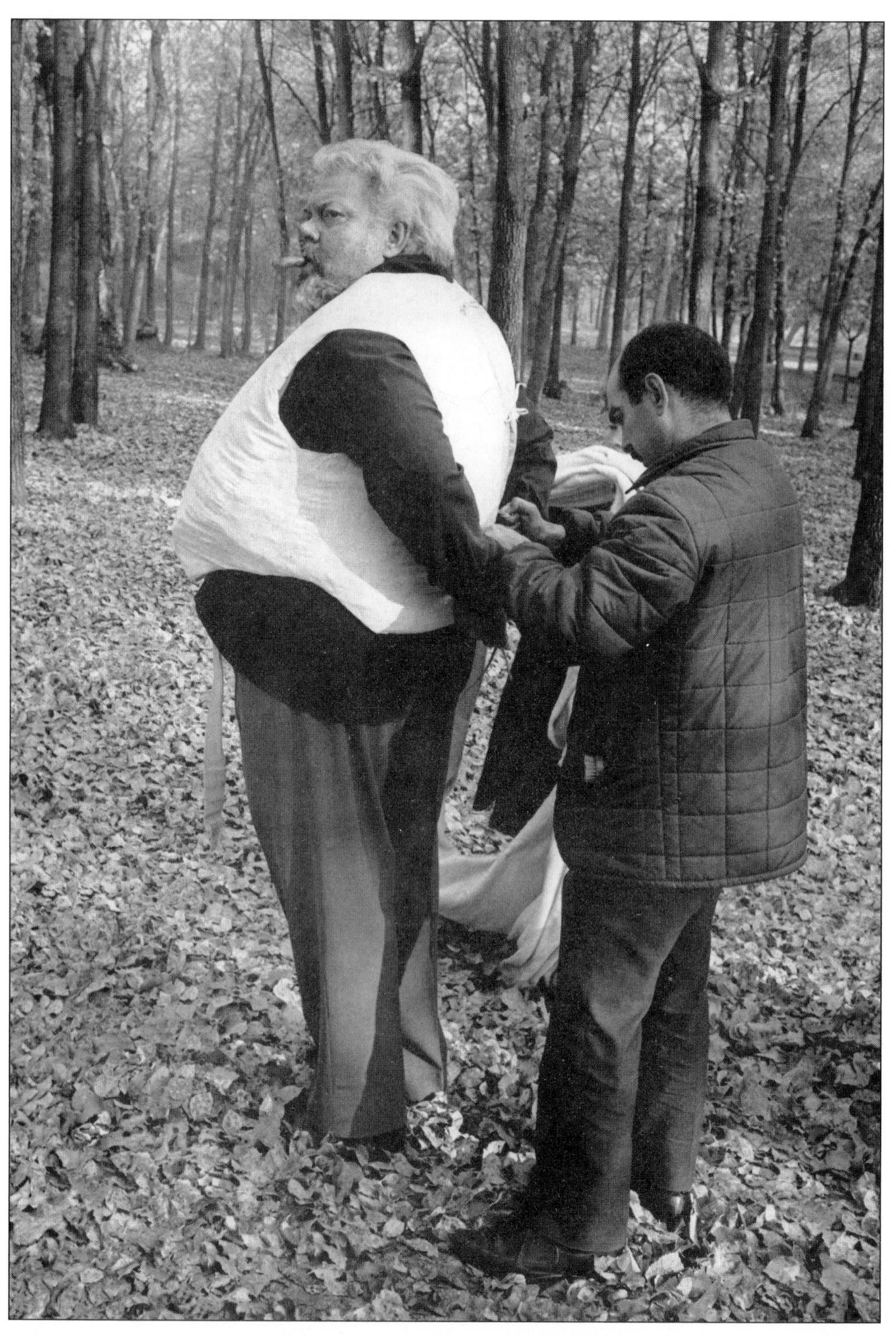

Chimes at Midnight film, location photograph,
Welles padding up in the forest, 1964 (Photograph Nicholas Tikhomiroff).

It is hard to imagine any way of working less congenial to Welles. That afternoon he announced that he had a terrible toothache. 'My dear boy,' said Edwards, 'you must see a dentist.' 'Yes, I think I should,' replied Welles. 'And so,' recalls Michael Lindsay-Hogg, 'Orson went to see his dentist. Who was in Rome.'[14] Welles reappeared two weeks later, by which time Edwards, working diligently, had staged the play as well as he could in the absence of the central character. They now finally cast the not-insignificant parts of Pistol (Rory MacDermot, a solid forty-five-year-old actor of the old school) and Hotspur, for whom they chose a startling young actor from Canada, Alexis Kanner, seventeen but claiming to be twenty-seven. He had just come from a season at the Birmingham Rep, in which, again lying about his age, he had played an acclaimed Caliban. He was a turbulent individual, possessed of what Baxter carefully described as 'raw unfocussed talent', and his arrival in the company introduced a new and dangerous energy into the proceedings. 'A mutinous character', Michael Lindsay-Hogg called him, and the relatively short part of Hotspur – dead at the interval – scarcely satisfied Kanner's huge need for attention and exposure. He concentrated on making the fight between him and Hal as life-threatening as possible, so much so that the official fight director walked out; he was never replaced.

Meanwhile Welles was unpicking all of Edwards's careful staging, discovering things and following his impulses. The first scene he did was with Keith Baxter; Edwards had staged it with Welles on one side of the stage and Baxter on the other. 'I can't play this scene like this,' said Welles. 'This is a scene where I've got to touch him and grab him.' For all Welles's elaborate courtesy, and his and Edwards's genuine affection for each other, he had no intention of being confined by preconceived moves. 'He redid everything that Hilton had tried to do,' remembered Thelma Ruby, 'he changed everything.'[15] The company generally felt a great sense of liberation when he returned to the rehearsal room. 'The real McCoy came from Orson,' Kanner remarked.[16] Not that his presence in the rehearsal room was by any means guaranteed, even after his return from Rome, though he did like to be present on Fridays when, according to Peter Bartlett, he would personally dispense the actors' salaries from a large brown parcel bag, in true actor-managerial spirit.

Early in February, Welles took a couple of days off for his appearance at the Oxford Union, where he had a whale of a time contesting the motion 'that this House holds America responsible for spreading vulgarity in Western society', moved by the noted humorist Stephen Potter, author of *Potter on America*, among other bestselling titles.

This was exactly the sort of tonic on which Welles thrived: the Union was even more crowded for the occasion than it had been the previous term, for the appearance of the Prime Minister. Welles comfortably saw the motion off, by 485 votes to 306. 'If Europe has lagged behind us in vulgarity,' he said, ' – and I think you must at least acknowledge that you have – it is not by virtue of niceties of feeling, it is largely because of two World Wars in which we in America have played a mainly expeditionary role. Now you are catching up with us, and all Europe is drunk with the same poison.'[17]

This was paradise for Welles – uncontested rhetorical flourishes in front of a thousand eagerly responsive people. After a very good dinner, he lingered at the Oxford and Cambridge boxing blues (being, he said, 'a great lover of the fancy') and seized the opportunity to offload into the eager ear of the *Oxford Times* some comments about the House Un-American Activities Committee: most of those sacked, he says, were in fact card-carrying communists. 'Not that that justifies sacking them; in a free country a man should be able to express any opinion. The people who disgusted me were the big boys who named their comrades just to keep their swimming pools.' He added more pithy observations about Hollywood, denouncing the 'utter incompetents who have been directors for thirty years, surrounded with such wonderful craftsmen that you can't go wrong, so long as you keep your mouth shut'. He didn't much care for movies in general, it appeared: it was something to do with his hatred of all machinery. 'It's different in the theatre,' he said. 'There anything can happen; it probably won't, but you believe it can. The actors remake it every night. At any moment they may take off, they may levitate.' In this well-lubricated vein, he embarked on a discussion of *The Third Man*, briskly dismissing Graham Greene's contribution to the film: 'The whole story, setting, and conception were Korda's. He just got Greene to write it – and I wrote my own part.' As for Reed: 'he is a real director, with a fine visual sense, though less sense of the architecture of a plot.' Coming from the director of *Mr Arkadin*, this was perhaps less wounding than it might otherwise have been. As for *Chimes at Midnight*, it was, he said, 'not the sort of thing a national theatre could do, but a maverick like me can get away with it'.

The maverick returned to London with his batteries recharged, but instead of rehearsing, he frequently retired to his room at the Hyde Park Hotel, whence he issued a stream of thoughts on the production. On 10 February, less than a fortnight before the show was due to open in Belfast, Welles confronted the tiresome reality that the costumier, Nathan's, had refused to supply the production with costumes or even go ahead with his own costume. His adrenalin was, as always, stirred by a crisis. He fired off a letter to Edwards with a radical proposal: what he called 'the modern dress or *un-dressed-up*' version of the production. 'The feeling should be that of the rehearsal just before the dress rehearsal.' To do it as the dress rehearsal itself – to *dramatise* it – would, he says, 'seem like self-plagiarism'; that idea had worked well enough with *Moby-Dick*, but he had a new idea for *Chimes at Midnight*. He would open the show by walking onto the empty stage as himself and talk to the audience, 'explaining our ideas and purposes, telling them about Shakespeare's theatre etc, etc, and preparing their minds for the unavoidable anachronisms, such as the sword-fight, by references to the striking clock in *Julius Caesar*, etc, etc.'[18]

We are back to *First Person Singular* territory. Back to Welles the conjuror, summoning up a production out of nothing – out of a basket, from which he would pluck a crown, noting that 'there are some things that never change'. In this way he would prepare the public, he says, not only for the extraordinary sequence of the 'crown on the pillow' when the King lies dying, but also for the coronation, the climactic event of the play. 'I also show, in a casual sort of a way, a couple of coronation robes; "This," I say, "is the only place where we will actually dress up, because the actors must have dressed up for it in Shakespeare's day, and people in real life dress up for it now. Nowadays, of course, they rent their robes – as we have – from Moss Brothers."' The idea was that the actors should wear the wardrobe 'most nearly approximating the station and function of the various characters insofar as the personal wardrobe of a present day company of actors might be expected to make this possible.' There was no reason to suppose, he said, that a character actor (playing, say, a Chief Justice) should not have striped trousers and a homburg hat in his personal wardrobe. This procedure, as he puts it, would become perfectly clear, if he explained it to the audience at the beginning. What he could not endure was the thought of actors pulling their costumes out of a skip, which was 'stagey and even a bit self-conscious and works directly against the kind of super-honesty which should be the whole purpose of this sort of interpretation'.

In the event, they never attempted these ideas – ideas that became commonplace in British theatre in the later 1960s and '70s. If Welles had had the time and the will, it could have resulted in something radical and very striking. Or not. Not all of Welles's notions were equally good: the pre-recorded dialogue he had so doggedly attempted to use on the films of *The Magnificent Ambersons* and *Macbeth* was a doomed idea. But when he really wanted to push an idea to its limits, the results could be extraordinary. This desperately underfunded and under-rehearsed production of *Chimes at Midnight*, however, was not a suitable occasion for experimentation. Instead, something very old-fashioned happened. Skips of old costumes from the well-loved television shows *Ivanhoe* and *Robin Hood* somehow arrived in the rehearsal room; the actors were invited to jump in and choose whatever they thought would work best for them. 'Some of the costumes were appalling,' recalled Aubrey Morris, 'but the great man himself adored the situation – he was in there like the rest of us, probing and digging. He made and cut a wonderful hat for me, and cut my hair. The great Genesis had begun. We worked through the night dressing and undressing. This was the real theatre I imagine Orson had always desired, glory from chaos.'[19]

And it was, too. They left the rehearsal room in London without ever once running the show; the actors had barely seen a glimpse of Welles's performance. On the rare occasions when he was present, he read from the text, never once putting the book down. Indeed, on the boat on which they all travelled together from Holyhead to Dun Laoghaire, Welles was seen, ensconced in his first-class apartment with Mrs Rogers, going over and over the lines with her. The stage manager had gone ahead a few days in advance to supervise the building of the set, which had been roughed out by Welles only a week earlier: fortunately it was simple, consisting of a series of rostra, with no moving parts, and a large number of spears draped with heraldic flags. It was built at Louis Elliman's Ardmore Film Studio in Dublin, which saved a welcome few quid, and was duly installed in the beautiful Opera House in Belfast – one of the greatest masterpieces of the greatest of the Edwardian theatre architects, Frank Matcham.

★

The company assembled in the foyer the morning after they arrived for a pep talk from Welles, who warned them that it was going to be tricky, but that they'd get there in the end, rather alarmingly citing his 1938 production of *Danton's Death* as an example of triumph over adversity: it had been the Mercury Theatre's biggest flop, at which three actors fell down the stage lift during the dress rehearsal, badly injuring themselves. There were no such catastrophes in Belfast – there was no stage lift, apart from anything else – but the technical rehearsal was a Welles special, lasting for twenty-two hours, with Welles and Edwards roaring away at each other and the company, Welles on stage, Edwards with a megaphone in the circle of the very large theatre, as they made the show on the hoof; Welles constantly rewriting and rearranging the script, with Mrs Rogers forever racing in and out with newly typed pages, to the despair of the stage management. Welles had taken against the stage manager, Alistair James, mostly because he was the one who had to say no to him, but also because he kept prompting Welles, due to his still very unsteady grip on the text. 'You cue me again and you're fired,' Welles roared at him on one occasion. 'We're all working up here and you just sit there doing nothing. Get up on the stage, Mr James, and get to work.'[20] The burden of actually running the show fell on the youthful shoulders of the assistant stage manager, Martin Tickner, just eighteen years old, who, having successfully discharged the challenging task of transporting a company of multiply demanding actors across the Irish Sea, was now wrestling not only with an endlessly changing proliferation of sound and light cues, but with the recalcitrant screen that the Opera House management insisted had to come in at the interval to show commercials.

Tickner had got a certain complex sequence wrong at least five or six times. He turned to Welles and said, 'Look, I'm terribly sorry, Mr Welles, I'm so tired I just don't know what I'm doing. I'll get it right eventually but I cannot do it now.' That, he said, seemed to spark off their relationship, 'because in a curious little way he seemed to admire somebody for turning round and saying that and being absolutely honest'.[21] The truth is, Welles was having a whale of a time and, with the exception of Alistair James and possibly Alexis Kanner, who was given to creating waves of negative energy whenever and in whatever manner he could, so was the rest of the company; this was not *Othello* in Newcastle. At two o'clock in the morning there was a break, and baskets of roast chickens and champagne were wheeled in. Micheál MacLiammóir, having just returned from America only to find himself immediately plunged into what he called 'the Welles vortex', had been sitting in the dark, brooding and observing, but now came down to mingle with everyone. Overhearing Edwards shouting at the actor playing Henry IV, poor deaf Reggie Jarman, and roaring 'to the left, Reggie, to the left', as Reggie resolutely marched to the right till someone yanked him in the correct direction, MacLiammóir murmured, in a voice audible on the other side of the River Lagan, 'you're the King of England, dear, not the fucking Wandering Jew'.[22]

In the hiatuses that occur at even the best-regulated technical rehearsals, Welles, hugely padded, with – inevitably – lifts in his shoes and clothed in a tentative selection of the garments he had pulled together for Falstaff, would (half to himself and half for the amusement of the company) perform a little soft-shoe shuffle, singing a ditty that went:

> Everyone loves the fellow who is smiling
> He brightens the day and lightens the way
> For you.
> He's always making other people happy
> Looking rosy when you're awful blue.[23]

The song had become a sort of mantra for him, especially when he was working with Edwards and MacLiammóir. He had first sung it at the Todd School at the age of eleven, in that year's revue, *Finesse the Queen*; the words were his own. His time at Todd, his discovery of the theatre and the unconditional approval from Skipper that he found there, made it one of his personal Merrie Englands: a period of Edenic innocence and uncomplicated happiness. And that little soft-shoe shuffle is oddly reminiscent of a haunting memory of his childhood sojourns in Grand Detour: there was a country store in the little town that had above it a ballroom with an old dance floor with springs in it. 'When I was little,' Welles told Peter Bogdanovich, 'nobody had danced up there for many years, but I used to sneak up at night and dance by moonlight with the dust rising from the floor . . .'[24]

The dreamy mood was abruptly broken when the technical rehearsal resumed and Michael Lindsay-Hogg – sword in hand and giving vent to a blood-curdling 'Aieeeee!', as very precisely directed by Hilton Edwards – hurled himself towards Welles, who was smoking his cigar, script in hand, desperately trying to make the lines stick in his mind, and only narrowly missed being impaled. Welles's voice roared out, 'I don't care if none of the music cues are working. I don't care if the stage manager is *sitting in the house*, when he should be backstage, working on the *music cues.* I don't care if some people are tired. This is the *theatre.* That's what happens. But, when at three o'clock in the morning, in Belfast in the North of Ireland, Michael Lindsay-Hogg tries to kill me, I quit.' Then he was gone, locked up in his dressing room. Lindsay-Hogg, who had felt that he and Welles had a special rapport, and who had begun to model his demeanour on Welles's – wearing the same bow ties tucked under his collar, smoking the same cigars, which had as often as not been given to him by Welles – was mortified. Suddenly MacLiammóir appeared at Lindsay-Hogg's side:

> 'He's such a monster sometimes. Oh, I could tell you some stories. But that's for another, happier time. What occurred had nothing to do with you or anything you did. At times, when we're depressed or tired, or hungry, we lash out and it's usually at someone we care about. You might say he needed an ally to help him release his fear. Yes, fear; he knows he's not really ready and he knows also that you're resilient and wise and talented and that you'd see it for what it was. Imagine how crushed another young actor might have felt to get that thrown at him.'

Not long after this act of mercy, MacLiammóir went to visit Welles in his dressing room, from which he emerged shortly afterwards to the sound of raised voices, slammed doors and broken china. Welles had tried to persuade MacLiammóir to take over the part of Henry IV; MacLiammóir had refused, and Welles had thrown the dread word 'betrayal' at him.[25]

In due course, the technical rehearsal continued. Welles, refreshed by having consumed an entire roast chicken and drunk a bottle of good red wine sent over from his hotel at three in the morning, was sufficiently restored to allow himself a huge guffaw of laughter at the sight of Lindsay-Hogg, in costume and make-up for his next character, the willing recruit, Francis Feeble, the woman's tailor. 'His tired eyes creased and he laughed as though he were more entertained by my makeup and appearance than by anything ever before in his life. The other actors laughed also and I felt my place regained. I was loved again.'[26] The rehearsal finally ended at eight in the morning. Because of the lateness of the hour, there was no chance of a run-through in the afternoon; besides, Thelma Ruby and Welles were due to go on television at 6 p.m. to publicise the opening. Welles pulled out of the interview and his place was taken by MacLiammóir, who may not have been deeply inclined to hymn the virtues of the man who had so recently denounced him as a traitor; it was, however, an Edmóir Production, so MacLiammóir managed a few honeyed words. Ruby went back to the theatre, and no sooner was she in costume than they were on. Anne Cunningham, dressed in something resembling academic uniform – mortar board and gown, with spectacles perched on her nose – briskly entered with a large tome purporting to be

Holinshed's Chronicles, from which she read selected passages. They were off.

Like many a Welles first night, this one passed in a blur of adrenalin, but for once it was all positive, once the cast were past the shock of Welles's physical appearance. 'We go out onto the stage before the curtain goes up,' said Thelma Ruby, 'and there's this stranger on the stage, he had never got into costume or make-up, ever. He had put on a false nose, a wig, padding, he was enormous anyhow, and he'd made himself twice the size and there was a person there that we had never worked with, we'd never run through the show with, we didn't recognise, he didn't look anything like himself.'[27] Even Alistair James, whom Welles had tormented, acknowledged that 'it was marvellous when we opened in Belfast, absolutely marvellous but that was mainly because Orson didn't know his lines very well and had to rely on absolutely everyone else in the company to get him through'.[28] At the end the audience roared its approval, and Welles made a warmly received speech in which he confessed that he'd been told that Belfast was a theatrical death-trap. 'Well,' he said, 'if this is a theatrical death-trap, it is baited with the most delectable cheese.'

The reviews were entirely approving. Taken together, they constitute perhaps the best set of reviews Welles ever had for anything in his career. 'Welles's Falstaff is a gigantic figure,' said the *Northern Whig*.[29] The Dublin *Irish Times* deeply admired Welles's 'wonderful presentation of Falstaff . . . everything was perfectly timed. It was a presentation which will be long remembered and who knows, may make Belfast audiences more critical of actors whom for want of a yardstick, we have labelled outstanding . . . it was a triumph for Hilton Edwards.'[30] The national press vied with the local, to praise the show: 'A towering Wellesian Première,' announced the influential Manchester *Guardian*, which found that Welles's proclaimed intention of providing a synthesis of the chronicle plays with Falstaff as its hero did less than justice to himself, both as compiler and as actor:

> His quite remarkable performance, and Hilton Edwards's production in this world premiere, are geared to a different purpose. They are notably directed to presenting the Plantagenet world as an Elizabethan understood it, and the genesis and development of the great Henry . . . [Welles's] Falstaff is no personality cult, as it could so easily have been. This is Shakespeare's Falstaff, the old philosopher-rake; he seems to have gone into the depths of the man's humorous soul for wisdom and then to utter it casually in a voice of incomparable richness.[31]

The London *Times* said that Welles 'gets every ounce of the philosophy, the ribaldry, the jesting; he changes with consummate skill from mood to mood and his was a performance that marks him as the ideal Falstaff . . . his superb acting did not dominate that of the others: it did not. What it doubtless did was to inspire the rest of the cast.'[32]

These are rave reviews. Any producer worth his salt would have built on them: great commercial triumphs have been constructed on far less. Who knows? Perhaps that first night in Belfast was one of those rare press nights where the god capriciously descends and sets the town on fire, only to beat a swift retreat the following night; perhaps the show, briefly bound together by a combination of terror and primitive survival instinct, then fell apart. As far as Welles was concerned, they had just begun. The following day he acted decisively on a matter that had been troubling him. Scarcely having been at rehearsals, most of the scenes he was not in had passed him by. Now that he could look beyond his own problems, he finally saw them, and did not care for much of what he saw. Most of all, he was appalled by the performance of Zinnia Charlton as Lady Percy. At 8 a.m. on the morning of the second performance she received a letter saying: 'I have decided to try Anne Cunningham as Lady Hotspur tonight. Orson.' Meanwhile, Anne Cunningham received a note saying she was not to play Chorus that night, but Lady Hotspur. The sacked actress appeared at the theatre and wailed at Orson. 'Why are you so upset?' he said. 'I've just cast you as Olivia in *Twelth Night*. You have that very special quality, repose. You're perfect for Olivia.'[33] In addition to playing Pistol, Rory MacDermot now took over as Chorus, wearing a cloak to conceal the book, because he had had no time to learn the part. That afternoon Welles rehearsed the Lady Percy scene with Cunningham and Kanner as Hotspur, demonstrating exactly how it should be done. 'I must say it was thrilling,' said Cunningham. 'Orson played Lady Percy brilliantly. I thought I'd never be able to match it.'[34] On she went that night. The following day, without a word of explanation, Welles cut the scene altogether – the scene he had set such store by; and that night, the third performance, after the interval, the two discarded Lady Percys, Anne Cunningham and Zinnia Charlton, made themselves up to the hilt, put on their evening dresses, sat in one of the boxes and watched the performance, with every sign of pleasure. Thereafter, Cunningham's role in the second half of the show was reduced to 'running about, screaming a lot',[35] while Charlton sat in her digs, waiting for *Twelfth Night* rehearsals to begin.

After a week of very good houses in Belfast, *Chimes at Midnight* opened at the majestic Gaiety Theatre in Dublin the following Monday, 29 February, and again the god descended. The show went brilliantly and the auditorium was in an uproar of enthusiasm. Welles stepped forward to make a speech; he was in a deeply emotional state, having last acted on stage in Dublin nearly thirty years earlier. 'Thirty years,' he said, 'is a good round figure – as I am tonight – but it is one year less than thirty since I first appeared with the Dublin Gate.' Then, perhaps rashly, he plunged into the fathomless bog of Irish theatre politics, taking up cudgels on behalf of his old colleagues Edwards and MacLiammóir, who were in exile from their own theatre – the victims, their supporters believed, of a coup by the current incumbent, the Earl of Longford. Welles declared that he felt himself to be an honorary Irishman, thanks to his past work with the Gate and his ongoing association with Edwards and MacLiammóir; as such, he wanted to express some criticism: why had Dublin Gate Productions no theatre of its own? This simple question was enough to turn the mood in the auditorium from one of unanimous approval to one of sharply divided partisanship, with insults being hurled from stalls to circle and up into the gods; an entirely satisfactory outcome, Welles felt. 'There were boos and shouts and cat-calls,' Keith Baxter recollected. 'Someone stood up and Orson said "Sit down." "By Christ, I won't sit down," roared back the man.'[36] Welles finally returned to the dressing room, moved and excited. But his tribute to his old mentors and current colleagues was not received by them as he had hoped.

The fracas in Belfast over Welles's attempt to persuade MacLiammóir to take over the part of the King had not ended with MacLiammóir's furious departure from Welles's dressing room. Welles had later added insult to injury by suggesting that if MacLiammóir didn't want to play the King, perhaps he might take on the role of Chorus; in this he was egged on by Edwards, who thought it deeply regrettable that the production was not availing itself of 'such a valuable personality as Micheál'. After the first night in Belfast, MacLiammóir had withdrawn to Dublin, whence he sent Welles a carefully meditated letter, which reveals the depth of his hurt and the deep complexities of the relationship between the three men. At the age of sixty, MacLiammóir had not entirely reconciled himself to no longer being the company's *acteur noble*; he seems, improbably enough, to have expected to be asked to play the barely post-adolescent Hal. To be asked to play the King at the last moment, and as a substitute for an inadequate actor of no profile, was bad enough; but to then be asked to play Chorus – a part as yet ill-defined in the script, but one that consisted largely of reciting chunks of Holinshed – was wholly inappropriate, MacLiammóir felt, to his position as *prima donna assoluta* of the Gate Theatre, whose many and storied triumphs, both national and international, were inextricably interlinked with his standing as a Great Actor. He had not much enjoyed recently playing second or even third fiddle to John Gielgud on Broadway, and he certainly hadn't come home to be further humiliated. MacLiammóir was not to be messed with, and Welles now found himself in the unusual position of being severely and eloquently criticised, as he himself had so severely and eloquently criticised others.

MacLiammóir's letter to Welles hovers excitingly between witty banter and a desire to inflict great pain. Edwards had informed MacLiammóir that Welles had been deeply hurt by his rejection of either part, MacLiammóir wrote, 'and I am astonished by this'. A couple of months earlier Welles had been talking of doing *The Duchess of Malfi* with MacLiammóir in the role of Ferdinand, only for him to be casually informed that Welles had changed his mind:

> I felt quite honestly that I had not only been let but flung down. But the resulting depression was purely professional. It did not affect my feelings about *you* at all. And I can't see why my much more reasoned failure to comply with every wish that flits through the shifting and fantastic caverns of your mind so that at a nod, a whistle, a risen finger, one must drop all other activities and fly to your aid (probably to discover on alighting, that the picture had changed once more and one's flight had been in vain). I can't see why, I say, your feelings for *me* should be affected. Hilton apparently can. He was in his usual condition of unhappy urgency when he rang me to give me your message and seemed to expect me to say I'd play Hotspur's wife for you, if necessary. But Hilton is more pliable than I, and probably *au fond* of sweeter fibre.[37]

Welles had persuaded Edwards, much against his instincts, to play Chorus in Dublin. 'I can't understand you want to push him to play any part you don't feel – having presumably cast the show yourself – is being done at the moment as it should be done. In Dublin of all places, the one city on earth where what he and I do is noted and gloated. Why do you?' MacLiammóir now goes for the jugular: 'Is it some remote shadow of Oedipus that hangs over us all? Is it that you enjoy putting people in positions impossible to maintain without distress or to complain against without embarrassment? Or is it that your very powerful imagination stops short at these places as British civilisation stops short at the table?' He believes, he says, that he knows what it is, 'though wild horses and all the torments of hell wouldn't drag it from me . . . and that is why I love you still and forgive you, as I hope that in the present case you forgive me.'

> The fact that Hilton and I are so proud to associate your name with ours should prove to you, if you need proof, that I am as anxious as you for the play to be a success wherever it may go: and that if *you* believed my playing the King would have helped you'd have got me to do it from the start, and that if I believed my doing Chorus would improve things now I *would* drop all and fly. Now don't be cross with me. It will only necessitate a reconciliation scene in about ten years' time, and then I shall be far too feeble to play it.

This is a letter full of harsh truths. MacLiammóir is, as Welles always maintained, distinctly feline – but he is fair, and rightly aggrieved. His cryptic hint at some sort of deep underlying disturbance in Welles is in the territory of Richard Fleischer's 'tragic genetic flaw' – an odd, if powerful, intuition of what would now no doubt be described as a personality disorder. Unquestionably Welles behaved in ways that were brutal, insensitive and exploitative. Most people either retired hurt, or let it wash over them. Micheál MacLiammóir was not such a person; you crossed him at your peril. The reconciliation scene he so amusingly imagined never came to pass. It was, in effect, the end of their friendship. Ten years later MacLiammóir wrote to Peter Bogdanovich that the fact that he and Welles were not on speaking terms was, 'alas, no Renoir illusion, but . . . I still love him and hope that one day maybe, tra-la, tra-la, tra-la . . .'[38] And so it was that Welles's genuinely heartfelt and tender speech at the Dublin opening of *Chimes at Midnight* fell on deaf ears. 'Afterwards, too long afterwards,' Ann Rogers noted in her diary:

> Michael Mac Liammóir came to his dressing room and just said 'Thank you.' 'You're welcome,' said Orson. 'You're welcome? Is that all you have to say?' says Michael. 'Yes, that's all.' 'You poor thing.' After Mac Liammóir left, Welles said 'I have waited for this and been looking forward to this for thirty years and now it is in, it's the greatest anti-climax of my life. I wish I was back in Kenosha.[39]

Oblivious of course to these backstage dramas, the press in Dublin was even more enthusiastic than it had been in Belfast. The *Irish Times* noted that the show brought 'a new actor of very considerable talent to Dublin in Keith Baxter, who conveys the dual and changing character of Hal better than I have ever seen it done'. It also gave Hilton Edwards 'a chance to use his virtuoso's magic once more, to create with a bare three-tiered stage, some stools, a table, spotlights and a few banners, a far more vivid illusion than could have been brought about with all the scenery in Irving's Lyceum'. The rest, the reviewer said, is Welles:

> a great sonorous wheezy ball of blubber . . . when Henry spurns him and there's nothing left for him but the babbling of green fields, the great besotted bag of wind takes his deflation with the tragic quality of a tawdry Lear. This is a performance and a production that actors will talk about for a long time. It's the most generous helping of full-blooded, unashamed acting on the grand scale that actors or their patrons out front could wish for, and schoolchildren in Ireland now abed will boast of seeing it, I hope, when Elvis is long forgotten.[40]

A sadly inaccurate prediction all round, as it turns out. With entirely characteristic perversity, the Dublin public, having read so much about the show, felt that it had seen it: they stayed away in droves. Nonetheless, Welles set about improving the production, if in somewhat erratic fashion: he would call the company, then not show up, or show up and find no one there because he had neglected to call them. Eventually Alistair James took to summoning the company at ten every day. When Welles discovered what he'd done, he erupted: 'This is cruel!' 'And I said, "Well, they're in digs, they've got no telephones, the landladies don't want them hanging around, they'd come in anyway to see if there's any mail." "No, no," insisted Welles, "that's cruel, they have to stay in their digs."'[41] If they weren't summoned by midday, then they knew they weren't on call; and if they were on call, then the assistant stage managers had to go out in taxis and collect them. 'Orson really took over unashamedly after we opened,' Thelma Ruby recollects. 'He had in mind that he was going to make a film and he wanted to experiment and make cuts and changes.'[42] Without even token consultations with Edwards, he constantly shifted the position of the great scene from *King Henry V* in which Falstaff's death is described by Quickly to Bardolph and Nym:

> A' made a finer end and went away an it had been any christom child; a' parted even just between twelve and one, even at the turning o' the tide: for after I saw him fumble with the sheets

> and play with flowers and smile upon his fingers' ends, I knew there was but one way; for his nose was as sharp as a pen, and a' babbled of green fields.

One night Welles placed it at the beginning of the play, so that, like many another Wellesian saga – *Kane*, *Othello*, *Mr Arkadin* – it began with a death. Only for a night: the following night it was the epilogue, ending the play with Bardolph's wonderfully earthy, deeply Shakespearean question: 'Shall we shog?' Chorus was another moveable feast: one night Hilton Edwards played the part in some sort of Jacobean robe with a ruff; another night he was in a dinner jacket, like the Chorus in Jean Anouilh's *Antigone*. Other nights, Rory MacDermot was back in harness; once, Welles himself played the part, nipping smartly back to his dressing room to pad up and make up as Falstaff.

At first Welles enjoyed himself, the whole rackety madness of it: Terence Greenidge missing virtually every entrance – 'I thought you said the Lord Chief Justice cometh?' busked Welles/Falstaff. 'Yes,' said Henry Woolf, as Nym, 'I *said* he cometh, but he cometh not' – and the soused extras lurching back from Naomi's pub across the road just in time for the coronation, grabbing their coronets and treading on Keith Baxter's cloak as he processed down the aisle. He loved sitting on the built-out apron of the stage, as the *Daily Mail* reported, delivering some of his soliloquies, 'as if he were a music hall comedian . . . chatting to the audience like Danny Kaye'.[43] But these pleasures began to pall as audiences dwindled and Welles started to move on in his mind. From a theatrical point of view, the demise of the stage version of *Chimes at Midnight* is another instance in Welles's life of a great missed opportunity. The fact that it clearly fed into the making of the film that, for many people, is Welles's masterpiece, is a consolation. But if the reviews – and the judgement of his fellow-actors – are anything to go by, it could have been an exceptional piece of theatre. Nearly a decade later, John Barton devised a piece for the RSC that he called *When Thou Art King*, which similarly charted the relationship between Falstaff and Hal; it was rich and funny and good. But though it had, in Brewster Mason, a splendidly vigorous and tender Falstaff, it didn't have Welles. This, it seems right to record, and with the qualification that he only gave the part his full attention intermittently, was the best of Welles on stage. It was Falstaff, not Othello or King Lear, that was truly his part of parts, and he seems to have brought his directorial imagination to bear on certain scenes to extraordinary effect.

'He had,' said Alexis Kanner of the great scene in Justice Shallow's orchard in Gloucestershire, 'the two tiniest actors in the world to play Shallow and Silence. And between them he looked like four people and they looked like two. And the three of them faced straight out, straight out front as he said it. "We have heard the chimes at midnight, Master Shallow". He had a way of saying it sometimes that it was like the tolling of a clock. Or the sound from a church tower, you know. It was the tolling of a bell. It had a kind of awful resonance like mortality.'[44] He suggested to Aubrey Morris that Silence should get totally drunk. 'Sobbing – singing – sobbing at his knees. It was a brilliantly directed scene,' said Morris. 'He would almost sob with Shallow and Silence at the line "We have heard the chimes at midnight."' Then Silence and Falstaff danced a minuet: 'he finally lifted me off my feet and danced with me as though I were a rag doll.'[45] It is the accepted view that Welles was depressed by the quality of the acting in the company, but many of the actors – Thelma Ruby, Leonard Fenton, Shirley Cameron, Anne Cunningham – went on to national fame; not much later Alexis Kanner played Hamlet for Peter Brook and gained a bit of a cult following in Patrick McGoohan's *The Prisoner*; Paddy Bedford became a Broadway star and Keith Baxter had a spectacular career on stage and film on both sides of the Atlantic. So why was Welles so restless during the production? One can only conclude that acting in the theatre, which he so often dreamed of, had limited charms for him in reality; it could scarcely compare with the orgasmic joy of making a film. He never acted on stage again.

★

The question of *Twelfth Night* hung in the air. It was still theoretically slated to be the second play of the tour, on which the Home Counties would be the next stop, and then London; then on, on: to Europe, Australia, the world. Louis Elliman, proprietor of the Gaiety, who had to a large extent bankrolled the production on the basis of this tour, needed to be reassured about progress. So halfway through the run in Dublin, a read-through of *Twelfth Night* was announced with some flourish. Zinnia Charlton looked forward to it more than most, since she had been kicking her heels, first in Belfast and then in Dublin, waiting for her chance to shine as Olivia; Anne Cunningham, now weary of screaming and running about, also approached it with great enthusiasm, as did the whole company; Thelma Ruby was longing to give her Maria. Peter Bartlett was not after all cast as Sebastian; that honour fell to Alexis Kanner. Baxter was Orsino; Edwards, Sir Toby. Welles outlined his notion of setting the play among the idle young rich on the brink of the First World War – 1912, to be precise – and described his design concept, in which the different scenes would be revealed by turning the pages of a large picture book. He neglected to tell them that this was the exact design of the production of the play he had done for the Todd troupers in 1932, while kicking his heels in Chicago after returning from his first Dublin season. He himself had played Malvolio in that long-ago production, in swashbuckling, Italianate make-up; the Malvolio he revealed that morning in Dublin was very different: 'It was', Martin Tickner remembered, 'most extraordinary. Sort of Cockney American. Cockney Orson.' Halfway through the read-through, they broke for tea; Welles did not return. That was the end of *Twelfth Night*.[46]

By now, Welles was restive. His concentration on the part was slipping; it took the presence in the audience of someone interesting for him fully to engage his faculties. Laurence Olivier's visit in early March produced exactly that effect: the company were astonished and delighted at the return of the Falstaff that Welles was capable of giving, but that Falstaff departed again with Olivier. Welles was looking for a way out. That way out nearly happened by chance. One evening, Kanner (who had been doggedly ratcheting up his personal rivalry with Keith Baxter) pushed the fight scene between Hotspur and Hal to dangerous levels of recklessness, which resulted in Baxter falling down the steps that led out of the orchestra pit; he was momentarily concussed. Hilton Edwards rushed backstage at the interval, ready to cancel the show and offer the audience their money back. Welles was appalled. 'Give them their money back??? I'll go on and tell them jokes.'[47] He was rather disappointed when Baxter recovered and insisted on going on for the second half. A plan started to form in Welles's mind. Towards the end of the run it was suddenly announced (to the public, not to the company) that on certain selected evenings *Chimes at Midnight* would be cancelled; instead he would perform a show he called *The Pleasure of Your Company* – essentially, *An Evening with Orson Welles* without the conjuring tricks: there would be stories, readings and a question-and-answer session. At designated performances, the announcement read, the event would be filmed for 'the first of Mr Welles's new TV Shows for the BBC', *Orson Welles Interviews the Irish and Vice Versa.*

On these evenings, most of the company chose to head off out of town for a glimpse of the beauties of Galway: Keith Baxter was detained to assist Welles, particularly in the evening given over to *Moby-Dick*, when Baxter had to run in and out of the auditorium crying, 'Hi there, the *Pequod*!' and suchlike sea-faring ejaculations. Welles's choice of items is testimony to the breadth of his reading: the Bible and James Thurber, Mark Twain and T.H. White – a substantial extract from *The Once and Future King*, which Leonard Fenton and Paddy Bedford were co-opted to read. But the real lure, it seems, was the question-and-answer sessions: not because the Dublin public had pressing queries for Welles, but because they were eager to appear on television. The stalls in the theatre had been boarded over so that the cameras could more easily be accommodated, and so that Martin Tickner could pass among them, handing them the microphone to speak into. But, Tickner reports, the cameras were only there for one night; at later performances the illusion was created by having a lot of bright lights. And he continued to pass the microphone around, even though it was not wired to anything.

However cavalier he might have been about *The Pleasure of Your Company,* Welles was quite serious about *Orson Welles Interviews the Irish*, which was to be the first of a new series along the lines of *Around the World with Orson Welles.* He interviewed John Huston (then living in Ireland) and other noted Irish figures for this pilot, but 'after the cameramen had been there about four or five days and they'd been brought over and had to drop everything in England,' said Ann Rogers, 'he gave me the dreadful job of telling them to disband and go back to England.' Nothing was ever seen of this material.

There was a distinct feeling in Dublin that, after a mere three weeks, Welles had outstayed his welcome. The first performance of *The Pleasure of Your Company* started twenty minutes late, reported the *Irish Independent*, and consisted of 'monotony in part one and the feeling of uncertainty in part two'. Elsewhere there were criticisms of Welles's observations on the state of the Irish theatre ('biting the hand that has never fed him', said one correspondent), and questions as to why, as a 'self-appointed Irishman', he had managed to include only one Irish actor, Paddy Bedford, in his company.[48] Time, Welles must certainly have felt, to move on. By now, the company knew they would not be moving on with him. *Chimes at Midnight* was in its final lap: despite the splendid notices, there would be no London season, there would be no world tour.

It had now been officially announced that Welles would be directing the British premiere of Eugène Ionesco's *Rhinoceros* at the Royal Court, with Olivier in the role that Jean-Louis Barrault had just so triumphantly created in Paris, which of course explained Olivier's unexpected visit to the show in early March. Cynics in the company may have bitterly recollected Welles's recent indignant statement to the press (actually delivered by Hilton Edwards) that rumours of his dissatisfaction with the *Chimes at Midnight* company were unfounded, and that the show would unquestionably be travelling to London. Had these same cynics known that Welles had been in negotiations over directing *Rhinoceros* with Oscar Lewenstein at the English Stage Company since October 1959, and that on 22 December of that year Welles had struck a deal with Lewenstein and Wolf Mankowitz whereby he, Welles, would put up one-third of the capitalisation for the production (the remaining two-thirds to be found by them), and that rehearsals would begin on 28 March, just two days after *Chimes at Midnight* closed,[49] they might indeed have felt that a lot of his apparently odd behaviour was understandable. They might also have felt that, as Thelma Ruby realised, and as Welles later confessed to Keith Baxter, *Chimes at Midnight* on stage had simply been an elaborate workshop for a future film.[50]

Had Hilton Edwards and Micheál MacLiammóir known that, their rage might have turned murderous. As it was, they were reduced, as always, whenever they dealt with Welles, to begging him for the money he had promised them. Even before the season ended, Edwards had written to Welles, 'I know that things have been very disappointing and in consequence your resources must be strained. This letter is therefore not a demand for cash so much as for information.'[51] Where, he wanted to know, should he send the bills that had come in under Dublin Gate Productions, and when might they expect settlement? 'As to my own affairs, I know that you will let me have cash when you can and I am content to leave it at that, just reminding you that I have never been able to build up any reserves and this is why I remain in weekly peril of being submerged . . .' This familiar woeful lament would turn shriller over the ensuing months.

But during the run, and despite the pointed absence of MacLiammóir from the social scene, there had been a great deal of conviviality around the show, for selected souls. Welles had taken to Baxter and Ruby in a big way, and young Lindsay-Hogg (returned from another failed attempt to take his preliminary exams at Oxford) was a regular visitor at the nightly suppers that Welles and Paola gave at Alfredo's restaurant, near the canal. On one of these post-show evenings at Alfredo's, when Hilton Edwards happened to be present, there was a curious eruption. At a nearby table sat the company performing Sam Thompson's radical play *Over the Bridge*, which had rocked the Ulster theatrical establishment, a play that dared to take on the full ugly truth of sectarianism in the dockyards. The play had been staged in defiance of the board of the theatre that had commissioned it, and a group of actors led by a firebrand player named James Ellis had broken away and triumphed with it. It was raw, harsh and of the minute and, there in Alfredo's, Jimmy

Ellis started attacking Edwards for producing something as passé and irrelevant as *Chimes at Midnight*. Two worlds of theatre confronted each other. And Welles, who at the age of twenty-one had exploded the theatrical norms of his day, now found himself, a quarter of a century later, being perceived as a representative of the theatrical old guard. On this occasion, in Dublin, it seemed to amuse him more than anything else. As the spat between Edwards and Ellis became more aggressive, Welles intervened, according to Aubrey Morris, 'like the Prince in *Romeo and Juliet*, pressing his somewhat substantial belly at the rebels – pushing them quite powerfully to their respective seats and adoring every moment of it'.[52]

Supper at Alfredo's was not normally so explosive. It was Welles at his happiest: regaling the table with his incomparable conversation, teasing his fellow-guests, ordering more and more mountains of food and flagons of wine, mostly for his own personal consumption. Lindsay-Hogg sat there, longing for something he could not entirely understand from this man whom he so oddly resembled, mirror images of each other: large, fleshy men, smoking their cigars, their bow ties tucked under their collars, with only twenty-five years separating them.

> One night, Orson said to me, 'It's always a good idea to start where things are fresh and you can make your own way quickly without interference.' I knew about the freedom he'd had when he made *Citizen Kane*, and how it never happened again. 'Mongolia,' he said. 'Mongolia?' I questioned. 'Yes,' Orson said emphatically. 'I hear they're starting up their own studio there. It's a fascinating place.' 'You've been there?' I asked. 'Sure, when I was your age.' I wondered if he were pulling my leg. I didn't want to be caught out, but why would he tease me, knowing I was so eager. 'Look into it,' he said sympathetically.[53]

Orson Welles was telling this young man, who longed above all other things to have Welles as his father, to go to Mongolia, during the run of the play he had fashioned into a story of fathers and sons, betrayal and abandonment. It could so easily have been. Welles and Lindsay-Hogg's mother, Geraldine Fitzgerald, had been extraordinarily close at the time Welles had more or less abandoned his first wife to her own devices, at the end of the 1930s and the beginning of the 1940s, just when Michael was born. Rumours were rife in the *Chimes at Midnight* company. Welles betrayed nothing in his behaviour towards Lindsay-Hogg that might suggest any greater bond between them. Lindsay-Hogg didn't know it, either, though he suspected it and hoped that it was so. Meanwhile, Welles put the boy under his spell. 'His knowledge, wit, insight, originality of view and opinion, compassion, depth of experience, heady highs, and frustrating harsh lows', writes Lindsay-Hogg in his deeply illuminating memoir, *Luck and Circumstance*, 'left one never wanting to be away from him, not to be out of his company. Then dinner would be over and he and Paola would go back to the Shelbourne Hotel and it would be as though something desirable and sustaining had been taken away and you'd feel a little deflated.'

The end of *Chimes at Midnight* was oddly marred by an absurd event. During the last week of the run, Anne Cunningham (her screaming and running about deemed dispensable) had been sent to an editing studio in Paris with the footage from *Orson Welles Interviews the Irish and Vice Versa*. She was about to return to Dublin when Mrs Rogers gave her Welles's instructions that she should go straight to London from Paris and stay there. But she had her clothes in Dublin, and all her effects, and her watch was at the repairer's. Besides, she didn't want to miss the last performance, and the promised party afterwards. So she took the decision to come back to Dublin after all and headed straight for the theatre, where she bumped into Welles in the wings. The instant he caught sight of her, he became apoplectic with rage; she rapidly retreated and kept out of his way for the rest of the evening.

The following day she made her way to the boat on which Welles and the company were ensconced, ready for departure to Holyhead. He spotted her at the bottom of the gangplank. What followed shocked everyone: Welles, at the top of the gangplank, with Paola and Beatrice and the Swiss nanny at his side, roared at her: 'You have no discipline, you will never work in the theatre again if you can't take a simple instruction like "Stay where you are."' Cunningham fought back her tears and then ran away, howling.[54] Next he turned on Mrs Rogers, who happened to be wearing a hat, which, she said, was like a sort of squashed mushroom. 'In spite of that hat,' Welles said, 'that makes serious conversation impossible,' he gave her a terrible dressing-down. 'You don't know how to carry out my instructions,' he bellowed. 'I told you that she was not to come back and you allowed her to come back and now you have spoiled everything.' Rogers had to go off, too, 'otherwise I would have cried and I didn't in front of anybody'.[55]

And so *Chimes at Midnight* ended, awash with tears and rage – rage provoked, Anne Cunningham thought, by her having 'disobeyed a ruling'. The man whose pathological dislike of authority had so often been his undoing would not allow his own authority to be questioned. Much later, as the boat chugged its way across the Irish Sea,

Welles came on deck and stood by Keith Baxter at the rail of the boat. 'That girl,' he said. 'I behaved badly.' Then, says Baxter, he emitted a great sigh, almost a cry of pain. 'When I'm angry. Never ask me why.' And then he told Baxter that he would be making a film of the play, and that he would never make it without him as Hal.[56]

So ended Welles's long career as an actor on stage. And now he was about to embark on his final production as a theatre director. One night at supper at Alfredo's he asked Michael Lindsay-Hogg if he would like to assist him on *Rhinoceros*. Lindsay-Hogg eagerly accepted. It was five years before he heard from Welles again.

CHAPTER SIXTEEN

More Rhino Roars

WELLES AND Ionesco had a little bit of history. In the summer of 1958, the London *Observer* published a pugnacious piece by its critic Kenneth Tynan, entitled 'Ionesco: Man of Destiny?', which challenged the French-Romanian dramatist's growing preeminence.[1] Tynan saw Ionesco as representing a dangerous departure from what he considered to be drama's essential realism and, worse, of being guilty of the thought-crime of political pessimism. Only two years earlier Tynan had been the cheerleader for the revolution in the British theatre that was initiated by John Osborne's *Look Back in Anger*, a play which had, at a stroke, smashed open the French windows and evacuated the drawing rooms of the typical West End drama, restoring the theatre to something resembling real life. It was, theatrically and in every other way, a period of upheaval in British life – prelude and harbinger to the profound transformations of the 1960s – and the English Stage Society at the Royal Court Theatre (where *Look Back in Anger* had first been performed) was instrumental in exploring the new freedoms suddenly opening up. It had wholeheartedly embraced Ionesco's early plays, *The Chairs* and *The Lesson*, which were by turns whimsical, surreal and sinister, revelling in the inanities of language and the nightmarish potential of inanimate objects. Partly, perhaps, because of their proximity to the British nonsense tradition, these proved immensely popular, both with the public and with the theatrical intelligentsia.

It was this popularity that troubled Tynan: the Royal Court seemed to be endorsing a cartoonish view of life that was far from progressive. 'M. Ionesco's theatre is pungent and exciting, but it remains a diversion. It is not on the main road.' The *Observer*, sensing a major controversy, gave Ionesco room to reply, which he did with great eloquence, explicitly renouncing any kind of political agenda; rejecting politics, indeed, as relevant to human needs. 'What separates us all from one another is simply society itself, or, if you like, politics. That is what raises barriers between men, this is what creates misunderstanding . . . if I may be allowed to express myself paradoxically,' he continued,

> I should say that the true society, the authentic human community, is extra-social – a wider, deeper society, that which is revealed by our common anxieties, our desires, our secret nostalgias. The whole history of the world has been governed by these nostalgias and anxieties, which political action does no more than reflect and interpret, very imperfectly. No society has been able to abolish human sadness, no political system can deliver us from the pain of living, from our fear of death, our thirst for the absolute; it is the human condition that directs the social condition, not vice versa.[2]

This was of course anathema to Tynan and anyone of a left-wing, or indeed a liberal, disposition; that decidedly included the management of the Royal Court Theatre: Oscar Lewenstein, for example, who had helped to found the English Stage Society and was on the board of the theatre, had been a member of the Communist Party until the Russian invasion of Hungary, just two years earlier.

Ionesco's statement, exactly as the always-mischievous playwright had intended, dumped the cat firmly among the pigeons, and various distinguished writers – John Berger, Philip Toynbee and others – weighed in on the side of art as a proactive agent for the improvement of mankind. Tynan again took up cudgels (the whole correspondence was given prominent coverage over an entire month of Sundays – those were the days), insisting that art and politics could not be divided: 'every play worth serious consideration is a statement . . . M. Ionesco correctly says that no ideology has yet abolished fear, pain or sadness. Nor has any work of art. But both are in the business of trying. What other business is there?' At this point, as Ionesco naughtily observed, 'an imposing personality' intervened: Orson Welles. 'As one of Mr Ionesco's enthusiasts,' wrote Welles, 'I felt that Mr Tynan rather overstated his case. A keen admirer is not a follower of a cult; and I did not like being told that to enjoy a play is necessarily to approve its message. When I applauded *The Chairs*, was I participating in a demonstration in favour of nihilism? This sounded far-fetched. After reading M. Ionesco's rebuttal to Mr Tynan, I am not so sure.' Welles continued with a spirited defence of the political significance of art:

> An artist's every word is an expression of a social attitude; and I cannot agree with M. Ionesco that these expressions are always less original than political speeches or pamphlets. An artist must confirm the values of his society; or he must challenge them. Giving, as he does, such emphasis to the wholly personal in art, to

> the individual, the unique, M. Ionesco surely knows better than to look for sanctuary among the authoritarians . . . He cannot hope to smuggle his own private world into a world where privacy is a crime, where the sovereign individual is an outlaw. He throws himself – frigidly aloof, proudly inviolable – on the mercy of the partisans of freedom . . . many freedoms everywhere are under siege, and all of them – including M. Ionesco's privilege to shrug his shoulders at politics – were, at one time or another, political achievements. It is not 'politics' which is the arch-enemy of art; it is neutrality, which robs us of the sense of tragedy.[3]

Welles elegantly articulates the argument against the apolitical stance. It is interesting, however, to note that, despite his lifelong interest in and commitment to politics, Welles's position as an artist is closer to that of Ionesco than that of Tynan. In his films, Welles had most eloquently presented the 'wider, deeper society, that which is revealed by our common anxieties, our desires, our secret nostalgias'; he too had shown how 'the whole history of the world has been governed by these nostalgias and anxieties, which political action does no more than reflect and interpret, very imperfectly'. *Touch of Evil* is drenched in a sense of *lacrimae rerum*, life's essential sadness, as was his stage production of *Chimes at Midnight* and as, supremely, his celluloid reimagining of it would be; no political action will alleviate the tragedy of a Quinlan or a Falstaff. Welles's profound melancholy was at odds with his commitment to political solutions. It is, of course, striking that his own – rather spasmodic – political activity was, with rare exceptions, unilateral and highly subjective.

It was in early October of 1959 that Oscar Lewenstein first approached Welles about the possibility of directing *Rhinoceros*, which had not yet been either published or performed. It was Ionesco's third full-length play; he had written it first as a short story, and then in November of 1958 he read the third act of the play in a public performance at the Vieux-Colombier Theatre in Paris. A radio broadcast of this, translated by Derek Prouse, went out on the BBC Third Programme in August 1959, by which time it had been promised, first to the Schauspielhaus in Düsseldorf, then to Jean-Louis Barrault for production at the Odéon-France Theatre. Lewenstein, having secured the English rights, invited Barrault to direct the play in English at the Royal Court Theatre, immediately after the French production, with the extraordinary American comic-turned-actor Zero Mostel in the central role of Bérenger; Mostel had just had a big success in London playing Leopold Bloom in *Ulysses in Night-town*. Barrault expressed huge enthusiasm for London and for Mostel, but for reasons unknown it proved impossible for him, so Lewenstein approached Welles. But Welles did one of his vanishing tricks. 'As you know,' Lewenstein wrote to Ionesco, 'it was supposed that I was going to meet Orson in Paris whilst I was over there, but not for the first time Orson succeeded in disappointing me. Despite the arrangement we had made to meet, I found that he was out of Paris when I should have been meeting him.'[4] As this sort of behaviour could always be expected of Welles, says Lewenstein, he has decided to offer the play instead to the noted British director Tyrone Guthrie, again with Mostel as Bérenger. Guthrie hesitated, so the net was cast wider, with Ionesco's approval, to include the most interesting directors of the day: Peter Brook, Joan Littlewood, Michel Saint-Denis and Peter Wood – and Welles came back into the frame again. After Guthrie turned it down, Brook was the front-runner, but he finally, reluctantly, turned it down at the end of November; Lewenstein then offered it to Welles, his original first choice, and Welles accepted.[5] Lewenstein drafted an agreement just before Christmas 1959, by which he and Wolf Mankowitz would find two-thirds of the capital, Welles the remaining third. Mostel would play Bérenger and rehearsals would begin on 21 March 1960; this would be a commercial production, in the West End.

Meanwhile, the play had its world premiere in Düsseldorf, directed by Karl-Heinz Stroux; bleak and terrible, the production was an overwhelming, if disturbing, triumph, the play's parable of the initially slow but rapidly increasing transformation of an entire community into rhinoceroses – the process of rhinocerisation, as Ionesco calls it – perceived as an unmistakable and deeply disturbing metaphor for what had happened in Germany only a quarter of a century before. The production presented the play, Ionesco said, 'as a stark tragedy with no concessions'.[6] Three weeks later Barrault's production was unveiled in Paris and was equally successful, though utterly different in tone: to Ionesco's great satisfaction, Barrault saw the play 'as a farce and a fantastic fable'. The production was much lighter and airier than the German version, at least to begin with: 'the town that first greets our eye is a veritable Dufy, bright and coloured and gay,' wrote Harold Hobson in the *Sunday Times*. 'Two long streets running away, past the town hall and the picturesque houses, into the romantic distance. Gradually the scene becomes more and more confined, more and more drab.'[7] The acting was surprisingly naturalistic, allowing the gradual transformation of society to happen moment by moment, though the production was quite explicit about the Nazi metaphor, which was true, to one degree or another, of all the productions that soon took place all over Europe; no one in any of those countries could have seen the play without being forcefully reminded of their recent history.

On the day of the play's Paris premiere, Welles and Lewenstein received alarming news: Zero Mostel had been knocked down by a bus in New York, his leg crushed. 'Both of us', wrote Lewenstein to Mostel, 'in the depths of despair at the thought that you might not be able to play in *Rhinoceros*.'[8] Amputation was proposed. In the event Mostel kept his leg, but he was four months in the Hospital for Joint Diseases in New York. Finally, Lewenstein wrote to him there, deeply regretting having to move on with the casting of Bérenger. 'I therefore had to try to find an alternative and was lucky enough', he says, slightly disingenuously, 'to get Laurence Olivier for the part.' If he was well enough in time, perhaps Mostel might be able to play the role of Jean, Bérenger's best friend – the first character in the play to succumb to rhinocerisation?[9] 'ROLE SWITCH DISAPPOINTING', cabled Mostel's agent, 'BUT ZERO WILL PLAY JEAN TO OLIVIER.' On the strength of this astonishing package, Welles (who had just come to the end of *Chimes at Midnight*'s chaotic London rehearsals and was about to sail to Belfast) signed his contract with untypical alacrity. 'Orson is designing the sets and working out some marvellous sound ideas,' Lewenstein told Ionesco, 'so that rhinoceroses can run all over the theatre.'[10]

After his startling triumph there three years earlier with *The Entertainer*, Olivier felt that he owed the Royal Court a play, so it was agreed that *Rhinoceros* would start there, with suitable provisions for a transfer, any income from which would be deeply welcome to a more than usually cash-strapped Welles. The moment Olivier's name was announced, sales at the box office at the Court went into overdrive; very soon, the small theatre was sold out for its four-week run. Welles, by now, was in Dublin, which is where Olivier came to see him for their little chat about the play. Ann Rogers picked him up at the station and took him for supper; then together they went to the Gaiety and saw *Chimes at Midnight*. Olivier was, said Rogers, 'appalled. Not with the acting, not with the play, but that the whole production was so makeshift.'[11] Welles had pulled out every stop on stage; so had the young actors. Olivier went backstage and chatted pleasantly to Keith Baxter and Alexis Kanner, the latter deeply anxious because Olivier had famously played a definitive Hotspur at the New Theatre during the war. The *Chimes at Midnight* fight was, Olivier said, the best fight he had ever seen on stage. Then he gave Baxter some helpful technical advice about his posture. 'Larry,' said Welles, laughing, 'don't start that actor-laddie stuff. You love giving actors notes guaranteed to screw them up.' (In fact, Baxter found the advice very useful.)[12] Olivier and Welles then posed a little for the cameras; the whole of the next day, 'like two Garbos,' according to the *Daily Mail*'s spies in Dublin, 'Sir Laurence Olivier and the bulky Mr Orson Welles wanted to be very much alone. They locked themselves in an hotel suite and didn't want to be disturbed.'[13]

They had much to talk about. Both men were anxious about the play they were about to do together. Olivier, with his urgent desire to be abreast of the modern movement, felt that it was something he should do, though he had no clear idea of how to play the part, or indeed what it all meant. Welles perhaps felt he knew all too well what it meant, its message spelled out in letters a mile high. He was already out of love with the play, finding it empty at its core, but he needed the work. And, indeed, Welles was looking forward to working with his old chum Larry again (which they had last done on the radio in March of 1939 in a dashing *Beau Geste*). Notwithstanding their rivalry as Shakespearean film directors – a rivalry Welles felt much more acutely than Olivier, since it was Olivier whose films were acclaimed as masterpieces – they had parted on perfectly pleasant terms after *Othello* at the St James, despite Welles's abandonment of the planned tour. A decade on, neither was perhaps in the best shape. Welles was frustrated and bored in equal measure by *Chimes at Midnight*, which had also made him no money whatever – in fact it had cost him a great deal; and there were no hopes of any potential film for him to direct. Olivier, for his part, had just completed a gruelling year of work in which he had played his famous Coriolanus at Stratford-upon-Avon while filming *The Entertainer* by day (in the course of which he had snapped his knee cartilage); straight after that, he had gone to America to direct Charlton Heston in *The Tumbler*, a creaky verse-play by his friend Benn Levy, which he had laboured over with typical energy and invention, but all to no avail: it had flopped spectacularly, closing on Broadway after four days. But all of this was merely the foreground to an intense private drama, featuring the irrecoverable collapse of Olivier's deeply troubled marriage to Vivien Leigh and the rapid burgeoning of his love for Joan Plowright, both of which had to be kept from the ever-prying eyes of the press on both sides of the Atlantic.

No doubt these matters were addressed during their day-long ensconcement in the Shelbourne Hotel (they didn't even appear for meals, marvelled the *Mail*). But the really urgent question was:

what were they going to do with the play? Welles had any number of ideas, the biggest of which was that he wanted to relocate it from France to England, an entirely understandable choice: setting it in France would have made it into a play about the French, suggesting that it was their problem, not ours, the exact opposite of what Ionesco had said in the Preface to the American edition of *Rhinocéros*. 'To understand the fundamental problem common to all mankind,' he said, 'I must ask myself what *my* fundamental problem is, what *my* most ineradicable fear is. I am certain then, to find the problems and fears of literally everyone. That is the true road into my own darkness, our darkness, which I try to bring to the light of day.'[14] However, there was a serious loss: clearly a great deal of the impact of the play when it was performed in Europe had been due to the continent's history of mass hysteria, of contagious collective paranoia, of uniformed regimentation. Even when the play was performed on Broadway not much later, America's recent history of McCarthyite collective hysteria informed the audience's experience of the play. But there had been no such event in modern British history. Changing the setting to England risked distancing the story, of turning it into an abstract sort of parable; nonetheless they decided to go down that path, and Welles, working from Derek Prouse's workmanlike translation, produced a script that was some way from Ionesco's original, both in tone and in meaning.

Welles also had ideas about the nature of Ionesco's dialogue, which plays variations on conversational banality in a highly structured, almost musical way. Welles was impatient with this procedure, so he thought to enliven it by overlapping the dialogue, as he had done to such brilliant effect on stage in *The Shoemaker's Holiday* and *Around the World*, and of course, most famously, in *Citizen Kane.* He sought to create the horror of the play primarily through sound – a thousand versions of thundering hooves, plus other, abstract sounds, which would give the impression of mankind being dragged backwards through a hedge. Olivier deeply admired Welles as a director and was no doubt encouraged by this plethora of ideas, which would surely swiftly coalesce into a coherent production, the way his own always did – all the elements fixed so that they could be repeated and honed to perfection.

Olivier went back to London. The casting process was conducted at long distance, but between the good offices of Laurence Olivier Productions (which now had 25 per cent of the action, as did each of the three other partners), Oscar Lewenstein and the Royal Court Theatre, a really splendid group of actors was assembled – distinguished stalwarts like fruity Gladys Henson; the great character comedian Miles Malleson; Alan Webb, veteran of many a Noël Coward production; brassy Monica Evans; and hatchet-faced Hazel Hughes. It was a very classy West End cast. There were two *Moby-Dick* veterans, Peter Sallis and Joan Plowright. When it became apparent that Zero Mostel was still *hors de combat*, they offered the pivotal part of Bérenger's friend Jean, now anglicised to John, to Peter Sellers, already on his way to comic superstardom; when he turned it down – 'it would have been wonderful prestige,' he told *Empire News*, 'but I couldn't understand a word of it'[15] – the great lantern-jawed Scottish comedian Duncan Macrae stepped up to the wire. There was even a refugee from *Chimes at Midnight*, Henry Woolf. Anne Cunningham had been promised a role, but, for obvious reasons, that role never materialised. As for costumes, set, light and sound – all those were to be in Welles's hands.

Time was now very short: as usual, there was no sign of any designs, so the Royal Court despatched one of its resident designers, Stuart Stallard, to Dublin, to elicit Welles's ideas from him. Welles proved typically elusive, refusing to answer his phone, not responding to notes left at the stage door or at the hotel, until finally Stallard was tipped off that he was taking the air on St Stephen's Green, which is where Stallard finally bearded him. In due course, as they sat together on a park bench, Welles reluctantly started to divulge his ideas; he and Stallard then repaired to the theatre, where they assembled some sort of a general idea of a set from bits of cardboard gummed together. The first act – a little French *place* in the original, with old men playing boules, all brightness and light – was now to be set in a pub (because what could be more English?) with a television set, on which the rhinoceroses would first appear. Welles had a very clear notion of the sort of light he wanted for the second act, when rhinocerisation starts in earnest: a great shaft of it in the centre of the stage, which presented its own design challenges. This second act, set in Bérenger's office, would be sparse, with banisters leading down to a staircase, plus a few filing cabinets; and the last act bare, apart from the rhinoceros heads.[16] The play has many technical challenges, not least the transformation of Jean/John into a rhinoceros in full view of the audience; these tricky problems were set aside for another day.

Welles left Dublin on 27 March; rehearsals commenced at the Royal Court on the 28th. They began as farce, but more Keystone Kops than Franco-Romanian absurdist. A press photographer was discovered lying on his back in the upper circle of the theatre: he claimed to be a member of the Royal Court Theatre's supporters' club, taking a snap for his Aunt Fanny. 'His and every one else's Aunt Fanny,' growled the press officer.[17] The papers knew perfectly well what was going on between Olivier and Plowright, but they wanted photographic evidence. Rehearsals were immediately transferred to a secret location in a church hall in Maida Vale in west London. Not quite secret enough: early on, a young vicar passed through, murmured a 'Good afternoon' and then disappeared. Someone's keen ears detected the click of a camera; the young man was discovered, Polonius-like, behind an arras, his camera confiscated and the film exposed by Welles personally. 'Go ahead and sue, you bum,' he told the quaking parson-paparazzo. This mania continued throughout rehearsals; it was dark glasses and headscarf for Plowright, secret entrances for Olivier. A strict embargo was placed on interviews. The *Express* grumpily noted the secrecy, the ban on publicity. The cast, it claimed, was working around the clock, 'driven, exhausted, by the driving, inexhaustible Orson Welles'.[18] The *Sunday Graphic* carried an aggressively unpleasant piece by a reporter who had been baulked of his story: 'The spectacle of two middle-aged gentlemen, one of them described as "the world's greatest actor," playing a silent hide-and-seek game with rhinoceroses round Sloane Square strikes me as being absurd. And somewhat pathetic.'[19] The *Graphic* was affronted that Welles's name was given equal billing with Olivier's. The aggressively lowbrow *News Chronicle* equally contemptuously expressed its resentment of Olivier's embrace of the avant-garde – 'a stunt', it said, 'pathetic' and 'absurd'.[20]

Meanwhile, all was not well within the sacred circle of art. It quickly became apparent that Olivier's working method was diametrically opposed to Welles's. Olivier always prepared a production some weeks before rehearsals began, wrote Joan Plowright, 'moving cardboard characters around on a model of the set and choreographing the entire play, before coming with a completed framework to present to the cast on the first day'. Only when the actors had mastered the structure would he allow them to make a contribution. As she well remembered from *Moby-Dick*, 'Orson liked to experiment in a hundred and one ways before making his choices and allowing some order to emerge from chaos.'[21] It was, in fact, rather more complex than that: what Welles liked to do was simultaneously change everything and rehearse specifics in obsessive detail. He pushed the cast to high comic stylisation. A great deal of time was spent on the overlapping dialogue, which needed to be very precise if it was to work. Their scripts, recalled Peter Sallis, began to look like orchestral scores. 'The number of different coloured dots, I start here when he says this, and she starts there when I say that.' Sallis called it 'dramatic punishment', but he 'loved it, I lapped it up', doing his damnedest to try to get it right according to what Orson wanted, as did Olivier and Plowright.[22] The older actors found it hard, but struggled on until they had mastered it, at which Welles started to rearrange it: a recipe for insanity. Even the stage manager, Paul Stone, trying to keep track of all this, objected: 'But yesterday you said—' 'Yesterday was yesterday,' growled Welles, menacingly. 'Today is today.'[23]

To compound the difficulty, Olivier was still far from clear how to perform his part. Bérenger, a character who reappears in four of Ionesco's plays, is (as has often been noted) a sort of Everyman, a bit of a dreamer, a bit of a boozer, a bit of a drifter, a bit sentimental. But when push comes to shove, he proves to be made of sterner stuff than might at first appear. The character is routinely described as a little man, but that is a reduction: he is an ordinary man, *un homme moyen sensuel*, a much more interesting proposition. He is an archetype, a modern *commedia dell'arte* character, not unlike Pulcinella – slothful, greedy, lustful, put-upon. He should have the warmth and the sloppiness of a lazy dog. This was very difficult for Olivier, who always sought a very sharply defined outline for his roles, precise and instantly recognisable. His concept of character was highly specific and realistic, always based on a kernel of observed truth, which he then, in a kind of choreography of character, physicalised. He was unable to find this kernel of truth for Bérenger, and thus unable to find the character's physical life, without which he was lost. Welles was unable to help him. Then one day, as Peter Sallis describes it, Olivier found his Bérenger:

> When we started rehearsing, Olivier just didn't know how to play it. He just used to turn up at rehearsals and sort of just say it, and then go away. And then there was one magical day when he turned up and all of a sudden, there it was, there was the character. He'd turned a page and there it was, this character. And from that point on he never let it slip. He had as firm a grasp of that character as anybody could ever have on anything.[24]

The only question was whether he had found the right character. Olivier's Bérenger was a little man – or, rather, his idea of a little man – which for him meant funny little man, a Chaplin or a Sid Field (the great music-hall comedian whom Olivier idolised). He reached for a theatrical type rather than a real type drawn from life. And of course he played that type superbly, to the hilt, physicalising it to the last detail and flick of his little finger: he was the little man to end all little men. But it cut against the meaning of the play. In fact, it stepped outside the play, became a source of fascination it itself, a masterly performance. But the character Ionesco wrote is a lazily reactive bloke who finds to his surprise that, because he is so very much himself, he has it in him to resist conformism. Olivier's performances, brilliant in themselves, often subverted the plays in which he appeared in this way. But he was now happy, because at least he knew what he was doing, which freed him up to observe what everyone else was doing. What he saw all around him was confusion and panic. It was at this point that Welles had started mucking around, as Sallis put it, with the overlapping dialogue, unpicking it, reshaping it. And this Olivier, and the older members of the company, could not endure: not knowing what they were doing. A sense of chaos and uncertainty set in, filling them with dread and anxiety. Alan Webb, Miles Malleson and Hazel Hughes all begged Olivier to take over. And he did, decisively and without hesitation. One morning at the beginning of the last week of rehearsal, he sidled up to Welles. 'You have to go away, Orson, baby,' Olivier told him. 'Not come to rehearsals because you're upsetting us all.'[25]

The shock of this for Welles is impossible to exaggerate – this banishment not just from his natural habitat, but from his kingdom, locked out from the rehearsal room, where for twenty-five years he had been a law unto himself. He had behaved, from an early age, like a classic actor-manager. There can only be one actor-manager in any rehearsal room, and on *Rhinoceros* that person was Laurence Olivier. Welles had sensed for some time that something was going on. Recently his old friend Pieter Rogers, now general manager of the Royal Court, had been helping him out with small services, among them taking dictation for Welles's correspondence: in one letter Welles told his correspondent that Olivier was destroying him. He became convinced, perhaps rightly, that Olivier, though accepting the notes Welles gave him 'like a good soldier',[26] was all the while taking the actors to one side behind his back and subtly (and sometimes not so subtly) modifying their performances. Welles had very little experience of directing Big Beasts like Olivier. Edward G. Robinson had been tricky, but that was on a film, and much more containable. In a rehearsal room, the structure of command is far more open, with all the actors present all the time; the atmosphere in the room – the same room, day in and day out – becomes deeply oppressive when things go wrong between the leading actor and the director. Sacking the troublesome actor is the usual recourse, but in this case, it was not an option; neither the producer nor the theatre would have supported Welles over Olivier. If anyone was going to have to go, it would be Welles.

Olivier had form in this manoeuvre: only five years before *Rhinoceros*, when he was playing Malvolio in *Twelfth Night* at Stratford, he had banished his director from the rehearsal room for being too fertile with ideas; that director happened to be John Gielgud. Welles was outgunned. He could have quit, but that would have incurred public humiliation; instead he beat as dignified a retreat as he could, coming to work every day and sitting in the workshops in Sloane Square for over a week: Orson Welles, world-conqueror, creative powerhouse, lord of misrule, incomparable bravura personality – beached. He was perfectly comfortable being there, with his friends the technicians, all of whom, despite his ever-changing and sometimes outrageous demands, had come to respect and even love him. 'Somebody with fresh ideas, blowing the dust away from the theatre,' said William Green, the Court's hard-bitten technical director. 'If he'd said to me, doing this production up in Yorkshire or anywhere, "Would you come?" I would have been thrilled to bits to go with him.'[27]

Welles now supervised the technical aspect of the production in great detail – more than he would have been able to do, had he been rehearsing with the actors: perhaps a little too much so. When Stallard asked him what they would put on the walls, Welles found a little bit of rhinoceros hide for them to reproduce as the pattern on the wallpaper. 'He felt that the audience would get this and it would be part of the rhinoceros going all the way round, and even I couldn't get it, I mean once it's blown up it's just an abstract sort of little bit of design.'[28] Welles personally dressed the set for John's bedroom with large ancestral portraits, blow-ups of photographs of Duncan Macrae, into which he painted, transforming Macrae into his grandmother or a general in the family. He personally painted a detailed and beautifully finished reproduction of Albrecht Dürer's rhinoceros on the front cloth. 'And I can remember a couple of times,' said Green, 'coming in to the Court and getting a member of staff to take the iron curtain up, and as the iron curtain went up, there was this big figure sitting at the easel painting. That was eight o'clock in the morning,'[29] – Welles the lonely dreamer, dancing again in the moonlight in Grand Detour.

He and the company were reunited for the technical rehearsals in the theatre. It was not a joyful reunion. Welles sat in the stalls loudly giving notes into a small tape-recorder, a pioneer Dictaphone; then, almost immediately, he and Olivier had a screaming fight over how Olivier should get off his bicycle – a clash of titans that it would have been interesting, if perhaps a little eardrum-threatening, to have witnessed. There were a thousand complex technical effects to achieve; William Green was convinced that Welles deliberately contrived that what was intended as a small release of dust over Olivier's head turned into an avalanche. But Welles had a more complex revenge up his sleeve, which many years later he confided to Kathleen Tynan:

> Larry came with the last big speech, when the rhinoceroses all come out of this wall, you know. And I said on the loud-speaker, 'Larry, I'm going to tell you how to play this scene.' And I knew I had his back up, but I knew what I had for him. 'As you get to this point in the line, you will suddenly realise that sitting over there in the audience is a rhinoceros. Then you will see another rhinoceros. And then you will realise that the theatre is full of rhinoceroses.' And I knew it was so good he had to take it, you know?[30]

And he did; every review drew attention to it. The lighting was of immense complexity, but that was as nothing compared to the sound. For this, Welles had summoned young Martin Tickner, his assistant stage manager from *Chimes at Midnight*, just before technical rehearsals began:

> I got a call from Ann Rogers on a Sunday saying 'Mr Welles wants you to come to the Star Sound Recording Studios straight away.' So I said, 'What, now?' and she said 'Yes, have your lunch or whatever and then come, can you meet him there for about three o'clock.' So I said, 'Well, what's this all about?' and she said 'He wants you to do the sound for *Rhinoceros* because he doesn't like any of the sound people at the Royal Court.' So I said, 'Ann, I've never been allowed to do sound,' and she said 'Orson says you would know how and you're to be his expert.' And I thought 'Oh my god, what have I been landed with?'[31]

Welles had assembled an extraordinary array of jazz drum-tracks, from his comprehensive knowledge of the territory: Art Blakey's *Drum Thunder Suite*; Louis Bellson's *Concerto for Drums*; *Alibi for Drums* by Thurston Knudson. They were originally recorded at 7½ rpm, then re-recorded at 3¾ rpm; sometimes he played them backwards. In addition there were recordings of actual rhinoceroses grunting, lavatory chains being pulled, crowds roaring:

> Orson greeted me warmly and said he was pleased that I was going to do this and I said, 'Well, hang on a minute, I don't know how to do this.' And he said, 'you'll just have to find out, won't you? I've told them that I'm bringing in my expert.' So, I rang a couple of friends and said how do I do this and how do I do that and got a vague sort of idea.

The following day the shy nineteen-year-old was introduced to the Royal Court Theatre's sound department as Welles's expert. 'I was in the very invidious position of being the expert who didn't know what the fuck he was doing.' He learned soon enough.[32]

★

That was Monday; the first night was on Thursday, with a dress rehearsal for the Friends of the English Stage Society the day before. When the tapes arrived from Star Sound, the cues – all 300 of them – were in the wrong order. They were still in the wrong order at the public dress rehearsal on the Wednesday. 'Just play anything,' said Welles, 'when there's a tape cue just play whatever's on the machine and hope for the best because at least it will give you an idea of where the cues come even if they're the wrong cues.' Which is what Tickner and his assistant did. 'I mean, it was chaos that evening and there were lavatory chains being pulled while rhinoceroses were running around and everything.'[33] They reconvened at 6 a.m. the following morning – the day of the press night – and finally, in the quiet and empty theatre, managed to get it into some semblance of what Welles wanted, though they didn't get round to setting the sound levels. A great deal of Welles's creative energy went into the sound: not only did it emerge from all over the auditorium, but one of the stage crew was on stage during the show, dressed in black, as in the Chinese theatre, holding a pole with a small speaker on the end of it, adding an extra rhinocerotic grace note to the soundscape.

The pressure on the first night was extreme. The company was insecure and overworked, the technical issues had scarcely been resolved, the stage manager had more or less reached a state of collapse through exhaustion. 'The only reason he got through the first night,' recollected the production photographer, John Timbers, 'was that he was one of the first people to pop pills in the sixties, amphetamines, I suppose, to keep him going.'[34] Out front, the audience was strictly monitored for possible press infiltration: despite vigilant scrutiny of first-night ticket applicants, wrote Virginia Fairweather, the Royal Court's press rep, 'the little theatre seemed to be stiff with narky journalists'.[35] Welles himself had been getting increasingly nervous over the days leading up to the first night: Mrs Rogers reported that he was drinking a great deal of coffee. 'I had relays of people taking four or five Thermos flasks over to an Italian Espresso café in a little alley off Sloane Square where they had real, very strong Espresso. How his heart stood it, I don't know, every day, and up to a bottle and a half to two bottles of good brandy, really good brandy.' Welles stood in the foyer prowling around before the curtain went up, as Noël Coward, the Earl of Harewood and Ionesco himself hurried into their seats. 'Don't leave me, don't leave me, stay with me,' he said to Rogers. She had a dozen small hand-towels in her holdall. 'He would wipe his face, which was sweating all over, and give it to me again wet and I would give him a dry one. That's how nervous he was.'[36] He had a job to do: the sound levels had not been set at the dress rehearsal. Welles duly went up to the dress circle, where, seated behind a black curtain, he had a microphone connected to a speaker in the room where Tickner was sitting off stage, Tickner recalled, 'saying up a bit, down a bit, and so on all the way through the show'.[37] This bizarre counterpoint to the action did not go unnoticed: 'SHH! DIRECTOR WELLES WHISPERS HIS WAY THROUGH THE PLAY'S OPENING NIGHT,' said a large headline in the *Daily Express* the following morning. 'He was whispering from the darkness: "More rhino roars. More! That's it."'[38]

Perhaps on account of this constant rumbling from the dress circle, things started to go wrong on stage – cues missed, overlapping dialogue out of kilter, lines forgotten – and at the interval Welles rushed backstage. Peter Sallis was sharing a dressing room with Miles Malleson, Duncan Macrae and Alan Webb. The door burst open, Sallis recalls. It was Welles. 'What the fuck,' he said, 'is going on here? There are only three people in the cast who are doing what I've asked them to do, and that is Laurence Olivier, Joan Plowright, and Peter Sallis.' Then he slammed the door and went back to the auditorium.[39]

Act Two continued in comparable chaos, till the end when Bérenger, the last human being not to succumb to rhinoceritis, is left alone. Olivier spoke his famous last lines (amended by Welles): 'People who try to hang on to their individuality always come to a bad end. Don't they? Don't they? Alright. Alright. I'll put up a fight, anyway.' Then he turned, looking out to the audience, who became very still, as Welles had predicted they would. Bérenger seemed suddenly to realise that the audience had become rhinoceroses too. 'Yes, I'll take on the whole lot of them – the whole lot of *you*! You! Oh God.' Blackout. The applause was only moderate.

Back in the Sallis/Malleson/Webb dressing room, there was another knock on the door. This time it was Noël Coward. 'What a perfectly bloody play,' he said, turning to a very small man who had come in with him. 'This is the author. He doesn't speak a word of English.' They departed, Ionesco beaming.[40] The cast eventually trailed away. Olivier had left by a private exit; Plowright from the front of house, unnoticed. What happened to Orson Welles is unrecorded. There was no party. There seemed very little to celebrate.

They were all in for a pleasant surprise the following morning: 'IONESCO PLAY ALL EASILY COMPREHENSIBLE,' said the headline of the *Times* review, palpably relieved.[41] Elsewhere – in the *Daily Mail* and the *Daily Express* – both play and production were ecstatically received: 'The chemistry of Sir Laurence Olivier's performance and Orson Welles's production explodes into a unique theatrical experience,' said the *Daily Mail*'s Robert Muller. 'The final closing-in of the herd is beautifully managed, the fireworks mount to a stupendous climax. The scene in which John turns into a rhinoceros must be one of the greatest coups of 20th century drama, and Mr Welles has squeezed it of every last drop of horror.'[42] Muller ended his review by demanding that Olivier extend the season. For Bernard Levin, in the *Daily Express*, the production was 'manifestly sharper, tighter, more inventive and more coherent than M. Jean-Louis Barrault's slack and careless Paris version . . . the truth is that Mr Welles and Sir Laurence have divined that *Rhinoceros* is not a comedy at all.'[43]

Elsewhere, there were cavils: Olivier was sometimes felt to be overcast for the role, which did not, many felt, ask enough of him. Welles's production was, in some quarters, denounced for its over-insistence: 'Sir Laurence Olivier plays with delicacy and strength,' said J. W. Lambert of the *Sunday Times*, who had seen and deeply admired Barrault's production and was having no truck with Welles's work: only Olivier, he thought, had resisted what he called 'the dreadful pressures of a production – by Orson Welles – which is throughout heavy-handed, careless and vulgar . . . [he] must take the blame for loss of effect in passage after passage. Ionesco's farcical counterpoint, in which the dialogue darts from character to character and group to group with ludicrous congruity, aspires to the condition of music but at present, in this production, rather resembles erratic small-arms fire. And the important sound effects are coarsely handled, deafening us from the start and spoiling the gradual swell of menace.'[44]

Several notices felt obliged to compare the production (and the play) with Harold Pinter's *The Caretaker*, which had opened the night before. '*Rhinoceros*', said the *Observer*, 'proved a sad disappointment, and *The Caretaker* the most dazzling evening to reach the London theatre this year . . . the fault is not Ionesco's and certainly not Olivier's. I suspect Orson Welles.'[45] The production had its fans – 'Orson Welles, as producer and designer, uses the full vocabulary of the theatre in a way that makes the average director's pidgin-language seem pitifully inexpressive,' said *Queen* magazine. 'We see the ground convulsed by the charges of a herd of rhinoceroses below the stage, tearing up banisters that suddenly disappear down the stair-well and so arousing the blood of a watching *bourgeoise* that she leaps down the well with a cry to join them, landing astride the back of a rhinoceros whom she recognises as her husband.'[46] On balance, though, Welles did not come out of it smelling of roses. In particular, he was thought not to have solved the great technical challenges, notably the on-stage rhinocerisation of John. 'We only get an impression of Jekyll becoming Hyde in the old stock-company manner,' said J.C. Trewin, 'and taking a quite unconscionable time about it.'[47] The acutest of the reviewers, Philip Hope-Wallace, of the *Guardian*, put his finger on the consequences of Welles's transposition of the action to England: 'a distinguished cast', he said, 'have become, in their Englishing, puppets from a little revue, mere types whose transmogrification into pachyderms carries no pathos or comic force. Moreover, the stilted, stylised, speedy playing takes all the edge off the horror. We ought to feel in the first act that we are dealing with "real" people. We feel no such thing.'[48] There was worse, much worse.

They cried all the way to the bank. Tickets, already at a premium, were now impossible to get, except on the black market. 'Sixteen shilling stalls for Ionesco's *Rhinoceros* at the Royal Court are being offered for two guineas,' lamented the *Evening Standard*.[49] Interest was unflagging: the *Standard* itself carried a three-part serialisation of Ionesco's original short story, while Robert Robinson had a facetious piece in the *Sunday Graphic* under the heading 'WHO IS IONESCO?' Something about the tiny dramatist really got under the skin of the British press. 'I met a man', wrote Robinson, 'who thought IONESCO was what the top bank of his typewriter keyboard spelled. I met another who said, Ionesco, ah yes, I did the bathroom with it. And yet a third who said, "Wait, wait, don't tell me, it's an anagram" . . . I am left wondering why meaningless has become so popular.'[50] But popular it was.

A transfer was inevitable, though Olivier was getting little pleasure from doing the show. They were just about to announce a limited run at the Strand Theatre in the West End, nearly three times the size of the Royal Court, when Vivien Leigh unleashed a bombshell, which instantly made international headlines: she was prepared, she said, to give Olivier a divorce so that he could marry Joan Plowright. It was the first time Plowright had been named in this context. The next day, therefore, *Rhinoceros* was all over the papers again; if anybody had failed to notice its existence before, they knew about it now. It did 99 per cent of its business during its eight-week run – better business, astonishingly, than *The Entertainer*, which was very good news for Welles, who was in some of his direst financial straits for a long time.

In the second week of rehearsal for *Rhinoceros* he had gone to see Pieter Rogers in his office at the Royal Court. 'Oh God,' he said. 'I can't cope.' He dictated a letter to be sent to one of his creditors: they were literally at the door. 'But there was nothing I could do. I couldn't go running to George or Oscar or Cecil Tennant and say Orson's having terrible financial troubles, because I'm sure they'd already been told that by Orson.'[51] Shortly afterwards, Welles was served with a bankruptcy petition filed against: 'George Orson Welles, actor, of South Eaton Square, formerly of Brown's Hotel, Dover St.' Bringing up the rear, Edwards and MacLiammóir, who were faced with piles of unpaid (and unpayable) bills from *Chimes at Midnight*, had instructed a new solicitor, Terence de Vere White, to pursue Welles; the new man proved unrelenting. Welles wrote a six-page letter to Edwards justifying his position. This letter was really, he said, in an uncomfortable covering note, written for the solicitor's eyes. 'I hope you'll appreciate . . . how impossibly difficult it is to write about money differences with a friend, without seeming unfriendly. Do please understand that I have no wish but to be very fair – even less than fair in my own behalf, and more than fair in yourself – if that should be necessary to the preservation of our own relationship.'[52]

The formal letter written for White's eyes is familiar in tone from the letters Welles had written to Edwards and MacLiammóir after *Othello*: a catalogue of misunderstandings; of excessive generosity on his, Welles's, part; of unthinking greediness on Edwards's part. He notes that he has lost upward of £8,000 on *Chimes at Midnight*, whose whole *raison d'être*, he says, was to help Dublin Gate Productions through a difficult spot. 'I've told you the awful total of my losses on *Chimes*. This all comes out savings, and really scrapes the bottom of the barrel. The only money I've earned for six months is some three hundred and fifty pounds for directing *Rhinoceros*. (Please note how much poorly I was paid for directing Olivier in London than you were for directing me in Dublin!)' It turns out, in fact, says Welles, on close examination of the figures, that – amazingly! – it is he, Welles, who is owed money, not the other way round. He proposes to send £500, not as payment, but as a loan, bearing in mind Edwards's and MacLiammóir's admittedly worse situation; and in closing, he reminds Edwards that he, Welles, was responsible for him getting the part of the Prophet Samuel in *David and Goliath.* Above all, he requests that they call off their legal eagle, as Welles calls him. 'What sincerely frightens me is that if I'm forced to deal with him, my only adequate defence must be costly to you and dangerous to a friendship which I value more than I can possibly say.' The whole episode is a dreadful warning about the pitfalls of entering into a business partnership with friends. The combination of Edwards and MacLiammóir's unworldliness and Welles's feckless-ness was more or less fatal to the relationship – a resolution was never achieved. Friendship was a difficult thing for Welles to main-tain at the best of times; his essentially restless nature forbade the element of constancy that is friendship's *sine qua non.*

The prospect of the transfer of *Rhinoceros* was encouraging, though scarcely the answer to all his problems; what he needed was a couple of fat film roles. Welles had avoided the Royal Court during the run there; his presence at the technical rehearsal for the transfer was token, a condition of his being paid. They had lost two actors en route to the West End: Alan Webb, who was replaced by Michael Gough; and Joan Plowright, for obvious reasons. Olivier feared that if she and Olivier appeared in the play together, there might have been protests during the show: divorce was still regarded as the devil's work by many people in the Britain of 1960. Plowright was replaced by the up-and-coming Maggie Smith (sufficiently unknown to be described in the newspapers as 'the twenty-five-year-old daughter of an Oxford pathologist');[53] she had scored a success at the Old Vic in *What Every Woman Knows* and a revue called *Share My Lettuce.* Her only recollection of Welles is of him sitting in the stalls, his long legs and large feet draped over the seats, shouting out instructions and swigging from a hip flask. Both Welles and Ionesco were disappointed when Olivier limited his commitment to the eight-week run at the Strand; attempts were made to lure another star. For a while it seemed as if the great English comedian Tony Hancock – an inspired idea for Bérenger – might take over, but he finally declined; then, casting their net rather wider, they toyed with the idea of the baby-faced slapstick comedian Charlie Drake. These ideas came from Welles, whose knowledge of British comedians was encyclopaedic. But no one wanted to follow Olivier. And so *Rhinoceros* came to an end.

It is impossible to know what the production might have been like if it had been conceived, executed and produced in calmer circumstances, because those circumstances were virtually unknown to Welles – were, indeed, possibly anathema to him. Despite its financial success, it was a wretched experience for virtually everyone involved in it. The unhappy stage manager had suffered a nervous collapse after the first night and been replaced; the actors never grew into their roles. And – though they maintained superficially cordial relations to the end – Welles was deeply shocked by his experience of Olivier. 'I've never known so monstrous and cunning and stupid an ego, except Chaplin's,' he told Kathleen Tynan in 1983. 'Very similar. And both, you know, tremendous figures in the 20th Century. And both curiously old-fashioned and peasant-like . . . but Chaplin didn't use people. Chaplin simply demolished them. Larry's more Machiavellian, you know.'[54]

And it is true: Welles was not like them. He never demolished or outwitted anyone. The only victim of his outbursts was himself. He lacked the will to power that both Chaplin and Olivier so overwhelmingly possessed, the instinct that told them they would not survive unless they had wiped out the opposition. Welles was, in a sense, more innocent than either man, or perhaps more aristocratic: he expected that things would come to him as of right; they knew that they would have to fight all the way for what they wanted. Welles relied on adrenalin and natural genius; they knew that work – fanatical and often repetitive work – was the way to succeed. Uncertainty was intolerable for them: the terrifying possibility of failure led them to take swift remedial action. Unlike Olivier, Welles could live with constant change; indeed, he could not live without it.

Though they were both acknowledged titans, Olivier, in the world's eyes, was the successful one, ascending to ever greater heights; Welles was the ruined, chaotic, wilful one, a wreck. Olivier was a titan, Welles the *Titanic*. It was, after all, Olivier – not Ionesco, and certainly not Welles – whom they had flocked to see. In his memoir, *Confessions of an Actor*, Olivier writes about *Rhinoceros* and his performance in it, and describes the brouhaha surrounding the production. Remarkably, though not entirely surprisingly, he never even mentions Welles's name. Likewise Ionesco, who saw the production twice – the last night and the first – and who describes many of the productions from the play's first year (French, German, Italian and American), makes no reference whatever to a production in which the man playing the leading part was the actor generally considered the greatest in the English-speaking world, and the man directing it was – well, Orson Welles.

CHAPTER SEVENTEEN

Welles on Trial

WELLES TURNED forty-five in 1960. By chance, at this climacteric, he was subjected to a great deal of very close scrutiny, in the newspapers and on television. It was time, it was clearly felt, to reopen the inquest on Welles. He seemed, to many people, to be a great deal older than he was. Precocious in everything, he already had the demeanour of a gnarled veteran, a battered warrior, a boxer on the ropes. Physically, he was in poor shape: it was about now that the battle for his waistline was lost; Welles, said Tynan, was now 'perilously fat'.[1] Though his status as a celebrity never faltered, his standing as a creative artist was low in the English-speaking world: his last four films as a director, *Macbeth*, *Othello*, *Mr Arkadin* and *Touch of Evil*, had been patronisingly dismissed and all had failed at the box office; his returns to the theatre, apart from the brief triumph of *Moby-Dick* in 1955, had been unsatisfactory in different ways: *The Blessed and the Damned* a patchy mess, *King Lear* an out-and-out disaster, *Chimes at Midnight* a *succès d'estime* seen by a mere handful of people in Ireland. His production of *Rhinoceros*, though a commercial success, was, by and large, disliked by the critics. It had been a protracted and very public fall from grace. The story of his supposed *dégringolade* had supplanted the earlier one of his prodigiousness: he now embodied the very idea of failure; this story only grew more fascinating to newspaper editors as the achievement of *Citizen Kane*, twenty years earlier, was more and more widely acknowledged, routinely topping international polls as the greatest film ever made. This complicated kind of fame – fame, not popularity – was one that translated into neither ticket sales nor job offers, except in the sphere where he least welcomed them: movie roles. These trickled in at a rate of two or three a year, in ever more obscure international co-productions, in which his various transformations – Tartar warlord, Venetian Renaissance historian, grotesque sea-captain – became increasingly preposterous.

However, quietly, steadily, an alternative narrative was gaining currency. In Europe – especially in France – Welles was regarded as self-evidently one of the greatest film directors of all time, a key artist of the twentieth century. The young *cinéastes* of *Cahiers du Cinéma*, soon to generate the *nouvelle vague*, were hypnotically fascinated by him, analysing every frame of his films with a forensic obsessiveness that kept him on the hop when he was interviewed by them. He hugely enjoyed the game of matching, and even exceeding, their speculations as to what he had meant by each *cadre*, every *découpage*. In effect, the inspired improviser who had made the films was a different man from the erudite panellist now discussing them; François Truffaut, one of the most acute of the *Cahiers* group, remarked that Welles's films were shot by an exhibitionist and cut by a censor; he might have added that they were then explained by a philosopher.

Welles's two long interviews with the magazine are wonderfully entertaining reading, and again offer a glimpse of his matchless conversation, ranging widely over history and philosophy, delighting in off-the-cuff definitions and provocative paradoxes. The man who emerges from these interviews is a master of self-expression and a model of intellectual self-confidence, which placed him in a different league from pretty well any other American film-maker. In fact young American *cinéastes*, in a host of small magazines, were beginning to offer their own revisionist views of Welles's position in cinema history. Not yet thirty, Andrew Sarris, fresh from a year in Paris hobnobbing with the *Cahiers* crowd, had thoroughly absorbed the *auteur* theory and, as early as 1956, had, under its influence, written a path-breaking essay about *Citizen Kane* and its creator with the suggestive title 'American Baroque' – exactly what the Italian critics had said of Welles (but in their case it was an insult). Welles was becoming an emblematic figure, a rallying point, in a way that no other American film-maker ever had, or ever would again. Already, at the age of forty-five, he had become a cause as much as a creator. The elegant cultural commentator Parker Tyler, in his puckish essay 'Orson Welles and the *Big* Experimental Film Cult', analysed Welles's paradoxical significance within the avant-garde film-making community:

> Simply what he is and has been makes Welles the quintessential type of Big Experimental Cult hero – always achieving failure yet bringing it off brilliantly, decking it with eloquence and a certain magnificence; fusing in each film the vices and the virtues appropriate to them. Welles is the eternal Infant Prodigy, and as such wins the indulgence of adult critics and the fervid

> sympathy of the younger generation, which sees in him a mirror of its own budding aspirations and adventurous near-successes.[2]

In 1959, an anonymous writer in *Contact* magazine wrote what amounts to an elegy for Welles, seeming to accept that he had been destroyed by the System. But if he was no longer a major force, he remained a continuing source of inspiration:

> His contribution will continue through the men he trained and influenced. If he was abused unnecessarily by those who looked with disdain upon imagination in the cinema and if he was therefore canonised by those who defend the abused, Orson Welles was not responsible for either the abuse or the defense. His interest was in making films. Yet history has given him a special place because he stood in the middle of a battle of ideals. And he will probably be remembered as the man who gave his life to introducing novelty to a mundane industry of the arts, and, through his baptism of fire, became a saint for the cinema.[3]

Perhaps the most significant event in the growth of an alternative American view of Welles was the season mounted at the Museum of Modern Art in New York in 1961 by the twenty-two-year-old actor-turned-film programmer Peter Bogdanovich; in the accompanying booklet, *The Cinema of Orson Welles*, Bogdanovich roundly asserted that though Welles had made just seven pictures that could fairly be called his own, there was a personal unity in his work that could only be found in the work of 'the very greatest poets of the cinema'. You could enter a Welles film at any point, he said, and know who had made it, not simply because of 'his darkly lyric imagery, his mysterious, brooding sense of the evil in the world, his remarkable technical ingenuity and originality, his witty, probing dialogue, or indeed his own physical presence as an actor', but because of what Bogdanovich calls 'the profound theme that runs through all his work, man as a tragic victim of the paradox between his sense of morality and his own dark nature'.[4] Welles's essential themes have always been and no doubt always will be the subject of debate; what Bogdanovich was saying, just as Sarris had said before him, was that as a film-maker Welles had a voice that was entirely uncorrupted by the formulaic, the routine, the conventional: he wholly lived up to the magisterial apophthegm he had enunciated to André Bazin: 'I believe a work is good to the degree that it expresses the man who created it.'[5]

In Britain there had always been an undertow of respect for Welles, starting with the very first monograph ever written about him – a surprisingly shrewd and remarkably accurate little book, given that its author, Roy Alexander Fowler, was a teenager writing in wartime Britain and that the book was published in 1946, when Welles himself was just thirty, and only *Citizen Kane*, *The Magnificent Ambersons* and *The Stranger* had been released. Since then, the British Film Institute's journal *Sight and Sound* had maintained a steady output of articles and analyses of Welles's work in which he was taken very seriously; and a younger generation of British film-makers, members of the Free Cinema and British New Wave schools, cheered him on as an iconoclast and renegade from the Hollywood system. Nor was he neglected by the arts establishment: at the BBC he had a crucial admirer in Huw Wheldon, who one week in March 1960 programmed a mini Welles festival, which consisted of showings of *Kane* and *The Magnificent Ambersons*, preceded by an hour-long interview of Welles by Wheldon on *Monitor*, BBC television's cultural flagship. It was heralded by a laudatory piece in the BBC's mass-circulation magazine *Radio Times* by the documentary film-maker Lindsay Anderson, already an Oscar-winner (for *Tuesday's Child*), a member of the Free Cinema movement, and before long to be a major film-maker in his own right. His article is ringingly headed 'He Asked the Impossible'.[6] All of this, in Britain in 1960, was tantamount to canonisation: even Wheldon – normally rather probing – was reverent in the presence of Welles. In the interview Wheldon gives Welles the chance to tell his story, which he does with inimitable charm, in a tone very different from the one he uses for Bazin and Bitsch and company at *Cahiers*. There is not a trace of anything highbrow in the air; he presents himself as a straightforward chap who likes to tell a good yarn. He dismisses what he calls 'the aesthetics of the cinema': 'I regard the whole bag of tricks of the cinema as being so petty and so simple and so uninteresting essentially. It's what a film says rather than a question of cinematic style and plastic shrinery, you know all this kind of special language that these people talk about in the cinema clubs; and I feel myself tremendously at odds with cinema clubs as much as with Hollywood.'[7]

Despite his reverential air Wheldon does tease Welles a little: after showing a clip of the great scene towards the end of *Citizen Kane* in which Susan Alexander struggles with a jigsaw puzzle while Kane paces restlessly in front of Xanadu's vast fireplace, he says, 'If I had made that, I would be terrified that I was just on the point of toppling over into farce, that I had made the fire too big, that I had made the room too large. Did you have this sort of anxiety?' 'No,' says Welles, 'because the room is that big.' 'What room is that big?' 'Awfully pompous answer – his room . . . I do feel that a man like Kane is very close to farce and very close to parody – very close to burlesque, and that's why I tried every sort of thing from sentimental tricks to an attempt at genuine humanity – to keep him always counterbalanced; but of course anybody who could build a place of that kind, you know, is very close to low comedy.' The impression left by the interview is one of complete transparency, of a trusting simplicity that has been baffled by the ways of the world; Welles candidly laments his apparent unemployability as a director. At the end of the interview Wheldon asks Welles how he would like to be remembered. He gets a surprisingly emotional and, for Welles, nearly inarticulate answer:

> Almost every American book on the cinema pricks the bubble and proves that what is said about me is a lie and I am no good. There is no book that says I am good in American literature; and I must say that talking about posterity . . . all I care about is, er, really my children, my grandchildren, if they ever say as I do, wondering about my grandfather who was a politician and a cabinet minister in America; and I would like to know more about him, and if somebody should ever want to know about me, which is the only posterity, I cannot take the rest of it seriously. I really wish there was something nicer that they could read about me.

Setting aside the fact that Welles's grandfather was not a politician, much less a Cabinet minister, and the slightly manipulative mention of his children, with whom he spent as little time as he could, his plea is the more remarkable for it having preceded by a good ten years the outcrop of books that called his whole career into question. The impression that he gives is of a man who underneath all the exuberance has been deeply hurt, and Wheldon was clearly both surprised and touched by the revelation. The response of reviewers was not warm: the *Daily Telegraph* called it 'disastrous'. It was felt that Wheldon had given Welles an easy ride.

Just slightly before the Wheldon interview was taped, Welles gave another one, in Paris, where he was staying in the swanky Meurice Hotel, this time to the Canadian actor/interviewer Bernard Braden.[8] Braden prefaces the interview by saying (in voice-over) that Welles is forty-five, 'which, for a Boy Wonder, is getting on a bit. Has he failed?' asks Braden. 'If so, at what? He is unique, one of the most stimulating and exasperating, exciting and erratic North Americans who ever made story-telling their trade' – a description which, if Welles had heard it, might not have displeased him too much. The tone is noticeably freer, Braden's questions much nimbler than Wheldon's: this is not the masterfully modest Welles of *Monitor*; he is not especially buoyant, looks heavy-featured and is often melancholy, sometimes on the brink of being aggressively defensive, cornered even, but finally expansive and uproarious. Braden's not unsympathetic but quick-fire questioning doesn't give Welles time to consider his responses; he says the first, often most revealing thing that comes into his head. Braden immediately touches a nerve with mention of exile: 'I don't think of myself as an exile,' protests Welles. 'I just happen to have lived abroad all my life. I'm from the mid-West.' 'What does the word "home" mean to you?' asks Braden. 'I have lots of homes. I would like to have one. It's a wonderful question: it may take me 40 years to think of the answer.' And then, out of nowhere, Welles says: 'Woodstock, Illinois' – the location of his old school, the Todd School for Boys. He reels off a list of great cities, including Peking ('I spent a lot of my childhood there'), then tells Braden, rather ruefully, that he lives in Rome 'because my wife's family is there – I'm longing to get away: it's turning into Philadelphia with spaghetti'. 'Does poverty bother you?' 'Oh yes, it's bothering me here, living in the Meurice Hotel.'

Braden quickly gets Welles talking candidly about his work – about his feeling, for example, that in the film of *Othello* he failed in the epileptic fit: 'I just cut to the seagulls.' He talks about directing, 'the most overrated job in the world,' he says. 'I know a lot of big directors that every actor knows are useless. Unless a director is something of a cameraman, something of a cutter, something of a writer, something of an actor – but a *lot* of a cameraman – he won't make any difference.' He has been lucky with actors, he says, but miserably unlucky with producers and money people. 'The scripts they send me are *terrible*.' Then, he says with striking simplicity, 'I would like to do something which would at least leave the art form or profession in question better for my having done it' – a remark at once more modest and more real than the sob story he fed Wheldon. There is huge melancholy here, alongside a glorious sense of absurdity; a helpless frustration allied to an immense sense of what might be; a genuine humility and a profound pride. But it is certainly not a portrait of a man on the brink of imminent achievement.

The following year Welles sat for a pen-portraitist with whom he had a much more complex relationship than either Wheldon or

Braden: Kenneth Tynan. It was Tynan's fourth major profile of Welles so far. This one – or rather these two; it was a diptych, spread over two issues – was for *Show* magazine.[9] The headline was not encouraging: 'Portrait of the legendary genius whose greatest production is, and always will be, his own life'. The first part is almost as much about Tynan as it is about his subject, but it provides a useful framework for the questions Tynan poses: why is the world so disappointed in Welles – why did we expect so much? Despite what Tynan clearly regards as the meagre accomplishments of the eighteen years since *Kane* – 'a handful of stylish thrillers, a couple of bombastic Shakespeare films, a few hit-or-miss stage productions, a number of self-exploiting television appearances, and several tongue-in-cheek performances in other people's bad films' – he bunches Welles with Chaplin, Cocteau, Picasso, Ellington and Hemingway as possessing 'a fixed international reputation that can never wholly be tarnished . . . the quickest ears prick up and the keenest eyes brighten at the advent of a new Orson Welles production – or rather manifestation, because one can never predict the form in which his talent will manifest itself.'

Welles offers him no clues as to what might be in the offing. Instead he fobs Tynan off with freewheeling fantasies, which Tynan reports, deadpan: he hardly lived in America till he was eighteen, he says; his father owned two factories, and tried to invent the aeroplane; his brother Richard 'upheld the family tradition of intelligent dilettantism' (he was actually in an asylum); he met Ravel and Stravinsky as a child; he sat down to dinner with Hitler when he was nine; during the war he was bundled out of the country under a false name 'to examine captured Nazi newsreels and other such filmic trivia'. This was going quite far, even for Welles; only one thing remained – to go further, so he adds that while he was on the mission he had an affair with Eva Perón. Inexplicably, having swallowed all that, Tynan capriciously decides to discredit an absolutely unimpeachable fact – namely, that Welles himself wrote Harry Lime's line about the cuckoo clock. Still trying to probe the question of Welles's failure to deliver what he promised, Tynan remarks on his proneness to 'depressions, onslaughts of gloom, spleen and sulks that the Middle Ages would probably have ascribed to the cardinal sin of *accidie*, which induces a sense of futility and a temporary paralysis of the will'. At such times, says Tynan, you feel that Welles has given up on people, but then, at the prospect of meeting Isak Dinesen, say, or Chou En-lai or Robert Graves, he revives: 'you feel kindled by his presence, by his mastery of rhetoric, by his uncalculating generosity'. Echoing what Michael Lindsay-Hogg had so keenly felt in Dublin, Tynan tells us that 'when he leaves a room, something irreplaceable and life-enhancing goes with him; something', he feels, 'that may eventually install him, given our luck and his help, in the special pantheon whose other occupants are Stanislavsky, Gordon Craig, Max Reinhardt, Jacques Copeau, and Bertolt Brecht'. For Tynan, and always excepting *Kane*, Welles remains – this genius without portfolio, as he calls him – just promising.

The *Playboy* profile perfectly encapsulates the absurdity of Welles's position: this peerless creature, this many-layered, multi-talented force of nature, this fountain of ideas, this cinematic wizard couldn't get a job. In a world where journeyman directors were churning out movies by the dozen, Orson Welles was a name on no one's lips or, indeed, lists. And then, after months of dreary alimentary travails and occasional stabs at *Don Quixote* (now known as *Don Quixote Flies to the Moon* and apparently, so he told Bernard Braden, finished and soon to be released), the wheel of fortune began to turn again in his favour.

★

In 1961, a production manager named Yves Laplanche decided to kick-start his career as a producer by acquiring the rights to some classic twentieth-century novels. Among them was Kafka's *The Trial*, for which he thought Welles would be the ideal director. Laplanche approached the producer Alexander Salkind (Franco-Russian, though technically Mexican), who had shown some entrepreneurial pluck by raising the money for *Austerlitz*, the seventy-year-old Abel Gance's sequel to his masterly and ceaselessly innovative *Napoléon* of thirty years earlier; as it happens, Welles had appeared in *Austerlitz* (playing Robert Fulton, American inventor of torpedoes), as had Vittorio De Sica; what interesting conversations the three colossi must have had during their tea-breaks. Salkind's immediate reaction to Laplanche's proposal was negative, but on touting the idea around among his investors, he found that he was able to raise the money ($1 million) without any difficulty. Needless to say, Welles was cock-a-hoop, but he was also astonished. 'It's a very expensive film, it's a big film,' an almost disbelieving Welles told Huw Wheldon in an extended *Monitor* interview devoted exclusively to the film:

> What's remarkable is that *The Trial* is being made by anybody! It's such an avant-garde sort of thing. Oh it's wonderful, and it's very hopeful. Five years ago there is nobody who could have made it, nobody who could have persuaded distributors or backers or

> anybody else to make it. But the globe has changed recently. There is a new moment in filmmaking and I don't mean by that that we're better filmmakers, but that the distribution system has broken down a little and the public is more open, more ready for difficult subjects.[10]

He was right: the European public, at any rate, was flocking to see avant-garde movies like *Hiroshima Mon Amour* and *Last Year At Marienbad*. Moreover, the stars were queuing up to appear in them; when Salkind started casting *The Trial* (co-producing with his father Michael), he signed up, in rapid succession, Jeanne Moreau, Romy Schneider and Elsa Martinelli, all of them as hot as cakes; Martinelli didn't even ask to see a script. Welles recruited some of his old *Arkadin* team, Suzanne Flon, Katina Paxinou and – almost a mascot for him now – Akim Tamiroff; Welles's wife Paola, bespectacled, had a scene as the court archivist. He wanted a big American name for Joseph K. and he found one immediately. Anthony Perkins, after his massive success with *Psycho*, was eager to explore the possibilities of working in Europe. He was the first American star, before Charles Bronson and Clint Eastwood, to become a major star in his own right in Europe. 'He would get two or three new scripts a week,' his agent noted with satisfaction. 'For the first time, French companies were prepared to pay an American star his American salary.'[11] Perkins made three films in quick succession with René Clément, Jules Dassin and Anatole Litvak; it was indeed the last-named who introduced Perkins to Welles, who immediately sent him the script of *The Trial*. 'Orson paid me the great compliment of saying he would like to know whether I would make the picture because if I wasn't going to make it, he wasn't going to make it either,' wrote Perkins. 'I'll never know if that's the way it really would have been or not, but I prefer to take it as the truth and I will always want to believe that.'[12]

For the role of the pompous, discursive lawyer Huld (renamed Hastler in the film) he approached Charles Laughton, their falling-out some quarter of a century earlier over Welles's withdrawal from the premiere of *Galileo* a distant memory. But Laughton was ill – terminally, though he didn't know it – and he declined the part; Jackie Gleason, whom Welles had courted to play the role of Mosca when he thought he was going to do *Volpone* fifteen years earlier at the City Center, was nervous of flying all the way to France, and so, with genuine reluctance, Welles himself took on the part. He had originally cast himself in the small but important role of the priest who, in the novel, recounts the story of a countryman who comes to the Gate of the Law with a complaint and is made to wait and wait until, many years later, he dies there, without ever having being admitted. Welles gave the role to a very young Michael Lonsdale, but stripped of the Gate of the Law story, which ended up in a very different place in the film – on Welles's lips, twice. The story, related by Welles in voice-over, became the prologue to the film, illustrated by striking black-and-white projections. Then, almost at the end of the film, K., encountering Hastler, who is of course his lawyer, finds himself standing in the light of the projector, as the Advocate briefly recapitulates the story – there is perhaps some sort of reference to the projection room at the beginning of *Kane*, some allusion to the art of film. It also puts Welles/Hastler, the representative of the law that has so tormented and failed K., back into the centre of the action.

Welles had worked exceptionally hard on the script over a period of six highly productive months, holed up with the family in Fregene. If *Rhinoceros* was the unhappiest job he ever had, worse even than *Mr Arkadin*, then *The Trial*, he claimed, was the happiest, though, interestingly, he had about as much sympathy for the source material as he had for *Rhinoceros.* He was no more admiring of Kafka than he was of Ionesco, and for much the same reasons: they both postulate an insane universe in which innocent Everyman is doomed; this was unacceptable to Welles, smacking of what Marxists used to call bourgeois despair. For him, man is guilty, but mankind is not doomed. The crucial difference in the two projects was that with *The Trial* he was uninhibited by a living author and could adjust the text as he chose, making it his own. He had no compunction, he told Huw Wheldon, about making alterations to a masterpiece when he put it on screen, 'because film is quite a different medium. Film should not be a fully illustrated, all-talking, all-moving version of a printed work, but should be itself, a thing of itself. It's a film inspired by the book, in which my collaborator and partner is Kafka. I've tried to make it my film because I think that it will have more validity if it's mine.'[13]

In fact, though he updated the story to the time of filming – 1962 – he stuck pretty faithfully to the narrative of the novel. What was radically different was his sense of the meaning of the material, and this fundamentally affected the way in which he shot it. Of the interpreting of *The Trial* there will never be an end: as a crucial twentieth-century text, it has been all things to all men, lavished with historical, political, psychological, theological and metaphysical exegeses. Welles's conception of Kafka was not far from Brecht's: Kafka, Brecht said, had described 'with wonderful imaginative power the future concentration camps, the future instability of the law, the future absolutism of the state *Apparat*'.[14] Echoing Brecht's words, Welles's official press release said, '*The Trial* is a contemporary nightmare, a film about police bureaucracy, the totalitarian power of the Apparatus, and the oppression of the individual in modern society. I've told the story of a particular individual. If you find a universal parable behind this story, so much the better.'[15]

The objection to this approach is that by allying the story so specifically to 'modern society', Kafka's very particular vision of human experience is diluted, or at the very least generalised. To say as Welles does: it's the state – it's the law – it's the police – it's society – that is at fault, is too easy. Kafka's theme is, famously, the frozen sea within us. This did not interest Welles. In a contemporary interview that he gave to the Anglo-French writer Jean Clay, he described two critical changes he had made to the novel. Firstly, he dismissed the endlessly debated question of what K. is supposed to have done, and whether indeed he has done it: 'Joseph K. belongs to the Apparatus – the Organisation – himself. He's an official. He's the head of a department. He too keeps people waiting, he too is arrogant and cloaked in a mystery of his own making. K. is a vain man and a climber. As a victim of the Apparatus, he tries to resist it but he's an accomplice just the same.' K., in Welles's script, is as guilty as hell: 'his crime is surrendering to the system that's destroying his individuality. Yet he tries to fight it. He represents the human condition today, half alive, half dead, conforming yet protesting. Like all of us.'[16] This had been Welles's theme for many years, at least since *Press Conference*, ten years earlier, but it most certainly was not Kafka's theme.

He introduced another startling change, he told Clay: in the novel, the two policemen who are responsible for executing him seem reluctant to kill him, hoping that he will seize their knife and do it himself. But K. lies there, unmoving. Finally, they twist the knife into his heart, twice, 'like a dog,' thinks K. to himself. 'It was as if,' says Kafka – it is the last line of the novel – 'the shame would outlive him.' Welles found this end to the book unacceptable. 'The murder seems to have the sanction of the victim. After the death of six million Jews, Kafka would not have written that. It seemed to me to be pre-Auschwitz.'[17] Moreover, it smacks of despair. 'I absolutely disagree with those works of art, those novels, those films that, these days, speak about despair,' Welles told *Cahiers du Cinéma* in 1964. 'I do not think that an artist may take total despair as a subject; we are too close to it in daily life. This genre of subject can be utilized only when life is less dangerous and more clearly affective.'[18] So in the screenplay he turns the tables on K.'s executioners. His K. dies with great spirit, laughing in their faces, as he says over and over again, 'You'll have to do it, you'll have to do it.' Welles refused to put his name, he said, 'to a work that implies man's ultimate surrender. Being on the side of man, I had to show him, in his final hour, undefeated.'[19] His changes are profoundly subversive: first, he makes K. guilty, an oppressor; then, at the end, he turns him into a hero. Kafka's purposes have been hijacked.

In addition, there is the question of casting. Giving a role to a particular actor can be a subversion all of its own. Antony Perkins's performance is a central part of Welles's reinvention of *The Trial*. The Josef K. of the novel is uptight, anxious, correct and prissy, obsessively compulsive and occasionally possessed of erotic eruptions, which only alarm him. Perkins's performance – inherently neurotic, though not notably anxious – does indeed suggest a man with a secret (not much acting called for there), but he has the soul of a poet. With his pale, haunted features, he has something of Pierrot Lunaire about him; he is almost balletic in his movements, elfin, occasionally skittish, voluptuously amorous when opportunity presents itself. As he races gracefully towards justice and then away from execution, he could be Orestes pursued by the Furies or Orpheus escaping the Thracian women; in his well-cut suit and floppy white shirt he is almost a figure from Tennessee Williams. It is a far cry from the novel's distressed and exasperated bank official.

The rest of the casting and the rest of the screenplay are straightforward and closely related to the novel; Welles invented only one scene, a sequence concerning K.'s encounter with a computer and the scientist who runs it, but at the eleventh hour, just before the premiere, he cut the scene, thus depriving the film of Katina Paxinou as the scientist, which can only be a source of regret.

★

As he worked on the script at home in Fregene, Welles had been in constant contact with the film's art department in Paris: he sent them fifty-four sketches he had drawn himself for sets, said one of the scenic artists. 'He never stopped saying, "Give me ten times as much."' They had to find hundreds of desks for K.'s office. 'I want it to run to the end of the world,' said Welles; for a corridor in a government office, he demanded a ceiling a mile and a half long.[20] The film would mostly be filmed in Yugoslavia, where the Salkinds had shot the bulk of *Austerlitz*; the interiors would be shot in Paris, at the Boulogne

Studios. During pre-production in Zagreb, in response to Welles's request for a technician, Salkind sent Edmond Richard, who had supervised the special effects on Gance's film. When he arrived, the recce had reached a standstill in the search for a large enough space to shoot Welles's office space, which would 'run to the end of the world'. Richard suggested a vast exhibition hall where he had worked on a film about Paganini. The hall was locked up, but with the aid of a bottle of slivovice and a roll of banknotes, all doors were opened to them: surveying the vast spaces of the Swedish and American Pavilions, Welles was enraptured; his eyes filled with tears. Richard had saved the day. Welles was delighted to discover that his saviour had been one of the team that had developed his favourite camera, the Caméflex: portable, easy to operate and simple to load. At the production meeting that night, Welles, without troubling to consult him, announced that Richard would be the director of photography for the film. 'I felt as if I'd been punched in the stomach,' said Richard.[21] He was thirty-four and had never shot a feature before. Welles had found his collaborator, his partner in crime; together they devised the visual language of the film.

Welles had three rules: first, the black-and-white should have maximum contrast: he had no interest in the fifty shades of grey offered by low-contrast negative; second, the light sources must never be identifiable in the shot; and finally, it must be possible to cut any two shots together, since their order in the film would only be decided at the editing stage. They used red filters, with high gamma, so that the contrast would be uniform throughout the movie. Using his felt-tip pen, Welles – who had, said Richard, 'a sense of synthesis rare among directors' – would sketch the shots, 'sculpting in light and shadow'. After rehearsing with the actors, he would break down their moves, using his hand-held Caméflex as a viewfinder, marking it all out methodically: 'first position here, plumb line, cross on the ground; second position, plumb line, cross on the ground'. Camera moves were invariably dictated by actors' moves. Their needs were always paramount; he would never allow them to be confined in any way because of the lighting. 'We need broad lighting,' he told Richard. 'We can't bother the actors with light.'

They started filming in Zagreb in March 1962, shooting the streets, the sewers, the brutalist architecture of the suburbs, the scene in the opera house, the church, the cathedral, the tribunal scene. Welles worked at high speed, constantly energising the unit. He was in his element, surrounded by collaborators, including the actors, whose work delighted him and who delighted in him. The producers kept a respectful distance, which was exactly how he liked it. They had their own problems to worry about: a tranche of the Yugoslavian funding fell through just as they were about to start shooting interiors in the Zagreb studios, so they had to go back to Paris to regroup. But there was no studio space available there, nor could they have afforded it, if there had been. Welles had a notion that a train-cleaning shed might be suitable; the producers approached SNCF, who were desolate to say that they were all in use, but wondered whether M. Welles might perhaps consider the Gare d'Orsay on the rue de la Légion d'Honneur? It was more or less abandoned, but perhaps something could be done with it? Welles's assistant, Marc Maurette, who had not been to the station since he was a little boy, went along to sound it out and saw some potential among the rats and the rubbish, noting with interest and admiration two enormous phalluses, one in blue and one in green, which had been drawn on the walls by one of the station's temporary residents; they later had them photographed for posterity.

This rather wonderful story of the discovery of the Gare d'Orsay as a location was too prosaic for Welles; he quickly invented a more romantic one, which his friend and colleague William Chappell (summoned out of the blue, never having acted in his life before, to play the painter Titorelli in the film) duly relayed to the readers of the London *Sunday Times*:

> Welles is a poor sleeper, and standing sleepless at five in the morning at the window of his hotel in Paris he became half-hypnotized by the twin moons of the two great clocks that decorate the deserted and crumbling Gare d'Orsay, that triumphantly florid example of the Belle Époque that looms so splendidly across the trees of the Tuileries gardens. He remembered that he had once been offered an empty station as a location, and his curiosity was aroused. By 7:30 he had explored the lunatic edifice, vast as a cathedral: the great vulgar corpse of a building in a shroud of dust and damp, surrounded and held together by a maze of ruined rooms, stairways and corridors. He had discovered Kafka's world.[22]

Whether lured by the twin moons or tipped off by Maurette, Welles certainly knew that this found space had everything he could ask for, and more. They took it for seven weeks. It possessed, he told Huw Wheldon, 'a kind of Jules Verne modernism that seems to me quite in the taste of Kafka.' It was also suffused with melancholy – filled, said Welles, with sorrow, 'the kind of sorrow that only accumulates in a railway station where people wait'. Kafka's story, he declared:

> is all about people waiting, waiting, waiting for their papers to be filled. It is full of the hopelessness of the struggle against bureaucracy. Waiting for a paper to be filled is like waiting for a train, and it's also a place of refugees. People were sent to Nazi prisons from there, Algerians were gathered there, so it's a place of great sorrow.[23]

Welles immediately determined to absorb as much of the station as possible, though it meant entirely redesigning the interior sequences. It meant, in fact, abandoning his cherished design concept for the film: he had envisaged the settings becoming less and less present, until by the end the story would have been played out in empty space. But he now had something much better, and he and his art director, Jean Mandaroux (the third; he had already sacked the first two), set to work liberating the building's manifold possibilities. They built a few sets within the shell of the station, but for the most part they preferred to use what was there: this 'Victorian nightmare of passageways and grillwork, dust, dirt, decay', as Perkins described it.[24] Once again, and this time definitively, Welles set out to create the massive, dank, dungeon world of Piranesi, but now within an M.C. Escher framework, where stairways lead upwards to landings on a lower level, where doors open onto other worlds. It is as if Lewis Carroll's Alice's had strayed into the dark underworld of the industrial revolution.

For Welles it became home, quite literally. He moved out of the Meurice and into the Hôtel d'Orsay, on the corner of the building; and everything to do with the film was located in the old station. It became his personal studio, a kind of medieval village filled with craftsmen and technicians and artists, all focused on one goal: the film, with Welles at the centre of it all, a sort of feudal overlord with a pot of paint in his hand. Whenever he could, he involved himself in creating the physical world of the film. One of the most striking features of the Gare d'Orsay was its magnificent glass roof, which it was impossible to cover up. This meant night shooting – and only night shooting – which suited Welles admirably: he would work in the cutting room (set up in a remote corner of the station behind great black drapes) from nine-thirty in the morning till eight at night, after which they would shoot until three. Perkins, who was in every single shot of the film, struggled to stay awake.

Welles would wear himself out, doing sleight-of-hand conjuring tricks to keep the actor conscious; once he hired a couple of guitarists to keep Perkins amused.

Welles was deeply solicitous of the actors' well-being. Most of them had no more than two or three days' shooting. He would happily rehearse a scene for as long as he and they thought necessary; shooting was once suspended for an entire day while he, Perkins and Romy Schneider worked on their difficult long scene in the Advocate's office. His patience with them was endless – which was all the more remarkable because, as Chappell wrote in the *Sunday Times*, 'in private life he is not patient, but often melancholy, moody, sometimes irritable. At work he is funny, apt, kind, coarse, didactic, generous, intolerant, sweeping, thoughtful: violently American and violently European by turns.' When the actors were ready, and only when they were ready, Welles would finalise the physical moves and show them to Richard and his crew, whom he would then allow as long as they needed to light it. Then, the preparatory work done, everything moved at high speed; he never did more than three takes, generally settling for one, plus one for good luck. The sound department's function was limited to providing guide tracks: the acoustics in the station were of course atrocious, so every single line in the film had to be redubbed, which was Welles's favoured practice anyway. In this manner the film proceeded apace; shooting finished four days ahead of time (though the bill for overtime accounted for any savings there might have been). 'Genius is not always ruinous,' noted *Film and Filming*'s Enrique Martinez, in his report on the shoot.[25]

To mark the end of this blissful period, Welles threw a party. There were still pickup shots to be done – in Madrid, in Rome – but he wanted to celebrate while everyone was together. There had been no such celebrations at the end of *Touch of Evil*, much less *Mr Arkadin* or *Othello*. But this had to be marked. *Time* magazine came to the party: 'when Welles stood, everyone stood,' it reported, starry-eyed. 'When he sat, cross-legged, like a giant Buddha on the floor, all eyes in the luxurious Paris apartment turned towards him. Through the whole long evening, he laughed, he talked, puffed on a cigar, listened to the gypsy singers, and downed endless jiggers of vodka.' At three in the morning, when two or three couples started for the door, he bellowed, 'You're not leaving already, my friends. The night is young. Play, gypsies, play, play, play!' The gypsies played, the guests stayed. 'Once again, and at long last,' said *Time*, 'Orson Welles was front and center . . . at forty-seven, the Boy

Wonder was a boy again.'[26] There was an inordinate amount of interest in this film, a sense that something very special was in the offing. Whole waves of journalists were despatched to find out what was up. Was Welles back on form? Reports from the editing suite were breathless: Jules Dassin and Anatole Litvak had seen some rushes and declared that they were witnessing 'the birth of a classic'. The conjunction of Welles and Kafka was part of the excitement: 'two shockers', as one paper put it.

Welles was unusually communicative with his interviewers. After a meal consisting of five copious courses, two bottles of red wine and many glasses of fifty-year-old cognac, Welles, obviously feeling he had turned a corner, confided to Jack Kobler of the New York *Saturday Evening Post*: 'It's rough to be thought of as the fellow who had it – once. I could easily have gone on the sauce. Then I found a solution. For years I'd been telling people they were wrong about Welles. Then I took a new tack. I'd give 'em a steely look and say, "You were right. Only I've changed." I haven't, of course. I'm just as good or as lousy as I ever was. But it worked. Hardly a day passes now that someone doesn't offer me a script.'[27] As for *The Trial*, in his mind it had become the film he had been dreaming about for years. It is acutely enjoyable to watch Welles in the process of working up his version of his own history, trying on the variants for size, until he settles on the most colourful one. For Jack Kobler he spins a tale about the genesis of the film, which he never repeated anywhere else: Alexander Salkind, in this variation, came to Welles to ask him to play a cameo in a planned film of *Taras Bulba*. The producer's eye lighted on the screenplay of *The Trial*, over which Welles had, he said, been toiling for fifteen years, and immediately asked him to direct it. So much for poor Laplanche (who is actually credited on the film as 'promoter'). 'What keeps you away from the States?' asks Kobler. Welles answers with some emotion: 'Don't get me wrong about me and my country. I'd give my eyeteeth to be there this minute. But I'm respected less there than anywhere else.' He quotes from memory Walter Kerr's ten-year-old dismissal of him as 'the world's youngest has-been'. 'Over here serious critics take me seriously.' Shrugging this off, Welles now really hits his inventive stride, telling a happily credulous Kobler that the year before, 'for a lark', he and Paola had toured Italy with a gypsy circus; Welles earned his keep as a clown. A beguiling thought. 'On such jaunts, he films documentaries, part family album, part travelogue, which England's BBC televises.' If only. And there is, it appears, a new film in the pipeline: *King of Paris*, about the Dumas dynasty, in which, says Welles, he will be playing both the grandfather, a mulatto general in Napoleon's army, and the son, author of *The Count of Monte Cristo*. 'Couldn't you play the grandson, too?' asks Kobler, getting into the swing of things and noting, through a haze of fifty-year-old cognac, that in some lights Welles looks awfully young. 'I might give it a shot,' says Welles, playfully.

Vintage Welles, with him at his most bonhomous, playing the much-loved role of Orson Welles to the hilt. At about the same time he gave another interview, to Jean Clay, noted author of innumerable elegant tomes on painters and painting; it counts as among the most revealing he ever gave to anyone. It could only have been because of his post-shooting euphoria that Welles allowed Clay to get under his skin in a way that almost no one else had ever done – not Tynan, with whom he was always understandably guarded; and certainly not the *Cahiers* team, who were often as obtuse as they were inaccurate. In their interview with him about *The Trial*, for example, they ask Welles whether the long travelling shot of Katina Paxinou dragging the trunk while Anthony Perkins talks to her is an *hommage* to Brecht.[28] Paxinou, it is true, was a famous Mother Courage, but the character who drags the trunk is Miss Pittl, played by Suzanne Flon, who never played anything by Brecht. Why, anyway, would Welles want to introduce such an *hommage* at such a time in his film? He doesn't even bother to correct them; it's not serious. But here in Paris, in June of 1962 at the end of his shoot, he took Jean Clay very seriously, and Clay returned the compliment. When Welles says he sees K. as guilty, Clay replies, 'If K. is guilty and you also depict him as the image of man, then your film fits into the Christian tradition of guilt and original sin.' Welles is unaccustomed to theological analyses from journalists and he rises to the bait, though not without bluster: 'There's no way today – perhaps there will be three centuries from now – to do anything that does not talk about innocence and sin or good and evil. I know that ever since the 19th century there has been writing in which God has been absent. But it has no literary value at all.' Clay brushes this enormity aside (farewell Dickens, goodbye Flaubert) and cuts to the chase: 'Are you a Christian?' Welles replies that he has great love and respect for religion, and great love and respect for atheism. 'What I hate are the agnostics: the people who refuse to make a choice.'

Too polite to point out that Welles has not answered the question, Clay steps back from the interview to attempt a *tour d'horizon* of this strangely ungraspable figure. Clay is baffled: 'Can anyone really know him? His private life is so public that it has become almost anonymous. Though he has been talked about since childhood, he has remained unknown.' There is no question of Welles's abilities, he says: he sees how Welles's collaborators respect him, and is astonished at his technical skill in editing: 'Technique?' Welles bellows, offering his familiar dismissal of his craft. 'Don't make me laugh. In the movies, just as in every other trade, you can learn the technique in four days . . . any amateur photographer knows enough technique to make a film.' But now he adds a new complaint: 'Technicians always try to manacle the creative artist and prevent him from taking risks.' This is Promethean Welles, bound by the forces that be; Welles as Gulliver, trammelled by the little people. All this, says Clay, is put forward with impressive energy: 'Welles has the physical and mental energy of three men.' 'On this point everybody agrees,' says Clay, carefully choosing his words: 'here is a man equipped to be a genius.' He describes Welles's lifestyle: 'he over-tips flagrantly, stays only in best hotels, rides in a chauffeur-driven Mercedes, has no trouble getting through his $1,000 per week allowance and in general lives by the adage quoted to me by his wife: "The more it costs, the cheaper it is."' Welles perfectly lives up to his myth. But is he sincere, wonders Clay, meticulously demolishing Welles's story about seeing the clock faces of the Gare d'Orsay; and then, more boldly, he asks, 'Is he a liar? He told me he was a descendant of the Norman conquerors and that his name was originally Vilibus.'

On the set, Clay sees him spreading energy and enthusiasm everywhere; he also witnesses an alarming outburst of rage. But, like Enrique Martinez of *Films and Filming*, he sees something else behind all this extrovert behaviour. Martinez had been permitted to observe filming. Every time Welles spotted him, he ordered the studio manager to throw him out, but Martinez kept creeping back, hiding behind boxes or filing cabinets. From this oblique vantage point, Martinez surprisingly noted that, 'in spite of giving himself the airs of genius and in spite of his enormous cigars and his appearance of ox-like strength, Orson Welles seemed to me to reveal a side of himself that was full of timidity, excessively sensitive and even fearful'. Clay, too, has sensed timidity in him: Welles works alone in Rome, says Clay, because he is afraid of new faces; he always tries to hire the same actors, the same technicians; he dreads the idea of a press conference, being afraid to walk into a crowded room. 'I consider my face an enemy,' Welles confesses. 'I don't want to be the man I am. It's sad for an actor not to have a nose. Even when I shave, I don't look in a mirror.' His wife tells Clay that

Welles has a collection of all the beards, false noses, sideburns, false teeth and other disguises he has ever used in his career. 'It so happens that I've always had the body of a man and the face of a baby,' says Welles. 'The two have to be harmonized, that's all.'

Frustrated by what he feels is a diversion, Clay quotes back at him a remark he once made about Picasso being a son of the sun, whereas he, Welles, is a son of the moon. Clay wants to know what that means. Welles refuses, angrily, to elaborate. He hates to be questioned, he says; 75 per cent of anything he says in any interview is a lie. Clay bravely persists: 'But if I've only got witty remarks—' 'I'm a medium,' barks Welles, 'not an orator. Like certain Oriental and Christian mystics, I think the self is a kind of enemy. My work is precisely what enables me to come out of myself. I like what I do, not what I am. Asking me questions is death to me. I'm fanatically against psychoanalysis. Freud kills the poet in man. He kills the contradictions – and they're essential to him. Until someone learns the secrets of the world, I demand that man should have the right to keep and encourage his contradictions.' Clay sticks to his guns, trying to get something concrete, quantifiable, out of him: 'Isn't a man's work a way of surviving death?' he asks. 'The idea of survival doesn't interest me,' says Welles. 'Being alive means not killing the tensions that one carries within oneself. On the contrary, a poet must seek out and cultivate his contradictions.'

Something clicks in Clay's mind. 'These ambiguities, internal clashes and tensions add up to something far more than a mere love of paradox,' he says. 'Look at his films; they reflect the strange dissociation of his personality, the contrast between what he could be – a monster – and what his intelligence and lucidity have made him: a humanist. A Nietzschean personality tempered with liberalism, a monster tamed by virtue of his own reason. Welles himself is a tumultuous combat that is reflected in his work. The tension is the key to the man. Through it, he becomes truly great.' His work, surmises Clay, is a psychodrama, a means for its creator to get a grip on himself by describing himself. The inner tension explains 'the impetuosity and the baroque seething' in Welles's style. But more important than this, says Clay, is that behind all this maelstrom of contradictory sentiments is 'a parallel to that moment in a bullfight when the crowd becomes hushed in anticipation of the death thrust. It is a zone of glacial silence.' Like the humans-turned-rhinoceroses in Ionesco's play, the sceptical, analytical Clay has begun to think like Welles, to talk like him. Tragic pessimism is at the root of Welles and his work, he says: 'there is only one standard by which to judge people: their attitude to death.' And there, says Clay, you have his message. 'It may be that the director of *The Trial*, if he can probe his own anxiety and settle his own fate more lucidly, will bring a new acuteness to his art. It may be that this man, to whom we owe some of the greatest moments in cinema, will in the future lift his song (as he calls it) to heights as yet unattained by the seventh art.'

This remarkable interview/profile demonstrates how deeply people were affected by Welles. It is a striking example of what might be called the Mounties school of journalism: Clay hangs in there till he gets his man. Usually Welles profoundly resists classification, tries to create a smokescreen, refuses self-analysis except as a kind of parlour game. But with Clay he doesn't fantasticate his past: he grapples with himself as an artist. Clay persuades Welles to give an account, however defensively, of his personal preoccupations, the things he thinks about most deeply. His delineation of Welles as being himself 'a tumultuous combat' that is reflected in his work comes very close to the mystery at the centre of Welles. Clay's notion that Welles needs to probe his own anxiety and settle his own fate more lucidly if he is to scale the heights is profoundly suggestive. Clay's encounter with Welles puts him in a majestic framework, away from the external and towards what is going on inside, changing the terms of reference from either the popular obsession with his versatility and flamboyance or the intellectuals' imputations of calculated cleverness, instead suggesting a depth and a disturbance within him predicated on profound contradictions.

⋆

It was to be the last acknowledgement of that kind that Welles would receive for some time. He edited the film with tremendous application, day and night, with a couple of assistants. Eventually, an outsider editor was brought in. Fritz Muller had some experience on Hollywood movies and had been working in Rome. When he entered the cutting room Welles roared, 'Who are YOU? And how did you get in here?' Muller told him he was the editor. 'Get out of here!!!' hollered Welles. 'Now!!!' Muller left, bewildered. Welles suddenly emerged from the station and called to him again. 'Who are you?' 'I've come to edit the film,' said Muller. 'Oh,' said Welles, 'you're not an Editor, you're a CUTTER. I thought you were a Newspaper Editor. You're a cutter. Well, come in. Let's get to work.'[29]

Once in the editing suite, Muller realised that chaos prevailed: his assistants were untrained, there were sacks of unlabelled film everywhere, and Welles, in cutting sequences together, had simply discarded the bits he didn't want. Muller told him that he had to reprint all the footage again and start from scratch, systematically. Welles agreed. He knew what he wanted, said Muller, but he had no idea how to get it. 'The challenge of editing any of Orson Welles's films,' he told the interviewer Peter Tonguette, 'was that he did not like script girls and he did not like the clapper boards. So one had to search and find and create source materials. Normally, you go by numbers and you find a take. But in this case, you couldn't. So the challenge was to try to find the pieces and put it together.'[30] He and Welles then worked closely and in harmony, until, predictably, they had a blazing row. Muller walked out; later Welles called him. '"You're the only man that knows how to talk to me," he said. I said, "What do you mean?" He said, "Well, nobody tells me to fuck off." I said, "Well, you probably scare people, but you don't treat people the way you should treat them."'[31] Welles worked obsessively, driving himself and everyone else, never satisfied. When he was exhausted, he would have a hot bath for twenty minutes and return refreshed. He was never satisfied, but the film began to takes shape.

He and Muller laboured especially hard on the sound. The Salkinds had allotted him a composer, Jean Drut, who had composed the score for *Austerlitz*, and Welles found himself at loggerheads with him, chiefly because he was not interested in Drut composing a score in any conventional sense: what he required were musical (or, to be more precise, sonic) building blocks, which he would re-assemble as required, at whatever speed he chose, played backwards if necessary. This was understandably dispiriting for a composer of some track record and unquestioned skills. Moreover Welles determined from an early point that he would use the then not especially familiar Adagio souped up in the 1940s by the musicologist Remo Giazotto from a fragment by Tomaso Albinoni. Its phoney religiose emotionalism must have suggested something specific to Welles, but he rarely uses it unadorned – most prominently at the very end of the film. Otherwise, as with the music Drut composed for him, he subjects it to every indignity imaginable, but the effect is curiously haunting, as the tune struggles against all sorts of other elements to assert itself – sometimes trudging backwards, sometimes emerging in tiny bursts. It's a curious musical ecology, contributing to the film's general sense of diffraction, often seeming to go its own way without reference to anything happening on the screen or in the narrative – part of Welles's ongoing experiment with sound, which had started on radio in the early 1930s. The dubbing of the dialogue was a huge task in itself. Perkins had the lion's share of it, and learned from Welles, he said, to love the process, coming to see that it was a chance to improve his performance; he became as skilled at it as Welles himself. Peter Sallis and other British actors were flown in to dub other characters. Welles, delighted to see Sallis again, showed him some favourite sequences from the footage:

> and he was, what he had always been I suppose, just a little bit of a child. He had a childlike delight in what he was doing and he wanted to share it with somebody, so he shared it with me, and I was flattered and pleased that he did.[32]

Welles dubbed many of the characters himself, as he had done on all of his films since *Othello*. The effect is to make Welles omnipresent; this is *First Person Singular* carried to new heights. It has been suggested that he embodies every aspect of the Law, but it is a little difficult to square that with his dubbing the Priest or, particularly, the painter, Titorelli, whom he endows with a slightly camp, rather sneering tone that seems at odds both with Billy Chappell's performance and with the character. Instead, it suggests a desire to stamp every second of the film with his own imprint, alongside a very human, Bottom the Weaver-like desire to play everyone. Complex as Welles was, one should never discount simple motives.

The film, in what was now almost a ritual with Welles, was entered for the Venice Film Festival and then withdrawn from it; in this case, it was replaced by another story of alienation and police brutality, *West Side Story*, co-directed by Robert Wise, Welles's editor on *Citizen Kane* and collaborator with the enemy (as he saw it) on *The Magnificent Ambersons* – a man from whose earnings the interest alone would have paid for every project Welles ever dreamed of. As the Paris premiere of *The Trial* approached, Welles lost faith in the one scene in the film that was entirely his invention, the one between Perkins and Katina Paxinou as the scientist, in which the computer (rather archly referred to as 'she') predicts that the one crime Joseph K. would be likely to commit would be suicide. Welles never really explained why it was cut; all his team thought it would work wonderfully, he said, but it didn't.

The Trial had a splendid premiere in Paris; in fact, it had two premieres in Paris, one in English and one in French. The French version was much criticised, but the English version was highly acclaimed. Welles's good feeling persisted; he was convinced that, as he told *Cahiers du Cinéma* in 1964, 'this is the best film I have ever made'. Then the English-language critics weighed in. The *New Yorker*'s Paris correspondent, the legendary Janet Flanner, writing under her nom de plume Genêt, described *The Trial* as 'the most expectantly awaited cinema event of the winter'. Her verdict was a mildly expressed presage of everything that was to come: 'as a film it is typical, talented, pure Welles', but 'there seems to be no emotion behind the film to squeeze the heart or inflame the brain'.[33] Brendan Gill, in the same magazine a few months later, at the time of the film's American release, noted that Kafka succeeds by the suppression of vivid images and that 'what a movie version of *The Trial* requires isn't exotic settings, weird camera angles, and voice echoing hollowly down improbable passageways but a bleak, bland ordinariness of film and sound, in which every setting, every action is precisely what it appears to be. Outrageous reasonableness is the iron rule and may not be violated. Have I sufficiently indicated', he purrs, 'that I think Orson Welles is the last man on earth who ought to have made a movie out of *The Trial*?'[34] From *Esquire* magazine came the same refrain: 'That Welles should have attempted *The Trial* shows an extraordinary lack of self-knowledge.'[35]

Six months later the film was released in England, having the misfortune to appear in the same week as Joseph Losey's *The Servant*, with its superb screenplay by Harold Pinter and its unsettling anatomisation of class differences; that, as well as Kafka, was used by the British critics to clobber *The Trial*. The *Times* headline was pretty explicit: 'ORSON WELLES FAILS WITH KAFKA'.[36] 'Technically, the film is masterful,' says the anonymous critic. 'And yet for most of the way it is just dull and lifeless.' Why? the critic asks. Not because it is not good Kafka: 'what matters here is whether it is good Welles'. It was not, according to *The Times*. 'Mr Welles has made bad films before and then surprised us all with his acrobatic powers of recovery, and will no doubt do so again. But meanwhile one is left by *The Trial* reflecting ruefully that it must, after all, take genius of a sort to make so little out of so much.' In *Sight and Sound*, normally very supportive of Welles, William S. Pechter laid into the film with a will:

> Though I had expected *The Trial* to be bad, I went to it truly hoping for the best. And in fact though I had expected it to be bad, bad as a mannerist painting can be bad, bad, for instance, as Welles's *Othello* is bad, I had not been expecting the worst; I had not expected that it might be boring. Orson Welles boring! And boring to stupefaction . . . for anyone familiar with Orson Welles's talents at their peak, even more shocking than how bad *The Trial* is, is how bad it looks: it looks like the dregs of Cinema 16.[37]

And in one of the few reviews to attempt even a modicum of analysis, Robert Hatch in *Horizon* noted that:

> *The Trial* goes astray because Welles is a romantic – and, I think, an optimist . . . in the book the law devours its most ardent disciple: in the picture the totalitarian police pick up a potential dissident (and quite properly, given the viewpoint). That is an idea for a picture, but it is not Kafka's idea. Nor did Kafka have it in mind to warn his public against the imminence of atomic war – he was dealing with a horror of the soul. The mushroom cloud at the end of the film is another example of the boy scout in Welles; he has never been able to pass a soapbox without jumping up for a brief exhortation.[38]

The disjunct between the joy in creating a work and the critical response is not unknown in the lives of artists, but here it is particularly violent, and particularly dismaying in contemplating Welles's personal trajectory. Fortune proved, after all, a cruel and fickle goddess. There was no respite; Welles was still being punished for being himself. It is pitiful. However, there is no question that *The Trial* – the film made under ideal conditions, the film in which there was no one to blame except himself, in which there could be no extended memos showing how he had been misunderstood and betrayed, the film that was his, from beginning to end – is a problematic film in his output. It has its partisans, but it has never sparked the sort of passionate defences and rehabilitations that even *Mr Arkadin*, god help us all, has attracted. As virtually every review, bad or indifferent, acknowledges, it is a staggering achievement, technically. Visually it is powerful, challenging, imaginative. The camera moves are superbly accomplished, the nightmare chases disturbing, the sense of space breathtaking. The film is filled with felicities: the deeply distressing sequences of the beating of the policemen; the Alice-in-Wonderland staging of the tribunal, in which K. first pleads his innocence; the numb faces of the extras who (not understanding English) so brilliantly suggest an absolute incomprehension of what is going on; the performances, especially of Tamiroff, who manages, yet again, to be grotesque and real in equal measure; and of Welles himself, his most relaxed, witty, fluid work as an actor for years (no prosthetics, phew). Welles's first appearance, lying on a bed, swathed in cigar smoke, in which he might as well be dead, is a brilliant *coup de théâtre*. Echoes of other Welles films abound: the courtroom scene in *The Lady from Shanghai*, the terrorisation of Janet Leigh in the motel in *Touch of Evil*, the projection-room sequence from *Citizen Kane* at different points inform the film with powerful resonances.

But amidst all the texture, the imagery and the energy, the story – the element to which Welles professed ultimate loyalty – has gone missing. As *The Times* remarked, whether it is Kafka-like or not is irrelevant: but the question of what we are given in its stead is. Welles consummately creates an anti-statist nightmare. But Kafka's darker, subtler parable of man's alienation from himself pierces you, disturbs you, frightens you. The film does none of these things, for all the vividness of its imagery and the force of its outrage against the forces of conformism. A single passage from the book, a moment absent from Welles's screenplay, shows what has been lost. It is the penultimate paragraph of the novel, as K. lies in the pit, awaiting – indeed expecting – his death at the hands of the police:

> The casement window flew open like a light flashing on; a human figure, faint and unsubstantial at that distance and height, forced itself far out and stretched its arms out even further. Who was it? A friend? A good man? One who sympathized? One who wanted to help? Was it one person? Was it everybody? Was there still help? Were there objections that had been forgotten? Certainly there were. Logic is of course unshakeable, but it cannot hold out against a man who wants to live.[39]

There is nothing in the film to touch this with its ambiguity, its fearful glimpse of hope, its human anguish. In his film of *The Trial* it is as if Welles had forgotten or dismissed what Joseph K. was actually experiencing. He wanted to make a film more than he wanted to make a film of *The Trial*. It is as if the possibilities of the language he was inventing had become more interesting to him than what he was trying to say in it. The last few minutes of the film, with the atomic mushroom rising up as the faux-Albinoni blares out, is truly dismaying in its banality. Perhaps this is what happens when you make a film just for the sake of making a film, from a book you do not admire: you have to bend your imagination so far that you end up involved in a purely mechanical exercise, however much fun it might have been to execute it.

Welles, for the good of his soul, needed to make a film that his heart was in. Fortunately, he did.

And meanwhile, he met a girl.

CHAPTER EIGHTEEN

Let's Have a Brainwash

WELLES'S MARRIAGE to Paola Mori was in many ways a great success. She was beautiful, organised, socially superb – both girlish and aristocratic – and an ideal mother; she kept house for Welles wherever they might be, and also provided him with the thing he had always lacked – a permanent base, a hearth – in her mother's home in Fregene, where he had installed the Moviolas, the essential tool of his trade, which Darryl Zanuck had given him in lieu of a salary for his performance in *Roots of Heaven*.

He, Beatrice and Paola constituted a happy unit, happy enough for Beatrice to remember it as an idyllic period, forever enshrined in the footage Welles shot for a remarkably free-form Italian television documentary entitled *In the Land of Don Quixote*, in which they behave like any loving family on holiday as they wander across Spain. But it was not enough. There is reason to believe that Welles was not monogamous; it was hard to break the habits of a lifetime. That was containable: Paola was a shrewd Italian wife and was not unaware of her husband's need for new stimulants, for his adrenalin fix. But then, unbeknown to her, he fell in love – deeply and, as it turned out, permanently. It was on the set of *The Trial* in Paris, in the Gare d'Orsay, that he met a sensationally beautiful, sexually provocative young art student called Olga Palinkaš, of mixed Hungarian and Croatian parentage. It was some years before they met again, but true to his essentially romantic nature, Welles kept the flame burning; when they were reunited, their relationship quickly developed into the most important relationship he ever had with a woman. He and Paola never divorced; for some years they maintained the surface of their relationship. Welles's new passion was a slow-burning thing, but as far as his heart was concerned, he was, to all intents and purposes, gone.

Meanwhile he continued to make his living in the usual way, financing or otherwise supporting the jobs that he really cared about. He made *In the Land of Don Quixote* (*Nella terra di Don Chisciotte*) for RAI early in 1961, just before writing the screenplay for *The Trial*. It is the longest thing he ever did, nine one-hour programmes, and it is curiously unmediated, having the distinct feeling of a home movie: the camera just runs. For once Welles, no doubt eager to fill up the nine hours, was able to resist intervening editorially. 'It's just a travelogue,' he told Juan Cobós, his assistant on *Chimes at Midnight*.[1] But he turns his camera on some very striking things, and his always interested eyes frequently light on charming, curious and sometimes breathtaking scenes. It is, in effect, a photo-album recording his fascination with the country he had first visited as a sixteen-year-old boy, but in which, out of deep detestation for Franco and his regime, he had avoided working until he shot *Mr Arkadin* there. (Welles might have mellowed somewhat towards the old man. At a press conference around this time he asked his audience of journalists: 'Which world statesman made movies? Franco: he made animated cartoons. Were they funny? No – but *at least he made them*.') For *In the Land of Don Quixote* Welles had specifically requested his producer on the series, his old chum Alessandro Tasca di Cutò, to hire a newsreel cameraman – someone with quick reflexes and a keen eye. Tasca had gone to the state newsreel organisation, NO-DO, which churned out the unending official footage of Franco that was compulsorily shown with feature films in Spanish cinemas, and found José Manuel De La Chica, with whom Welles had a very amicable relationship, to the extent that a high percentage of the footage of *In The Land of Don Quixote* was shot by De La Chica on his own; indeed, some of the material in the series is actually lifted from the NO-DO archives.

The nine programmes cover most of the tourist high points: the Prado, Seville, Toledo, Granada and further afield – the Bodega Della Domecq in Jerez de la Frontera; Cadiz and Palos, whence Columbus sailed to America; Gibraltar, Malaga and the Mediterranean coast. Inevitably there is a long bullfighting sequence of a decidedly gory nature showing the bull's slow demise, and an interesting section in which the glamorous young El Cordobés prepares for a fight. Almost all of the footage is silent. Ardent Wellesian sleuths can detect motifs from his output, past and yet to come. But there is no coherence to it; it's just one damned thing after another. Even if Welles had wanted to whittle down the material, transform it, bring some poetry to it, somehow render it truly cinematic, properly Wellesian, the absence of his personal charisma on screen, relating directly to the audience, would have made it all but impossible. Tasca suggested to RAI that Welles should narrate it himself, in Italian, a language that he spoke poorly, but pronounced perfectly.

They not only declined the offer, but re-edited the material, rewrote the commentary and hired another actor, Arnoldo Foà (Inspector A. in *The Trial*) to read it. History repeating itself: his work jerked away from him yet again.

But Welles shed no tears: he got exactly what he wanted out of the project: namely, money, which enabled him to commit yet more of his fleeting inspirations for *Don Quixote* to film. 'As soon as he was ready to shoot, Orson would call Akim Tamiroff, who always came straightaway,' reported Cobós. 'He'd put on the Sancho Panza costume and jump straight onto the donkey.'[2] Tamiroff was on his own this time; his master, Francisco Reiguera, by now ancient and frail, was stranded in Mexico, still barred from Franco's Spain. *In the Land of Don Quixote* thus bought Welles more material for his cinematic sketchbook. But it gave him something else: a good working knowledge of the Spanish landscape. He used the programme as an excuse to visit potential locations for the film that was already germinating in his mind, *Chimes at Midnight*. He had decided to shoot it in Spain, firstly because he believed that only there would he find some credible semblance of the medieval world, the world of old Catholic England – and secondly because, as he sometimes claimed, Spain was the last country in the world that still believed in black-and-white film, in which form his film would unquestionably be shot. He was actively seeking financial backing for it, but the money was slow to materialise. Once again, it looked as if he would have to raise it himself.

To which end, the prospect of decent payment loomed gratifyingly in the form of Dino De Laurentiis's wildly ambitious venture to film the Bible. Each episode was to be directed by a different titan of the cinema: Bresson was going to direct *Genesis*, Visconti *Joseph and His Brothers*, and Welles *Jacob and Esau*. A photograph that was taken for De Laurentiis's press release shows the three masters standing rather uncomfortably together; the caption reads: 'The Magnificent Three'. It all began to unravel very quickly. Bresson was dumped early on, when he told De Laurentiis that the screenplay would be in Hebrew and Aramaic, and that there would be no animals in Noah's Ark, just their footprints in the sand; Visconti simply stepped away; but Welles's section, telling the vexed tale of the twins who founded warring nations, got quite close to being filmed. Keith Baxter was cast as Jacob and was duly flown to Rome for make-up tests; he had to age from seventeen to ninety. The tests were personally conducted by Welles, 'gluing on beards and eyebrows,' reported Baxter, 'waxing out hair on my scalp for the old man, curling and highlighting and lavishly slapping on eye-shadow and false eyelashes for the teenager'. Welles, like the nineteenth-century actor-manager that he was, revelled in all of this. '"The thing about film, Keith," he said, wielding the make-up sticks like a painter, "is that you can get away with a great deal more than people think. Confidence is all that matters"'[3] – a profoundly characteristic observation.

De Laurentiis's confidence in Welles failed not over his version of the Jacob story, which, according to Baxter, was 'both moving and hilarious, and always reverent' in its delineation of Jacob's transformation 'from a really odious teenager on the make into the archetypal Jewish patriarch',[4] but in his approach to the savage story of Abraham and Isaac, an episode that Welles took on when Ingmar Bergman turned it down. He had a vivid take on the story, predictably rejecting any submission to destiny on the boy's part. If Welles would not allow Joseph K. to acquiesce in his own demise, why should he let Isaac? 'I saw nothing in the story,' he told *Cahiers du Cinéma*, 'which meant that Isaac should be a willing sacrifice.'[5] He planned to shoot the picture on the barren slopes of Vesuvius, 'in that ashy ominous landscape,' according to Baxter, 'with Isaac running for his life, falling, stumbling, screaming in terror as his father pursued him with a knife'.[6] It should be, said Welles, 'a brutal, terrible scene'. This conception, however, ran up against Catholic theology. For the Church, the story foreshadows the Crucifixion, with Isaac prefiguring Jesus's self-sacrifice: to show him fearful or resistant would be heretical. Isaac had to be – or be willing to be – a Lamb of God. Welles wouldn't budge, nor would De Laurentiis.

In the end the great producer threw in the towel, replacing his bevy of troublesome titans and their fancy ideas with one tested buccaneer director, John Huston, who would also narrate and play Noah – exactly what Welles would have liked to have done: Huston and Welles treading parallel paths yet again. Welles claimed that Huston used his screenplay for *Abraham: The Sacrifice*, but, as shot, the sequence does not in any way match Welles's or Baxter's description of what he planned. One of the most enterprising sections of Huston's movie, it is filmed entirely in stills and is silent (apart from a massively throbbing score, which won its composer an Oscar); at no point does Isaac run away from his father. Nonetheless Welles cheerfully pocketed a large sum of money for his work on the film, the exact amount revealed in one of his best jokes, to the *New York Post*, which had asked him why he wanted to make the film. 'An angel came to me and said unto me: "Orson, bow down before de

Laurentiis and sign for $200,000."' It would have been interesting to have seen what the author of *Miracle in Hollywood*, that savage satire of religiose cinema, would have made of the project. From any perspective, it is one of the more regrettable of the many projects to have got away from Welles. It is almost equally vexing that he never filmed his script for *Jacob and Esau*, in view of the fact that, as the Angel Peniel with whom Jacob wrestles, Welles had cast the recently defected Russian ballet dancer Rudolf Nureyev – 'twenty-three years old, sensationally callipygous', as Keith Baxter appreciatively describes him, 'with a mane of untidy blond hair, the physique of an athlete and the movements of a tiger'. Added to all of which Welles would have had a decent budget, something he was never again to command. It is true that at the time all he really wanted to film was *Chimes at Midnight*, but from his earliest days at RKO, when Mercury Productions were exploding with projects, he had had his eye on various sections of the Bible, from both New and Old Testaments; Noah was a permanent presence on his list of potential projects. It is especially frustrating that, at a time when he was writing his screenplay for *Chimes at Midnight* and reflecting deeply on the matter of fathers and sons, he came so close to telling one of the most terrible of all such stories, of a child so very nearly slain by his father, out of obedience to his god.

Later that year of 1963, Welles lumbered onto the screen in one of the most wretched of all the many wretched films in which he appeared, the sadly misnamed *Marco the Magnificent*, playing, as the narration has it, 'a wise old Jew', Marco Polo's tutor, Akerman. It is a brilliant performance, vocally – a wonderfully observed Yiddish accent – but the make-up is lamentable, featuring a recycling of his Macy's Santa Claus beard and another impossibly aquiline nose, and there is nothing whatever that he or anyone could have done with the scene, or indeed with Horst Buchholz as Polo; one can only hope that he made a great deal of money from it.

He alleviated the humiliation and boredom by moonlighting on another, much less lucrative but infinitely more rewarding engagement, arriving at the crack of dawn on the train from Paris, still in Akerman's nose and beard, to be swept off to a location deep in the Roman countryside, then raced back to Paris three days later. The film for which he made such strenuous efforts was the catchily titled *Let's Have a Brainwash: RoGoPaG*, one of the portmanteau films fashionable in Italy in the Sixties, this one named after its quartet of distinguished directors, Roberto Rossellini, Jean-Luc Godard, Pier Paolo Pasolini and Ugo Gregoretti. Comprising four films, announces the title-sequence, 'whose authors limit themselves to recounting the joyous end of the world', *RoGoPaG* mounts a bilious assault on Italy in the early 1960s; it was put together by Pasolini's regular producer, Alfredo Bini, and it is Pasolini's contribution, *La Ricotta*, that has stood the test of time, its thirty-four minutes a startling and savage allegorical attack on modern Italy's abandonment of its proletariat, fobbed off with the tacky baubles of consumerism.

Pre-dating Pasolini's masterpiece *The Gospel According to St Matthew* by a year, *La Ricotta* concerns the making of a film about the Crucifixion; Welles was cast as the director or, rather, according to the credits, 'The Director', of the film; for Welles, in 1963, there seemed to be no escaping the Good Book. The action focuses on its stars (Laura Betti among them), its director (Welles) and, crucially and centrally, its extras: the story concerns one of them, Stracci, playing the Good Thief crucified alongside Jesus. Desperately hungry, Stracci (his name means rags in Italian) hides the rations he gets from the film's caterers; coming back to enjoy them, he finds a dog has got there before him. Stracci sells the dog to a passer-by, and with the money he buys a large cream cheese (the eponymous ricotta); in a break from filming, he shoves it into his mouth in a kind of frenzy. His fellow-extras start throwing him bits of food, cheering him on in his frenzied eating marathon. At the height of it, he's called back to the set: it's the last scene, he's on the cross and the producers' invited guests are descending, paparazzi in tow, to watch the filming. Before the cameras roll, an assistant director makes him repeat his one line – 'Lord, when you get to heaven, remember me to your Father' – after which, unnoticed by anyone, he dies. Welles arrives to shoot the scene, the spectators gather round, Welles cries '*Motore!*', the cameras roll – and nothing happens. He says it again; again nothing. When he realises what's happened, they cut Stracci down and Welles muses: 'Poor Stracci: he had to die to remind us that he was ever alive.'

Instinct with Pasolini's characteristic poetry, both visual and verbal, *La Ricotta* has as many narrative strands as it has visual styles: the film-within-the-film (which features reconstructions of the Crucifixion after Pontormo and Rosso Fiorentino) is shot in saturated Technicolor; the scenes with the extras hanging around are done in newsreel colour film; the rest is in black-and-white, with two sequences comically speeded up. The music is sometimes baroque, sometimes pop, often by Verdi ('Libiamo', of course), played by a brass band at varying tempos. It all hangs together perfectly, including the very striking sequences featuring Welles as The

Director, which, in yet another change of idiom, paint a lightly satirical portrait of the artist as Marxist intellectual, which somehow, improbably but entirely convincingly, merges aspects of both Welles and Pasolini. Pasolini cast Welles because he was by now the iconic representative of the whole tribe of Director-Geniuses, more so than Hitchcock, Renoir or Bergman – more so, even, than Ford or DeMille, von Stroheim or von Sternberg, Fellini or Antonioni or Rossellini; he was the man, after all, who made *Citizen Kane*, by now universally acknowledged as the epitome of *auteur* film-making. In the film Welles plays himself, exactly as Pasolini had written him: as a philosopher-director, a whimsical, erudite, reflective provocateur. This is the Welles of the *Cahiers du Cinéma* interviews, rather than hands-on Welles, Welles the human tornado, the maker of props, the applier of make-up, the designer of sets, the wielder of the Caméflex. He was very happy with the script, said his co-star, Pasolini's close friend Laura Betti. 'He changed nothing, he asked for no changes. He got it in one.'[7] He wore no make-up for the part, always significant in a Welles performance.

He is first discovered, immediately after we have seen the half-naked extras twisting and shouting in the summer sunshine, sitting – as Welles sometimes sat on his own sets – in a sort of meditative trance, almost comatose, eyes glazed, communing with his inner world, script in hand, wearing a huge black trench coat in the middle of the baking Roman countryside. Finally he murmurs a phrase: 'The crown.' This is taken up by assistant directors, runners, gaffers, grips, prop men, even the extras: 'The crown! The crown!! The crown!!!' As the world of the film springs to life around him, Welles continues to sit, semi-glazed, in which state he is approached by a reporter, with whom he deals in a playfully provocative manner, much as Welles himself dealt with reporters. He allows the hapless man only four questions: the first is 'What is this project trying to express?' 'My intimate, profound and traditional Catholicism,' replies Welles, with a ghost of a smile, his eyebrows delicately expressing the absurdity of his reply – he, a notorious Marxist. Welles was not a Marxist, of course; Pasolini was. Welles was not a Catholic (though he sometimes whimsically claimed to have been brought up as one); Pasolini, naturally, had been, and expressed profound respect for the Bible narratives, as – of course – did Welles. 'What do you think of Italy?' asks the journalist, for his second question. 'The most illiterate masses and the most ignorant bourgeoisie in Europe,' says Welles, and the remark could so easily have come from his own mouth. 'What d'you think of death?' quizzes the journalist. 'As a

Marxist I never give it any thought,' says Welles-Pasolini. The journalist has used up three of his four questions. Finally he asks, 'What do you think of our great director, Fellini?' Again you can see Pasolini and Welles simultaneously in the wicked reply: 'He . . . dances.' Pause and then, definitively: 'He dances.'

The journalist starts to go. The Director calls him back: 'I am a force of the past,' he says, explaining to the baffled hack that the words are from a poem in which the poet describes certain ancient ruins whose style and history no one understands any more, and certain hideous modern buildings that everyone, alas, understands perfectly well. He reads from the printed screenplay of Pasolini's film *Mamma Roma*, which contains a number of Pasolini's poems; the ecstatic words – Italian Whitman – conveying a dynamic sense of the past, an urgent sense of loss, an insistent longing for wholeness, which must have echoed powerfully for Welles himself, 'the man of many nostalgias':

> Tradition is my only love. I come from ruins, churches, altarpieces, forgotten hamlets in the Apennines and the foothills of the Alps where our brothers dwelled. I walk the via Tuscolana like a madman, the Appian Way like a dog without a master. I behold the twilight and the mornings over Rome, over Ciocaria, over the world like the first acts of post-history, which I witness by privilege of birth from the furthest edge of some buried past age . . . and I . . . wander, more modern than any modern, in search of brothers who are no more.

The Director asks the journalist whether he's understood a word of what he's just said. 'Write this down,' he says. 'You understand nothing because you're an average man, right? But do you know what an average man is? He's a monster. A dangerous criminal, a conformist, a colonialist, a racist, a slave trader, a political cynic.' The Director idly asks the journalist whether he has a heart condition, then explains his question: if the journalist dropped down dead, it would be good pre-publicity for the film. 'You don't exist anyway. Capital acknowledges the existence of labour only insofar as it serves production. And the producer of my film is also the owner of your newspaper. Good-bye.' Welles puts on his spectacles; rising from his chair, he turns its back towards us. On it is written '*Regista*' – 'Director'. He reverts to his catatonic-laconic style of directing – 'Nail them to the cross. Leave them nailed down. Unnail them' – until he finally tears himself away to dally with the beautiful people who have come to witness the filming. With no particular enthusiasm, he goes to the cross to direct the man whom he doesn't yet know is dead; his manner when he realises what has happened is wonderfully complex and ambiguous. Together with his Hastler in *The Trial*, this performance seems to betoken a new style of playing for Welles, which is highly personal and compelling in an entirely novel way: there is a certain mystery about it, a held-back quality, which speaks of depths rarely touched upon in the rest of his work as an actor (always excepting Harry Lime). It is spellbinding rather than dominating; it seeks neither to charm nor to impress. Welles has finally arrived at the sort of acting he always admired, but which he almost never achieved on film: he uses himself, imposing nothing, simply being, thus harnessing the force not only of his personality, but of his prodigious inner life.

How did this come about? Welles and Pasolini got on wonderfully well, though Pasolini spoke no English, and Welles only a little Italian. 'He sensed that [Pasolini] was a great personage,' said Bini, 'but I can't say he understood much.'[8] The cinematographer, Tonino Delli Colli, said of Welles that 'he did everything Pier Paolo told him to, without argument ever, or attempting to change anything'.[9] From the beginning, with *Accatone*, Pasolini had worked with amateur actors: 'I didn't do anything,' he told James Blue. 'I didn't tell them anything. In fact, I didn't even tell them precisely what characters they were playing. Because I never chose an actor *as an interpreter*. I always chose an actor *for what he is*. That is, I never asked anyone to transform himself into anything other than what he is.' He approached Welles in the same way:

> He played himself. What he really did was a caricature of himself. And also because Welles, in addition to being an actor, is also an intellectual so I used him as an intellectual director rather than as an actor. Because he's an extremely intelligent man, he understood right away and there was no problem. He brought it off well . . . it was a very brief and simple part, with no great complications. I told him my intention and I let him do as he pleased. He understood what I wanted immediately and did it in a manner that was completely satisfying to me.[10]

According to Bini, Pasolini offered every one of his subsequent films to Welles: each time Welles toyed with the idea, but he never accepted. *La Ricotta* was a one-off, a superb and happy conjunction of his own and Pasolini's artistic and intellectual universes. One might quarrel with Pasolini's view that Welles caricatures himself in the film: he did that in many of his film performances, but not here. Here he subtly and wittily comments on himself, and on the position and function of the director.

Interestingly, Pasolini and his producer, Bini, fell out over *La Ricotta*. Unnoticed by Bini, Pasolini had named one of the more unsavoury characters after a local public prosecutor with whom they had clashed. The film was duly banned, and Bini had to pay an enormous fine – nearly $1 million in current terms. 'At least Pasolini could have warned me, no?' said Bini plaintively. The matter was resolved very elegantly when Pasolini wrote a poem for Bini about what he calls the father-producer, who, Pasolini concedes in the poem, was on this occasion right, but who is at heart a mercenary. Bini was delighted with the poem; and he and Pasolini continued to make films together. Too bad Welles never wrote John Houseman a poem.

★

Back, then, to Welles's main focus: raising finance for *Chimes at Midnight*. It is evident that he was hoping to raise a sizeable chunk of money – inevitably period films cost more. The costumes (often for large numbers of people), the settings, the props involved in re-creating another world do not come cheap. And, unlike *Othello*'s Mediterranean setting, this is a northern world, in which people are apparelled to the gills. Very little money – very little interest – was forthcoming.

In June of 1964, in the midst of working on the screenplay, Welles wrote to Keith Baxter, 'Why don't we go quietly ahead sometime this year with our own family-sized production of *Chimes*? There probably wouldn't be sixpence in it for any of us, but it would certainly be fun and, I think, worthwhile . . . what are your plans?'[11] Baxter needed little persuading: he had had a highly successful career since the end of *Chimes at Midnight* in Dublin, 'but there was never any doubt', he wrote, 'that the handle which first opened all the doors was the name of Orson Welles'; he remained passionately keen to be in the film. He heard nothing, and then a sensational telegram arrived in late September of that year: 'HAVE JOHN GIELGUD AS THE KING STOP MARGARET RUTHERFORD AS MISTRESS QUICKLY STOP JEANNE MOREAU AS DOLL TEARSHEET STOP AM PLAYING FALSTAFF STOP PLEASE COME LOVE ORSON.' Baxter was on the next flight out. When he arrived at Welles's villa, he was taken aside by Ann Rogers, who was now in residence in the villa, along with Paola, Beatrice, the German governess and a parrot. 'He's with the producers,' she whispered. 'They've been here all morning. I think the film is cancelled.'

Fortunately not. Welles had first attempted to set up the film in Yugoslavia; this failed. Then he found some Spanish money from a company called Producciones Cinematográficas MD; this fell through. Finally he met a producer, a thirty-something young man called Emiliano Piedra, who wanted Welles to direct *Treasure Island* for him and play Long John Silver. Welles saw his chance and agreed to do it, but only if he could shoot *Chimes at Midnight* at the same time, sharing some of the locations and doubling up some of the cast. Only a deeply inexperienced producer would have agreed to such an insane scheme; but Piedra did. He had exactly one producing credit to his name, an early spaghetti-western called *Badmen of the West*. Welles, of course, had been there before, twenty years earlier: *The Magnificent Ambersons* and *Journey into Fear* were shot side-by-side, but then he had the weight and resources of RKO behind him; and *Journey into Fear* was, nominally, at any rate, directed by somebody else.

It is impossible to be certain whether Welles thought he could actually bring this off, and whether it was more than an elaborate ploy. There is no question that he loved *Treasure Island*, as he loved all such stories; it was, indeed, the subject of only the second broadcast of the *Mercury Summer Theatre of the Air* a quarter of a century earlier, one of the most spirited of that great series. 'I don't care how young you are,' says Welles in his irresistible introduction to the programme, 'nothing charms, nothing ingratiates, nothing wins like a one-legged, double-barrelled buccaneer with a ring in his ear, a handkerchief on his head and a knife between his teeth.' Welles then proceeds to play, with timber-shivering relish (if a somewhat indeterminate sense of geography – Essex? Hackney? Nova Scotia?), not only that very same double-barrelled buccaneer but also the cabin-boy Jim Hawkins, an imaginative doubling, which he was not proposing to repeat on film.

The making of the film had every appearance of credibility. There was even a schedule memo for *Treasure Island*, meticulously typed up by Mrs Rogers, which has an unimpeachable air of authority about it:

> *Treasure Island* shoots Oct 5, *Chimes at Midnight* Oct 12. Oct 24th: boat sequence in *Treasure Island* finished. Crew works as 2nd Unit on *Chimes at Midnight*. Nov 26th the 2nd Unit begins shooting *Treasure Island* as well as *Chimes at Midnight*, and the boy playing

> *Jim Hawkins* returns to work. Dec 9th: on this day we begin shooting in Alberque both *Treasure Island* and *Chimes at Midnight* for a period of three days; then on Dec 23rd, 2nd Unit is disbanded. *Chimes at Midnight* is now virtually completed for its principal photography. Four days off, then *Treasure Island* resumes on Dec 27th, for six weeks. After which, pick-up shots for *Chimes at Midnight* in Avila.[12]

Apart from its almost demented ambitiousness, there is a rather serious flaw in this schedule: very few of the actors contracted for *Chimes at Midnight* would be there for longer than a few weeks, and some of them only for a few days. Welles had not in fact mentioned the existence of *Treasure Island* to any of his actors: John Gielgud, who was only available for three weeks, was perfectly innocent of the fact that, as well as King Henry IV, he was slated to play Squire Trelawney; Tony Beckley had no idea that during his four weeks' shooting he was down not just for Poins, but also for the treacherous Israel Hands; nor had Keith Baxter been told that he would be incarnating Squire Livesey. Fernando Rey, playing the Earl of Worcester, may or may not have been informed that he would be making an appearance in Admiral Benbow's Inn. One actor was specifically hired for *Treasure Island* – McIntosh Ferguson, to play Jim Hawkins; there were rumours of the participation of Robert Morley and Hugh Griffith. And there was a director for the film – the second unit director for both films, but with special responsibility for *Treasure Island*. This was Jesús Franco, something of a buccaneer himself, a cinematic jack-of-all-trades who had been a composer, a screenwriter and an assistant director on more than twenty films, before graduating to directing; modelling his output on that of the Hammer House of Horror, he almost immediately scored a hit with *The Awful Dr Orloff*; by the time he encountered Welles he had ten films under his belt, including *Vampiresas*, *Death Whistles the Blues* and *Symphony for a Sadist*; when they met, he and Welles hit it off immediately.

That night Franco read the script Welles had given him; the following day Welles told him he'd reread it and that it was 'junk'. Instead he gave Franco a copy of the novel – 'the best script ever written' – and told him just to go and shoot exteriors. In fact they did considerably more than that: they followed the schedule memo, beginning with all the scenes on board the *Hispañiola* (in reality a boat built for Samuel Bronston's *John Paul Jones* five years earlier). They started with a couple of days at the then barely cultivated

Bay of Calpe near Alicante, including a scene featuring young Fergusin as Jim Hawkins, Beckley as Israel Hands and Welles himself as Silver, but, according to Franco, Welles was nervous of the boat, so in the end it was just Fergusin and Beckley who shot: the material still exists, in sumptuous Technicolor, and is energetic, with Beckley a bearded and wild-eyed Hands, unrecognisable from his slim and sardonic Ned Poins. After the second day, the *Hispañiola* sailed off for a fortnight of location shooting, after which it disappeared into a cinematic Bermuda triangle, taking *Treasure Island* with it. By then the tornado that was *Chimes at Midnight* was blowing at full force, and it never let up till Christmas.

CHAPTER NINETEEN

Fathers and Sons

WELLES NEVER germinated a project more deeply, or over a longer period. *Chimes at Midnight* was, as he told his old friend Alessandro Tasca, the film's executive producer, 'the picture he had in his heart'. From his days at Todd as an infant Reinhardt, to the last days of the Mercury Theatre, to his return to Ireland – that is to say, from *Winter of Discontent* in 1929, to *Five Kings* in 1939, to *Chimes at Midnight* on stage in 1960 – this was the story that, Ancient Mariner-like, he had to tell: the story of a surrogate father and son, of profound friendship and deep rejection, of trust given without qualification and betrayed without sentiment. Welles's story was not merely personal; it embodied, for him, the human situation: above all, it was about mankind's universal and central experience, the loss of innocence. Nothing stirred him, moved him or grieved him more, and he strove, over more than thirty years, to find the perfect form in which to tell that story, a form that could encompass both the personal and the universal. The circumstances in which he filmed were almost perversely difficult (to say nothing of the surreal dimension of the phantom film of *Treasure Island*) and yet for once everything, or nearly everything, worked in his favour. Heart and mind, form and content, casting and location, technology and manpower – all meshed perfectly.

He worked for many months on the screenplay; in the midst of that work, in July of 1964, his former guardian, Dr Maurice Bernstein, died after a fall from a ladder while pruning a tree. They were still in regular contact. Bernstein was one of Welles's two surrogate fathers: since childhood, even before his father's death, Welles had always called him Dadda. Welles's mother had been Bernstein's lover after she broke up from Welles's father, and perhaps even before. Dadda's various ménages were deeply unstable as he moved from mistress to mistress – sometimes, it seemed, for financial rather than erotic or amorous reasons. Money, as it happens, was often a vexed issue between Dadda and Welles: Welles always felt that Dadda had cheated him over his father's inheritance, due when he was twenty-one and never fully paid; once Welles went to Hollywood, Dadda never ceased begging him for financial help (though he was a highly successful physician in Los Angeles), or indeed giving him pointed advice about how he should conduct himself, both professionally and personally. And yet the love Welles felt for him was deep, and when Ann Rogers brought him the news of Dadda's death, he withdrew to a dark room and did not emerge for two days. Strict, fussy, demanding and emotionally invasive, Dadda was nothing like Welles's own father; their relationship was immensely complex. It was Dadda who first attached the dread word 'genius' to the young Orson, who encouraged journalists to write about him, who planted ideas of future greatness in his head; he seems to have been obsessed by the boy, as well as having intensely proprietorial feelings about him. He was both loving and exigent, strict but adoring, a stifling combination containing within it strong elements of emotional blackmail, of love conditional on certain behaviour. And Welles, though diligent about keeping in touch and always punctilious in observing Christmas and birthdays, seems to have experienced claustrophobic feelings around him. And now his grief at Dadda's death was such that he needed to lock himself away in a darkened room.

Welles's feelings for his other surrogate father, Roger – 'Skipper' – Hill, his former headmaster, and the man he always described as having saved him, were far simpler. With his belief that you would only learn from the things you loved doing, Skipper had much more in common with Welles's happy-go-lucky natural father Dick. Welles's relationship with Skipper was utterly straightforward (though Welles once naughtily told him at a public symposium in Los Angeles that 'I was the boy you could have had'). No, they simply loved each other, sustaining each other over the years via long and affectionate telephone calls from wherever in the world Welles might be; this continued till Welles's death. Though Skipper had a high appreciation of Welles's worth, and was full of dreams for the great good that he could do in the world, there was no attempt to pressure him into being professionally ambitious, just simple celebration of his gifts and his achievements. For his part, Welles saw Skipper as a model, a perfectly balanced man, productive, wise and generous; the marriage between Skipper and his wife Hortense was, to Welles, the *beau idéal* of what relationships between men and women should be. They were his family, a source of stability to which he regularly addressed himself.

As for Dick Welles, Welles romanced him into being a dreamer, an inventor, the intimate of artists and statesmen, a man born out of his time – 'My Father Wore Black Spats' is the title of the piece

Welles wrote about him in *Vogue* magazine – but in reality, after his early retirement, he became a full-time hedonist, deeply devoted to the pursuit of pleasure. He gave Welles an education in the pleasures of life – food, drink, travel, girls, entertainment – and loved his boy unconditionally. But his love was not sufficient for Welles, who banished him.

For a while, after the death of Welles's mother Beatrice, and before Dick's gin-sodden demise, these three men – Dadda, Skipper and Dick – took joint responsibility for Welles. It was the formative period of his life, setting up the tensions and contradictions of his future. The feelings he had for these three very different fathers were at the core of his being, and although he always disavowed any autobiographical element in his work, in *Chimes at Midnight* it is unavoidably present.

★

The screenplay completed, Welles was ready to go, firing on all cylinders. Then a small dark cloud on the distant horizon suddenly loomed very large, threatening to engulf the project. *Mr Arkadin* had had a disastrous commercial history in Spain and in Britain, where, in a version without flashbacks, it had changed its name to *Confidential Report*; it another version it had been seen, without great enthusiasm, in Cannes and in Germany. As far as America was concerned, the putative distribution company gave up trying to release the film there. In the wake of that failure, in September 1961 Louis Dolivet, or rather Filmorsa, had filed a suit against Welles for breach of contract and unprofessional behaviour, including 'unskilful and inefficient performance of duties' during filming:

> Defendant attended night clubs almost every night and consistently reported late for work. This caused regular shooting schedules to be abandoned. The defendant did not restrict his drinking to night clubs. On a number of occasions he appeared on the set in an intoxicated condition and on some occasions brought liquor with him onto the set.[1]

The damages claimed were $750,000. Welles rebutted the charges, claiming they employed 'blunderbuss, catch-all phraseology, naked generalizations, unsupported inferences and patent irrelevancies'. The case rumbled on inconclusively. Finally, in October 1962, the film reached America, in a provisional version that closed almost as soon as it had opened. There was a legal lull, and then in June 1964 a pre-trial hearing of *Filmorsa v. Orson Welles* was announced. The case, already widely reported in the newspapers,[2] wasn't going to go away. The consequences of this were likely to be disastrous for Welles.

On 2 September, 1964, two weeks before Welles began to shoot *Chimes at Midnight*, he wrote Dolivet an abject letter. 'Dear Louis,' it began, 'this is written to a very successful man by one who is close to being a failure.' He reviewed his melancholy situation, earning his living as an actor, doing only what he calls 'occasional bits', the special appearances of which he reckons he has played four in the previous ten years. His last full-length part was in 1959 (in *Compulsion*). But acting is not his proper job. 'I call myself a director.' As a director he has directed only two pictures since 1954, an average, he notes, of one picture every five years. "I'm hanging on by my fingers, and I don't think I could survive another failure," he says. "If I had to return to New York I would fall into their hands; there would be no escape."

He tells Dolivet that he is – 'frankly' – desperate. 'The slightest bad publicity – the vaguest hint of trouble in America' – will wreck the Spanish picture deal that has taken so long to put together.

> At my age – and with all the years of failure behind me – this could well be my last real chance. Louis, if you don't call it off this lawsuit will ruin me.

All begging letters, he says, are shameless, so he regrets that he has to invoke the name of their old, close friendship. 'I do wish,' he ends, 'that I were the one who could give proof of the loyalty of an old friendship, instead of having to ask for it.'

It worked; Dolivet must have been touched by Welles's letter, or perhaps he felt that, finally, he had made his point. On 10 September he replied to Welles to tell him that he would call off the lawsuit; the next day, Dolivet wrote to his lawyers to that effect. Welles generally preferred not to talk about *Mr Arkadin*; sad though its failure was, perhaps even sadder from Welles's point of view was the failure of his relationship with Dolivet, who, having known nothing about film production before he met Welles, had gone on, very successfully, to produce Jacques Tati's inspired *Mon Oncle*. Welles had been perfectly happy to accept Dolivet as his political mentor, but could not tolerate him as his producer. Another road not taken; another potential partnership bust. Meanwhile, *Chimes at Midnight* was safe.

★

The screenplay with which they started filming in October 1964 was a distillation of everything Welles had learned about the plays and about the characters over the years, but it had taken on a new colour. The final version of *Chimes at Midnight* on stage in Dublin traced the arc of *Henry IV*, *Parts One* and *Two*: Act One moving from the explosive energy of the angry barons, through the chivalric splendour of Hotspur's challenge and culminating in the King's mastery of the situation, as Falstaff and Hal dance the antic hay; Act Two, by contrast, showing the slow physical decline of both Falstaff and the King, as the political situation becomes ever more mired in a brutal war of attrition, until Hal is finally ready to rule as Henry V. The stage show concluded, as the film does, with the scene from *Henry V* in which Falstaff's followers ponder his death, and the death of everything he represented. Welles's screenplay begins, not with death itself, but with intimations of mortality, a sequence that sets the tone for the entire film. It features a snippet from a scene in *Part Two* of *Henry IV* in which three very old gentlemen, Justices Shallow and Silence and Sir John Falstaff, pad through the snow, ruminating as they go on the passing of time. Falstaff, in particular, descends into a pit of melancholy, the word 'old' tolling mournfully through the scene: 'Old, old, Master Shallow.' Welles speaks the title-line of the film – 'we have heard the chimes at midnight, Master Shallow' – in no spirit of nostalgia, but as if describing funeral bells.

It is a remarkable start to the film, effective and affecting, and it is very different from the dynamic way in which both *Five Kings* and the Irish *Chimes at Midnight* had begun. It starts with a dying fall, swiftly succeeded in the screenplay by the braying of trumpets and the thunder of hooves, but from the very start it sets a potent tone of lament, and – joyous though the film often is – it is the lamentation that lingers. This will be a film about age and about loss and about the passage of time. It is noteworthy that Welles sets it in winter, to compound all these things: Shakespeare's scene is set in high summer ('it is hot, Master Shallow'). In Dublin they had tried many alternative openings, including beginning with the scene that ends the film, 'Falstaff is dead . . . the king has killed his heart.' Had Welles started the film that way, it would have had Wellesian form: both *Kane* and *Othello* start at the end, as, arguably, does *Mr Arkadin*. But opening with Falstaff's death would have made the film all about Falstaff; as it stands, it is about much bigger things than the death of one man. The stage version was skilfully but linearly done, with due respect for Shakespeare's progression of the action.

In the screenplay Welles goes to work with a vengeance with the scissors and paste, snipping a line here and a line there, redistributing speeches, conflating characters, taking *Parts One* and *Two* of the play and shuffling them up like a deck of cards; it is quite brilliantly done, a collage of genius, kaleidoscopic in its portrayal of the characters, their world and the actions in which they are involved; with his strong musical instinct, Welles rearranges the text into an endlessly varying pattern of ensembles, arias, duets, trios and quartets, which form a through-composed whole. It is also quintessentially filmic, never still, ever-moving, breathing, changing direction.

For it to work, Welles needed skilled, nimble, flexible actors, and he could scarcely have improved the cast he had assembled. Securing John Gielgud was a great coup, though in fact his career on stage was at something of a low ebb, and his film career had not yet fully established itself. Two years earlier he had had a spectacular flop on stage as Othello, in an over-designed and under-imagined production by Franco Zeffirelli; on the other hand, his one-man show *The Ages of Man* had confirmed him, if any confirmation were needed, as the outstanding living speaker of Shakespeare. What people were perhaps beginning to forget was the brilliance of his conception and interpretation of character – his Hamlet, Cassius, Prospero, Lear, Angelo, Richard II, to name a handful, were all as psychologically acute as they were beautifully spoken. Henry IV, line for line and scene for scene, is one of the greatest of Shakespearean roles, but it is rarely attempted by a great actor because the King disappears from the play for long sections of the action; this is to be regretted, because the success of the play (and the success of Welles's screenplay) is entirely dependent on the three-way transaction between King, Hal and Falstaff; if the King is dull or blustery or commonplace, there is no contest and it is impossible to rejoice at Hal's growth to authority. Gielgud inhabits the part with a seething inner energy, extraordinary emotional intensity and a flawless command of the King's volatility; it was – of all people – Lee Strasberg, high priest of the Method, evangelist of content over form, who said that when he saw Gielgud acting, he heard Shakespeare think; and if ever a demonstration of this uncommon capacity were required, here it is, preserved for all time. Indeed, one has the unnerving sensation that he might be making it up. But he isn't; every word, every syllable is perfectly placed. On his first day of filming Gielgud was called on to speak the famous speech that ends 'Uneasy lies the head that wears a crown' in a single shot, on two cameras, which he did on the first take and without rehearsals, crying out triumphantly, 'I said all the words in the right order!'

Hal, of course, was Keith Baxter, whose irresistible élan is utterly natural and spontaneous, and his Celtic relish of language delicious; but the watchful, mindful brain is always there at work, underneath all the youthful charm. The deep brilliance of the performance is rooted in his off-screen relationship with his two fathers in the film. Baxter idolised Gielgud as an actor, and their dealings with each other on screen are coloured by that: Gielgud is Baxter's father-in-acting, and this informs Hal's growing understanding and admiration of his father's qualities; he hangs on his every word. With Falstaff, his experience of playing the role on stage with Welles, and their private friendship, give Baxter great freedom with him, both physically and mentally. The playfulness and tactility are clearly liberating for Welles too, who is rarely seen getting involved in actual bodily contact with male actors: here the horseplay and the sheer affection are human, warm, unforced, and the rejection of Falstaff palpably upsetting, both for Hal and for Baxter. Occasionally, off-screen or off-stage factors colour a performance, not necessarily for the better; in this case they immeasurably enrich the film. The tug-of-war between the central trio is manifest.

For the rest, Welles gathered around him a choice selection of actors who were both vivid and experienced and created amongst themselves, however briefly they might have been on board, a sense of company: Alan Webb, whom Welles had directed in *Rhinoceros*, was a reedy, sharp-nosed Shallow; Norman Rodway, a brilliant new young Irish actor, witty and eruptive as Hotspur; Michael Aldridge, a West End stalwart, displayed unexpected fantasy and extravagance as Pistol; Tony Beckley, straight from the nascent RSC, was dark and sour as Poins; Andrew Faulds, soon to be a Labour MP, played the part of the Earl of Westmoreland, to which he brought the vigour and barely masked aggression that his opponents in the House of Commons later came to fear. Then there was Jeanne Moreau, enchanted by Welles, as were some women whom he didn't personally desire – Marlene Dietrich was another – here seemingly much more at ease than in *The Trial*, a credible and genuinely sexy tart at the Boar's Head, deeply touching in her devotion to Falstaff; and Margaret Rutherford as Mistress Quickly, as unlikely a whore-mistress as could be found on the face of the planet, and one, moreover, endowed with an inexplicable and freely roaming Irish accent, but who is somehow perfectly and properly at home in Welles's Merrie England.

Two of the aristocracy were played by Spaniards, and Hotspur's

Welsh wife was Franco-Russian (Marina Vlady, very successfully dubbed). Falstaff's witty little page was Welles's nine-year-old daughter, Beatrice. Apart from Baxter, the only other survivor from the Irish *Chimes at Midnight* was Paddy Bedford, nominally playing Bardolph, but disappointingly without Bardolph's single most notable characteristic, his incandescent nose. A final piece of casting was Hilton Edwards as Justice Silence. Right at the beginning of shooting, Edwards succumbed to influenza and begged to be allowed to withdraw from the film, to which Welles agreed without argument, no doubt conscious that his reasons for wanting to be released were as much emotional as physical: nothing had been resolved between Welles and his old colleagues on the financial front, and a bad taste still lingered. MacLiammóir, in particular, was implacable, despite the transformation of his professional life and financial situation with the triumphant premiere, just six months after the end of the run of *Chimes at Midnight*, of his one-man show, *The Importance of Being Oscar*, directed by Edwards, which became a huge international hit. Dublin Gate Productions, of which Welles was still theoretically a board member, was now solvent at last, but Orson Welles was no part of its plan for the future.

When Edwards left the film, a panic to cast Silence then ensued. Marlene Dietrich was roped in to find someone from among her vast acquaintance, but she failed to come up with anyone; then Welles had a sudden inspiration: the distinguished Anglo-American actor Ernest Milton, acclaimed as the Hamlet of his generation and now, at seventy-five, in semi-retirement. Somehow Welles got hold of his number and booked a call to England; he and his fellow-actors, according to Michael Aldridge, gathered around the phone in the local Spanish post office until eventually they heard Milton's telephone being lifted. 'I have a person-to-person call for Mr Ernest Milton from Mr Orson Welles in Spain,' said the operator. There was a pause. Then they heard Milton's extraordinary fluting voice: 'I don't want to speak to him,' after which the receiver went down.[4] The explanation for this brush-off lies in a now quite widely circulated BBC interview on the subject of *Hamlet*, which Welles had given a year earlier to the ever-supportive Huw Wheldon.[5] It was a three-way conversation between Welles, Peter O'Toole (who was then playing the part at the new National Theatre) and, theoretically, Milton. O'Toole and Welles hit it off wonderfully, roaring appreciatively at each other's gags and nodding sagely at each other's aperçus and barely acknowledging Milton's existence, when he attempted to express his reflections on a lifetime's experience of doing the play.

His observations, full of poetic locutions and quivering sensibility, must indeed have seemed hopelessly old-fashioned to O'Toole and Welles in 1963; but heard now, they have a fragile imaginative intensity which you would have to go many miles to see on any stage today. Milton looks increasingly battered by the discourtesy of his fellow-actors; Welles, in particular, keeps his shoulder firmly turned away from him. This was so striking that there was critical comment the following day from television reviewers. It would seem that Welles was simply over-excited by the youthful O'Toole; he was now more and more engaged by the rising generation of actors, keen to work with them, to be associated with them. Despite his bulk, he was feeling revitalised, his appetite for directing and acting renewed. Hope was in the air.

Whatever the reason for the brush-off, the result was that the world was denied Ernest Milton's Silence. Prompted by Paola, Welles eventually offered the part to the very high-profile Italian actor Walter Chiari – leading light of the *dolce vita* crowd in Rome, erstwhile star of *Bonjour Tristesse* and *The Little Hut*, lover of Ava Gardner and fluent and witty English-speaker. Welles seems to have taken against him immediately, until one lunchtime Chiari told a story featuring a man with a stutter. Welles immediately saw the possibilities of the stutter for Silence; thereafter Chiari never finished a line in the part – a brilliant idea that brings forth an exquisitely lugubrious performance from him, a man doomed to be unheard.

This initial hostility towards Chiari, not unconnected with his Via Veneto glamour and his egregious reputation as a ladies' man, was rare; the other actors on the film unanimously reported Welles's benevolence, energy, sheer sense of fun. 'Working with him,' said Margaret Rutherford, 'is like walking where there's only sunshine.'[6] Alan Webb was astonished that Welles even stuck on his false nose for him. 'He wanted to do everything,' reported Michael Aldridge. 'We re-designed my costume together. He's the only film director I know who knows how to deal with actors.'[7] Amongst other things, Welles knew – he, of all people, knew – the importance of lunch. When the break was due, said Jeremy Rowe, playing Prince John of Lancaster, Welles would always appear, 'personally and proudly', with a trolley laden with food for the cast, chosen by him.[8] At the end of the longest day he would travel miles on the promise of a good meal. One night the dialogue director, Michael Knox, told him about a restaurant of which he had heard good reports. It was seventy miles from where they were staying in Pamplona, but Welles would not be deterred. Along steep, winding paths they chugged for over four hours; when they finally reached the restaurant, it was closed. Knox miraculously found another, which opened specially for Welles, because they recognised him. They stayed till the small hours of the morning. 'This restaurant saved your ass, boy,' growled Welles.[9]

His greed for food was identical to his appetite for work; in the famous words of Théophile Gauthier, he was a man for whom the visible world existed. Pierre Billard came to watch the filming and saw how powerfully Welles responded to his surroundings, the ancient buildings, the landscape – and the actors. 'This verve, and this gluttonous appetite for effects, are characteristic of Welles as he rediscovers the delights of creation. Tireless on the set, he moves about with disconcerting agility, even in the bulky padding which he wears for Falstaff's girth, and develops his *mis-en-scène* as changes of lighting bring him new ideas.'[10] Norman Rodway remarked that he seemed to carry the whole film in his head. 'Or he'd say, "Follow me, I'm looking for a shot" and improvise from there.' But for Welles, directing was by no means a solitary activity. Juan Cobós, his assistant on *Chimes*, noted that once the actors' basic positions had been established, he would ask them again and again whether they were comfortable with their movements, 'and all their ideas about what is more or less natural are listened to and discussed'.[11] This combination of freedom and a sense of participation in the final result was particularly liberating for Gielgud, who, with his teeming imagination, had never felt entirely comfortable within the storyboarded confines of most filming. Welles removed any sense of pressure from him, encouraging him in his own ideas, with which he was notoriously fecund. Thirty years later, by which time he was a major film star, Gielgud recollected his time on *Chimes at Midnight* as the most enjoyable he'd ever spent on a film.[12] Welles invited the actors to see the rushes every night after filming: there would be wine, the rushes would be shown and discussion ensued. 'There was no mystique,' wrote Keith Baxter. '"Film-making is so boring!" he'd cry, "come on, let's have some fun!"'[13]

Above all, Welles created energy on the set, and for that alone, actors – who spend so much of their time on a movie repining in limbo – were deeply grateful. 'He had a pressing, physical need not to waste time or energy,' wrote Cobós in *Cahiers du Cinéma* shortly after filming had come to an end:

> His speed was literally alarming. As they followed Welles on his swift traversal of the woods of Castille, the large team assembled

> by the producer looked more like people making a documentary than a complex, serious film. No sooner had Welles shouted 'That's it! That's the one!' than he was moving the camera to the next position.[14]

This is what Welles adored: the gallant, the democratic, the all-in-it-together, the romantic way, which he had tried to create in the theatre (with sometimes inspired results) and hoped to be able to bring to film-making, a medium which, because of the large sums of money involved, almost immediately lost its playfulness, its innocence. The idea of innocence is at the heart of *Chimes at Midnight*, and innocence is what Welles was trying to restore to the process of making movies. For that to happen, everyone had to go along with it, willingly endorsing his assumption of the role of the crazy captain of a mad enterprise. You don't question the captain, you commit to him, and then he's the best person on earth. But if you don't commit, then he's stranded – it won't work, he loses confidence, becomes grumpy, difficult and not very good; this is what happened on *Mr Arkadin*. Believe in him, on the other hand, and Welles is everything you want him to be, and more.

And he made sure that on *Chimes at Midnight* he was surrounded by believers: his baby producer, Emiliano Piedra, who sometimes put his foot down – 'shoot everything you want to shoot on Friday and Saturday, Orson, because on Sunday I'm taking the set down' – but who had absolute faith in the film; Alessandro Tasca di Cutò, the Sicilian prince who was his executive producer and, in some way mysterious to both men, his blood-brother; Edmond Richard, the director of photography, able effortlessly to translate Welles's every impulse into practice; Juan Cobós, attentive to his needs and inventive in dealing with them; Jesús Franco, who after *Treasure Island* had sunk without trace, made his second unit a swift and effective adjunct to *Chimes*; Mrs Rogers, impeccable, untiring, utterly devoted, typing out the twenty-fifth, the thirty-seventh, the fifty-fifth version of the screenplay; Mickey Knox, the dialogue director, whom Welles had given the job because when they were working together on *Marco Polo* he had told Welles after a take, 'You did it better on the first take,' and explained why; Billy Chappell, veteran of *Moby-Dick* and *The Trial*, who could whip a random group of actors into crack movers at a second's notice.

'We few, we happy few, we band of brothers' – that might have been the epigraph for Welles's filming; these were the conditions in which he wanted to work; the only ones, indeed, in which he could work: no studio Big Brother peering over your shoulder, no union regulations, no bossy technicians telling you what you can and can't do, no pompous stars demanding trailers and billing – nobody saying 'no'. The band of brothers put up with a lot on *Chimes at Midnight*: there was throughout an absence of lavatories, 'so one walked into piles of shit on every corner,' said an uncomplaining Gielgud,[15] just as earlier, as reported by Keith Baxter, he had responded with equanimity (quickly developing into positive enthusiasm) to the discovery that the only costumes available had been discarded from other movies: 'These tights are a bit smelly,' says Gielgud. 'Maybe it's just mildew. Shall I catch something from them? I've never had Spanish Fly and I don't want Spanish Crabs. I've always had good legs. Larry's are spindly, but he has hair. How do I look?' Baxter convinced Gielgud that the lack of armour was a profound statement on Welles's part: the King, Baxter reasoned, was an ascetic who had already renounced all the vanities of this world, even armour. For himself he assembled, out of a skip somehow purloined from the Samuel Bronston Company, an ensemble consisting of knitted chain-mail tights and a suede jerkin worn by Jayne Mansfield in *The Sheriff of Fractured Jaw*, embroidered with piping from the harness on Stephen Boyd's horse's from *The Fall of the Roman Empire*.[16] The weather was bitter, especially when they were filming in the ruined abbey of Cardona. 'There was no glass in the windows and the November air poured in,' said Gielgud in an interview. 'I was wearing tights and a dressing gown and practically nothing else for my death scene. I would sit on my throne with a tiny electric fire to warm my feet while Orson spent his last pesetas sending out to buy brandy to keep me going.'[17]

They worked mad hours. Andrew Faulds, playing Westmoreland, was appalled by the clear flouting of Equity rules, but by the end, when they ran out of time, he told Baxter: 'Tell Orson I'll come back; I don't even have to be paid.' They needed to be on their toes, because if the perfect location and light for a particular sequence suddenly materialised, Welles would seize the moment, abandoning what he was doing. They took the entire wardrobe for the film with them to every location, in case inspiration struck. On one occasion they were in the middle of shooting the Gadshill robbery scene, when Welles suddenly announced that they would shoot the extraordinary scene in which Hal tells his buddy Poins, 'My heart bleeds inwardly that my father is so sick: and keeping such vile company as thou art hath in reason taken from me all ostentation of sorrow . . . what wouldst thou think of me, if I should weep?' To which

Poins replies, 'I would think thee a most princely hypocrite.' Welles had always seen the scene played, he said, on water, but the location they had found had become unavailable at the last moment, so he shot something else. Now, on this early November morning, shooting the immensely complex Gadshill robbery scene in a huge park in the centre of Madrid, inspiration suddenly struck. 'There is in the middle of the Casa de Campo,' recalled Keith Baxter:

> a perfectly horrible boating lake and it is only this deep if that, and it's bounded by a road, a public road which cars flash past, but this was November and it was about nine in the morning and there was a mist and you couldn't see where the water stopped and the sky began. 'We have two minutes to shoot this, Keith,' he said, 'Sit on that wall.' I said, 'I hope I remember it.' 'We will have somebody shouting the lines,' he said.[18]

The relevant costumes were swiftly summoned and the actors thrown into them, and in two minutes the scene was done. It betrays no hint of the madness of the circumstances of the shooting: it is an impeccable, idyllic vision against which the bitter, tense scene plays. It is another of Welles's miraculous conjuring tricks, a perfect demonstration of his conviction that a scene should start with the bare minimum. 'Poetry suggests things that are absent, it evokes more than what you see,' he told *Cahiers du Cinéma* in 1967, apropos of *Chimes at Midnight*. 'And the danger in cinema is that, in using a camera, you see everything, everything is there. What one must do is succeed in evoking, in making things emerge that are not, in fact, visible, in bringing about a spell.'[19] Not for the first time, he echoes his friend Jean Cocteau – not someone with whose work Welles's is often compared. Cocteau's great watchword, 'I am a lie that tells the truth', could have been Welles's own motto. He never took the easy way out, the literal way. He had so few opportunities to make films that he determined to make every moment, every scene he ever shot, creative – poetic – in some measure.

Welles's unceasing stimulation of energy and imagination was all the more remarkable in that he was not in good health. Gielgud, ever observant, despite the unstopping cascade of words emerging from his mouth, noted that Welles was suffering from eczema and couldn't wash his hands; Jeremy Rowe observed that he had a gall-bladder condition, which was deeply uncomfortable. Both of these conditions were associated with, if not caused by, his now monumental girth. Welles was, on and off during the course of shooting, on a diet, but it was a delusory one. Paola would prepare healthy, simple dishes for him for the following day, putting them in the refrigerator at night, but in the small hours of the morning, reported Billy Chappell, whose room was between Welles's bedroom and the kitchen, Welles would pad back and forth, till by dawn the fridge was empty. At lunchtime Welles's plate was always piled high, filled with the finest delicacies, and when he had finished, 'not only would he have seconds,' reported Jeremy Rowe, 'but he would routinely push the left-overs from his crew and cast's plates onto his own'. It is hard to disagree with Rowe's conclusion that 'he was trying to feed something which can't be fed; he ate to stifle his insecurities'.[20]

Those insecurities were real enough: Welles was particularly anxious about working with Gielgud. 'Do you think John will think me a fool?' he asked Baxter, before Gielgud arrived. 'No actor can touch him in Shakespeare. I don't want him to think me just a trickster.'[21] But Gielgud adored working with Welles: 'such wonderful fun,' he said forty years later. The unprecedented pleasure he took in filming with Welles led him to suggest other projects on which they might work. They tried to buy the rights to *Death in Venice*, but they had already been taken; next, Gielgud proposed *The Tempest* to Welles, having for many years been obsessed by trying to film the play. Gielgud would of course have been Prospero, with Welles as Caliban, and Benjamin Britten was to have written the music. 'I was enormously impressed and fascinated by his talent as a director,' Gielgud wrote to Britten after *Chimes at Midnight*, 'even more in working with him than when I had seen his work on screen.'[22] Among Welles's countless fleeting projects that came to naught, this is one to regret bitterly.

Such was Welles's insecurity in front of his fellow-actors that, whenever he could, he avoided being filmed with them, preferring once again – as he had done on all his films since *Othello* – to shoot as much of his part as possible in single shots after they had all departed. Edmond Richard described to François Thomas how, even then, Welles had to have his lines chalked up on a blackboard. 'He had a very elegant way of looking into the wings, as it were, to see the line.'[23] Jeanne Moreau quickly became aware of Welles's reluctance to play the part. Having waited two or three days to do a certain scene with him, she eventually asked why they were waiting. 'My little make-up suitcase is lost,' he said. 'I can't do any scenes till it's found. We'll start with the reverse shots of you, the close-ups.' The next day she spotted the errant make-up kit hidden under a settee. 'Oh look!' she shrieked. 'Don't say it,' hissed the make-up assistant. 'He has stage-fright. He hid it himself.' When they got to the scene in which Doll jumps up and down on Falstaff in the bed, she rehearsed it with another actor; Welles finally installed himself on the bed for the take, but when Moreau leaped onto him, he shouted, 'Cut, cut, you've destroyed my nose – we can't shoot this scene today.'[24]

As a director, on the other hand, he was absolutely confident and free. His constant improvisations on the set were only possible because he had planned it all so carefully. He decided that the film should have the texture of a woodcut (as it happens, when the film was released in England at the Academy, the leading art-house cinema of the time, the poster consisted of a superb woodcut of Welles); to achieve that texture, he used red and blue filters, and had the wood on the set darkened with a blowtorch. The light source, Thomas observes, is often given prominence, magnified by mirrors, 'concentrated into a single ray filled with aluminium powder' – all done, then, quite literally with smoke and mirrors. Welles himself designed and personally supervised the construction of a model of the Boar's Head Tavern, Falstaff's centre of operations; Richard and the crew were more than a little sceptical about its usefulness, but it turned out that Welles had calculated every angle, every entrance, for specific effects. 'He'd visualised the whole thing in his head. And everything was in forced perspective; every entrance and exit was trapezoidal.'[25] Like everything in all of Welles's films, it was a trick; even the height of the tables in the tavern was cheated. The difference is that in *Chimes at Midnight* Welles takes pains to conceal the trick: there is very little *Shazam!* about the film, in which – as in *The Magnificent Ambersons*, but rarely in the rest of his work – he eschews stylisation, not interposing himself between the spectator and the film by conscious distortion. It seems to unfold naturally and humanly, though in fact this naturalness was achieved by an infinity of ingenious devices on the part of Welles and his associates; for once, he chooses to use art to conceal art.

Of no part of the film was this more true than the great battle sequence, which is a miracle of cutting and pasting, of cheating and faking, but whose effect is of a fierce and sickening verisimilitude, making Olivier's Agincourt and even Eisenstein's Battle on the Ice, by which Olivier was so obviously inspired, seem like something of a tea party by comparison, tame and almost balletic. Welles knew he only had the use of the Casa del Campo in the centre of Madrid for a few days, and 150 Spanish cavalrymen for even less – for a single day, in fact – so he planned it in great detail, to make sure he would have enough material for the four sections of the battle that Thomas says he had identified: slow and tense beginning, brutal and ever-accelerating battle, one-to-one combat, and aftermath. Most unusually for him, Welles storyboarded the whole sequence, to make the framings he wanted clear to the whole camera crew.

It was deepest November, and the weather was filthy. Welles had already lined up smoke and wind machines; as the rain fell more and more heavily, he had the fire brigade, which was standing by, turn their hoses on the soil to generate even more mud. He used three hand-held cameras to cover the action, plus another on a crane; according to Edmond Richard, they changed the speed of the film as they shot. 'To give the fake clubs some weight, we slowed the film down; as the horses entered we speeded up.' The proximity of the horses made it very dangerous. Richard got hit by a flying hoof and was taken to hospital 'pissing blood', as he said;[26] Welles took over his camera. No time for sentimentality: *carpe diem* was the motto. Falstaff is of course at the centre of the battle, or rather he does everything he can to absent himself from the centre, comically avoiding engagement whenever possible, weaving in and out of the hurly-burly like a great big ball in the middle of a rugby scrum; needless to say, it was never Welles in the armour, always an extra (rather nimbler than Welles, in fact). Conscious of time and the brief opportunity he had to use the extras playing the rival armies, Welles raged and roared, riling everyone; when the pressure got too great, Richard would get his gaffer to fake a short-circuit, which calmed everyone down for a little while.

The huge mass of material they shot that November of 1964, plus some later pickups made early the following year, was toiled over unceasingly by Welles, even before filming was complete, and drove the editorial team, headed by Fred Muller, his editor on *The Trial*, to the point of collapse – in Muller's case, beyond it; Welles had literally to pick him up off the floor and carry him downstairs. On this extremely raw material – 'you can't imagine . . . how sad the beginning and end of each shot was,' Welles told Leslie Megahey, 'pitiful in all the wrong senses of the word. Showing a lot of tired gypsy extras turning around, wondering where they were gonna eat'[27] – Welles worked, demonically possessed, day and night, to create a wholly original texture and rhythm for the sequence, a fluidity and an instability created by speeding up and slowing down the film, excising every other frame, using the tiniest fragments of the footage, introduced almost subliminally. This, as Welles so often said, is where the film was made. It was crucial for the story he wanted to tell that the duel that results in the death of Hotspur should signal the end of the chivalric age, and the subsequent battle the beginning of the modern – the end, of heroism, of honour, of dignity, of Merrie England, in fact. Welles's Battle of Shrewsbury is thus deliberately and consciously anachronistic, owing as much to Mons as it does to the medieval period: it is muddy, messy, bloody, at times farcical, but ultimately tragic. How, one feels at the end, can England – the world, indeed – ever recover from this ugly slaughter? While editing, he listened to medieval music to shape his sense of the film, and Francesco Lavagnino, with whom he had worked so successfully on *Othello*, supplied a splendidly sturdy score, which Welles treated with his usual freedom, as on *Othello* and equally effectively, speeding it up, cutting it down, stringing random bits together.

He left shooting the denouement of the film till last, laying the crew off before Christmas 1964 and resuming with a much-slimmed-down crew in late January 1965 until March. Of the leading actors, only Keith Baxter was retained, and the end of filming was an emotional business for both men. Edmond Richard reports that when they shot Hal's coronation, Welles was exhausted, having sprained his ankle in the dance scene in the tavern. 'He'd lived his film, and when we saw him come into the church, throw himself at the feet of the new king, and be rejected by him, the whole set wept. We'd seen the guy emptied out. He'd given everything he had to give, he'd lived the character.'[28] As well as the end of the story, it was the core of Welles's performance, the re-enactment of the great betrayal that, in *King Henry IV, Parts One* and *Two*, comes twice: the first time as farce, the second as tragedy. It is unquestionably the most personal performance Welles ever gave, in the most personal film he ever made. Paradoxically, it is also the one he least dominates.

Falstaff, unlike every other character he ever played, is essentially reactive: throughout the action (in Welles's version of the story) he is a satellite to Hal's star; he is also – again, in Welles's version – in physical decline. Despite the astounding brilliance of the battle sequence, and indeed of much of the film, one is not conscious of the directorial presence imposing itself on the material. In this film, though as usual Welles dubs several of the characters, it is subtly and delicately done, so that only the closest scrutiny can detect it: it is not part of the expressive gesture of the piece that we should identify the voices as Welles's, as it seems to be in *The Trial*. He doesn't even narrate the film himself, instead importing the ripely eccentric voice of Ralph Richardson, who becomes a character in his own right – the chronicler Holinshed. The film permits of more perspectives than Welles's movies habitually do; it is, in Leo Braudy's terminology, a more open film than Welles was wont to make, and therefore, perhaps, a more Shakespearean one than his versions of either *Macbeth* or *Othello.* The characters seem to live their own lives, breathe their own breath, independently of the concept of the film. Its theatricality, which is all-pervading, is entirely cinematic – that is to say, the camera participates in the theatricality of the protagonists, but does not present it to the audience. We are drawn into the game-playing world of these people, not expected to applaud it.

Out of impossibly skimpy materials, Welles has created an entirely and consistently credible world. The epitome of this is his magicking, out of the three remaining walls of the abbey at Cardona, the church in which the coronation takes place. It appears massive and solid, a result of superb lighting and a feeling of perpendicularity evoked by the shafts of the crowd's banners. It is a consummate work of craftsmanship: apart from anything else, on the strength of it alone Welles deserves to be known as one of the greatest set decorators film has ever known. His formidable technical brilliance is entirely at the disposal of the material, of this story he so deeply wanted to tell.

As for his own performance, it is inarguably one of the finest things – if not *the* finest thing – he ever did as an actor. *Qua* Shakespeare, it is, to put it mildly, a remarkably personal conception of Falstaff. On the face of it, Falstaff is a slumming aristocrat who knows no shame, a drunk and a gourmandiser, who believes that the world owes him a living, who has had the extraordinary good fortune to fall in with the heir to the throne, and who leads for a while a charmed existence as a result. Behind this engaging rogue seems to lie a much bigger figure. His titanic energy and majestic self-confidence put him in the realm of myth, allying him to characters like the Greek satyr Silenus and the Egyptian god Bes, prodigious imbibers who act as tutors to young gods (Dionysus, in the case of Silenus) and who are summarily discarded when the god (or sometimes the king) matures and has no further need of them. But a strong and, to some scholars, compelling connection has also been made between Falstaff and the figure of the Vice, the devil's emissary, in the medieval morality plays. It is therefore an astonishing leap for Welles to have decided that Falstaff is essentially benevolent, telling Kenneth Tynan that he was 'the only great character in dramatic literature who is also good'. Pressed by Tynan, he agrees with Auden's even more extreme view that Falstaff was a Christ-figure. Later in the interview Welles describes him as 'the prince's spiritual father, who is a kind of secular saint'.[29] This is remarkably counter-intuitive stuff. In fact, Welles does not appear to play Falstaff as either saintly or even especially good. He does, however, play him as sweet and tender, in relation both to his regular whore, Doll Tearsheet, and, of course, to young Hal, whom he pretty well idolises (though he is not above insulting him behind his back and deploring his lack of honesty). It is love – Falstaff's love of Hal – that is, for Welles, at the centre of the man; and it is love that sanctifies him. Like the woman taken in sin in St Luke's Gospel, Falstaff's sins are forgiven him, because he has loved.

It is incontestably one of Welles's very best, richest, most detailed, most human performances; whether it is strictly Shakespeare's Falstaff is neither here nor there. It is also patently autobiographical. 'Falstaff has to live by his wits, he has to be funny,' as Keith Baxter observed. 'He hasn't a place to sleep if he doesn't get a laugh out of his patron.' Welles often despairingly referred to his obligation to go through what he called his Dancing Bear routine – the all-singing, all-laughing, all-dancing Orson Welles routine – if he was to be allowed to make a film. Baxter made it explicit: 'There are many things of which Falstaff is culpable of which you could not accuse Welles. His terrible betrayal and dishonesty, which was not true of Orson. But Falstaff needed to duck and dive and to scheme and to plan and always living on the edge of no money at all – but being adored. That's very much Welles.'[30] His Falstaff is a self-portrait, both justification and apologia: greed sanctified, mendacity hallowed, rascality blessed; he is both child and fallen monarch, an exiled citizen of Eden. He is life, he is laughter, he knows no laws, he bows to no king. He is playfulness incarnate; he liberates us all from our straitjackets. He is indispensable. 'Banish Jack, and banish all the world.'

Over and beyond that is the question of betrayal. If, as Welles claimed, he bore all his life the guilt of having let his father die alone and in despair, then perhaps there is something in the unexpected way in which Welles's Falstaff seems to accept, maybe even to embrace, his punishment at the hands of the young King that suggests acceptance of some sort of sacrificial role, as proposed by Auden.[31] This same emphasis on Falstaff's goodness in Welles's performance sometimes robs the character's pithy and often savage utterances of their force. The famous speech in which Falstaff deconstructs the notion of honour, denuding it of its fabled majesty

– 'what is honour? . . . can it set to a leg? No. Or an arm? No. Or take away the grief of a wound? No' – is spoken by Welles in a vein of reflective and rather rueful irony. Many of the speeches with which, in Belfast and Dublin, he had amused and provoked the audience, his legs dangling raffishly over the edge of the stage, are, in the film, given rather inward performances, often as muttered soliloquies rather than as bitter or profane jokes. It is a somewhat sanitised, slightly subdued Falstaff, though superb in melancholy and deeply poignant in rejection. Falstaff's deluded assurance to his companions after being dismissed – 'I shall be sent for soon. At night' – one of the most heartbreaking lines even Shakespeare ever wrote, is deeply, personally upsetting, in a way that Welles's performances rarely are.

It is interesting that, in speaking of the film to Leslie Megahey, Welles again used religious terminology: 'If I wanted to get into heaven on the basis of one movie, that's the one I would offer up.'[32] But maybe that is just another way of saying what Sandro Tasca said of it: 'it was the picture he had in his heart.'

CHAPTER TWENTY

Genius Without Portfolio

WELLES HAD been cutting the film from the first day of shooting. *Chimes at Midnight* is the most tightly edited of all his films. As he cut tighter and tighter, he was in danger of making it incomprehensible. 'One day in the lift,' reported Tasca, 'he talked to me about a scene he had been editing for two days; then he concluded: "I want to shorten it." I replied: "If you keep shortening it, you will be the only person who understands what it is about; the audience won't understand a thing". He went berserk and shook his fist. I shook mine and he growled: "Now you want to tell me how to edit".'[1] Later, says Tasca, Welles restored much of what he had cut. He was in the dangerous realm of infinite possibilities. Fred Muller, Welles's editor, felt that 'because he knew what was happening, he got bored. And he didn't allow for an audience who saw it for the first and only time to absorb what was happening before going into the next scene. He was on the next step before the first step was completed.'[2] And on *Chimes at Midnight* he had a bigger editing team than he had ever had: eight cutters and a sound editor, Peter Parasheles, who, like Muller, toiled around the clock, day in and day out. One night, Welles invited Parasheles to supper with Paola and Beatrice, regaling him with vintage anecdotes, after which Parasheles went back to work in the editing suite, finally going home at about 1.30 a.m. Welles was furious: he had expected him, newly energised by the food and the fine talk, to work through the night, and refused to speak to him for a week.[3] He drove himself, and everyone else, like a man convinced that this was his last chance of immortality.

Principal photography had been due to finish in December of 1964, but by the time the crew was laid off at the end of the month there was still a great deal to be shot, notably the crucial scenes between Hal and Falstaff. Welles sent Keith Baxter off to Morocco to cool his heels over Christmas and into January, and then they resumed, continuing to pick up shots until March of 1965. This portion of the filming was paid for by the maverick producer Harry Saltzman; Piedra had finally run out of money. Saltzman was then riding high on the success of the early James Bond films, as well as the Tony Richardson films *Look Back in Anger* and *The Entertainer*, part of the English new wave that Saltzman had made possible, in collaboration with Welles's old partner Oscar Lewenstein and his company, Woodfall Films. Saltzman stumped up the not inconsiderable sum of $750,000. Had it not been for this investment, said Saltzman's widow, 'it would have just been one more movie by Welles that was never completed', a sobering thought, although in truth, up to this point, all of Welles's films – with the spectacular exceptions of *It's All True*, abandoned and to a large extent destroyed by RKO, and his intensely personal *Don Quixote*, already ten years in the making – had been completed: incompletion lay in the future.

But Saltzman's investment was critical. The saviour of *Chimes at Midnight* was a man after Welles's own heart: at the age of seventeen he had run away to join the circus; before long he had become a circus impresario. During the Second World War he was part of the Psychological Warfare Division – what better training for being a film producer? – and subsequently helped to found UNESCO's film division. Then movies beckoned. After his initial success with Bond, it all blew up in his face, though not before he had bought out (and wound up) the illustrious London theatre management, H.M.Tennent. But if Saltzman had saved *Chimes at Midnight*, he had also condemned it to decades of confusion in the matter of rights, by selling on his share in the film to a distribution company, which then sold it on to another, resulting in the film being blocked for many years from public exhibition, and even from reproduction on cassette or DVD. For many years Welles's masterpiece was a film largely unknown to the movie-going public, who now, with the recent resolution of these problems, can at last form a more balanced view of his achievements.

From the beginning, the film's commanding position in his output was confirmed by those who saw it before its release. In August 1965, Welles's friend Darryl Zanuck, who fifteen years earlier did for *Othello* what Saltzman had just done for *Chimes at Midnight*, wrote to Welles to say how 'deeply moved and emotionally thrilled by your film' he was;[4] it was, Zanuck continued, 'far and away the best film in this category I have seen', by which he presumably means that it surpassed not just Welles's two essays in Shakespearean adaptation, but Olivier's three – perhaps even including Kozinstev's remarkable *Hamlet*, which had been released in America the previous year. Putting his money where his mouth was, Zanuck went on to propose that Welles's representatives at 20th Century Fox should immediately travel to Europe to see the film: 'Please cable me at the St Regis Hotel in New York the date so they can arrange their plans accordingly.' This very direct offer was presumably forestalled by Saltzman's distribution arrangement with Welles. Nothing came of it, a deeply regrettable fact: Zanuck's intervention could have transformed the film's fortunes in America. 'My congratulations on a masterful job,' Zanuck, no hyperbolist, ended his letter.

The following year Welles entered the film for Cannes and, by a supreme effort of willpower, didn't withdraw it. He was, as ever, reluctant to let the film go, hoping to implement yet more editing refinements. To some extent every director feels this, but with Welles it was a physical grief to send his celluloid child out into the world in what he thought was not a fully achieved form. And it is true that, especially in the area of sound, *Chimes at Midnight* is far from perfect technically; sometimes, too, the limitations of the physical setting are apparent. But it was still, despite these flaws, exactly the film Welles wanted to make – except that he had meant Falstaff to be funnier. Somehow, in the making, it had turned out otherwise: 'having made a story, a film, which contains Falstaff's rejection and death,' he told Kathleen Tynan, 'I felt I had to prepare for it from the very first moment of the film.'[5] He was not displeased by the way the film had turned out, just surprised.

It was the twentieth year of the Cannes Festival and both Welles and *Chimes at Midnight* were honoured with the award of a special Grand Prix to celebrate the occasion. 'This was the Festival,' a French commentator noted, 'which crowned King Orson.'[6] Jean Marais read the citation: 'Orson Welles, for his contribution to World Cinema'. Welles shook him warmly by the hand, kissed Sophia Loren, Chair of the Jury, and was given the award itself – bizarrely, by a youthful and properly bashful Raquel Welch. In the newsreel footage, King Orson seems genuinely delighted and touched. It was a notably lightweight festival: the Palme d'Or was shared between Claude Lelouch's monosodium-glutamate *Un homme et une femme* and a now-forgotten Italian film by Pietro Germi, *Signore e Signori*, known in the English-speaking world (insofar as it is known at all) as *The Birds, the Bees and the Italians*; the Special Jury Award went to *Alfie*. *Chimes at Midnight* also shared the Award for Outstanding Technical Achievement with a short film, *Skaterdater*. All very gratifying. Welles got into the prevailing merry mood, throwing a picnic for the press immediately after the warmly received film was projected.

First responses across the Channel were highly laudatory: 'Olé For Citizen Falstaff,' said the *Daily Mail*, alluding to the film's technically

Spanish provenance. 'Rich, rare, rewarding – the most ambitious and most successful film that Welles has created since *Citizen Kane*. His battle . . . is a swirling, massive affair which outdoes anything in this line before – not excluding Olivier's *Henry V*.'[7] But transatlantic reactions were much more guarded: describing him as 'that American International journeyman filmmaker Orson Welles', *Variety* described him as trying 'to veer from the theatrical in creating visuals . . . he succeeds sometimes and at other times detracts from the language or replaces life and content by showiness and overdone angles'. Its verdict on the film's commercial potential was not exactly positive (or particularly coherent): 'film looms mainly on arty house possibility for abroad on its Shakespearean backdrop . . . an irritating, so personal but knowing Shakespearean pic'.[8] Much more damagingly, Bosley Crowther, who was covering Cannes for the *New York Times*, casually dismissed the film. He returned to the fray at greater length on its American release: nothing, he said, had made him change his mind about what he called 'a big, squashy, tatterdemalion show'. For a start, he couldn't understand the actors, especially Welles's basso profundo, as he put it, 'which he seems to direct into his innards rather than through his lips'. The performance, said Crowther, ranged between a farcical conception of the character and a mawkishly sentimental one. 'He makes him a sort of Jackie Gleason getting off on one of his homilies when he gives his great apostrophe to honour . . . and he chokes up like an opera grandma when he is suddenly banished by the new Henry V.' In closing, he notes, sneeringly, that Welles has always wanted to play Falstaff. 'Now he has had his chance. Those who are interested may see him at the Little Carnegie.'[9]

The most striking aspect of the review is the absolute contempt that underlies it. Welles had committed an unforgivable crime in American eyes: he had failed, but refused to give up. He was just irritatingly *there*, a constant reminder of the disappointment he had caused. Crowther's reaction to Welles, and that of many of his colleagues, was an urgent underlying desire to put him out of his misery – and them out of theirs. These reviews brought Welles close to despair. His perennial dream of going home, of working in the American film industry, were scuppered yet again.

The British reviews of the same year, 1967, were rather more nuanced, but it scarcely mattered to Welles. It couldn't influence his career. Robert Robinson in the *Sunday Telegraph*, in a generally hostile review, made an important point about Welles's approach, which Robinson felt was too detailed – 'a pocky nose, a spastic eye' – to do justice to the grandeur, the scale of Falstaff. 'What came out of the consciousness of everybody will not be found in merely natural surroundings.'[10] But Welles had spent a lifetime in film creating figures that were larger than life: for once, and for very personal reasons, he chose to discover the human dimension. It may not be exactly what Shakespeare had in mind, but it is richly and authentically true to life. In her piece in the *Spectator*, Penelope Houston homed in on exactly what Welles was trying to do:

> Welles's Falstaff becomes a man play-acting on borrowed time, until the prince chooses to bring down the curtain. Falstaff stumbling about the battlefield, a mammoth sardine in his armour, or beaming under a saucepan-lid crown, or enlisting his amateur retinue, is the happy, doomed innocent-at-large . . . underlying every intimation of mortality, leaving him vulnerable as a foolish fond old man.

Welles, she says, presents Falstaff less as a great comic presence than as a concept – 'the old England, dying and betrayed'. Welles's Maytime England comes through, she continues, 'as a sad, lost dream, a memory for garrulous old women and quavering old men who once heard the chimes at midnight'.[11]

But it is this doomed yearning for the non-existent past, the *saudades* for an imaginary yesteryear, that gives the film its great originality. It purveys not an active longing for something joyous, but an Edenic, a prelapsarian hankering, as of something snatched away from one, an innocence defiled, banishment from paradise. This is a quintessentially Wellesian experience, the thing that gives the film its strange emotional power, creating a world that is exactly and expertly poised, as Crowther said, between the farcical and the sentimental – a Chekhovian world, in fact, awash with tears of laughter and sudden pangs of heartache. Another English critic, John Coleman, acutely pinpointed the absurdist quality of Welles's Falstaff, 'in dark, swollen armour – the spitting image of Jarry's Ubu . . . I suspect', added Coleman, 'that this is a film we shall return to with increasing admiration and affection. The Welles Falstaff has more subtlety than may meet the purist's eye.'[12]

Even in America, despite the body-blow of the *New York Times*'s outright dismissal of the film, there was a groundswell of enthusiasm, nowhere more eloquently expressed than by Pauline Kael during her brief and rebellious tenure at the *New Republic*. By the time she wrote the piece, the film had closed: '*Falstaff* [the film's title everywhere but in England] came and went so fast,' she wrote, 'there was hardly time to tell people about it, but it should be back (it should be around forever) and it should be seen.' She chose the occasion to offer a revisionist view of Welles's career, dismissing the idea that he suffered from lack of discipline; on the contrary, she says, he was scuppered because of the size of his imagination. She describes the 'atmosphere of anxiety' surrounding him, comparing him, in an appraisal that would have delighted Welles, with his friend, the great French director so decisively rejected by Hollywood, Jean Renoir. Welles's removal to Europe, said Kael, had deprived him of his greatest asset as a director: 'his sound'. To compensate, she says, he developed great visual virtuosity, as a result of which his work 'is often spoken of as flashy and spectacular as if this also meant cheap and counterfeit . . . but there's life in that kind of display: it's part of an earlier theatrical tradition that Welles carries over into film, it's what the theatre has lost, and it's what brought people to the movies'. Describing him as 'the one great creative force in American film in our time, the man who might have redeemed our movies from the general contempt in which they are (for the most part, rightly) held', Kael laments that, as 'an expatriate director', his work only reaches the art-house audience. 'And he has been so crippled by the problems of working as he does, he's lucky to reach that. The distributors of *Falstaff* tested it out of town before risking Bosley Crowther's displeasure.'

She is frank about the poor technical quality of the first twenty minutes of the film, the problems of sound and synch – 'you may want to walk out' – but then, Kael says, 'the movie begins to be great'. And she has something very original to say about Welles as an actor, finding that he has always been betrayed by – of all things – his voice:

> It was too much and too inexpressive; there was no warmth in it, no sense of a life lived. It was just an instrument to be played, and it seemed to be the key to something shallow and unfelt in even his best performances, and most fraudulent when he tried to make it tender.

But in *Chimes at Midnight*, she says, he seems 'to have grown into his voice. He's not too young for it anymore, and he's certainly big enough. And his emotions don't seem fake anymore; he's grown into them, too. He has the eyes for the role. Though his Falstaff is short on comedy, it's very rich, very full.' The battle sequence, she says, is totally unlike anything Welles has ever done, 'indeed unlike any battle ever done on screen before. It ranks with the best of Griffith, John

Ford, Eisenstein, Kurosawa – that is, with the best ever done.' It's so good, she says, because of course there is no dialogue; Welles is unhampered by sound. 'It's the most brutally sombre battle ever filmed.' But because of 'technical defects due to poverty, Welles's finest Shakespearean production to date – another near masterpiece, and this time so very close – cannot reach a large public'.[13]

This is perhaps the best, the frankest, the most sympathetic account of *Chimes at Midnight* – and of Welles's entire career – to have appeared during his lifetime. That it came from the pen of a woman whom he had cause at the end of his life to regard as his nemesis is an irony lost on no one. The film has had no commercial run in an American cinema since Kael wrote the review, forty-five years ago, which of course has done nothing to transform its fortunes.

In Europe – in France, particularly – it was accorded the acclaim due to a self-evident masterpiece. Jean-Louis Comolli, in *Cahiers du Cinéma*, instantly homed in on the film's essential theatricality:

> That tavern, with its long tables and its benches, its common room, the gallery that runs along the upper floor, where from time to time curious women come scantily dressed, to lean over, is a kind of theatre in the round, in which the actors are not far from spectators when they are not both at once.[14]

Even the throne room is theatrical, 'cleverly tiered, lighted from the side by beams of light that could be those of spotlights. On the one hand, the tragedy of power, on the other, its comedy.' Falstaff and the King are doubles and reversed images: Hal 'rehearses with one what he then plays with the other, all the more proud in the tavern because he is ashamed in the palace . . . Falstaff, the King and Hal are all equally histrionic.' It is this aspect of the film that makes it seem like a *summum* of Welles's work, a culmination of his life's professional obsessions: Shakespeare, film, theatre. Roger Planchon, the great French theatre director, remarked that critics would understand Welles better if they were more familiar with the works of William Shakespeare. But *Chimes at Midnight* is not filmed theatre: it is the sort of film Shakespeare might have made, had he had the medium at his disposal. And Welles's great themes resound more richly and fully in it than anywhere else in his work: the exaltation of innocence, the corruption of power, the inevitability of betrayal. Comolli, in his *Cahiers* review, drew attention to something very striking: the obsession with humiliation, as he puts it, which is in every Welles film, but especially in *Chimes at Midnight*.

'*Falstaff* is the film of masochism . . . the son humiliates the father whether the latter is absent or present, whether he speaks to him or acts a performance of him, as the father humiliates himself in the son. Only one person is duped, Falstaff. But that is precisely', says Comolli, 'where one finds Welles's imperious obstinacy at carrying his cross.'

It was a cross. By this stage of his life, aged fifty, Welles had assumed a symbolic role in American life: 'In his deeply melancholy *Chimes at Midnight* Orson Welles plays the old gormandizer and carouser with all the empathy of an exiled, outcast, abused and unappreciated entertainer,' wrote Georgia Brown in the *Village Voice*. 'If the Falstaff story is a cautionary tale, warning us about banishing play and carnival at one's peril, Welles treats his own ritual sacrifice as foregone fact.'[15] The glib, churlish reception (with few exceptions) of his best film had only confirmed that Welles had become the portly embodiment of failure, the American dream gone horribly wrong; it is striking how many of his films are about one American dream or another, all turned sour. The dream Welles had embodied, the dream of the young genius, the dashing conquistador of every medium, was now utterly expunged. At the very moment at which he delivered his most mature, most complex, most human film, when he was at his absolute prime as a film-maker and at his zenith as an actor, he was deemed by the pundits to be on creative Skid Row. The story he was telling – 'the world from Falstaff's point of view', in Gore Vidal's inspired phrase – was not one America wanted to hear.[16]

He never again completed a film in America; he never again completed a full-length film anywhere. But he never, ever stopped, not for one waking moment, trying to tell stories he believed mattered, in the way in which he wanted to tell them, always striving to progress a medium that he felt had hardly begun to fulfil its potential. Twenty years lay ahead of him in which, till he drew his dying breath, Welles served his restless daemon, experimenting, exploring, pointing a way forward. His life underwent a huge transformation. He returned to America, though he would always go back to Europe, where he was treated as a titan, though not a titan in whom many people wished to invest. In his native land he continued to be regarded as a Cautionary Tale, the Man Who Stuck his Tongue Out at Hollywood. In pursuit of the sort of celebrity that he mistakenly thought would encourage backers, Welles became an over-familiar figure on television, occupying rather too much of the guests' couch, rather too often; he dismayed his admirers by making risible commercials for inferior products. As Shakespeare's Henry IV says of Richard II, he was 'lavish of his presence, common-hackney'd in the eyes of men, became stale and cheap to vulgar company'. His physical shape was mocked; sometimes he even descended to making fat jokes against himself. He became, as he put it, a dancing bear.

But underneath it all, and sustained by a relationship with a woman unlike any other relationship with any other woman he had known in his long lifetime of womanising, he was thrusting out towards unknown regions, dreaming celluloid visions, unceasingly toiling over the chance to extend the ribbon of dreams, as he had so memorably described film-making. It was an epic journey to match the epic of his first fifty years, and the fact that there was so little to show for it is at once tragic and oddly inspiring: there is a nobility, a selflessness to the quest. *Chimes at Midnight* proved not to be a harbinger of anything; Welles sailed off in other directions. But not before he had secured his place in heaven.

ORSON WELLES'S PERFORMANCES AS AN ACTOR, 1948–1965

Year	Film	Role
1949	*Black Magic*	Cagliostro
	The Third Man	Harry Lime
	Prince of Foxes	Cesare Borgia
1950	*The Black Rose*	Bayan
1951	*Return to Glennascaul*	Narrator/Himself
	Le Petit Monde de Don Camillo	Narrator
1952	*Trent's Last Case*	Sigsbee Manderson
1953	*L'Uomo, la bestia e la virtù*	Captain Perella, the Beast
	Si Versailles M'Etait Conté	Benjamin Franklin
	King Lear	King Lear
1954	*Trouble in the Glen*	Sanin Cejadory Mengues
1955	*Three Cases of Murder*	Lord Mountdrago
	Napoléon	Hudson Lowe
1956	*Moby Dick*	Father Mapple
	Out of Darkness	Dramatic narrator
	Ford Star Jubilee	Oscar Jaffé
1957	*Man in the Shadow*	Virgil Renchler
1958	*The Long, Hot Summer*	Will Varner
	The Vikings	Narrator
	South Seas Adventure	Narrator
	The Roots of Heaven	Cy Sedgewick
1959	*High Journey*	Narrator
	Les Seigneurs de la forêt	Narrator
	Compulsion	Jonathan Wilk
	Ferry to Hong Kong	Captain Hart
1960	*David and Goliath*	King Saul
	Crack in the Mirror	Hagolin, Lamerciere
	Austerlitz	Robert Fulton
1961	*La Fayette*	Benjamin Franklin
	King of Kings	Narrator
	I Tartari	Burundai
1962	*Ro.Go.Pa.G.*	The Director
1963	*The V.I.P.s*	Max Buda

1964	*The Finest Hours*	Narrator
1965	*A King's Story*	Narrator
	La Fabuleuse aventure de Marco Polo	Akerman, Marco's Tutor

THE BLESSED AND THE DAMNED
A double bill by ORSON WELLES

Opening performance: Théâtre Édouard VII, Paris, 15 June, 1950

Production, design and costumes by ORSON WELLES

THE UNTHINKING LOBSTER

Cast in order of appearance:

Miss Prat	SUZANNE CLOUTIER
Roland Zitz	JAMIE SCHMITT
Jake Behoovian	ORSON WELLES
Lender Plaice	GEORGE LLOYD
Manny Burns	MARVIN FRANK
The Archduke	FRÉDÉRIC O'BRADY
Letitia Pottle	JENNIFER HOWARD
Hal Sprokett	LEE ZIMMER
Television assistants	ANDRE DAHL and HERBERT MACHIZ
The Archbishop	HILTON EDWARDS
The Archangel	HELENA HUGHES
The voice of Alexandra Sporcaccione	LUCIO ARDENZI
First servant	EDWINA HAZARD
Second servant	HELENE REMY
Third Servant	ASTRID DUBOIS

TIME RUNS
Based on the works of MILTON, DANTE and MARLOWE

Music by DUKE ELLINGTON

Cast in order of appearance:

The choir:	EARTHA KITT
	ROSALIND MURRAY
	TOMMIE MOORE
Doctor John Faustus	ORSON WELLES
Mephistopheles	HILTON EDWARDS
First man	LEE ZIMMER
A woman	JENNIFER HOWARD
Second man	JAMIE SCHMITT
Third man	MARVIN FRANK
Fourth man	HERBERT MACHIZ

AN EVENING WITH ORSON WELLES

Opening performance: Frankfurt, 7 August 1950

TIME RUNS
By ORSON WELLES, based on the works of MILTON, DANTE and MARLOWE

Directed by ORSON WELLES
Lighting by HILTON EDWARDS
Music by DUKE ELLINGTON

Cast:

The Girl	EARTHA KITT
The Man	MICHEÁL MACLIAMMÓIR
Dr John Faustus	ORSON WELLES

Onlookers: JANET WOLFE, LEE ZIMMER, SAMUEL MATLOWSKY

Magic performed by ORSON WELLES

AN EPISODE FROM THE IMPORTANCE OF BEING EARNEST
By OSCAR WILDE

Directed by HILTON EDWARDS

Mr Algernon Moncrieff	ORSON WELLES
Lane the Butler	LEE ZIMMER
Mr John Worthing	MICHEÁL MACLIAMMÓIR

Songs performed by EARTHA KITT

A SCENE FROM KING HENRY VI PART THREE
By WILLIAM SHAKESPEARE

Directed by HILTON EDWARDS

Henry VI	MICHEÁL MACLIAMMÓIR
Prison Guard	LEE ZIMMER
Richard, Duke of Gloucester	ORSON WELLES

OTHELLO

By WILLIAM SHAKESPEARE

Opening Performance: St James Theatre, London, 18 October 1951

Production by ORSON WELLES
Music by FRANCESCO LAVAGNINO
Designed by MOTLEY
Stage Manager DIANA BODDINGTON

Cast in order of appearance:

Othello	ORSON WELLES
Desdemona	GUDRUN URE
Roderigo	BASIL LORD
Iago	PETER FINCH
Brabantio	KEITH PYOTT
Cassio	JOHN VAN EYSSEN
The Duke	AUBREY RICHARDS
Lodovico	EDWARD MULHARE
Emilia	MAXINE AUDLEY
Montano	MICHAEL WARRE
Bianca	DIANNE FOSTER
The Herald	AUBREY RICHARDS

MOBY DICK

By ORSON WELLES, adapted from *Moby-Dick* (novel) by HERMAN MELVILLE

Opening performance: Duke of York's Theatre, London, 14 June 1955

Associate Producer WILLIAM CHAPPELL
Music Composed by ANTHONY COLLINS
Musical Effects by RICHARD JOHNSON and T BLADES
Stage Decorations by MARY OWEN

Cast in order of appearance:

A young actor/Ishmael	GORDON JACKSON
A young actress/Pip	JOAN PLOWRIGHT
A stage manager/flask	PETER SALLIS
An assistant stage manager/Bo'sun	JOHN GRAY
A second assistant stage manager/ Tashtego/Captain of the *Rachel*	JOHN BOYD-BRENT
A stage hand with a harmonica/ Portuguese sailor/Dagoo	JOSEPH CHELTON
Other stage hands	PHILIPPE PERROTET HARRY CORDWELL DAVID SAIRE
A middle-aged actor/Stubb	WENSLEY PITHEY
An experienced actor/Peleg/ old Cornish sailor	JEFFERSON CLIFFORD
A serious actor/Starbuck	PATRICK MCGOOHAN
A very serious actor/Elijah/ ship's carpenter/old Bedford sailor	KENNETH WILLIAMS
An actor–manager/Father Mapple/ Ahab	ORSON WELLES

KING LEAR

By WILLIAM SHAKESPEARE

Opening performance: New York City Center of Music and Drama, 12 January 1956

Production by ORSON WELLES
Costumes by ROBERT FLETCHER
Stage Settings by THEODORE COOPER

Electronic sound by OTTO LUENING and VLADIMIR USSACHEVSKY
Music by MARC BLITZSTEIN

Cast:

King Lear	ORSON WELLES
King of France	ROBERT BLACKBURN
Duke of Burgundy	WALTER MATHEWS
Duke of Albany	SORRELL BOOKE
Duke of Cornwall	THAYER DAVID
Earl of Kent	ROY DEAN
Earl of Gloucester	LESTER RAWLINS
Edgar, son to Gloucester	ROBERT FLETCHER
Edmund, bastard son to Gloucester	JOHN COLICOS
Lear's Fool	ALVIN EPSTEIN
Curan	TOM CLANCY
Oswald, Steward to Goneril	FRANCIS CARPENTER
Old Man, tenant to Gloucester	JACK ARONSON
Servant to Cornwall	ROBERT BURR
Doctor	WALTER MATHEWS
Captain to Edmund	ROBERT BURR
Gentleman to King Lear	JACK ARONSON
Goneril	GERALDINE FITZGERALD
Regan	SYLVIA SHORT
Cordelia	VIVECA LINDFORS

CHIMES AT MIDNIGHT

Opening performance: Grand Opera House, Belfast 24 February, 1960
Opening performance: Gaiety Theatre Dublin, 29 February 1960

Staged by HILTON EDWARDS

Cast in order of appearance:

Chorus	RORY MACDERMOT
King	REGINALD JARMAN
Northumberland	TERENCE GREENIDGE
Worcester	AUBREY MORRIS
Hotspur	ALEXIS KANNER
Westmoreland	STUART NICHOL
Lancaster	PETER BARTLETT

Gower	ALAN MASON
Page to Gower	JOHN SOUTHARN
Prince Hal	KEITH BAXTER
Falstaff	ORSON WELLES
Poins	PATRICK BEDFORD
Bardolph	LEONARD FENTON
Nym	HENRY WOOLF
Peto	PETER BARTLETT
Francis, a Drawer	LEE HARRIS
Mistress	THELMA RUBY
Sherriff Fang	RORY MACDERMOT
Snare	WILLIAM STYLES
Lord Chief Justice	TERENCE GREENIDGE
Attendant to Lord Chief Justice	KEITH MARSH
Doll Tearsheet	SHIRLEY CAMERON
Pistol	RORY MACDERMOT
Justice Shallow	KEITH MARSH
Justice Silence	AUBREY MORRIS
Mouldy	LEONARD FENTON
Shadow	LEE HARRIS
Wart	CHARLES ARMSTRONG
Feeble	ALAN MASON
Bullcalf	STUART NICHOL
Davy	PATRICK BEDFORD
Guard to Worcester	ALAN MASON

RHINOCEROS
By EUGÈNE IONESCO, translated by DEREK PROUSE

Staged and designed by ORSON WELLES

Cast in order of appearance:

Bessie, a barmaid	MONICA EVANS
Berenger	LAURENCE OLIVIER
John	DUNCAN MACRAE
A grocer	HENRY WOOLF
The grocer's wife	MARGERY CALDICOTT
A lady with a cat	HAZEL HUGHES
A logician	GEOFFREY DUNN
An old gentleman	MICHAEL BATES
A publican	WILL STAMPE
Daisy	JOAN PLOWRIGHT

Duddard	ALAN WEBB
Mr Butterfly	MILES MALLESON
Bottard	PETER SALLIS
Mrs Beef	GLADYS HENSON
A fireman	PHILIP ANTHONY

OTHELLO (1952)

Directed by ORSON WELLES

Writing credits (in alphabetical order) JEAN SACHA (uncredited), WILLIAM SHAKESPEARE (play), ORSON WELLES (uncredited)
Produced by JULIEN DERODE (associate producer), WALTER BEDONE (producer), PATRICE DALI (producer), ROCCO FACCHINI (producer), GIORGIO PAPI (producer), ORSON WELLES (producer)
Music by ALBERTO BARBERIS and FRANCESCO LAVAGNINO

Cast in order of credits:

Iago	MICHEÁL MACLIAMMÓIR
Roderigo	ROBERT COOTE
Othello	ORSON WELLES
Desdemona	SUZANNE CLOUTIER
Brabantio	HILTON EDWARDS
Lodovico	NICHOLAS BRUCE
Cassio	MICHAEL LAURENCE
Emilia	FAY COMPTON
Bianca	DORIS DOWLING
Desdemona (voice) (uncredited)	GUDRUN URE

TOUCH OF EVIL (1958)

Directed by ORSON WELLES
Written by ORSON WELLES
Produced by ALBERT ZUGSMITH
Music by HENRY MANCINI

Cast:

Mike Vargas	CHARLTON HESTON
Susan Vargas	JANET LEIGH
Police Captain Hank Quinlan	ORSON WELLES
Police Sergeant Pete Menzies	JOSEPH CALLEIA
'Uncle' Joe Grandi	AKIM TAMIROFF
Marcia Linnekar	JOANNA MOORE
District Attorney Adair	RAY COLLINS
Mirador Motel Night Manager	DENNIS WEAVER
Pancho	VALENTIN DE VARGAS
Al Schwartz	MORT MILLS
Manelo Sanchez	VICTOR MILLAN
Risto	LALO RIOS
Pretty Boy	MICHAEL SARGENT
Blaine	PHIL HARVEY
Zita	JOI LANSING
Chief Gould	HARRY SHANNON
Tana	MARLENE DIETRICH
Strip-Club Owner	ZSA ZSA GABOR

MR ARKADIN (1955)

Directed by ORSON WELLES
Written by ORSON WELLES (story and screenplay)
Produced by LOUIS DOLIVET and ORSON WELLES
Music by PAUL MISRAKI

Cast:

Gregory Arkadin	ORSON WELLES
Burgomil Trebitsch	MICHAEL REDGRAVE
Mily	PATRICIA MEDINA
Jakob Zouk	AKIM TAMIROFF
The Professor	MISCHA AUER
Raina Arkadin	PAOLA MORI
Sophie	KATINA PAXINOU
Bracco	GRÉGOIRE ASLAN
Thaddeus	PETER VAN EYCK
Baroness Nagel	SUZANNE FLON
Guy Van Stratten	ROBERT ARDEN
Marquis of Rutleigh	JACK WATLING
Oscar	FRÉDÉRIC O'BRADY

Woman in apartment	TAMARA SHAYNE
Secretary	TERENCE LONGDON
Parisian woman with bread	ANNABEL BUFFET
First Policeman – Munich	GERT FRÖBE
Second Policeman – Munich	EDUARD LINKERS
General Martinez	MANUEL REQUENA

THE TRIAL (1962)

Directed by ORSON WELLES
Screenplay written by ORSON WELLES based on the novel by FRANZ KAFKA
Produced by ROBERT FLORAT (associate producer), ALEXANDER SALKIND (producer) and MICHAEL SALKIND (producer)
Music by JEAN LEDRUT

Cast:

Josef K.	ANTHONY PERKINS
Inspector A	ARNOLDO FOÀ
Second Assistant Inspector	JESS HAHN
First Assistant Inspector	BILLY KEARNS
Mrs Grubach	MADELEINE ROBINSON
Marika Burstner	JEANNE MOREAU
Deputy Manager	MAURICE TEYNAC
Irmie	NAYDRA SHORE
Miss Pittl	SUZANNE FLON
Policeman	RAOUL DELFOSSE
Policeman	JEAN-CLAUDE RÉMOLEUX
Examining Magistrate	MAX BUCHSBAUM
Man in leather	CARL STUDER
Uncle Max	MAX HAUFLER
Leni	ROMY SCHNEIDER
Chief Clerk of the Law Court	FERNAND LEDOUX
Bloch	AKIM TAMIROFF
Hilda	ELSA MARTINELLI
Bert the law student	THOMAS HOLTZMANN
Courtroom guard	WOLFGANG REICHMANN
Titorelli	WILLIAM CHAPPELL
Priest	MICHAEL LONSDALE
Albert Hastler – The Advocate/ Narrator	ORSON WELLES

CHIMES AT MIDNIGHT (1965)

Produced by ÁNGEL ESCOLANO (producer), EMILIANO PIEDRA (producer), HARRY SALTZMAN (producer) and ALESSANDRO TASCO DI CUTÒ (executive producer)
Music by FRANCESCO LAVAGNINO

Cast:

Falstaff	ORSON WELLES
Doll Tearsheet	JEANNE MOREAU
Mistress Quickly	MARGARET RUTHERFORD
Henry IV	JOHN GIELGUD
Kate Percy	MARINA VLADY
Mr Silence	WALTER CHIARI
Pistol	MICHAEL ALDRIDGE
Ned Poins	TONY BECKLEY
Prince John	JEREMY ROWE
Shallow	ALAN WEBB
Worcester	FERNANDO REY
Prince Hal	KEITH BAXTER
Henry 'Hotspur' Percy	NORMAN RODWAY
Northumberland	JOSÉ NIETO
Westmoreland	ANDREW FAULDS
Bardolph	PATRICK BEDFORD
Falstaff's Page	BEATRICE WELLES
Narrator (voice)	RALPH RICHARDSON

TELEVISION PRODUCTIONS

ORSON WELLES'S SKETCHBOOK

Transmitted April–June 1955

Directed by HUW WHELDON
Produced by HUW WHELDON
Series film editing by HAZEL WILKINSON (3 episodes) and WILLIAM MORTON (2 episodes)
Cameraman EDWARD LLOYD

AROUND THE WORLD WITH ORSON WELLES

Transmitted September–December 1955

Directed by ORSON WELLES
Written by ORSON WELLES
Produced by LOUIS DOLIVET (7 episodes), ROLAND GILLETT (2 episodes) and JOHN JONES (2 episodes)
Cinematography by ALAIN POL
Sound department JACQUES CARRÈRE

FOUNTAIN OF YOUTH

Transmitted 16 September 1958

Directed by ORSON WELLES
Screenplay written by ORSON WELLES, based on the story 'Youth From Vienna' by JOHN COLLIER
Produced by DESI ARNAZ (executive producer) and ORSON WELLES (producer)
Cinematography by SIDNEY HICKOX

Cast:

Journalist	MARJORIE BENNETT
Journalist	MADGE BLAKE
Albert Morgan	BILLY HOUSE
Alan Brody	RICK JASON
Stella Morgan	NANCY KULP
Carolyn Coates	JOI LANSING
Humphrey Baxter	DAN TOBIN
Host/narrator	ORSON WELLES

PORTRAIT OF GINA (1958)

Directed by ORSON WELLES
Written by ORSON WELLES
Produced by LEONARD H. GOLDENSON

Cast in order of credits:

ORSON WELLES
GINA LOLLOBRIGIDA
VITTORIO DE SICA
ANNA GRUBER
PAOLA MORI

Nella Terra di Don Chisciotte (In the Land of Don Quixote) (1964)

Shown on RAI TV
Directed by ORSON WELLES
Written by ORSON WELLES
Produced by ALESSANDRO TASCO DI CUTÒ
Music by JUAN SERRANO

NOTES

CHAPTER 1

1. Chaplin, 22nd November 1947, quoted in Alberto Anile, *Orson Welles in Italy*. Indiana University Press, 2013.
2. Richard Wilson, letter to Orson Welles, 24th March 1948, Lilly Library Orson Welles Archive.
3. Richard Wilson letter to Orson Welles, 8th March 1948, Lilly Library Orson Welles Archive.
4. Anile, *Orson Welles in Italy.*
5. Emanuele Rocco, 'Il Pranzo della Pace', *Tempo*, 20–27 December 1947, quoted in Anile, *Orson Welles in Italy.*
6. James Naremore, 'The Trial: Orson Welles vs. the FBI', *Film Comment*, 27, No. 1, January–February 1991.
7. Frank Brady, *Citizen Welles: A Biography of Orson Welles*. Scribner, 1989.
8. Richard Fleischer, *Just Tell Me When to Cry: A Memoir*. Carroll and Graf, 1993.
9. Samuel Blumenfeld, *L'Homme Qui Voulait Être Prince: Les Vies Imaginaires de Michal Waszynski. Grasset*, 2006.
10. Bob Breen, telegram to Orson Welles, 29th May 1947.
11. *Edinburgh Evening Despatch*, 26th May 1948.
12. Alessandro Tasca di Cutò, *A Prince in America*. Sellerio, 2004.
13. Lea Padovani, interviewer unknown, n.d., Lilly Library Orson Welles Archive.
14. Harriet White Medin, 'Othello, Desdemona and Me', *Video Watchdog*, 23, May–June 1994.
15. Rita Kohler, *Fragments on Life with Orson Welles, 1947–1949* (unpublished). Courtesy of Ann Percival.
16. Ibid.
17. Ibid.
18. The director of the film, Henry King, had been informed that Welles didn't start work until midday, and then worked through the night. 'I said, if an actor is going to work with me in a picture, he's going to start at 9.00 or 8.00 . . . if he has a day off, I'll give it to him.' Welles surprised King by turning up every day at work, in full costume and make-up. Quoted in *Henry King: Director – From Silents to 'Scope Directors*, Guild of America, 1996.
19. Quoted in Anile, *Orson Welles in Italy.*
20. Ibid.
21. *Daily Variety*, 8th September 1948.

22. Kohler, *Fragments on Life with Orson Welles.*
23. Ibid.
24. Sir Alexander Korda, letter to David Selznick, 23rd September 1948, quoted in Charles Drazin, *In Search of the Third Man.* Methuen, 1999.
25. Graham Greene, *The Third Man.* Viking, 1950.
26. Guy Hamilton, conversation with the author, 2009.
27. Guy Hamilton, quoted in Drazin, *In Search of the Third Man.*
28. Greene, *The Third Man.*
29. Quoted in Brigitte Timmerman, *The Third Man's Vienna.* Shippen Rock Publishing, 2005.
30. Cole Lesley, *The Life of Noël Coward.* Jonathan Cape, 1976.
31. Kohler, *Fragments on Life with Orson Welles.*
32. Elizabeth Montagu, *Honourable Rebel: The Memoirs of Elizabeth Montagu, Later Elizabeth Varley.* Montagu Ventures, 2003.
33. Ibid.

CHAPTER 2

1. Elizabeth Montagu, *Honourable Rebel: The Memoirs of Elizabeth Montagu, Later Elizabeth Varley.* Montagu Ventures, 2003.
2. Ibid.
3. Jonathan Lynn, correspondence with the author, June 2014.
4. Micheál MacLiammóir, *Put Money in Thy Purse.* Foreword by Orson Welles. Methuen, 1976.
5. Ibid.
6. Rita Kohler, *Fragments on Life with Orson Welles 1947–1949.*
7. Betsy Blair, *The Memory of All That: Love and Politics in New York, Hollywood, and Paris.* Alfred A. Knopf, 2003.
8. Nicholas Shakespeare, 'Journey to the End of the World', *Daily Telegraph Magazine*, 16th October 1993.
9. *New York Times*, 9th June 1949.
10. George Fanto, *Reminiscences of Working with Orson Welles*, from his unpublished memoir, *Hungarian Life.*
11. Ibid.
12. MacLiammóir, *Put Money in Thy Purse.*
13. Alberto Anile, *Orson Welles in Italy.* Indiana University Press, 2013.
14. Blair, *The Memory of All That.*
15. Alexandre Trauner, interview with O. Eyquem, September 1984.
16. Ibid.
17. MacLiammóir, *Put Money in Thy Purse.*
18. Jean-Pierre Berthomé, 'The Labyrinths of *Othello*', in *Orson Welles at Work.* Phaidon, 2008.
19. Oberdan Troiani, quoted in Anile, *Orson Welles in Italy.*
20. Ibid.
21. Ibid.
22. Fanto, *Reminiscences of Working with Orson Welles.*
23. Blair, *The Memory of All That.*
24. Fanto, *Reminiscences of Working with Orson Welles.*
25. MacLiammóir, *Put Money in Thy Purse.*
26. Fay Compton, diary entry, written during the making of *Othello* (unpublished). Courtesy of Joe Pelissier.
27. Ibid.
28. MacLiammóir, *Put Money in Thy Purse.*

CHAPTER 3

1. Fay Compton, diary entry, written during the making of *Othello* (unpublished). Courtesy of Joe Pelissier.
2. Ibid.
3. Alvaro Mancori, quoted in Alberto Anile, *Orson Welles in Italy.* Indiana University Press, 2013.
4. Alexandre Trauner, interview with O. Eyquem, September 1984.
5. Alvaro Mancori, quoted in Anile, *Orson Welles in Italy.*
6. Fay Compton, *Othello* diary.
7. Ibid.
8. Orson Welles, letter to Hilton Edwards and Micheál MacLiammóir, quoted in Christopher Fitzsimmons, *The Boys: A Double Biography*. Nick Hern Books, 1994.
9. Mancori, quoted in Anile, *Orson Welles in Italy.*
10. George Fanto, *Reminiscences of Working with Orson Welles*.
11. Orson Welles, letter to George Fanto, 19th February 1950, Lilly Library Orson Welles Archive.
12. Truman Capote, letter to Andrew Lyndon, 1st November 1949.
13. *Le Parisien Libéré*, 3rd May 1950.
14. *L'Aurore*, 4th May 1950.
15. *France-Soir*, 5th May 1950.
16. Jennifer Howard, letter to the author, September 1989.
17. Eartha Kitt, *Tuesday's Child*. Cassell, 1957.
18. Ibid.
19. Jennifer Howard, letter to the author, September 1989.
20. John L. Williams, *America's Mistress: The Life and Times of Eartha Kitt*. Quercus, 2013.
21. *New Leader*, September 30th 1950.
22. René MacColl, *Daily Express*, 17th June 1950.
23. Jean Cocteau, programme essay for *The Blessed and the Damned*, June 1950.
24. Georges Beaume, 'Orson Among Us', programme note for *The Blessed and the Damned*, June 1950.
25. Jean-François Reille, *Arte*, 7th July 1950.
26. Art Buchwald, 'Paris After Dark', *International Herald Tribune*, 22nd June 1950.
27. Francis Koval, *Sight and Sound*, December 1950.
28. Daniel Farson, *Sacred Monsters*. Bloomsbury, 1988.
29. Williams, *America's Mistress*.

CHAPTER 4

1. Micheál MacLiammóir, *Each Actor on His Ass*. Methuen, 1952.
2. Ibid.
3. Kenneth Ames, 'Orson Puzzles the Long Haired', *Daily Telegraph*, 6th September 1950.
4. Orson Welles, 'Thoughts on Germany', *The Fortnightly Review*, May 1951.
5. MacLiammóir, *Each Actor on His Ass.*
6. Hilton Edwards, letter to Orson Welles, 30th September 1950.
7. Hilton Edwards, letter to Orson Welles, 13th October 1950.
8. Francesco Lavagnino, unattributed interview, Lilly Library Orson Welles Archive.
9. *Corriere della Sera*, 29th November 1950.

10. Fay Compton, diary entry, written during the making of *Othello* (unpublished). Courtesy of Joe Pelissier.
11. David Robinson, *The Times*, October 1992.

CHAPTER 5

1. *Picture Post*, 21st April 1951.
2. Elaine Dundy, *Life Itself!* Virago, 2001.
3. Leslie Megahey, 'The Orson Welles Story', *Arena*, 18th May 1982.
4. Harry Alan Towers, taped statement, March 1990.
5. Margaret Harris, interview with the author, 1990.
6. Maxine Audley, interview with the author, 1990.
7. Gudrun Ure, interview with the author, March 1989.
8. Oreste Tesei, *Oggi*, 13th September 1951, quoted in Alberto Anile, *Orson Welles in Italy*. Indiana University Press, 2013.
9. Orson Welles, 'Thoughts on Germany', *The Fortnightly Review*, October 1951.
10. Elaine Dundy, *Finch, Bloody Finch: A Biography of Peter Finch*. Michael Joseph, 1980.
11. Peter Wilsher, *Newcastle Evening News*, 27th September 1951.
12. *Newcastle Chronicle*, 3rd October 1951.
13. Peter Wilsher, *Newcastle Evening News*, 27th September 1951.
14. Gudrun Ure, interview with the author, March 1989.
15. *Newcastle Evening News*, 2nd October 1951.
16. *Newcastle Evening Chronicle*, 2nd October 1951.
17. Brian Blacklock, letter to the author, 19th September 1999.
18. *Manchester Guardian*, 9th October 1951.
19. *Manchester Evening News*, 9th October 1951.
20. *Oldham Chronicle*, 9th October 1951.
21. Diana Boddington, interview with the author, November 1989.
22. W. A. Darlington, *Daily Telegraph*, 19th October 1951.
23. P. L. Mannock, *Daily Herald*, 19th October 1951.
24. C. V. Curtis, *The Stage*, 24th October 1951.
25. Stephen Williams, *Evening News*, 19th October 1951.
26. Harold Hobson, *Sunday Times*, 21st October 1951.
27. T. C. Worsley, *New Statesman*, 19th October 1951.
28. Ibid.
29. Percy Harris, interview with the author, September 1989.
30. Christopher Morahan, interview with the author, September 1989.
31. Laurence Olivier, quoted in Peter Noble, *The Fabulous Orson Welles*. Hutchinson, 1956.
32. *News Chronicle*, 19th October 1951.
33. Kenneth Tynan, *Evening Standard*, 19th October 1951.
34. Ibid.
35. Dundy, *Life Itself!*
36. Kenneth Tynan, letter to Julian Holland, 4th March 1942.
37. Kenneth Tynan, 'The New Playboy of the Western World', *King Edward School Chronicle*, 1943.
38. Kenneth Tynan, letter to Julian Holland, 19th May 1944.

39. Kenneth Tynan, *The Sketch*, 24th October 1951.
40. Ibid.
41. Orson Welles, interview with Kathleen Tynan, 12th February 1983.
42. Maxine Audley, interview with the author, September 1989.
43. Gudrun Ure, interview with the author, March 1989.
44. Harry Alan Towers, taped statement, 1990.
45. Alberto Moravia, *Europeo*, 12th December, quoted in Anile, *Orson Welles in Italy.*
46. Alberto Mondadori, *Epoca*, 8th September 1951, quoted in Anile, *Orson Welles in Italy.*
47. Angelo Solmi, *Oggi*, 13th December 1951, quoted in Anile, *Orson Welles in Italy.*
48. Moravia, *Europeo*, quoted in Anile, *Orson Welles in Italy.*
49. Vittorio Bonicelli, *Il Tempo*, 15th December 1951, quoted in Anile, *Orson Welles in Italy.*
50. Laurence Olivier, letter to Orson Welles, 13th November 1951.
51. Orson Welles interview with Kathleen Tynan, 12th February 1983.
52. Christopher Fitzsimmons, *The Boys: A Double Biography*. Nick Hern Books, 1994.

CHAPTER 6

1. Michael Stern 'Wine, Women and Money', *True*, August 1953.
2. James Naremore, *The Magic World of Orson Welles.* Oxford University Press, 1978.
3. Orson Welles and Peter Bogdanovich, ed. Jonathan Rosenbaum, *This Is Orson Welles*. HarperCollins, 1992.
4. Eric Bentley, *New Republic*, 3rd October 1955.
5. Jean Desternes, *Débat sur le réalisme*, September 1948.
6. Francis Koval, *Sight and Sound*, December 1950.
7. Michael Kustow, *Peter Brook: A Biography*. Bloomsbury, 2005.
8. Peter Noble, *The Fabulous Orson Welles*. Hutchinson, 1956.
9. Ibid.
10. Ibid.
11. Lucio Fulci, quoted in Alberto Anile, *Orson Welles in Italy.* Indiana University Press, 2013.
12. Tatti Sanguineti, quoted in Anile, *Orson Welles in Italy.*
13. Orson Welles, 'The Third Audience', delivered August 1953, printed in *Sight and Sound* January–March 1954.
14. Richard Negri, interview with the author, 1989.
15. Peter Williams, *Dance and Dancers*, October 1953.
16. William Hickey, *Daily Express*, 8th September 1953.
17. John Barber, *Daily Express*, 8th September 1950.
18. *Daily Telegraph*, 8th September 1950.
19. *Times Educational Supplement*, 11th September 1953.
20. All quoted from Peter Noble, *The Fabulous Orson Welles*. Hutchinson, 1956.
21. Val Adams, 'Random Notes on a Shakespearean Rehearsal', *New York Times*, 18th October 1953.
22. Letter to the author from David Thomas, to whom Saudek told the story.

23. Robert MacCauley, interviewed by Richard France.
24. *Newsweek*, 26th October 1953.
25. Peter Brook, introductory essay to the reissue of *King Lear* on DVD.
26. Philip Hamburger, *The New Yorker*, 31st October 1953.
27. John Crosby, *Herald Tribune*, 19th October 1953.
28. Philip Minoff, *Cue*, 29th October 1953.
29. Ibid.
30. Ibid.
31. Ibid.
32. Richard Watts Jr, *New York Post*, 19th October 1953.

CHAPTER 7

1. Sergio Leone, quoted in Alberto Anile, *Orson Welles in Italy*. Indiana University Press, 2013.
2. Orson Welles and Peter Bogdanovich, ed. Jonathan Rosenbaum, *This Is Orson Welles*. HarperCollins, 1992.
3. Orson Welles, 'For a Universal Cinema', *Film Culture*, No. 1, January 1955.
4. Ralph Waldo Emerson, *Essays: First Series*. James Munroe, 1841.
5. Robert Arden, interview with the author, 1989.
6. Orson Welles, *Mr Arkadin* (screenplay).
7. Orson Welles (attributed), *Mr Arkadin* (novel), W.H.Allen, 1956.
8. Gary Giddins, *New York Sun*, 11th April, 2006.
9. Orson Welles (attributed), *Mr Arkadin* (novel), introduction by Robert Polito, new edition as part of the Criterion Collection edition of the film, 2006.
10. Parker Tyler, 'Orson Welles and the Big Experimental Film Cult', *Film Culture*, No. 29, Summer 1963.
11. Patricia Medina, *Laid Back in Hollywood: Remembering*. Belle Publishing, 1998.

CHAPTER 8

1. Huw Wheldon, letter to his father, quoted in Wynn Wheldon, *Kicking the Bar*. Unbound, 2016.
2. *TV Mirror*, April 1955.
3. *Daily Telegraph*, April 1955.
4. *Evening News*, London.
5. Kendall Macdonald, 'Orson Welles Will Star for Rival TV', *Evening News*, 26th April 1955.
6. John Gielgud, quoted in Jonathan Croall, *John Gielgud: Matinee Idol to Movie Star*. Methuen Drama, 2011.
7. *Daily Mail*, 9th May 1955.
8. Duffield, outline for *Moby-Dick*, in *Antepast*, 1947, Lilly Library Orson Welles Archive.

CHAPTER 9

1. John Huston, *An Open Book*. Macmillan, 1980.
2. Ibid.
3. Wolf Mankowitz, interview with the author, 1989.
4. Press release, May 1955.
5. Joan Plowright, *And That's Not All*. Weidenfeld & Nicolson, 2001.
6. Ibid.
7. Patrick McGoohan, interview with Arnold Hano, *TV Guide*, 1977.

8. Gareth Bogarde, interview with the author, 1989.
9. Ibid.
10. Plowright, *And That's Not All.*
11. Wolf Mankowitz, interview with the author, 1989.
12. Oscar Lewenstein, interview with the author, 1989.
13. Plowright, *And That's Not All.*
14. *Daily Mail*, 4th June 1955.
15. Kenneth Williams, *Just Williams: An Autobiography*. JM Dent & Sons, 1985.
16. Kenneth Williams, *Diaries*, ed. Russell Davies. HarperCollins, 1993
17. Patrick McGoohan, interview with Arnold Hano, *TV Guide*, 1977.
18. *Daily Telegraph*, 13th June 1955.
19. Gareth Bogarde, interview with the author, 1989.
20. Peter Sallis, interview with the author, 1989.
21. *New York Times*, 16th June 1955.
22. Elizabeth Frank, *News Chronicle*, 17th June 1955.
23. *Daily Mail*, 17th June 1955.
24. John Barber, *Daily Express*, 17th June 1955.
25. *The Times*, 17th June 1955.
26. T. C. Worsley, *Financial Times*, 18th June 1955.
27. Richard Watts Jr, *New York Times*, 12th July 1955.
28. Robert Otway, *Sunday Graphic.*
29. Eric Bentley, *New Republic*, July 1955.
30. Kenneth Tynan, *Observer*, 19th June 1955.
31. Peter Hall, in conversation with the author, June 1980.
32. Plowright, *And That's Not All.*
33. Peter Sallis, *Fading Into the Limelight*. Orion, 2006.
34. Williams, *Just Williams.*
35. Plowright, *And That's Not All.*
36. Ibid.
37. John Houseman, *Front and Center*. Simon & Schuster, 1979.
38. *Punch*, November 1955.
39. Wolf Mankowitz, interview with the author, 1989.
40. Ibid.
41. Ann Rogers, interviews with the author, 1989–1998.
42. *New York Times*, 9th July 1955.
43. Richard Wilson, letter to Orson Welles, 1949.

CHAPTER 10

1. Alain Pol, *The Dominici Affair.* La Huit, 2000.
2. Orson Welles, interview with André Bazin and Charles Bitsch, *Cahiers du Cinéma*, June 1958.
3. Lael Wertenbaker, 'Orson Welles: Nasty, Enchanting', *Keene Sentinel*, 16th October 1968.
4. Associated-Rediffusion, press statement.
5. L. Marsland Gander, *Daily Telegraph*, 5th November 1955.
6. Kenneth Williams, *Diaries*, ed. Russel Davies. HarperCollins, 1993.
7. Christopher Lee, interview with Lawrence French, wellesnet.com, 13th June 2009.
8. Peter Sallis, taped statement.

CHAPTER 11

1. Ann Rogers, notebook entry, 30th October 1955.
2. Michael Moynihan, *News Chronicle*, 30th November 1955.

3. Ibid.
4. Walter Kerr, *Theatre Arts*, September 1951.
5. Don Ross, 'Welles is Back in Full Crisis', *New York Herald Tribune*, 8th January 1956.
6. *Ed Murrow Show*, broadcast, 25th November 1955.
7. *New York Herald Tribune*.
8. Richard Maney, *Fanfare: The Confessions of a Press Agent*. HarperCollins, 1957.
9. Eric A. Gordon, *Mark the Music: The Life and Work of Marc Blitzstein*. St Martin's Press, 1989.
10. Orson Welles, 'The Return of the Prodigy', interview in *Cue*, 14th January 1956.
11. Proposal for *King Lear*, 1947, Lilly Library Orson Welles Archive.
12. Orson Welles, 'Tackling King Lear', *New York Times*, 8th January 1956.
13. Alvin Epstein, interview with the author, 1989.
14. Orson Welles, interview with Saul Levison, *World-Telegram*, 30th November 1955.
15. John Maxtone-Graham, interview with the author, 1989.
16. Ibid.
17. Eric Bentley, 'New Republic', 1956, collected in *In Search of Theatre*. Dobson, 1954.
18. John Maxtone-Graham, interview with the author, 1989.
19. Geraldine Fitzgerald, interview with the author, 1989.
20. Michael Lindsay-Hogg, *Luck and Circumstance*. Alfred A. Knopf, 2011.
21. Julian Barry, interview with Museum of Broadcasting.
22. John Maxtone-Graham, interview with the author, 1989.
23. Alvin Epstein, interview with the author, 1989.
24. John Maxtone-Graham, interview with the author, 1989.
25. Ibid.
26. Barbara Leaming, *Orson Welles: A Biography*. Viking, 1985.
27. Quoted in George Oppenheimer (ed.) *The Passionate Playgoer.* Viking, 1958
28. Alvin Epstein, interview with the author, 1989.
29. Brooks Atkinson, *New York Times*, 13th January 1956.
30. Richard Watts Jr, *New York Herald Tribune*, 13th January 1956.
31. Henry Hewes, 'No Great Shakes', *Saturday Review*, 14th January 1956.
32. Walter Kerr, *New York Herald Tribune*, 13th January 1956.
33. Wolcott Gibbs, *The New Yorker*, 21st January 1956.
34. Richard Hayes, *Commonweal Magazine*, 17th January 1956.
35. Paula Laurence, interview with the author, 1989.
36. Geraldine Fitzgerald, interview with the author, 1989.
37. Viveca Lindfors, interview with the author, 1989.
38. John Maxtone-Graham, interview with the author, 1989.
39. Alvin Epstein, interview with the author, 1989.
40. Sorrell Booke, interview with the author, 1989.
41. John Maxtone-Graham, interview with the author, 1989.
42. Ibid.
43. *New York Times*, 1st February 1956.

44. Brooks Atkinson, *New York Times*, 22nd January 1956.
45. George Jean Nathan, *New York Journal-American*, 21st January 1956.

CHAPTER 12

1. Bart Whaley, *Orson Welles: The Man Who Was Magic*. Lybrary.com, 2011.
2. 'Willard', *Daily Variety*, 23rd February 1956.
3. Whaley, *Orson Welles: The Man Who Was Magic*.
4. Ben Walters, 'Arrested Development: How Orson Welles Tried to Revolutionize Television, and Why Television Wouldn't Let Him', Culturalformations.org.
5. Desi Arnaz, *A Book*. Morrow, 1976.
6. Ben Walters, 'Arrested Development'.
7. John Collier, *Fancies and Goodnights*. Doubleday, 1951.
8. Arnaz, *A Book*.
9. Ben Walters, 'Arrested Development.'
10. Harriet Van Horne, *New York World-Telegram and Sun*, 17th September 1958.
11. Arnaz, *A Book*.
12. Jim Brochu, *Lucy in the Afternoon: An Intimate Memoir of Lucille Ball*. New English Library, 1990.
13. Todd McCarthy and Charles Flynn, eds, *Kings of the Bs: Working Within the Hollywood System, An Anthology of Film History and Criticism*. E. P. Dutton, 1975.
14. Jack Arnold, interview with Lawrence French, wellesnet.com, 24th August 2006.

CHAPTER 13

1. Todd McCarthy and Charles Flynn, eds, *Kings of the Bs: Working Within the Hollywood System, An Anthology of Film History and Criticism*. E. P. Dutton, 1975.
2. Orson Welles and Peter Bogdanovich, ed. Jonathan Rosenbaum, *This Is Orson Welles*. HarperCollins, 1992.
3. Charlton Heston, interview with the author, 1990.
4. Charlton Heston, *An Actor's Life: Journals, 1956–1976*, entry for 8th January 1957, ed. Hollis Alpert. E. P. Dutton, 1978.
5. Charlton Heston, *In the Arena: The Autobiography*. HarperCollins, 1995.
6. Ibid.
7. Ibid.
8. Janet Leigh, interview, 18th September 1998.
9. Dennis Weaver, *Working with Welles*, Directors' Guild of America.
10. Mercedes McCambridge, *The Quality of Mercy: An Autobiography*. Times Books, 1981.
11. Welles and Bogdanovich, ed. Jonathan Rosenbaum, *This Is Orson Welles*.
12. Transcript of a press conference on *Touch of Evil*, Brussels International Fair, 1958.
13. Heston, *In the Arena*.
14. Press release, Universal International, notes.
15. Ibid.
16. Heston, *An Actor's Life*, entry

for 25th March 1957.
17. Ibid., entry for 30th March 1957.
18. Ibid., entry for 1st April 1957.
19. Orson Welles, editing notes for Virgil Vogel, Lilly Library Orson Welles Archive.
20. Henry Mancini, *Did They Mention The Music?: The Autobiography of Henry Mancini*. McGraw-Hill, 1989.
21. Heston, *An Actor's Life*, entry for 17th June 1957.
22. Ibid.

CHAPTER 14

1. Orson Welles, interview with André Bazin, *Cahiers du Cinéma*, 1958.
2. Charlton Heston, *An Actor's Life: Journals, 1956–1976*, entry for 4th November 1957, ed. Hollis Alpert. E. P. Dutton, 1978.
3. Rick Schmidlin, interview with Lawrence French, wellesnet.com, 8th October 2008.
4. Heston, *An Actor's Life*, entry for 7th November 1957.
5. Orson Welles, letter to Charlton Heston, 8th November 1957.
6. Heston, *An Actor's Life*, entry for 12th November 1957.
7. Edward Muhl, letter to Orson Welles, 12th November 1957.
8. Ann Rogers, interview with the author, August 1998.
9. Orson Welles, letter to Charlton Heston, 17th November 1998.
10. Heston, *An Actor's Life*, entry for 19th November 1957.
11. Orson Welles, letter to Charlton Heston, 20th November 1957.
12. James Naremore, letter to the author, March 2015.
13. Orson Welles, memorandum to Edward Muhl, 5th December 1957.
14. Orson Welles, letter to Charlton Heston, early December 1957.
15. Charlton Heston, interview with the author, November 1990.
16. Heston, *An Actor's Life*, entry for 11th November 1957.
17. Orson Welles and Peter Bogdanovich, ed. Jonathan Rosenbaum, *This Is Orson Welles*. HarperCollins, 1992.
18. Gerald Weales, 'The Twilight of an Aging Prodigy', *The Reporter*, 18, No. 13, 1958, quoted in Sarah Nilsen, *Projecting America, 1958: Film and Cultural Diplomacy at the Brussels World's Fair*. MacFarlane & Company, Inc., 2011
19. Stanley Kaufmann, 'Whither Welles', *New Republic*, 26th May 1958.
20. Howard Thompson, 'Orson Welles Is Triple Threat in Thriller', *New York Times*, 22nd May, 1958.
21. Welles and Bogdanovich, ed. Jonathan Rosenbaum, *This Is Orson Welles*.
22. Janet Leigh, unattributed interview, 18th September 1998.
23. Welles and Bogdanovich, ed. Jonathan Rosenbaum, *This Is Orson Welles*.
24. Nilsen, *Projecting America, 1958*.
25. *Los Angeles Times*, April 1958.
26. Nilsen, *Projecting America, 1958*.
27. Orson Welles, interview with André Bazin and Charles Bitsch, *Cahiers du Cinéma*, June 1958.

28. Richard Fleischer, *Just Tell Me When To Cry: A Memoir*. Carroll and Graf, 1993.
29. Lewis Gilbert, *Desert Island Discs*, BBC Radio 4, 25th June 2010.
30. Fleischer, *Just Tell Me When To Cry*.

CHAPTER 15

1. Richard Barr (Dick Baer), letter to Orson Welles, 24th March 1947.
2. *Vogue Magazine*, French edition, December 1982–January 1983.
3. Orson Welles, letter to Hilton Edwards, late July 1959.
4. Orson Welles, letter to Hilton Edwards, 20th July 1959.
5. Hilton Edwards, letter to Orson Welles, late July 1959.
6. *Daily Telegraph*, 29th September 1959.
7. Hilton Edwards, letter to Eric Glass, 10th December 1959.
8. Hilton Edwards, letter to Orson Welles, 18th January 1960.
9. Leonard Fenton, interview with the author, 1989.
10. Anne Cunningham, interview with the author, 1989.
11. Peter Bartlett, interview with the author, 1989.
12. Keith Baxter, interview with the author, 1989.
13. Thelma Ruby, interview with the author, 1989.
14. Michael Lindsay-Hogg, *Luck and Circumstance*. Alfred A. Knopf, 2011.
15. Thelma Ruby, interview with the author, 1989.
16. Alexis Kanner, interview with the author, 1989.
17. *Oxford Times*, 3rd February 1960.
18. Orson Welles, letter to Hilton Edwards, 10th February 1960.
19. Aubrey Morris, letter to the author, June 1989.
20. Alistair Davidson, interview with the author, 1989.
21. Martin Tickner, interview with the author, 1989.
22. Micheál MacLiammóir, quoted in Christopher Fitzsimmons, *The Boys: A Double Biography*. Nick Hern Books, 1994.
23. Michael Lindsay-Hogg, interview with the author, 2007.
24. Orson Welles and Peter Bogdanovich, ed. Jonathan Rosenbaum, *This Is Orson Welles*. HarperCollins, 1992.
25. Lindsay-Hogg, *Luck and Circumstance*.
26. Ibid.
27. Thelma Ruby, interview with the author, 1989.
28. Alistair Davidson, interview with the author, 1989.
29. *Northern Whig*, 24th February 1960.
30. *Irish Times*, 25th February 1960.
31. 'A Towering Wellesian Première', *Manchester Guardian*, 25th February 1960.
32. *London Times*, 26th February 1960.
33. Alistair Davidson, interview with the author, 1989.
34. Anne Cunningham, interview with the author, 1989.
35. Ibid.
36. Keith Baxter, interview with the author, 1989.
37. Micheál MacLiammóir, letter to Orson Welles, 1960.

38. Micheál MacLiammóir, letter to Peter Bogdanovich, quoted in FitzSimmons, *The Boys*.
39. Ann Rogers, diary entry, 1st March 1960,
40. *Irish Times*, 1st March 1960.
41. Alistair Davidson, interview with the author, 1989.
42. Thelma Ruby, interview with the author, 1989.
43. H. R. Jeans, 'Sometimes You Feel It Could Be Danny Kaye', *Daily Mail*, 24th February 1960.
44. Alexis Kanner, interview with the author, 1989.
45. Aubrey Morris, letter to the author, June 1989.
46. Martin Tickner, interview with the author, 1989.
47. Ibid.
48. Godfrey Quigley, letter in *Irish Times*, 1st March 1960.
49. Oscar Lewenstein, letter to Orson Welles, 22nd December 1959.
50. Keith Baxter, *My Sentiments Exactly*. Oberon, 1998.
51. Hilton Edwards, letter to Orson Welles, 18th March 1960.
52. Aubrey Morris, letter to the author, June 1989.
53. Lindsay-Hogg, *Luck and Circumstance*.
54. Anne Cunningham, interview with the author, 1989.
55. Ann Rogers, interview with the author, 1989.
56. Baxter, *My Sentiments Exactly*.

CHAPTER 16

1. Kenneth Tynan, 'Ionesco: Man of Destiny?', *Observer*, 22nd June 1958.
2. Eugène Ionesco, *Observer*, 29th June 1958.
3. Orson Welles, *Observer*, 13th July 1958.
4. Oscar Lewenstein, letter to Eugène Ionesco, 5th October 1959.
5. Oscar Lewenstein, letter to Orson Welles, 22nd December 1959.
6. Eugène Ionesco, *Notes and Counter-Notes*. John Calder, 1964.
7. Harold Hobson, *Sunday Times*, 3rd April 1960.
8. Oscar Lewenstein, letter to Zero Mostel, 20th January 1960.
9. Oscar Lewenstein, letter to Zero Mostel, 20th February 1960.
10. Oscar Lewenstein, letter to Eugène Ionesco, 20th February 1960.
11. Ann Rogers, interview with the author, 1989.
12. Keith Baxter, *My Sentiments Exactly*. Oberon, 1998.
13. *Daily Mail*, 9th March 1960.
14. Eugène Ionesco, 'Preface to the American edition of *Rhinocéros*', November 1960.
15. Peter Sellers, *Empire News*, 27th March 1960.
16. Stuart Stallard, interview with the author, 1989.
17. Virginia Fairweather, interview with the author, 1989.
18. *Daily Express*, 21st April 1960.
19. Robert Otway, *Sunday Graphic*, 24th April 1960.

20. *News Chronicle*, 24th April 1960.
21. Joan Plowright, *And That's Not All*. Weidenfeld & Nicolson, 2001.
22. Peter Sallis, taped statement, 1989.
23. William Green, interview with the author, 1989.
24. Peter Sallis, taped statement, 1989.
25. Ibid.
26. Barbara Leaming, *Orson Welles: A Biography*. Viking, 1985.
27. William Green, interview with the author, 1989.
28. Stuart Stallard, interview with the author, 1989.
29. William Green, interview with the author, 1989.
30. Orson Welles, interview with Kathleen Tynan, 12th February, 1983.
31. Martin Tickner, interview with the author, 1989.
32. Ibid.
33. Ibid.
34. John Timbers, interview with the author, 1989.
35. Virginia Fairweather, interview with the author, 1989.
36. Ann Rogers, interview with the author, 1998.
37. Martin Tickner, interview with the author, 1989.
38. 'Shh! Director Welles whispers his way through the play's opening night', *Daily Express*, 29 April 1960.
39. Peter Sallis, taped statement, 1989.
40. Ibid.
41. *The Times*, 29th April 1960.
42. Robert Muller, *Daily Mail*, 29th April 1960.
43. Bernard Levin, *Daily Express*, 29th April 1960.
44. J.W. Lambert, *Sunday Times*, 1st May 1960.
45. Alan Pryce-Jones, *Observer*, 1st May 1960.
46. Hugh Siriol-Jones, *Queen*, 11th May 1960.
47. J. C. Trewin, *Illustrated London News*, 14th May 1960.
48. Philip Hope-Wallace, *Guardian*, 29th April 1960.
49. *Evening Standard*, 6th May 1960.
50. Robert Robinson, *Sunday Graphic*, 1st May 1960.
51. Pieter Rogers, interview with the author, 1989
52. Orson Welles, letter to Hilton Edwards, 19th May 1960.
53. *Birmingham Mail*, 23rd May 1960.
54. Orson Welles, interview with Kathleen Tynan, 12th February 1983.

CHAPTER 17

1. Kenneth Tynan, *Show Magazine*, October–November 1961.
2. Parker Tyler, 'Orson Welles and the Big Experimental Film Cult', *Film Culture*, No. 29, Summer 1963.
3. Anonymous, 'A Saint for the Cinema', *Contact*, Winter 1960.
4. Peter Bogdanovich, 'The Cinema of Orson Welles', *MOMA*, 1961.
5. Orson Welles, interview with André Bazin, *Cahiers du Cinéma*, 1958.
6. Lindsay Anderson, 'He Asked the Impossible', *Radio Times*, 11th March 1960.
7. Orson Welles, BBC television interview with Huw Wheldon, 13th March 1960.

8. Bernard Braden, television interview with Orson Welles, June 1960.
9. Kenneth Tynan, *Show Magazine*, October–November 1961.
10. Orson Welles, BBC television interview with Huw Wheldon, 16th September 1962.
11. Robert Hussong, quoted in Charles Winecoff, *Split Image: The Life of Anthony Perkins*. Dutton and Dial, 1996.
12. Antony Perkins, quoted in Winecoff, *Split Image*.
13. Orson Welles, BBC television interview with Huw Wheldon, 16th September 1962.
14. Bertolt Brecht, quoted in Stefan Kanfer, 'The Malady Was Life Itself', *Time Magazine*, 18th July 1983.
15. Press release, *The Trial*, 1962.
16. Jean Clay, 'Orson Welles on Trial', *Realités*, December 1962.
17. Ibid.
18. Orson Welles, 'A Trip to Don Quixoteland', interview with Juan Cobós, Miguel Rubio, and J.A. Pruneda, *Cahiers du Cinéma*, June–July 1964; English edition, *Cahiers du Cinema in English*, No. 5, 1966.
19. Jean Clay, 'Orson Welles on Trial', *Realités*, December 1962.
20. Ibid.
21. Edmond Richard, quoted in Jean-Pierre Berthomé and François Thomas, *Orson Welles at Work*. Phaidon, 2008.
22. William Chappell, *Sunday Times*, 27th May 1962.
23. Orson Welles, BBC television interview with Huw Wheldon, 16th September 1962.
24. Antony Perkins, quoted in Winecoff, *Split Image*.
25. Enrique Martinez, 'The Trial of Orson Welles', *Films and Filming*, October 1962.
26. 'Prodigal Revived', *Time Magazine*, 28th June 1962.
27. John Kobler, *Saturday Evening Post*, 8th December 1962.
28. Welles, 'A Trip to Don Quixoteland', *Cahiers du Cinema in English*.
29. Fred Muller, interview with the author, 2011.
30. Fred Muller interview with Peter Tonguette, in *Orson Welles Remembered: Interviews with His Actors, Editors, Cinematographers and Magicians*. McFarland, 2006.
31. Fred Muller, interview with the author, 2011.
32. Peter Sallis, *Fading into the Limelight*. Orion, 2006.
33. Genêt (Janet Flanner), *The New Yorker*, 12th January 1963.
34. Brendan Gill, *The New Yorker*, 2nd March 1963.
35. Dwight Macdonald, *Esquire*, July 1963.
36. 'Orson Welles Fails with Kafka', *The Times*, 12th November 1962.
37. William S. Pechter, *Sight and Sound*, Winter 1962.
38. Robert Hatch, 'Adult Prodigy', *Horizon*, July 1963
39. Franz Kafka, *The Trial*, translated by Idris Parry. Originally published in Germany, 1925. This edition published by Penguin Classics, 2000.

CHAPTER 18

1. Juan Cobós, *In the Land of Don Quixote*, 18th June 2008, wellesnet.com.
2. Ibid.
3. Keith Baxter, *My Sentiments Exactly*. Oberon, 1998.
4. Ibid.
5. Orson Welles, 'A Trip to Don Quixoteland', interview with Juan Cobós, Miguel Rubio, and J.A. Pruneda, *Cahiers du Cinéma*, June–July 1964; English edition, *Cahiers du Cinema in English,* No. 5, 1966.
6. Baxter, *My Sentiments Exactly*.
7. Laura Betti, interview for the booklet accompanying the *Eureka*! edition of *RoGoPaG*, 2012.
8. Alfredo Bini, ibid.
9. Tonino Delli Colli, ibid.
10. Pier Paolo Pasolini, interview by James Blue, *Film Comment*, 1965.
11. Orson Welles, letter to Keith Baxter, June 1964, quoted in Baxter, *My Sentiments Exactly*.
12. Ann Rogers, *Chimes at Midnight/Treasure Island* memorandum, Autumn 1964.

CHAPTER 19

1. *New York Herald Tribune*, 29th September, 1961.
2. *New York Times*, 29th September, 1961.
3. Orson Welles, letter to Louis Dolivet, 2nd September 1964. Gray Film Archives, Paris.
4. Roger Sansom, letter to the author, September 1998.
5. 'Orson Welles, Peter O'Toole and Ernest Milton discuss *Hamlet*', interview with Huw Wheldon, *Monitor*, BBC Television, 27th October 1963.
6. Margaret Rutherford, quoted in Keith Baxter, *My Sentiments Exactly*. Oberon, 1998.
7. Alan Webb and Michael Aldridge, quoted in Orson Welles interview with Kathleen Tynan, *Sunday Times.*
8. Daniel Sollé, letter to the author, 9th April 1998.
9. Michael Knox, unattributed interview, Dublin Gate Collection, Northwestern University, Illinois Archive.
10. Pierre Billard, *Sight and Sound*, Spring 1965.
11. Juan Cobós, *Cahiers du Cinéma*, April 1965.
12. John Gielgud, conversation with the author, 1994.
13. Baxter, *My Sentiments Exactly*.
14. Juan Cobós, *Cahiers du Cinéma*, April 1965.
15. John Gielgud, interview with Brian Case, *Time Out*, August 1991.
16. Baxter, *My Sentiments Exactly*.
17. John Gielgud, interview with Brian Case, *Time Out*, August 1991.
18. Keith Baxter, interview with the author, 1989.
19. Orson Welles, interview, *Cahiers du Cinéma*, September 1967; English edition, *Cahiers du Cinéma in English*, No. 11.
20. Daniel Sollé, letter to the author, 9th April 1998.
21. Baxter, *My Sentiments Exactly*.
22. John Gielgud, letter to Benjamin Britten, quoted in *John Gielgud: From Matinee Idol to Movie Star*. Methuen Drama, 2011.

23. Edmond Richard, quoted in Jean-Pierre Berthomé and François Thomas, *Orson Welles at Work*. Phaidon, 2008.
24. Jeanne Moreau, 'The Orson Welles Story', BBC Arena television interviews, 1982, quoted in Marianne Gray, *La Moreau: A Biography of Jeanne Moreau*. Little Brown, 1994.
25. Edmond Richard, quoted in Berthomé and Thomas, *Orson Welles at Work*.
26. Ibid.
27. Orson Welles, interview with Leslie Megahey, BBC Arena television interviews, 1982.
28. Edmond Richard, quoted in Berthomé and Thomas, *Orson Welles at Work*.
29. Orson Welles, interview with Kenneth Tynan, 'A conversation with the protean actor-writer-producer-director and Falstaffian bon vivant', *Playboy Magazine*, March 1967.
30. Baxter, *My Sentiments Exactly*.
31. W. H. Auden, 'The Prince's Dog', *The Dyer's Hand, and Other Essays*. Faber & Faber, 1963.
32. Orson Welles, interview with Leslie Megahey, BBC Arena television interviews, 1982.

CHAPTER 20

1. Alessandro Tasca Di Cutò, *A Prince in America*. Sellerio, 2004.
2. Fred Muller, interview with Peter Tonguette, in *Orson Welles Remembered: Interviews with His Actors, Editors, Cinematographers and Magicians*. McFarland, 2006.
3. Peter Parasheles, interview with Peter Tonguette, in *Orson Welles Remembered*.
4. Darryl F. Zanuck, letter to Orson Welles, 10th August 1965.
5. Orson Welles, unpublished interview with Kathleen Tynan, June 1965.
6. V. C. Thomas, *Festival de Cannes*, 1966.
7. David Lewin, 'Olé For Citizen Falstaff', *Daily Mail*, 10th May 1966.
8. *Daily Variety*, 18th May 1966,
9. Bosley Crowther, *New York Times*, 20th March 1967.
10. Robert Robinson, *Sunday Telegraph*, 26th March 1967.
11. Penelope Houston, *Spectator*, 31st March 1967.
12. John Coleman, *New Statesman*, 24th June 1967.
13. Pauline Kael, *New Republic*, 24th June 1967.
14. Jean-Louis Comolli, 'Jack Le Fataliste', *Cahiers du Cinéma*, August 1967.
15. Georgia Brown, *Village Voice*, 30th June 1992.
16. Gore Vidal, 'Remembering Orson Welles', *New York Review of Books,* 1st June 1989.

BIBLIOGRAPHY

Anile, Alberto translated by Marcus Perryman, *Orson Welles in Italy*. Indiana University Press, 2013.

Arnaz, Desi, *A Book*. Morrow, 1976.

Auden, W. H., *The Dyer's Hand & Other Essays*. Faber & Faber, 1963.

Baxter, Keith, *My Sentiments Exactly*. Oberon, 1998.

Bentley, Eric, *In Search Of Theatre*. Dobson, 1954.

Berthomé, Jean-Pierre & François Thomas, *Orson Welles at Work*. Phaidon, 2008.

Bessy, Maurice translated by Ciba Vaughan, *Orson Welles*. Crown Publishers, 1971.

Blair, Betsy, *The Memory of All That: Love and Politics in New York, Hollywood, and Paris*. Alfred A. Knopf, 2003.

Blumenfeld, Samuel, *L'Homme Qui Voulait Être Prince: Les Vies Imaginaires de Michal Waszynski*. Grasset, 2006.

Brady, Frank, *Citizen Welles: A Biography of Orson Welles*. Scribner, 1989.

Brochu, Jim, *Lucy in the Afternoon: An Intimate Memoir of Lucille Ball*. New English Library, 1990.

Capote, Truman ed. Gerald Clarke, *Too Brief a Treat: The Letters of Truman Capote*. Random House, 2004.

Croall, Jonathan, *John Gielgud: Matinee Idol to Movie Star*. Methuen Drama, 2011.

Drazin, Charles, *In Search of the Third Man*. Methuen, 1999.

—, *Korda: Britain's Only Movie Mogul*. Sidgwick & Jackson, 2002.

Dundy, Elaine, *Finch, Bloody Finch: A Biography of Peter Finch*. Joseph, 1980.

—, *Life Itself!*. Virago, 2001.

Farson, Daniel, *Sacred Monsters*. Bloomsbury, 1988.

Fitzsimons, Christopher, *The Boys: A Double Biography*. Nick Hern Books, 1994.

Fleischer, Richard, *Just Tell Me When to Cry: A Memoir*. Carroll and Graf, 1993.

Gordon, Eric A., *Mark the Music: The Life and Work of Marc Blitzstein*. St Martin's Press, 1989.

Gray, Marianne, *La Moreau: A Biography of Jeanne Moreau*. Little Brown, 1994.

Heston, Charlton, *In the Arena: The Autobiography*. HarperCollins, 1995.
—, *An Actor's Life: Journals, 1956–1976*, ed. Hollis Alpert. E. P. Dutton, 1978.
Higham, Charles, *Orson Welles: The Rise and Fall of an American Genius*. St Martin's Press, 1985.
Ionesco, Eugène translated by Donald Watson, *Notes and Counter-Notes*. John Calder, 1964.
Jason, Rick, *Scrapbooks of My Mind: A Hollywood Autobiography*. Strange New Worlds, 2000.
Kitt, Eartha, *Tuesday's Child*. Cassell, 1957.
Leaming, Barbara, *Orson Welles: A Biography*. Viking, 1985.
Lindfors, Viveca, *Viveka-Viveca*. Bonniers, 1978.
Lindsay-Hogg, Michael, *Luck and Circumstance*. Alfred A. Knopf, 2011.
MacLiammóir, Micheál, *Each Actor on His Ass*. Methuen, 1952.
—, *Put Money in Thy Purse: The Filming of Orson Welles' 'Othello'*. Foreword by Orson Welles. Methuen, 1976.
Mancini, Henry, *Did They Mention the Music?: The Autobiography of Henry Mancini*. McGraw-Hill, 1989.
McCambridge, Mercedes, *The Quality of Mercy: An Autobiography*. Times Books, 1981.
McCarthy, Todd & Charles Flynn, eds, *Kings of the Bs: Working Within the Hollywood System, An Anthology of Film History and Criticism*. E. P. Dutton, 1975.
Nilsen, Sarah, *Projecting America, 1958: Film and Cultural Diplomacy at the Brussel's World Fair*. McFarland, 2011.
Noble, Peter, *The Fabulous Orson Welles*. Hutchinson, 1956.
Plowright, Joan, *And That's Not All*. Weidenfeld & Nicolson, 2001.
Rosenbaum, Jonathan, *Discovering Orson Welles*. University of California Press, 2007.
Sallis, Peter in collaboration with John Miller, *Fading Into the Limelight*. Orion, 2006.
Tarbox, Todd, *Orson Welles and Roger Hill: A Friendship in Three Acts*. BearManor Media, 2013.
Tasca di Cutò, Alessandro, *Un Principe in America*. Sellerio, 2004.
Timmerman, Brigitte, *The Third Man's Vienna: Celebrating a Film Classic*. Shippen Rock Publishing, 2005.
Tonguette, Peter Prescott, *Orson Welles Remembered: Interviews with His Actors, Editors, Cinematographers and Magicians*. McFarland, 2006.
Welles, Orson & Peter Bogdanovich ed. Jonathan Rosenbaum, *This Is Orson Welles*. HarperCollins, 1992.
Whaley, Bart, *Orson Welles: The Man Who Was Magic*. Published as eBook, Lybrary.com, 2011.

Wheldon, Wynn, *Kicking the Bar.* Published as eBook, Unbound, 2015.
Williams, John L., *America's Mistress: The Life and Times of Eartha Kitt.* Quercus, 2013.
Williams, Kenneth, *Just Williams: An Autobiography*. Dent, 1985.
—, *Diaries*, ed. Russell Davies. HarperCollins, 1993.
Winecoff, Charles, *Split Image: The Life of Antony Perkins*. Dutton and Dial, 1996.
Wood, Bret, *Orson Welles: A Bio-Bibliography*. Greenwood Press, 1990.

PICTURE CREDITS

Welles in Paris, 1950 (photo by Robert Doisneau/Gamma-Rapho/Getty Images).

Welles as Faustus and Eartha Kitt as Helen of Troy (photo by ullstein bild/ullstein bild via Getty Images).

Welles being listened to by Carol Reed during filming for *The Third Man*, 1950 (photo by Popperfoto/Getty Images).

Harry Lime, cornered (photo by Donaldson Collection/Michael Ochs Archives/Getty Images).

Gielgud as Sherlock Holmes, Welles as Moriarty, Ralph Richardson as Dr Watson, London, 1955 (photo by Hulton Archive/Getty Images).

Welles as Hank Quinlan in *Touch of Evil*, 1958 (photo by Universal Studios/Newsmakers).

Chimes at Midnight location photographs, 1964 (© Nicolas Tikhomiroff/ Magnum Photos).

All other images from author's personal collection.

ACKNOWLEDGEMENTS

FIRST OF all, I have to thank Dan Franklin of Jonathan Cape, for sticking with the ever-expanding book through thick and thin, across its many volumes, accommodating with superhuman tolerance the impossible schedule of a writer who is on first call to several other professions. Secondly, deep gratitude and sympathy to Katherine Ailes, my ever-vigilant and always good-humoured editor, who took with apparent relish to the experience of chapters emerging suddenly and without warning at erratic intervals, and endured with perfect equanimity the orgy of radical rewriting which I like to undertake at the last possible moment. My agent Maggie Hanbury has as ever been angelically serene, bravely passing on terrible messages of delays and Radical New Thinking without a qualm. Her American counterpart, Robin Straus, has been nothing but supportive, and my American editor, Rick Kot, has been nothing but patient and encouraging. The Wellesian scholars have, as ever, been generous, forthcoming and stimulating: my deep thanks to François Thomas, to Robert Fischer, to Stefan Drössler of the Munich Film Museum, to Jonathan Rosenbaum, and as always, to James Naremore. Rick Schmidlin and Michael Dawson, both involved in Wellesian reconstructions, have been wonderfully helpful, as has Todd Tarbox. My interviewees, whom I list below, have been a source of unending illumination and amusement; I must single out Charlton Heston, who gave most generously of his time, shared his archive with me, sent me photocopies of crucial documents, while Keith Baxter – who did me the honour of agreeing to play King Henry IV when I played Falstaff in *Chimes at Midnight* onstage at the Chichester Festival Theatre – is one of the key witnesses to Welles, with total recall and shrewd judgement. Kate Percival let me read Rita Ribolla's wonderful diary, and Joe Pelissier lent me the handwritten diary of his grandmother, Fay Compton, which added greatly to the sum of knowledge about the film of *Othello.* Finally, my secretary Fiona Wilkins became a one-woman Welles bureau, downloading, typing, scanning, sleuthing, all above and beyond the call of duty. This book owes a lot to her.

INTERVIEWEES AND THEIR RELATIONSHIPS TO WELLES

ARDEN, Robert	MR ARKADIN
AUDLEY, Maxine	OTHELLO
BARTLETT, Peter	RHINOCEROS
BAXTER, Keith	CHIMES AT MIDNIGHT
BEDFORD, Patrick	CHIMES AT MIDNIGHT
BODDINGTON, Diana	OTHELLO
BOGARDE, Gareth	MOBY-DICK
BOOKE, Sorrell	KING LEAR
CHAPPELL, William	MOBY-DICK/THE TRIAL/ CHIMES AT MIDNIGHT
CORDWELL, Harry	MOBY-DICK
CUNNINGHAM, Anne	CHIMES AT MIDNIGHT
DAVIDSON, Alisdair	RHINOCEROS
EPSTEIN, Alvin	KING LEAR
FAIRWEATHER, Virginia	OTHELLO/RHINOCEROS
FANTO, George	IT'S ALL TRUE/OTHELLO/ THE BLESSED AND THE DAMNED
FENTON, Leonard	CHIMES AT MIDNIGHT
GREEN, William	RHINOCEROS
HESTON, Charlton	TOUCH OF EVIL
JACKSON, Gordon	MOBY-DICK
KANNER, Alexis	CHIMES AT MIDNIGHT
KRONSHAW, Bill	Friend
LACEY, Jackie	CHIMES AT MIDNIGHT
LEWENSTEIN, Oscar	MOBY-DICK/RHINOCEROS
LINDFORS, Viveca	KING LEAR
LINDSAY-HOGG, Michael	CHIMES AT MIDNIGHT
MACAULEY, Alistair	KING LEAR (TV)
MACDOWALL, Roddy	MACBETH
MANKOWITZ, Wolf	MOBY-DICK
MARGOLIS, Henry	MOBY-DICK/KING LEAR

NEGRI, Richard	LADY INTO ICE
NOBLE, Peter	Biographer
PROUSE, Derek	RHINOCEROS
ROGERS, Ann	Secretary
ROGERS, Pieter	RHINOCEROS
RUBY, Thelma	CHIMES AT MIDNIGHT
SALLIS, Peter	MOBY-DICK
STALLARD, Stephen	RHINOCEROS
THEOBALD, Peter	RHINOCEROS
TICKNER, Martin	RHINOCEROS
TIMBERS, John	RHINOCEROS
TOWERS, Harry Alan	HARRY LIME
URE, Gudrun	OTHELLO
WIDHOFF, Françoise	OTHER SIDE OF THE WIND
ZIMMER, Lee	THE BLESSED AND THE DAMNED

INDEX